CHINA'S NEW SOURCES OF ECONOMIC GROWTH

vol. 1

Reform, Resources, and Climate Change

Other titles in the China Update Book Series include:

1999 China: Twenty Years of Economic Reform
2002 China: WTO Entry and World Recession
2003 China: New Engine of World Growth
2004 China: Is Rapid Growth Sustainable?
2005 The China Boom and its Discontents
2006 China: The Turning Point in China's Economic Development
2007 China: Linking Markets for Growth
2008 China's Dilemma: Economic Growth, the Environment and Climate Change
2009 China's New Place in a World of Crisis
2010 China: The Next Twenty Years of Reform and Development
2011 Rising China: Global Challenges and Opportunities
2012 Rebalancing and Sustaining Growth in China
2013 China: A New Model for Growth and Development
2014 Deepening Reform for China's Long-Term Growth and Development
2015 China's Domestic Transformation in a Global Context

The titles are available online at press.anu.edu.au/publications/series/china-update-series

CHINA'S NEW SOURCES OF ECONOMIC GROWTH

vol. 1

Reform, Resources, and Climate Change

Edited by Ligang Song, Ross Garnaut,
Cai Fang and Lauren Johnston

Australian National University
PRESS

社会科学文献出版社
SOCIAL SCIENCES ACADEMIC PRESS(CHINA)

Published by ANU Press
The Australian National University
Acton ACT 2601, Australia
Email: anupress@anu.edu.au
This title is also available online at press.anu.edu.au

National Library of Australia Cataloguing-in-Publication entry

Title: China's new sources of economic growth : reform, resources and climate change. Volume 1 / editors: Ligang Song, Ross Garnaut, Cai Fang, Lauren Johnston.

ISBN: 9781760460341 (paperback) 9781760460358 (ebook)

Series: China update series ; 2016.

Subjects: Economic development--China.
Sustainable development--China.
Climatic changes--Government policy--China.
China--Economic policy--2000-

Other Creators/Contributors:
Song, Ligang, editor.
Garnaut, Ross, editor.
Cai, Fang, editor.
Johnston, Lauren, editor.

Dewey Number: 330.95106

Cover design and layout by ANU Press

Contents

Part II: Resources, Energy, the Environment and Climate Change

Figures

Tables

Contributors

Ross Garnaut
Professional Research Fellow in Economics, University of Melbourne, Melbourne

Cai Fang
Vice President, Chinese Academy of Social Sciences, Beijing

Ligang Song
Crawford School of Public Policy, The Australian National University, Canberra

Lauren Johnston
Research Fellow, Melbourne Institute of Applied Economic and Social Research, Faculty of Business and Economics, University of Melbourne, Melbourne

Guo Zhenwei
National Health and Family Planning Commission of China, Beijing

Wang Meiyan
Institute of Population and Labour Economics, Chinese Academy of Social Sciences, Beijing

Xiaolu Wang
National Economic Research Institute, China Reform Foundation, Beijing

Yixiao Zhou
Curtin Business School, Curtin University, Perth

Harry X. Wu
Institute of Economic Research, Hitotsubashi University, Tokyo

Yiping Huang
National School of Development, Peking University, Beijing

Yan Shen
National School of Development, Peking University, Beijing

Jingyi Wang
National School of Development, Peking University, Beijing

Feng Guo
National School of Development, Institute of Internet Finance, Peking University, Beijing

Wing Thye Woo
Economics Department, University of California, Davis; Institute of Population and Labor Economics, Chinese Academy of Social Sciences, Beijing; Jeffrey Cheah Institute on Southeast Asia, Sunway University, Kuala Lumpur

Xin Meng
Research School of Economics, College of Business and Economics, The Australian National University, Canberra

Sen Xue
Research School of Economics, College of Business and Economics, The Australian National University, Canberra

Jinjun Xue
Economic Research Centre, Graduate School of Economics, Nagoya University, Japan

David Dollar
Senior Fellow, John L. Thornton China Center, The Brookings Institution, Washington DC

Xing Liu
Research Fellow, China Center for Health Economic Research, National School of Development, Peking University, Beijing

Maorui Yang
Research Fellow, China Center for Health Economic Research, National School of Development, Peking University, Beijing

Xiang Zhang
Research Fellow, China Center for Health Economic Research, National School of Development, Peking University, Beijing

Zhenya Liu
School of Finance, Renmin University of China, Beijing; Department of Economics, University of Birmingham, United Kingdom

Danyuanni Han
Department of Economics, University of Birmingham, United Kingdom

Shixuan Wang
Department of Economics, University of Birmingham, United Kingdom

Ivan Roberts
International and Economic Research Departments, Reserve Bank of Australia, Sydney

Andrew Zurawski
International and Economic Research Departments, Reserve Bank of Australia, Sydney

Biliang Hu
Professor of Economics, Dean of Emerging Markets Institute, Beijing Normal University, Beijing

Jia Luo
Industrial and Commercial Bank of China, Beijing

Chunlai Chen
Crawford School of Public Policy, The Australian National University, Canberra

Bingqin Li
Crawford School of Public Policy, The Australian National University, Canberra

Haimin Liu
China Steel Industry Development Research Institute, Beijing

Can Wang
Department of Environmental Planning and Management, Tsinghua University, Beijing

Xinzhu Zheng
Department of Environmental Planning and Management, Tsinghua University, Beijing

Kathleen Buckingham
Research Associate, World Resources Institute, Washington DC

ZhongXiang Zhang
College of Management and Economics, Tianjin University, China

Fergus Green
Grantham Research Institute on
Climate Change and the Environment,
London School of Economics,
United Kingdom

Nicholas Stern
Grantham Research Institute on
Climate Change and the Environment,
London School of Economics,
United Kingdom

Xiaoli Zhao
School of Business Administration,
China University of Petroleum,
Beijing

Jianxin Wu
School of Economics and Institute
of Resources, Environment and
Sustainable Development Research,
Jinan University, Guangzhou, China

Yanrui Wu
Economics, Business School,
University of Western Australia,
Perth, Australia

Xiumei Guo
Curtin University Sustainability
Policy Institute, Faculty of
Humanities, Curtin University,
Perth, Australia

Acknowledgements

The China Economy Program gratefully acknowledges the financial support for the *China Update 2016* provided by Rio Tinto through the Rio Tinto–ANU China Partnership, as well as the coordination provided by Program Manager Elizabeth Buchanan, and our colleagues at the East Asia Forum at The Australian National University. The 2016 *China Update* book is the 16th edition in the *China Update* book series and we wish to thank Tim Lane for his unwavering support for the research unit. We sincerely thank our contributors from around the world for their valuable contributions to the book series and the *Update* events throughout these years. Thanks also go to the ANU Press team, notably Lorena Kanellopoulos, Emily Tinker and Jan Borrie, for the expeditious publication of the book series, and to Social Science Academic Press (China) in Beijing for translating and publishing the Chinese versions of the *Update* book series to make the research work available to the readers in China.

Abbreviations

ADB	Asian Development Bank
ADBI	Asian Development Bank Institute
AfDB	African Development Bank
AIIB	Asian Infrastructure Investment Bank
APF	aggregate production function
APPF	aggregate production possibility frontier
BIS	Bank for International Settlements
BIT	bilateral investment treaty
BRICS	Brazil, Russia, India, China and South Africa
C&P	commodities and primary input materials
CAR	capital adequacy ratio
CBRC	China Banking Regulatory Commission
CCICED	China Council for International Cooperation on Environment and Development
CCR	command-and-control regulation
CDB	China Development Bank
CDM	Clean Development Mechanism
CE	choice experiment
CFIUS	Committee on Foreign Investment in the United States
CIP	China Industrial Productivity
CISA	China Iron and Steel Association
CLSA	Credit Lyonnais Securities Asia
CPCCEs	commuting-related per capita carbon dioxide emissions
CPI	consumer price index
CSIC	Chinese Standard Industrial Classification
CSMAR	China Securities Markets and Accounting Research Database
CSRC	China Securities Regulatory Commission
CULS	China Urban Labour Survey
DF	Dickey–Fuller
DPSIR	Driving Force-Pressure-State-Impact-Response
EBIT	earnings before interest and tax
EBITDA	earnings before interest, tax, depreciation and amortisation
EP	Equator Principles

EPFI	Equator Principles Financial Institution
ETS	emissions trading scheme
EXIM Bank	Export–Import Bank of China
FDI	foreign direct investment
FGD	flue-gas desulphurisation
FYP	Five-Year Plan
gce/kWh	grams of standard coal consumed per kilowatt hour
GCP	gross city product
GDP	gross domestic product
GFC	Global Financial Crisis
GHG	greenhouse gas
GICS	Global Industry Classification Standard
GMM	generalised method of moments
GNI	gross national income
GOAR	getting old after getting rich
GOBR	getting old before getting rich
GRP	gross regional product
GS	government subsidy
GSADF	generalised sup augmented Dickey–Fuller test
GW	gigawatt
HSR	high-speed rail
hukou	household registration
IADB	Inter-American Development Bank
IBRD	International Bank for Reconstruction and Development
ICBC	Industrial and Commercial Bank of China
ICT	information and communication technology
IDA	International Development Association
IDA	index decomposition analysis
IEA	International Energy Agency
IFDI	Internet Finance Development Index (Peking University)
IMF	International Monetary Fund
INDC	intended nationally determined contribution
IPAT	impact, population, affluence and technology
IPCC	Intergovernmental Panel on Climate Change
IPR	intellectual property rights
IT	information technology

LCCDI	low-carbon city development index
LMDI	logarithmic mean Divisia index
M&A	merger and acquisition
MBR	market-based regulation
MDB	multilateral development bank
MEP	Ministry of Environmental Protection
MNL	multinomial logit
MOFCOM	Ministry of Commerce
MPS	material product system
MRV	measurement/monitoring, reporting and verification
NBS	National Bureau of Statistics
NDRC	National Development and Reform Commission
NEA	National Energy Administration
NPL	non-performing loan
NPV	net present value
OBOR	'One Belt and One Road'
ODI	outward direct investment
OECD	Organisation for Economic Co-operation and Development
OLS	ordinary least squares
OPEC	Organization of the Petroleum Exporting Countries
P2P	peer-to-peer
PAA	prefecture level and above
PBC	People's Bank of China
PE	price-to-earnings
PEC	primary energy consumption
PO	poor–old
R&D	research and development
RBA	Reserve Bank of Australia
RIETI	Research Institute of Economy, Trade and Industry
RMDB	regional multilateral development bank
ROE	return on equity
RPL	random parameters logit
RUMiC	Rural–Urban Migration in China
S&P	Standard & Poor's
SADF	sup augmented Dickey–Fuller test
SAR	semi-autonomous region

SCE	standard coal equivalent
SCE	state-controlled enterprise
SDA	structural decomposition analysis
SF&F	semifinished and finished goods
Shibor	Shanghai Interbank Offered Rate
SME	small and medium-sized enterprise
SNA	System of National Accounts
SOB	state-owned bank
SOE	state-owned enterprise
SPC	State Power Corporation
STAR	smooth threshold autoregressive
STIRPAT	stochastic impact by regression on population, affluence and technology
tce	tonnes of standard coal equivalent
TFP	total factor productivity
TPCCE	transport-related per capita carbon dioxide emission
TPP	Trans-Pacific Partnership
TWh	terawatt-hours
UN	United Nations
UNFCCC	United Nations Framework Convention on Climate Change
UNFCCC COP21	United Nations Framework Convention on Climate Change Conference of Parties
UPCCE	urban system-related per capita carbon dioxide emission
WRI	World Resources Institute
WTO	World Trade Organization
WTP	willingness to pay
WWF	World Wide Fund for Nature

1. China's New Sources of Economic Growth: A supply-side perspective

Ross Garnaut, Cai Fang, Ligang Song and Lauren Johnston

Introduction

The Chinese economy has continued to absorb massive pressures for structural change since the publication of *China's domestic transformation in a global context* (Song et al. 2015). The increasing scarcity of labour and rising labour costs foreshadowed in *The turning point in China's economic development* (Garnaut and Song 2006) have continued to constrict the old Chinese strengths linked to exports of labour-intensive manufactures. The overhang of excessive investment in infrastructure and heavy industry from the aftermath of expansion to counteract the Global Financial Crisis (GFC) and the debt that funded it requires large structural change independent of the longer-term pressures. The ageing of the Chinese population deriving from low fertility in the reform period has generated special challenges of growing old before getting rich (Johnston et al., Chapter 10, this volume). Global and domestic environmental imperatives have forced a reshaping of priorities for economic development and exerted their own pressure for change away from the old pattern of investment-led growth. Meanwhile, China grapples with the special challenges of transition from the ranks of the world's middle-income countries into the developed world—the challenge of escaping the 'middle-income trap'.

The Chinese Government has remained committed to the directions defined in China's new growth model. The new directions have shaped the Five-Year Plan (FYP) for 2016–20.

The changes in China have taken place within a troubled international economy. Growth in the developed economies has remained weak since the descent into the GFC from late 2007. Developing countries beyond China demonstrate a wide range of experiences. Many continue to grow reasonably strongly through the troubles of the developed world. But the many developing and transitional economies specialising in commodity exports that were carried high by the Chinese resources boom from early in the century to 2011—Brazil, Russia, South Africa, Nigeria and others large and small—have fallen on hard times under China's new model of growth. World trade has expanded less rapidly than output over recent years, removing a source of economic expansion in China and elsewhere.

Savings are well above investment through the developed world and China, generating the lowest market-determined long-term interest rates ever. The Federal Reserve Bank of the United States has moved only tentatively to haul in the most expansionary monetary policy in history. Other central banks through the developed world continued to ease monetary policy in an attempt to lift growth in incomes and output. Investment remains weak, generating a tendency everywhere for economic growth to remain below what had once been regarded as attainable rates. Weak business investment has been the effect and the cause of the lowest productivity growth in modern times—in the developed world and, recently, in China.

Global economic growth fell to 1.5 per cent with the onset of the GFC in 2008 and declined further to –2.1 per cent in 2009. The latter outcome would have been lower still but for the powerful fiscal and monetary expansion that restored Chinese growth to historically strong rates by the end of that year. Global growth recovered briefly in 2010 to an old normal rate of 4.1 per cent, but settled at rates below any sustained period since the middle of the twentieth century: 2.8 per cent in 2011, and then to 2.3 per cent (2012), 2.4 per cent (2013), 2.5 per cent (2014) and 2.4 per cent in 2015.

So China's structural change has been occurring through challenging international circumstances. When slumping demand in the industries supplying the high investment in the later years of investment-led growth in China generated sharp increases in exports of surplus steel and other products, the developed world responded with the strongest protectionist reaction of the twenty-first century. The political consequences of stagnant real incomes in the United States and Europe threaten to further weaken the international environment for Chinese growth.

China's economic growth continued to slow through 2015 and the first half of 2016—as it has done consistently since 2011: the annual growth rate fell to 7.7 per cent in 2012 and 2013, and then further, to 7.3 per cent in 2014 and 6.9 per cent in 2015.

China's new model of economic growth, now embraced as the 'new normal' by the Chinese leadership and embodied in state planning, is meant to generate slower growth, which is a natural accompaniment of a lower investment share of expenditure. Over the past year, there have been periodic fears within Chinese and foreign business and wider communities that Chinese growth is slowing more rapidly than sought by policy. This has generated periods of market disruption and awkward government responses.

China's economic slowdown is part of a deceleration throughout the more prosperous parts of the world, but also has its own causes and characteristics. This book examines the special structural features of economic change in China, which will determine whether the economy and society experience a smooth transition to high-income country status—or remain mired in the middle-income trap.

China's domestic transformation in a global context (Song et al. 2015) drew attention to a then recent tendency for Chinese growth to come overwhelmingly from growth in the capital stock. Low fertility from early in the reform period had removed increases in the labour force as a significant source of economic growth. This had long been anticipated—together with the many consequences of an ageing population. What had not been anticipated was the decline in total factor productivity (TFP) growth—the reverse of what was required for smooth implementation of the new model of growth. A decline in the rate of investment—required within the new model of growth—would be associated with a large decline in the rate of growth in output unless it was accompanied by a large lift in productivity. There were no signs of such a lift.

The broad macroeconomic story has not changed much over the past year. There are large practical difficulties in measuring TFP growth and those who attempt to measure this dimension of development in China may not have it exactly right. But with the negligible TFP growth continuing in 2014, in the best estimates that we have, there is no reasonable doubt that there is a problem in contemporary economic development in China.

The anticipated decline in rates of growth in the capital stock together with the absence of productivity and labour force growth remove the potential for fiscal and monetary expansion to raise the rate of growth in output for any sustained period.

In standard growth accounting terms, the Chinese adjustment required by the new model of growth involves a moderate deceleration of aggregate growth, contributed by a cessation of growth in the labour force, a large decline in the growth in the capital stock and some acceleration of the growth in TFP. China has to achieve these outcomes within a set of policies that change fundamentally the old negative relationship between economic growth and environmental degradation.

China's new sources of economic growth: Volume 1—Reform, resources and climate change looks closely at each of these elements of the Chinese adjustment. Here we outline some of the big demographic changes affecting growth in the labour force, the drivers of growth in the capital stock and the influences on TFP. We then outline the ways in which each of the book's chapters advance our understanding of the Chinese adjustment.

From Lewis to Solow: China's demographic transition

China's strong growth in the first several decades of the reform era is now the world's leading example of growth in a surplus-labour economy, as analysed by Lewis (1954) and applied to Taiwan by Fei and Ranis (1964) and to Japan by Minami (1973). In the Lewis-type labour-surplus economy, rapid growth in a highly productive and initially small modern sector (mostly urban and industrial) is supported by the flow of labour from the countryside. Average productivity is much lower in the rural than in the dynamic modern sector, and marginal productivity is lower still.

The flow of labour from the countryside does not greatly increase the supply price of labour for a long period—in China's case, from 1978 until about 2006. Wages are anchored by the large number of people in the countryside who offer themselves for modern-sector employment at the going wage rate.

Wages increase more slowly than productivity in the modern sector of the economy. The profit share of income rises, supporting high rates of saving. The tendency for wages to lag behind productivity growth supports high returns on investment, encouraging the investment of the increase in savings in the modern sector of the economy.

Productivity growth at a national level is supported strongly by the shift of people from low-productivity rural to high-productivity modern economic activity. It is supported by the accretion of skills in the growing modern economy, which cannot proceed at a similar rate in the rural sector.

In the first several decades of the reform era, the structure of China's population was increasingly favourable for high rates of growth in output per person.

The One-Child Policy of the reform era reinforced and extended beyond the most prosperous centres the general experience of humanity for fertility to fall as incomes rise with economic growth. The ratio of child dependants to members of the labour force fell. This added a 'demographic dividend' to other forces contributing to rapid economic growth: the high growth of the capital stock and high productivity growth. The demographic dividend, however, provided only a temporary boost to growth in output; eventually, low fertility flows through to low and negative growth in the labour force and to an increase in aged dependence.

When a country enjoys an extended period of growth in its working-age population, alongside a fall in the dependency ratio—the ratio of the sum of the age groups 0–14 and 60-plus over the age group of 15–59 years—the potential rate of growth is higher than it would otherwise be. The demographic dividend affects growth through several channels and, whatever the rate of growth, the increase in the ratio of the labour force to total population leads directly to increased average income per person.

The period of Lewisian surplus labour came to an end through the second half of the first decade of the new century. In a large, diverse country, the end of the labour surplus came not as a 'turning point' but as a 'turning period'. The rate of increase in wages accelerated unevenly but broadly through the country. During 2004–15, the growth rate of migrant worker wages was 10.7 per cent per annum. Facing pressures from labour shortages and rising labour costs, firms substituted capital for labour in industrial processes. The relative importance of labour-intensive industries shrank as their international competitiveness declined and the relative importance of more technologically sophisticated and capital-intensive industries increased. The economy-wide effect was a higher capital/labour ratio and a fall in the return to capital. China's average return to capital fell from 24.1 per cent in 2004 to 14.7 per cent in 2013 (Bai and Zhang 2014).

The Lewisian stage of economic growth has given way to a neoclassical or Solow stage of growth. Cessation of growth and, recently, a decline in the number of people in the conventional 'working age' group remove an important source of growth in total output. The deceleration in the rate of increase in movement of people from the countryside to the modern economy removes a major source of productivity growth. Lower labour force and productivity growth reduce the incentive to invest. Economic growth comes to rely more heavily on investment in human capital—increases in the education levels and skills of the labour force—and more demanding sources of productivity growth embodying innovation and relying on flexible and sophisticated capital and goods and services markets.

In the neoclassical 'Solow' economy, supply-side reforms to improve the quality of markets and to allow restructuring towards more productive economic activities hold the key to enhancing potential economic growth (Cai 2016).

One important area of supply-side reform relates to removal of obstacles to full utilisation of labour supply. This can slow the loss of the demographic dividend.

The working-age population (aged 15–59) has been falling in absolute terms since 2012. It is estimated that the growth rate of the economically active members of the population aged 15–59 will become negative from 2018. It is therefore important to find ways of utilising as completely as possible the available labour supply, particularly in high-productivity sectors. A 1 percentage point increase in the labour participation rate in 2015 would have corresponded to nine million additional economically active people in 2015. Reform of the *hukou* (household registration) system in a way that would lead to more complete absorption of migrants into urban life offers a chance to raise the labour participation rate.

The recent relaxation of family planning laws allows families now to have two children. Over time, this will modify the age structure of the population by lifting the fertility rate, which sits at about 1.5 births per woman—far from the replacement level of 2.1. A gradual increase in the fertility rate due to a shift in family planning policies would help to raise China's potential growth rate in the future. To ensure that higher fertility does not lead to a decline in female labour force participation, it will be necessary to improve child care and to expand investment in public-oriented infrastructure such as affordable housing, which can reduce the costs of raising children. Chinese policy is moving towards parents being left to choose how many children they have. There is likely to be some lift in fertility rates for a while, but not by much if China follows the experience of other East Asian countries.

Aoki (2012) found from the East Asian growth experiences that, in the current Solow phase of Chinese development, growth is strongly driven by the accumulation of human capital. There are strong links—at least during certain periods of development—between the formation of human capital and a country's potential growth rate. Manuelli and Seshadri (2014) suggest that the contribution of human capital to economic growth could be even higher than that of increases in productivity. China has greatly increased its expenditure for education and training in recent years and this will contribute to offsetting the effects on growth of a declining labour force.

Changes in productivity

TFP growth has many sources. The transfer of labour from agriculture to industry was particularly important in China under the old model of growth. This process in China has slowed rapidly in recent years. Data from the National Bureau of Statistics (NBS various years) suggest that in the period 2005–10 the rate of increase in the number of rural migrant workers moving to cities was an average of 4 per cent and then fell to 1.3 per cent in 2014 and to just 0.3 per cent in 2015.

Institutional barriers that result from the *hukou* system have brought forward the slowing of growth in rural–urban migration. The *hukou* system prevents large numbers of migrant workers becoming permanent urban residents with full access to social security and education benefits. With rural workers having more market power than previously, and consumption a more important source of growth in demand, these institutional residency hurdles have become more costly.

Reforms to the *hukou* system could slow the decline in the rate at which rural migrant workers move to cities. While labour market reforms would help to hold up growth in TFP as rural–urban migration slows, only the continual improvement of institutions can generate sustained increases in TFP. One new impetus for growth is advancement in science and technology.[1] Another is reform to increase the efficiency with which resources are allocated[2] through institutional changes including improvement of markets. This is referred to as the 'reform dividend'.

Measures to reap a reform dividend include nurturing markets for goods, capital, labour and natural resources including the environment. They include reform of the structures of state-owned enterprises (SOEs), regulations with respect to market entry and exit, policies to encourage entrepreneurial activities including innovation, financial and banking system reform and local government system reform, especially with respect to local public finances. One contemporary policy challenge is how to handle 'zombie firms' associated with overcapacity in several industries.

Macroeconomic policy and the role of investment

The Chinese Government has committed itself to maintaining growth at over 6.5 per cent per annum through the current FYP to 2020, and to do this with little or no growth in the labour force and a much lower rate of growth in the capital stock. This can only be achieved by reform to accelerate growth in TFP. But neither the reform nor the acceleration of growth in TFP is currently a prospect.

As growth slows, the government will come under pressure to increase the rate of growth above the rate of increase of the economy's supply capacity through fiscal and monetary expansion. This can succeed only temporarily. And the attempt will artificially increase investment, as this is the main channel through which fiscal and monetary expansion works. The increase in investment cuts across reform of markets and institutions and feeds back into lower growth in TFP. It is therefore self-defeating.

1 We are going to cover the issues of human capital, technological change and innovation for growth of the Chinese economy in the 2017 China Update book on *China's new sources of economic growth* (Volume 2).

2 In recent Update books, we have put strong emphasis on supply-side reform and restructuring. For example, the 2010 book discusses China's next 20 years of reform and development; the 2012 book covers the issues of rebalancing and sustaining growth in China; the 2013 book touches on the issues of a new model for growth and development; and the 2014 book focuses on deepening reform for China's long-term growth and development.

How, then, can the government resolve the problem posed by potential growth falling below the desired rate? Only by accelerating reform and accepting the possibility of growth falling short of announced goals, at least for a while.

Equity and environmental amenity

China's rebalancing of growth to reduce reliance on investment and to increase TFP at a time of demographic change that is unfavourable to growth is complicated by the simultaneous requirement for more equitable and less environmentally damaging patterns of growth.

The rebalancing and sustenance of growth is complicated but not contradicted by the equity and environmental goals. The reform of the *hukou* system is favourable to labour force and productivity growth as well as to equity. The spread of high-quality education through the countryside and to all urban residents improves both growth and equity.

The macroeconomic adjustment associated with the shift from surplus to increasingly scarce and valuable labour is an inevitable outcome of successful growth over a long period. This is forcing rebalancing along lines favoured by the government and is powerfully favourable for promoting equity in income distribution.

In the early reform period, the concentration of investment in regions that were favourable for economic growth supported rapid economic growth for the national economy. Independently of regional policy, it was the coastal provinces that were in the best position to take advantage of early opportunities for increased integration into the international economy. The coastal provinces and cities experienced rapid growth through the first quarter-century of reform and drew away from inland provinces in average incomes. Now, the faster growth of provinces in central and western China is favourable both for overall growth and for inter-regional equity.

The long-term problem of regional imbalances in development has eased in China since early in the Turning Period. The deceleration of growth in the eastern region started earlier (since 2007) than other regions and the trend continues. The central and western regions' growth rates and contributions to gross domestic product (GDP) have tended to increase continually since 2000, narrowing the regional gaps in growth and development. The deceleration of growth for the central and western regions began about 2012, dragging down the overall growth. However, as latecomers to development, the central and western regions have greater potential than the coastal provinces for continued growth for some time.

While growth that pays no attention to pressure on the global and domestic environment—as in the old model of Chinese economic growth—is consistent with rising economic welfare for a while, beyond some point it undermines the ecological basis for growth in living standards. China had passed that point in 2011 when the Chinese leadership committed the country to a 'new normal' in economic affairs. There is a fundamental sense in which the breaking of the nexus between growth in economic output and degradation of the natural environment is a precondition for sustained economic growth—appropriately defined in human welfare terms.

The Chinese government has made large efforts to weaken the link between economic growth and global and local environmental degradation. Areas of large progress include improving energy efficiency, reducing and capping coal use and reducing resource intensities in production, arresting the deterioration in air and water quality in regions where degradation had been most severe, developing renewable and other new low-emissions sources of energy, and experimenting with models of 'green growth' in some of the regions. Continued progress will require judicious use of both market (such as the establishment of an emission trading system to reduce the use of greenhouse gases (GHGs)) and regulatory (such as implementation and more stringent enforcements of the state regulations on resource exploration and development, air, soil and pollution, land and water use and conservation) mechanisms. Both market and regulatory mechanisms are being applied extensively to changing the relationship between economic growth and pressure on the environment. But the environmental challenges that China still faces are enormous.

This year's book, built around the theme of China's new sources of economic growth, covers many of the issues discussed in this introductory chapter. Here we provide a guide to the content of the following chapters of the book.

The book has two parts. Part I has 11 chapters covering Reform and Macroeconomic Development. In this summary, we divide these into three sets of chapters: Growth in the 'New Normal'; Growth and the Demographic Transition; and Financial Market Performance and Reform. Part II has 8 chapters covering Resources, Energy, the Environment and Climate Change.

Part I: Reform and Macroeconomic Development

Growth in the 'new normal'

Four chapters provide perspectives of recent and prospective overall growth performance, looking at changes in the broad aggregates, including TFP. Garnaut (Chapter 2) updates his (Garnaut 2015) assessment of recent progress under the new model of growth, focusing on the objectives to which the Chinese government has attributed greatest importance. Wang and Zhou (Chapter 4) examine alternative futures for the Chinese economy, depending on the approach to building the new model of growth. Wu (Chapter 5) analyses rates of growth in TFP across industry sectors and draws implications for expectations of growth performance. Wing (Chapter 7) examines links between public finances and risks to growth and reaches strong conclusions about the importance of removing the 'soft budget constraints' left over from earlier in the reform era.

Garnaut (Chapter 2) notes how the fundamental changes in economic strategy defined in earlier Update books (from Garnaut et al. 2013) as the new model of economic growth, are now officially described as the 'new normal'. He sees limited progress on only one of the most prominent of the government's ambitions for the new model of growth. The greatest changes in trajectory relate to the modification of the relationship between economic growth and pressure on domestic and global environmental amenity and stability. China is ahead of its international commitments on reductions in GHG emissions—and needs to be if there is to be any hope of global warming being contained within the limits defined by the United Nations (UN) meeting on climate change in Paris in December 2015. China made rapid progress on the goal of relying more on domestic demand and less on growth in exports and a trade surplus in the immediate aftermath of the GFC, but has fallen back almost to pre-crisis rates of surplus in the past year. There is slight progress in shifting from investment demand to consumption, and so far only limited progress on structural reform to unleash more rapid TFP growth. There has been early but as yet modest progress on reversing the earlier tendency towards greater inequality in the distribution of income.

Wang and Zhou (Chapter 4) use growth accounting techniques to analyse the sources of China's strong economic growth until 2011, the slowdown since then and the prospects under various policy scenarios. They see excessive investment and inadequate consumption as being the largest of several contributors to slower TFP growth from the early twenty-first century. At first this effect on total growth was obscured by loose monetary policy, which promoted more investment to compensate for lower growth from other sources. This was eventually self-defeating, leading to overcapacity in industries supplying the investment industries—spectacularly for steel and cement—and to economic underperformance. Continuation of recent policies is likely to lead to financial crisis within a few years, and to major underperformance against announced goals. In these circumstances, growth would be likely to slump to an average of 2.9 per cent per annum for 2016–20 and 4.4 per cent per annum for 2020–30. China would be caught in the middle-income group of countries, rather than making the transition to a high-income country. Strong reform to build institutions that support a rapid shift of resources to more productive uses and technological improvement, together with cessation of monetary policies that artificially maintain high levels of investment and inhibit consumption, would lead to a transition to developed country status. Within uninhibited reform policies to raise productivity, growth of around 6.2 per cent per annum could be expected for 2016–20, and higher still in 2020–30.

Wu is one of the stalwarts of measuring TFP growth in China. He has taken this work a step further in Chapter 5. He applies a new technical approach to estimate China's reform era TFP growth. China's industries are aggregated into eight groups according to the extent of the role of government in decisions. Simply by adopting nominal output weights for industries, Wu derives new estimates of historical GDP growth, with an average growth rate of 8.94 per cent for the whole reform period 1980–2012, which is lower than the double-digit official figure. TFP accounted for less than one of those percentage points, and was especially low in industries most subject to government intervention, for example, the 'energy' industries. TFP growth reached its highest level in the 1990s (1.63 percentage point contribution to annual average growth). TFP growth eased from the turn of the century, influenced by the rapid expansion of investment in state-connected industries in the fiscal and monetary expansion in response to the East Asian Financial Crisis. TFP growth then collapsed after 2007, as a result of the even larger fiscal and monetary expansion in response to the recessionary pressures from the GFC.

Amid rising pessimism as to China's growth trajectory, Wing (Chapter 7) identifies some of the characteristics of the Chinese economy that led to current challenges. Like Wang and Zhou (Chapter 4) and Wu (Chapter 5), he highlights the role of the expansionary policies in response to the GFC in inflating the roles of state-connected enterprises, increasing investment to levels that were counterproductive to development, and cutting across the structural reforms that are necessary for sustained strong growth. In outlining important structural reforms that would help to entrench dynamism into China's economy, Wing focuses on the need for China to dramatically rein in the soft-budget constraint to ensure fiscal sustainability. Correcting manager incentives, broader labour market reform and land reforms, and a strong push toward a more innovative economy are all policies that would help to China to move toward becoming a developed economy. But they will not be implemented unless the state is able to constrain the growth of state-connected industries that are responsible for low productivity, excessive debt and vulnerability to financial instability.

Growth and the demographic transition

Three chapters discuss ways in which two dimensions of China's demographic transition affect China's growth prospects. Cai et al. (Chapter 3) focus on the headwind to growth from the end of the demographic dividend and see reform of the *hukou* system as an important offset to this supply-side cause of deceleration of growth. Meng et al. (Chapter 8) discuss how inhibitions on permanent urban settlement of migrants reduces propensity to consume, and therefore cuts across government goals of increasing the contribution of consumption to increases in demand. Johnston et al. (Chapter 10) examine an old anxiety about the early Chinese transition—about getting old before rich—and gives us reason to reconsider old expectations.

Cai et al. (Chapter 3) discuss the critically important population and labour market dimensions of supply-side constraints on Chinese growth. Alongside excessive investment in industries favoured by the fiscal expansions in response to the East Asian Financial Crisis late in the twentieth century and the GFC 2007–08, China's demographic transition and labour market turning period have been the most important source of the slowdown in TFP in recent years. This chapter explores these dimensions of the growth deceleration in rich detail. The slowdown in transfer of people from rural (not only, or now even mainly, agricultural) to urban employment has been a major source of productivity growth through many channels. Its slowing exacerbates the drag on TFP and output growth that was bound to come with the end of the demographic dividend. Reform of residency rights (the *hukou* system) could allow the continued flow of workers from rural to urban areas over the next decade to help in the balancing of the relatively rapid ageing of China's urban populations. Reform would also contribute to the necessary increase in investment in human capital. Together with allowing working migrants plus families access to urban social security, this can support China's transition to consumption-led growth. It would be an important support for China's transition from upper-middle income to high-income status. The authors encourage Chinese policymakers to eliminate institutional barriers that deter labour supply and TFP growth and to set a target for the growth rate that is aligned with China's stage of development.

Meng et al. (Chapter 8) study the constraints that inhibit rural-to-urban migrants from being more responsive to the needs both of their own families and consequently of the needs of China's economy. The current system of denying access to subsidised education and health services in the rural–urban migrants' cities and towns of residence enforces family separation, the need to split incomes and to increase precautionary savings. Meng and colleagues find that migrant consumption rises with the length of urban residence but that peak consumption is seldom reached thanks to residence restrictions prohibiting long stays. Internal migration reforms are thus fundamental to the next phase of China's economic transition, which relies on much greater contributions of consumption to demand growth.

Johnston et al. (Chapter 10) take a fresh look at a subject that has generated much anxiety in China about the prospects for successfully graduating to developed country status: an unusually strong and early demographic transition is causing China to grow old before average incomes reach high levels. Population ageing has been associated with decline in the share of the population that is of working age since around 2011. Since the early 1980s it has been feared that China's unique 'one child policy' and resulting premature population ageing would inhibit China's transition to a high per capita income economy. This chapter sheds a different light on 'getting old before getting rich'. The studies of transitions into the high-income group of countries that are presented in this chapter show that China is not alone in seeking to rise to high average incomes with an ageing population. China is one of about 30 developing countries with ageing populations. Four countries have recently entered the high-income group despite having an ageing population. The success rate for transition to high-income status is lower for developing countries that have younger population structures. Ageing in developing countries may have a political economy upside: countries that have grown old before becoming rich are more likely to establish fiscally sustainable social security and taxation systems than developed countries that grew old after becoming rich. In the 'old first' countries like China, retirement programs are being established with reference to the fiscal constraints of high age dependence, low ratios of work-age to total population, longer life expectancies and more modest expectations of living standards.

Financial market performance and reform

Four chapters discuss the related questions of financial market efficiency in allocating resources, and changes in industry structure in ways required for the new model of growth. Dollar (Chapter 9) looks at direct foreign investment in China. Roberts and Zurawski (Chapter 12) illuminate complex changes in financial intermediation in China and the need for continuing reform. Huang et al. (Chapter 6) tell a remarkable story of financial innovation in China, in ways that open our eyes to the possibility of China moving the frontier of global efficiency. Liu et al. (Chapter 11) show how weaknesses in the financial sector have combined with other features of the Chinese economic transition to trigger dramatic stock exchange collapses in 2008–09 and 2014–15.

Two-way direct foreign investment is now an important feature of the Chinese economy. Dollar (Chapter 9) describes the extraordinarily rapid rise of China as a source of international investment over recent years. China is now the second largest international creditor, and is soon to be the first. Until a few years ago, China's investment abroad was very different from that of the established developed creditor countries. It mainly took the form of investing monetary reserves in the official securities of the United States and, to a lesser extent, other developed countries. China's investment abroad is now moving rapidly towards a more normal pattern, with direct foreign investment rapidly becoming more prominent. Dollar notes that Chinese direct investment seems to be characterised by indifference to governance standards in host countries. Dollar argues that China is much more closed than developed countries to inward direct foreign investment and that there would be benefits to both China and its partners in correcting this imbalance.

Roberts and Zurawski (Chapter 12) examine closely the pattern of indebtedness that has emerged recently in Chinese business and the economy. They observe that a rapid build-up in corporate leverage since the late 2000s is fuelling fears for financial stability and growth within and beyond China's borders. Discussion of leverage in China tends to emphasise the role of recent stimulus policies, especially through the financing of investment by SOEs. Analysis of non-financial companies on mainland public stock exchanges shows that SOEs account for the lion's share of overall leverage. However, this masks broader heterogeneity. There is emerging evidence of deleveraging. Private firms have tended to contribute more to leveraging since 2012, especially in the real estate and construction sectors, while mining, utilities and services have reduced their proportionate contribution. Sophisticated analysis throws interesting light on a complex reality. Results from a fixed-effects panel regression suggest a negative association between leverage and profitability and a positive correlation with firm size, collateral and industry leverage patterns. Weaker state-sector profitability and a shift in industry composition towards more highly leveraged sectors such as real estate and construction may explain much of the upward trend in leverage over recent years. Slow adjustment in firm behaviour could make it difficult for China's corporate sector to achieve a rapid deleveraging.

Liu et al. (Chapter 11) look closely at the two crashes in Shanghai's A-share stock market, around 2008 and 2014. This chapter uses new, more efficient econometric techniques to study these dramatic episodes in the wider context of movement of this Shanghai stock market. Different methods of analysis are assessed, and the most promising applied. Analysis of the two crashes covers November 2006 to January 2009, and May 2014 to July 2015. The two episodes have common characteristics in terms of bubble formation, development and bursting. In both, irrational behaviour, including noise trading and herding behaviour, plays a big part in the dynamics of boom and bust. The absence of a broad array of investment opportunities for Chinese investors and some features of government policies both encourage that irrationality.

Huang et al. (Chapter 6) describe an exciting development of global significance: the rapid emergence of internet banking. Internet finance has a history of more than a decade in China. It includes both information technology (IT) companies providing financial services and financial institutions applying IT to their more traditional services. The speculator rise of internet finance in China has been spurred by financial sector market failure that has resulted in limited access for small firms and low-income households. Huang and colleagues expect internet finance to become an increasingly effective tool for promoting inclusive finance, and that this will help to stimulate consumption, innovation and job-creation. Good outcomes depend upon the building of good infrastructure including for big data, qualified financial professionals and a regulatory approach that manages the balance between risk control and healthy innovation.

Part II: Resources, Energy, the Environment and Climate Change

Sustainable development is a prominent theme of the new model of growth. Eight chapters look at progress and challenges in different areas with implications for sustainable development. The strongest focus is on climate change and reduction in carbon emissions. Liu and Song (Chapter 14) tell the story of problems and so far limited success in adjustment to the realities of the new model of growth in the steel industry—one of the two industries (the other being coal) that are subject to greatest pressure in the new model because of their contribution to carbon and other emissions, as well as because they are inputs to investment goods industries that are meant to decline. Hu et al. (Chapter 13) discuss the promotion of new forms of urban development as one of many approaches to reducing carbon emissions. Zhang (Chapter 17) discusses the ambitious concept of 'ecological civilisation', which has entered official discourse alongside the new model of growth. Green and Stern (Chapter 18) describe and assess Chinese targets for reducing GHG emissions and policies for reaching them in the context of recent Chinese commitments to the international community. Zhao (Chapter 19) draws attention to the complex interrelationship between electricity sector regulation and the attainment of competing environmental and more traditional economic goals. Wu et al. (Chapter 20) look at links between policies on urban density and GHG mitigation. Buckingham (Chapter 16) looks at reforestation of the Loess Plateau as a wider environmental matter that also has implications for carbon sequestration. Finally, Wang and Zheng (Chapter 15) draw attention to the special problems of water management that are arising with sustained economic growth, and to some of the important links between water and energy.

Liu and Song (Chapter 14) analyse progress in adjustment of one of the pillars of the old model of growth, in the different circumstances of the 'new normal'. The investment-led growth that reached its highest levels from early this century to 2011 required huge expansion of the steel industry. The decline in rates of growth and the investment share of the economy has drastically reduced demand for steel. In steel, coal and cement more than any other industries, the new model of growth requires far-reaching adjustment. China became the world's largest steel producer in 1996. Steel production increased more than six times in a decade and a half, in response to the old pattern of China's growth. China became a net exporter of steel from 2006. Within the new model of growth, domestic steel consumption peaked in 2013. Steel production, however, kept rising until 2015, causing a glut of steel that has affected world markets, caused dozens of trade disputes and massive protectionist responses in the developed countries. The overshoot by Chinese steel producers reflects issues in the structure of the industry, especially with respect to firm size, ownership (roughly equally shared between state and private) and location (proximate to the coast or inland). Reform has proven to be difficult, being delayed by continued distortions in the financial sector. Steelmaking is also under pressure from the high priority of environmental objectives. Fundamental reform and retrenchment of uncompetitive plants is a precondition of return to profitability.

The creation of energy efficient and low-carbon urban hubs is now central to China's sustainable economic growth. By 2020 some 60 per cent of China's citizens are expected to live in cities, compared to just 18 per cent in 1978. Hu et al. (Chapter 13) evaluate China's official low-carbon city pilots along five dimensions: economic growth, energy utilisation, city construction, government support and residential consumption. Cities in the south are ahead of cities in the north in reducing carbon emissions, but the overall level of low-carbon development remains consistently low. To achieve the reorientation required by government objectives and commitments to the international community, further adjustments to policy are required, to develop market support for energy savings, research and development in urban transformation, strategic industry development and the wider use of energy-efficient technologies in China's cities.

Zhang (Chapter 17) examines the emergence of new elements of climate change and energy policy to reconcile continued growth with acceptable domestic and international environmental outcomes. China's government faces intense pressure at home and abroad to reduce its environmental footprint. Since late 2012, this agenda has been driven by the national goal to become an 'ecological civilisation'. This chapter introduces China's energy and environmental goals, and the 10 related mitigation policies and measures. The latter include mandating the closure of small, energy-inefficient electricity plants, and low sulphur requirements for thermal power plants. Other initiatives include the low-carbon city development pilot program, and the wide range of incentives for investment in renewable energy. These have brought victories in immediate battles, but not yet in the war to establish a low-carbon economy.

Green and Stern (Chapter 18) describe the dramatic changes in Chinese policy and outcomes on the relationship between economic activity and GHG emissions that have played a central role in a more positive global outlook on containment of global warming. Most important of all the many changes, China's coal consumption again fell significantly in 2015 after a fall in 2014. It is possible that China's coal consumption reached a peak in 2013, after contributing most of the growth in global coal use from the turn of the century to 2011. This transition away from coal is the result of changes in the structure of China's economy and a far-reaching set of policies. Both are acting to change energy efficiency and the energy supply mix and also the dynamics of energy demand. The trajectory of growth in China's total primary energy consumption has fallen dramatically, from a compound annual rate of more than 8 per cent per year between 2000–13 to less than 1 per cent year-on-year in 2015. The outlook for China's carbon dioxide emissions has changed even more dramatically over the last few years. A less than 2°C mitigation pathway for the world climate system has become feasible, creating a chance for realisation of the goals of the global climate agreement signed by 195 countries in Paris in December 2015.

Zhao (Chapter 19) looks at issues of central importance to implementation of China's climate change objectives: environmental standards, encouragement of low-emissions energy and electricity reform. China's electricity generation sector has been the world's largest since 2011. Coal-fired generation accounts for 70 per cent of installed thermal power capacity and 75 per cent of generation, which is more than double the share in the United States. Together with the high scale of production, this has brought massive environmental externality costs, of national and international consequence. Since the mid-1990s, the government has experimented with firm and consumer-level market mechanisms and reforms for improving the efficiency and reducing the externalities of China's electricity industry. This chapter presents the results from modelling of Chinese consumer willingness to pay via in their monthly electricity bill for clean energy, and from analysing the results of a survey of the opinion of power generation plants on the effects of various policies on the efficiency of their operations. Market-based regulation has been useful, but is less effective for being imperfectly coordinated with command-and-control mechanisms. Despite continuing massive change, China's electricity sector remains in transition.

Wu et al. (Chapter 20) look at how the density of Chinese cities affects carbon emissions. In March 2014, Premier Li Keqiang announced to China's national legislature that China would declare war on pollution like it did war on poverty. Ensuring that China has energy-efficient low-carbon cities is a big battle in that war. Flagship initiatives moving China in this direction include the Top 1,000 Enterprises Energy Conservation Action Program, the 10,000 Enterprises Conversation Low Carbon Action Program, and mandatory closure of small and inefficient power plants. This chapter discusses China's energy and environmental goals and policy measures, with a focus on the low-carbon urban development experimentation that began in July 2010 in five provinces and eight cities. Green transportation, industry and household energy efficiency and optimisation of space lie at the heart of the bigger agenda to ensure that cities that are housing an increasingly large majority of China's citizens over time will contribute to sustainable development.

In Chapter 16, Buckingham looks at one of many reforestation programmes in China: the reforestation of the Loess Plateau. Historic forest loss has made China one of the world's most forest-deficient countries and also the world's largest importer of timber and wood-based products. Rapid environmental development has also caused widespread damage to soils and water supply. On the other hand, China now has the highest rate of afforestation in the world, and forestry goals also recently began to feature in the FYP. China's post-2020 climate commitments include increasing forest cover by 50–100 million hectares in order to create a 1-gigaton carbon sink. Lessons from a more than two-decade restoration project, in China's Loess Plateau offer a seminal reforestation study and broader policy reference point. Other initiatives have been less successful, partly because forest cover tends to be higher in poorer areas, whose residents battle for their own survival first.

Wang and Zheng (Chapter 15) look at China's challenges and strategies for confronting water shortage. The dynamics of water withdrawal and energy consumption are sensitive to common influences, but few studies have explored these trends together. Wang and Zheng undertake a panel data analysis of 36 industrial sectors 2002–12, and find that the two dominant factors driving water and energy consumption—economic scale and resource intensity—interact with each other. Sectors growing more strongly economically made more effort to improve resource efficiency, of both water and energy. Growth of some industrial sectors including smelting and electricity production led to rising energy and also water consumption. Optimal policymaking to reduce water and energy consumption would take into account the many interactions between the two.

References

Aoki, M. (2012), Five phases of economic development and institutional evolution in China, Japan and Korea, in M. Aoki, T. Kuran and G. R. Roland (eds), *Institutions and comparative economic development*, Basingstoke, UK: Palgrave Macmillan.

Bai, C. and Zhang, Q. (2014), The rates of return to capital and the analysis of the determinants, *The World Economy*, 10: 3–30.

Cai, F. (2016), *Understanding the slowdown of the Chinese economy: A supply-side perspective*, Working Paper, Beijing: Chinese Academy of Social Sciences.

Cai, F. and Lu, Y. (2013), The end of China's demographic dividend: The perspective of potential GDP growth, in R. Garnaut, F. Cai and L. Song (eds), *China: A new model for growth and development*, Canberra: ANU E Press.

Fei, J. C. H. and Ranis, G. (1964), *Development of the labor surplus economy: theory and policy*, Homewood, Ill.: Richard D. Irwin for the Economic Growth Center, Yale University.

Garnaut, R. (2015), The new model of growth and the global resources economy, in L. Song, R. Garnaut, F. Cai and L. Johnson (eds), *China's domestic transformation in a global context*, Canberra: ANU Press.

Garnaut, R., Cai, F. and Song, L. (eds) (2013), *China: A new model for growth and development*, Canberra: ANU E Press.

Garnaut, R. and Song, L. (eds) (2006), *The turning point in China's economic development*, Canberra: ANU E Press.

Lewis, W. A. (1954). Economic development with unlimited supplies of labour. *Manchester School of Economic and Social Studies*, Vol. XXII (May), pp. 139–191.

Manuelli, R. and Seshadri, A. (2014), Human capital and the wealth of nations, *The American Economic Review*, 104(9): 2736–2762.

McMillan, M. S. and Rodrik, D. (2011), *Globalization, structural change and productivity growth*, NBER Working Paper No. 17143, Cambridge, Mass.: National Bureau of Economic Research.

Minami, R. (1973), *The turning point in economic development: Japan's experience*, Tokyo: Kinokuniya Bookstore.

National Bureau of Statistics (NBS) (various years), *China Statistical Yearbook*, Beijing: China Statistics Press.

Song, L., Garnaut, R., Cai, F. and Johnson, L. (eds) (2015), *China's domestic transformation in a global context*, Canberra: ANU Press.

The Conference Board (2015), *The Conference Board total economy database: Summary tables*, New York: The Conference Board. Available from: conference-board.org/data/economydatabase/.

Part I: Reform and Macroeconomic Development

2. Mostly Slow Progress on the New Model of Growth

Ross Garnaut

We said in the introductory chapter to the 2013 China Update book that contemporary changes in economic policy and structure were so comprehensive and profound they represented a new model of Chinese economic growth (Garnaut et al. 2013a). The new model had conventional economic and more subtle institutional dimensions. We (Garnaut et al. 2013b) and Huang et al. (2013) explored the former and Dwight Perkins explored the institutional changes (Perkins 2013).

The new model encompassed a moderately lower rate of growth of output (around 7 per cent, compared with around 10 per cent, on average, over the first 11 years of the century); a shift in resource allocation from investment to consumption and, within consumption, some increase in the relative importance of services; reversal of the tendency within the old model for growth towards greater inequality in income distribution; reduction in the adverse environmental impacts of economic growth, globally in relation to climate change and locally in relation to air and water quality; and reform of economic institutions so these outcomes would be achieved within an economy that was more market-oriented and more deeply integrated into the international economy.

I said in Chapter 2 of the 2015 book that China up to the end of 2014 was moving in the directions required by the new model of growth in terms of the main macroeconomic parameters, but that progress was slow and in its early stages. One exception to the generally slow progress was in the transformation of the environmental impact of growth, where a new trajectory of change had been established. It was too early to tell whether there had been positive progress on the qualitative, institutional dimensions of change, but there certainly had not been decisive movement to that time.

This chapter takes another look at progress to date, discussing some of the main official statements and private debates about the economy over the past year, examining some of the main changes in the economy against the objectives of official policy.

Official statements and policy on the new model of growth

The main elements of the Thirteenth Five-Year Plan (FYP) (2016–20) were agreed to at the fifth plenary session of the Chinese Communist Party's Eighteenth Central Committee in October 2015. The plan outline was approved by the National People's Congress in March 2016 and comes into effect this year. The full planning documents await release by ministries, provincial and local governments and other public institutions. Official statements on the new plan, including in the Premier's report to the National People's Congress in March, have revealed its main elements to the public.

The new FYP is an evolutionary document. It builds on and expands earlier official statements on the new model of growth and provides us with the most elaborate statement to date on its content and implementation. An early goal is to build a moderately prosperous society by 2020, with per capita output doubling from 2010 to 2020. Implementation of what the Chinese President and Communist Party have called the 'China dream' (Xi 2012) will be achieved in an international context. This will see 'the great revival of the Chinese nation … to stand more firmly and powerfully among all nations around the world and make a greater contribution to mankind' (Xi 2012). These themes were reiterated in the Thirteenth FYP proposal.

There will be a shift from investment to consumption, alongside a shift in the balance from exports towards domestic demand. The services share of the economy will rise from about half in 2015 to 60 per cent over the five years. Lower investment logically accompanies the lower goals for economic growth. The government remains committed to doubling total output and per capita income over the decade 2011–20. A rapid start early in the decade means that this can now be achieved with gross domestic product (GDP) growth in the range of 6.5–7 per cent over the period, with 6.5 per cent a minimum target.

The statements about the FYP expand on themes that are well known from official statements back to the beginning of the decade and from the Twelfth FYP—growth will: be of 'higher quality'; emphasise equitable distribution of income ('inclusive growth'); minimise negative environmental impacts ('green growth to build an ecological civilisation'); rely on markets at home and abroad; and deepen China's engagement with the international economy.

'Higher-quality' growth will come from an emphasis on innovation, with high reliance on science and technology and advanced use of the internet. By 2020, 60 per cent of economic output will come from applications of science and technology, which will be accompanied by decommissioning of much capacity in heavy industries such as steel and coal. More than RMB100 billion has been put aside to assist employees affected by structural adjustment in steel and coal to prepare for and find new jobs. There is a protectionist tinge to some of the goals for industry structure and industrial development, with some emphasis on developments of 'national champion' firms in important industries.

Inclusive growth and equity in income distribution will be pursued through improvement of infrastructure and services in rural and other poorer regions and extension of social security protections from some urban residents to the whole of the population. Seventy million people will be lifted from poverty, completing the process of removing poverty in China. The proportion of people enjoying 'middle incomes' will be increased and the incomes of people in the lower echelons of the distribution increased. Urbanisation will be one of the instruments of inclusive growth, with the proportion of urban residents rising from 55 per cent to 60 per cent of the population. The '*hukou*' system of residential permits will be reformed, with all urban residents having access to urban services and barriers to movement to cities removed. The one-child limit will be raised to two children per family, which is expected to ease the growing challenges of an ageing population.

Perhaps the largest and most important policy developments relate to 'green growth' and the development of an 'ecological civilisation'. China will build a low-carbon economic system. Officials' performance indicators will be restructured to wean society from the old singular emphasis on increased output to include reference to environmental effects. There is strong emphasis on improving domestic water and air quality and conserving the natural environment throughout China. High energy efficiency, recycling of materials and increasing the proportion of energy generated from renewable sources are prominent goals. The transport sector will be restructured to rely on low-carbon technologies. There is strong commitment to meet goals on greenhouse gas (GHG) emissions articulated by President Xi Jinping in his joint statement with US President Barack Obama in Beijing in November 2014, as developed in China's statements at the United Nations (UN) meeting on climate change in Paris in December 2015. The innovation in the Xi–Obama statement was its acceptance of a limit on emissions. However, the announced limit—peaking by 2030 and earlier if possible—was not ambitious given what Chinese mitigation efforts were already achieving. There will be a national permit system to constrain emissions and a national water management system. Commercial logging of forests is to be banned.

The FYP repeats and extends the emphasis in earlier policy statements on greater use of markets for domestic and international transactions. This will require development of a rule of law and credibility in judicial processes. The proportionate role of state entities in the economy will be reduced.

There are considerable statements about deepening international integration. Two-way movements of foreign direct investment (FDI) will be encouraged, with restrictions on entry of FDI limited by a 'negative list' and commitment to foreign enterprises being subject to national treatment. China will participate in international financial liberalisation, through making the Chinese yuan convertible on the capital account and removing barriers to its use as an international currency. Barriers to international trade will be reduced by facilitating transactions in border areas and through multilateral trade agreements and bilateral investment agreements. China's initiatives in facilitating investment in infrastructure related to trade and development through the 'One Belt and One Road' program, the Asian Infrastructure Investment Bank (AIIB), the Silk Road Fund and the new Development Bank will be important vehicles for promoting deeper integration of the Chinese economy into the global economy (Callaghan and Hubbard 2016). China will participate actively in global economic governance and in the making of rules for international exchange.

The announcements over the past year and, in particular, the FYP consolidate and extend the directions set since 2011, which involved greater departures from established directions of development when they were embodied in the Twelfth FYP (2011–15). The China Update group had to invent a name for the change of direction when it was first apparent—calling it the new model of Chinese growth. It now has an official name: the 'new normal'. How is performance within the new normal shaping up?

Economic growth outcomes and prospects

Chinese GDP increased by 6.9 per cent in 2015—the lowest rate of growth since 1990, but within the 'new normal' range (Figure 2.1). Among many signs of weakness, wages rose more slowly than in recent years. The weak impulse of growth became more evident early in 2016. GDP growth in the year to the March quarter fell to 6.7 per cent, with many market participants and analysts expressing anxiety about growth continuing to fall until it was well below the official target range. Premier Li Keqiang seemed to be setting out to remove these concerns in his March statements after the National People's Congress, which underlined the importance of meeting the target rate of growth.

In an economy in which market dynamics are important to total investment and consumption, how can the government be confident of delivering on its aim to maintain growth at 6.5 per cent per annum or higher? The short answer is that it cannot be certain that it can do so while maintaining progress on structural reform within the new model of growth.

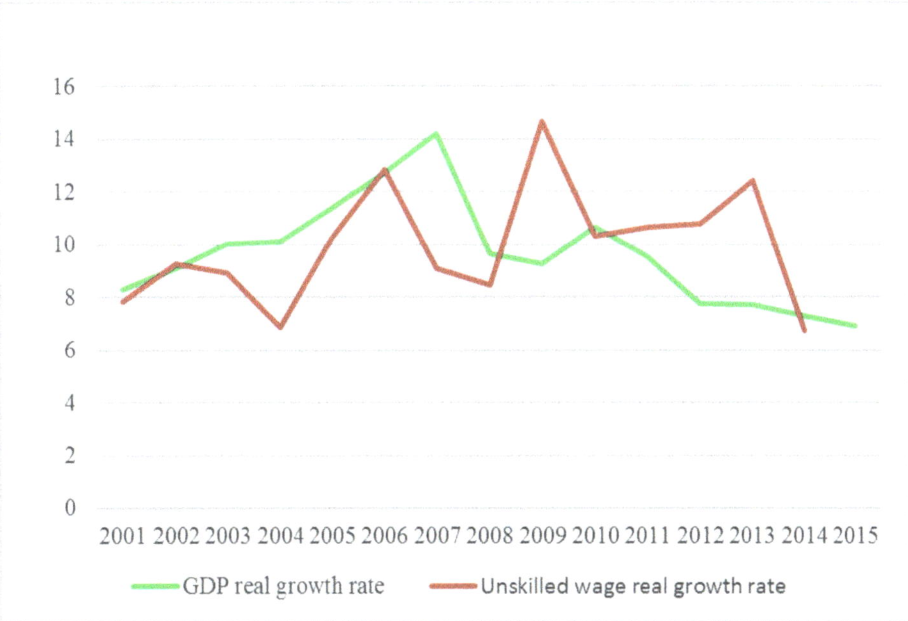

Figure 2.1 GDP real growth rate and unskilled wage real growth rate

Sources: World Bank (various years); NBS (various years).

In the short term, there is a risk that the anticipated decline in business investment as a share of economic output will proceed more rapidly than the anticipated increase in consumption. The government will then face a choice between reverting to fiscal and monetary expansion to maintain growth in demand or maintaining the pace of structural reform. Fiscal and monetary expansion in the forms favoured in earlier years tends to increase the role of public enterprises and the public sector more generally, increases the indebtedness of public institutions, reduces reliance on market exchange and slows reform of institutions that are important in the new model of growth. Certainly, the immense Keynesian fiscal and monetary expansions that insulated China from the worst effects of the East Asian Financial Crisis of 1997–99 and the Global Financial Crisis (GFC) of 2008 extended the life of an old, obsolete and, in important ways, damaging model of growth.

The new model of economic growth embodies structural change at an immense scale. One can define a possible path of smooth adjustment that would see rapid but gradual offsetting changes in the main growth parameters that together ensure the continuation of reasonably strong growth in output, employment and incomes of most people. But it is possible—maybe likely—that intended investment falls for longer than intended consumption rises. On the supply side, productivity may not rise to compensate sufficiently for lower contributions from other sources of growth in output and incomes. In either case, but probably more quickly and immediately damaging where the shortfall is on the demand side, there would be disruption of growth in output and incomes. Disruption would introduce risks of financial or political dislocation compounding the initial loss of growth momentum.

The possibility of rough adjustment has loomed large over the past year. There has been anxiety that the fall in business investment—in particular, in relation to urban real estate—had been proceeding more rapidly than the increase in consumption, with contractionary consequences. There were signs in late 2015 and early 2016 that declining activity in urban real estate and associated heavy industry was leading to lower growth than anticipated in official statements. Concern about excessive reduction in the trajectory of growth led to substantial compensatory fiscal and monetary expansion and to some public debate about whether there had been reversion to an emphasis on growth at the expense of institutional reform. The Communist Party—undoubtedly from the highest authority—sought to bring the debate to an end with a prominent article in the *People's Daily* in May on the importance of holding firm to structural change associated with reform.

Smooth adjustment was challenged through 2015 by declining values and associated panic in the Shanghai and Shenzhen stock markets. Official intervention to halt the fall through suspension of trading and official purchase of stocks initially increased uncertainty and exacerbated the panic. The interventions were a setback for reform to build a more market-oriented economy. The main long-term legacy is probably an acceptance for the future that arbitrary interventions in markets are likely to do more harm than good.

Adjustment to the new model of growth requires for a while an absolute reduction in total investment and not just a fall in the investment share of expenditure. Change in the required level of investment—and therefore demand for inputs into investment—depends not on the rate of growth in the economy, but on changes in the rate of growth. The rate of growth of output is expected to fall by about one-third within the new model of growth—from about 10 per cent per annum to 6.5–7 per cent (and eventually to lower levels). In the absence of changes in the productivity-related influences that determine the capital–output ratio, the level of investment can be expected to fall by a similar proportion. Consumption has to rise quickly and by a large amount to maintain domestic demand that is consistent with maintenance of the new, lower potential rate of growth.

The new model of growth is meant to rely much more heavily on expansion of domestic demand and less on international demand as revealed in growth in net exports. There was large and rapid progress in reducing net exports (the trade surplus) and also the current account surplus as domestic investment increased in the fiscal and monetary expansion in response to the GFC. Over the past two years, there has been some reversal of this tendency. Weak domestic demand has been partially compensated by an increase in the trade surplus.

The tendency since 2013 for the trade surplus to rise again from the much lower levels after the GFC strengthened in 2015 (Figure 2.2). The trade surplus has increased to levels that put in doubt progress towards one of the central macroeconomic objectives of the new model of growth: increased reliance on domestic rather than international demand. There was a major correction to the hugely excessive surpluses immediately before the GFC, but the lift in the surplus over the past two years has removed half of the early progress. The current account surplus has not increased in line with the trade surplus, partly because of diminished earnings on overseas investments in the contemporary environment of low global interest rates.

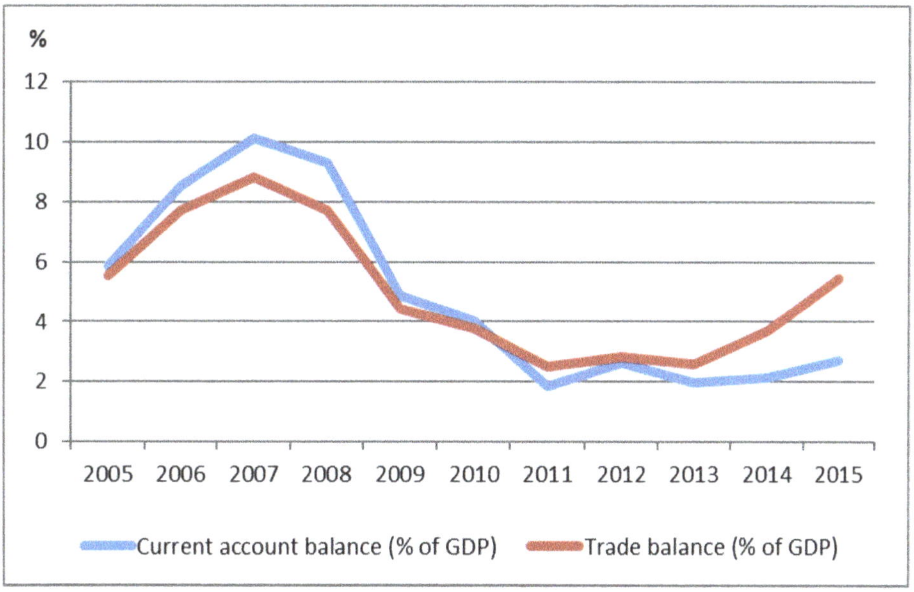

Figure 2.2 Trade and current account balances

Sources: World Bank (various years); State Administration of Foreign Exchange (2015); and NBS (various years).

Some aspects of China's international economic strategy are designed to underpin a continuing trade surplus and to reduce the pressures for domestic structural change. This will help to keep the scale of structural adjustment within manageable limits. The developed countries and China in recent times share a tendency for total savings to exceed investment. Capital outflows from these countries have tended to be disproportionately among themselves rather than to lower-income developing countries. Larger movements of capital to lower-income economies would support growth and employment in the developed countries themselves, as well as supporting higher levels of growth in developing countries. Capital flows from developed to developing countries would be most valuable to the home and host countries if they were concentrated in long-term investments in income-generating infrastructure. Higher levels of infrastructure investment in developing countries, in turn, would help to hold up demand for capital goods and inputs into construction and so reduce the amount of structural change that is necessary in the developed countries and China as a result of lower growth rates and investment levels.

The big barrier to higher levels of investment from the developed countries and China in the developing countries has been the absence of institutions to support confidence in market exchange and reduce perceptions of risk around such transactions. Private markets alone have not been able to provide the necessary confidence in high levels of investment in infrastructure from developed to developing countries. China's strong focus on the building of institutions for channelling investment from itself and other high-income countries to developing countries—the AIIB, the new Development Bank, the Silk Road Fund and the financial institutions being established around the 'Belt and Road' initiative—can be seen as filling this gap. Already China's efforts have spurred increased activity in developed countries in channelling funds to support infrastructure investment in developing countries—for example, through increased Japanese support for the lending of the Asian Development Bank.

It is possible that the scale of international investment supported by the new public lending institutions could end up being large enough to make a larger trade surplus—with higher proportions of capital goods and materials—a permanent feature of Chinese macroeconomic balance. This would ease the extent of domestic contraction of industries supplying capital goods within China within the new model of growth. If China's example were influential internationally, it could be helpful to the maintenance of employment and growth in the developed countries at a time of macroeconomic stress. It would be strongly supportive of development in low-income countries.

Figure 2.3 shows only modest progress in reducing the investment share and raising the consumption share of expenditure. It is change in the right direction, but slowly. A question arises: if the investment share of expenditure remains near where it was before the high point of the old model of growth, why has growth in output fallen by one-third? The answer is that total factor productivity (TFP) growth is much lower than it was. Much contemporary investment is wastefully deployed. This spoils the objective of the new normal to apply a larger part of the benefits of growth to increases in consumption and, more broadly, to raising the living standards of the Chinese people.

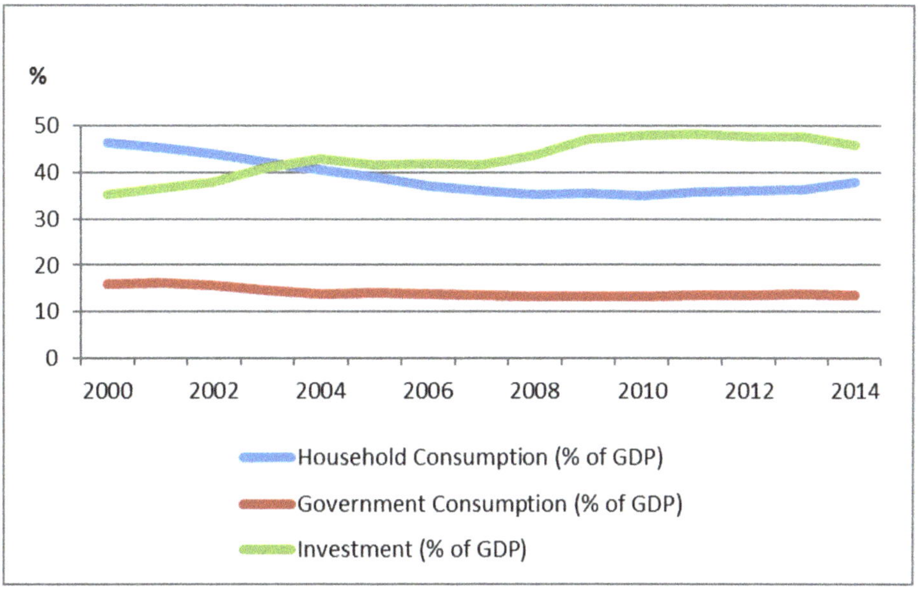

Figure 2.3 Consumption and investment share of GDP

Source: NBS (various years).

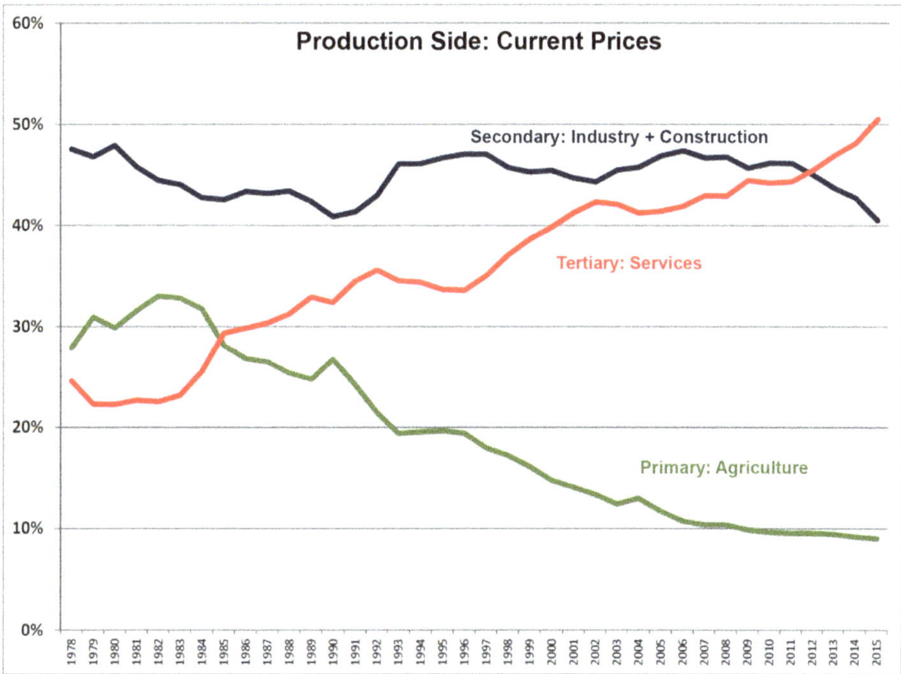

Figure 2.4 Composition of GDP (per cent)

Source: Naughton (2016).

Figure 2.4 shows a rapid increase in the services share of output when all goods and services are valued at current prices. The tendency emerged early in the reform period and has accelerated within the new model of growth since 2011. Naughton (2016) has noted that the increase in the services share is smaller when production is measured in constant prices. That is commonly the case in economies experiencing rapid growth in real wages and does not remove the significance of the major structural change that is taking place.

Institutional change and productivity growth

In the medium and longer terms, there is great uncertainty about the rate of TFP growth that will be achieved under the new model.

Smooth adjustment to a lower but reasonably strong growth rate, as envisaged in the new normal, would require the maintenance or even some acceleration of TFP growth back to levels preceding the GFC to offset part of the declines in the contributions of growth to the capital stock and labour. Rising real wages introduce pressure to raise productivity. The focus on improvement of the institutions for market regulation and exchange can raise productivity. The focus on increased investment in education within the new model of growth combines with the large decline in the school-age population to greatly improved labour quality, which shows up as increased TFP. Success in raising productivity growth depends especially on the institutional reforms discussed by Perkins (2013) in his contribution to this series. It depends on maintenance of openness to the international economy in all of its dimensions. It requires far-reaching financial system reform to allow capital to move quickly and in large quantities to its most productive uses. Strong growth in TFP requires acceptance of rapid changes in the composition of economic activity in line with rapidly changing comparative advantage. It requires improvement of market institutions, including through increased transparency and reliability of state mechanisms for regulating legal relations between the state and private entities and among private businesses. These improvements require strengthening of rights to intellectual and other property. Success in maintaining and lifting productivity growth requires easy and low-cost transfers of economic information within China and between Chinese and overseas individuals and enterprises.

Most of these requirements are accepted within the new normal model of Chinese growth—accepted, but difficult to apply.

There has been some progress in some areas of institutional and market reform but not much and not in many areas. And, in some areas requiring relatively free access to information through the internet, there has been retrogression. There has not yet been any sign of a lift in the low rates of productivity growth that emerged in the aftermath of the fiscal and monetary expansions of 2008 and 2009, which were discussed in Chapter 2 of the 2015 China Update volume. Indeed, data for 2014 have repeated the bleak story from 2013: there was no increase at all in TFP growth, with growth in output coming almost entirely from increases in the capital stock. Measurement is difficult, but good enough for us to be confident that TFP growth remains well below rates that were typical of the first three decades of reform (Figure 2.5).

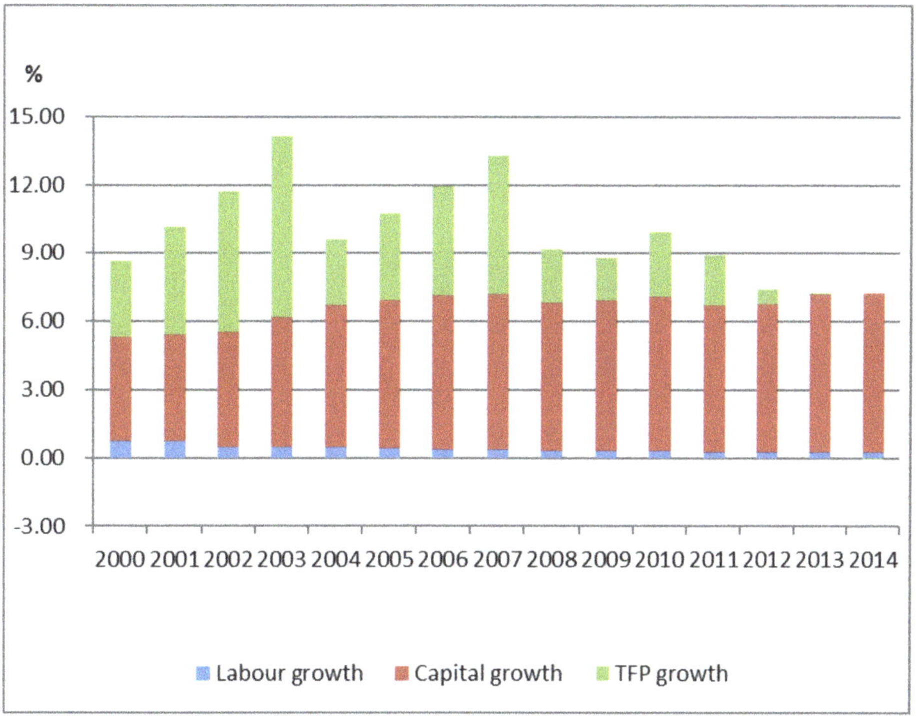

Figure 2.5 Contributions of components of GDP growth

Source: The Conference Board Total Economy Database (2015).

The continued—indeed, increased—reliance on growth in the capital stock with the implementation of the new normal would have massive effects on the industrial structure of demand. In particular, investment uses metals and energy far more intensively than consumption, so that sharply lower investment means a slump in demand for the products of heavy industry that had central roles in the old model of growth. Coal, steel and cement are the most prominent of the industries subject to lower demand growth—with coal also affected by the shift to low-emissions sources of power generation that follows the elevation of environmental amenity among national objectives. The need for contraction in production capacity of steel and coal figures prominently in the 2016 planning documents and official statements. The slow progress so far in reducing the investment share of GDP suggests that the greater part of adjustment to the new normal remains in the future.

The slowing of the rate of urbanisation after the turning period of Chinese economic development induces deceleration in growth in demand for all of the infrastructure required by a growing urban population, including housing and transport infrastructure. As with demand for investment goods, this induces an absolute fall in demand for many goods that occupied a large place within the old model of growth. This is an important part of the current anxiety about oversupply of housing in many Chinese cities—an oversupply that is transmitted with acceleration into industries like steel and cement, which supply inputs into real estate and infrastructure development.

The massive structural adjustment required by the new model of growth compounds risks of disruption that emerged in the mature stage of the old model of growth. The unprecedentedly high investment shares of GDP channelled disproportionately through state agencies led to overinvestment in some areas of heavy industry and infrastructure. Provincial and local government sponsorship of real estate developments in particular had been associated with strong growth in revenue during the later years of the old model of growth. Financial institutions that had provided funds for infrastructure and heavy industry are vulnerable to the deterioration in the fortunes of these mainstays of the old growth model—as are provincial and local governments, whose revenues came to depend excessively on new urban development during the period of rapid, investment-led growth. The pullback in investment in urban development and heavy industry under the new model has led to severe imbalances in local government finances and vulnerability on the balance sheets of many financial institutions (Yu 2009; Wong 2015). Financial reform is necessary for success in transition to the new model of economic growth, but is inhibited by the fragility of financial institutions deriving from the lending patterns of the era of investment-led growth.

Little or no progress seems to have been made in dealing with the accumulation of public debt, most importantly, at subnational government level.

The labour supply contribution to growth was small but positive early in the century and has since shrunk to negligible levels. That it remains slightly positive in the face of a decline in the population age cohorts that are conventionally considered to be the years of employment reflects some increase in labour force participation rates.

The growth in the capital stock has been the major contributor to growth in output through this century so far, with 2003 the only exception. Its absolute contribution to growth reached a high plateau in about 2006 and has remained there since, despite the contrary expectations from the new model of growth.

The low levels of TFP growth since the fiscal and monetary expansions in response to the GFC in 2008 were noted for the period to 2013 in last year's book. The data show that they continued through 2014 (Figure 2.5). There is no sign of a change in 2015. Economic development since 2011 has been characterised by greater reliance on increases in the capital stock than at any time in the reform period from 1978.

In a scenario of smooth adjustment to China's new model of growth, steady or rising contributions from increased productivity could have offset a decline in the capital contribution. Here the evidence points to the reverse: since the GFC of 2008, productivity growth has declined markedly and economic growth is now more reliant than ever on growth in the capital stock. The successful transition to lower but strong growth within the new model of growth requires this to be corrected. There is as yet no sign of correction.

Progress on inclusive growth

There has been modest movement in the desired directions for most of the measures contemplated in the new model of growth for their contribution to equity in income distribution.

The powerful labour market pressures for reduced inequality through the growth in wages relative to other incomes have diminished since 2013 as weaker labour demand growth has moderated the growth in real wages (Figure 2.1). Nevertheless, labour market developments have been contributing substantially to reduction of overall inequality as measured by the Gini coefficient (Figure 2.6). China's new model of growth—or, more generally, contemporary economic circumstances—has secured a reversal of the powerful tendencies for income disparities to widen in the quarter-century from the mid-1980s.

The extension of social security arrangements to a higher proportion of urban residents and gradually to rural residents has begun, but, to date, it is a modest beginning.

Local resistance to breaking down restrictions on migrants' rights has been strong and has slowed implementation of *hukou* reforms.

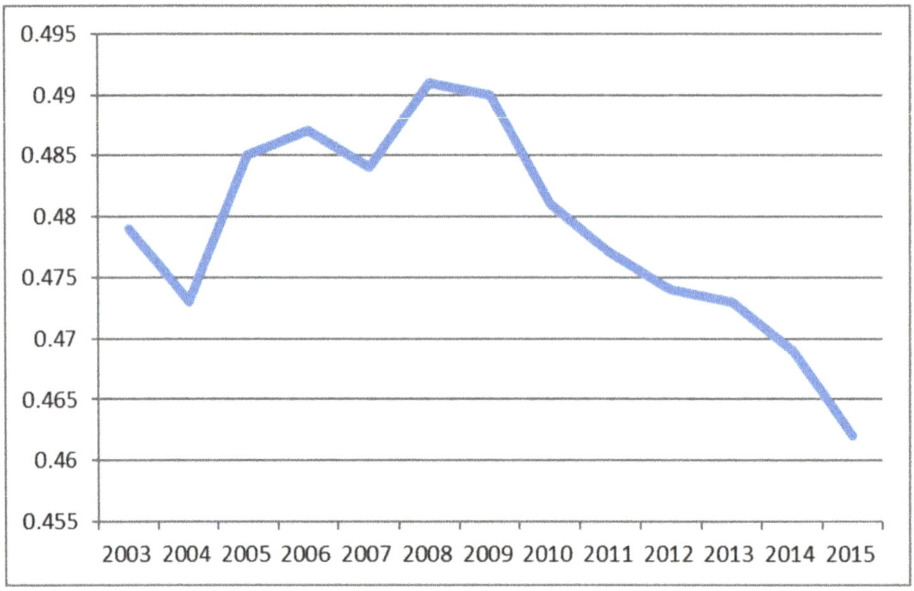

Figure 2.6 Gini coefficient in China

Source: NBS (various years).

Environmental effects of growth

The old model of growth had a devastating impact on the natural environment of China and the world. The growth in Chinese GHG emissions through the first 11 years of this century accounted for most of the substantial global increase. Chinese emissions greatly increased the urgency of global action on climate change. And yet there was no inclination to change China's contribution to the global problem before 2009.

The Chinese contribution to global emissions came primarily from coal; China contributed virtually the whole of the large increase in global coal consumption in the first 11 years of this century (Figure 2.8). At the same time as growing Chinese coal use heightened the urgency of global action on climate change, it imposed immense pressures on local air quality. This generated large public health problems and pressures for reform (Garnaut 2015).

China continues to make great progress on reducing the global and domestic environmental impacts of economic growth. This is the clearest example so far of success in the new model of growth.

Changes in the growth model have reduced the rate of growth in demand for energy. Policies motivated by domestic and global environmental concerns have radically reduced the importance of coal as a source of energy. These effects from the energy sector have been reinforced by reduced emphasis on investment in heavy industry and infrastructure with its intense use of metals (especially steel) and cement, the manufacture of which utilises coal intensively.

Table 2.1 records the continuing progress in reducing the electricity intensity of economic activity and the importance of fossil fuels in the generation of electricity. China aims to greatly increase the efficiency with which it uses energy in economic activity. Success in this aim is evident in Table 2.1, where the rate of growth in electricity demand has been well below the rate of GDP growth since 2012. Note that the decline in coal use in 2014 and 2015 is greater than the reduction in thermal power generation, for two reasons. First, while thermal power generation is mostly coal, there has been an increase in thermal generation from zero emissions (biomass) and lower emissions (gas) sources. Second, the continued replacement of less environmentally efficient by larger and more environmentally efficient coal generation plants has led to steady reduction in the amount of coal used per unit of power generated (and also some reduction in carbon emissions per unit of coal used).

Table 2.1 Electricity generation by source, 2010–15

	Quantity (million Mwh)						Rise over previous year %					
Year	Total	Thermal	Hydro	Nuclear	Wind	Solar	Total	Thermal	Hydro	Nuclear	Wind	Solar
2010	4228	3416	687	75	49	0	14.9	13.4	20.1	6.7	78.9	73.7
2011	4731	3900	668	87	74	1	11.9	14.2	–2.7	16.7	49.9	459
2012	4986	3925	856	98	103	4	5.4	0.6	28.1	12.7	39.1	412
2013	5372	4222	892	112	138	9	7.7	7.6	4.2	14.3	34	125
2014	5573	4205	1070	126	156	23	3.3	–0.4	20	12.5	13	155.6
2015	5605	4097	1114	166	157	38	0.6	–2.6	4.1	31.7	18.6	65.2

Source: China Electricity Council (various years).

More than the whole of the increase in electricity generation has come from non-thermal sources, with zero emissions, since 2013. Hydro-electricity remained the most important source of zero-emissions power. Weather limited the growth in hydro-electric generation in 2015, although investment in capacity continued at a rapid rate. Hydro-electric output can be expected to return to reasonably strong growth in future years. Wind was the second-largest source of zero-emissions energy again in 2015, with the rate of growth in supply rising despite the increased scale of generation. Nuclear power output returned to strong growth, in response to the resumption of investment in new capacity after the initial review of safety and policy spurred by the Fukushima disaster in Japan. Solar power again grew more rapidly than any other source of electricity, although the rate of growth continues to moderate as the level of output increases.

To the extent that the 'thermal power' category in Table 2.1 is read as a proxy for coal generation, the table underestimates the decline of emissions from electricity generation. While coal contributes most to thermal generation, there is an increasing contribution from biomass with zero emissions and from gas with much lower emissions than coal. This has displaced a small part of coal generation. Coal use in electricity generation has fallen more rapidly than thermal power output.

Chinese emissions from industry are also large by global standards. The high levels of investment in the old model of growth made China the locus of about half of steel and cement production, the manufacture of both of which uses coal intensively.

Figure 2.7 shows how China contributed almost all of the growth in global steel use from the turn of the century until the new model of growth changed the pattern of demand in 2012. Steel consumption reached its peak in 2013, and has since fallen significantly. Figure 2.7 shows how this caused global consumption of steel to stagnate in 2014 and 2015 despite modest growth in demand elsewhere.

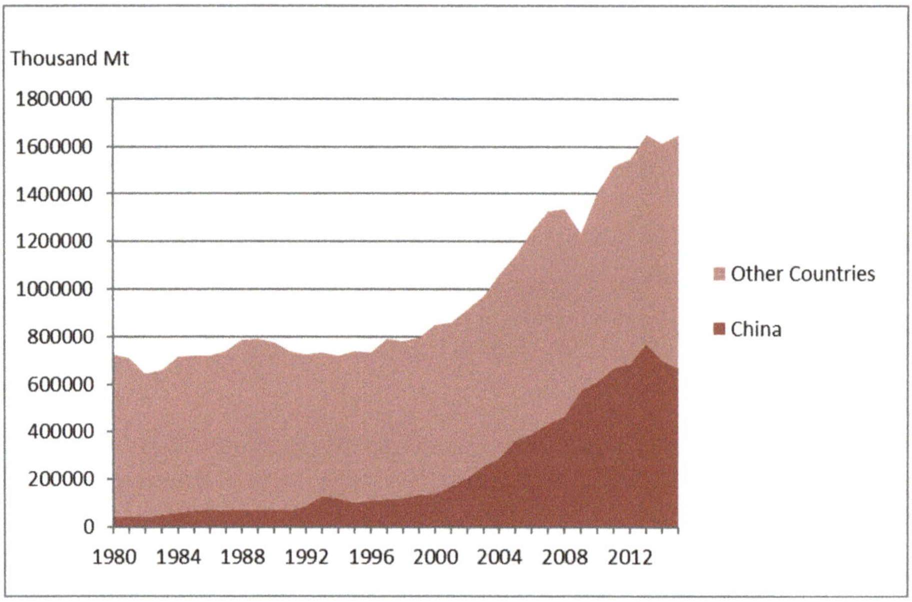

Figure 2.7 Steel consumption in China compared with other countries

Sources: World Steel Association (2015); and author's estimation.

Chinese steel production fell over these years, but much less rapidly than consumption. The difference was poured on to world markets, depressing steel prices below the cost of production in China and elsewhere. This generated a visceral protectionist reaction in much of the world. The increase in protection against Chinese steel imports into developed countries in 2015 and early 2016 is the most important retreat into protectionist policy in the global economy in the twenty-first century.

The environmental pressures from the use of coal in steelmaking and the losses being incurred by most steel enterprises have caused the Chinese Government to seek large reductions in steel output and manufacturing capacity. The reduction in capacity is being sought from use of blast furnaces. The environmental objectives of the FYP favour recycling of steel, and electric arc production from scrap is likely to steadily increase in importance through and beyond the period of transition to the new model of growth. The FYP and other policy statements have spoken of a reduction of 100–150 million tonnes of steelmaking capacity, which would make a substantial contribution to achieving the balance between global supply and demand. It is possible—I would say likely—that Chinese steel production from blast furnaces reached its all-time peak in 2013.

The declines in coal-based power generation and in steel and cement production are the main sources of a dramatic change in trajectory in Chinese coal use. After contributing nearly all of the growth in global coal consumption from the turn of the century to 2012, China has contributed its full share of a decline in coal use since then (Figure 2.8). GHG emissions probably fell in China and the world in 2015, for the first time outside recessionary circumstances in the major emitting countries. The reduction in Chinese coal use was the most important contributor to the decline in global emissions.

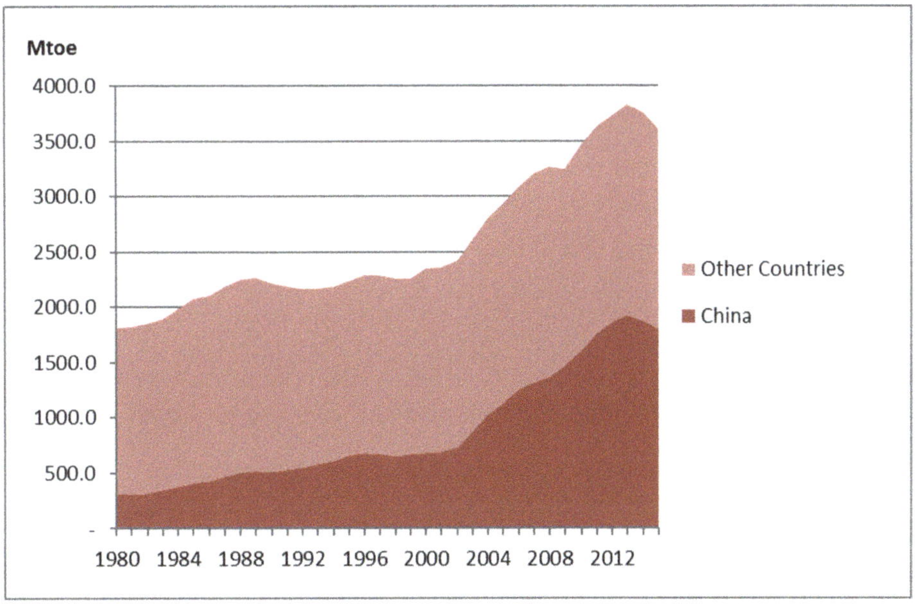

Figure 2.8 Coal consumption in China compared with other countries

Sources: BP (2015); and author's estimation.

The changes are of great importance to the quality of the Chinese domestic environment and to the prospects for the world avoiding extremes of human-induced climate change. China has arrested growth in coal use and emissions well in advance of its commitments to the international community in Beijing and Paris. However, while the turnaround in China's use of coal and its output of GHGs is of immense value to China and the global community, the levels of emissions remain well above reasonable assessments of the natural environment's capacity to absorb them without large problems.

The FYP envisages systematic efforts to apply science and technology to reducing carbon emissions throughout the economy. In the transport sector, the focus is on shifting from liquid and gaseous fossil fuels to zero-emissions electricity as a source of energy. Current plans envisage China having five million electric cars on the road by 2020 and increasing rapidly in number after that. This would provide the scale for mass production within China and reduction in costs for consumers everywhere, just as rising Chinese use and production of photovoltaic panels has reduced the costs of solar energy in all countries.

The recent progress in reducing Chinese coal use and GHG emissions is of extraordinary dimension, but it has to be only the beginning of a continuing effort. The implementation of the Paris agreement on climate change mitigation will require an intensification of the recent reduction in carbon emissions, until net emissions have been reduced to zero in the third quarter of the century.

China has made a start on the transition to its new model of growth. In terms of environmental impact, it has made a much larger start than close observers a few years ago would have thought possible. But all elements of transition have a long way to go.

As Premier Li Keqiang said in March 2016, the transition is a difficult one and it would be surprising if there were no disruptive bumps in the road.

References

BP (2015), *Energy charting tool*, London: BP. Available from: bp.com/en/global/corporate/about-bp/energy-economics/energy-charting-tool.html.

Callaghan, M. and Hubbard, P. (2016), The Asian Infrastructure Investment Bank: Multilateralism on the Silk Road, *China Economic Journal* 9(2): 116–139.

China Electricity Council (various years). Available from: www.cec.org.cn/guihuayutongji/tongjxinxi/.

The Conference Board Total Economy Database (2015). Available from: www.conference-board.org/data/economydatabase/index.cfm?id=27762.

Garnaut, R. (2015), The new model of growth and the global resources economy, in L. Song, R. Garnaut, F. Cai and L. Johnston (eds), *China's domestic transformation in a global context*, Canberra and Beijing: ANU Press and Social Sciences Academic Press.

Garnaut, R., Cai, F. and Song, L. (eds) (2013a), *China: A new model for growth and development*, Canberra and Beijing: ANU E Press and China Social Sciences Academic Press.

Garnaut, R., Cai, F. and Song, L. (2013b), China's new strategy for long-term growth and development: Imperatives and implications, in R. Garnaut, F. Cai and L. Song (eds), *China: A new model for growth and development*, Canberra and Beijing: ANU E Press and China Social Sciences Academic Press.

Huang, Y., Fang, F., Xu, P. and Xin, G. (2013), The new normal of Chinese development, in R. Garnaut, F. Cai and L. Song (eds), *China: A new model for growth and development*, Canberra and Beijing: ANU E Press and China Social Sciences Academic Press.

National Bureau of Statistics of China (NBS) (various years), *China statistical yearbook*, Beijing: China Statistics Press. Available from: www.stats.gov.cn/english/Statisticaldata/AnnualData.

Naughton, B. (2016), *Rebalancing, restructuring and reform: China 2016*, Sydney: Reserve Bank of Australia. Available from: rba.gov.au/publications/confs/2016/pdf/rba-conference-2016-naughton.pdf.

Perkins, D. H. (2013), New institutions for a new development model, in R. Garnaut, F. Cai and L. Song (eds), *China: A new model for growth and development*, Canberra and Beijing: ANU E Press and China Social Sciences Academic Press.

State Administration of Foreign Exchange (2015), Annual Report of State Administration of Foreign Exchange. Available from: www.safe.gov.cn/wps/portal/english/Home.

Wong, C. (2015), Can Xi Jinping's reforms be implemented? Let's look at China's fiscal architecture, Presentation to Centre for Contemporary Chinese Studies Academic Seminar, University of Melbourne, Melbourne, 5 March.

World Bank, World Development Indicators. Available from: data.worldbank.org/country/china.

World Bank (various years), World Development Indicators. Available from: data.worldbank.org/data-catalog/world-development-indicators.

World Steel Association (2015), *Crude steel production 2014–2015*, Brussels: World Steel Association. Available from: worldsteel.org/statistics/crude-steel-production.html.

Xi, J. (2012), Speech to the Politburo Standing Committee Members' meeting, 12 November 2012. Available from: www.bbc.com/news/world-asia-china-20338586.

Yu, Y. (2009), China's policy responses to the global financial crisis, *The 2009 Snape Lecture*, Melbourne: Australian Productivity Commission. Available from: pc.gov.au/news-media/snape-lectures/yongding.

3. New Urbanisation as a Driver of China's Growth

Cai Fang, Guo Zhenwei and Wang Meiyan

Introduction

The Chinese economy has experienced a substantial slowdown in growth since 2012. Colligating its pace, extent and duration, this slowdown is unprecedented since reforms were initiated in the late 1970s. A massive stimulus package implemented by the Chinese Government during the 2008–09 Global Financial Crisis had some shock impacts on growth but had no effect on the growth trend. China's gross domestic product (GDP) growth rate fell from its peaks of 14.2 per cent in 2007 and 11.3 per cent across the Eleventh Five-Year Plan (FYP) period (2006–10) to 6.9 per cent in 2015 and 7.8 per cent across the Twelfth FYP period (2011–15). Critically, this slowdown has not yet bottomed out in a manner consistent with usual macroeconomic fluctuations.

The slowdown of the Chinese economy—like the slowdown of the world economy—has thus become a topic of focus and increasing concern among economists. The matter is also important given China's particular stage of development—that is, upper-middle income status. China's capacity to tackle the challenges raised by the slowdown will determine whether it avoids or falls into the 'middle-income trap'—an even bigger theme in development economics. Adopting sound policies to navigate through the slowdown requires clear and prescient judgement of the economic situation.

Based on conventional wisdom and analysis, both international and domestic economic advisors to the Chinese Government tend to attribute the slowdown to a cyclical phenomenon caused by demand-side shocks. This idea is comparable with previous macroeconomic events that have occurred since reforms began in 1978, leading to a prescription of loose macroeconomic policies in hopes of stimulating investment. Lin (2011) cites two reasons for supporting this type of policy. First, he links the sharp decline in China's exports to the sluggish growth of the world economy and global trade, and notes that these are both external, demand-side factors. Second, by drawing comparisons between China's present development stage (per capita GDP as a percentage of the US GDP) and other East Asian economies at a similar point in per capita income history, he asserts that the window for achieving catch-up growth remains open to China, as does, therefore, potential for high growth. This relates to the fact that China's present per capita income—at 20 per cent of the per capita GDP of the United States—is only the equivalent of Japan in 1951, Singapore in 1967, Taiwan in 1975 and South Korea in 1977. For these economies, across the 20-year period after reaching this same share of US GDP per capita, the annual growth rate was 9.2 per cent in Japan, 8.6 per cent in Singapore, 8.3 per cent in Taiwan and 7.6 per cent in Korea. It is believed China, too, will be able to maintain this regional historical growth potential of at least 8 per cent.

This method of drawing development stage comparisons between East Asian economies does, however, overlook the effect of population on economic growth. In China's case, this means 'growing old before getting rich', whereas the other economies got rich before the population aged. Incorporating demographics into this type of comparison of East Asian growth precedents may shift the relative growth potential in the years after China reaches GDP per capita levels that are one-fifth of those of the United States.

Taking the year in which the working-age (15–59 years) population peaks (and falls thereafter) as the reference point,[1] China is not far behind its advanced East Asian counterparts. Specifically, China in 2010 is equivalent to Japan in 1990–95 and on par with Korea in 2010–15 and Singapore's forecast for 2015–20. Adding in the dependent population tails allows for comparison of the population dependency ratio—the ratio of the population aged 14 and under and 60 and over to the working-age population—which is commonly used as a proxy indicator for the demographic dividend. Comparing China's population dependency ratio trend with that of advanced East Asian economies, there are evident turning points from a fall to a rise in those economies—but these came when GDP per capita was much higher than the same dependency ratio levels in China (Figure 3.1). In Japan, the dependency ratio reached a point of inflexion in the early 1970s and did not rise significantly until the 1990s. However, in the case of China, South Korea and Singapore, there is relative synchronicity in the movement of the total population dependency ratio.

In sum, so far we have underscored that relative to China's cross-country per capita GDP level experience, its demographic transition has taken place much more quickly. As a result, China exhausted its demographic dividend much earlier in the development process than did today's high-income East Asian economies. Therefore, in assessing China's growth potential herein, the relatively rapid exhaustion of the demographic dividend—which was an important factor in 30 years of rapid GDP growth—should be taken into account. Accounting for the impact of demographic transition trends on the factors spurring economic growth, Cai and Lu (2013) estimate China's GDP potential growth. The estimated average potential growth rate is 9.66 per cent over the period 1979–94,

1 Data used for the comparison are from UN (2011).

10.34 per cent over 1995–2010, 7.55 per cent over 2011–15 and 6.20 per cent over the period 2016–20. According to their methodology for calculating the growth rate, supply-side factors—such as labour supply, human capital accumulation and total factor productivity (TFP) growth—and not demand-side factors produce this growth slowdown.

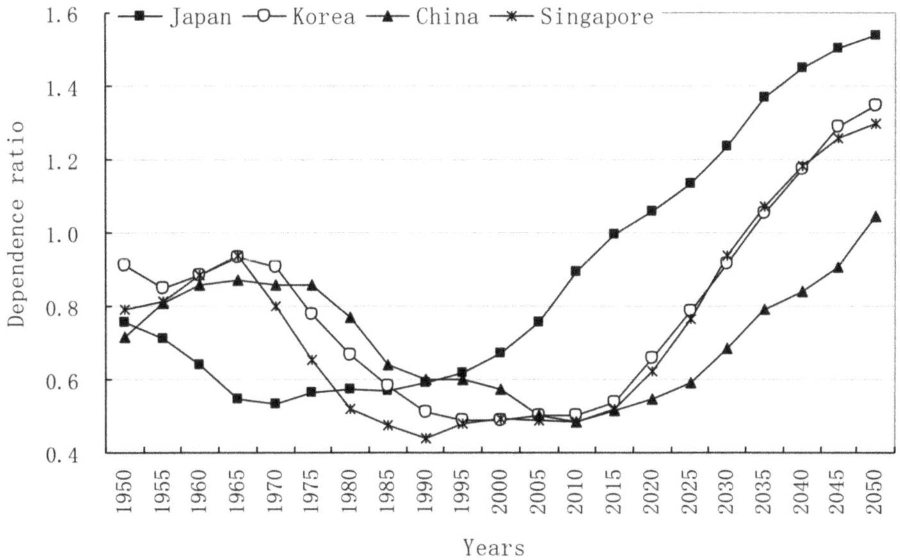

Figure 3.1 Comparison of population dependency ratio changes in selected countries

Source: UN (2011).

Some economists explain the slowdown of the Chinese economy by applying a convergence framework, which builds on the idea that as income levels converge towards high income, the opportunities for catch-up-style rapid growth diminish. Barro (2016), for example, asserts that no country, including China, can forever escape the 'iron law of convergence' of a 2 per cent growth rate. He thus predicts an imminent plunge in China's growth rate, from 6 per cent towards 3–4 per cent. In that case, China is unlikely to meet its official growth target, which is set to enable the country's per capita GDP to cross the threshold from upper-middle income to a high-income economy in the near future. Pritchett and Summers (2014) also predict that China's growth rate will revert to the world mean—namely, 5 per cent in the period 2013–23, followed by an average of 3.3 per cent over the decade starting in 2023. Despite some researchers having sought to identify country-specific factors (for example, Eichengreen et al. 2013), most predictions are part of an attempt to reveal a universal slowdown law, and thus generally ignore China-specific factors, including by failing to identify

China's potential to sustain a reasonable level of growth in the near future. Most forecasters, even if unintentionally, tend to offer pessimistic theses and negative bets on China's near-term growth potential.

So far, we have presented China-specific data and research on the supply-side factors that help to contextualise and explain the growth slowdown. In turn, we argue that policymakers in China should not seek a V-shaped rebound akin to expectations of recovery that follow classical business cycle theories. Instead, they should seek to eliminate institutional barriers that deter labour supply and TFP growth and target a growth rate that aligns with China's development stage. Such a rate would decline over time as smoothly and gradually as possible. The level and rate of decline should be sufficient to guarantee an L-shaped growth trajectory such that China completes the transition from upper-middle income to high-income economy status.

One intended structural driver of this type of economic growth is urbanisation and, in particular, reform of the residential registration (*hukou*) system. In 2014, the Chinese Central Government (CPC and the State Council 2014) issued a national plan promoting a new round of urbanisation. As it defined a people-centred urbanisation rather than focusing just on the expansion of urban areas, it was called 'new urbanisation'. The demand-side role that new urbanisation can play in stimulating growth has been studied intensively within China. In *The government work report, 2016*, Premier Li Keqiang (2016) notes that new urbanisation offers the highest potential to drive domestic consumption and growth. Wang and Cai (2015) quantified the potential contribution of consumption and saving shifts that would take place were migrants given full access to local public services and market opportunities in their adopted cities—that is, if migrants were granted full urban *hukou*.

This chapter views this 'new' urbanisation as an important component of supply-side structural reforms. It specifically discusses the potentially significant role that urbanisation, and *hukou* reform especially, can play in enhancing labour force participation and TFP growth, and hence in preserving China's growth momentum.[2] The next section of this chapter outlines the role that urbanisation and migrant workers have played in China's reform-era growth so far. The third section explores more deeply the dynamic composition and contribution of those migrant workers. Importantly, it draws attention to the impact of China's *hukou* system, which is inhibiting Chinese migrant mobility and security and, in the presence of rising labour supply constraints and rising dependency ratios, is increasingly inhibiting China's economic growth.

2 Unless specifically cited, population figures used in this chapter are the predictions of one of the authors. For details of these predictions, see Guo (2016).

Urbanisation in China's reform-era growth miracle

China's unprecedented growth since reforms began in the late 1970s offers a story of successful Lewis-type dual-economy development. Decomposition of growth sources over this period identifies the distinctive properties of China's growth: an unlimited and therefore guaranteed labour supply, accumulation of human capital, a high savings rate, high return to capital and allocative efficiency of resources via labour mobility (contributing greatly to TFP increases) (Cai and Zhao 2012). Because these sources of growth arise from a favourable stage of demographic transition, they are recognised as forming a demographic dividend. Less well recognised is the fact that this demographic dividend-supported growth was accompanied by an equally transformative process of urbanisation. In 1978, China's urbanisation rate was 17.9 per cent. This had increased to 54.8 per cent by 2014, meaning an annual increase of 3.2 per cent. This reflects the largest peacetime population movement in human history (Roberts et al. 2004).

This transfer of labour from the agricultural sector and rural areas to non-agricultural sectors and urban areas in China also underwrote the world's fastest sustained period of economic growth in the past three decades. To understand China's urbanisation experience, one has to understand the millions of migrant workers and the institutional settings in which they conduct their lives. In what follows, we more closely examine China's recent urbanisation and labour migration from the perspective of their capacity to drive economic growth.

Contribution to labour supply

Urbanisation driven by labour migration in China has, first, helped the country meet the strong demand for labour across the urban sectors. The unlimited flow of labour has been embodied in the outflows of surplus agricultural labour on one hand and inflows of migrant workers to urban sectors via urbanisation on the other. Given that the population ages at a faster rate in urban areas than in rural areas (which have a higher total fertility rate) and that the urban sector expands more quickly than the agricultural sector and rural economy in general, labour migration from rural to urban areas is inevitably related to economic opportunity.

In fact, in parallel with a peak in the working-age population, the number of urban workers with local *hukou* peaked in 2010, and has been declining since. In turn, any observable increase in total urban employment comes from the contribution of continual rural-to-urban migration. Utilising a variety of statistical sources and by making some necessary assumptions,[3] we summarise the composition of urban employment over the period 2001–14 in Table 3.1.

Table 3.1 Composition of urban employment (million)

	Covered by official statistics				Not covered
	Urban *hukou* (1)	Migrants (2)	Total (3)	Annual change (4)	Migrants (5)
2001	232.33	7.07	239.40	-	76.92
2002	239.04	8.76	247.80	8.40	95.94
2003	245.53	10.86	256.39	8.59	103.04
2004	251.33	13.43	264.76	8.37	104.80
2005	256.71	16.60	273.31	8.55	109.18
2006	274.74	21.56	296.30	22.99	110.56
2007	282.56	26.97	309.53	13.23	110.00
2008	287.53	33.50	321.03	11.50	106.91
2009	291.57	41.65	333.22	12.19	103.68
2010	294.94	51.93	346.87	13.65	101.07
2011	294.74	64.40	359.14	12.27	94.23
2012	291.34	79.68	371.02	11.88	83.68
2013	284.04	98.36	382.40	11.38	67.74
2014	271.99	121.11	393.10	10.70	47.10

Source: Cai (2016).

The data in Table 3.1 identify trends that may clarify some common points of confusion about China's urban employment figures. While Column 1 shows the decline in the number of employed *hukou*-holding urban residents from 2011, the number of migrant workers included in urban employment statistics increased (Column 2). The resulting change in total urban employment, shown as the percentage difference between Columns 2 and 3, increased from 3 per cent in 2001 to 30.8 per cent in 2014. The absolute contribution made by migrant workers to the urban worker pool that has in turn sustained the absolute expansion of total urban employment (Column 3) accounts for annual growth of urban employment in the range of several million to more than 10 million workers (Column 4). Column 5 presents the difference between the total number of migrant workers and those who are statistically included, suggesting there

3 For details, please see the explanation on Table 3.2 in Cai (2016).

remains a large though declining share of migrant workers outside official urban employment statistics, which continue to understate the migrant contribution to urban employment.

A scrupulous person may, however, identify a statistical trick in the urban employment numbers—that is, the inclusion of a higher share of migrant workers in the official statistical pool that drives recent numerical increases in urban employment. Otherwise, the current natural growth of the economically active population (3.8 million in 2014) could not support the expansion of urban employment. This does not necessarily imply that official statistics are evidence of data fraud. In reality, in recent years, as more and more migrant workers have signed employment contracts that increase their job security and participation rate in social insurance programs, they are more likely to be viewed as formal employees by their employers and be reported as such to statistical authorities. Such a change in statistical categorisation implies two things. One, as a result of strengthening labour market regulations, the formality of migrant workers' employment in urban sectors has increased. Two, since some of the increased number of urban workers are not really 'new entrants', but are reclassified migrant workers, the increase in urban employment reflected in the statistics does not indicate high growth prospects.

Preventing diminishing return to capital

Urbanisation has helped sustain China's high savings rate and therefore high return to capital (for example, Bai et al. 2006), making an overwhelming contribution to high-speed growth (Cai and Zhao 2012). Compared with rural workers who remain in rural areas and local urban workers, rural–urban migrant workers are, on average, significantly younger—for two reasons. First, the general experience of labour migration indicates that migrant workers are more advantaged in human capital endowment and other demographic features when compared with workers who remain in rural areas. Second, because China's demographic transition towards an ageing population has taken place earlier in urban than in rural areas, urban residents holding local *hukou* are significantly older than newly arriving rural–urban migrant workers. Attracted by the more productive and more developed urban sector (which has a higher per capita income), rural–urban migrants have helped to shape a more productive population structure by lowering the urban dependency ratio and helping to maintain a higher savings rate for the economy as a whole.

Using data from China's sixth national census, conducted in 2010, we compute and then compare the age structure difference between urban residents with local *hukou* and migrants without urban *hukou* (Figure 3.2). The data show that while the native urban population has aged rapidly, migrant arrivals have helped to mitigate the scale of urban ageing. Our calculations suggest that the native population produces a dependency ratio of 0.43, and migrants have a dependency ratio of 0.18. Bringing these figures together, current migration can reduce the urban dependency ratio to 0.35.

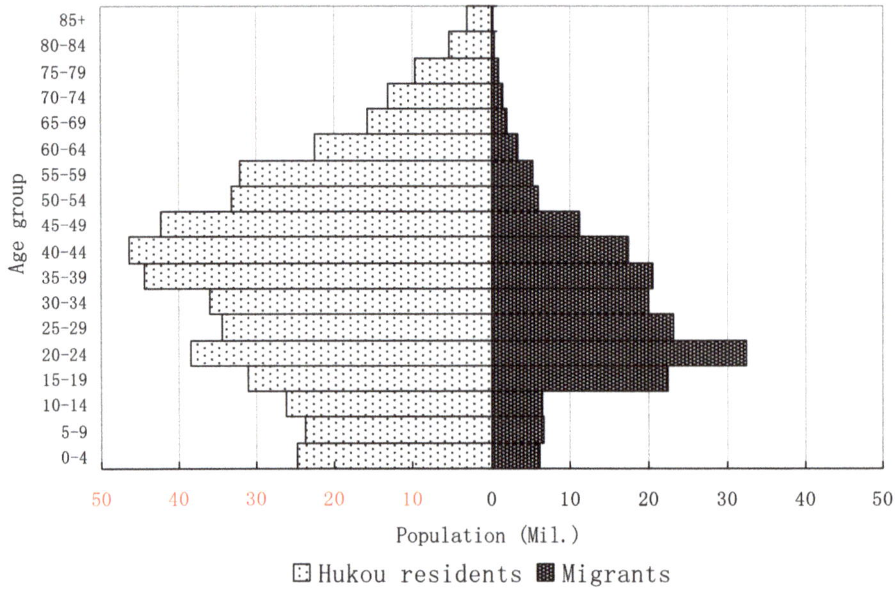

Figure 3.2 Age structures of *hukou* residents and migrants in urban areas, 2010

Source: NBS (2011).

Massive internal labour migration has helped the Chinese economy enjoy an unlimited supply of labour during most of the reform period, until the 'Lewis turning point' arrived in the early 2000s (Cai 2016: 3), preventing the phenomenon of diminishing return to capital of neoclassical growth theories and commonly seen in developed economies. In turn, studies have shown that throughout the reform period, Chinese growth produced a high return to capital (Bai et al. 2006) and that, as a result, physical capital accumulation made an overwhelming contribution to economic growth (Cai and Zhao 2012).

Improving the human capital of the urban workforce

In general in China, the contribution of migrant workers to enhancing levels of human capital in the urban labour force has been neglected. This relates to the common observation that migrant workers are, on average, less educated than the native residents and generally are able to assume only unskilled work. On average, it is statistically evident that, in China, migrant workers do indeed have fewer years of schooling than their urban counterparts. According to the

China Urban Labour Survey (CULS)[4] data, the average years of schooling for a migrant worker were 9.5 compared with 12.1 for local urban workers. The difference of 2.6 years is statistically significant.

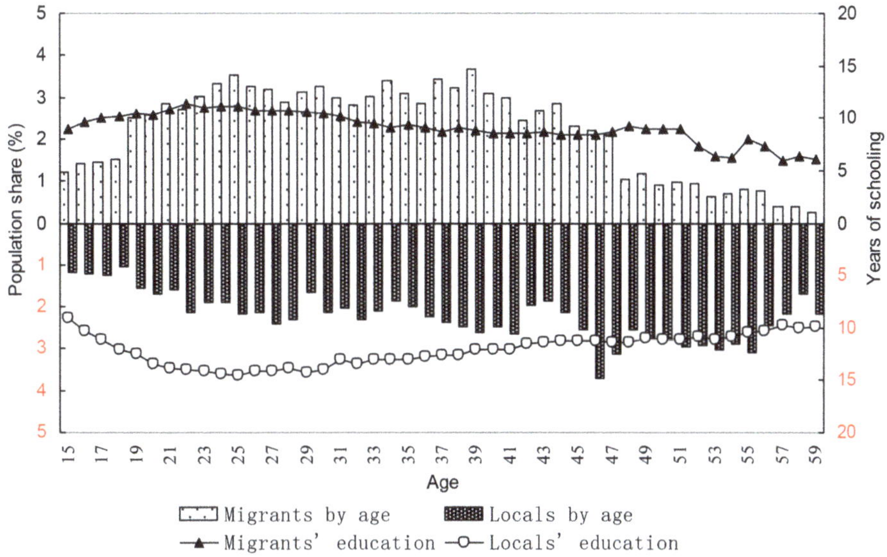

Figure 3.3 Population and education by age: Migrant and urban local workers

Source: Based on authors' calculations using CULS data.

Taking into account the different age distribution structures of the two groups of workers provides an alternative conclusion as to the contribution of migrant workers to the human capital of the urban workforce. For example, within the CULS study, the median age of the sample is 33 for migrant workers and 40 for local urban workers. Figure 3.3 shows the two groups' age distribution and years of schooling by age. Divided around a base point of zero, the upper part of the figure presents information on migrant workers and the lower half offers local urban worker information. As migrant workers are relatively young—and since younger groups in China have generally attained more years of schooling than older workers—migrant workers are displacing older urban workers with a level of education lower than the arriving migrants. This in turn serves to improve the overall human capital of the urban workforce, even though young migrant workers are less educated than young urban native workers. For example, if a migrant worker aged 21–25 years, who has, on average, attained 13.3 years of

4 The China Urban Labour Survey (CULS) was conducted in Shanghai, Wuhan, Shenyang, Fuzhou, Xi'an and Guangzhou by the Institute of Population and Labour Economics at the Chinese Academy of Social Sciences in 2010. In each city, a proportional population sampling approach was used to select 700 households of urban residents and 600 households of migrants in a two-stage procedure. In our analysis, only observations of migrants without urban *hukou* were included.

schooling, takes a vacancy created by a retiring local urban worker aged 55–59 years with average attained schooling of 10.1 years, the net human capital gain to the urban working population can be substantial.

Reallocative efficiency of resources

According to Kuznets (1957), the central purpose of sectoral reallocation is to move resources from low-productivity sectors to high-productivity sectors, and therefore to increase allocative efficiency. In the context of this chapter, the transfer of surplus labour from lower productivity agriculture to more productive employment in non-agricultural sectors, in general, reflects a Kuznets progress that improves productivity (see Aoki 2012). This type of reallocation of labour up the productivity ladder underlies the recent relatively good performance of productivity in Asia (McMillan and Rodrik 2011), and specifically forms an important part of China's reform-era labour productivity growth (Bosworth and Collins 2008). It thus contributes significantly to the story of China's growth over the period (Du 2014).

To understand the allocative efficiency of labour in China, one first must understand the allocation of labour among sectors. There have been questions about National Bureau of Statistics (NBS) data on agricultural employment. Thanks to Du and Wang (2010), there is reason to believe that the official statistics overstate the share of the workforce that is in agriculture. They modify the definition of an agricultural labourer from the yearly base to a monthly base and the result of the recalculation is that the estimated share of rural labour in 2009 decreases by 13.4 per cent. Thereafter, Cai (2016) constructed an agricultural labour force data series spanning the period 1978–2014 (Figure 3.4). This shows that, by 2014, the actual share of agricultural labour was at least 10 percentage points lower than what the NBS had reported.[5] In Figure 3.4, we treat the difference between the estimated and officially reported numbers of agricultural labourers as a 'residual'. In reality, such a residual of labourers is likely to divide itself between serving to enlarge the secondary and tertiary sector labour pools or returning to the agricultural sector when macroeconomic shocks hit the job market in urban areas. As a result of rapidly enhanced mechanisation and rising labour productivity in agriculture, however, the primary sector serves less and less as a pool for absorbing surplus labour. It is thus more likely that residual labourers are absorbed into the secondary and tertiary sector labour pools.

5 This estimate is almost identical to the results of similar work using a different data source by Brandt and Zhu (2010).

To summarise, this section has provided an overview of the mechanics of and selective issues in the transfer of labour over 30 years in China. That transfer—from low-productivity regions and sectors to higher productivity sectors and regions—was complemented by relative high population growth in rural areas and the fact that the young across China are, on average, better educated than the old. Thus, although young rural workers are, on average, less educated than urban workers, rural–urban migrants tend to be young and often replace older, less-educated urban workers. This also helps to lower the dependency ratio in China's higher productivity urban areas, and so is a more efficient allocation of labour resources. Advancing modernisation of the agricultural sector also increases the push factor of rural labour into the urban sector, where it has proven easier to find industrial and service sector jobs during periods of negative employment market shocks.

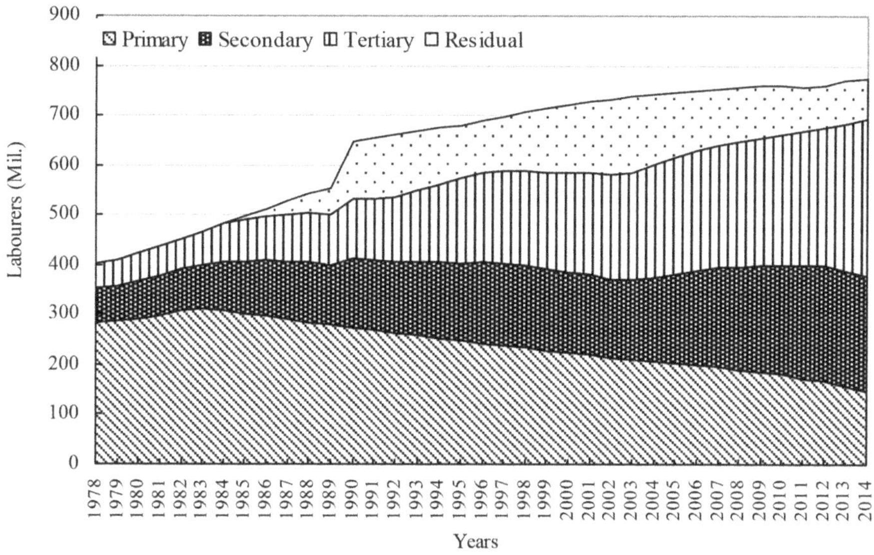

Figure 3.4 Estimates of actual labourers by sector

Source: Authors' estimations based on NBS (various years [a]) and Du and Wang (2010). For technical details, see Cai (2016).

Decomposing urbanisation's migrant foundations

Urbanisation—as the relative expansion of the share of urban population against the non-urban population—has two sources of growth: natural population growth (of the native population) and mechanical growth (of migrants). As China's urban areas are characterised by low birth rates relative to rural areas, the urbanisation process is in turn heavily dependent on rural–urban migration. The scale of this migration is a unique feature of China's demographic and economic transitions, and is embodied by a tide of migrant workers pushing forward the boundaries of urban residence.

The official definition of 'resident urban population' refers to those who live in cities for at least six months and migrant workers who have left their home township for at least six months. Since 96 per cent of migrant workers enter various tiered Chinese cities, they are statistically counted among (de facto) the urban resident population, though they are not de jure urban residents as they do not hold the associated local and urban residential permit, known as a *hukou*. By comparing official urbanisation data with migrant worker survey data, we can roughly sketch the contribution of the growth in numbers of migrant workers to total urban resident numbers.

According to data published by the NBS (various years [a], [b]), in 2014, there were 749 million de facto urban residents, including 168 million migrant workers and 581 million residents holding an urban *hukou*. This produces an official urban residency rate of 54.8 per cent. Among these urban residents, *hukou*-holders contributed 42.5 percentage points to the urbanisation rate and migrant workers contributed 12.3 percentage points. That is, between 2004 and 2014, migrant workers made up 24.2 per cent of the increase in the de facto urban population.

In what follows, we provide a further breakdown of the constituent components of the urban resident population. We focus on the migrant workers' contribution to urban population expansion by analysing the composition of China's total urban population. As a result of data limitations, we focus on incremental population decomposition of urban residents in 2010, the last year for which census data are available.

We first break down increases in the urban population—namely, of de facto urban residents. This reveals that a process of mechanical increase led the rise in this type of urban residence. According to NBS data, the resident urban population increased by 24.7 million, of which the net natural increase was 3.9 million people—18.2 per cent of the total. The net mechanical increase, however, was 20.8 million, accounting for 84.2 per cent of the total.

Second, we decompose the mechanical increase of the urban population into non-*hukou* migration (mainly migrant workers whose *hukou* stays with their hometown) and *hukou* migration (where the *hukou* changes from rural to urban status). There are two scenarios for those who have changed their *hukou* status.

First, some residents changed their *hukou* status from rural to urban but did not change their residence geographically. Second, some people migrated from rural to urban areas and their *hukou* status change reflects this move.

From Ma et al. (2014), we find the relative distribution of migrant movement between places—rural-to-rural, urban-to-urban, urban-to-rural and rural-to-urban—within the total increase of non-*hukou* migrants. We then estimated there were 127.6 million non-*hukou* rural–urban migrants in 2009 and 133.9 million in 2010. The difference between the two numbers comprises an increase in non-*hukou* rural–urban migrants of 6.3 million people. In other words, non-*hukou* rural–urban migrants, the majority of whom are migrant workers and their accompanying family members, contributed to one-quarter of urban resident growth in 2010.

Third, we decompose rural–urban migrants who changed their *hukou* status. These migrants were the difference between the total mechanical increase in urban residents and the increase in non-*hukou* rural–urban migrants. They numbered 14.5 million and contributed 58.6 per cent to urbanisation in 2010. Based on population sampling data of one per 1,000 people in 2014 (Guo 2016), we extrapolated that in 2010 there were 1.23 million cross-regional migrants who changed their *hukou* and 13.2 million 'in situ migrants' who changed their *hukou*. 'In situ migration' with changed *hukou* refers to the phenomenon in urbanisation in which an outer suburban resident is granted an urban *hukou* even though the location of their residence has not changed. This typically happens when there is an alteration of the administrative division or rezoning.

Finally, we can additionally categorise the 7.53 million rural–urban (cross-regional) migrants into two groups: those with a *hukou* change and those without a *hukou* change. The estimation from the most recent census data shows that in 2010 there were 1.23 million migrants whose *hukou* changed, 16.3 per cent of the total, and 6.3 million whose *hukou* did not change, or 83.7 per cent.

Building on the estimation results presented in Table 3.2, we now summarise the findings. First, mechanical population growth is the dominant driver of urbanisation as measured by residency changes. Second, non-*hukou* migrants, who are mainly migrant workers, make up one-quarter of urbanisation-related residence shifts. Three, in situ migration, which is a change to *hukou* status by virtue of an administrative change, has also made a significant contribution to urbanisation, although typically it does not involve a job or a residence change for those 'migrants'. Fourth, the existing *hukou* system still functions as an institutional obstacle by restraining individual migration behaviour and the broader migration process. Migrants with both *hukou* status and geographic change, who apparently are not officially defined as migrant workers, account for only a small fraction of rural–urban migrants. This makes the present urbanisation pattern in China an atypical one.

Table 3.2 Composition of incremental urban population, 2010

<table>
<tr><td rowspan="4">Total:
24.66 m.
(100%)</td><td colspan="4">Natural growth: 3.9 m. (15.8%)</td></tr>
<tr><td rowspan="3">Mechanical growth:
20.76 m. (84.2%)</td><td colspan="2">Non-hukou migrants: 6.3 m. (25.5%)</td><td rowspan="2">Cross-regional migrants: 7.53 m. (30.5%)</td></tr>
<tr><td rowspan="2">Hukou migrants:
14.46 m.
(58.6%)</td><td>Cross-regional migrants with hukou change:
1.23 m. (5.0%)</td></tr>
<tr><td colspan="2">In situ migrants with hukou status change:
13.23 m. (53.6%)</td></tr>
</table>

Source: Authors' estimations.

The characteristics of China's urbanisation process outlined in Table 3.2 are broadly attributable to China's *hukou* system, which is a legacy of the planned economy. On the surface, the impact of the *hukou* system is to divide Chinese residents into rural and urban groups, as well as into provincial and subregional identities. Closer examination of *hukou*-related residence dynamics, however, suggests that the *hukou* system also segments urbanisation itself as well as urban residents into unusual policy treatment groups, as outlined herein. This means urban residents have unequal access to jobs, job security, social security and other public services such as education. Ultimately, this impedes the Kuznets process, as characterised by labour migration. In other words, it impedes the very process of reallocation of resources that underpins structural change, which in turn supports economic growth.

New urbanisation as a reform dividend

Judging by both population trends and existing patterns within urbanisation, China's urbanisation rate will slow in future years. *The national plan on new urbanisation (2014–2020)* (CPC and State Council 2014) predicts that the residential urbanisation rate will be about 60 per cent in 2020. Combining this projection with population predictions, it is possible to simulate China's urbanisation scenario up to 2030 (Table 3.3).

Given trends in the movement of migrant workers around China, the assumption of an annual increment of several million—or even over 10 million—rural–urban migrants is unrealistic. Therefore urbanisation targets based on these forecasts are likely to end up being aborted.

Table 3.3 Simulated prediction of residential urbanisation (million, percentage)

	Total population	Urban population	Urbanisation rate	Rural–urban migrants
2015	1,375	766	55.7	11.97
2016	1,382	782	56.6	11.25
2017	1,392	800	57.5	10.86
2018	1,400	817	58.3	10.78
2019	1,407	833	59.2	10.60
2020	1,413	848	60.0	10.29
2021	1,417	862	60.8	10.11
2022	1,421	875	61.6	9.80
2023	1,424	888	62.3	9.93
2024	1,427	900	63.1	9.43
2025	1,429	911	63.8	9.23
2026	1,431	922	64.5	8.94
2027	1,432	932	65.1	8.85
2028	1,432	942	65.8	8.33
2029	1,432	951	66.4	8.03
2030	1,431	959	67.0	7.64

Source: Authors' estimations.

Moreover, the characteristics of migrant workers themselves are also subject to change. In Chinese official documents, migrant workers are often called 'transferred agricultural labourers'; however, few contemporary migrants are transferring from agricultural production. Agricultural labourers are these days more likely to fall into a disadvantaged demographic category, and are less likely to enjoy the same opportunities as the average migrant workers, who, in contrast, are mostly junior and senior high school graduates from China's rural areas, aged between 16 and 19 years old. This population group, whether defined by residential location or *hukou* registration, peaked in 2014, and began to shrink in 2015. In Figure 3.5, we plot this demographic change by residential classification, which confirms the dramatic drop after 2014. Similarly, the growth in numbers of migrant workers will lose momentum—a transition that is also evident in Figure 3.5. According to NBS data, the annual growth rate of numbers of migrant workers declined from 4 per cent over the period 2005–10 to 3.7 per cent in 2011, 3 per cent in 2012, 1.7 per cent in 2013, 1.3 per cent in 2014 and 0.4 per cent in 2015. Such a trend will not only retard the momentum of urbanisation, but also further lower the potential growth rate.

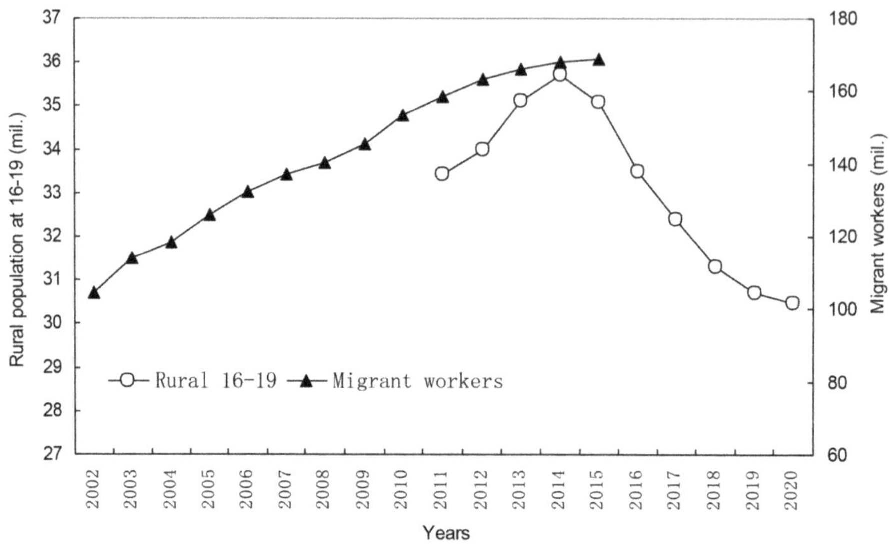

Figure 3.5 Changing trends of youth and outbound migrant workers in rural areas

Source: Authors' calculations based on NBS (2015[b]) and population predictions.

Constrained by the *hukou* system, the present flow of rural labourers to urban areas in China is not a one-way permanent migration but instead an iterative pattern of movement between two areas. The declining number of (younger) migrants means that soon the increasing number of (older) returning migrants will outnumber city-bound migrants. This inevitably will result in further labour shortages in urban sectors. The specific consequences could include: 1) more rapid convergence of China's manufacturing unit labour costs towards their counterparts in developed countries owing to wage increase pressures surpassing positive change in labour productivity; 2) slower human capital accumulation as a result of there being fewer new and relatively educated entrants to the labour market to replace the older, less educated workers leaving the labour market; 3) further diminished return to capital as the labour supply becomes more limited; and 4) a reverted Kuznets process that will suppress TFP growth.

Du (2014) reports that as China's urbanisation rate slowed, the contribution of labour reallocation to economic growth also decreased—from 27.2 per cent in 2001–03 to 9.1 per cent in 2010–12. For policymakers, the important line of inquiry is whether and how China's urbanisation rate will find its momentum again and, in so doing, continue to support China's now moderately high growth rate. An alternative question is how China can engineer a higher rate of mechanical growth in urbanisation. Before answering that question, let us examine the conditions needed for the Chinese economy to sustain long-term growth, and how those conditions might be created.

Here we have presented the case that the ongoing slowdown of the Chinese economy reflects a decreasing potential growth rate that is itself a product of supply-side factors. Among these, the disappearance of the demographic dividend is important. In turn, all reforms that can eliminate institutional obstacles to labour supply and TFP growth are urgently needed. China's working-age population peaked in 2010. The economically active population is expected to peak in 2017. That turning point has several implications. One, as the momentum of quantitative growth of labour attenuates, the sectoral and regional reallocation of labour—for example, increasing non-agricultural labour force participation—is the only way to maintain labour supply. Two, given the present patterns of urbanisation are no longer sustainable, *hukou* reform that grants migrant workers and their family members legitimate local residency, including equal access to public services, will spur a more stable, socially insured and inclusive form of urbanisation. Three, any structural reforms that increase the labour supply will also improve reallocative efficiency (TFP). The three points all suggest that transforming migrant workers from guest workers to full local citizens via implementation of *hukou* reform and new urbanisation may help to generate a new type of reform dividend that can, in turn, instigate increased growth.

In addition to human capital accumulation, a fertility rate rebound and other potential reform dividends, Cai and Lu (2013) especially identify the labour force participation rate and TFP as key drivers to substantially raise the potential growth rate in China. Their simulation, based on a production function model, provides two scenarios in terms of prospective reform dividends across the period 2011–20. First, an annual increase of 1 percentage point in the non-agricultural labour force participation rate could add a 0.88 percentage point to the potential annual growth rate. Second, a 1 percentage point increase in the average growth rate of TFP per annum could lift the growth rate by 0.99 percentage points.

Conclusion and policy recommendations

China's rapid urbanisation has contributed to unprecedented economic growth during the reform period. The failure to grant rural–urban migrants permanent urban residency has, however, left this important transformative group of workers in a vulnerable limbo with respect to access to public services.

It has also undermined the stable flow of labour into urban sector vacancies. Therefore, while the population growth-driven demographic dividend may be beyond its contemporary peak, in the ongoing absence of *hukou* reform, the demographic dividend and the role played by urbanisation retain uncaptured efficiency gains. As China's demographic transition deepens in the direction of ageing, urbanisation will inevitably slow, and possibly even stagnate, and thus no longer support economic growth as it did before.

With appropriate policy adjustments, however, China is positioned to make more of its demographic potential. Earlier, we outlined how urbanisation can be driven by population growth and also by structural policy approaches. Acceleration of the transformation of migrant workers into full and equal urban residents will in turn help to capture the benefits of this next phase of urbanisation in China, and thus become the next driver of economic growth.

Reform of the *hukou* system has long been a topic in academia, and there is now wide consensus that it should be at the top of the reform agenda among policymakers. Why, then, has the reform process so far made little progress? In what follows, we try to explore the reasons for the slow pace of reform, which we believe have implications for other areas of reform.

First, the dividend attached to such reforms has not been truly recognised. Central and local governments are immediately concerned about growth rates. Demand-side stimulus policies are considered to offer a tangible means of generating quick returns, whereas supply-side measures—say, structural reforms—often take longer to prove effective and that effectiveness is also difficult to link to particular policy action. In this context, Chinese governments, central and local, tend to encourage urbanisation's economic growth dividend in relatively selective and traceable ways. One, boosting urbanisation by stimulating investment offers more tangible incentives to local governments. Such motives, however, may tempt governments to overorientate their stimulus policies towards the demand side. Two, urbanisation policies that directly affect the incubation of local middle-income groups and also the expansion of domestic consumption motivate governments to push forward with reforms. Some vested interest groups may even resist *hukou* reform, preferring instead to enjoy a more exclusive urban environment. Three, the benefits of enhancing labour force participation and TFP via *hukou* reform are simply not understood or fully appreciated.

Second, respective responsibilities for different levels of government in any *hukou* reform process have not been clearly defined. This leads to problems, such as agreeing how to share costs and benefits. The Central Government has begun open discussions about the issue of splitting the costs of *hukou* reform. In *The national plan on new urbanisation (2014–2020)*, for example, one chapter outlines the division of administrative rights and corresponding fiscal expenditure responsibilities, and also how various levels of government should be responsible for providing public services, especially in the case of areas where relatively high numbers of migrant workers have settled as residents (CPC and the State Council 2014). Unfortunately, the statement remains general, even vague, and has not explicitly allotted the potential costs and benefits among central, provincial and municipal governments in accordance with their expenditure responsibilities. Moreover, it gives no explicit indications as to the relevant participants in the reform, and therefore means local governments lack the necessary incentives and have even been denied their institutional ability to implement *hukou* reform.

Third, these misunderstandings and incomplete directives serve to encourage local governments to revise their own more local decisions about where to draw tangible and intangible urban boundaries. For example, China's larger cities, which are the main destination for labour migration, typically provide better basic public services, which means the costs of *hukou* reform for these governments would be heavier. In addition, these costs are borne at the municipal government level, but such governments cannot enjoy all the benefits delivered by the entry of migrant workers. They therefore lack the incentive to permanently settle migrant families as local citizens with equal rights. All the while, the Central Government has formulated several urbanisation principles, such as placing strict restrictions on the expansion of municipalities with a population size of more than five million people and on any large city increasing in size; it is also encouraging the development of medium-sized and small cities. On that basis, local governments are expected to direct urbanisation by strengthening *hukou* restrictions in large cities, while relaxing *hukou* settlement only in small cities.

To accelerate China's next phase of urbanisation, the Thirteenth FYP calls for a raising of the *hukou*-holding rate in urban areas—that is, increasing the proportion of the long-term resident population holding a local *hukou*. If the incentive mechanisms do not change, however, local governments may attempt to meet this policy directive simply through in situ migration, which is the result of a geographic boundary redrawing, rather than physical migration. In situ migration is the opposite of the intention of new urbanisation as an ongoing driver of economic growth.

In general, economic history points to high urbanisation levels being an outcome of development and thus indicative of modernisation. For countries in the transition from middle-income to high-income status, urbanisation is a useful way of sustaining economic growth and dynamism. For China in particular, the proposed new urbanisation is expected to deliver a return to several areas of structural reform that aim to correct institutional distortions in resource allocation. But, like any process of reform, this new urbanisation requires design and input at the highest levels, which would solve all three problems mentioned above, and therefore unlock the related growth dividend.

References

Aoki, M. (2012), Five phases of economic development and institutional evolution in China, Japan and Korea, in M. Aoki, T. Kuran and G. R. Roland (eds), *Institutions and comparative economic development*, Basingstoke, UK: Palgrave Macmillan.

Bai, C.-E., Hsieh, C.-T. and Qian, Y. (2006), *The return to capital in China*, NBER Working Paper No. 12755, Cambridge, Mass.: National Bureau of Economic Research.

Barro, R. J. (2016), *Economic growth and convergence, applied especially to China*, NBER Working Paper No. 21872, Cambridge, Mass.: National Bureau of Economic Research.

Bosworth, B. and Collins, S. M. (2008), Accounting for growth: Comparing China and India, *Journal of Economic Perspectives*, 22(1): 45–66.

Brandt, L. and Zhu, X. (2010), *Accounting for China's growth*, Working Paper No. 395, Toronto: Department of Economics, University of Toronto.

Cai, F. (2016), *China's economic growth prospects: From demographic dividend to reform dividend*, Cheltenham, UK: Edward Elgar.

Cai, F. and Lu, Y. (2013), The end of China's demographic dividend: The perspective of potential GDP growth, in R. Garnaut, F. Cai and L. Song (eds), *China: A new model for growth and development*, 55–73, Canberra: ANU E Press.

Cai, F. and Zhao, W. (2012), When demographic dividend disappears: Growth sustainability of China, in M. Aoki and J. Wu (eds), *The Chinese economy: A new transition*, Basingstoke, UK: Palgrave Macmillan.

Central Committee of the Communist Party of China (CPC) and the State Council (2014), *The national plan on new urbanisation (2014–2020)*, Beijing: The State Council. Available from: gov.cn/gongbao/content/2014/content_2644805.htm.

Du, Y. (2014), Labor market changes and the new economic growth, *China Opening Journal*, (3): 31–35.

Du, Y. and Wang, M. (2010), New estimate of surplus rural labor force and its implications, *Journal of Guangzhou University (Social Science Edition)*, 9(4): 17–24.

Eichengreen, B., Park, D. and Shin, K. (2013), *Growth slowdowns redux: New evidence on the middle-income trap*, NBER Working Paper No. 18673, Cambridge, Mass.: National Bureau of Economic Research.

Guo, Z. (2016), From demographic transition to population equilibrium, *Population Research*, (1): 57–68.

Kuznets, S. (1957), Quantitative aspects of the economic growth of nations II: Industrial distribution of national product and labor force, *Economic Development and Cultural Change*, 5(Supplement): 3–110.

Li, K. (2016), *The government work report, 2016*, Beijing: People's Publishing House.

Lin, J. Y. (2011), China and the global economy, *China Economic Journal*, 4(1): 1–14.

Ma, X., Duan, C. and Guo, J. (2014), A comparative study on four types of floating population, *Chinese Journal of Population Science*, (5): 36–46.

McMillan, M. S. and Rodrik, D. (2011), *Globalization, structural change and productivity growth*, NBER Working Paper No. 17143, Cambridge, Mass.: National Bureau of Economic Research.

National Bureau of Statistics (NBS) (2011), *Major figures on 2010 population census of China*, Beijing: China Statistics Press.

National Bureau of Statistics (NBS) (various years [a]), *China Statistical Yearbook*, Beijing: China Statistics Press. Available from: stats.gov.cn/.

National Bureau of Statistics (NBS) (various years [b]), *Migrant worker monitoring survey report*, Beijing: China Statistics Press. Available from: stats.gov.cn/.

Pritchett, L. and Summers, L. H. (2014), *Asiaphoria meets regression to the mean*, NBER Working Paper No. 20573, Cambridge, Mass.: National Bureau of Economic Research.

Roberts, K., Connelly, R., Xie, Z. and Zheng, Z. (2004), Patterns of temporary labor migration of rural women from Anhui and Sichuan, *The China Journal*, 52: 49–70.

United Nations (UN) (2011), *World population prospects: The 2010 revision*, CD-ROM edn, Population Division, Department of Economic and Social Affairs, New York: United Nations.

Wang, M. and Cai, F. (2015), Destination consumption: Enabling migrants' propensity to consume, in L. Song, R. Garnaut, F. Cai and L. Johnston (eds), *China's domestic transformation in a global context*, Canberra: ANU Press.

4. Forecasting China's Economic Growth by 2020 and 2030

Xiaolu Wang and Yixiao Zhou

Introduction

From the late 1970s, China enjoyed an annual average growth rate of 9.9 per cent for more than three decades. This followed the introduction of reform and opening-up policies in 1978. In recent years, however, growth has slowed, to only 6.9 per cent in 2015. This study analyses the causes of this slowdown and forecasts China's economic growth from 2016 to 2020, and projects China's growth to 2030.

A voluminous literature has identified the main reasons for China's rapid economic growth in the past 30 or more years. First, the transition towards a market economy improved resource allocation and increased economic efficiency. Second, rapid capital accumulation driven by high savings fuelled economic growth. Third, openness to trade and investment enhanced economic efficiency and enabled the economy to enjoy its comparative advantage in labour-intensive industries. Fourth, with China moving into a fast line of industrialisation and urbanisation, there was significant change in economic structure, the allocative efficiency of factors was greatly enhanced and increasing demand exercised a strong pull on economic growth. Fifth, China enjoyed rapid growth of its labour force during the 1980s and 1990s, led by a demographic boom that arrived at the same time as a demographic boom in developed economies, which drove faster growth in both.

The pattern of growth that drove that miracle has, however, broadly run its course. That pattern also helps to explain why the Chinese economy is now burdened with severe structural imbalances that are causing growth to slow.

Four factors are worth special attention.

First, the savings and investment rates have been rising continuously. High investment has led to increasingly severe overcapacity in some sectors. In 2014, China's annual capital formation rate was as high as 46 per cent, while private consumption was a mere 38 per cent of gross domestic product (GDP). Unlike in the early stages of China's development and the reform era, overcapacity now significantly lowers the productivity of capital.

Second, for a long period in the past, the government interfered too much with resource allocation. Corruption was rampant and the size of government was expanded. These are important factors that lower efficiency and therefore slow growth.

Third, economic growth requires a stable macroeconomic environment and prudent macroeconomic policies. But since the outbreak of the Global Financial Crisis (GFC) in 2008 and the subsequent monetary easing measures by the People's Bank of China (PBC), the debt leverage ratio (the ratio of total debt to GDP) has continued to climb. Calculation based on incomplete information from the central bank's social financing statistics suggests that the leverage ratio escalated from 126 per cent in 2008 to 211 per cent in 2015. An excessively high leverage ratio lowers the allocative efficiency of financial resources, heightens financial risk and threatens long-term economic growth.

Finally, a couple of other factors also played a role in the slowdown of the economy. Demand growth for China's exports dropped off a cliff, and this brought an end to the export-led model of growth, forcing China to rely more on domestic consumption; and China passed its peak working-age population share in 2011, reducing labour supply.

In this study, we build a growth model for the Chinese economy to analyse the contribution of the growth in factor inputs and total factor productivity (TFP) to China's economic growth. TFP growth is defined as the sum of the contribution of technological progress and allocative effect, led by various institutional and structural factors. Data spanning more than six decades since the foundation of the People's Republic of China are used to obtain a longitudinal perspective. The rest of the chapter is structured as follows. Section two presents the results of growth accounting based on the model estimates. Section three discusses the impact of demand-side issues on economic growth. Section four forecasts future economic growth based on the results in sections two and three. Section five summarises the main findings and draws policy implications from the analysis.

Growth determinants on the supply side: An empirical model

The study of economic growth often relies on the neoclassical growth model (Solow 1956) and the human capital growth model (Romer 1986; Lucas 1988). Both models establish the functional relationship between factor inputs and output (GDP) and can be empirically tested with econometric methods.

China's growth experience is complex, and it may not be enough to focus just on factor inputs. In the past 30-plus years, institutional reforms and structural changes in China have had a significant impact on TFP and economic growth. Analysis in the literature of economic growth in transitional economies typically incorporates a few institutional or structural variables into the model, such as the urbanisation rate, the non-state share in the economy and foreign shares in capital stock (Collins and Bosworth 1996; Chen 1997; Bosworth and Collins 2008; Zhu 2012). As these examples show, each study has a different emphasis, with some emphasising the role of openness to trade and investment and others highlighting the role of market-oriented reforms.

In the following analysis, we build a growth model amended from that of Lucas (1988). This model incorporates human capital, physical capital and several important institutional and structural variables. This model enables us to comprehensively analyse the impact on growth of a number of factors relating to TFP, including technological progress, market-oriented reform, urbanisation, trade expansion, foreign investment, government administrative costs, the consumption rate and the leverage ratio. Time-series data from 1950 to 2014 are used.

The growth model adopted in this study is defined in Equation 4.1.

Equation 4.1

$$Y = AK^{a_1} H^{a_2} H_a^{a_3} R^{a_4} e^{f(x)}$$

In Equation 4.1, Y is real GDP; A is a constant representing the base level of TFP; K is fixed capital stock; H is human capital stock; H_a is the average education level of the labour force, which is used to estimate the externality of human capital; R is the research and development (R&D) capital stock accumulated from R&D expenditure; and $f(x)$ is a subfunction composed of several institutional and structural variables that affect TFP. It is defined as Equation 4.2.

Equation 4.2

$$f(x) = a_5 m + a_6 u + a_7 i + a_8 d + a_9 g + a_{10} l + a_{11} c + a_{12} c^2 + a_{13} T$$

In Equation 4.2, m is the share of the non-state (that is, private) economy; u is the urbanisation rate defined by the ratio of urban population to the total population; i is the foreign capital share in total capital; d is the foreign trade dependency rate defined as the ratio of total trade value in GDP; g is the ratio of government's administrative cost defined as the share of total government-related budgetary expenditure in GDP; l is the leverage ratio, defined as the ratio of total debt over GDP; c is the consumption rate, defined as the ratio of total consumption to GDP, and c^2 is its quadratic term; and T is a time trend to capture possibly unexplained TFP. More explanations of these variables are given below.

The econometric model used herein is obtained through substituting Equation 4.2 into Equation 4.1 and taking a logarithm of both sides of the equation. Variables H_a and T are dropped after initial analysis due to statistical insignificance. R&D capital, lnR, lacks statistical significance and is substituted by its first difference term, $DlnR$. The consumption rate and its quadratic term are lagged by one period to avoid the possible bicausality problem. To correct the discrepancy caused by autocorrelation, the Prais-Winsten AR (1) method is used in the regression.

In this study, capital stock is calculated with the perpetual inventory method, using data for fixed-asset investment and fixed capital formation since 1950 (unless otherwise indicated, all data are from NBS n.d., various years). We found errors in the two data series in opposite directions in recent years. Therefore, combining these two datasets to calculate fixed capital stock could reduce the discrepancy. Estimation of the initial capital stock in 1950 was with reference to Chow (1993). Considering the acceleration of depreciation in the reform period, rising composite depreciation rates are adopted when we calculate capital stock after 1978. The composite depreciation rate rose from the minimum value of 3.3 per cent to 10 per cent in recent years.

Human capital is measured as total effective labour, which is calculated as the weighted sum of the number of graduates from all levels of educational institutions, using years of schooling as the weights. Uncompleted study and non-degree vocational education are also taken into account in building this data series.

R&D capital stock is calculated with the perpetual inventory method, using annual R&D expenditures. Since a large part of R&D expenditure is already counted in fixed assets investment, this variable is not considered as an input but as a mean to measure the contribution of technological progress to TFP.

The share of the non-state (private) sector in GDP is not available, and therefore is represented by the share of total sales of non-state firms in industry. Since the statistical definition of these firms was changed several times, data were adjusted accordingly for comparability.

The urbanisation rate is the share of urban residents in the total population. The trade dependency ratio is the ratio of the sum of import and export values to GDP. Foreign capital share is the ratio of foreign capital stock in total fixed capital stock. Foreign capital is calculated with the perpetual inventory method, using foreign investment data from total investment in fixed assets statistics.

The government administrative cost refers to the share of administrative expenditure (a component in budgetary expenditure) in GDP. Due to changes in budgetary accounting, the item 'expenditure for general public services' is used with adjustment from 2007 onwards. The leverage ratio is the ratio of total debt to GDP, data for which are from the PBC's social financing statistics (PBC n.d.). These do not offer full coverage of debt for firms, government and residents, but are an approximate substitute. The consumption ratio is the ratio of final consumption to GDP.

Table 4.1 presents the model estimation results. The adjusted R^2 and t-statistics show that the model has strong explanatory power.

Table 4.1 Modelling results (dependent variable: log GDP)

Regressor	Symbol	Estimates	t-statistics
Log capital	$lnK_{(t)}$	0.3882	2.65*
Log human capital	$lnH_{(t)}$	0.4717	3.87**
Log R&D capital in first difference	$DlnK_{r(t)}$	0.7205	8.97**
Urbanisation rate	$u_{(t)}$	3.5321	3.08**
Non-state share in the economy	$m_{(t)}$	0.4422	4.89**
Foreign share in capital stock	$k_{f(t)}$	3.2299	4.01**
Trade dependency ratio	$d_{(t)}$	0.2734	1.71'
Government administrative cost	$g_{(t)}$	−13.4858	−4.67**
Leverage ratio	$l_{(t)}$	−0.2978	−2.91**
Consumption rate	$c_{(t-1)}$	3.8383	1.97'
Squared consumption rate	$c^2_{(t-1)}$	−2.8982	−2.07*
Constant	C	−2.8279	−3.85**
Adjusted R^2	Adj. R^2	0.997	
Observations: 64			

** statistically significant at 1 per cent
* statistically significant at 5 per cent
' statistically significant at 10 per cent
Source: Authors' estimations.

Based on the estimates in Table 4.1, we carry out a growth-accounting exercise to calculate the factor contribution and impact of institutional and structural elements on GDP growth. Total factor contribution is the sum of the contribution from capital and human capital. The contribution from TFP is the sum of contributions from all remaining variables. Table 4.2 therefore contains a comprehensive decomposition of TFP.

It is observed from the modelling result that the signs and magnitudes of the residual term change irregularly. Together with the insignificant *T*, it suggests that there is no systematic omission of variables and the residuals are likely to reflect statistical errors in the raw data. Taking this into account, we exclude the residual term from the TFP calculation.

Table 4.2 Growth accounting results for different periods (annual growth rate, per cent)

	1953–78	1979–90	1991–2000	2001–10	2011–14
GDP growth rate	6.1	9.0	10.4	10.5	8.1
Total factor contribution	6.0	5.8	5.5	6.3	6.5
Capital	2.9	3.4	4.0	5.1	5.4
Human capital	3.1	2.5	1.5	1.2	1.1
Total TFP	0.3	2.4	5.3	2.3	0.7
R&D capital	0.0	–0.4	0.9	0.1	–0.7
Urbanisation	0.7	2.5	3.5	4.9	4.3
Non-state share	–0.6	0.8	0.5	0.9	0.5
Foreign share in capital	0.0	1.0	1.2	–1.1	–1.3
Trade dependency	0.0	0.5	0.3	0.3	–0.6
Government cost	0.4	–0.9	–0.8	–0.4	0.5
Consumption rate	0.2	0.0	0.0	–0.9	0.5
Leverage ratio	–0.4	–1.0	–0.2	–1.5	–2.4
Residual	–0.1	0.8	–0.4	1.9	0.8

Notes: The contribution of foreign share in capital is negative because a fall in the share lowers economic growth. The contribution from government costs is positive because a fall in this enhances economic growth. A similar situation applies to the other variables. In some periods, the sum of individual terms differs slightly from the GDP growth rate due to the rounding of numbers.

Source: Calculated based on the estimates in Table 4.1 and data from NBS (n.d.).

The main findings of our growth accounting are as follows.

First, capital is still playing the most important role in driving economic growth. Its contribution to growth has been on the rise, reaching over 5 percentage points in recent years. However, compared with earlier findings by Wang (2000) and Wang et al. (2009), it can be seen that the productivity of capital has fallen significantly as capital elasticity has dropped from around 0.50 to 0.39. The sum of the output elasticity of capital and human capital is significantly below one, indicating that the economy has changed from constant returns to scale to decreasing returns to scale. The fall in the productivity of capital is due mainly to overcapacity, indicating overinvestment that weakens the contribution of capital to economic growth.

Second, the contribution of human capital to economic growth decreases significantly over different periods. This is caused by the slowdown in labour force growth. In this study, human capital is measured as total effective labour that is enhanced by education. Slowing labour force growth reduces the rate of human capital accumulation. In recent years, despite the increases in workers' years of education, this has not fully compensated for the deceleration in labour force growth.

Third, R&D capital, *lnR*, lacks statistical significance and is substituted by its first difference term, *DlnR*, which is positive and significant at the 5 per cent level. This implies that R&D capital has a positive impact on economic growth only when R&D capital grows at an accelerated rate. The results indicate that this occurred only in the 1990s. Since growth in R&D capital proxies for technological progress, the result implies that technological progress has not yet become one of the main drivers of TFP and economic growth.

Fourth, urbanisation plays a major role in TFP growth, and has contributed more than 4 percentage points to the GDP growth rate in recent years. The large contribution comes from the allocative effect of factors moving from the low-productivity agricultural sector to high-productivity urban non-agricultural sectors, which improves the overall efficiency of resource allocation and contributes to economic growth. This can be considered on the basis of the Lewis (1954) model. This effect is also a result of increased market orientation, as the market is an effective mechanism by which to facilitate resource reallocation between urban and rural areas and thus to expedite urbanisation during the reform period.

Fifth, the efficiency of the non-state (private) sector was higher than the state sector throughout the reform period from 1978. With a 1 percentage point increase in the share of the non-state sector, TFP rises by 0.44 percentage point. Rapid growth of the non-state sector has been contributing more than 0.5 percentage point to TFP and economic growth every year since reforms began. Like urbanisation, this can also be attributed to market-oriented reforms that enhance economic efficiency through improving resource allocation and incentive mechanisms.

Sixth, the combined contribution of foreign capital and foreign trade to TFP reached 1.5 percentage points in the 1980s and 1990s, which shows that productivity of foreign capital is higher than that of domestic capital and trade enhancement improves resource allocation. In recent years, however, their combined contribution became negative, due mainly to falls in the share of foreign investment and the trade dependency ratio. Furthermore, as the technological gap between domestic firms and frontier firms narrows, the growth effects of foreign investment and foreign trade tend to weaken.

Seventh, during the reform period until 2010, government administrative costs, measured as the ratio of the administrative expenses in the government budget to GDP, have been on the rise, lowering TFP by 0.4 to 0.9 percentage point each year. This shows that low efficiency of government administration, as well as inappropriate government intervention in the market, negatively affects the efficiency of resource allocation. Examples of inappropriate intervention include providing favourable policies for certain industries, causing excess firm entry and consequently excess supply in industries in which it has occurred. For instance, government encouragement in earlier periods and stimulus policies during 2008–10 are chiefly responsible for the serious overcapacity in the iron, steel and cement industries. Preferential government policies during the Twelfth Five-Year Plan caused more serious overcapacity in photovoltaic and wind power industries. Since 2012, a strong anticorruption campaign has reduced government administrative costs to some extent. This is found to contribute 0.5 percentage point to TFP growth in recent years. Whether government reform can be effectively implemented in the future will determine the future contribution of this factor.

Eighth, based on the regression results, the contribution of the consumption rate (share of total consumption in GDP) to TFP growth and economic growth is characterised by an inverted-U curve (Figure 4.1). In this figure, the horizontal axis is the consumption rate and the vertical axis indicates its growth effect on logarithm GDP. The consumption rate that maximises the growth effect is at 66 per cent, corresponding to a savings rate of 34 per cent. This implies that a consumption rate either higher or lower than 66 per cent will cause losses in efficiency, lowering economic growth. This empirical finding supports the theoretical extrapolation of the 'golden rule saving rate' in the growth literature (Barro and Sala-i-Martin 1995). Barro and Sala-i-Martin (1995: 21) clearly state that 'an economy that oversaves is said to be dynamically inefficient'.

During the period 2001–10, the consumption rate fell by more than 10 percentage points while the saving rate rose by a corresponding amount. This change cut TFP by 0.9 percentage point per annum (Table 4.2). During the period 2011–14, the consumption rate picked up slightly and contributed to TFP by 0.5 percentage point per annum. However, the consumption rate was still a mere 51 per cent in 2014, significantly below the optimal value of 66 per cent (Figure 4.1). This indicates that economic growth will benefit from reform and structural adjustment measures that help boost the consumption rate and lower the saving and investment rates towards their respective optimal values (note that too much government investment increases rates of both savings and investment).

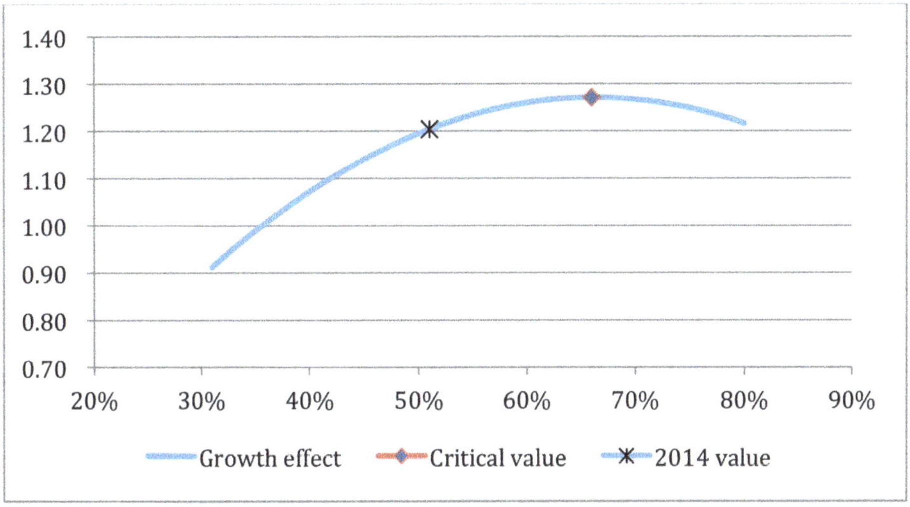

Figure 4.1 Simulating the growth effect of the consumption rate

Source: Authors' simulation based on model estimates.

Ninth, the hike in the leverage ratio has had negative impacts on efficiency and growth in all subperiods. In recent years, the leverage ratio has shot up dramatically, reducing TFP growth by more than 2 percentage points per annum. A high leverage ratio has become the major unfavourable and risky condition in the economy. Monetary easing and excess credit supply for long periods have led to overinvestment and lower efficiency in the economy. It is critical to maintain neutral monetary policies and a lower leverage ratio in the future, both to enhance efficiency and to prevent a financial crisis.

To summarise the above findings, the contribution from TFP was significantly higher in the reform period than in the pre-reform era. Since 2000, however, the TFP contribution has been dipping continuously, reaching a low of 0.7 percentage point per annum in recent years. The main causes, besides the subdued effects of slower foreign investment and trade growth, include the following: rising government administrative costs and increasing government intervention; excessive falls in the consumption rate (or excessive rises in saving and investment rates); and a significant rise in the leverage ratio. These factors act as a drag on economic efficiency and greatly offset the positive contribution of urbanisation and market oriented reforms to TFP. The fall in government administrative costs and the rise in the consumption rate in recent years have had some positive effects, although these are largely offset by the negative impacts from the rising leverage ratio.

The demand-side effect

The growth effect of the consumption rate found in the previous section can be thought of as a supply-side effect as it changes TFP. Nevertheless, this phenomenon can also be analysed from the demand side and, in fact, only via demand-side analysis can we disentangle the mechanisms through which this variable impacts on TFP.

Keynesian economics shows that when total investment is lower than total savings in an economy and when trade is in balance, aggregate demand is lower than aggregate supply and therefore the economy is in disequilibrium. In this situation, either government investment or an expansion of money supply to stimulate investment can increase aggregate demand and revitalise economic growth. This theory, however, does not take into account how the effectiveness of such demand management policies depends on the initial investment rate. It implicitly assumes that investment demand and consumption demand are perfectly substitutable with each other. In fact, this assumption only holds approximately in the short run and loses efficacy in the medium and long runs.

Suppose an economy like China has had high rates of savings and investment before the monetary authority implements expansionary policy to further stimulate investment. In the short run, new investment projects, such as new production lines and new factories, will increase the demand for investment goods and labour input, and thus lift economic growth. However, when these investment projects are complete, production capacity will expand, increasing aggregate supply. If consumption and net export shares in GDP remain unchanged, a new imbalance between aggregate supply and aggregate demand will arise, requiring further demand expansion to balance the supply increases. The government may fear that growth could stall without these expansionary measures.

Continued expansionary policies raise the savings rate and ever-rising rate of investment and production capacity through various mechanisms. Expansionary policies enjoy only conditional success. They can have the desired positive early expansionary effects and negative longer-term consequences.

To be more specific, for high-saving and high-investment economies, the longer-term cost of expansionary monetary policy is an increasing mismatch between rapid expansion of production capacity and insufficient increase in consumption demand.

Expansionary fiscal policies that are not used for investment in industrial sectors may not have these costs. More effective directions for expansion of government-connected expenditure include investment in infrastructure and environmental protection, payments for public services and social security, transfer payments to populations in poverty and reduction of firms' fiscal burdens. Expansionary policies through these mechanisms can help to rebalance the economic structure, especially between consumption and investment.

China has had high rates of savings and investment for a long period. However, between 2000 and 2010, the savings rate as a share of GDP further rose by about 15 percentage points, to 51 per cent in 2010. The investment rate rose by about 13 per cent to 47 per cent. The consumption rate dropped from 64 per cent to 49 per cent during the same period (Figure 4.2). By 2010, China's saving rate was higher than the world average by about 30 percentage points, and the consumption rate was below the world average by 30 percentage points. The high investment and low consumption rates aggravate industrial overcapacity and lead to a fall in productivity.

The rapid fall in the utilisation rate of industrial capacity in China has been identified by several studies in the literature (Figure 4.3).

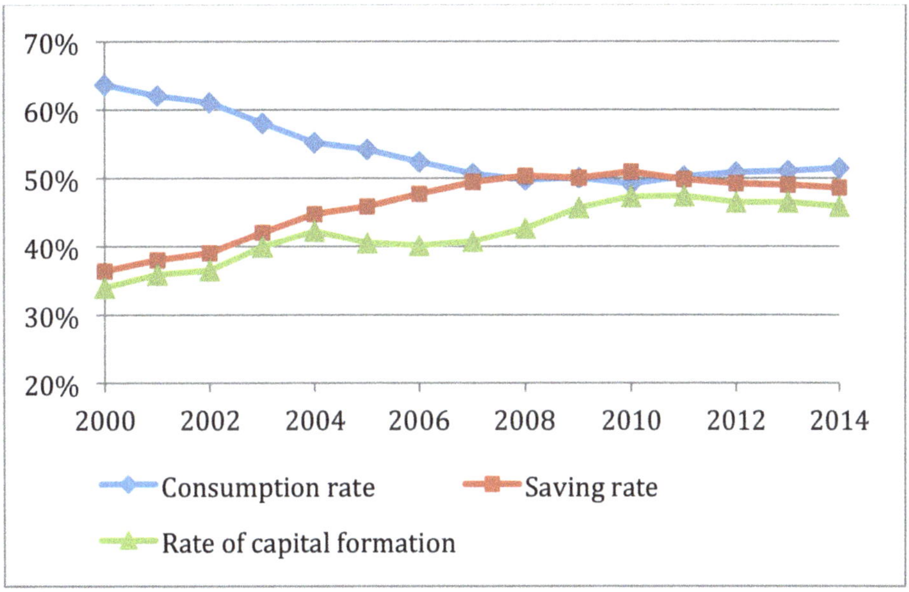

Figure 4.2 Trends of the savings rate, investment rate and consumption rate, 2000–14 (per cent)

Source: GDP accounts by expenditure approach, NBS (n.d.).

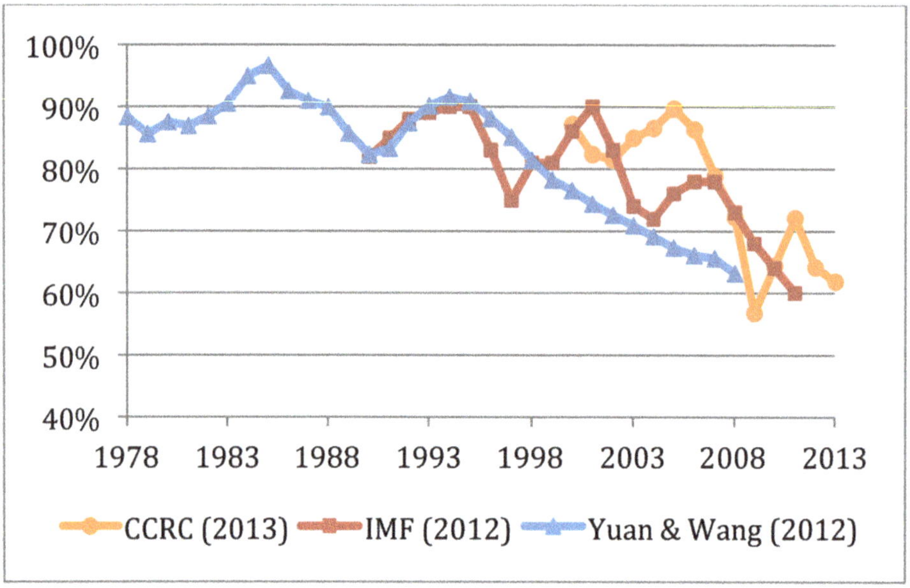

Figure 4.3 The downward trend of the utilisation rate of industrial capacity, 1978–2013 (per cent)

Source: Reproduced from China Credit Rating Co. Ltd (2013).

The excessive investment and inadequate consumption demand provide the main reasons for the significant drop in TFP and the slowdown of economic growth in China. What causes the structural imbalance between consumption, saving and investment? The answer is unequal income distribution and resource misallocation. Continuous widening of income gaps, inflation of real estate prices and massive turbulence in capital markets all tend to dampen the public's consumption demand. Irrational government expenditure at various administrative levels—excessive government investment, insufficient provision of public services and incomplete coverage of social security networks—cause excessive savings and investment and inadequate consumption.

In current circumstances, continued monetary easing to stimulate investment can worsen the structural imbalance and not be conducive to economic growth. During the GFC, the dramatic expansion of government investment and great easing of money supply in China boosted growth only in the short run. Economic growth weakened shortly afterwards, showing the decreasing effectiveness of stimulus policies.

In 2015, Money and Quasi-Money (M2) grew by 13.3 per cent—twice the nominal GDP growth (6.4 per cent). Monetary policy is still too loose. Excess money supply will further lift the leverage ratio, expand the size of non-performing loans for the commercial banks and threaten the stability of the macroeconomy.

Given the excessively high current savings and investment rates, the emphases of macroeconomic policy should be redirected from stimulating investment to improving public services, social security systems and income distribution. This would support rather than counteract the necessary rebalancing of the demand structure between investment and consumption.

Growth forecasts for 2020 and projections for 2030

The growth accounting and demand-side analysis in the previous two sections enable us to forecast growth to 2020 and to project growth to 2030 by considering the important influences on growth in factor supplies and TFP.

There are uncertainties about the influences on economic growth, especially those related to policy options. We consider three different scenarios.

Baseline scenario

The baseline scenario assumes that most growth determinants (including factor inputs, institutions and policies) generally continue past trends. One exception is made: to prevent a financial crisis, the monetary authority slows the injection of liquidity and places a modest constraint on the rise of the leverage ratio. However, the possibility of financial crisis in the future cannot be totally ruled out. Here we simply assume that there will be no financial crisis in the periods under consideration.

The paths of changes in some other factors are also adjusted moderately to reflect our conjectures about the most likely developments. It is assumed that:

1. The savings and capital formation rates continue to fall slowly. The government continues to invest in infrastructure but the scale of such investment is restricted by the government budget and the availability of effective investment opportunities. Changes in the growth rate of capital stock lag behind changes in the growth rate of investment. The growth rate of capital stock was 14 per cent, on average, between 2011 and 2015, and is presumed to slow to 10 per cent between 2016 and 2020 and 7.3 per cent between 2021 and 2030.

2. The education level of the labour force continues to increase at a constant speed, but the growth rate of the labour force turns negative in the next five years. The annual growth rate of human capital stock therefore drops from 2.4 per cent, which has been the level for the past five years, to 2 per cent between 2016 and 2020 and 1.5 per cent between 2021 and 2030.
3. With the slowdown of the economy, the increase of the urbanisation rate slowed in the past five years, decreasing from 1.4 percentage points to 1.2 percentage points per annum. It is assumed to be 0.8 percentage point per annum between 2016 and 2020 and 0.6 percentage point per annum between 2021 and 2030.
4. The degree of market orientation continues to rise but its pace slows. It is assumed that the share of the non-state economy in industrial value added increases by 4 percentage points from 2014, reaching 83 per cent in 2020 and 88 per cent in 2030.
5. Growth accounting results in previous sections show that the net growth rate of R&D investment slowed in recent years, exerting a negative impact on economic growth. This, however, might be a short-term phenomenon. It is assumed that the growth rate of R&D investment does not fall in the next few years and accelerates after 2020, thus contributing 0.5 percentage point to TFP in the later period.
6. It is expected that, along with expansion in the size of the economy, the trade dependency ratio continues to fall at the same rate as the past several years. It drops by 13 percentage points between 2014 and 2020 and by another 10 percentage points between 2021 and 2030, bottoming out at 19 per cent. The share of foreign capital in total capital drops by 1 percentage point in the next five years and plateaus after 2020.
7. Government administrative costs as a share of GDP have fallen in the past two years thanks to the anticorruption campaign. This change makes a positive contribution to TFP. The trend is expected to continue in the next two or three years. Whether it will continue in the longer term depends on the extent to which further institutional reforms take place. We assume that the share will be stable after 2018.
8. The consumption rate has picked up slightly in recent years, making a positive contribution to economic growth. However, due to the current growth slowdown and the associated deceleration of increases in real wages, the consumption rate is assumed to increase by only 0.2 percentage point per annum in the next five years and then by 0.3 percentage point per annum after 2020.
9. In the past several years, the leverage ratio rose rapidly, by 10 percentage points per annum, enlarging financial risks in the economy. We assume that monetary policy will be adjusted to some extent, limiting the rise of the

leverage ratio to 6 percentage points per annum to reach 230 per cent in 2020. It is assumed to increase by 3 percentage points per annum after 2020, to reach 260 per cent in 2030. We assume no financial crisis occurs during these periods, and only consider the negative impact of a high leverage ratio on economic efficiency.

Our simulation indicates that, in the above circumstances, future economic growth weakens to 5.3 per cent per annum in 2016–20—so missing the government's target of doubling GDP in 2020 from the level of 2010. Between 2021 and 2030, structural adjustment and technological progress raise the growth rate to 5.5 per cent per annum.

Crisis scenario

In the crisis scenario, it is assumed that the trends of various factors after 2015 are similar to those in scenario one, but with no adjustment to monetary policy. The leverage ratio shoots up quickly and exceeds 260 per cent in 2020. During this period, a financial crisis is a high probability.

With a rapid rise in the leverage ratio, commercial banks' non-performing loans accumulate, and may eventually exceed the limit that banks and the government can handle. A financial crisis then erupts. It is assumed that the following situation emerges in 2018:

1. A large portion of bank funds is taken up by the increasing amounts of non-performing loans, leading to an overall repayment failure in the banking system. Debt crisis occurs.
2. Banks cannot continue to finance the real economy, forcing enterprises into increased reliance on informal credit sources. This causes a dramatic increase in interest rates in the market, raises firms' operation costs and leads to more and more losses and bankruptcy of firms. The chain reaction drives the economy into recession. Investment decreases and foreign capital flies out of the economy. Both manufacturing production and employment shrink. The urbanisation process and growth in household incomes stagnate.
3. Government fiscal revenue is seriously affected and huge budgetary deficits arise, turning fiscal policy from expansionary to contractionary, further lowering aggregate demand and causing social crisis due to the shortfall in public spending.
4. Government may pursue even looser monetary policy to stimulate the economy. However, due to overcapacity and lack of effective investment opportunities, monetary easing is less and less effective in promoting growth. Instead, such policies bring forward the bursting of financial bubbles.

5. Since previous overinvestment has already squeezed out effective space for further investment, the effect of fiscal and monetary expansion is limited. The economy could be stuck in depression for several years. The rapid recovery that occurred after 2009 will not be repeated.
6. Because of the importance of China in the world economy, the crisis has a significant impact on the world economy. This feeds back negatively on China's export prospects and economic activity.
7. The blow to the real economy during the crisis reduces aggregate activity while monetary supply keeps expanding, probably leading to stagflation and aggravating social instability and conflict.

The crisis scenario could lead to an overall stagnation for the economy between 2019 and 2021. With some time lag, the investment slowdown during the crisis reduces growth of the stocks of capital and human capital over the longer term. Urbanisation slows and household consumption is seriously affected.

The crisis has long-lasting negative impacts on economic growth after the crisis, changing the growth trajectory during the period 2021–30. During 2020–30, the following would seem to be a plausible combination of outcomes. The average growth rate of capital stock falls to 5.8 per cent, 1.5 percentage points lower than in the base scenario. The growth rate of human capital stock decreases to 1.2 per cent, 0.3 percentage points lower than in the baseline scenario. R&D investment is retarded, making no significant contribution to TFP. Urbanisation slows, progressing at an annual increase of 0.5 percentage point. The consumption rate recovers even more slowly, increasing by 0.2 percentage point per annum.

In the past in China, rising levels of non-performing loans have exerted a negative impact on economic conditions but have not caused a full-blown financial crisis. There are several reasons, however, why crisis could take place in the circumstances that we are considering. First, the leverage ratio has reached an unprecedentedly high level. Second, there was much greater leeway to deal with debt crisis in the past than today. Before the 1998 East Asian Financial Crisis, the leverage ratio had been falling for several consecutive years. Furthermore, plenty of effective investment opportunities in infrastructure were available at that time, leaving much room for expansionary fiscal policy to work. During the GFC, there was still room for implementing both fiscal and monetary stimulus, but these conditions no longer exist.

The simulation result indicates that, in the crisis scenario, GDP grows at 2.9 per cent on average between 2016 and 2020 and there could be two to three years of stagnation or negative growth during this period. From 2021 to 2030, the GDP growth rate recovers to 4.4 per cent per annum, which is a short-term recovery and will not be sustained. In 2030, the growth rate is expected to fall back to around 3 per cent.

Reform and rebalancing scenario

In the reform and rebalancing scenario, we assume that the government pushes through reform and structural rebalancing in three key areas to bring the economy on to a healthy development path. Other conditions in this scenario are the same as those in the baseline scenario.

Deleveraging

It is assumed that through good government policies and the efforts of firms, the trend of a rising leverage ratio ceases within the next two or three years. The leverage ratio does not surpass 210 per cent in 2020 (starting from 200 per cent at the end of 2015) and falls to 180 per cent or less—a relatively safe level—by 2030. To achieve this, the following outcomes are necessary:

- Monetary policy becomes neutral, bringing liquidity growth in line with GDP growth.
- Non-performing loans are stripped and cleared.
- 'Zombie firms' are purged or reset and the 'soft budget constraint' problems of local governments are solved. Firms are given equal opportunities for market competition and governments behave in line with the legal framework.
- Financial and capital markets are better regulated and channels for the financing of small and medium-sized firms are widened.

Rebalancing the consumption-saving structure through institutional reforms

Income distribution is improved through fiscal reform and public policy adjustment, so the consumption rate rebounds by 13–14 percentage points in the next 15 years to reach about 65 per cent in 2030, and the saving rate falls to around 35 per cent.

To achieve this, the following reforms and policy adjustments are required:

- The fiscal system is reformed, transforming the focus of government expenditure on public services and reducing inefficient government investment and excessive administrative expenditure. The household registration system is reformed and full coverage of social security systems is provided. Public expenditure is increased on education, medical services and public housing for rural–urban migrants and in less-developed regions. The education system is reformed to improve effectiveness and quality.

- State assets are partly mobilised to complement the shortage in social insurance funds and to lower the social security contribution burden for firms.
- Income inequality is reduced through reform of resource and income taxes and the fiscal transfer payment system and by levying property tax. The income gap between competitive and monopolistic industries is reduced through reform of business income tax and the promotion of market competition.

Reforming the government administrative system and lowering administrative costs

Overstaffed government organisations and high government administrative costs breed corruption and exert negative impacts on market competition and economic growth. The anticorruption campaign in the past two or three years has played a positive role in reducing administrative costs. To maintain this positive impact, it is critical to implement reform of the administrative system, raise transparency and legalisation of policies, streamline government institutions and reduce government intervention in the market.

It is assumed that, through government reforms, administrative costs as a share of GDP fall at the same rate as in the past few years until 2020, and then at half that rate from 2020 onwards.

Simulation results show that reforms and adjustment in the above three areas have a positive impact on medium- and long-term economic growth. However, deleveraging and shedding 'zombie firms' have some negative impact on growth performance in the short and medium runs. The latter effect is assumed to lower the growth rate by 0.5 percentage point during the period 2016–20 and continues in the first few years of the period 2021–30 to lower the average growth rate by 0.2 percentage point.

The combined result of the above positive and negative factors is that the growth rate between 2016 and 2020 increases from 5.3 per cent (the rate in the baseline scenario) to 6.2 per cent. Growth accelerates to 7.5 per cent from 2021 to 2030 after the downward pressure on economic growth is overcome. This growth rate is higher than commonly expected. This could be achieved not by stimulus policy, but rather by efforts to implement reforms and structural rebalancing.

Table 4.3 and Figure 4.4 present the forecasts for economic growth under the three scenarios.

The three scenarios differ significantly from each other. In the reform and rebalancing scenario, in 2030, GDP will be greater than that in the baseline scenario by 26 per cent, and greater than that in the crisis scenario by 58 per cent. GDP can reach RMB188 trillion (2014 constant price) or US$29 trillion based on the exchange rate of RMB6.5 per US dollar. Per capita GDP reaches US$20,000 (considering real renminbi appreciation, per capita GDP would be higher). China will become a high-income country by 2030.

Table 4.3 Forecast of future economic growth: Three scenarios (growth rate and ratio changes per annum, per cent)

	Baseline scenario		Crisis scenario		Reform and rebalancing scenario	
	2016–20	2021–30	2016–20	2021–30	2016–20	2021–30
Total factor contribution	4.7	3.5	4.1	2.8	4.7	3.5
Capital	3.8	2.8	3.2	2.2	3.8	2.8
Human capital	0.9	0.7	0.9	0.6	0.9	0.7
Total TFP	0.6	2.0	–1.3	1.6	1.5	4.0
R&D capital	0.0	0.5	0.0	0.0	0.0	0.5
Urbanisation rate	2.8	2.1	1.8	1.8	2.8	2.1
Share of non-state economy	0.3	0.2	0.3	0.2	0.3	0.2
Foreign capital share	–0.5	0.0	–0.7	0.0	–0.5	0.0
Trade dependency ratio	–0.6	–0.3	–0.6	–0.3	–0.6	–0.3
Consumption rate	0.2	0.3	0.1	0.2	0.5	0.5
Government administrative costs	0.2	0.0	0.2	0.0	0.4	0.2
Leverage ratio	–1.8	–0.9	–2.4	–0.3	–0.9	0.9
Adjustment	0	0	0	0	–0.5	–0.2
GDP growth rate	5.3	5.5	2.9	4.4	6.2	7.5

Note: The sum of the total contribution from TFP and from factor inputs may be slightly different from the forecast GDP growth rate due to the rounding of numbers.

Source: Authors' forecasts.

In the crisis scenario, in 2030, GDP would reach only RMB119 trillion and GDP per capita would be about US$12,700. Based on the criterion at that time, China would still be a middle-income country, which implies that China will fall into the middle-income trap in the next 15 years.

The baseline scenario lies between the above two scenarios. In this scenario, in 2030, GDP reaches RMB149 trillion or US$15,900 per capita. It is very likely that China will still not be a high-income country in 2030.

The main differences between the reform and rebalancing scenario and the other two scenarios relate to whether or not there is: 1) deleveraging and lowering of financial risks; 2) improved income distribution through reforms to lift the consumption rate and lower the savings and investment rates; and 3) government reform to lower administrative costs and promote market competition.

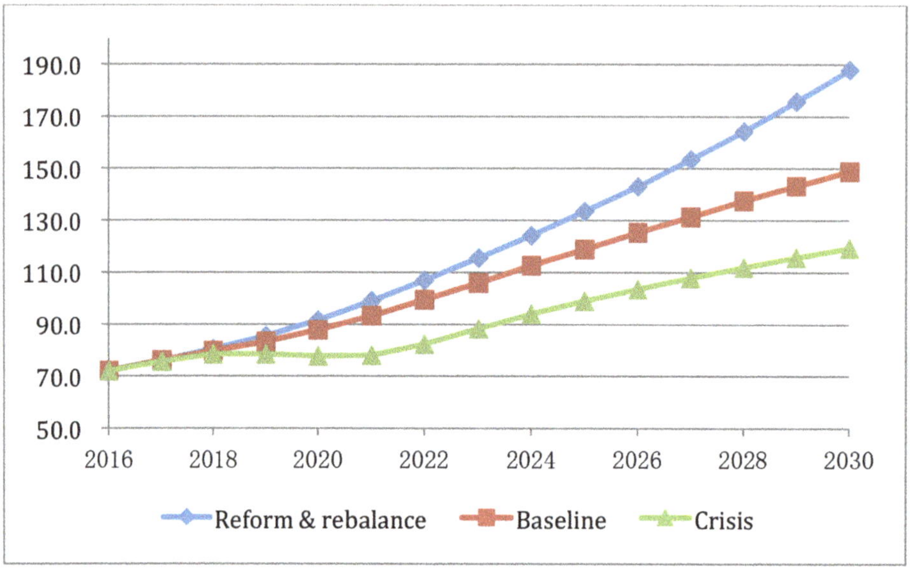

Figure 4.4 Future economic growth: Three scenarios (RMB trillion, 2014 constant price)

Source: Simulation results from Table 4.3.

Conclusion

This study quantitatively analyses the contribution to economic growth of factor inputs and the positive and negative impacts on TFP of institutional and structural factors.

Our growth accounting exercise finds that the contribution of capital to economic growth has been rising throughout various periods, but the productivity of capital has fallen significantly in the past decade, changing the overall economy from constant returns to scale to decreasing returns to scale.

Growth accounting also shows that TFP is significantly higher during the reform period than the pre-reform period. The main driver of TFP growth is not technological progress, but improvement in resource allocation resulting from institutional and structural changes, including development of the non-state economy, openness to trade and investment and rapid urbanisation. In recent decades, however, TFP has dropped significantly, for three main reasons: first, rising government administrative costs; second, the drop in the consumption rate and excessive investment; and third, the rapid rise in the leverage ratio, which reduces financial efficiency. Easing these three constraints is the key to putting China on a path to emerge from the middle-income trap and become a high-income country by 2030.

Demand-side analysis clarifies that the fall in TFP is closely linked to insufficient domestic consumption demand. Consumption demand and investment demand are not perfect substitutes for each other, especially in the medium and long runs. In particular, when the initial investment rate is very high, continued monetary easing to stimulate investment causes an increasing imbalance between investment and consumption, resulting in insufficient domestic consumption demand, overcapacity and falling productivity of capital. Monetary policy needs to be restored to neutrality and fiscal policy should shift from focusing on government investment to improving public services, social security systems and income distribution to lift the low consumption demand.

Based on the results of growth accounting and simulation, we forecast future trajectories of economic growth in three scenarios subject to different policy options.

In the baseline scenario, as a natural extension of past trends, economic growth continues to slow and the government's goal of doubling GDP between 2010 and 2020 are not achieved. In 2030, China's GDP per capita is around US$15,900, which means that China is unlikely to be a high-income country at that time.

The crisis scenario emerges if monetary policy is not adjusted and the leverage ratio continues to increase rapidly. In this case, financial crisis is likely to occur, pushing the economy into stagnation for years, with negative impacts lasting for a long period. In 2030, China is not a high-income country and has fallen into the middle-income trap.

The third scenario considers that reform speeds up and economic structure is rebalanced through measures including deleveraging, improving income distribution to revitalise consumption, lowering government administrative costs and enhancing market mechanisms via government reforms. It is forecast that the GDP growth rate could be maintained at 6.2 per cent per annum between 2016 and 2020 and lift to 7.5 per cent between 2021 and 2030. China becomes a high-income country before 2030. This indicates that the economy is on a development path that is sustainable and more beneficial to public welfare.

References

Barro, R. and Sala-i-Martin, X. (1995), The golden rule of capital accumulation and dynamic inefficiency, in R. Barro and X. Sala-i-Martin, *Economic Growth*, New York: McGraw-Hill.

Bosworth, B. P. and Collins, S. M. (2008), *Accounting for growth: Comparing China and India*, NBER Working Paper No. 12943, Cambridge, Mass.: National Bureau of Economic Research.

Chen, E. K. Y. (1997), The total factor productivity debate: Determinants of economic growth in East Asia, *Asia-Pacific Economic Review*, 11: 18–38.

China Credit Rating Co. Ltd (2013), Assessing the overcapacity of China's manufacturing sector: An optimal-input decision model, [in Chinese], *Special Report*, 40.

Chow, G. C. (1993), Capital formation and economic growth in China, *The Quarterly Journal of Economics*, (August): 809–842.

Collins, S. M. and Bosworth, B. P. (1996), Economic growth in East Asia: Accumulation versus assimilation, *Brookings Papers on Economic Activity*, 82: 964–980.

International Monetary Fund (IMF) (2012), *People's Republic of China 2012 Article IV consultation*, IMF Country Report No. 12/195.

Lewis, W. A. (1954), Economic development with unlimited supplies of labour, *The Manchester School*, 22(May): 139–192.

Lucas, R. E. (1988), On the mechanics of economic development, *Journal of Monetary Economics*, 22(1): 3–42.

National Bureau of Statistics (NBS) (various years), *China Statistical Yearbook*, Beijing: China Statistics Press.

National Bureau of Statistics (NBS) (n.d.), Homepage, NBS, Beijing. Available from: stats.gov.cn/.

People's Bank of China (PBC) (n.d.), Homepage, PBC, Beijing. Available from: pbc.gov.cn/.

Romer, P. M. (1986), Increasing returns and long-run growth, *Journal of Political Economy*, 94(5): 1002–1037.

Solow, R. M. (1956), A contribution to the theory of economic growth, *Quarterly Journal of Economics*, 70(1): 65–94.

Wang, W. and Yuan, M. (2012), Modeling China's capacity utilisation rate and its application, [in Chinese], *Statistics and Decision Making*, 20: 82–84.

Wang, X. (2000), The sustainability of China's economic growth and institutional reforms, [in Chinese], *Economic Research*, 7(2000).

Wang, X., Fan, G. and Liu, P. (2009), Transformation of China's growth pattern and sustainability of economic growth, [in Chinese], *Economic Research*, 1(2009).

Zhu, X. (2012), Understanding China's growth: Past, present, and future, *Journal of Economic Perspectives*, 26(4): 103–124.

5. Accounting for the Industry Origin of China's Growth and Productivity Performance, 1980–2012

Harry X. Wu[1]

Introduction

The substantive slowdown of the Chinese economy in the wake of the 2008–09 Global Financial Crisis (GFC) has added fuel to the long-running debate about the sustainability of China's growth model. Despite the government's unprecedented stimulus package, the official statistics—although often accused of exaggerating the real growth performance, especially in times of crisis (Wu 2014b)—show that China nearly halved its pace of growth, from 13.5 per cent per annum in 2005–07 to about 7 per cent per annum in 2013–15 (NBS 2015: 64–65).[2] While economists have been divided on the nature of the slowdown and the choice of macroeconomic policy, one issue is not so controversial: to achieve sustainable growth, China needs to shift from an input-driven to a productivity-led growth model. This study offers new light on China's post-reform productivity performance, taking into account the role of the government.

In this context, an important question is that while the government has (so far) solved the growth problem since the reform period—particularly in alleviating the scale of the post-GFC growth slowdown—it is unclear whether it has also promoted genuine productivity growth. To ascertain the answer, we explore the *industry origin* of the economy's growth and productivity performance—

1 This study is an update of my 2014 China Update paper on China's industrial total factor productivity (TFP) growth and also a substantial extension of that paper to include all non-industrial sectors. Results similar to those of this study are also reported in the Reserve Bank of Australia (RBA) 2016 China Conference (Wu 2016) and Asian Development Bank Institute (ADBI) 2015 China Conference (Wu 2015a). I am indebted to helpful comments and suggestions on this and/or earlier versions from Kyoji Fukao, Xuehui Han, Mun Ho, Yiping Huang, James Laurenceson, Peter Robertson, John Simon, Ligang Song, Marcel Timmer, Rod Tyers, Yong Wang, Wing Thye Woo and Yanrui Wu, as well as participants at conferences and seminars at ADBI, The Australian National University, Asian KLEMS, Institute of Developing Economies, National School of Development at Peking University, RBA, Shanghai Jiao Tong University, Hong Kong University of Science and Technology and the University of Western Australia. Reported in this chapter are interim results of the China Industrial Productivity (CIP)/KLEMS Database Project supported by the Asian Industrial Productivity Program of the Research Institute of Economy, Trade and Industry and the Institute of Economic Research of Hitotsubashi University. The usual claims apply.

2 The national accounts statistics of this source extend to 2014. The growth estimate for 2015 is based on preliminary estimates available from the National Bureau of Statistics website: stats.gov.cn/tjsj/zxfb/201601/t20160119_1306083.html.

an approach that differs from the one more frequently used in the literature, which concentrates on the aggregate economy. The role of the government can be captured, though indirectly, by the productivity performance of state-monopolised or influenced industries. After all, government interventions are often made through industry-specific policies and supportive institutional arrangements.

This study is both an update and a substantive extension of my 2014 China Update chapter on China's industrial total factor productivity (TFP) growth. Using the latest version of the China Industrial Productivity (CIP)/KLEMS database, which now includes the production accounts of 37 industries economy-wide for the period 1980–2012, I can comprehensively cover all non-industrial sectors of the Chinese economy in this growth accounting exercise.

The rest of the chapter is organised as follows. Section two is a conceptual discussion of the industry-specific role of the government in the context of supporting an economy-wide industry grouping. Section three introduces the Jorgensonian approach to accounting for the industry origin of aggregate growth and productivity performance. Section four proposes an industry-specific grouping strategy to distinguish economic activities by degree of market or non-market environment, the latter defined by the level of government intervention. Section five presents and discusses the results, and section six provides a conclusion.

Considering the role of the government

One important change since the reform period is that government interventions are no longer all-encompassing as they were in the central planning era, which completely abandoned the market. They have, however, become more industry-specific through subsidisation, administrative interference or some combination of both. Subsidies can be made in direct or indirect form. Direct subsidies come with administrative interference that aims to compensate for output losses. Indirect subsidies, in contrast, seek mainly to reduce the producer cost of inputs including energy, land, environment, labour and capital (Huang and Tao 2010). Administrative interference serves the government's interests or strategic plans by controlling or influencing output prices and business operations ranging from managing personnel to the choice of technology. To explore the role of government, we may need to consider distinguishing industries that are subject to different types of government intervention, directly or indirectly, through inputs from other regulated industries.

I argue that whether or to what extent the government uses administrative interference or different types of subsidisation depends on the distance of an industry from the point of final demand, especially the international market. Indirect subsidies have been used by local governments mainly to promote export-oriented manufacturers that make semifinished and finished goods. Most of these downstream industries are labour intensive and therefore crucial for China to reap its demographic dividend in a timely fashion. However, the government tends to get directly involved in upstream industries such as energy and primary input materials that are deemed strategically important in supporting downstream industries. This is illustrated in a flow chart (Figure 5.1) simplified for the industrial economy only.

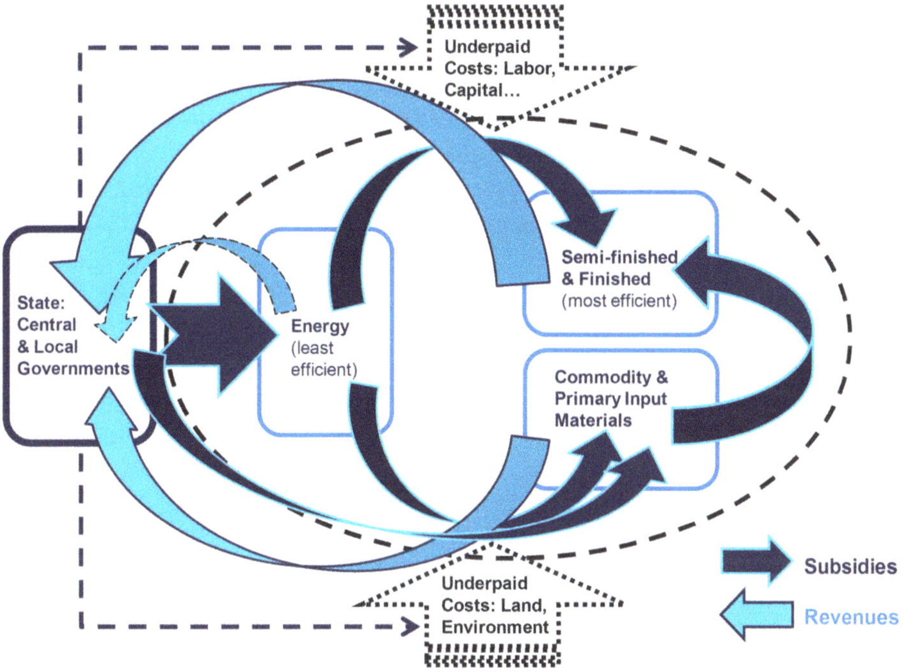

Figure 5.1 'Cross-subsidisation' in Chinese industry: An exploratory flow chart

Source: Author's illustration.

To understand the behaviour of enterprises in such a policy environment and the implications for efficiency improvement and productivity growth, our hypothesis is that industries supported mainly by indirect subsidies are more efficient and productive than those receiving direct subsidies for losses with administrative interference. In the former case, enterprises may still behave like market competitors even though their competitiveness is arbitrarily enhanced. Upstream industries such as oil companies and electricity providers are traditionally dominated by state-owned enterprises (SOEs) and do not conform to China's comparative advantage. Their assumed 'strategic importance' gives them strong bargaining power in negotiating for government support. In return, they accept controls from the authorities. This distorts their behaviour and acts as a disincentive to efforts for efficiency and innovation.

Figure 5.1 illustrates that the nature of government interventions and subsidies is ultimately a form of 'cross-subsidisation'. The key to sustaining it is that downstream industries must be able to grow more rapidly and relatively more efficiently than upstream industries and the public revenues generated from downstream industries must cover direct subsidies. The cost of negative externalities—that is, the cost that cannot be internalised due to subsidies—must be borne by the public. These negative externalities also play a role in resource misallocation.

To investigate the TFP performance of industries within this interventionist environment, I categorise the 37 CIP industries into eight groups (see Table A5.1), guided by the degrees of government intervention, either direct or indirect. The first step in that process is to divide the 24 industries in the industrial sector into three groups: 'energy', including coalmining, petroleum and utilities; 'commodities and primary input materials' (C&P), such as basic metals, chemicals and building materials; and 'semifinished and finished goods' (SF&F), such as clothing, electrical equipment and machinery. C&P and SF&F have been the key drivers of China's post-reform growth. According to their 'distance' from final demand, the 'energy' group is located upstream, followed by C&P, with SF&F the closest to the final consumer market. The SF&F group will therefore, and as conjectured, be most inclined to receive indirect government intervention.

The non-industrial sectors are divided into five groups, although their locations in the production chain cannot be easily defined. Among them, the agricultural sector serves final demand and also provides intermediate inputs to food processing and manufacturing industries and as such can be an important channel for indirect policies. Similarly, construction delivers both investment and consumer goods. Services are further divided into three subgroups: Services I, consisting of state-monopolised services of important intermediate input industries such as financial intermediaries, transportation and telecommunication services; Services II, covering the remaining market services, which are mainly final demand providers; and Services III, denoted by 'non-market services', including government administration, education and health care.

Further exploring the three industrial groups, the 'energy' group remains largely monopolised, if not completely in the hands of large, Central Government-owned enterprises, due to its 'strategic importance'. Firms in this group can easily access public resources but are subject to strong administrative interference. The C&P group is also considered important for downstream industries and hence is heavily influenced though less characterised by state ownership. The third industrial group, the SF&F group, consists of all downstream industries including not only private and foreign enterprises, but also SOEs, particularly in heavy machinery industries. The competitive nature of these industries makes it difficult for the government to directly interfere in business decisions. On average, SF&F is more labour intensive than the other groups and therefore more in line with China's comparative advantage. We therefore conjecture that the productivity growth of SF&F will be faster than that of 'energy' and C&P.

Accounting for industry origin of TFP

The aggregate production function (APF) is a widely adopted approach to TFP analysis. It is also implicitly subject to stringent assumptions that for all (underlying) industries 'value-added functions exist and are identical across industries up to a scalar multiple' and 'the aggregation of heterogeneous types of capital and labour must receive the same price in each industry' (Jorgenson et al. 2005b: 364–365). Given heavy government intervention and institutional setups that cause market imperfections in China, this approach is inappropriate for the growth accounting exercise in the Chinese economy. This study instead adopts Jorgenson's aggregate production possibility frontier (APPF) framework, incorporating also Domar weights to more accurately account for the contributions of individual industries to the growth of aggregate inputs and output.

The APPF approach in growth accounting abandons the strong assumption of the APF approach that all industries are subject to the same value-added production function (Jorgenson 1966). The Domar-weighted aggregation was later adopted into the APPF framework in Jorgenson et al. (1987) to exercise direct aggregation across industries to account for the role of American industries in the changes in aggregate inputs. It has since been used in Jorgenson et al. (2005a, 2005b) to quantify the role of information technology (IT)-producing and IT-using industries in the US economy. The approach is now the international standard and has also been applied to the Chinese economy in Cao et al. (2009) and Wu (forthcoming).

To illustrate this methodology, I begin with a production function where industry gross output is a function of capital, labour, intermediate inputs and technology indexed by time. We use individual industries as building blocks as this allows us to explicitly trace the sources of the aggregate productivity growth and input accumulation to the underlying industries. For the industry-level production function given by Equation 5.1, each industry, indexed by *j*, purchases distinct intermediate inputs, capital and labour services to produce a set of products.

Equation 5.1

$$Y_j = f_j(K_j, L_j, M_j, T)$$

In this equation, *Y* is output, *K* is an index of capital service flows, *L* is an index of labour service flows and *M* is an index of intermediate inputs purchased from domestic industries and/or imported. Note that all input variables are indexed by time but this is suppressed for notational convenience.

Under the assumptions of competitive factor markets, full input utilisation and constant returns to scale, the growth of output can be expressed using the translog functional form as the cost-weighted growth of inputs and technological change (Equation 5.2).

Equation 5.2

$$\Delta \ln Y_j = \bar{v}_j^K \Delta \ln K_j + \bar{v}_{jt}^L \Delta \ln L_j + \bar{v}_j^M \Delta \ln M_j + v_j^T$$

In this equation, $\bar{v}_i^K$, $\bar{v}_i^L$ and $\bar{v}_i^M$ are two-period averages of nominal weights of input $v_j^K = \frac{P_j^K K_j}{P_j^Y Y_j}$, $v_j^L = \frac{P_j^L L_j}{P_j^Y Y_j}$ and $v_j^M = \frac{P_j^M M_j}{P_j^Y Y_j}$, respectively. Under constant returns to scale, $v_j^K + v_j^L + v_j^M = 1$, which is controlled by industry production accounts in nominal terms. Each element in the right-hand side of Equation 5.2 indicates the proportion of output growth accounted for, respectively, by the growth of capital services ($\bar{v}_j^K \Delta \ln K_j$), labour services ($\bar{v}_j^L \Delta \ln L_j$), intermediate materials ($\bar{v}_j^M \Delta \ln M_j$) and TFP ($v_j^T$).

One of the advantages of Equation 5.2 is that it can better account for each input service by different types. For example, it can account for labour services provided by different types of labour with specific demographic, educational and industrial attributes, as shown in pioneering studies by Griliches (1960), Denison (1962) and Jorgenson and Griliches (1967). It has relaxed the usual strong assumption that treats the numbers employed or hours worked as homogeneous measures of labour input. The growth of total labour input can therefore be defined as a Törnqvist quantity index of individual labour types (Equation 5.3a).

Equation 5.3a

$$\Delta \ln L_j = \sum_h \bar{v}_{h,j} \Delta \ln H_{h,j}$$

In this equation, $\Delta \ln H_{h,j}$ indicates the growth of hours worked by each labour type, *h* (with specific gender, age and educational attainment), and its cost weights, $\bar{v}_{h,j}$, given by two-period average shares of each type in the nominal value of labour compensation controlled by the labour income of industry production accounts.

The same user-cost approach is also applied to *K* and *M* to account for the contribution of different types of capital asset (Z_k) and intermediate input (M_m) in production with type-specific, two-period average cost weight defined as $\bar{v}_{k,j}$ and $\bar{v}_{m,j}$, respectively (Equations 5.3b and 5.3c).

Equation 5.3b

$$\Delta \ln K_j = \sum_k \bar{v}_{k,j} \Delta \ln Z_{k,j}$$

Equation 5.3c

$$\Delta \ln M_j = \sum_m \bar{v}_{m,j} \Delta \ln M_{m,j}$$

It should be noted that Equations 5.2 to 5.3c also explicitly express the methodological framework for the CIP industry-level data construction that is linked to and controlled by the national production and income accounts. This point will be discussed again in relation to the data issues in the following section.

Using the value-added concept, Equation 5.2 can be rewritten (Equation 5.4).

Equation 5.4

$$\Delta \ln Y_j = \bar{v}_j^V \Delta \ln V_j + \bar{v}_j^M \Delta \ln M_j$$

In this equation, V_j is the real value added in *j* and v_j^V is the nominal share of value added in industry gross output.

By rearranging Equations 5.2 and 5.4, we can obtain an expression for the sources of industry value-added growth (that is, measured in terms of input contributions) (Equation 5.5).

Equation 5.5

$$\Delta \ln V_j = \frac{\bar{v}_j^K}{\bar{v}_j^V} \Delta \ln K_j + \frac{\bar{v}_j^L}{\bar{v}_j^V} \Delta \ln L_j + \frac{1}{\bar{v}_j^V} v_j^T$$

Growth of aggregate value added by the APPF approach is expressed as weighted industry value added in a Törnqvist index (Equation 5.6).

Equation 5.6

$$\Delta \ln V = \sum_j \bar{w}_j \Delta \ln V_j$$

In this equation, w_j is the share of industry value added in aggregate value added. By combining Equations 5.5 and 5.6, we generate a new expression of aggregate value-added growth by weighted contribution of industry capital growth, industry labour growth and TFP growth (Equation 5.7).

Equation 5.7

$$\Delta \ln V \equiv \sum_j \bar{w}_j \Delta \ln V_j = \sum_j \bar{w}_j \frac{\bar{v}_j^K}{\bar{v}_j^V} \Delta \ln K_j + \bar{w}_j \frac{\bar{v}_j^L}{\bar{v}_j^V} \Delta \ln L_j + \bar{w}_j \frac{1}{\bar{v}_j^V} v_j^T$$

Through this new expression, we have introduced the well-known Domar weights to the aggregation (Domar 1961)—that is, a ratio of each industry's share in total value added (w_j) to the proportion of the industry's value added in its gross output (v_j^V).

If we maintain the stringent assumption that capital and labour inputs have the same marginal productivity in all industries, we can define aggregate TFP growth (Equation 5.8).

Equation 5.8

$$v^T \equiv \sum_j \bar{w}_j \Delta \ln V_j - \bar{v}^K \Delta \ln K - \bar{v}^L \Delta \ln L$$

However, this assumption is not likely to hold, in particular in China, as argued above. It is therefore interesting to look at the differences in the two measurement approaches. By subtracting Equation 5.7 from Equation 5.8 and rearranging, we can demonstrate how the aggregate TFP growth relates to the sources of TFP growth at the industry level and to the effect of factor mobility across industries (Jorgenson et al. 2005b) (Equation 5.9).

Equation 5.9

$$\begin{aligned} v^T = & \sum_j \frac{\overline{w}_j}{\overline{v}_j^V} v_j^T \\ & + \sum_j \overline{w}_j \frac{\overline{v}_j^K}{\overline{v}_j^V} \Delta \ln K_j - \overline{v}_K \Delta \ln K \\ & + \sum_j \overline{w}_j \frac{\overline{v}_j^L}{\overline{v}_j^V} \Delta \ln L_j - \overline{v}_L \Delta \ln L \end{aligned}$$

In this equation, the *reallocation* terms in the second and third brackets can be simplified (Equation 5.9a).

Equation 5.9a

$$v^T = \sum_j \frac{\overline{w}_j}{\overline{v}_j^V} v_j^T + \rho^K + \rho^L$$

Equation 5.9 expresses the aggregate TFP growth in terms of three sources: Domar-weighted industry TFP growth, reallocation of capital and reallocation of labour across industries. This Domar weighting scheme ($\overline{w}_j / \overline{v}_j^V$), originated by Domar (1961), plays a key role in the direct aggregation across industries under the Jorgensonian growth accounting framework. A direct consequence of the Domar aggregation is that the weights do not sum to unity, and this implies that aggregate productivity growth amounts to more than the weighted average of industry-level productivity growth (or less, if negative). This reflects the fact that productivity change in the production of *intermediate inputs* not only had an 'own' effect, but also leads to price changes in downstream industries, and that effect accumulates through vertical links. As elaborated by Hulten (1978), the Domar aggregation establishes a consistent link between industry-level productivity growth and aggregate productivity growth. Productivity gains of the aggregate economy may exceed the average productivity gains across industries because flows of intermediate inputs between industries contribute to aggregate productivity by allowing productivity gains in successive industries to augment one another. The same logic can explain productivity losses.

The next two terms reflect the impact on aggregate TFP growth of the reallocation effect of capital (ρ^K) and labour (ρ^L) across industries. Each of the reallocation terms is obtained by subtracting the cost-weighted aggregate factor (capital or labour) input growth from the Domar-weighted input growth across industries. It should be noted that both theoretically and methodologically, when these terms are not negligible, it indicates that industries do not face the same factor costs, which suggests a violation of the assumption of the widely used aggregate approach. However, one should not expect a significant reallocation effect in an economy where there is a well-developed market system. This is an especially useful analytical tool for the Chinese case, where strong government interventions in resource allocation may have caused severe market distortions.

Data and periodisation

The CIP database

This study has benefited from a new economy-wide, industry-level dataset that was constructed by the ongoing CIP Project. It is beyond the scope of this chapter to provide an extensive history of studies of the data.[3] I refer interested readers to three working papers for details (Wu 2015b; Wu and Ito 2015; Wu et al. 2015).

In the CIP Project, the principles of industry data construction adhere to the underlying theory and data constraints as expressed in Equation 5.2 and Equations 5.3a–c. This implies that the industry-level data are linked to and consistent with the national production and income accounts of China.

Some features of the CIP data should be noted. For the classification of industries, we in principle adopt the 2002 version of the Chinese Standard Industrial Classification (CSIC/2002) and reclassify the economy into 37 industries (see Appendix Table A5.1). The reconstruction of the Chinese national accounts is based on different versions of official national accounts compiled under the material product system (MPS) before 1992 and the United Nations System of National Accounts (SNA) thereafter. To construct a time series of Chinese input–output accounts for the period 1981–2010, we use China's SNA input–output accounts that are available for every five years since 1987 and an MPS input–output table for 1981 that is converted to an SNA-type table (Wu and Ito 2015).

3 The CIP project is based on Wu's China Growth and Productivity Database project, self-initiated in 1995 and heavily involved in Angus Maddison's work on China's aggregate economic performance from 1912 and manufacturing, mining and utility industries from 1949 (see Maddison 1998, 2007; Maddison and Wu 2008). The CIP project began in 2010, aiming to extend Wu's earlier work to all non-industrial sectors under the KLEMS framework.

Nominal accounts are deflated by industry-level producer price indices (PPIs), constructed using official PPIs for the agricultural and industrial sectors and the consumer price index or its components for service industries (Wu and Ito 2015). The work reported in this chapter, however, still uses the single deflation approach, assuming changes in input prices are the same as changes in output prices—similar to the Chinese national accounts. This choice results from a lack of price data, and is used instead of the double-deflation approach that would otherwise be preferred.[4]

For the required labour data, following earlier studies that analysed the industrial sector only (Wu and Yue 2003, 2010, 2012), CIP has established economy-wide employment series (in both the numbers employed and the hours worked) and compensation matrices for 37 industries. 'Workers' refers to both employees and those who are self-employed (farming households and self-employed retailers and transporters), cross-classified by gender, seven age groups and five educational levels (see Wu et al. 2015).

The construction of net capital stock at the industry level proved most challenging. CIP has reconstructed annual investment flows by industrial sector using official gross capital stock data at historical costs, but it has to adopt the official investment series estimates for the non-industrial sectors. The results are yet to be reconciled with the national accounts gross fixed capital formation data. Industry-specific investment deflators are constructed using the PPIs of investment goods industries and the nominal wage index of construction workers (H. Wu 2008, 2015a). The industry-specific depreciation rates are estimated based on asset service lives and declining balance values used in the US national accounts, following the approach developed by Hulten and Wykoff (1981).

Periodisation

To better examine the productivity impact of major policy shifts on the Chinese economy, I divide the entire period covered by the current version of the CIP data, 1980–2012, into four subperiods: 1980–91, 1992–2001, 2002–07 and 2008–12. The first subperiod, 1980–91, is characterised by decollectivisation in agriculture and planning-market double-track price reform with more operational autonomy in the industrial sector. The subperiod ended with the rising inflation that helped to trigger the 1989 Tiananmen Square political turmoil.

4 See Wu and Ito (2015) for preliminary growth estimates at the industry level using the double-deflation approach.

The second subperiod, 1992–2001, began with Deng Xiaoping's call for bolder and deeper reforms in 1992 and the official adoption of the so-called socialist market economy in 1993. Wider opening up to Western technology and foreign direct investment drove a new wave of investment in export-oriented manufacturing capacity. Meanwhile, due to the deregulation of private activities, new private firms absorbed huge numbers of state-owned industry employees who lost their jobs in the SOE reforms of the 1990s. However, this also resulted in serious overinvestment. The East Asian Financial Crisis (1997–98) hit the Chinese economy hard and, from 1998, China entered a four-year period of deflation.[5]

The third subperiod, 2002–07, began with China's entry to the World Trade Organization (WTO) in late 2001, and is characterised by counteracting forces. On one hand, WTO entry induced further opening to foreign trade and direct investment, which directed the Chinese economy further towards the market system. On the other hand, consolidated and enlarged state corporations experienced resurgence in the name of protecting national interests in a time of accelerating globalisation. Growth-motivated local governments were meanwhile pressured to undertake rapid urbanisation and heavy industrialisation.

The final subperiod, 2008–12, broadly characterises the aftermath of the GFC. The unprecedented fiscal stimulus package from both central and local governments substantially enhanced the role of SOEs. Separating this period from others helps to examine differences in productivity performance between state and non–state-dominated industries at the time of the crisis.

Results and discussion

Sources of growth in the APPF framework

We now examine China's aggregate TFP performance in the APPF framework. The results are summarised in Table 5.1. According to our estimates, the Chinese economy achieved real output growth of 8.94 per cent per annum in 1980–12. Until the GFC, the SF&F group was the top contributor to growth, followed by Services II (market). In the wake of the crisis, SF&F was marginally overtaken by Services II. On average, over the years 1980–2012, SF&F contributed over one-quarter of real output growth, Services II contributed about 20 per cent and agriculture, C&P and Services I (state monopoly) together contributed nearly

5 China's retail price index declined from 380.8 in 1997 (1978 = 100) to 346.7 in 2003; meanwhile, the producer price index declined from 315.0 to 299.3 (NBS 2014: 123).

40 per cent. The estimated aggregate TFP growth was 0.83 per cent per annum. However, the TFP performance was highly unstable over time, with the highest growth achieved in 1991–2001 (1.63) and the worst in 2007–12 (–2.06).[6]

Table 5.1 Growth in aggregate value added and sources of growth in China, 1980–2012*

	1980–91	1991–2001	2001–07	2007–12	1980–2012
	Industry contributions to value-added growth				
Value-added growth due to (%):	7.61	9.04	11.00	9.23	*8.94*
Agriculture	*1.75*	*1.18*	*0.50*	*0.65*	*1.17*
Construction	*0.38*	*0.64*	*0.68*	*0.73*	*0.58*
Energy	*–0.06*	*0.33*	*0.74*	*0.30*	*0.27*
Commodities & primary materials	*0.90*	*1.49*	*1.57*	*1.31*	*1.28*
Semifinished & finished goods	*1.87*	*2.65*	*2.72*	*2.01*	*2.29*
Services I	*0.92*	*0.64*	*1.47*	*1.20*	*0.98*
Services II	*1.45*	*1.74*	*2.39*	*2.35*	*1.86*
Services III (non-market)	*0.39*	*0.37*	*0.94*	*0.67*	*0.53*
	Factor contributions to value-added growth				
Value-added growth due to (%):	7.61	9.04	11.00	9.23	*8.94*
Capital input:	*5.00*	*6.15*	*8.63*	*9.30*	*6.71*
Stock	*5.00*	*6.22*	*8.71*	*9.30*	*6.75*
Capital quality (composition)	*–0.01*	*–0.07*	*–0.08*	*0.00*	*–0.04*
Labour input:	*1.39*	*1.26*	*1.19*	*1.98*	*1.40*
Hours	*1.34*	*0.88*	*0.71*	*0.34*	*0.92*
Labour quality (composition)	*0.05*	*0.38*	*0.48*	*1.65*	*0.48*
Aggregate TFP	*1.22*	*1.63*	*1.19*	*–2.06*	*0.83*

* Contributions are share-weighted growth rate in percentage
Source: Author's estimates.

Of the 8.94 per cent annual output growth rate for the entire period, the contribution of capital input was 6.71, labour input was 1.40 and TFP 0.83. This means that 64 per cent of the real value-added growth relied on capital input, 27 per cent relied on labour input and 9 per cent relied on TFP growth. The contribution of capital input increased from 46 per cent in the 1980s to 71 per cent post–WTO accession and nearly 100 per cent in the wake of the GFC. On the other hand, the contribution of labour inputs declined from 38 per cent in the 1980s to 19 per cent post WTO accession. This trend reversed after

6 Contact the author for the estimated TFP growth of individual industries.

the GFC and the contribution of labour inputs rose back to 26 per cent—largely attributed to quality improvement rather than hours worked. The contribution of the quality of capital was, on average, insignificant.[7]

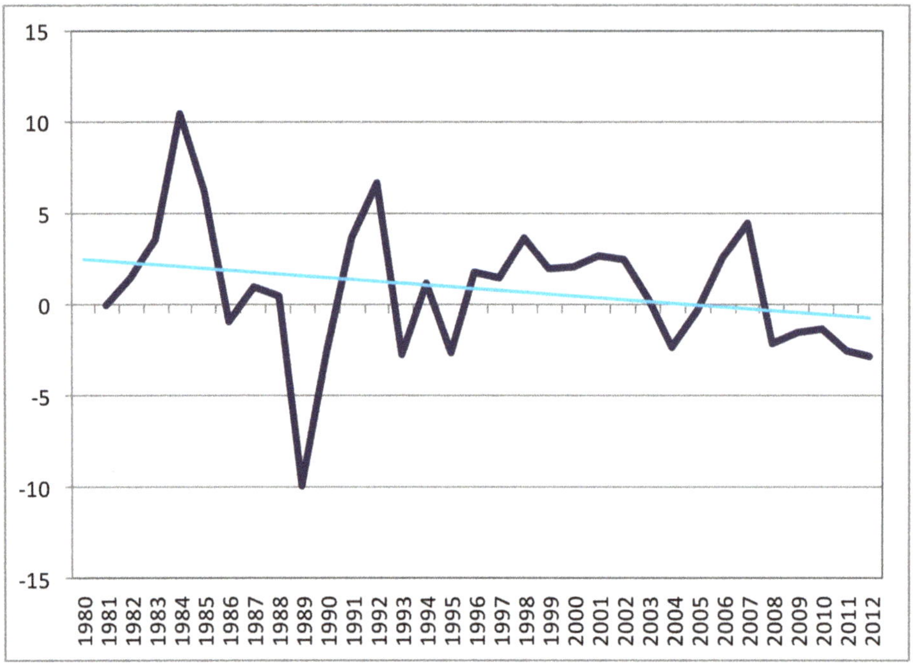

Figure 5.2 TFP growth in China: An APPF approach

Note: 1980 = 100.

Source: Constructed from results shown in Table 5.1.

Constructed using empirical results, Figure 5.2 shows that China's TFP growth was not sustained. In the period 1980–2012, it followed a declining trend. China's first TFP drive was observed from the early to mid-1980s and was associated with successful agricultural reform and the kick-off of nationwide industrial reforms, yet it was short lived. Thereafter, the growth of TFP slowed significantly before collapsing sharply around the 1989 political crisis. The post-crisis TFP recovery was short. The only period that saw stable and sustained TFP growth was 1996–2002. China's post–WTO accession period saw only a short resurgence of TFP growth, in 2006–07, which was interrupted by the GFC. There is little sign that the decline in TFP will shift any time soon.

7 This might be due to the limited set of asset types ('structures' and 'equipment') available in the current CIP database. If a distinction between information and communication technology (ICT) and non-ICT assets could be made, a higher measured contribution is expected.

Table 5.2 presents the results of a decomposition of China's aggregate value added per hour worked into changes in capital deepening, labour quality (composition) and TFP. This enables us to separate the contribution of hours worked from the contribution of genuine labour productivity improvement and its sources. The Chinese economy benefited significantly from the increase in hours worked: the so-called demographic dividend. The dividend, however, declined over time, from 2.83 per cent per annum in 1980–91 to 0.73 per cent per annum in 2007–12. Although value added per hour worked increased from 4.78 to 8.50 per cent per annum, it appeared to be relying increasingly on capital deepening, from 3.51 to 8.91 per cent per annum. More importantly, the growth of labour productivity was not necessarily in line with the pace of capital deepening if we compare the results for 2007–12 with those for 2001–07, and this suggests serious disequilibrium and misallocation of resources that were likely caused by increasing overinvestment.

Table 5.2 Decomposition of aggregate labour productivity growth in China*

	1980–91	1991–2001	2001–07	2007–12	1980–2012
	Growth rates				
Value-added growth (APPF)	7.61	9.04	11.00	9.23	*8.94*
Value added per hour worked	*4.78*	*7.29*	*9.44*	*8.50*	*7.02*
Hours	*2.83*	*1.75*	*1.57*	*0.73*	*1.93*
	Factor contributions				
Value added per hour worked	4.78	7.29	9.44	8.50	*7.02*
Capital deepening	3.51	5.28	*7.77*	8.91	*5.71*
Labour quality (composition)	*0.05*	*0.38*	*0.48*	*1.65*	*0.48*
TFP growth	*1.22*	*1.63*	*1.19*	*–2.06*	*0.83*

* Contributions are weighted growth in percentage
Source: Author's estimates.

The industry origin of aggregate TFP growth

To explicitly account for differences across industries and their impact on China's aggregate TFP performance, we now introduce Domar weights to the exercise, following the studies of the US economy by Jorgenson et al. (2005a, 2005b). The results presented in the first line of Table 5.3 are estimated with the stringent assumption that marginal productivities of capital and labour are the same across all industries, and are the same as those presented in Tables 5.1 and 5.2. As expressed in Equation 5.9, using Domar weights, the aggregate TFP growth rate can be decomposed into three additional components: 1) the change of Domar-weighted aggregate TFP; 2) the change of capital reallocation; and 3) the change of labour reallocation. Let us first focus on the first component in Table 5.3, the most important finding of the study.

Table 5.3 Domar-weighted TFP growth and reallocation effects in the Chinese economy*

	1980–91	1991–2001	2001–07	2007–12	1980–2012
Aggregate TFP growth	1.22	1.63	1.19	–2.06	*0.83*
1. Domar-weighted TFP growth	0.60	1.72	0.54	–2.10	*0.52*
Agriculture	*0.99*	*0.75*	*0.82*	*0.68*	*0.83*
Construction	*–0.05*	*0.12*	*0.29*	*0.04*	*0.08*
Energy	*–0.76*	*–0.24*	*–0.32*	*–0.49*	*–0.47*
Commodities & primary materials	*–0.50*	*0.77*	*0.20*	*–0.27*	*0.07*
Semifinished & finished goods	*0.30*	*1.35*	*0.50*	*–0.35*	*0.57*
Services I (market monopolies)	*0.25*	*–0.59*	*0.28*	*–0.02*	*–0.05*
Services II (market)	*0.31*	*–0.42*	*–0.79*	*–0.97*	*–0.33*
Services III (non-market)	*0.06*	*–0.03*	*–0.43*	*–0.71*	*–0.18*
2. Reallocation of K (ρ^K)	0.28	–0.09	–1.03	–0.01	*–0.12*
3. Reallocation of L (ρ^L)	0.35	0.01	1.68	0.06	*0.44*

* Growth in per cent per annum and contribution in percentage points
Source: Author's estimates following Equation 5.9.

On average, across the entire period 1980–2012, China's TFP growth estimated with the Domar weights is 0.52 per cent per annum, which is much slower than the aggregate TFP growth of 0.83. This implies a net factor reallocation effect of 0.44, which will be discussed later. Table 5.3 also shows the contribution of each industrial group to the Domar-weighted annual TFP growth. The highest contributor to the Domar-weighted aggregate TFP growth was agriculture, which contributed 0.83 percentage points. The SF&F group also did relatively well over time (0.57), followed by construction (0.08). The worst performer was the 'energy' group (–0.47), followed by Services II (–0.33) and Services III (–0.18). Such a sharp contrast in TFP performance across industry groups can also be observed over different subperiods. In general, this suggests that treating individual industries as homogeneous within growth accounting may be substantially distorting our understanding of the productivity performance of the Chinese economy.

As was earlier elaborated, the subperiods for examination are set around policy regime shifts that may shed important light on the role of the government. The agricultural sector benefited most from reforms in the 1980s, especially the decollectivisation of farming and deregulation of rural township–village enterprises. According to our analysis, it specifically contributed 0.83 percentage points to the Domar-weighted TFP growth at 0.52 per cent per annum. Even in the last of our subperiods (2008–12), which was affected by the GFC, it was still the most important contributor (0.68 percentage points) to the Domar-weighted TFP growth (–2.10 per cent per annum). What is possibly surprising is that, although this group's share in nominal gross domestic product (GDP) has been declining over time (see Table 5.1), its contribution to the Domar-weighted TFP growth has remained high throughout the period. This is suggestive of a process in which the agricultural sector is still releasing capital (including land) and labour that have a marginal productivity below the sector's average. By shedding these 'surplus' factors, the average productivity with which factors are used is still growing. Clearly, however, this cannot be a long-run source of growth, as this structural shift is temporary. Future growth must come from the manufacturing and services sectors.[8]

The period 1991–2001 saw the most rapid TFP growth, at 1.63 per cent per annum by Domar weights, and despite the impact of the East Asian Financial Crisis (1997–98) and the subsequent period of deflation in 1998–2003 (see footnote 7). The SF&F group was the most important contributor (1.35 percentage points), followed by the C&P group (0.77 percentage points), driven by unprecedented state sector reforms and opening to foreign trade and direct investment, which allowed the market to play an increasing role in resource allocation. The productivity performance of the construction industry also turned positive for the first time (0.12 percentage points) and even the productivity decline of the 'energy' group slowed substantially, to –0.24 from –0.76 percentage points in the previous period (1980–91).

Despite these group effects, I nevertheless find that China's accession to the WTO at the end of 2001 was accompanied by a slowdown rather than an acceleration of TFP growth: 0.54 per cent per annum in 2001–07, which is less than one-third of the 1.72 achieved over 1991–2001. This puzzling result may be supported somewhat by the observed increasing interventions by local governments in the 2000s aiming to promote local urbanisation and heavy industrialisation (see J. Wu 2008). Table 5.3 shows that in 2001–07, the contribution of SF&F and C&P to TFP growth reduced considerably, from 1.35 to 0.50 percentage points and from 0.77 to 0.20 percentage points, respectively. It also shows that the contribution of construction and state-monopolised Services I (transportation, telecommunications and financial services), both of which are engineered and promoted by the government, significantly increased, from 0.12 to 0.29 percentage points and from –0.59 to 0.28 percentage points, respectively.

8 I am indebted to Marcel Timmer for discussion of the role of Chinese agriculture in the productivity performance of the aggregate economy.

In the wake of the GFC, China's Central Government implemented a RMB4 trillion stimulus package that was also accompanied by RMB18 trillion worth of projects driven by local government financing vehicles. In the face of this stimulus, China's TFP growth declined by –2.10 per cent per annum from 2007 to 2012. Since most of the stimulus package projects were in infrastructure development, construction groups experienced nearly zero TFP growth. Similarly, Services I suffered least (–0.02 percentage points) in terms of productivity decline. The most recent development shows that while the effect of the unprecedented government cash injection has quickly abated since 2012, there are increasing signs that China's surplus capacity in manufacturing is worsening and may take many years to recalibrate to a new, sustainable equilibrium.

The effect of factor reallocation

The slower Domar-weighted TFP growth (0.52) compared with the aggregate TFP growth (0.83) implies that above 60 per cent of the aggregate TFP growth is attributable to productivity performance within individual industries while a less than 40 per cent share goes to the reallocation of capital and labour. Following Equation 5.9, Table 5.3 shows that this effect consists of a positive labour reallocation effect (ρ^L) of 0.44 percentage points and a negative capital reallocation effect (ρ^K) of –0.12 percentage points.

It should be noted that a reallocation effect of such magnitude is typically not observed in market economies. Empirical work on the US economy over the period 1977–2000 by Jorgenson et al. (2005b) showed that first, the reallocation effect was generally negligible and second, if it was non-negligible for some subperiods, the capital and labour reallocation effects generally moved in opposite directions. Jorgenson et al. (1987) also reported the reallocation of capital was typically positive and the reallocation of labour was typically negative for the US economy for the period 1948–79. This is because capital grew more rapidly in industries with high capital service prices and hence high returns on capital, whereas labour grew relatively slowly in industries with high marginal compensation.

In the case of China, the much larger magnitude and unexpected signs of capital and labour reallocation effects have two important implications. First, individual industries indeed face significantly different marginal factor productivities. Second, this suggests that there are barriers to factor mobility that cause misallocation of resources in the economy. The flipside is that corrections to the distortions can potentially be productivity enhancing, which might be good news in terms of the much talked about and long-awaited structural reforms.

I also find that the effect of labour reallocation remained generally positive over time. This may suggest that the labour market was much less distorted than the capital market, having benefited from increasing labour mobility along with reforms. Notably, the post–WTO accession period experienced the most significant gain from labour reallocation (1.68 percentage points over 2001–07), which underwrote the rapid expansion of export-oriented, labour-intensive industries that were then in line with China's comparative advantage.

The case of capital reallocation is different. The early reform period was the only period that saw a positive effect on TFP growth from capital reallocation (0.28 percentage points over 1980–91). The partial removal of the distortions inherited from the central planning period was part of the story. The TFP growth here has, however, since turned negative, especially following China's WTO accession (–1.03 percentage points over 2001–07), likely because of the enhanced role of the government in supporting the state sector's resurgence in upstream industries.

Nevertheless, the results for the post-crisis period from 2008 to 2012 covered in the data deserve greater attention. As shown in Table 5.3, during this period and in contrast with the earlier period, the reallocation effect in both capital and labour approaches zero—that is, 0.06 compared with 1.68 percentage points in the case of labour and –0.01 compared with –1.03 in the case of capital. This rather unusual outcome likely reflects government intervention to keep the economy intact following the external shock. If this finding is true, China's unprecedented government stimulus package did enhance the existing structure of the economy in terms of resource (mis)allocation.

Conclusion

This chapter explores the industry origin of China's aggregate growth and productivity performance for the reform period 1980–2012 using the newly constructed CIP database, and by adopting the Domar aggregation-incorporated Jorgensonian growth accounting framework. This approach provides a highly appropriate analytical tool for investigating the industry origin of aggregate productivity and the effect of resource reallocation across industries in the Chinese economy.

Our preliminary results show that China achieved TFP growth of 0.83 per cent per annum for the entire period 1980–2012. This means that compared with an industry-weighted value-added growth rate of 8.94 per cent per annum, TFP growth accounted for about 9.3 per cent of average GDP growth. This is a result that is much smaller than all previous productivity studies on the Chinese economy based on the aggregate approach—for example, about 40 per cent contribution estimated by Bosworth and Collins (2008) and by Perkins and Rawski (2008). Our finding is, however, also small when compared with the only work in the literature applying the same approach but specifically to the period 1982–2000 (Cao et al. 2009). The finding herein is in fact about one-third of their result of 2.51 per cent per annum. The differences could come from data construction, measurement, classification and coverage (for example, we have 11 service sectors whereas Cao et al. put everything in one sector).

At the industry group level, and as conjectured, we find that in general industries less prone to government intervention, such as agriculture and the semifinished and finished manufactures, tended to have higher TFP growth rates than those industries subject to direct government intervention, such as the 'energy' group. The fact that the SF&F group maintained positive TFP growth while the 'energy' group experienced persistent TFP declines suggests the existence of 'cross-subsidisation' between upstream and downstream industries in which the government plays different roles to serve its own strategies.

We also found strong effects from factor input reallocation across industries that significantly address the key issue of resource misallocation in the ongoing policy debate. On the one hand, the magnitude of this reallocation effect reflects barriers to factor mobility in the economy and, on the other hand, it suggests potential gains from market-driven reallocation. Institutional deficiencies in the Chinese economy that allow governments at all levels to intervene in resource allocation at their discretion are responsible for resource misallocation, measured here by diminished TFP growth. Therefore, disentangling government from business and allowing the market to correct the cost structure of industries will be important for solving China's structural problems. Indeed, 'restructuring' for healthy and sustainable growth is the most crucial and challenging pillar of the 'Liconomics' agenda. But there is no such thing as the 'right structure', and certainly not without allowing more market-based resource allocation across industries.

References

Bosworth, B. and Collins, S. M. (2008), Accounting for growth: Comparing China and India, *Journal of Economic Perspectives*, 22(1): 45–66.

Cao, J., Ho, M. S., Jorgenson, D. W., Ren, R., Sun, L. and Yue, X. (2009), Industrial and aggregate measures of productivity growth in China, 1982–2000, *The Review of Income and Wealth*, 55(SI 1) (July).

Denison, E. F. (1962), *The sources of economic growth in the United States and the alternative before us*, New York: Committee on Economic Development.

Domar, E. (1961), On the measurement of technological change, *Economic Journal*, 71(284): 709–729.

Griliches, Z. (1960), Measuring inputs in agriculture: A critical survey, *Journal of Farm Economics*, 40(5): 1398–1427.

Huang, Y. and Tao, K. (2010), Factor market distortion and the current account surplus in China, *Asian Economic Papers*, 9(3): 1–37.

Hulten, C. R. (1978), Growth accounting with intermediate inputs, *Review of Economic Studies*, 45(3): 511–518.

Hulten, C. R. and Wykoff, F. C. (1981), The measurement of economic depreciation, in C. R. Hulten (ed.), *Depreciation, inflation, and the taxation of income from capital*, Washington, DC: The Urban Institute Press.

Jorgenson, D. W. (1966), The embodiment hypothesis, *Journal of Political Economy*, 74(1): 1–17.

Jorgenson, D. W. (1990), Productivity and economic growth, in E. R. Berndt and J. E. Triplett (eds), *Fifty years of economic measurement: The jubilee of the conference on research in income and wealth. Volume 54*, Cambridge, Mass.: National Bureau of Economic Research.

Jorgenson, D. W., Gollop, F. and Fraumeni, B. (1987), *Productivity and US economic growth*, Cambridge, Mass.: Harvard University Press.

Jorgenson, D. W. and Griliches, Z. (1967), The explanation of productivity change, *Review of Economic Studies*, 34(3): 249–283.

Jorgenson, D. W., Ho, M. S. and Stiroh, K. J. (2005a), Growth of US industries and investments in information technology and higher education, in C. Corrado, J. Haltiwanger and D. Sichel (eds), *Measuring capital in a new economy*, Chicago: University of Chicago Press.

Jorgenson, D. W., Ho, M. S. and Stiroh, K. J. (2005b), *Information technology and the American growth resurgence. Productivity. Volume 3*, Cambridge, Mass.: MIT Press.

Maddison, A. (1998), *Chinese economic performance in the long run*, OECD Development Centre, Paris.

Maddison, A. (2007), *Chinese economic performance in the long run, 960–2030*, OECD, Paris.

Maddison, A. and Wu, H. X. (2008), Measuring China's economic performance, *World Economics*, 9(2): 13–44.

National Bureau of Statistics of China (NBS) (2014), *China Statistical Yearbook*, Beijing: China Statistics Press.

National Bureau of Statistics of China (NBS) (2015), *China Statistical Yearbook*, Beijing: China Statistics Press.

Perkins, D. H. and Rawski, T. G. (2008), Forecasting China's economic growth to 2025, in L. Brandt and T. G. Rawski (eds), *China's great economic transformation*, Cambridge: Cambridge University Press.

Timmer, M., van Moergastel, T., Stuivenwold, E., Ypma, G., O'Mahony, M. and Kangasniemi, M. (2007), *EU-KLEMS growth and productivity accounts. Version 1.0. Part I: Methodology*, Paris: OECD.

Wu, H. X. (2008), Measuring capital input in Chinese industry and implications for China's industrial productivity performance, 1949–2005, Presentation to World Congress on National Accounts and Economic Performance Measures for Nations, Washington, DC, 12–17 May.

Wu, H. X. (2013), How fast has Chinese industry grown? The upward bias hypothesis revisited, *China Economic Journal*, 6(2–3): 80–102.

Wu, H. X. (2014a), *China's growth and productivity performance debate revisited: Accounting for China's sources of growth in 1949–2012*, The Conference Board Economics Working Papers EPWP1401, New York: The Conference Board.

Wu, H. X. (2014b), The growth of 'non-material services' in China: Maddison's 'zero-labour-productivity-growth' hypothesis revisited, *The Economic Review*, 65(3) (July): 265–283.

Wu, H. X. (2015a), China's institutional impediment to sustainable productivity growth, presentation to ADBI International Conference of 'Implications of Possible PRC Growth Slowdown for Asia', 25–26 November.

Wu, H. X. (2015b), *Constructing China's net capital stock and measuring capital service in China*, RIETI Discussion Papers 15-E-006, Tokyo: Research Institute of Economy, Trade and Industry. Available from: rieti.go.jp/en/ publications/ summary/15010007.html.

Wu, H. X. (2016), Productivity hurdle to China's sustainable growth or institutional impediment to raising China's productivity, presented at Reserve Bank of Australia Annual Conference on Structural Change in China and Implications for Australia and the World, Sydney, 16–18 March.

Wu, H. X. (forthcoming), On China's strategic move for a new stage of development: A productivity perspective, in D. W. Jorgenson, M. P. Timmer and K. Fukao (eds), *The world economy: Growth or stagnation?*, Cambridge: Cambridge University Press.

Wu, H. X. and Ito, K. (2015), *Reconstruction of China's national output and income accounts and supply–use and input–output accounts in time series*, RIETI Discussion Papers 15-E-004, Tokyo: Research Institute of Economy, Trade and Industry. Available from: rieti.go.jp/en/publications/summary/15010005.html.

Wu, H. X. and Shea, E. Y. P. (2008), China: Institutions, domestic financial architecture and macro volatility, in J. M. Fanelli (ed.), *Macroeconomic volatility, institutions and financial architecture*, Basingstoke, UK: Palgrave Macmillan.

Wu, H. X. and Yue, X. (2003), Sources of quality change in the labour input of Chinese industry, 1955–2000, presented at Western Economic Association International Pacific Rim Conference, Taipei.

Wu, H. X. and Yue, X. (2010), Accounting for labor input in Chinese industry, presented at the 31st IARIW General Conference, St Gallen, Switzerland.

Wu, Harry X. and Yue, X. (2012), *Accounting for labor input in Chinese industry, 1949–2009*, RIETI Discussion Papers, 12-E-065, Tokyo: Research Institute of Economy, Trade and Industry.

Wu, H. X., Yue, X. and Zhang, G. G. (2015), *Constructing employment and compensation matrices and measuring labour input in China*, RIETI Discussion Papers 15-E-005, Tokyo: Research Institute of Economy, Trade and Industry. Available from: rieti.go.jp/en/publications/summary/15010006.html.

Wu, J. (2008), *The choice of China's growth model*, [in Chinese], Shanghai: Yuandong Book Press.

Wu, J. (2013), Towards a proper analytical framework for studying the engine of China's growth, in Boyuan Foundation (ed.), *China's opportunities and challenges in the next ten years*, Beijing: China Economy Press.

Xu, C. (2011), The fundamental institutions of China's reforms and development, *Journal of Economic Literature*, 49(4): 1076–1051.

Appendix 5.1

Appendix Table A5.1 CIP/China KLEMS industrial classification and code

CIP code	EU-KLEMS code	Grouping	Industry	
1	AtB	Agriculture	Agriculture, forestry, animal husbandry & fisheries	AGR
2	10	Energy	Coalmining	CLM
3	11	Energy	Oil & gas extraction	PTM
13	23	Energy	Petroleum and coal products	PET
25	E	Energy	Power, steam, gas and tap water supply	UTL
4	13	C&P	Metal mining	MEM
5	14	C&P	Non-metallic minerals mining	NMM
8	17	C&P	Textile mill products	TEX
12	21t22	C&P	Paper products, printing & publishing	P&P
14	24	C&P	Chemicals and allied products	CHE
16	26	C&P	Stone, clay and glass products	BUI
17	27t28	C&P	Primary & fabricated metal industries	MET
6	15	Finished	Food and kindred products	F&B
7	16	Finished	Tobacco products	TBC
9	18	Finished	Apparel and other textile products	WEA
10	19	Finished	Leather and leather products	LEA
23	34t35	Finished	Motor vehicles & other transportation equipment	TRS
24	36t37	Finished	Miscellaneous manufacturing industries	OTH
19	29	Semifinished	Industrial machinery and equipment	MCH
11	20	SF&F	Sawmill products, furniture, fixtures	W&F
15	25	SF&F	Rubber and plastic products	R&P
18	27t28	SF&F	Metal products (excluding rolling products)	MEP
20	31	SF&F	Electrical equipment	ELE
21	32	SF&F	Electronic and telecommunications equipment	ICT
22	30t33	SF&F	Instruments and office equipment	INS
26	F	Construction	Construction	CON
29	I	Services I	Transport, storage & postal services	T&S
30	71t74	Services I	Telecommunications & postal	P&T
31	J	Services I	Financial intermediation	FIN
27	G	Services II	Wholesale and retail trades	SAL
28	H	Services II	Hotels and restaurants	HOT
32	K	Services II	Real estate services	REA

CIP code	EU-KLEMS code	Grouping	Industry	
33	71t74	Services II	Leasing, technical, science & business services	BUS
37	O&P	Services II	Other services	SER
34	L	Services III	Public administration and defence	ADM
35	M	Services III	Education services	EDU
36	N	Services III	Health and social security services	HEA

Notes: This is based on Wu's series of works to reclassify official statistics reported under different CSIC systems adopted in CSIC/1972, CSIC/1985 and CSIC/1994 (see Wu and Yue 2012; Wu and Ito 2015). The current Chinese classification system, CSIC/2011, largely conforms to the two-digit-level industries of the International Standard Industrial Classification of All Economic Activities (ISIC, Rev. 4) and can be reconciled with the EU-KLEMS system of classification (see Timmer et al. 2007).

6. Can the Internet Revolutionise Finance in China?

Yiping Huang, Yan Shen, Jingyi Wang and Feng Guo

Introduction

The Chinese term for 'internet finance' was coined by Ping Xie and Chuanwei Zou (2012) at the 2012 Annual Conference of the China Finance 40 Forum. It now enjoys a place in public discourse alongside such phrases as 'digital finance' and 'fintech', which are often used outside China. The context for the use of 'internet finance', however, is somewhat richer, as internet finance can refer to both information technology (IT) companies providing financial services, such as WeChatPay, and financial institutions applying IT to their more traditional services, such as the e-ICBC service of the Industrial and Commercial Bank of China (ICBC). Narrow definitions of internet finance nonetheless embrace a wide range of activities, including third-party payment, online lending, direct sales of funds, crowd-funding, online insurance and banking and digital money. Our discussion in this chapter focuses on the potential of internet finance in China.

Internet finance has been operating in China for more than 10 years. AliPay was launched in 2004 and CreditEase was established in 2005. Most people, however, regard the launch of Yu'ebao, an online sales platform for money market funds established by Alibaba's Ant Financial Services in June 2013, as the point from which the recent explosive development of internet finance in China began. Public sentiment towards internet finance has moved the full gamut from fever pitch to fear. Extreme feelings—from exuberance to pessimism—are common among the public and in the market. Often such sentiments do not represent the true picture. As scholars, we have a responsibility to study the innovation, revealing the key risks and recommending sensible policies regardless of market sentiment.

This chapter attempts to shed some light on the central question of whether China's new internet finance economy reflects real innovation or a superficial bubble. We first describe recent developments in internet finance using some of the findings of the newly constructed Peking University Internet Finance Development Index (IFDI). We then try to identify the key factors contributing to the surge in internet finance, by drawing lessons from China's past financial reform. We also attempt to assess potential risks associated with internet finance and discuss implications for the guiding regulatory framework through a case study of peer-to-peer (P2P) lending platforms.

Our main arguments can be summarised as follows. The rise of internet finance in China has been triggered by at least three factors. First, repressive financial policy produces an undersupply of financial services, especially for small and medium-sized enterprises (SMEs) and low-income households. This leaves a hole in the financial market. Second, regulator tolerance has provided space for internet finance to emerge and grow. And, third, IT tools, especially mobile terminals and big data analysis, increasingly offer effective ways for internet finance to increase its efficiency and control financial risk. In short, there are many legitimate explanations for the emergence of internet finance.

Some critiques express fear that internet finance is an attempt to rewrite financial laws rather than merely a utilisation of new technological tools to facilitate existing financial transactions. For example, Mingshun Li, chief executive officer of an internet finance company in China, announced that his enterprise would start a revolution as it can safely lend money to every part of the heating market.[1] Information technologies are in fact likely to be widely applied to all types of financial transactions, but only some types of internet finance will survive. These will be those that effectively solve real problems for financial transactions—for example, Zhima Credit, a credit-collecting company launched by Ant Financial that has set up an individual credit evaluation system.

We believe that far from being a threat to the traditional finance industry, internet finance will increasingly become an effective tool with which to promote inclusive finance and thus also increase the size and reach of financial services. Internet finance, that is, can play a supplementary role, enhancing traditional financial transactions and extending financial services to areas that traditional finance has not yet embraced. For example, internet finance may facilitate inclusive finance by providing market-based services to financially underserviced SMEs and low-income households. The most successful cases of this to date involve taking advantage of either large numbers of mobile terminals, such as AliPay, or analyses of available data, such as WeBank's Weilidai. Internet finance itself also faces challenges and risks, including serious investment bubbles and widespread Ponzi schemes. If uncontrolled, these risks could destroy the entire industry. In response, some local governments have already prohibited registration of new P2P platforms.

Healthy development of internet finance requires at least three necessary conditions. The first is good infrastructure, including big data, integrated credit information and effective market discipline. The second is a troupe of qualified financial professionals. And the third is a regulatory framework that strikes the balance between controlling risk and encouraging innovation.

1 Available from: economy.gmw.cn/2016-05/13/content_20091004.htm.

Recent developments

Internet finance is a relatively new development even though its impact has already been felt in many areas and at least several well-known institutions have emerged. The most widely used internet finance service is probably third-party payments. In China, this market is already dominated by two players, AliPay and WeChatPay, which at the end of 2015 had more than 270 million and 200 million active users respectively. Another active area is online lending, which includes both P2P platforms and online micro credit. CreditEase is ranked as the largest P2P firm in the world, although it prefers to call itself a marketplace firm, because its borrowers include SMEs as well as individuals. Its platform Yirendai listed on the New York Stock Exchange at the end of 2015. That same year, P2P lending reached RMB1 trillion. Ant Financial's Mayiweidai and WeBank's Weilidai are also both rapidly expanding online lending businesses.

In this chapter, we introduce some outstanding types of internet finance. First, internet payments are the most well-developed business, with a history going back more than 10 years. Founded by the Alibaba group, AliPay is an online payment services provider that allows individuals and businesses to make secure online payments. AliPay is used primarily by buyers and sellers engaging in e-commerce transactions, and it is also the main payment method on its sister site Taobao. Second, money market funds or online direct investment funds are investment funds sold directly through a platform of internet companies. Such companies act as no more than an intermediary and the money is actually handled by traditional, heavily regulated funds. The most famous online direct investment fund in China is Yu'ebao, launched by Alibaba in 2013. Third, P2P has been one of the most explosive sectors of internet finance since 2014. There are more than 4,000 platforms in China, attracting nearly three million people to lend their money (Huang et al. 2016). There are also famous P2P platforms outside China, such as Lending Club, Prosper and OnDeck.

Online direct investment fund sales are also quite active, with the best-known such product being Yu'ebao. Tianhong Investment Fund, which manages a money market fund for Yu'ebao, had assets worth RMB500 billion within a year of Yu'ebao's launch, becoming the largest investment fund in China. The previous top-ranked firm, the China Investment Fund, took 17 years to reach the same asset size. Following the sharp decline of interbank market rates in 2014, Ant Financial launched another platform, Zhaocaibao, with the aim of selling wealth management products and investment funds. At the end of 2015, the market size for such investment products reached an estimated RMB1 trillion.[2] There are also a number of crowd-funding platforms, among which the

2 Data source: wdzj.com (one of the leading P2P lending information websites in China).

most prominent are Angel Crunch and Demo Hour. Two online banks, WeBank and MyBank, also received their operating licences in 2015, but growth has been limited by regulatory restrictions on the remote opening of bank accounts in China.

To advance systematic measurement of China's internet finance industry, Peking University's Institute of Internet Finance developed the Peking University IFDI, with assistance from Ant Financial Services. The IFDI, which was launched in December 2015, is a monthly measure that begins in January 2014 and is disaggregated across 31 provinces and 335 prefecture-level cities. It comprises a weight of six subindices for the main business categories of internet finance: investment (10 per cent), money market funds (25 per cent), insurance (15 per cent), payment (30 per cent), lending (15 per cent) and credit rating (5 per cent) (Guo et al. 2016).

The six indices correspond to the business categories that are commonly taken as the principles used for index calculation—namely, representativeness, feasibility, divisibility and expandability. The January 2014 nationwide index is normalised to 100 and indices of other times or districts are based on that. An increase in the index means development in that district or business category (Guo et al. 2016).

The results indicate that between January 2014 and December 2015, the nationwide IFDI increased from 100 to 386 (Figure 6.1). The average month-on-month growth rate was 5.8 per cent in 2014 and increased to 6.7 per cent in 2015. Among the six business categories, payments and money market funds, represented by AliPay and Yu'ebao respectively, enjoyed relatively slow growth, probably as they were already more mature than the other firms. The boom in P2P lending from 2014 is driven mainly by the investment subindex (Figure 6.1). Insurance fluctuation implies that it was more limited and heavily influenced by e-commerce sales.

There was also very wide interprovincial variation in terms of both levels of internet finance activities and their pace of growth (Figure 6.2). Specifically, the activity levels of seven relatively more developed provinces, as measured by gross domestic product (GDP) per capita, exceeded the national average. The provinces with relatively low levels of internet finance activities, however, were the ones that showed modestly faster growth rates in both 2014 and 2015, suggesting a possible trend of convergence over time.

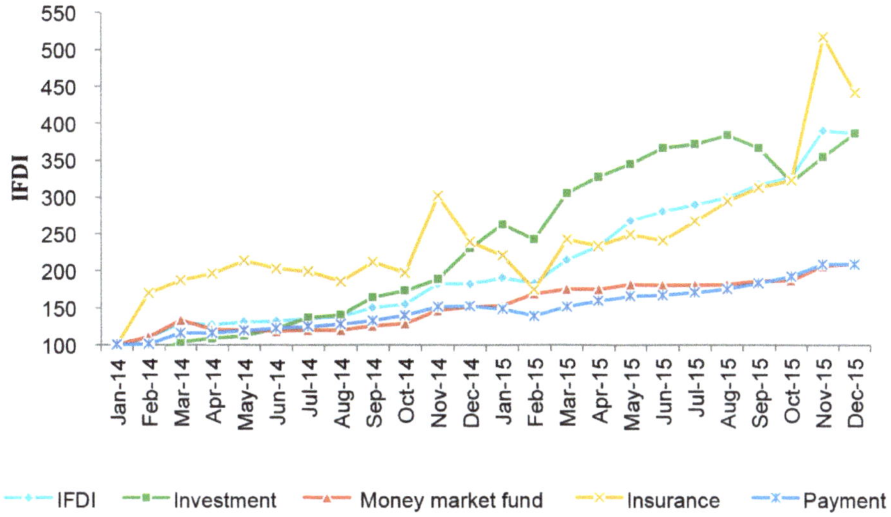

Figure 6.1 IFDI: Aggregated and by subsector, 2014–15

Source: Guo et al. (2016).

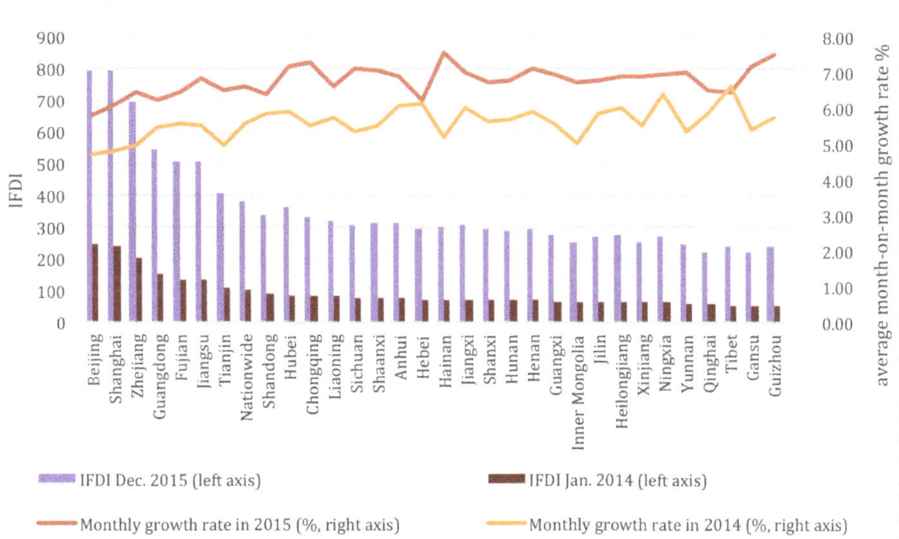

Figure 6.2 IFDI: Provincial subindices and growth, 2014–15

Source: Guo et al. (2016).

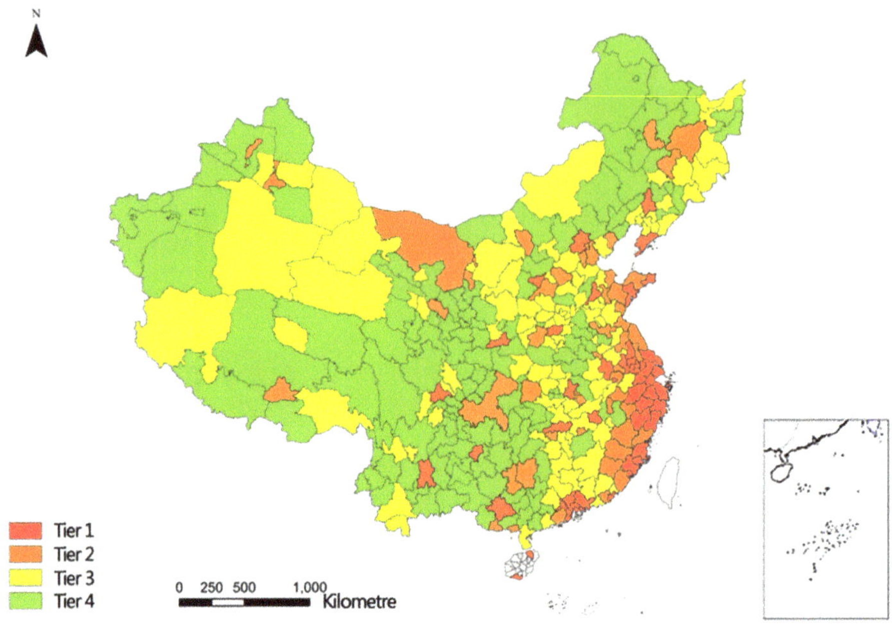

Figure 6.3 IFDI: Subindices by prefecture-level cities, December 2015

Source: Guo et al. (2016).

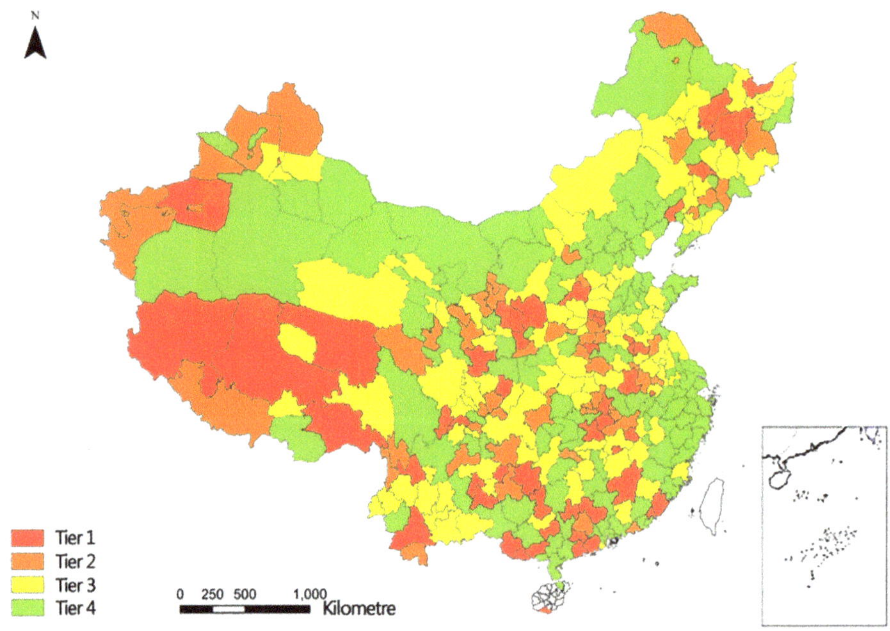

Figure 6.4 IFDI: Growth of subindices by prefecture-level cities, 2014–15

Source: Guo et al. (2016).

Disaggregating the index to the prefecture level reveals that most cities with high IFDIs are in the eastern coastal region, especially the Yangtze River Delta and the Pearl River Delta (Figure 6.3). This is suggestive of a positive correlation between levels of internet finance and levels of economic development among cities. But the pattern is less clear for prefecture-level IFDI growth rates. In general, coastal cities also experienced relatively slower growth (Figure 6.4), a trend that is consistent with the provincial data that show coastal cities tend to be more economically developed. This is a trend that requires further empirical validation.

One interesting—and important—question concerns the relationship between internet finance and traditional finance, and the extent to which the former complements or substitutes for the latter. We use the proportion of outstanding loans from financial institutions as a share of GDP as an indicator of the development of traditional finance. By utilising prefecture-level data, we find the correlation coefficient between the stated indicator of traditional finance and IFDIs is 0.59 (Figure 6.5). We also find that higher rates of mobile phone penetration increase IFDIs at the prefecture level, with a correlation coefficient of 0.74 (Figure 6.6).

Disaggregated indices for age groups show clearly that internet finance is driven mainly by young people, especially those born in the 1980s and 1990s (Figure 6.7). Use of internet finance by those who were born in the 1990s is, in general, slightly more advanced than for those who were born in the 1980s. There is one exception, however, in that the latter group uses internet finance for investment more than the former.

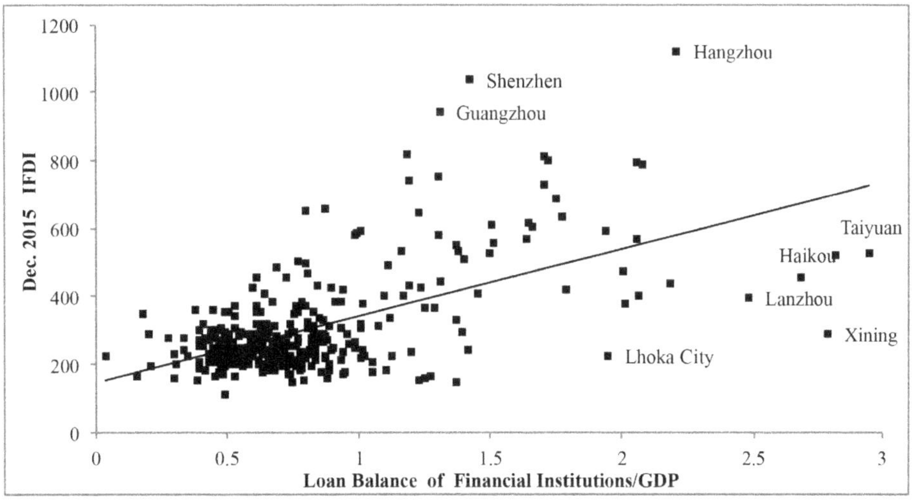

Figure 6.5 Relationship between traditional finance and IFDI at the prefecture level

Source: Guo et al. (2016).

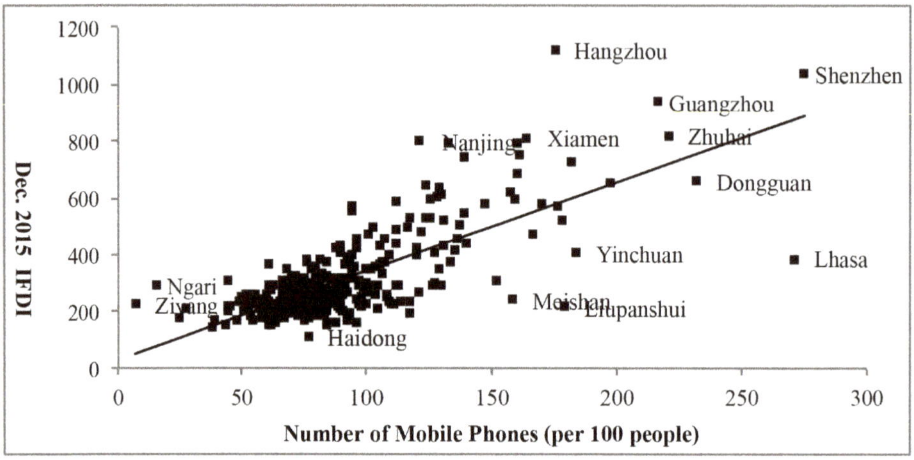

Figure 6.6 Prefecture-level relationship between mobile phone penetration and IFDI

Source: Guo et al. (2016).

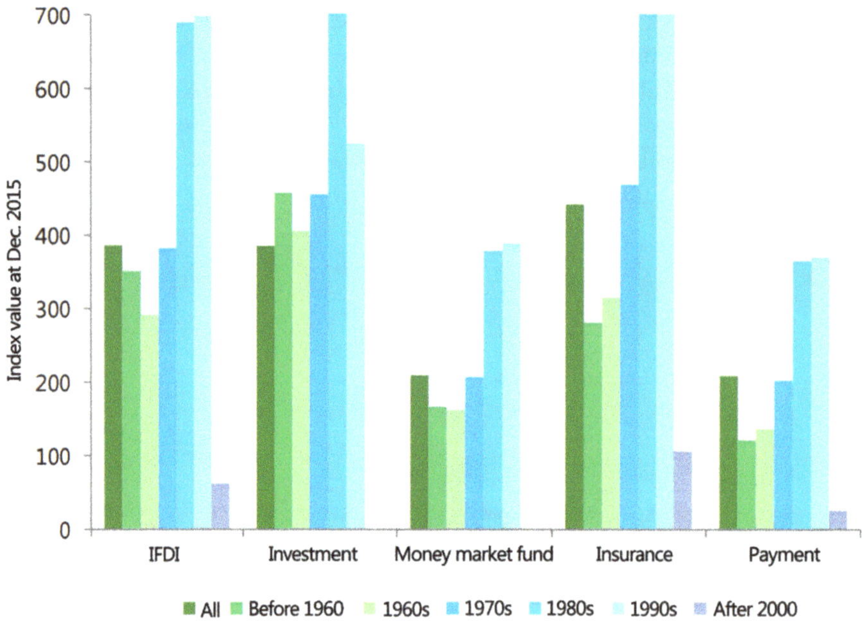

Figure 6.7 IFDI: Subindices by age group, December 2015

Source: Guo et al. (2016).

Innovation or bubble?

Despite the rapid development of internet finance over the past several years, debate about its future never goes away. Optimists, like Ping Xie, argue that internet finance represents the third type of financial intermediation, after direct and indirect financing, and that it could completely revamp traditional financial industries. Others point out that internet finance is mainly a Chinese phenomenon and is actually a product of regulatory arbitrage, which could therefore evaporate once financial regulations tighten to levels equivalent with those in advanced economies. From mid-2015, as internet finance grew and the associated risks escalated, evidenced by growing numbers of problematic P2P lending platforms, these pessimistic assessments gained traction among financial industry practitioners, scholars and even government officials. Qilun Wu, a famous financial commentator on Chinese microblogging website Weibo, has written an article saying P2P lending is a Ponzi scheme. A lot of people share Wu's opinion, however, they may voice it less aggressively.[3] Is internet finance really just a bubble? Before jumping to conclusions, one should first understand the trends and logic underlying the boom in the sector in China.

Three important factors: Light regulation, underservicing and transaction facilitation

We see at least three important factors. The first is that regulators have adopted a light approach. Internationally, commentators have noted that it is almost impossible for trade and manufacturing companies to be granted finance-related operating licences in many countries, including the United States. In China, however, selective online shopping firms, such as Alibaba and Jingdong, and social media platforms such as Tecent have received permission to supply financial services. Without this friendly regulation, it would not have been possible for internet finance in China to reach current levels of activity.

The second factor is financial underservicing, especially with respect to SMEs and average households. In pre-reform China, there was just one monolithic financial institution: the People's Bank of China (PBC). This served as both the central bank and a commercial bank. Funds transfer and allocation were guided mainly by the central plan. Financial institutions played only a very supplementary role. The reform period of the past 38 years, however, has witnessed significant developments in and transformation of the financial sector. Modern China has a significant, relatively established financial industry with a complete set of financial institutions and very large volumes of financial assets (Huang et al. 2013).

3 Available from: weibo.com/ttarticle/p/show?id=2309403966351516530359.

The government does, however, continue to intervene in the functioning of the financial system, as is the case in advanced countries. An International Monetary Fund index of financial repression measuring the extent of policy distortions with respect to restricting market-based movement of the interest rate, exchange rate and funds, finds that financial policy distortion in China is among the most severe globally (Abiad et al. 2008). One direct consequence is financial industry bias in favour of certain groups of (potential) customers. For instance, state-owned enterprises (SOEs) still receive proportionately greater access to bank credits and other funding thanks to ownership bias. Funding constraints are common globally for SMEs, but the problem is exaggerated in China. About 70 per cent of SMEs and probably a similar proportion of individuals do not receive decent financial services (Zhang 2014). Typically, to access finance, SMEs have to go to informal markets, where funding costs are often at least four times higher than those in the formal sector, such as from commercial banks.

Regulator tolerance of internet finance may relate to issues such as the undersupply of financial services to certain groups in China. It may be a way of testing new models of financial service provision. Development of inclusive finance has been a key policy objective of China's government for some years, and aims to improve the provision of market-based, commercially sustainable financial services to underserviced enterprises and individuals. Developing inclusive finance is, however, very difficult. Policymakers probably see hope in using the internet as a tool with which to facilitate inclusive finance. Certainly, many SMEs and low-income individuals have enthusiastically embraced new forms of internet finance, such as WeChatPay, Yu'ebao and Yirendai. For instance, since few university students are warmly welcomed by commercial banks because of their relatively low level of deposits, and also given their familiarity with mobile technologies, they have become very loyal and capable users of internet finance services.

The third factor is the extraordinary potential for internet technologies to facilitate financial transactions. In essence, the central challenge underlying any financial transaction can be summarised as information asymmetry. The most important function of financial intermediation is, therefore, risk pricing. In this sense, the reasons the financial industry discriminates against certain groups of customers and why development of inclusive finance is so difficult can be explained within a cost–benefit analysis framework. For instance, SME financing difficulty is common because they usually have fewer hard data, fewer assets to use as collateral and also a higher probability of failure. Due-diligence costs for these enterprises could be prohibitive. Many commercial banks and other financial institutions therefore find it cost ineffective to service such customers. Should they do so, the financing costs would correspondingly be prohibitively high, which might not be legal under certain regulations or could simply inhibit the SME from borrowing.

The internet may shift these asymmetries, as it has two important features that traditional financial institutions normally do not: a mobile terminal and big data analysis. China is home to 785 million active smartphones (National Bureau of Statistics of PRC 2015). Together, these provide an effective means for internet companies or financial institutions to identify potential customers. Third-party payment services and direct sale of funds businesses are built primarily on internet connections to smartphones.

Big data analysis, if applied efficiently, can help reduce information asymmetry and also in part replace the otherwise labour-intensive due-diligence process. For instance, Ant Financial's online lending is based on data analyses from some one million shops and 300 million individual accounts on various online shopping platforms of its parent company, Alibaba. The shops' business and cash flows and individuals' spending behaviour and other habits offer reliable information about their credit risks, especially if they have been with Alibaba's platforms for several years. Through analysis of this data, Ant Financial is able to quickly and cost-effectively preapprove loan quotas for qualified shops and individuals. If the shops or individuals with preapproved loan quotas activate the application, it takes Ant Financial less than three minutes to put borrowed funds into the applicant's AliPay account. No face-to-face meeting is required (Figure 6.8).

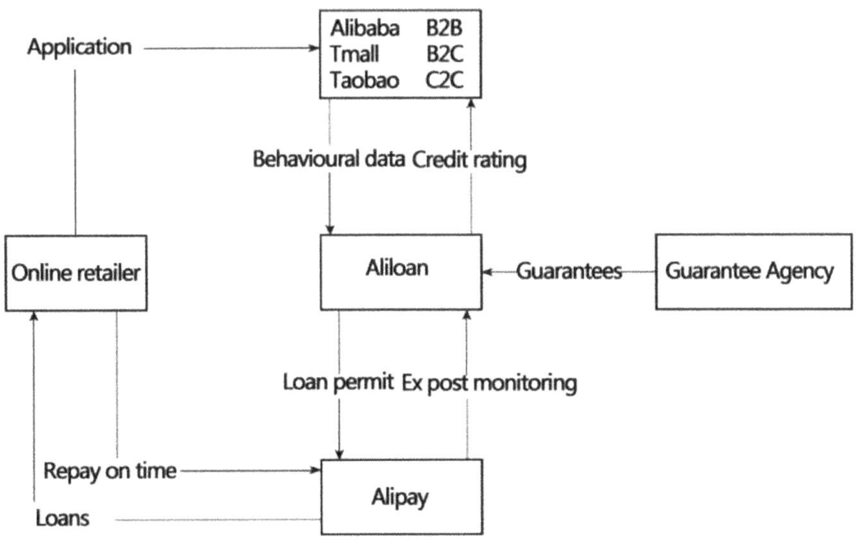

Figure 6.8 Flow chart for Ant Financial online lending

Source: Xie (2015).

WeBank has essentially done the same thing for its service, Weilidai, except that it relies mainly on WeChat social media data. By analysing WeChat users' addresses, active chat groups, WeChatPay spending behaviour and habits of red envelope distribution during festivals (at Chinese New Year WeChatPay allows users to send electronic gifts of cash instantly using the same social media service), WeBank also preapproves individual loan quotas. If the individuals decide to activate the application, WeBank undertakes the lending in cooperation with commercial banks because, at this stage, WeBank does not have its own bank customers. To increase commercial banks' confidence in this type of risk evaluation, WeBank often contributes 20 per cent of funding for loans.

Ant Financial and WeBank assess credit risks by analysing in-house data on potential customers. Zhejiang-based Zuoli Kechuang Micro-Finance, which is a listed company on the Hong Kong Stock Exchange, also offers online loans but does not possess the same customer database. Instead, it relies on three sets of external data: 1) potential customers' main bank account transactions; 2) telephone bills with detailed call records; and 3) the PBC's personal credit information printed by a credit applicant.

In other words, a distinct advantage of internet finance over traditional finance is that it substantially reduces due-diligence costs. As a result, financial transactions that would otherwise be commercially unviable in the traditional financial industry are enabled. More importantly, the long-tail feature of internet technology implies that, once the system is established, the marginal cost of servicing additional customers is close to zero. Therefore, the internet has a natural fit with the evolution of more inclusive finance in China. In this sense, internet finance is indeed a real innovation, and not a passing bubble as some fear.

This suggests that internet finance has the potential to add real value to financial transactions, especially via enabling commercially profitable transactions from demand for credit that previously was commercially unviable. Whether this potential can turn into real business, however, is dependent on several conditions, the most critical of which is the internet's ability to continue to reduce information asymmetry for financial transactions. For internet finance to work, institutional market participants need to have sufficient understanding of finance, access to internet channels, a quality dataset and data analysis capacities. Against these straightforward criteria, we conclude that many practitioners of internet finance in China today are probably not ideally qualified. Moreover, this fact, rather than the core of the industry itself, is why the internet finance industry is suffering from bubbles and scandal at present.

Case study of P2Ps

The development of P2P lending in China has been rapid in the past several years. As shown in Table 6.1, the number of P2P platforms increased 19 times, from 200 in 2012 to 3,858 in 2015. During this same period, P2P trading volume skyrocketed from RMB21.2 billion to RMB982.8 billion, and outstanding loans surged from RMB5.6 billion to RMB547.8 billion. At the end of 2014, P2P lenders in the United States generated $6.6 billion in loans, and in Europe this number was $3.9 billion (BI Intelligence 2015; Wardrop et al. 2015). In comparison, Chinese P2P lenders generated $41.3 billion. In other words, China already has the world's largest P2P industry in terms of trading volume.

Even though the P2P industry remains tiny compared with formal banking balances (RMB93.95 trillion at the end of 2015), it nonetheless affects a large number of investors and borrowers. In April 2016, P2P platforms in China had 2.98 million active investors and 800,000 borrowers (Table 6.1, columns 6 and 7). Therefore, the sharply increased number of financial collapses of P2P platforms has generated great concern among the general public. Specifically, the number of problematic P2P platforms skyrocketed from 16 in 2012 to 1,598 in April 2016 (Table 6.1, column 3). In other words, some 40 per cent (1,598 of 4,029) of P2P platforms were problematic in 2016. A platform is identified as problematic if it records at least one of the following difficulties: termination of operation, failure to cash out, cheating, loss of contact, police interference or platform shutdown.

Table 6.1 Chinese P2P platforms at a glance

(1) Year	Platforms		(4) Trading Vol (Billion)	(5) Balance (Billion)	(6) Investors (Thousand)	(7) Borrowers (Thousand)
	(2) All	(3) Problem				
2012	200	16	21.2	5.6	51	19
2013	800	92	105.8	26.8	250	150
2014	1,575	367	252.8	103.6	1,160	630
2015	3,858	1,263	982.3	439.5	2,980	780
2016*	4,029	1,598	522.8	547.8	2,980	800

* Data for 2016 cover January–April only.
Source: wdzj.com/.

On the other hand, P2P lending in China does provide room for investors to reap higher returns and for borrowers to access funds at lower costs. In Figure 6.9, we compare several interest rates in China, with 'P2P lending' denoting the composite investors' interest rates in all P2P platforms. After earlier oscillations, the P2P investor interest rate decreased from above 20 per cent in 2013 to about 10 per cent at the end of 2015. Compared with returns from an online investment fund like Yu'ebao, the one-week Shanghai Interbank Offered Rate (Shibor) and the three-month bill rate from the PBC, which all fluctuated around 5 per cent, P2P platforms appear to provide investors a higher return. For borrowers, this compares favourably with the 20 per cent lending rate charged for informal finance (Wenzhou private lending in Figure 6.9).

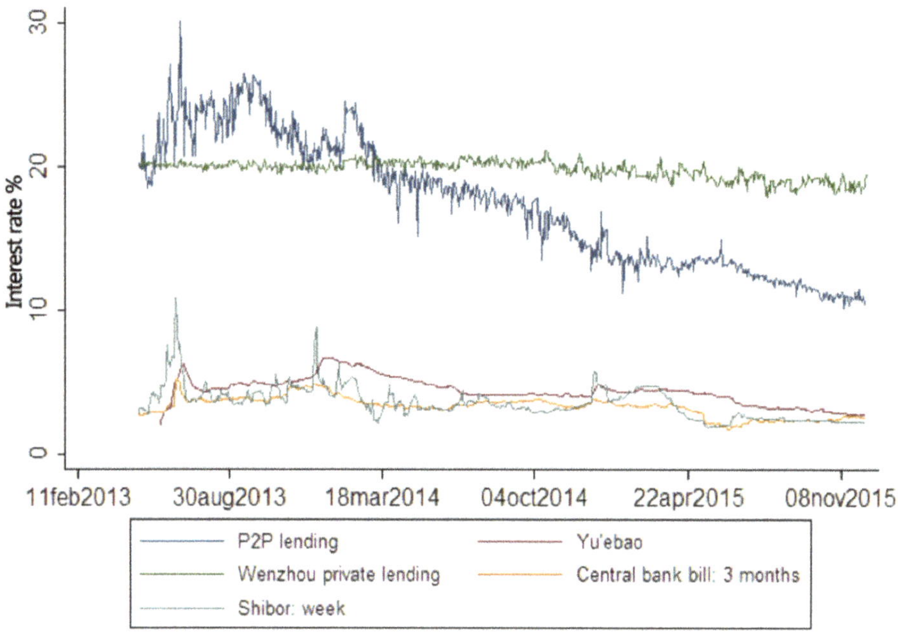

Figure 6.9 Comparison of P2P composite interest rates with others

Notes: P2P lending = the composite investors' interest rates in all P2P platforms; Yu'ebao = online investment fund rate managed by Alibaba; WenZhou private lending = a representative lending rate of informal finance in China; Central Bank bill three months = rate of three-month bill from PBC; Shibor = weekly Shanghai Interbank Offered Rate.

Source: Huang et al. (2016).

Given that the development of P2P lending has so far expedited financial innovation, increased capital allocation efficiency and encouraged competition, for some years China's regulators have taken a lenient stance towards the industry. In fact, it has so far been unclear which regulatory authority should be responsible for P2P platforms. The first official document relating to the industry, 'Guidance on promoting the healthy development of internet banking', was released only in July 2015. This designated the China Banking Regulatory Commission (CBRC) as the main regulatory authority. On 28 December 2015, the regulatory authorities revealed a draft of proposed rules for regulating the P2P industry. The announcement compels online lenders to act as information intermediaries only and not as credit intermediaries, and also prohibits leveraged outside funding. On the other hand, no minimum registered capital was stipulated. Local financial authorities will be the main regulating authority and are expected to both register and supervise P2P lenders. Under this type of regulatory scheme, P2P platforms will not need to hold a special licence and there will be no specific requirements on deposits or management of funds. Supervision will rely on organisations such as micro-loan associations.

Some might question whether the P2P industry will prosper or go astray amid such a light regulatory scheme characterised by no licensing requirements, no minimum entrance requirements and with industry associations as the main regulatory authority. To shed light on this uncertainty, we use all publicly available P2P platform-level data to study the characteristics of problematic platforms and to identify the risk factors of this industry.

Using a big-data approach, we extract and integrate all publicly available P2P platform datasets from the four major P2P information platforms up to the end of 2015. After cleaning the outliers and crosschecking, we obtained a dataset of 3,439 P2P platforms with registered capital, among which there are 1,048 problematic platforms. Data points collected include establishment date, registered capital, date the platform became problematic, the nature or type of problems, whether or not a platform has a guaranteed investor, the structure of the loan term, investor interest rate, projects in which the platform has invested, location, whether the platform offers customer service, VIP (very important person) services, toll-free call services and so on. As all the data were collected on 8 December 2015, the life of some platforms may be curtailed. In other words, when we observe a life of 30 days in the data, it could be for two reasons: one is the platform stayed active for only 30 days, from the date it first went online until the day it became problematic; two, it was online on 8 November 2015, active on 8 December 2015 and we do not know how long it will survive. Our estimation method needs to deal carefully with this issue. We therefore use the Kaplan–Meier nonparametric estimator to study the survival probabilities of the various platforms with different perspectives, and then use duration estimation to consider all risk factors together.

Our analyses unveil a number of important findings:

- **First, problematic platforms survive for an increasingly short duration.** In Figure 6.10, we compare the survival durations of normal platforms and problematic platforms. Overall, 18 per cent of the 192 problematic platforms survived for less than 30 days; 55 per cent lasted less than half a year; and over 80 per cent stayed in the industry for less than a year. In contrast, over 38 per cent ([979 + 215 + 118]/3,439) of normal platforms survived for more than one year and over 60 per cent lasted more than half a year. In particular, our duration analysis indicates that compared with platforms established before 2012, on average, more recently established platforms have shorter lives and suffer a higher probability of becoming problematic platforms.

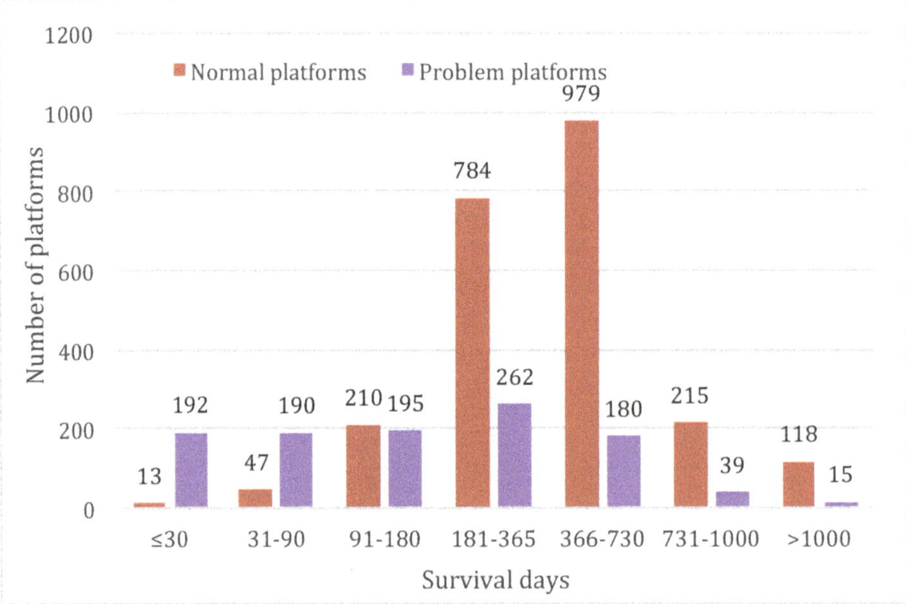

Figure 6.10 Average number of operating days of normal platforms and problematic platforms

Source: Huang et al. (2016).

- **Second, problematic platforms are not concentrated in particular regions.** If one studies only Figure 6.11a, where darker regions indicate the presence of more problematic platforms, it is easy to conclude that problematic platforms are concentrated in coastal areas, and especially in the provinces of Shandong, Guangdong and Fujian. Taking into account the fact that coastal regions have more platforms than inland areas, from Figure 6.11b, one can infer that there is no particular regional pattern in problematic platform distribution. This is consistent with the characteristics of internet finance; as transactions are operated through the internet, regional differences will be smaller than for enterprises focusing their business in local areas. So the distribution of problematic platforms should be studied together with their relative share among all platforms.

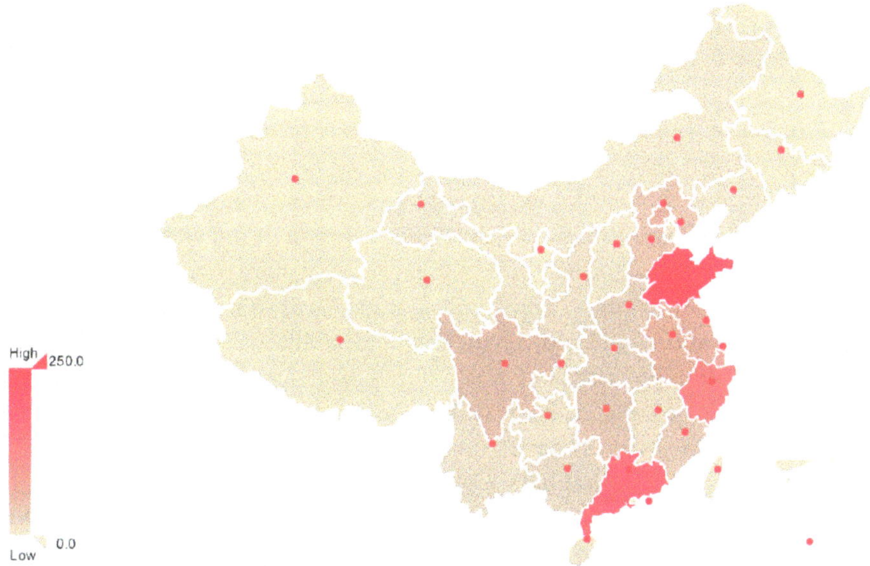

Figure 6.11a Regional distribution of all problematic P2P platforms

Source: Huang et al. (2016).

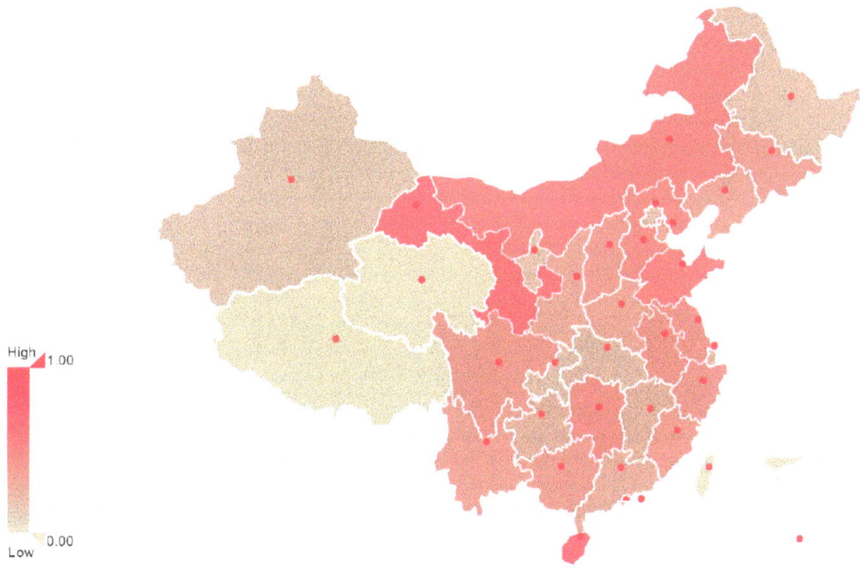

Figure 6.11b Regional distribution of proportions of problematic platforms

Source: Huang et al. (2016).

- **Third, missing information on registered capital or low registered capital signifies a high platform risk.** Figure 6.12 compares the survival probabilities of three platform types: those missing registered capital, those with less than RMB30 million in registered capital and those with more than RMB30 million in registered capital. The horizontal axis shows the survival days and the vertical axis shows the probability. Platforms missing registered information are highly risky, as demonstrated by the sharp drop in their 200-day survival probability, to around 25 per cent. In other words, given four newly established platforms, three will not survive more than 200 days if they are missing information on registered capital. Platforms with less registered capital also tend towards a lower survival probability. One-fifth of platforms with more than RMB30 million in registered capital are problematic, but this ratio drops to 37.2 per cent for platforms with less than 30 million. Similarly, platforms missing actual capital information or with a low ratio of actual capital to registered capital have lower survival probabilities.

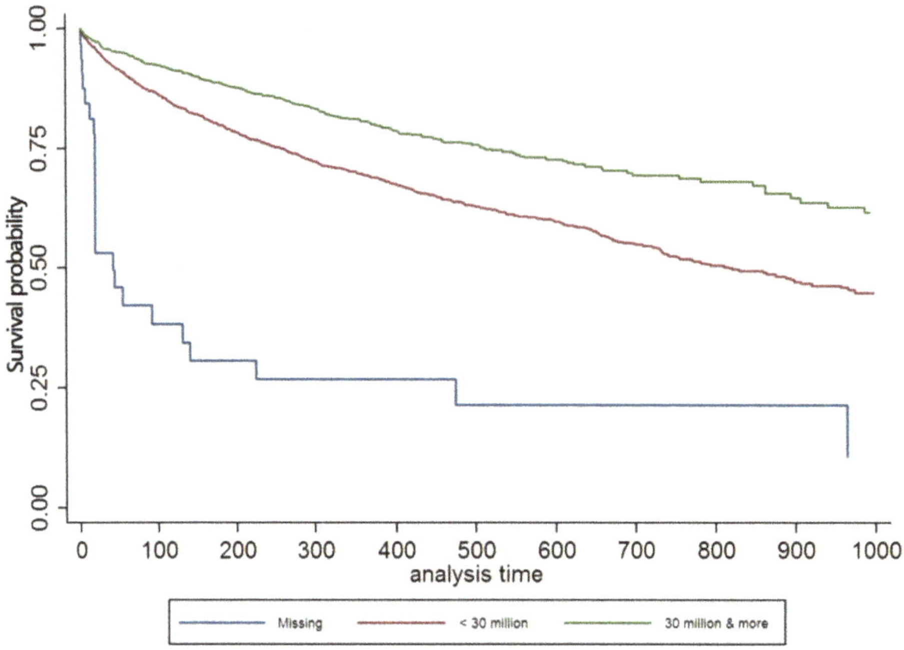

Figure 6.12 Survival probability and registered capital

Source: Huang et al. (2016).

- **Fourth, highly risky platforms are often missing interest rate information, have a narrow transaction interest rate range or offer unusually high or low interest rates.** Of the problematic platforms, 77.5 per cent are missing information on investor interest rates. If a platform offers only one interest rate, it is highly likely to be a problematic platform. It is no surprise that problematic platforms have demonstrated higher probabilities to promise investors interest rates higher than 20 per cent. In Figure 6.13, however, we show that platforms offering rates of less than 8 per cent are also highly risky. Some 60 per cent of problematic platforms offer interest rates lower than 8 per cent. For example, in 2015, the Ezu Bao platform was charged with illegally raising about $7.6 billion in funds. The data show that Ezu Bao did offer an interest rate of 6 per cent for some of its financial leasing projects before the crackdown. As investors can easily buy wealth management products with an annual return of less than 8 per cent, when P2P platforms offer such interest it is highly likely the transactions that ensue are fake and hence the platform bears high risk. Similarly, platforms offering only one interest rate are dubious.

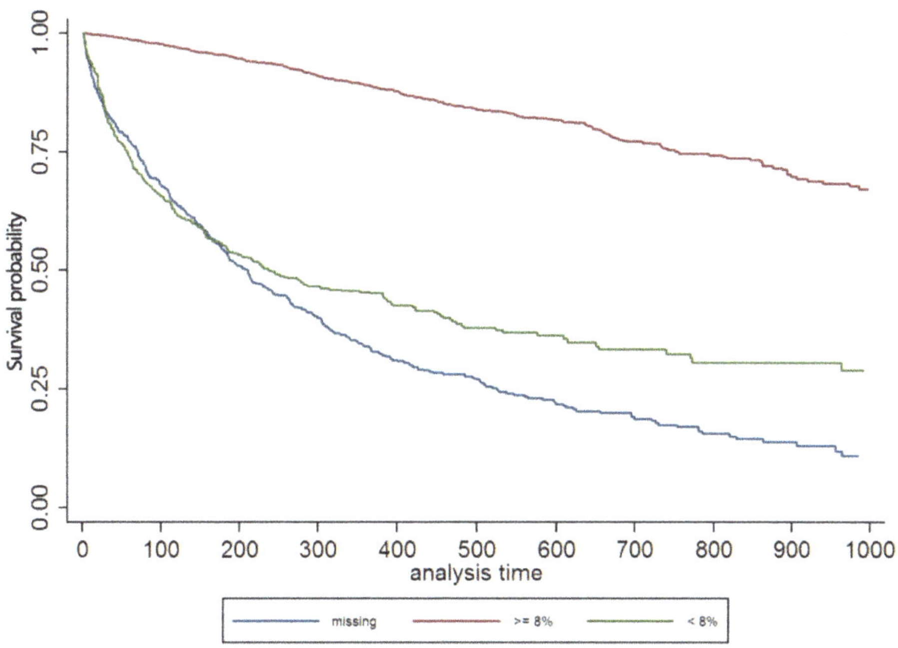

Figure 6.13 Survival probabilities for platforms with interest rates lower or higher than 8 per cent

Source: Huang et al. (2016).

- **Fifth, platforms without reliable third-party assurance are highly risky.** What matters for the reliability of a platform is not how many types of assurance it has, but whether it is assured by a reliable insurance company or bank. For those with (without) such assurances, 3 per cent (14 per cent) is the problematic threshold.

- **Finally, platforms guaranteeing both principal and return are highly risky.** If a platform promises its investors that both the principal and the interest are 100 per cent secured, its probability of being a problematic platform is 20.7 per cent—a rate that is 12 per cent higher than for firms not offering such promises. Such guarantees will, naturally, increase a P2P platform's costs. There may also be an adverse selection issue—that is, platforms that are having financial difficulties and that are desperate for funds tend to be the ones providing investors such offers, which are unsustainable in the long run.

The above findings are important for understanding the risks associated with P2P platforms. Investors, for example, should stay away from risky platforms and realise that platforms are less risky when they have a longer survival time, adopt a strategy for complete information disclosure, provide appropriate interest rates, maintain diversified interest rate term structures and have acquired assurances from banks or insurance companies. An investor should avoid platforms missing key information such as registered capital, interest rates and term structure, and promising full guarantees towards both principal and interest.

Implications for regulation

Our review and analysis reveal two important features of the development of internet finance in China. First, it fills an important gap in the market by extending financial services to customers who are insufficiently serviced by the traditional financial industry. Second, it also facilitates financial transactions in general by lowering costs and reducing risks through better use of customer analytics data—by reducing information asymmetry. On these two counts, we see that internet finance offers genuine innovation. If these features can be further improved and strengthened, internet finance should survive, especially as a form of more inclusive finance, whether or not regulations are tightened significantly. It is in fact even possible that China is leading a new product cycle globally in this pioneering area.

As with any young but promising new industry, the risks are high for China's internet finance sector. Many investors, for example, chase quick money through either blind optimism or Ponzi schemes. At the end of the twentieth century, the United States also experienced a collapse of its internet bubble, but there was real and lasting innovation: a number of global leaders such as Google and Amazon rose from the ashes. At this stage, there are no guarantees that internet finance will even survive, as was the case with selective internet-based IT platforms 15 years ago.

To ensure healthy development of internet finance, important conditions need to be met in at least three areas. The first requires there to be a set of 'infrastructure' facilities. At the minimum, this requires a network of mobile terminals or the ability to analyse available data, or both. Strictly speaking, big data still does not exist in China. The government may need to introduce a policy framework to both make useful data publicly accessible and safeguard individuals' privacy. A credible and integrated credit reporting system for individuals and SMEs would also be valuable for internet finance credit allocation decisions.

The second condition concerns regulation of financial qualifications for industry participants. At the moment, there are three groups of professionals working in this sector: financial professionals, IT experts and others. The essence of internet finance is the financial transaction. Therefore, it is vital for internet finance professionals to have a good understanding of finance, especially the related risks. According to our limited observations, a lot of problems in the internet finance sector were created by professionals who did not understand or respect basic financial rules and principles.

The third condition relates to a regulatory framework that strikes a balance between encouraging innovation and controlling risks. Internet finance is finance, and financial transactions need to be appropriately regulated. Both too little and too much regulation could hinder the otherwise beneficial evolution of internet finance.

Here we make a preliminary assessment of the regulatory framework for P2P proposed by the CBRC in December 2015, which itself was based largely on analytical findings for problematic P2P platforms described in section four. The first relates to the macro side of managing the dynamic emergence of new internet-based informal lending agencies. The second relates to the micro side of these institutions, and ensuring they have the necessary qualifications and systems to take appropriate risk controls.

On the first point, at the baseline, the credit reporting system is at an early stage of development and social trust remains low in China. In this environment, the merit of treating the P2P platform as a pure information intermediary in China has not yet been ascertained. As information intermediaries, P2P platforms should not engage in activities appropriate to credit intermediaries. However, the majority of borrowers in P2P platforms are individuals and SMEs, and the majority of investors are individuals. In fact, most internet finance platforms are not capable of providing sufficient and accurate information to help investors make investment decisions, and they are therefore de facto credit intermediaries. As long as the credit reporting system is not significantly improved there will be no change to this situation, even if all platforms changed their names to include 'information intermediary' after the requirements of the regulatory authority. Moreover, if regulatory authorities insist that P2P platforms should be information intermediaries, they will have to enforce one of two alternative strategies. The first would be to crack down on all platforms that are not information intermediaries, which would in effect terminate the industry; the second would be to tolerate a majority of these platforms undertaking what are illegal transactions until a substantial financial collapse makes the headlines, after which it would be relatively easy and necessary to impose legal constraints on the industry.

Second, since most P2P lending platforms are not qualified information intermediaries and such platforms are numerous, it may not be deemed appropriate to implement a framework of no minimum capital requirements, only requiring platforms to register with local regulatory authorities and to be supervised by organisations like industrial associations. On the other hand, if it remains obvious that regulation will not check the qualifications of those operating a P2P business, most platforms will simply continue to operate until they become problematic.

Data from the first four months of 2016 show that risks in the internet finance industry appear to be increasing, despite the announcement of a draft regulatory scheme announced in December 2015. Huang et al. (2016) identified that more recent platforms have higher failure probabilities. Besides bad platform management, the advance of more prominent platforms and apparent promises of returns may have tempted others to engage in Ponzi scams. While some of these scams will be uncovered and legal action taken, the losses for investors are often hard to recover. Given these potential losses, it would be inappropriate to treat such situations as opportunities to educate investors, as the P2P industry is not like the capital market. That is, it does not have an established and complete regulatory framework on cooperative governance, transaction conditions and information disclosure. From this perspective, a strategy of not taking preventative regulatory action against perceivable and probable losses is hard to justify to the general public.

Third, what consequences will investors bear if local financial authorities become the major regulators? Such arrangements govern micro-loan companies; however, P2P platforms are different from micro-loan companies in several aspects. First, micro-loan companies typically do not operate across regions, but P2P platforms, operating through the internet, commonly execute transactions across multiple regions. Figure 6.3 indicates that problematic platforms show no region-specific patterns. In addition, when disputes between platforms and investors need to be tackled via legal channels, if the plaintiffs are scattered across provinces, the internet platforms will need to go through the courts in a series of different provinces. Second, the sources of funds for formal micro-loan companies are the capital and donations of their shareholders, and funds are often from no more than two banks. In contrast, for P2P platforms, the majority of investors are individuals with potentially inadequate financial education to appreciate the risks they are taking, individually or systemically. The interactions of internet and individual investors could potentially rapidly propagate risks to a much larger scale. Further, local financial offices may not have the appropriate equipment, knowledge or sufficient resources to effectively regulate platforms within their jurisdiction.

If a consensus can be reached from this analysis, it is to recommend authorities revise the internet finance regulations in the following areas. First, we suggest the CBRC be made responsible for the formulation, coordination and implementation of related regulatory policies. Second, minimum qualification requirements for P2P platforms should be specified—for example, there should be a threshold of registered capital for new P2P entrants. Such requirements will not contradict the policy of encouraging financial innovation, but will offer a necessary check to protect vulnerable investors. It would also help the industry grow in a healthy direction by restricting the entrance of unqualified platforms into the market. Even where such platforms are considered as information intermediaries, there should still be requirements regarding registered capital and platforms should be supervised as to whether actual capital is injected over time. If internet finance platforms are considered credit intermediaries, higher capital standards should be set. The regulatory framework should also prohibit certain transactions and set up rules that regulate borrowing qualifications, project types, loan term structure, interest rate ranges and so on. Third, strict information disclosure rules should be established. For platforms unable to provide key information, or failing to update information in a timely manner, the authorities should limit their operations or revoke their operational eligibility.

References

Abiad, A., Detragiache, E. and Tressel, T. (2008), *A new database of financial reforms*, No. 2008–2266, Washington, DC: International Monetary Fund.

BI Intelligence (2015), Peer-to-peer lending markets: The leading countries for alternative finance and the next high-growth markets, *Business Insider*, 16 May.

Guo, F., Kong, S., Wang, J., Cheng, A., Yuan, F., Shao, G., Wang, F. and Yang, J. (2016), *Peking University internet finance development index*, May, Institute of Internet Finance, Beijing: Peking University.

Huang, Y., Shen, Y. and Wang, J. (2016), Analyses and thoughts on individual online lending and its regulatory framework, [in Chinese], *Comparative Studies*, 2(2016).

Huang, Y., Wang, X., Wang, B. and Lin, N. (2013), Financial reform in China: Progress and challenges, in Y. C. Park and H. Patrick (eds), *How finance is shaping the economies of China, Japan, and Korea*, 44–142, New York: Columbia University Press.

National Bureau of Statistics of PRC (2015), Statistical Communiqué of the People's Republic of China on the 2015 National Economic and Social Development.

Wardrop, R., Zhang, B., Rau, R. and Gray, M. (2015), *Moving mainstream: The European alternative finance benchmarking report*, Cambridge: University of Cambridge.

Xie, P. (2015), Fundamental theory of internet finance, Lecture notes, November, Institute of Internet Finance, Peking University, Beijing.

Xie, P. and Zou, C. (2012), Research on business models of internet finance, [in Chinese], *Financial Research*, (12).

Xie, P., Zou, C. and Liu, H. (2014), *Handbook of internet finance*, Beijing: Renmin University Press.

Zhang, W. (2014), Study on Chinese commercial bank credit financing problem on small and micro enterprises, [in Chinese], Doctoral dissertation, University of International Business and Economics, Beijing.

7. The Necessary Demand-Side Supplement to China's Supply-Side Structural Reform: Termination of the soft budget constraint

Wing Thye Woo[1]

China in the news in the first half of 2016

After uncharacteristically low real gross domestic product (GDP) growth in 2015 (6.9 per cent—below the official target of 7 per cent), 2016 began with much international media attention drawn to the weakness of China's economy. In an interview, for example, George Soros proclaimed that 'a hard landing is practically unavoidable for China', and added that this was also the root cause of global financial market turmoil (Bielski 2016). The *International New York Times* then ran worrisome China-related stories on its front page on three consecutive days: 'Fears about China's economy fester at Davos' (Stevenson 2016), 'China's woes deflate hopes for economic rise in Africa' (Onishi 2016) and 'Investigation fuels doubts about growth data in China' (Bradsher 2016).

The *Wall Street Journal* (2016a) and the *Financial Times* (Wildau 2016) also stoked investors' concerns about China's internal weakness and external belligerence by running front-page stories with the headlines 'China faces dilemma over yuan' and 'China mouthpiece warns Soros against shorting renminbi', respectively. The same issue of the *Wall Street Journal* also ran, on page two, the alarmist story headlined 'China's working-age population sees biggest-ever decline' (Burkitt 2016).

Pessimism about China's economic outlook deepened in January 2016 when the World Bank lowered its growth rate projections for China and the rest of the world from January 2015 for 2016–17. This unexpected slowdown in the growth rates of most countries (for example, the anticipated US growth rate for 2016 was reduced from 3 per cent to 2.7 per cent) also reduced the room that would allow Chinese policymakers to induce growth through exports in the 2016–17 period.

1 wtwoo@ucdavis.edu.

The sense of doom and gloom about China also revived attention to earlier allegations that the real situation in the country was in fact far more negative again, but had been hidden by official manipulation of economic data. Investment houses Capital Economics and Lombardi Street disputed the official growth rates for each quarter of 2015. Their alternative estimates for the annual growth rate in 2015 were about 4.3 per cent and 3.1 per cent, respectively, compared with the official figure of 6.9 per cent (Russell and Lai 2015).

In the first quarter of 2016, China started further easing of its monetary policy to counter the widely perceived dire picture of its economic growth. In response, the *Wall Street Journal* (2016b) editorialised on the danger of 'China's bond bubble', and Nobel Laureate Paul Krugman announced in an interview:

> China scares me. China has a huge adjustment problem. They have an economy that is based upon unsustainable levels of investment and needs to radically shift from investment to consumption. They don't seem to be managing it. They have a large internal debt problem and a government that doesn't seem to be thinking clearly about it. At this point their response to economic difficulty seems to be to crack down on the financial press and to tell them to write happy stories. (Martens 2016)

Foreign media concerns about the course that China's economy was taking and the nature of its economic management found their domestic counterparts in China itself, on the front page of the *People's Daily* on 8 May 2016. The article quoted an unnamed 'authoritative' official as 'saying that boosting growth by increasing leverage was like *growing a tree in the air* and that a high leverage ratio could lead to a financial crisis' (Xin 2016a). The *South China Morning Post* interpreted the article as heralding an impending 'big economic policy shift'.

This prediction was validated the following day when the *People's Daily* ran on its front page an article written by Xi Jinping that expounded on the need for 'supply-side structural reform':

> China could not rely on 'stimulating domestic demand to address structural problems such as over-capacity', he said. 'The problem in China is not about insufficient demand or lack of demand, in fact, demands in China have changed, but supplies haven't changed accordingly,' Xi said. He gave the example of Chinese consumers shopping overseas for daily products such as electric rice cookers, toilet covers, milk powder and even baby bottles to show that domestic supply did not match domestic demand. Xi said [that China] faced 'outstanding problems of unwieldiness, puffiness and weakness'. 'The main symptom is limited innovation, and that's the Achilles heel of China's [macro] economy,' Xi said. (Xin 2016b)

We agree with the assessment that supply-side structural reform is the most effective way to address China's present economic problems. In this chapter, we will identify some of the major structural reforms that would entrench dynamism in China's economy and also seek to emphasise that better demand-side management is required for this entrenchment to be successful. Specifically, on the demand side, China needs to expunge the soft budget constraint from the economic system (or greatly reduce its frequency and size) if supply-side structural reforms are to generate the desired outcomes.

Sizing up the dimension of the supply-side problem

A most persuasive case for supply-side structural reform is instinctively made when one looks at Table 7.1, which shows the production capacity and utilisation rate in seven major heavy industries in China: crude steel, cement, flat glass, oil refining, electrolytic aluminium, paper and paperboard and shipbuilding. The increase in production capacity for these heavy industries over the period 2008–14 ranged from 36 per cent (shipbuilding) to 111 per cent (electrolytic aluminium). Five of the seven industries experienced increases of over 60 per cent. The most disturbing indicator in Table 7.1, however, is that there was also a drop in the capacity utilisation rates in the six industries for which these data are available. For example, the production capacity of crude steel rose from 600 million tonnes in 2008 to 1.1 billion tonnes in 2014, reflecting an increase of 77 per cent over the six years; however, the utilisation rate in the industry dropped significantly, from 80 per cent to 71 per cent. In fact:

> [An analyst] has calculated that from 2004 to 2014, global steel production increased by 57 per cent—China contributed a staggering 91 per cent to this increase. As a result, its steel industry now accounts for more than half of global output, or more than twice the combined output of the next four biggest steel makers: Japan, India, the US and Russia. (European Union Chamber of Commerce in China 2016: 16)

Table 7.1 Production capacity and utilisation rates in selected heavy industries, 2008–14

	Capacity (million ton)			Utilisation Rate	
	2008	2014	% increase	2008	2014
Crude steel	644.0	1,140.0	*77.0*	80	71
Electrolytic aluminium	18.1	38.1	*110.5*	78	76
Cement	1,870.0	3,100.0	*65.8*	76	73
Oil refining	391.0	686.0	*75.4*	80	66
Flat glass	650.0	1,046.0	*60.9*	88	79
Paper & paperboard	89.0	129.0	*44.9*	90	84
Shipbuilding	28.8	39.1	*35.8*		

Source: European Union Chamber of Commerce in China (2016).

Similarly, the production capacity of China's cement industry climbed 66 per cent between 2008 and 2014, from 1.9 billion tonnes to 3.1 billion tonnes, while its utilisation rate dropped from 76 per cent to 73 per cent. The scale of the expansion in the production capacity of the cement industry in China is captured well by the observation that 'according to data from China's National Bureau of Statistics and the US Geological Survey, in just two years—2011 and 2012—China produced as much cement as the US did during the entire 20th century' (European Union Chamber of Commerce in China 2016: 1).

It is instructive to note that the observed excess capacity phenomenon exists in these Chinese industries only because China has become a large economy in global terms. If China had remained as it was in 1980—a price-taker in international markets (that is, the textbook case of a competitive agent)—then it could have continuously enjoyed 100 per cent capacity utilisation. Each of these industries would simply have exported its surplus products (leftover from domestic consumption) and China would not face complaints from its trade partners. Today, however, China is so big that the rest of the world cannot absorb the exports from its excess capacity without significant loss of employment in their own industries. At the same time, to export surplus capacity, Chinese firms would have had to accept such price reductions for their exports that only short-run marginal costs and not long-run total costs could be covered.

In short, potential antidumping measures by China's trade partners alongside potentially large price declines are the reasons China cannot export away pervasive excess capacity in its economy. China is now such a big player in global markets that exports can no longer be used as the safety valve in macroeconomic stabilisation. Global prices for imported inputs would rise whenever China's demand increased and global prices for its exports would fall whenever its supply expanded. Such behaviours would also elicit criticisms abroad about China's mercantilist practices and the negative environmental spillovers being generated.

The immediate outcome from the significant excess production capacity in so many industries is that many related firms are unable to service the bank loans that were used to finance that capacity expansion. The investment house Credit Lyonnais Securities Asia (CLSA) has put the non-performing loan (NPL) ratio of the banking system in the range of 15–19 per cent, compared with the official estimate of 1.6 per cent (Yu 2016). The CLSA estimate has the value of NPLs equivalent to 10–15 per cent of GDP. Meanwhile, the consultancy Oxford Economics has put the value of China's NPLs at the high end of that range, 14 per cent of GDP (O'Brien 2016).

The return of non-performing loans to economic centre stage

The phenomenon of a high NPL ratio is an old one in China, but it has not been seen for almost a decade. In 1998, Nicholas Lardy (1998) brought great international attention to this issue by warning of possible bank runs in China. Table 7.2 shows the NPL ratio of the four largest state-owned banks (SOBs) in 1998 was 48 per cent and the capital adequacy ratio (CAR) was about 5 per cent. In response, then premier Zhu Rongji initiated a process of bank recapitalisation that would incrementally raise the CAR to 8 per cent by 2004 and reduce the NPL ratio to a low level by 2006 by having state-owned asset management companies buy a large amount of the NPLs at original face value. The main reason this bank recapitalisation effort stretched over eight years was because it involved reinvesting the bank profits that were created by financial regulation to keep a large gap between the lending rate and the deposit rate.

Table 7.2 Financial conditions of the domestic commercial banks, 1996–2005

	1996	1998	2001	2002	2003	2004	2005
Proportion of Non-Performing Loans (NPLs, %)							
Big four banks	40.0	48.0	31.1	26.5	20.4	15.6	10.1
Whole financial system				30.2			37.4
Whole financial system				30.2			28.2
Average Capital Adequacy Ratio (CAR, %)							
Big four banks	4.4	>8.0	5.0		approx 8.0		>8.0

Source: Author's estimates.

In fact, there was never a serious possibility of a bank run or a banking system collapse in the late 1990s and early 2000s. This was because the owner of the banks was the Ministry of Finance, and it was solvent. The value of state assets could easily guarantee the safety of the bank deposits. In turn, Chinese people had no rational reason to want to put their savings under their mattresses.

Since there was no real danger of the NPLs inducing a financial crisis, it is interesting to ask why Zhu Rongji bothered cleaning up the balance sheets of the SOBs. The reason is that in 1998 China had made enough progress in its negotiations with the United States on its application for World Trade Organization (WTO) membership that agreement was within reach. Policymakers were aware that WTO membership would require that national treatment be given to foreign banks after a short transition period—that is, the many discriminatory regulations against foreign banks that reduce their domestic competitiveness would have to end. The presence of a high NPL ratio among Chinese banks would mean, ultimately, that SOBs could easily be pushed into bankruptcy.

To see how WTO membership would threaten the SOBs, consider the minimum cash flow requirement of a domestic bank (assuming that the required reserve ratio is zero) (Equation 7.1).

Equation 7.1

$$r_D D = r_L [D - NPL]$$

In this equation, r_D is the deposit rate, r_L is the lending rate and D is the amount of the deposit.

Now if NPL = (1/3)D and r_D = 4 per cent, the minimum lending rate charged by the domestic bank is 6 per cent, r_L = 6 per cent.

If the newly entered foreign bank has no NPLs, it would be able to entice the entire customer base of the domestic bank to switch by setting its deposit rate marginally higher than that of the domestic bank and its lending rate a little lower, such as r_D = 4.2 per cent and r_L = 5.8 per cent.

To provide incentives to the SOBs to guard against the creation of new NPLs, the presidents of the four largest SOBs were advised that if their respective NPL ratios were to rise for three consecutive years, they would be dismissed. It was rumoured that the president of each SOB would then inform provincial-level bank chiefs that if the NPL ratio for the province were to increase for two consecutive years, the provincial chief would be replaced. The result was that the interval over which the NPL ratio could rise would progressively shorten with each step down the organisational hierarchy, so there was a new and higher level of scrutiny and caution about extending new loans. This was perhaps another important reason the NPL ratio declined rapidly between 1998 and 2006, and stayed low through the first term of the Hu Jintao–Wen Jiabao administration (2002–07).

In retrospect, the first-term Hu–Wen administration laid the basis for the creation of NPLs in later years. In a careful examination of the 'credit availability of listed firms in China between 2003 and 2011', Herrala and Jia (2015: 164) found 'that favoritism of state-owned firms in access to credit grew continuously more pronounced until at least 2011. In other words, this pattern continued even after the accommodative policies in response to the first phase of the 2008–09 global financial crisis had abated.' The growth rate of total bank loans in 2002–07 (Hu–Wen's first term) was a little higher than in 1997–2002 (Jiang Zemin–Zhu's last term), but the proportion of loans going to enterprises with significant state ownership was much higher in 2007 than in 2003.

The growth rate of bank loans jumped noticeably at the end of 2008 following then premier Wen Jiabao's return from the first G20 Summit held to formulate a collective response to what was correctly anticipated to be a near global economic meltdown, the Global Financial Crisis (GFC). The resolution of the G20 summit was that it was the responsibility of every country to undertake macrostimulus because any country doing it alone would soon be running large trade deficits and would be forced to end the macrostimulus prematurely.

In December 2008, Wen Jiabao announced plans to inject into the Chinese economy an annual macrostimulus of 7 per cent of GDP in 2009 and 2010 to reach a target annual growth rate of 8 per cent. To prevent the significant waste that had been generated in earlier episodes of macrostimulus, the focus was to bring forward investment projects—that is:

- To undertake investments in important hard infrastructure such as roads, bridges, ports, high-speed rail and telecommunications.
- To develop the 'industries of tomorrow', such as alternative energy industries (for example, solar power).
- To increase housing construction to accelerate urbanisation (rural-to-urban migration).

This announcement of expansionary policy in December 2008 reversed the semi-austerity policy that was in force in September 2008. After the end of the important Party Congress in October 2007, during which changes took place among the top leadership, the Chinese Government set out to lower the pace of economic growth to ensure continued price stability. GDP had grown by over 10 per cent annually throughout the period 2003–07.

The International Monetary Fund (IMF), meanwhile, predicted a growth rate of 6.7 per cent in both 2009 and 2010, which was lower than Wen Jiabao's target of 8 per cent. Given the severity of the GFC, the IMF also predicted that even a coordinated macrostimulus effort could only blunt the output collapse, and that offsetting it completely was out of the question.

Our prediction in February 2009 for China's economy that year fell between the two forecasts:

> China's growth in 2009 is likely to lie closer to Premier Wen's 8% target than to the IMF's projection of 6.7% … The state-owned banks (SOBs) will be happy to obey the command to increase lending because they cannot now be held responsible for future nonperforming loans. The local governments and the state-owned enterprises (SOEs) can now satisfy more of their voracious hunger for investment motivated by the soft-budget constraint situation where the profits would be privatized and the losses socialized. The stimulus package will [therefore] work well … The price … will be paid later by the recapitalization of the SOBs and a more depleted natural environment. (Woo 2009)

As it turned out, actual GDP growth exceeded Wen Jiabao's expectations as well as our own by quite a large margin. Unlike in almost every other G20 country, in China, macrostimulus prevented a slowdown from occurring at all, and this moved several typically very critical China analysts to praise Chinese policymakers for their masterful Keynesian countercyclical management.

In presenting our prediction for 2009, we had referred to the concept of the soft budget constraint, and explained this as an investment situation where the profits would be privatised and the losses socialised. An alternative definition of the *soft budget constraint mechanism* in terms of outcome is the *practice of institutionalised bailout* by a state where this is adopted with bias towards state-controlled enterprises (SCEs). This practice presents a moral hazard problem that results in blind investment demand by the SCEs and a complacent willingness by SOBs to supply funds for related investments. The bias of the Hu–Wen administration in promoting state capitalism (Herrala and Jia 2015) at the expense of the private sector served to enlarge the investment shares of local governments and SCEs and, importantly, thereby also increased the scope for soft budget constraint behaviour in the economy.

Pervasive soft budget constraint behaviour reappeared in China at the end of 2008 when the SCEs and SOBs were tasked with preventing an economic downturn. The complete abandonment of Zhu Rongji's micro-incentive of holding SOB presidents accountable for an upward trend in the NPL ratio facilitated GDP growth in 2009 (9.2 per cent) that was almost equal to that of 2008 (9.6 per cent) and GDP growth in 2010 that soared to 10.6 per cent.

This re-emergence of the pervasive soft budget constraint is the cause of the large amount of excess capacity in China's heavy industries today, and also of the serious NPL problem in the SOBs.

The relative lack of concern about financial sustainability from 2008 onward is encapsulated in the example of investment in railways. While there is no doubt that the expansion of the railway system, including the high-speed rail (HSR) service, is a much-needed infrastructure investment in a continent-sized country that has many densely populated areas, it is possible to fault the large investments in the intermediate input industries. The point is that no prudent cement (steel) enterprise would have increased production capacity to supply the amount of cement (steel) required to build the railways in the short specified period.

Table 7.3 shows the length of railways and highways in operation in 2002, 2008 and 2014. The network of railways increased by 32,100 km in 2008–14 from 7,800 km in 2002–08—a fourfold increase (Column A in Table 7.3). Most impressively, China's HSR began service in April 2007 with less than 700 km of track and, in less than a decade, China 'has the world's longest High-Speed Rail (HSR) network with over 19,000 km (12,000 mi) of track in service as of January 2016, which is more than the rest of the world's high-speed rail tracks combined, and a network length of 30,000 km (19,000 mi) is planned for 2020' (Wikipedia 2016).

Table 7.3 Length of transportation routes (1,000 km)

	Total Railways in Operation (A)	National Electrified Railways (B)	High Speed Railway (C)	Total Highways (D)	Expressways (E)
2002	71.9	17.4	na	1,765.2	25.1
2008	79.7	25.0	0.7	3,730.2	60.3
2014	111.8	36.9	16.5	4,463.9	111.9

Note: High-speed rail service was introduced in China on 18 April 2007.
Source: NBS (2015).

The increase in the network of electrified railways and the expressways network in the 2008–14 period was also substantially greater than in the 2002–08 period. It was roughly 1.5 times in both cases (columns B and E in Table 7.3).

Table 7.4 Two recent estimates of net TFP growth

Ding Lu (forthcoming)	
1996–2000	2.30%
2001–2005	2.92%
2006–2010	3.65%
2011–2015	0.71%
Harry Xiaoying Wu (2016)	
1991–2001	1.72%
2001–2007	0.54%
2007–2012	–2.10%

Note: Net TFP growth = aggregate TFP growth – growth effects from the reallocation of capital and labour.
Source: Taken from Lu (forthcoming) and Wu (2016).

The magnitude of the increases in both high-quality railways and high-quality roads in the six-year period 2008–14 reinforces our point that a prudent cement (steel) enterprise, before accepting orders for its product, would have had to think carefully about the use for its additional production capacity after the transportation projects were finished—that is, the underlying long-run demand for cement (steel). The prudent owner of the cement (steel) firm would therefore have negotiated with the railway company to arrive at some combination of the following three actions:

1. The cement (steel) firm would accept only a portion of the original order from the railway company (hence requiring the latter to import cement/steel).
2. The cement (steel) firm would deliver the contracted amount over a longer period (thereby forcing the railway company to lengthen the construction period).
3. The cement (steel) firm would deliver the contracted amount at a price that reflected the longer-term prospective rapid depreciation or write-off of future excess capacity.[2]

Because the largest Chinese cement producers are SCEs, however, the objective of the SCE manager is to maximise his career ahead of maximising profits for the SCE. Career maximisation means that the SCE manager will obey orders promptly and consistently, and recognise that the first priority is to contribute to the fulfilment of the targets in the national plan—for example, to construct 15,800 km of HSR lines in the next six years. The SCE manager has no direct or

2 We are grateful to Lauren Johnston for this third point.

immediate incentive to negotiate with the railway company to reduce the size of the order, to deliver the product over a longer period or to charge a price that would reflect the long-run costs of such a short-term surge in output.

Moreover, it is always to the benefit of the manager of a state-controlled cement (steel) factory to have the factory grow under his watch because this signals that he is capable of managing bigger projects. If he is lucky, he will be transferred to oversee more important projects before the railway project is completed. If not, he can count on the soft budget constraint mechanism to come to the rescue of the SCE.

Financial instability, fiscal crisis, zombie firms and low TFP growth

By the beginning of 2014, knowledgeable analysts had started warning about the worsening levels of excess capacity and the inevitable appearance of NPLs. Since NPLs are avoidable if the SCEs can pay back the loan principal they will be unable to service in the near future, the government began instructing the SCEs to issue new shares and pay back bank loans with the proceeds. Simultaneously, the government started promoting the stock market to the general public as a good investment vehicle for savings. The result of this talking up of the stock market was that the Chinese stock market climbed steeply—a rise that was itself helped by stock market manipulation by some large investment funds. The Shanghai Stock Market Index rose 150 per cent between June 2014 and June 2015.

The dramatic stock market boom ended badly in the form of an equally dramatic crash that began on 12 June 2015. The Shanghai Stock Market, specifically, had lost one-third of its value by 12 July 2015. The reason for the reversal of stock prices is obvious. What rate of return could an SCE pay on its equities when it could not afford to pay the average loan rate? The rate of return on this SCE's shares has to be lower than the average loan rate. This understanding would inevitably prevail and the stock bubble would then end. The attempt in 2014–15 to use the stock market to forestall the NPL problem resulted instead in financial market instability.

Ultimately, the Chinese Government would be forced to remove the NPLs from the balance sheets of the SOBs to prevent foreign banks driving the SOBs out of business by charging a lower margin between the deposit rate and the lending rate (as explained earlier). The important question therefore becomes how much of a burden would this recapitalisation of the SOBs be to the fiscal sustainability of the state?

For brevity, in the rest of this section, we will use the term 'debt' as shorthand for 'government debt'. Fiscal sustainability is possible only when the debt–GDP ratio does not continue to increase indefinitely—that is, the ratio does not follow an explosive path. So, fiscal sustainability is possible only when the debt–GDP ratio can ultimately converge to a finite steady-state value.

Fiscal sustainability is also, however, at risk where the equilibrium debt–GDP ratio is perceived to be very high. Where this ratio is very high, a large share of state revenue will be used to service the debt, creating a fiscal crisis in the financing of state programs. The European Union has adopted the safety standard of a debt–GDP ratio no higher than 60 per cent. For poor developing countries, the World Bank's Heavily Indebted Poor Country Initiative regarded a ratio of between 30 per cent and 50 per cent as the threshold, depending on the strength of the country's institutions.[3]

The mathematical condition for the existence of an equilibrium debt–GDP ratio is given by Equation 7.2.

Equation 7.2

$$y > r$$

In this equation, y is the trend growth rate of real GDP and r is the real interest rate on government debt.

When $y > r$, the steady-state equilibrium (debt/GDP) value ratio is shown as Equation 7.3.

Equation 7.3

$$(\text{Debt/GDP})_{\text{steady-state}} = (f + b)/(y - r)$$

In this equation, f is the primary fiscal deficit rate (state expenditure excluding debt service – state revenue)/GDP, and b is (increase in NPLs in SOBs)/GDP, because the state will take over the NPLs when it recapitalises the SOBs.

We will now look at the role of NPLs in influencing the equilibrium debt–GDP ratio by using Equation 7.4.

Equation 7.4

$$(\text{Debt/GDP})_{\text{steady-state}} = (f + b)/(y - r)$$

3 We thank Lauren Johnston for pointing this out to us.

The average value of the long-term growth rate (y) for the 1978–2011 period is above 9.5 per cent. Since the growth slowdown began in 2012, the government has called this new growth phase the 'new normal' economic era, and this is usually taken to mean a long-term growth rate of about 7 per cent. For example, after 2015, growth came in at 6.9 per cent, and the government's target for growth in 2016 was set within the range of 6.5–7 per cent.

The historical value for the primary deficit of the Chinese state budget (f) is usually between 2 and 3 per cent. The NPL-generation process that led to the NPL ratio being 48 per cent in 1998 gave an annual NPL creation rate (b) of 6 per cent of GDP. The real interest rate is in the historical range of 3–7 per cent.

Under the 'optimistic scenario', in which y is 8 per cent, f is 2 per cent and r is 3.5 per cent, we find:

- $(\text{Debt/GDP})_{\text{steady-state}}$ = 178 per cent when b = 6 per cent
- $(\text{Debt/GDP})_{\text{steady-state}}$ = 111 per cent when b = 3 per cent
- $(\text{Debt/GDP})_{\text{steady-state}}$ = 67 per cent when b = 1 per cent.

Under the 'new normal economy scenario', in which y is 6.8 per cent, f is 2 per cent and r is 3.5 per cent, we find:

- $(\text{Debt/GDP})_{\text{steady-state}}$ = 242 per cent when b = 6 per cent
- $(\text{Debt/GDP})_{\text{steady-state}}$ = 152 per cent when b = 3 per cent
- $(\text{Debt/GDP})_{\text{steady-state}}$ = 91 per cent when b = 1 per cent.

The simulations under the optimistic scenario reveal that the only time the equilibrium debt–GDP ratio is anywhere close to 60 per cent (the EU benchmark) is when b is 1 per cent, which is very much below the historical value of 6 per cent.

The simulations under the new normal economy scenario emphasise that fiscal sustainability is not assured even in the case of b = 1 since the lower growth rate of 6.8 per cent has made it impossible for the economy to grow out of its debt. *In short, under the present new normal growth phase, the soft budget constraint must be eliminated completely for fiscal sustainability to be possible.*

The term 'zombie firm' was coined to describe a firm that continues to operate despite being unable to service its loans at the market interest rate. Zombie firms show profits only thanks to receipt of various types of subsidies—for example, concessionary interest rates on loans and bank debt being converted to equities held by the banks. Tan et al. (forthcoming) find that zombie firms have lower TFP growth rates than non-zombie firms.

The growing presence of zombie firms since 2008 coincides with the downward trend in the growth rate of net TFP established in two recent studies: Lu (forthcoming) and Wu (2016).[4] Lu (forthcoming) found China's net TFP growth rate of 0.71 per cent over the 2011–15 period was the lowest since 1996. The net TFP rate was 2.3 per cent in 1996–2000, 2.92 per cent in 2001–05 and 3.15 per cent in 2006–10. Wu (2016) made similar findings, estimating that net TFP had grown 1.72 per cent in 1991–2001, 0.54 per cent in 2001–07 and –2.10 per cent in 2007–12. This is an alarming development for China. Technological innovation is the ultimate engine of economic growth.

The economic policy agenda

China's growth target in the new normal economy is 7 per cent. The World Bank predicted in January 2016 that the growth rate in 2016 would be 6.7 per cent, and 6.5 per cent in 2017. As growth in 2015 was 6.9 per cent, China faces the possibility of a three-year period of below target and progressively slowing growth. This is the context of the present animated discussion in China and abroad about what can and must be done to bring China's growth back to the 7 per cent trajectory. The two most common sets of policy actions that have been proposed are: demand-side macrostimulus via fiscal policies; and supply-side structural reform.

We know from experience that macrostimulus has immediate impacts, while structural reforms are effective over a longer period and can also involve short-term risks of output contraction. In China's case at present, however, these two sets of instruments may in fact present the choice between short-run growth stability and long-run stagnation on one hand and, on the other, below target growth in the short run and avoidance of the middle-income trap in the long run.

The most direct demand-side measures to deal with excess capacity are:

1. To create additional investment demand to use up excess capacity. This has to be investment and not consumption demand because heavy industrial products cannot be eaten. However, more infrastructure investments and/or more cement and steel factories are desirable only if their rates of return equal those of private investments, or are at least non-zero.
2. To extend financial subsidies to expand production and then put the output into inventory. Again, this measure is sensible only if the rate of return is at least non-zero.

4 Net TFP growth = aggregate TFP growth – growth effects from the reallocation of capital and labour.

The most direct supply-side measures to deal with excess capacity are:

1. To shut down excess capacity, but this will create unemployment.
2. To retool factories to use the excess capacity to produce other products. The problem with this is that most equipment in heavy industries is highly task-specific.

We support the present policy preference for prioritising supply-side structural reform. This is because the macrostimulus of state-directed investments during the 2003–13 period: 1) crowded out private sector growth and; 2) served as a lifeline for economically inefficient zombie firms (Tan et al. forthcoming).

The four most important components of supply-side structural reforms are:

1. To set up an adequate social safety net for laid-off workers.
2. To establish an effective retraining program for the laid-off workers.
3. To give the market mechanism a more decisive role in factor markets (the markets for capital, land and labour) in China (Woo and Zhang 2009).
4. To strengthen national innovation (Fu et al. forthcoming).

The first two reforms—safety nets and retraining programs—are crucial not only for political and moral reasons but also for a fast-growing economy to endure. A fast-growing modern economy requires a changing composition of skills in the labour force. China must therefore accelerate the integration and coverage of its fragmented social safety net into a comprehensive national system and scale up and strengthen retraining programs.

Retraining programs, it must be emphasised, work only if the state funds and monitors them adequately; otherwise they are just another form of welfare delivery. Lifelong learning is important for an ageing society such as China's. If China succeeds in establishing effective retraining programs, it will become a model for the rest of the world, which has been grappling mostly unsuccessfully with this problem.

Reforms should also occur concurrently in the three factor markets because of the seriousness of the situation in all three. Capital market reform must start with the recognition that physical infrastructure is no longer the foremost binding growth constraint. This means that the task of the financial system should no longer be to channel savings cheaply towards funding government investment projects. Instead, the state must now promote the establishment of private small and medium-sized banks because these are the most effective vehicles to support the growth of small and medium-sized enterprises (SMEs) and of rural firms.

Land reform is particularly important in rural areas. Privatisation of rural land to the current leaseholders will provide collateral for them to become entrepreneurs and/or will free them to move to cities permanently. At present, most urban land is owned by the state. An advantage of this is that it is relatively feasible to construct public housing for the new migrants under a system of future home ownership (as practised in Singapore). After 10 years, the new migrants would have the first right to buy the public housing units at the original construction price. Such migration and greater labour market flexibility will, however, need to be supported by a rapid phasing out of the household registration (*hukou*) system and of the restrictions on labour movement to the large and more developed coastal cities such as Shanghai and Guangzhou.

Enhancing innovation is the most important supply-side reform in the long run. National innovation performance is a complex interaction of capabilities, incentives and institutional factors. A country's capabilities—that is, technological efforts, human capital and physical investment—define the best that can be achieved in innovation. Incentives at the macro and micro levels guide the use of these capabilities and stimulate their expansion, renewal and disappearance. These incentives help to determine the efficiency with which these capabilities are used. More fundamentally, both factors (capabilities and incentives) operate within an institutional framework—for example, legal institutions (including intellectual property rights (IPR) protection and economic regulation) and educational institutions. These institutions set the rules of the game and, through this, alter capabilities and incentives.

There are two main bottlenecks in China's innovation capabilities. The first is creativity, because the Chinese education system emphasises respect for and attention to existing knowledge and doctrine, rather than fostering critical thinking and challenging existing limits. The state is aware of this problem and has been seeking to implement fundamental changes. The task now is to accelerate and greatly extend this root-and-branch reform of the education system (from the nursery level up).

The second major bottleneck lies in unequal access to resources for innovation and the need for greater support of SMEs (which form the most dynamic sector in the economy) and also the private sector in general (the most efficient innovator in the economy). The basic problem that SMEs face the world over (even in developed economies) is greater difficulty in accessing financial resources. Therefore, even with a more liberalised financial sector in China, the government needs to set up targeted SME innovation funds and information support systems. Innovative experimentation with internet finance and the related credit rating assessment may support this process.

In terms of incentives, the fundamental task for government is to allow price signals from competitive markets to guide resource allocation. For China, the primary task here is to implement reform of the factor markets, as identified earlier in this section. The government must persist in reducing its intervention in the business and commercial sectors, except in cases of well-known market failures—for example, supporting basic research because it faces high risks and uncertainties and requires long-term investment to be sustained.

China, as a middle-income country, must establish two institutions to entrench innovation within its economic system. The first is a strong system of IPR institutions, which would:

- Strengthen the diffusion of outside knowledge into China. At the same time, it is hard to dismiss the frequent statements by foreign investors and multinational enterprise managers that relatively weak IPR protection in China discourages them from using the most advanced technology in their production in the country.
- Further encourage indigenous innovation inside China.

The second important institution required to boost China's capability in innovation is that of external engagement in technology. The government should integrate China deeper into the global innovation system by enhancing existing efforts to:

- strengthen programs in international innovation collaboration and international knowledge co-production
- encourage international technology acquisition through cross-border mergers and acquisitions by offering financial and diplomatic assistance
- actively attract highly skilled world-leading researchers for innovation projects in China
- actively participate in the global standard-setting activities of international organisations.

It is important to end this chapter by making the point again that supply-side structural reforms cannot work to their full potential—and might even be undermined—if the soft budget constraint mechanism (that is, the practice of institutionalised bailouts) is not eliminated on the demand side. The existence of the soft budget constraint guarantees the existence of excess capacity and zombie firms. A crude but previously effective instrument with which to curb the overinvestment proclivity of local governments and SCEs is to hold the top management of the SOBs accountable for the appearance of NPLs.

Efficient curbing of soft budget constraint behaviour will require that the career-maximising practices of SCE and SOB managers are shifted to match the long-run profit-maximising practices adopted by owners of private firms in a modern market economy. Both demand-side reform (the termination of the soft budget constraint) and supply-side structural reforms are necessary to induce this convergence in practice. Structural reforms will correct the incentives faced by China's managers and government officials—mainly as a result of changing the composition of ownership in China towards the enlargement of SMEs; and also by reducing the share of adjustment costs borne by labour when the production structure has to change to accommodate demand-side changes. Government officials will have less incentive to soften the budget constraints of production units and firm managers will have less political clout to demand the softening of their budget constraints.

References

Bielski, V. (2016), George Soros says 'hard landing practically unavoidable' for China's economy, *Sydney Morning Herald*, 22 January. Available from: www.smh.com.au/business/markets/george-soros-says-hard-landing-practically-unavoidable-for-chinas-economy-20160121-gmbh1w.html.

Bradsher, K. (2016), Investigation fuels doubts about growth data in China, *International New York Times*, 27 January.

Burkitt, L. (2016), China's working-age population sees biggest-ever decline, *Wall Street Journal*, 22 January.

European Union Chamber of Commerce in China (2016), *Overcapacity in China: An Impediment to the Party's Reform Agenda*. Available from: www.europeanchamber.com.cn/en/publications-overcapacity-in-china.

Fu, X., Hou, J. and Woo, W. T. (forthcoming), Technological innovation policy in China: The lessons, and the necessary changes ahead, *Economic Change and Restructuring*.

Herrala, R. and Jia, Y. (2015), Toward state capitalism in China, *Asian Economic Papers*, 14(2) (Summer): 163–175.

Lardy, N. (1998), *China's unfinished economic revolution*, Washington, DC: Brookings Institution.

Lu, D. (forthcoming), China surmounting the middle-income trap: The impact of capital formation and demographic transition on growth potential, *Asian Economic Papers*.

Magnier, M. (2015), China's better-than-expected GDP prompts skepticism from economists, *Wall Street Journal*, 19 October.

Martens, C. (2016), Paul Krugman: What's going on in China right now scares me, *Business Insider Malaysia*, 25 February. Available from: businessinsider.my/paul-krugman-interview-china-greece-brexit-2016-2/?r=US&IR=T#McDZDFz8kyDyHAXo.97.

National Bureau of Statistics (NBS) (2015), *China statistical yearbook 2015*, Beijing: China Statistics Press.

O'Brien, M. (2016), China's debt bubble is getting only more dangerous, *The Washington Post*, 16 May.

Onishi, N. (2016), China's woes deflate hopes for economic rise in Africa, *International New York Times*, 26 January.

Russell, K. and Lai, R. (2015), Why China is rattling the world, *New York Times*, 26 August. Available from: nytimes.com/interactive/2015/08/26/business/-why-china-is-rattling-the-world-maps-charts.html.

Stevenson, A. (2016), Fears about China's economy fester at Davos, *International New York Times*, 22 January.

Tan, Y., Huang, Y. and Woo, W. T. (forthcoming), Zombie firms and the crowding-out of private investment in China, *Asian Economic Papers*.

Wall Street Journal (2016a), China faces dilemma over yuan, *Wall Street Journal*, 25 January.

Wall Street Journal (2016b), China's bond bubble, [Editorial], *Wall Street Journal*, 23 February.

Wikipedia (2016), High-speed rail in China, *Wikipedia*. Available from: en.wikipedia.org/wiki/High-speed_rail_in_China.

Wildau, G. (2016), China mouthpiece warns Soros against shorting renminbi, *Financial Times*, 27 January.

Woo, W. T. (2009), China in the current global economic crisis, in *China's role in the origins of and response to the global recession*, Hearing before the US–China Economic and Security Commission, 111th Congress (first session), Washington, DC, 17 February.

Woo, W. T. and Zhang, W. (2009), Time for China to move from macro-stability to macro-sustainability: Making macro-stimulus work and maintaining its effects, *Journal of the Asia Pacific Economy*, 15(4) (November): 349–368.

Wu, H. X. (2016), China's institutional impediments to sustainable growth: A productivity approach, Presentation to Reserve Bank of Australia Conference, Sydney, 17 March.

Xin, Z. (2016a), China heading for big economic policy shift, says mystery 'authoritative' source in People's Daily, *South China Morning Post*, 9 May.

Xin, Z. (2016b), Xi Jinping's stance on China's economy laid bare as he distances hallmark policy from Western-style supply-side economics, *South China Morning Post*, 10 May.

Yu, X. (2016), China's real bad debt ratio at least nine times the official number and still growing, *South China Morning Post*, 6 May.

8. Consumption and Savings of Migrant Households: 2008–14

Xin Meng, Sen Xue and Jinjun Xue[1]

Introduction

China's economic growth can be divided into two phases: the export-oriented phase and the domestic demand-driven phase. The main dividing point is the onset of the Global Financial Crisis (GFC). In late 2008 and early 2009, China's exports fell by more than 20 per cent, which alerted Chinese policymakers to the unreliability of growth depending purely on exports. Government spending on domestic infrastructure was the main driver of China's economic recovery from the GFC. Thereafter, many other policies were enacted to stimulate domestic demand, including increasing public sector wages and agricultural price subsidies, increasing public holidays to encourage tourism, providing subsidies for farmers to purchase electrical goods and cars and speeding up social insurance reform to reduce precautionary savings. To date, the transition from export-led to domestic demand-driven growth is ongoing, and its success, to a large extent, depends on household consumption and saving responses.

China has an unusually high household saving rate. Studies on Chinese household savings have largely concluded that this relates to precautionary saving motives (Meng 2003; Chamon et al. 2013; Choi et al. 2014). In the pre-reform era, urban residents enjoyed cradle-to-grave social welfare coverage. In the 1990s, market-oriented reform gradually eroded these free public services and social security, and left households responsible for funding their own needs. Reforms to housing, education, pensions and health care required households to be more forward-looking and more cautious. As a result, household savings in cities increased dramatically from the mid-1990s onwards (for example, Meng 2003; Cai et al. 2012; Chamon et al. 2013; Choi et al. 2014). While education reform affected rural households, the main factor impacting on rural savings was the change from communal welfare provision to the household

1 We would like to thank Bob Gregory for his helpful comments and Yubing Xiang for her excellent research assistance. The paper was written when Xin Meng was visiting the Economic Research Centre of Graduate School of Economics, Nagoya University. She would like to thank the Centre for providing the research facilities and environment. Xin Meng and Sen Xue are in the Research School of Economics at The Australian National University. Email: xin.meng@anu.edu.au and sen.xue@anu.edu.au. Jinjun Xue is in the Economic Research Centre, Graduate School of Economics, Nagoya University and is Chief Scientist at the Center of Hubei Cooperative Innovation for Emissions Trading System (CHCIETS). Email: setsu@soec.nagoya-u.ac.jp.

responsibility system. Before these reforms, for example, elderly individuals in rural areas were looked after by the commune with a low level of welfare provision. After the household responsibility system was introduced, most commune-provided 'social welfare' disappeared. Households needed to save for their lean days (Cai et al. 2012). On top of this, another important saving motive in rural areas relates to the marriage prospects of one's offspring—in particular, sons. The implementation of the One-Child Policy, together with the traditional preference for having sons, created an acute imbalance in the sex ratio, mostly in rural China, which substantially increased the cost of marriage and generated precautionary savings motives in parents (Wei and Zhang 2011).

To date, there have been almost no studies discussing the savings and consumption behaviour of migrants in China, even though rural–urban migrants make up about 40 per cent of the urban labour force. This chapter begins to fill this gap.

In general, people living in urban areas spend more of their income than their rural counterparts and people living in large cities spend more than those in small cities. This is not only because urban dwellers have higher incomes, but also because urban centres provide more options for consumption, which, in turn, generate demand. Data from the Rural–Urban Migration in China (RUMiC) project have shown that migrants in cities spend more than their counterparts living in rural areas (see Figure 8.1) and this is the case for all subcategories of consumption (see Figure 8.2). Thus, one way to move towards transformation from an export-led to a domestic demand-driven development strategy ought to be to encourage more migration, especially in an economy in which unskilled labour is in short supply in cities. The Chinese Government has so far not fully realised the link between migration and consumption-driven growth. This can be seen from the slow progress made in helping more people to migrate, encouraging them to migrate to large cities and helping those workers who have already migrated to settle permanently in cities. It is also evident in the developing small-city urbanisation strategy implemented since 2014.

In this chapter, we examine whether the policies encouraging consumption implemented so far have had any impact on the consumption and saving behaviour of rural–urban migrants and what are the potential constraints on increasing the consumption of migrant workers.

The rest of the chapter is organised as follows. The next section discusses current institutional restrictions on migration and how these affect migrant consumption and saving behaviour. Section three presents the data and the general patterns of migrant consumption and saving over the period 2008–14. Section four investigates the evolution of migrant precautionary saving behaviour, and section five concludes and provides some policy implications.

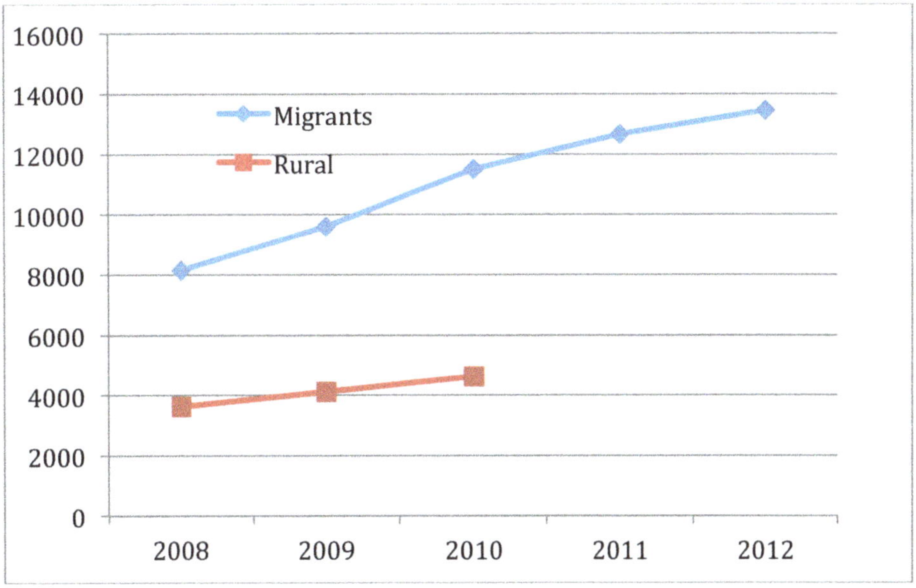

Figure 8.1 Comparison of annual per capita expenditure: Rural and migrants

Source: Migrant Household Survey of the RUMiC Project, 2008–12 wave, and Rural Household Survey of the RUMiC Project, 2008–10 wave.

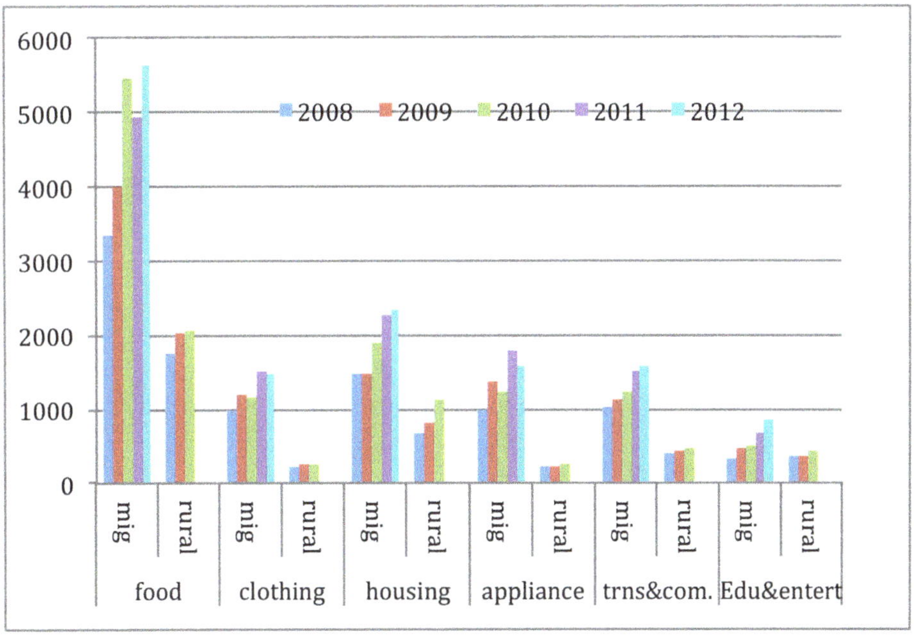

Figure 8.2 Comparison of detailed consumption items: Rural and migrants

Source: Migrant Household Survey of the RUMiC Project, 2008–12 wave, and Rural Household Survey of the RUMiC Project, 2008–10 wave.

Background

Migrants in China are, in general, treated as 'guest workers'. Despite their significant contribution to economic growth, they are restricted in the type of job they can obtain and in their access to urban social services in the destination cities, including access to education, health care, unemployment benefits and pensions. These restrictions prevent migrant workers from staying in cities in the long run and also from bringing their families to the cities (Du et al. 2006). Inevitably, migrants do not regard the city they are working in as their 'home' and this, to a large extent, affects their consumption behaviour. Migrants have always been thought of as a group who come to cities to make and save money so that eventually they can go back to their rural home to build a better life. Consequently, they work hard, spend less and save more.

In recent years, the Chinese Central Government has realised the drawbacks of the 'guest worker' system and has introduced new laws and regulations to protect migrants' benefits and increase their access to urban services. These attempts to eliminate discrimination against migrants have had rather limited success for systemic reasons. Consider children's schooling as an example. Although the Central Government has announced policies that mean migrant children should be treated in the same way as local urban kids and should be allowed to enrol in urban public schools, it was expected that funding for the education of these children would be provided by local governments. However, local governments' priority is to provide the best services for their local constituents and they are therefore reluctant to implement the policy (Chen and Feng 2013). As a result, most migrants leave their school-aged children in their hometown. The same situation occurs with regard to other services and welfare provisions for migrants.

In general, over the past eight years, there have been some improvements in social services and welfare provision for migrants, but the pace of improvement is rather slow. For example, although the Labour Contract Law implemented in 2008 clearly requires all employers to pay social insurance for migrant workers, until 2014 only 30 per cent of migrant workers had either pension or health insurance, and less than 26 per cent had unemployment insurance (RUMiC survey results). In terms of children being left behind in rural hometowns, in 2008, nearly 60 per cent of children aged 15 and below were left behind, and by 2014 the figure had reduced to 51 per cent. That is, even in 2014, almost half of migrants' children were still being left behind in rural areas.

In these circumstances, the consumption and saving behaviour of migrants should be very different from that of their urban- and rural-resident counterparts, largely because of the unsettled nature of their 'guest worker' status.

Data and general trends in consumption and savings

The data used for this study are from the RUMiC surveys for 2008 to 2014. The survey is conducted annually in 15 cities in nine provinces. These cities include coastal migrant destination cities, such as Guangzhou, Shenzhen, Dongguan, Shanghai, Wuxi, Nanjing, Hangzhou and Ningbo, as well as major interior destination cities: Chengdu, Chongqing, Wuhan, Hefei, Bengbu, Zhengzhou and Luoyang. The sampling of the RUMiC survey differs significantly from any other household surveys of migrant workers in China, which mainly sample migrants at urban residential addresses. Because of China's internal migration policy, many migrants move to the city alone and do not have their family with them, making it more likely that they live in factory dormitories or other workplace-based accommodation. Even if migrants come to the city with their families, the high rental costs have deterred them from living in urban residential accommodation. As a result, the normal urban household survey is more likely to offer a biased sample of migrant workers. To avoid this potential bias, RUMiC adopted a sampling frame that is based on a census of potential migrants' workplaces.[2]

The RUMiC is designed to be a longitudinal survey, which follows migrants over time. However, due to the nature of the population—which is young and mobile—the attrition rate has been high. In particular, in 2009, when the GFC reduced China's exports by 20 per cent and forced many migrants to return home, the attrition rate was about 63 per cent. The attrition rate has been reducing gradually since 2009, from 63 per cent to 35 per cent in 2014. To maintain the original sample size, each year the RUMiC team creates a random refreshment sample, the 'new-household sample'. Thus, apart from 2008, in each subsequent year, the RUMiC survey has had two subsamples: one traces part of the previous year's sample ('old-household sample') and one draws a new random sample ('new-household sample'). The new-household sample gives us a representative picture of migrants in general, while the old-household sample presents the dynamic picture of migrant life and work (Meng 2013).

2 For detailed discussion of the RUMiC sampling procedure, see Gong et al. (2008).

General patterns and the distributional perspective

We first examine the patterns over time of income, consumption and saving. All the income and expenditure variables are deflated by provincial urban consumer price indices (CPIs) using 2008 as 100. We also adjust for migrant household size (number of household members living in the same address in the city) to obtain per capita values. In addition, following the convention in the literature, we trim the top and bottom 1 per cent of the sample based on income, expenditure and saving variables. The saving rate is defined as Equation 8.1.

Equation 8.1

$$SR_i^1 = \frac{Inc_i - Cons_i}{Inc_i}$$

In the equation, SR_i is the saving rate for household *i*, Inc_i is household *i*'s annual income and $Cons_i$ refers to its annual consumption expenditure. Because of the special nature of the population we examine (migrants), we also define a second saving rate variable (Equation 8.2).

Equation 8.2

$$SR_i^2 = \frac{Inc_i - Cons_i - Remit_i}{Inc_i}$$

In this equation, $Remit_i$ indicates migrant households' total annual remittances. In the survey, there are four components of household saving: 1) investment saving (purchase of security and stocks, housing purchase and investment in family business); 2) remittances; 3) transfers and other non-consumption expenditure; and 4) residual saving, which should comprise households' annual increments in deposits and cash-in-hand. The first three components form household non-consumption expenditure, while the last component can be obtained by subtracting total household consumption expenditure and non-consumption expenditure from household income.

Table 8.1 reports summary statistics for real per capita income, consumption expenditure, non-consumption expenditure, remittances and the two saving rates defined above. The first panel of the table presents the total sample information while the next two panels report for the top and bottom 20 percentile samples based on per capita real income. Over the past seven years, migrant per capita real income increased by 9 per cent per annum, and the growth rate for the low-income group was lower, at 7 per cent per annum. Real per capita consumption expenditure increased by 8 per cent per annum, on average, but it was much higher for the low-income group (10 per cent per annum) than for the high-income group (5 per cent). Real per capita non-consumption expenditure increased, on average, by 5 per cent per annum but the growth occurred mainly at the top of the distribution. The bottom two decile households actually had a reduction in non-consumption of 4 per cent per year over the period, while the top two decile households had an increase of 8 per cent per year. Remittances also followed the same pattern as non-consumption expenditure, with the low-income group sending less of their income home relative to the earlier years, while the high-income group sent more. If we examine the value of remittances, the top income group is sending three to 10 times the amount of money back to their rural homes as their low-income counterparts. The last two columns of the table present the two saving rates, with and without remittances. Over the seven years, the average SR_1 has been hovering around 36 to 38 per cent, but there is huge diversity in savings across different income groups. The top two income decile households saved about 40 per cent at the beginning of the period and more than 50 per cent at the end of the period. The low-income group, however, had a reduction in their saving rate, dropping from 27 per cent at the beginning to 10 per cent at the end of the period. Excluding remittances from savings, the average saving rate increased over the period from 23 per cent in 2008 to 26 per cent in 2014. But most of the increase in savings is due to the top income group's saving.[3]

We now turn to year-on-year changes and plot log real per capita consumption and savings against log real per capita income by year. The upper panel of Figure 8.3 presents these unconditional relationships and shows that between 2010 and 2011 there seems to be a 'structural' change, with much steeper (flatter) consumption (saving) and income relationships in the earlier years (2008–10) than in the later years (2011–14). The clearest structural change can be observed in consumption and savings, which differ between the two periods for the high- and low-income groups. In both cases, the early year curves intercept with later year curves, suggesting an opposite change between the two periods for the high- and low-income groups.

3 We also present the same summary statistics for the new-household sample (see Appendix Table A8.1), and the patterns are almost the same as for the total sample.

Table 8.1 Household income, consumption and saving: Full sample

Total sample	Real per capita income	Real per capita consumption	Real per capita non-consumption	Real per capita remittances	Saving rate	Saving rate excluding remittances	No. of observations
2008	16,225	9,838	3,412	2,266	0.370	0.228	4,731
2009	18,780	12,172	3,975	2,819	0.330	0.192	4,981
2010	20,911	13,505	3,247	2,071	0.334	0.238	5,126
2011	24,001	13,292	3,571	2,361	0.385	0.292	4,967
2012	24,374	13,834	3,867	2,659	0.377	0.273	4,922
2013	27,504	15,697	5,459	3,723	0.364	0.243	4,332
2014	29,004	16,471	4,713	3,463	0.361	0.256	4,223
Average annual growth	0.087	0.076	0.047	0.062			
Top 20% income group:							
2008	29,218	16,534	5,476	3,675	0.431	0.303	
2009	32,694	20,250	8,194	5,688	0.379	0.208	
2010	37,100	23,094	5,602	3,540	0.375	0.277	
2011	42,769	20,041	6,403	4,299	0.523	0.421	
2012	43,547	20,916	7,155	4,993	0.511	0.394	
2013	49,668	23,219	1,0914	7,947	0.523	0.360	
2014	51,753	23,622	9,090	7,269	0.536	0.393	
Average annual growth	0.085	0.052	0.075	0.102			

Total sample	Real per capita income	Real per capita consumption	Real per capita non-consumption	Real per capita remittances	Saving rate	Saving rate excluding remittances	No. of observations
Bottom 20% income group:							
2008	7,846	5,596	2,075	1,105	0.268	0.130	
2009	9,142	6,938	1,438	889	0.225	0.132	
2010	9,659	7,330	1,454	735	0.228	0.154	
2011	10,255	83,95	1,446	629	0.145	0.085	
2012	11,115	90,18	1,889	948	0.160	0.072	
2013	12,070	10,427	1,958	852	0.104	0.037	
2014	12,362	10,708	1,554	756	0.102	0.044	
Average annual growth	0.067	0.097	–0.040	–0.053			

Source: RUMiC survey, 2008–14.

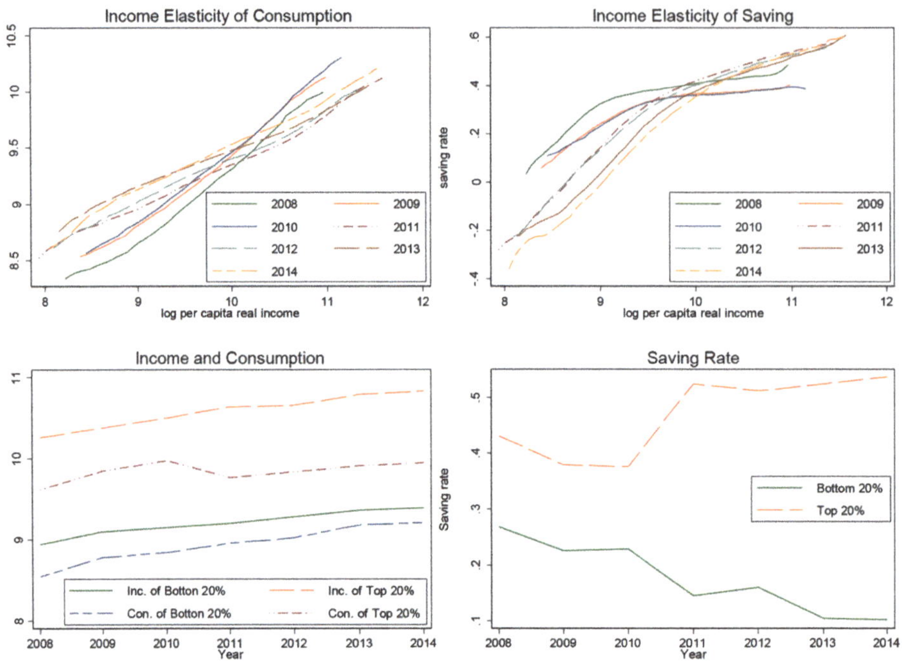

Figure 8.3 Consumption and saving by income, 2008–14

Source: Migrant Household Survey of the RUMiC Project, 2008–14 wave.

To further understand these changes, we plot the average log consumption and savings rates for the top and bottom 20 percentiles in the bottom panel of Figure 8.3. The left bottom panel (income and consumption) reveals that for both high- and low-income groups real per capita income has been increasing, but the real consumption change over time differs significantly between the two groups. The major difference happens between 2010 and 2011, where there is a significant reduction in real per capita consumption for the top two decile income groups. Meanwhile, for the bottom income group, real per capita consumption has been increasing continuously and, at the end of the period, the rate of increase in consumption seems to be faster than the rate of increase for income. This difference is probably one of the causes of the structural change we observed in the upper panel of the figure.

Next, we examine the detailed consumption and saving items to identify the major consumption component that generated the structural change. In particular, we examine food, health, education, housing and other expenditure within consumption. Figure 8.4 presents the itemised consumption levels for the top and bottom 20 percentile households. There are a few general points worth noting. First, food consumption is the single most important item for migrant workers, and is more than double the level of the second most important item, housing. Second, the change in consumption between 2010 and 2011 seems to occur mainly because of the food consumption change in the top income group. Why does this happen? We examined the change in general and food prices over this period and discovered that between 2010 and 2011 food prices increased dramatically and, within food, the price of meat changed the most (see Figure 8.5). Not only did meat prices increase significantly between 2010 and 2011, but also, this came after a drop in meat prices between 2008 and 2010. The pattern observed in our food consumption graph (Panel 1 of Figure 8.4) seems to coincide very well with the food price pattern. In particular, the consumption level of the top income group, who are likely to consume more meat, seems to have been affected the most by the change in meat prices—increasing when the meat price dropped and reducing when meat prices increased. The middle income group was also affected somewhat, whereas the bottom group—who presumably are not large consumers of meat—was the least affected. A possible explanation is that due to the sharp increase in meat prices, the top income group began to substitute other food for meat, which generated lower overall food consumption levels for this group. For the poor, however, perhaps they were already eating basic foods so food substitution is unlikely and their food consumption levels were unaffected between 2010 and 2011. After 2011, the prices of food and meat increased much more slowly, which would explain why food consumption in general for all income groups has been increasing.

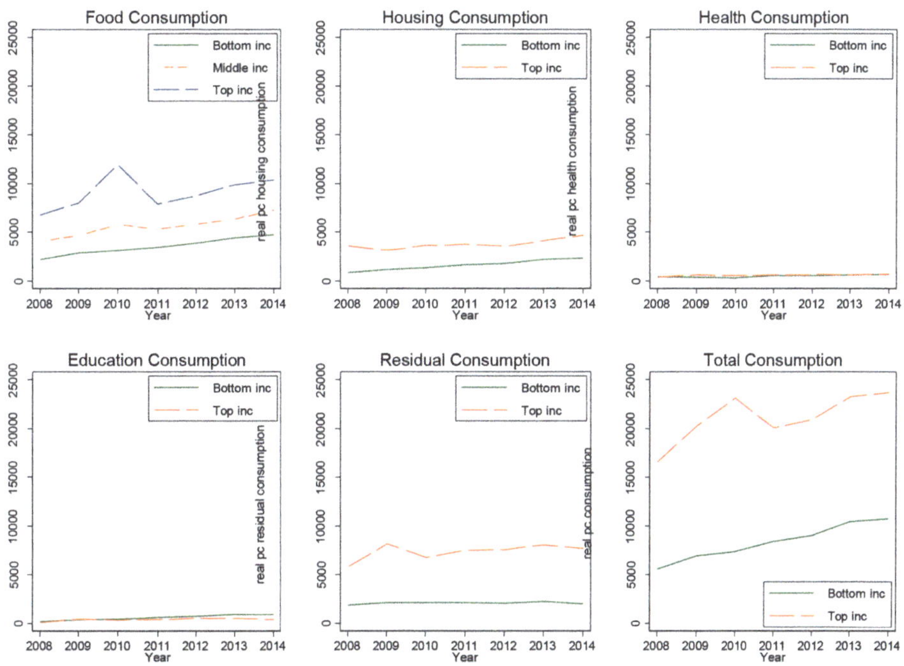

Figure 8.4 Consumption components for bottom and top income groups, 2008–14

Source: Migrant Household Survey of the RUMiC Project, 2008–14 wave.

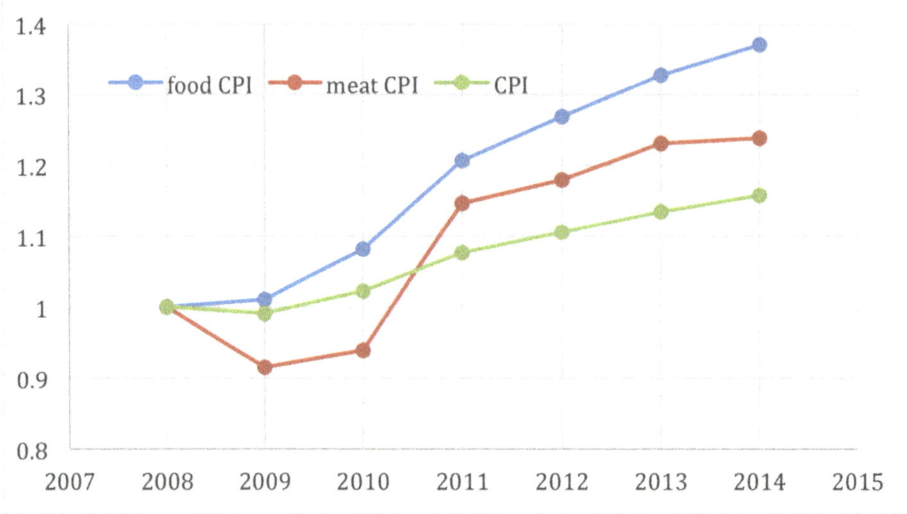

Figure 8.5 Price indices, 2008–14

CPI = consumer price index

Source: National Bureau of Statistics (various years).

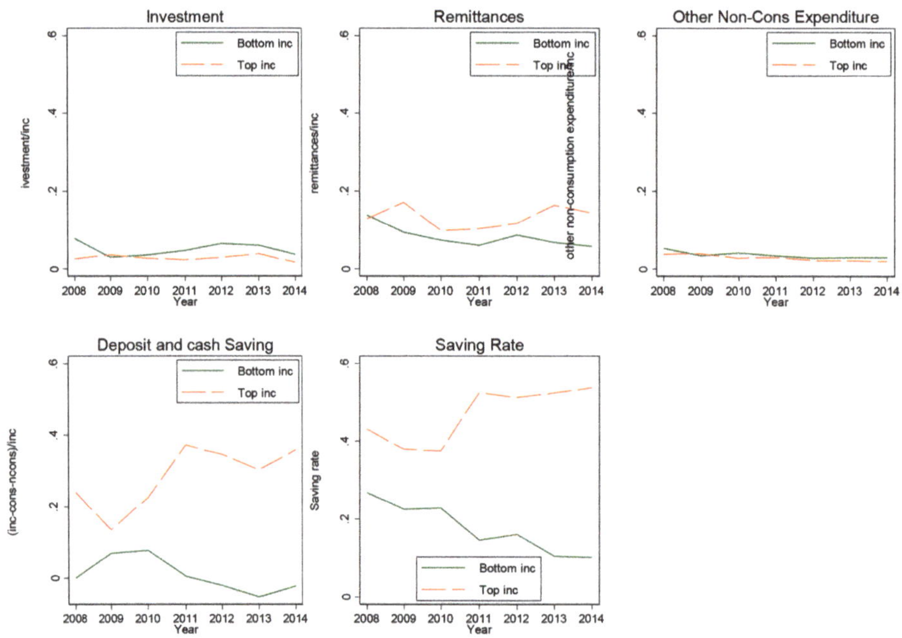

Figure 8.6 Saving components for bottom and top income groups, 2008–14

Source: Migrant Household Survey of the RUMiC Project, 2008–14 wave.

For the saving rate, we look at investment (stock market, housing purchase and production-related investment), remittances, other non-consumption expenditure as well as residual savings (increments in bank deposits and cash-in-hand). Figure 8.6 reveals that the saving increase for the top income migrant group was not used for investment, nor did it go to other non-consumption expenditure. Although remittances increased slightly, they reduced again in 2014. It seems the majority of the increase in the top income group's saving went into residual savings, suggesting a strong precautionary motive.

Migration restrictions and the consumption/saving pattern

In this subsection, we examine the pattern of consumption and savings in response to migration restrictions. To this end, we examine two sets of institutional restriction indicators: 1) whether migrants with family members left behind behave differently than their counterparts without family members left behind; and 2) whether migrants with social insurance have different behaviour relative to their counterparts without social insurance. For the first indicator, we divide our sample into three household types: 1) households whose head is married and either their children or their spouse is left behind in a rural village; 2) households whose head is married but without a spouse or children left behind; and 3) households whose head is single. The indicator for households' social insurance status is set to one if the household head has either a pension or health insurance, and zero otherwise.

Table 8.2 presents income level, consumption and remittance shares of income and saving rates with and without remittances for these five types of household groups. Panels A to C investigate consumption and saving patterns for households with and without members left behind, whereas panels D and E compare consumption and saving patterns for household heads with and without a pension and/or health insurance.

Table 8.2 Household income, consumption and saving for different groups: Full sample

	Real per capita income	Real per capita consumption	Remittances as % of income	Saving rate	Saving rate excluding remittances	No. of observations
Single:						
2008	16,884	10,676	0.106	0.357	0.247	2,175
2009	20,231	13,399	0.114	0.332	0.223	2,183
2010	22,505	15,140	0.087	0.319	0.232	2,249
2011	26,279	14,914	0.082	0.394	0.314	2,008
2012	26,512	15,649	0.091	0.382	0.292	1,756
2013	31,553	18,980	0.117	0.367	0.251	1,414
2014	34,275	20,186	0.107	0.383	0.282	1,187
Average annual growth	0.107	0.095				
No family left behind:						
2008	13,274	8,413	0.050	0.313	0.262	1,037
2009	14,621	10,340	0.106	0.260	0.166	1,278
2010	16,446	10,885	0.038	0.291	0.251	1,380
2011	18,155	10,976	0.044	0.306	0.259	1,515
2012	19,541	11,725	0.057	0.319	0.257	1,673
2013	21,447	13,145	0.058	0.293	0.240	1,666
2014	22,517	13,917	0.051	0.292	0.244	1,824
Average annual growth	0.078	0.075				

	Real per capita income	Real per capita consumption	Remittances as % of income	Saving rate	Saving rate excluding remittances	No. of observations
With family left behind:						
2008	17,298	9,609	0.232	0.426	0.177	1,519
2009	20,193	11,949	0.228	0.387	0.168	1,520
2010	22,633	13,463	0.156	0.397	0.234	1,497
2011	26,965	13,468	0.158	0.454	0.296	1,444
2012	27,275	14,061	0.170	0.438	0.267	1,493
2013	30,991	15,384	0.226	0.456	0.238	1,252
2014	33,605	16,677	0.200	0.444	0.247	1,212
Average annual growth	0.010	0.082				
With insurance:						
2008	18,530	11,045	0.131	0.385	0.259	1,094
2009	21,205	13,912	0.155	0.325	0.181	1,283
2010	22,841	14,784	0.111	0.338	0.228	1,511
2011	27,439	15,355	0.116	0.391	0.278	1,569
2012	26,250	14,746	0.126	0.393	0.271	1,830
2013	29,369	16,849	0.149	0.374	0.237	1,664
2014	31,291	17,771	0.133	0.375	0.255	1,578
Average annual growth	0.078	0.070				

	Real per capita income	Real per capita consumption	Remittances as % of income	Saving rate	Saving rate excluding remittances	No. of observations
Without insurance:						
2008	15,532	9,474	0.142	0.365	0.219	3,637
2009	17,939	11,568	0.147	0.332	0.196	3,698
2010	20,104	12,970	0.093	0.333	0.242	3,615
2011	22,413	12,340	0.088	0.382	0.299	3,398
2012	23,264	13,294	0.097	0.368	0.274	3,092
2013	26,341	14,979	0.125	0.358	0.247	2,668
2014	27,640	15,696	0.109	0.353	0.256	2,645
Average annual growth	0.086	0.075				

Source: RUMiC survey, 2008–14.

We first compare households with and without members left behind. Of the three groups, single households have had the most income growth, averaging 11 per cent annually. This rate for married households without and with members left behind is 8 per cent and 10 per cent, respectively. In terms of per capita income level, the married household heads without members left behind are also the ones with the lowest real per capita income. However, this is probably an artefact of the households without members left behind having, on average, 3.2 members living in cities, while this number for single households is 1.1 and for households with members left behind it is 1.6 people. Real per capita income should be lower for this group.

The second column of the table presents real per capita consumption and its annual growth rate at the bottom row. It shows that for singles and households without members left behind, their annual growth in consumption is only slightly (no more than 1.2 percentage points) lower than their income annual growth rate, suggesting a high consumption share and low savings for these two groups. For households with members left behind, however, their consumption growth rate is 2 percentage points below their average income growth rate. In fact, the share of consumption as a proportion of income for the other two groups was about 60 per cent in 2014; for households with members left behind, it was only 50 per cent—10 percentage points lower.

Going across to Column 3, we also observe that the proportion of income remitted is more than 10 percentage points higher among households with members left behind than for the other two types of households. Even the single households remit more than households without members left behind. Finally, columns 4 and 5 present the saving rates with and without remittances. Once again, households with members left behind save the most, and single households have a lower saving rate than them, but higher savings than households without members left behind. In the early years, households with members left behind sent almost 60 per cent of their savings home as remittances, but this has gradually reduced to 40–45 per cent. For singles, about one-third of their savings goes to remittances, whereas remittances account for only about 15 per cent of savings for households without members left behind.

Turning to panels D and E of Table 8.2, we observe very limited differences in income and consumption growth. However, households without insurance have a much larger increase in the saving rate excluding remittances than households with insurance, indicating a greater need to save in the city in recent years.

Household characteristics

We also present summary statistics for household characteristics that may be related to household consumption and saving behaviours. The top panel of Table 8.3 presents the characteristics for the total sample and the second panel reports the same variables for the new-household sample. The table shows that, in 2008, migrant household heads were about 30 years of age and, over time, there has been a gradual increase in the average age. About 60–69 per cent of household heads are male. In the early years, there were more single people in the sample than there are now. In 2014, for example, about 72 per cent of household heads were married (including cohabitation). This may be due to the fact that our total sample includes a large proportion of the panel households and married people are more likely to stay longer in cities. When we examine the average of the new sample, we find that the proportion of household heads who are married has also increased, but not to the extent suggested by the total sample.

The majority of heads of migrant households have education to junior high school level or below. There is some increase in the proportion of household heads who are self-employed—from 19 per cent in 2008 to 31 per cent in 2014. However, this phenomenon is confined mainly to the 'old-household' sample. For the new-household sample, the proportion increased only slightly—to 22 per cent in 2014. Perhaps those who are self-employed are more likely to stay in the city longer and are therefore more likely to be tracked. The variable 'number of years since first migrating' is based on the information migrants provided on the year when they first migrated. This may be an exaggeration of their actual years of migration due to the frequent churn of Chinese migrants between cities and their home village, but it is the best information we can find. Based on this information provided from the new-household sample, over time, the length of stay in cities seems to be increasing from 7–8 to 9–10 years.

The average size of migrant households in the city has also increased, from 1.7 to two people, confirming that more family migration is occurring now than in the past. More importantly, from our data, it seems that there has been a reduction in the proportion of households who leave their children or spouse behind. Based on the new-household sample data, in 2008, only 38 per cent of families with children brought their children with them when they migrated. This had increased to 52 per cent by 2014. Similarly, the proportion of married migrants who left their spouse behind has reduced—from about 40 per cent to about 30 per cent.

Table 8.3 Summary statistics of household characteristics

Total sample	2008	2009	2010	2011	2012	2013	2014
HH head age	30.45	31.28	31.5	32.16	33.43	34.74	35.97
HH head is male	0.69	0.67	0.66	0.62	0.62	0.63	0.62
HH head is married	0.54	0.56	0.56	0.60	0.64	0.67	0.72
HH head has junior high school or below education	0.66	0.63	0.61	0.63	0.64	0.63	0.65
HH head is self-employed	0.19	0.22	0.22	0.24	0.26	0.29	0.31
HH no. of years since first migrating	7.75	8.37	8.16	9.25	10.52	11.27	12.33
Family size	1.67	1.73	1.77	1.88	1.97	2.06	2.19
Total no. of migrant children for HH with children	0.49	0.59	0.58	0.68	0.71	0.76	0.79
Total no. of children left behind for HH with children	0.80	0.72	0.64	0.63	0.62	0.58	0.57
Total no. of children for HH with children	1.29	1.31	1.22	1.31	1.33	1.34	1.35
Proportion of spouses left behind if married	0.35	0.33	0.32	0.30	0.27	0.26	0.23
HH head with pension insurance	0.20	0.22	0.24	0.27	0.33	0.35	0.34
HH head with health insurance	0.12	0.15	0.25	0.23	0.30	0.34	0.33
2008 or new sample:							
HH head age	30.45	30.52	30.27	30.24	31.42	32.62	34.39
HH head is male	0.69	0.65	0.64	0.61	0.61	0.62	0.6
HH head is married	0.54	0.51	0.48	0.48	0.55	0.58	0.63
HH head has junior high school or below education	0.66	0.62	0.59	0.63	0.62	0.60	0.64
HH head is self-employed	0.19	0.18	0.16	0.17	0.17	0.21	0.22
HH no. of years since first migrating	7.75	7.70	6.50	7.68	8.8	9.03	10.33
Family size	1.67	1.58	1.54	1.60	1.73	1.70	1.89
Total no. of migrant children for HH with children	0.49	0.50	0.41	0.53	0.54	0.54	0.65
Total no. of children left behind for HH with children	0.80	0.79	0.69	0.77	0.8	0.79	0.71
Total no. of children for HH with children	1.29	1.3	1.1	1.29	1.34	1.32	1.36
Proportion of spouses left behind if married	0.35	0.40	0.40	0.39	0.34	0.38	0.29
HH head with pension insurance	0.20	0.21	0.19	0.25	0.35	0.30	0.29
HH head with health insurance	0.12	0.15	0.22	0.19	0.34	0.30	0.29

HH = household

Source: RUMiC survey, 2008–14.

Finally, in terms of social insurance coverage, there has been a steady improvement among migrants; however, the speed of this improvement is slow. For example, at the beginning of the survey period, about 20 per cent of household heads had pension insurance, either provided by their employer or purchased by the household head. This increased to about 30 per cent in 2014. The high-income households had much more success in this area than their low-income counterparts, which could be related to the fact that a significantly larger proportion of the low-income group is self-employed. But, by any account, the figures presented in our new-household sample (the current representative sample) suggest that the access rate for the top income group is about 35 per cent, which is still very low.

All these household characteristics should have an important influence on migrants' consumption and saving behaviour.

Understanding migrant consumption and saving

In this section, we examine what factors influence migrant household consumption and saving behaviour. We estimate Equation 8.3.

Equation 8.3

$$Y_{ijt} = \alpha + f(ln(inc)_{ijt}) + \delta X_{ijt} + \gamma W_{ijt} + c_{jt} + \epsilon_{ijt}$$

In this equation, subscripts i, j and t refer to household, city and year, respectively; Y is a vector of dependent variables in which we are interested, including log of real per capita consumption and saving rate; $ln(inc)$ is log real per capita income; X is household characteristics related to permanent income, such as household heads' education level, age and its squared term, gender of the household head and whether or not the head is self-employed. Because the purpose of this chapter is to understand how institutional restrictions on migration affect migrant household consumption behaviour, we do not pay too much attention to separately identifying permanent and transitory incomes, but simply control for some determinants of permanent income. W is a vector of variables, which proxies the impact of the current institutional restrictions on migrant households, including whether the household head is married or single, family size, the total number of children the household has, and the number of children left behind, whether or not the spouse of the household head is left behind, and two dummy variables indicating whether the household head has pension or health insurance. C is a vector of city*year fixed effects, which should control for all the year–city varying fixed factors that could affect individuals' spending, such as the price effect, which is not fully captured by the provincial-level CPI. Finally, ϵ_{ijt} is the household random error term. Our main interest is to examine the impact of institutional restrictions on household consumption and saving behaviour (γ). The $f(\cdot)$ allows a nonlinear relationship between income and the outcome variables. Equation 8.3 is first estimated using the parametric functional form, where we observe a mean relationship between $ln(inc)$ and the outcome variable, because the main purpose here is to examine the coefficients on other variables, in particular γs. Later in the chapter, we also estimate the semiparametric function of Equation 8.3 to examine the potential nonlinear relationship between income and outcome variables using the Yatchew (1997, 1998) method.

Main results

Table 8.4 presents the results from parametric estimation of Equation 8.3. Panels A and B report results using the total sample and the new-household sample, respectively. The two dependent variables used are log real per capita consumption and the saving rate. The results from the two samples are largely consistent. The discussion below focuses on the total sample results unless there is a significant difference in the results.

Table 8.4 Regression results: Consumption and saving

	Panel A: Total sample			Panel B: 2008 and new-household sample		
Variables	Log real per capita consumption	Log consumption excluding insurance	Saving rate	Log real per capita consumption	Log consumption excluding insurance	Saving rate
Log(real per capita income)	0.608***	0.605***	0.252***	0.679***	0.677***	0.209***
	[0.006]	[0.006]	[0.004]	[0.008]	[0.008]	[0.005]
HH head age	–0.000	–0.001	0.000	0.000	0.000	–0.001
	[0.002]	[0.002]	[0.001]	[0.002]	[0.002]	[0.001]
HH head age squared	–0.000**	–0.000**	0.000**	–0.000**	–0.000**	0.000**
	[0.000]	[0.000]	[0.000]	[0.000]	[0.000]	[0.000]
HH head is male	–0.036***	–0.035***	0.019***	–0.025***	–0.024***	0.014***
	[0.005]	[0.005]	[0.003]	[0.006]	[0.006]	[0.004]
HH head years of schooling	0.012***	0.012***	–0.008***	0.011***	0.011***	–0.006***
	[0.001]	[0.001]	[0.001]	[0.001]	[0.001]	[0.001]
HH head is self-employed	0.186***	0.182***	–0.113***	0.176***	0.174***	–0.108***
	[0.006]	[0.006]	[0.004]	[0.009]	[0.009]	[0.006]
HH head years since first migrating	0.005***	0.005***	–0.003***	0.006***	0.006***	–0.004***
	[0.001]	[0.001]	[0.001]	[0.001]	[0.001]	[0.001]
HH head years since first migrating squared	–0.000**	–0.000**	0.000**	–0.000*	–0.000*	0.000**
	[0.000]	[0.000]	[0.000]	[0.000]	[0.000]	[0.000]
Household size	–0.052***	–0.053***	0.035***	–0.025***	–0.027***	0.018***
	[0.004]	[0.004]	[0.003]	[0.006]	[0.006]	[0.004]
HH head is married	–0.069***	–0.069***	0.029***	–0.071***	–0.071***	0.031***
	[0.009]	[0.009]	[0.005]	[0.012]	[0.012]	[0.007]

	Panel A: Total sample			Panel B: 2008 and new-household sample		
Variables	**Log real per capita consumption**	**Log consumption excluding insurance**	**Saving rate**	**Log real per capita consumption**	**Log consumption excluding insurance**	**Saving rate**
Total number of children	0.056***	0.055***	–0.038***	0.054***	0.055***	–0.038***
	[0.006]	[0.006]	[0.004]	[0.009]	[0.009]	[0.006]
Total no. of children left behind	–0.106***	–0.106***	0.064***	–0.100***	–0.102***	0.062***
	[0.006]	[0.006]	[0.004]	[0.010]	[0.010]	[0.006]
Dummy for spouse left behind	–0.053***	–0.053***	0.018***	–0.053***	–0.054***	0.019**
	[0.009]	[0.009]	[0.005]	[0.012]	[0.012]	[0.007]
HH head with pension insurance	0.023***	0.017**	–0.011***	0.024**	0.020**	–0.012**
	[0.007]	[0.007]	[0.004]	[0.009]	[0.009]	[0.006]
HH head with health insurance	0.052***	0.041***	–0.030***	0.049***	0.043***	–0.027***
	[0.007]	[0.007]	[0.005]	[0.010]	[0.010]	[0.006]
Dummy for new-HH sample	0.000	0.002	0.000			
	[0.005]	[0.005]	[0.003]			
City–year fixed effects	Yes	Yes	Yes	Yes	Yes	Yes
Observations	33,282	33,282	33,282	17,526	17,526	17,526
R-squared	0.483	0.478	0.236	0.502	0.500	0.209

HH = household
*** $p < 0.01$
** $p < 0.05$
* $p < 0.1$

Notes: The dummies indicating the missing entries in years since first migrating and self-employment are included in the regressions. Robust standard errors are in parentheses. RUMiC survey, 2008–14, waves are used.

On average, the income elasticity of consumption is about 0.61–0.68. The income elasticity of saving is about 0.21–0.25, controlling for the vector of permanent income-related variables (X). We also tried to estimate two-step regression using X to predict permanent income and taking the residual as the transitory component of income; the coefficient obtained for the permanent component of income is about 0.91, while the coefficient on the residual component is 0.58, which is roughly the same as what is observed here. Note that, in general, migrants are a very low-paid group, and consuming a large proportion of transitory income could be seen as rational behaviour.

The age of the household head has an inverted-U shaped relationship with consumption, while education and self-employment are positively correlated with consumption (and opposite to saving). Male-headed households consume less and save more.

The years since first migrating also have an inverted-U shaped relationship with consumption, but the turning point does not occur until migrants stay in the city for 36 years (see Figure 8.7). Thus, the longer the migrants stay in the city, the more their consumption level increases in the first 36 years of their working life. This probably is an assimilation process in terms of their consumption behaviour. Recall that due to institutional restrictions on family migration, Chinese internal migrants are less likely to stay long in cities. Based on our data, the median years of migration currently stands at eight, while the mean years of migration is about 11; both are way below the point at which migrants' consumption level starts to taper. From this point of view, the institutional restrictions on migration limited migrants' city consumption. Given the large number of migrants working in cities and the significant difference between individuals' consumption in city and rural areas (see Figures 8.1 and 8.2), the aggregated effect on reduction in consumption from shortened duration of migration should be significant.

Household size has a negative relationship with per capita consumption, perhaps because larger families need to spend less per capita on 'public goods' within the family. Controlling for household size, married household heads relative to those who are single are spending less regardless of whether or not their spouse is living within the household. Perhaps married households have more to take care of and are more concerned about their future. Households with more children consume more, but, controlling for the total number of children, households with children left behind are consuming less and saving more. For every additional child left behind, migrant households in the city will reduce their per capita consumption by 5 per cent (10.6 per cent – 5.6 per cent). Similarly, for migrants who are married and have left their spouse behind, their household per capita consumption will be reduced by 12.2 per cent (6.9 per cent + 5.3 per cent). These are very large effects, indicating the impact of the family migration restrictions on migrant household consumption and saving behaviour.

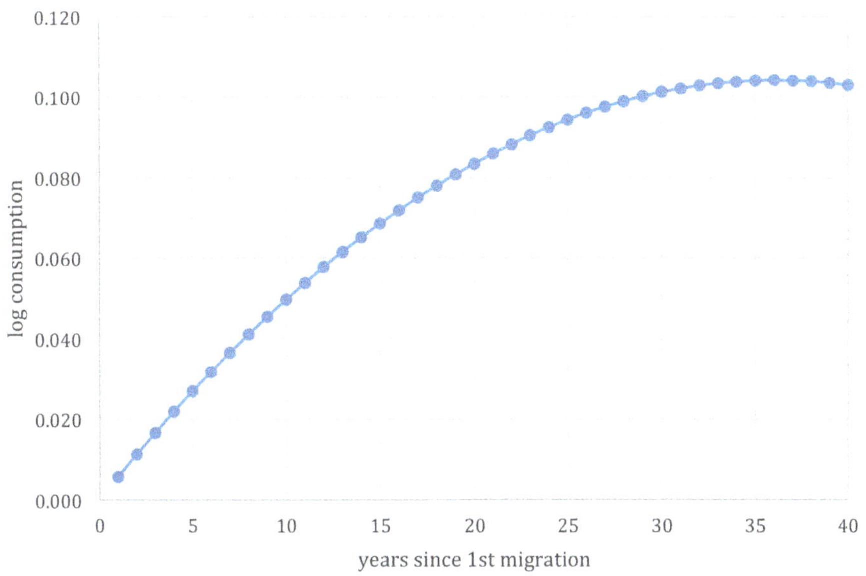

Figure 8.7 Migration duration and consumption

Source: Authors' own estimation based on results presented in Table 8.4.

Finally, whether or not the migrant household head has pension or health insurance is also related to their consumption pattern. One concern is that some insurance payments are included in the measure of consumption and therefore the idea that those who have insurance spend more is only an artefact of the data. To test this, we calculated the per capita consumption excluding insurance payments and reran the regression (the second column in each panel), and the results are largely consistent. This seems to suggest that individuals with social insurance have less to worry about and hence are willing to spend more. In other words, those without social insurance are saving more due to the precautionary motive. Indeed, if a household head does not have health or pension insurance, the family's per capita consumption reduces by 6–8 per cent.

We also estimated Equation 8.3 using the semiparametric method to examine whether the marginal propensity to consume (save) is similar for the high- and low-income groups, controlling for all the permanent income-related variables, institutional related variables as well as city–year fixed effects. The results are shown in Figure 8.8. The general pattern of the consumption and income relationship presented in Panel A of Figure 8.8 seems to be consistent with that revealed from the unconditional relationship presented in Figure 8.3: over time, the relationship between income and consumption becomes flatter, due mainly to the low-income group spending less and saving more than in the early period.

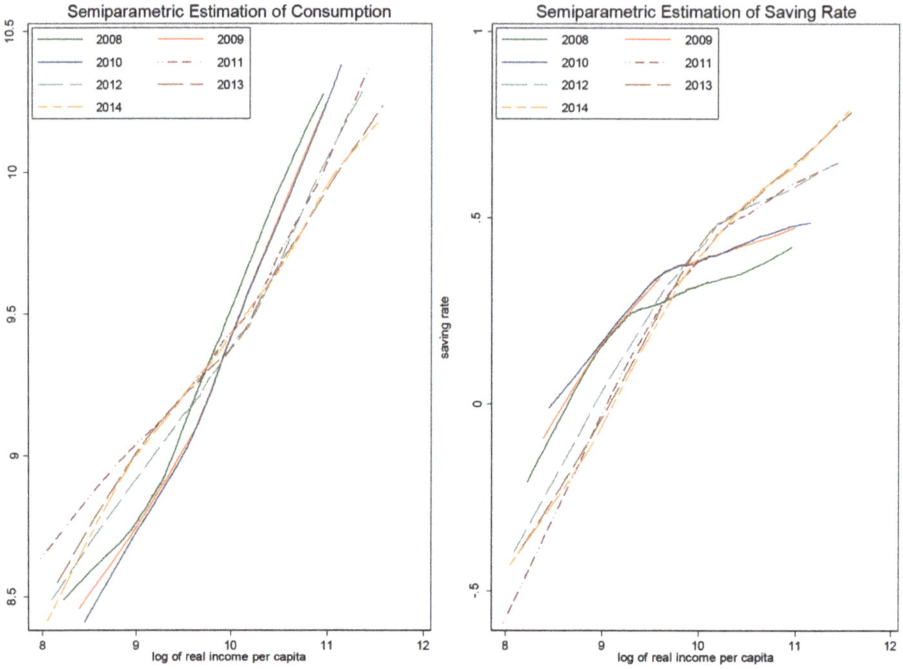

Figure 8.8 Semiparametric relationship between income and consumption and saving

Source: Authors' own estimation.

Finally, we estimate the log real per capita consumption and saving rate equations for the top and bottom 20 percentile households separately (see Table 8.5). We find that among the low-income group, the income effect on consumption is flatter than among the high-income group: a 10 per cent increase in income increases the low-income group's consumption by 4.7 per cent, while the rate is 6.9 per cent for the high-income group. Naturally, when compared with the saving rate, the income effect is reversed: higher for the low-income group and lower for the high-income group. The marginal propensity to save among low-income households is 0.44, while for the high-income group it is 0.14. These results coincide well with the unconditional relationship presented in Figure 8.3, where we see that the income elasticity to saving curve becomes flatter for the high-income group. Moving to the important variables that proxy for institutional restrictions, we find that the results are very similar to those found in the total sample estimation. The additional information we find here is that the impact of children left behind is slightly larger among the high-income group than among the low-income group. Regarding social insurance coverage, the effect is almost the same for the two groups; however, because social insurance coverage for the low-income group is almost half that for the high-income group, policy to improve social insurance coverage at the lower end of income distribution among migrants may be more effective in increasing the level of migrants' city consumption. Note that we include only two variables to indicate social insurance coverage; the unmeasured social insurance coverage could be the reason for the higher saving propensity among the poor than among the high-income group.[4]

Table 8.5 Consumption and saving: Top and bottom income groups

	Log(per capita real consumption)		**Saving rate**	
	Lowest income	**Highest income**	**Lowest income**	**Highest income**
Log(real per capita income)	0.474***	0.688***	0.443***	0.140***
	[0.016]	[0.024]	[0.014]	[0.012]
HH head age	0.002	–0.004	–0.000	0.003
	[0.003]	[0.005]	[0.002]	[0.003]
HH head age squared	–0.000	–0.000	0.000	–0.000
	[0.000]	[0.000]	[0.000]	[0.000]
HH head is male	–0.017*	–0.075***	0.016**	0.038***
	[0.009]	[0.012]	[0.007]	[0.006]
HH head years of schooling	0.008***	0.014***	–0.007***	–0.007***
	[0.002]	[0.002]	[0.001]	[0.001]
HH head is self-employed	0.126***	0.201***	–0.098***	–0.095***
	[0.010]	[0.015]	[0.008]	[0.008]
HH head years since first migrating	0.004*	0.004	–0.003*	–0.002
	[0.002]	[0.003]	[0.002]	[0.001]
HH head years since first migrating squared	–0.000	–0.000	0.000	0.000
	[0.000]	[0.000]	[0.000]	[0.000]
Household size	–0.042***	–0.122***	0.038***	0.058***
	[0.006]	[0.013]	[0.005]	[0.006]
HH head is married	–0.063***	–0.072***	0.024	0.035***
	[0.023]	[0.018]	[0.017]	[0.009]

4 Often such insurance is highly correlated; including them separately generates a strong multicollinearity problem.

	Log(per capita real consumption)		Saving rate	
	Lowest income	Highest income	Lowest income	Highest income
Total number of children	0.033***	0.047**	–0.025***	–0.022**
	[0.008]	[0.020]	[0.007]	[0.010]
Total no. of children left behind	–0.086***	–0.098***	0.064***	0.045***
	[0.011]	[0.019]	[0.009]	[0.010]
Dummy for spouse left behind	–0.089***	–0.090***	0.040***	0.037***
	[0.020]	[0.022]	[0.015]	[0.011]
HH head with pension insurance	0.014	0.007	–0.010	–0.002
	[0.015]	[0.015]	[0.012]	[0.008]
HH head with health insurance	0.043***	0.046***	–0.024*	–0.022***
	[0.016]	[0.016]	[0.013]	[0.008]
Dummy for new-HH sample	0.041***	0.003	–0.026***	0.000
	[0.011]	[0.012]	[0.008]	[0.006]
City–year fixed effects	Yes	Yes	Yes	Yes
Observations	6,705	6,478	6,705	6,478
R-squared	0.398	0.304	0.254	0.216

HH = household
*** $p < 0.01$
** $p < 0.05$
* $p < 0.1$

Notes: The dummies indicating the missing entries in years since first migrating and self-employment are included in the regressions. Robust standard errors are in parentheses. RUMiC migrant, 2008–14, waves are used.

To sum up, we find that there are many channels through which institutional restrictions on migration exert a negative impact on migrants' city consumption. These channels include shortened duration of migration, children and other family members left behind due to the lack of social services provision in cities for migrants and their families, as well as precautionary saving generated by lack of social welfare coverage.

Saving and remittances

The above analyses are based on migrants' city consumption, and savings include remittances. Although migrants spent less than they would have in cities had they been treated more equally with their city counterparts, part of their 'savings'—that is, remittances—is spent in rural areas. Hence, this type of reduction in consumption may not necessarily reduce aggregated domestic demand. For example, the reason migrants with children left behind are spending less themselves in cities is because they need to send more remittances to their children back home, which will eventually be spent in rural areas.

Here, we would like to mention three points. First, as shown in Figures 8.1 and 8.2, on average, individuals spend more in the city than in rural areas. Thus, had the family members left behind been brought to cities, the spending would be greater. Second, Zhu et al. (2012) used data from about 1,500 households in two rural provinces to show that the marginal propensity to save out of remittances using ordinary least squares (OLS) regression is over 0.9, and, even with IV, it still stands at 0.3–0.6, which is high.[5] Third, whether or not the institutional restrictions on migration affected only migrant spending in cities because of increased remittances rather than a general change in consumption and saving patterns is an empirical question. To understand this issue a little better, we examine saving patterns by subcategories of savings, including investment, remittances, residual savings (increments in deposits and cash savings) and total saving excluding remittances. The first two items plus other non-consumption expenditure add up to the total non-consumption expenditure. The residual saving is obtained by subtracting consumption expenditure and non-consumption expenditure from income.

Because many households do not have all the subitems of the non-consumption expenditure and many have negative saving components, these variables have a large number of zero or negative values. We first examine the distribution of these variables to determine how they should be estimated. Among our total sample of migrants over seven years, only 12 per cent of observations had any investment savings. We therefore estimate a linear probability model, which examines what household characteristics are associated with having any investment savings (the dependent variable is a dummy that takes the value of one if the observation has any investment savings and zero otherwise). For the remittances variable, about 40 per cent of observations have negative or zero values, whereas for deposits and cash-in-hand, 22 per cent of observations have negative values. For these variables, the econometric literature generally resolves the problem of skewed distribution by taking inverse hyperbolic sine transformations of the variable to make them less skewed before estimating the regression using OLS (for example, Carroll et al. 2003; Cobb-Clark and Hildebrand 2006; Meng 2007). Thus, when using remittances and deposits–cash as dependent variables, Equation 8.3 may be written as Equation 8.4.

5 The validity of the IV and the estimation strategy used in their study, though, are debatable.

Equation 8.4

$$g(Y_{ijt}) = \tilde{\alpha} + \tilde{\beta}\ln(inc)_{ijt} + \tilde{\delta}X_{ijt} + \tilde{\gamma}W_{ijt} + \tilde{c}_{ijt} + \tilde{\epsilon}_{ijt}$$

The inverse hyperbolic sine transformation is defined as Equation 8.5.

Equation 8.5

$$g(Y_{ijt}) = sinh^{-1}(\theta Y_{ijt})/\theta = ln[\theta Y_{ijt} + (\theta^2 Y_{ijt}^2 + 1)^{\frac{1}{2}}]/\theta$$

In this equation, θ is a damping parameter.[6] To interpret the results, the marginal effect for each variable is calculated and the calculation is based on a formula. For example, to calculate the marginal effect of X on Y, we need to calculate $Y/\partial X = \tilde{\beta}[(\theta Y)^2 + 1]^{1/2}$ where the first term is the estimated coefficient and the second term is $\partial Y/\partial g(Y_{ijt})$.

The estimated results for investment, remittances, the residual saving rate and the saving rate excluding remittances are reported in Table 8.6. Column 1 presents the probability of the household having any investments. We find that every 1 per cent increase in income increases the probability of investing by 0.074 per cent, whereas a household head who is self-employed has a 14.5 per cent higher probability relative to his wage/salary-earning counterparts to invest, which is the largest impact in the investment equation. Having a child or a spouse left behind reduces the investment probability, but only the coefficient for children left behind is precisely estimated. Households whose heads are covered by pension and/or health insurance are more likely to invest than household heads who are not covered.

Table 8.6 Regression results from subitems of savings

	Investment coefficient	Remittance Coefficient ME at mean		Residual saving rate Coefficient ME at mean		Saving rate excluding remittance coefficient
	(1)	(2)	(3)	(4)	(5)	(6)
Log(real per capita income)	0.074***	479.273***	1394.89	0.236***	0.241	0.263***
	[0.005]		[13.784]		[0.005]	[0.005]
HH head age	0.002*	9.599*	27.94	–0.003**	–0.003	–0.002*
	[0.001]		[4.924]		[0.001]	[0.001]
HH head age squared	–0.000	–0.131**	–0.38	0.000***	0.000	0.000***
	[0.000]		[0.065]		[0.000]	[0.000]

6 In this study, we take θ = 0.001 for remittances and θ = 1.2 for the residual saving rate to make the residuals close to normal distribution.

	Investment coefficient	Remittance Coefficient ME at mean		Residual saving rate Coefficient ME at mean		Saving rate excluding remittance coefficient
	(1)	(2)	(3)	(4)	(5)	(6)
HH head is male	–0.003	84.378***	245.58	0.004	0.004	0.005
	[0.004]		[11.469]		[0.004]	[0.003]
HH head years of schooling	0.002**	–4.506**	–13.12	–0.008***	–0.008	–0.008***
	[0.001]		[2.027]		[0.001]	[0.001]
HH head is self-employed	0.145***	–116.289***	–338.45	–0.132***	–0.135	–0.097***
	[0.006]		[14.384]		[0.005]	[0.005]
HH head years since first migrating	0.001	12.510***	36.41	–0.005***	–0.005	–0.005***
	[0.001]		[3.273]		[0.001]	[0.001]
HH head years since first migrating squared	–0.000	–0.299***	–0.87	0.000***	0.000	0.000***
	[0.000]		[0.108]		[0.000]	[0.000]
Household size	0.030***	–166.214***	–483.75	0.051***	0.052	0.061***
	[0.004]		[8.121]		[0.004]	[0.003]
HH head is married	0.006	295.939***	861.31	–0.031***	–0.032	–0.025***
	[0.006]		[22.809]		[0.006]	[0.006]
Total number of children	0.009*	81.176***	236.26	–0.052***	–0.053	–0.048***
	[0.005]		[12.701]		[0.005]	[0.005]
Total no. of children left behind	–0.011*	374.706***	1090.55	0.011**	0.011	0.004
	[0.006]		[14.897]		[0.005]	[0.005]
Dummy for spouse left behind	–0.010	273.430***	795.80	–0.053***	–0.055	–0.050***
	[0.007]		[20.576]		[0.007]	[0.006]
HH head with pension insurance	0.012**	20.011	58.24	–0.020***	–0.020	–0.010**
	[0.006]		[18.075]		[0.006]	[0.005]
HH head with health insurance	0.034***	–27.625	–80.40	–0.029***	–0.030	–0.026***
	[0.006]		[19.199]		[0.006]	[0.005]
Dummy for new-HH sample	–0.023***	–106.793***	–310.81	0.030***	0.031	0.022***
	[0.004]		[13.641]		[0.004]	[0.004]
City–year fixed effects	Yes		Yes		Yes	Yes
Observations	33,282		33,282		33,282	33,282
R-squared	0.110		0.279		0.167	0.170

HH = household
*** $p < 0.01$
** $p < 0.05$
* $p < 0.1$

Notes: The dummies indicating the missing entries in years since first migrating and self-employment are included in the regressions. Robust standard errors are in parentheses. RUMiC survey, 2008–14, waves are used.

The results of the remittances equation (coefficients presented in Column 2 and the marginal effect in Column 3) show that every 1 per cent increase in income increases remittances by RMB14. The largest impact on remittances is related to family composition. First, married migrants remit RMB861 more than those who are single. Second, for those who are married and have children, every additional child will increase their remittances by RMB236. On top of this, migrants with children left behind send the most money back home: one additional child left behind increases remittances by RMB1,091. Furthermore, a household head with a spouse left behind sends home RMB796 more than a married migrant whose spouse is in the city with her/him. Intuitively, if a married migrant has a child and a spouse left behind, he would remit RMB2,984 = 861 + 236 + 1,091 + 796 more back home than his single counterparts. This is a very large amount—almost 1.1 times average real per capita remittances for the whole sample and, over the eight years, 86 per cent of the 2014 average per capita remittances. Contrary to the positive effect on remittances of family members being left behind, if a migrant has a larger family in the city, one additional city family member reduces remittances by RMB484. Self-employed people are less likely to send remittances home and perhaps this is due to their city investment needs (see the result on the investment equation).

Columns 4 and 5 of Table 8.6 report the coefficients and marginal effects evaluated at the mean value from the residual saving rate ((*income* – *cons* – *nconsexp*)/*income*) equation. The average residual saving rate over the seven years is about 19 per cent. Most independent variables, except the gender of the household head, are statistically significantly correlated with the residual saving rate and most signs are reasonable. In particular, age has a U-shaped relationship and education is negatively associated with the residual saving rate. Those who are self-employed put more money into investments but less into residual savings (deposits or cash-in-hand). Households with social insurance are putting less money in residual savings and remittances, but are more likely to invest. Taking the residual saving rate, for example, the results suggest that if the household head does not have pension or health insurance, he/she would save 4.9 percentage points more in deposits and cash savings, which accounts for 26 per cent of the average residual saving rate. Note that the majority of these are related to health insurance. It makes sense that households without insurance would put more money into deposits and cash. Without health insurance, one would need to put money aside in case of bad luck. The results on family composition suggest that marriage status, number of children and the dummy for a spouse left behind are all negatively related with residual saving; most of these migrants' money went into remittances. However, having children left behind is positively associated with the residual saving rate, although the magnitude is small. An additional child being left behind increases the residual saving rate by 1 percentage point, which is about 5 per cent of the average residual saving rate. It is not clear why migrants would put more money aside when they have children left behind; perhaps this is used in preparation for the children eventually coming to the city to join them. Whatever the reasons, migrant households with children left behind are saving more than others. In the RUMiC survey for 2013 and 2014, we asked migrants to rank the type of social services they thought were the most important condition for them to stay in the city permanently. About 36 per cent (the largest proportion) ranked childcare and children's education as the most important among the eight types of services listed, suggesting the importance of children's education to migrants.

Finally, in Column 6, we present the results for the saving rate excluding remittances. The results are very similar to those obtained from the residual saving regression.

Thus, in general, it is true that households with family members left behind are mostly sending their money back to rural villages. Although Zhu et al. (2012) suggest a high saving rate from remittances, testing whether this is the case for our sample is beyond our ability and the scope of this chapter. What we can say, based on our results so far, is that for migrants with family members left behind, and conditional on them spending less and saving more, they also substitute within saving items, such as reducing the probability to invest. It is also interesting to see that families with children left behind are putting more money aside. More importantly, the lack of social insurance coverage among migrants also reduces investment and increases cash savings.

Conclusion

China's future development will rely heavily on domestic demand, which, in turn, relies heavily on the urbanisation process. To a large extent, however, China's existing institutional setting, which restricts permanent settlement of rural–urban migrants, could be detrimental to its smooth transition from an export-oriented to a domestic demand-driven economic growth path.

In this chapter, we use seven years of RUMiC survey data to demonstrate how these institutional restrictions directly curbed the consumption of 166 million migrant workers. In particular, migrants with family members left behind are consuming considerably less in cities than their counterparts who brought their family members with them to the city. More importantly, migrants without social insurance are the major precautionary savers. Consider that even in 2014 less than 35 per cent of household heads were covered by either health or pension insurance. Resolving the problem of social insurance coverage for migrant workers could contribute significantly to an increase in domestic demand.

Among migrant workers, it is the low-income group that has very low levels of social insurance coverage. In 2014, the social insurance coverage level for households in the bottom 20 income percentile was half that for the top 20 income percentile households. We also find the saving propensity is much higher among the poor than among the top income group. It could therefore be the case that precautionary saving among the poor is higher. Consequently, promoting social insurance among the poor should have a significant impact on consumption.

References

Cai, F., Giles, J., O'Keefe, P. and Wang, D. (2012), *The elderly and old age support in rural China*, Washington, DC: The World Bank.

Carroll, C. D., Dynan, K. E. and Krane, S. D. (2003), Unemployment risk and precautionary wealth: Evidence from households' balance sheets, *Review of Economics and Statistics*, 85(3): 586–604.

Chamon, M., Liu, K. and Prasad, E. (2013), Income uncertainty and household savings in China, *Journal of Development Economics*, 105: 164–177.

Chen, Y. and Feng, S. (2013), Access to public schools and the education of migrant children in China, *China Economic Review*, 26: 75–88.

Choi, H., Lugauer, S. and Mark, N. C. (2014), *Precautionary saving of Chinese and US households*, NBER Working Paper 20527, September, Cambridge, Mass.: National Bureau of Economic Research.

Cobb-Clark, D. A. and Hildebrand, V. A. (2006), The wealth and asset holdings of US-born and foreign-born households: Evidence from SIPP data, *Review of Income and Wealth*, 52(1): 17–42.

Du, Y., Gregory, R. and Meng, X. (2006), The impact of the guest-worker system on poverty and the wellbeing of migrant workers in urban China, in R. Garnaut and L. Song (eds), *The turning point in China's economic development*, Canberra: ANU E Press.

Gong, X., Kong, S., Li S. and Meng, X. (2008), Rural–urban migrants: A driving force for growth, in L. Song and W. Woo (eds), *China's Dilemma*, Canberra: ANU E Press.

Meng, X. (2003), Unemployment, consumption smoothing, and precautionary saving in urban China, *Journal of Comparative Economics*, 31(3): 465–485.

Meng, X. (2007), Wealth accumulation and distribution in urban China, *Economic Development and Cultural Change*, 55(4): 761–791.

Meng, X. (2013), Rural–urban migration: Trend and policy implications (2008–2012), in R. Garnaut, F. Cai and L. Song (eds), *China: A new model for growth and development*, Canberra: ANU E Press.

National Bureau of Statistics (various years), 'Consumer Price Indices', Beijing: China Statistics Press. Available from: data.stats.gov.cn/easyquery.htm?cn=C01.

Wei, S.-J. and Zhang, X. (2011), The competitive saving motive: Evidence from rising sex ratios and savings rates in China, *Journal of Political Economy*, 119(3): 511–564.

Yatchew, A. (1997), An elementary estimator of the partial linear model, *Economics Letters*, 57(2): 135–143.

Yatchew, A. (1998), Nonparametric regression techniques in economics, *Journal of Economic Literature*, 36(2): 669–721.

Zhu, Y., Wu, Z., Wang, M., Du, Y. and Cai, F. (2012), Do migrants really save more? Understanding the impact of remittances on savings in rural China, *The Journal of Development Studies*, 48(5): 654–672.

Appendix 8.1

Table A8.1 Household income and expenditure: New sample

2008 or new sample	Real per capita income	Real per capita consumption	Real per capita non-consumption	Real per capita remittances	Saving rate	Saving rate excluding remittances	No. of observations
2008	16,225.42	9,837.508	3,411.86	2,266.32	0.37	0.22	4,731
2009	19,000.90	12,183.36	3,669.57	2,675.58	0.34	0.21	3,268
2010	21,619.83	14,184.54	2879.3	2,021.38	0.32	0.23	2,732
2011	24,531.56	13,362.47	3,375.64	2,294.48	0.39	0.30	2,144
2012	25,050.38	13,787.52	3,056.88	2,195.42	0.39	0.31	1,742
2013	28,943.50	16,388.13	5,353.05	4,147.01	0.37	0.24	1,453
2014	29,726.80	16,278.42	4,593.63	3,769.61	0.38	0.27	1,456
Average annual growth	0.090	0.075	0.043	0.075			
Top 20% income group:							
2008	29,218.17	16,533.60	5,476.37	3,675.41	0.43	0.30	
2009	32,531.97	20,227.77	7,564.03	5,356.82	0.37	0.21	
2010	37,387.77	24,048.33	4,646.83	3,208.73	0.35	0.26	
2011	42,070.16	19,361.46	6,045.42	3,995.87	0.53	0.43	
2012	41,974.11	19,524.46	4,419.41	3,276.06	0.52	0.44	
2013	48,222.10	22,274.89	1,1031.6	8,482.42	0.53	0.35	
2014	50,506.49	22,122.55	8,694.94	7,476.69	0.55	0.40	
Average annual growth	0.081	0.042	0.068	0.107			

2003 or new sample	Real per capita income	Real per capita consumption	Real per capita non-consumption	Real per capita remittances	Saving rate	Saving rate excluding remittances	No. of observations
Bottom 20% income group:							
2008	7,846.04	5,595.98	2,075.09	1,104.80	0.26	0.13	
2009	9,397.13	6,909.44	1,242.66	851.379	0.25	0.16	
2010	9,894.18	7,644.64	1,251.12	823.272	0.21	0.13	
2011	10,458.27	8,930.17	1,417.30	703.143	0.10	0.03	
2012	11,241.73	9,516.81	1,787.61	727.825	0.12	0.05	
2013	12,140.89	11,416.75	1,550.31	998.772	0.03	–0.04	
2014	12,564.55	10,458.46	1,322.49	745.757	0.14	0.08	
Average annual growth	0.07	0.09	–0.06	–0.05			

Source: RUMiC survey, 2008–14.

9. China as a Global Investor

David Dollar[1]

China's economic rise is one of the factors creating strains in the international financial order. China is already the largest trading nation and the second-largest economy, and it is likely to emerge in the next few years as the world's largest net creditor. Currently in second place, China had an estimated $2.4 trillion in net foreign assets by the end of 2015, compared with Japan's $3.6 trillion. Increases in net foreign assets come through current account surpluses. In the four years ending in 2015, China's cumulative current account surpluses amounted to about $1 trillion—far larger than Japan's $200 billion. If those trends continue, it is simple arithmetic that China will become the largest net creditor around 2020.

While China is already the second-largest net creditor, the pattern of its external assets and liabilities is unusual. In mature creditors such as Germany and Japan, private companies and households hold most of the foreign assets. In China, on the other hand, the most important foreign asset has been international reserves accumulated by the central bank, mostly invested in US Treasury bonds and similar instruments. In the past couple of years, however, this pattern has started to change.

China's reserves peaked at about $4 trillion at the end of 2014. Since then, the People's Bank of China has sold some reserves, but the country as a whole is still accumulating net foreign assets, as evidenced by the large current account surplus. What is new is that the overseas asset purchases are coming from the private sector and state enterprises, not from the official sector. The Institute for International Finance estimated that the net private capital outflow from China was $676 billion in 2015 (an estimate that includes outward investments by China's state enterprises, which, strictly speaking, are not 'private'; the point is to distinguish between official holdings of foreign assets at the central bank and more commercial transactions) (Donnan 2016). As investment opportunities diminish in China, owing to excess capacity and declining profitability, this commercial outflow of capital is likely to continue at a high level.

1 David Dollar is a Senior Fellow in the John L. Thornton China Center at the Brookings Institution. Helpful suggestions on an earlier draft came from my Brookings colleagues Barry Bosworth, Bruce Jones, Homi Kharas, Ken Lieberthal, Eswar Prasad and Mireya Solis. My research assistant, Wei Wang, prepared the data and graphs. Gail Chalef provided important assistance in preparing the chapter for publication. My research on Chinese investment in Africa is supported in part by a grant from the Carnegie Corporation of New York. Brookings recognises that the value it provides is in its absolute commitment to quality, independence and impact. Activities supported by its donors reflect this commitment. The views in the chapter are my own.

Much of the commercial outflow consists of direct investment (greenfield investments plus mergers and acquisitions). China's Ministry of Commerce (MOFCOM) is the best source of information about the breakdown in China's overseas direct investment. Chinese officials refer to outward direct investment as ODI to distinguish it from inward direct investment. This chapter will use that convention. MOFCOM reports the annual outflow of ODI and the accumulating stock of China's outward investment. Frankly, its numbers seem a bit low given the macroeconomic estimates of capital outflow from China. In recent years, MOFCOM has reported ODI flows a bit above $100 billion per year, accelerating to above $200 billion in 2014. The cumulative stock roughly tripled between 2010 and the end of 2014, reaching nearly $900 billion (Figure 9.1).

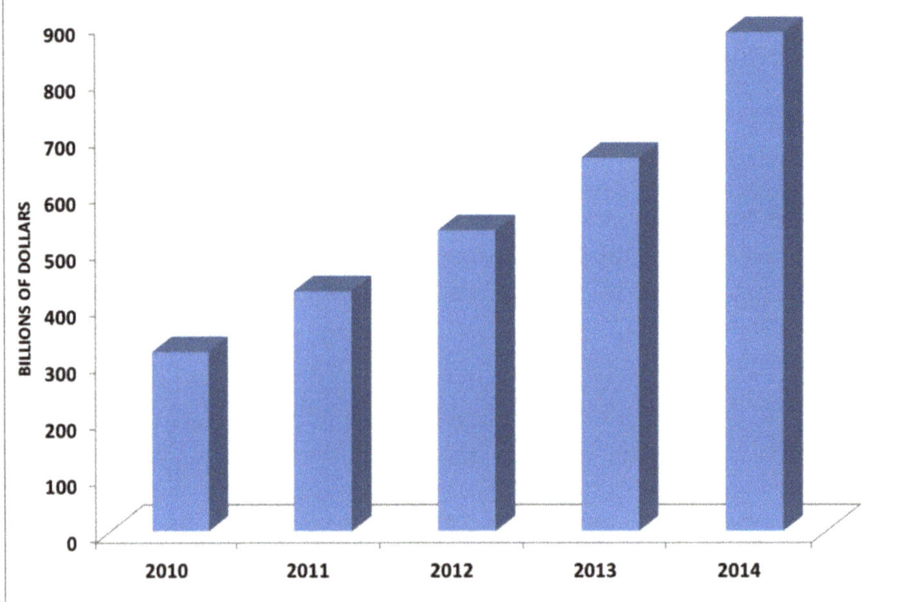

Figure 9.1 The stock of China's ODI expands rapidly

Source: Ministry of Commerce of China (2014).

MOFCOM also reports the allocation of ODI to major recipient economies. About half of China's ODI goes to Hong Kong. This is almost certainly not the ultimate destination for all of this investment; China should work to improve its statistics to reflect the ultimate destination of its overseas investments. One of the obvious recommendations of this chapter is that China makes an effort to improve the statistics on its ODI. There is ample evidence that this is one of the important developments in the world economy today: the emergence of China as the world's largest creditor, with a significant portion of its investment going to direct investment. In general, recipient countries welcome direct investment so it would be smart for China to invest in better data that more accurately reflect its role in global investment.

In addition to direct investment, there is significant overseas lending, primarily through the Export–Import Bank of China (China EXIM Bank) and the China Development Bank (CDB). This lending will show up as portfolio investment in the balance of payments. In recent years, each bank has been lending about $100 billion overseas. Some of the overseas investment by China takes place under the rubric of the 'One Belt and One Road' (OBOR) initiative. OBOR is Xi Jinping's vision for expanded infrastructure and other investment along the traditional Silk Road route through Central Asia as well as along the maritime route south from China through South-East Asia to South Asia and on to Africa and Europe. However, the actual amounts involved in OBOR investment so far appear small. Looking at the list of the top 10 destinations for China's ODI, leaving aside Hong Kong, the top three are the United States, Australia and the United Kingdom, none of which is involved in OBOR. Also in the top 10 are France, Canada and Germany. Most foreign direct investment (FDI) in the world goes to advanced industrial economies and the same can be said for China's ODI. The only OBOR-involved countries among China's top 10 investment destinations are Russia, Indonesia and Kazakhstan.

That a developing country is emerging as the world's largest investor is an interesting phenomenon that raises the following questions: to what extent is Chinese investment similar to other foreign investment and to what extent, if any, is it challenging global norms and practices? I argue that there are three ways in which Chinese investment differs from the existing norms and practices: 1) Chinese investment is relatively, though not absolutely, concentrated in poor governance environments; 2) China, in general, does not subscribe to global standards of environmental and social safeguards; and 3) China itself remains relatively closed to foreign investment in many sectors, in contrast to its partners in both the developed and the developing worlds. As China gains more experience as a global investor, it is likely that Chinese investment will, in some ways, become more typical, that it will reshape global norms in other areas, but that it may remain at odds with global practices to some extent.

Chinese investment and governance

China has drawn attention to itself through some large investments in countries that have poor governance, such as the Democratic Republic of the Congo and Angola in Africa and Venezuela and Ecuador in Latin America. At the same time, the United States is the single biggest destination for China's ODI, with a stock of $38 billion at the end of 2014. This section examines the general relationship between Chinese ODI and governance.

A natural point of departure is the relationship between FDI overall and governance.[2] The stock of FDI in the world is around $20 trillion and most of it has come from the Western industrial economies. Much FDI is in fact cross-investment among advanced economies. Of the 10 largest recipients of FDI, eight are advanced economies: United States, United Kingdom, France, Germany, Canada, Spain, the Netherlands and Australia. The two emerging economies on the list are China (number two after the United States) and Brazil.

The best predictor of how much FDI a country has received is its market size as measured by total gross domestic product (GDP). One of the main motivations of direct investment is to get close to markets to understand demand trends and to provide after-sales services. There is also a certain amount of FDI that is in search of natural resources. This trend is not that strong globally, but it can be important within regions. Among African countries, for example, natural resource rents as a share of GDP are a good predictor of how much FDI a country has received.

After controlling for market size and natural resource wealth, FDI is strongly attracted to better governance environments. Figure 9.2 shows the correlation between the stock of FDI and an index of property rights and the rule of law for 152 countries. The index, from the *Worldwide governance indicators*, 'captures perceptions of the extent to which agents have confidence in and abide by the rules of society, and in particular the quality of contract enforcement, property rights, the police, and the courts, as well as the likelihood of crime and violence' (Kaufmann and Kraay 2015). The figure shows a partial scatter after controlling for total GDP and natural resources rents. The index has a mean of zero and a standard deviation across countries of 1.0, so that one standard deviation better on rule of law is associated with 62 per cent more FDI. There are other aspects of governance—notably, political indicators such as measures of democracy and civil liberties. In general, measures of political governance and economic governance are highly correlated across countries. In examining investment and growth, economic measures tend to perform better. It makes intuitive sense that the profitability of investment would be higher in an environment of better property rights and rule of law, and that such environments would attract more investment, other things being equal.

2 The data in this section come from Dollar (2015).

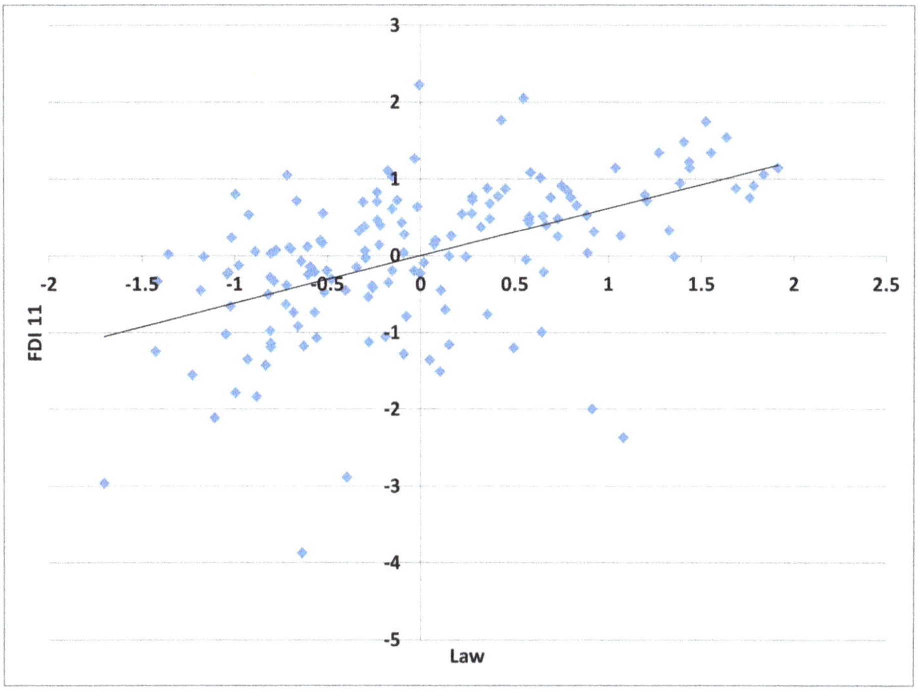

Figure 9.2 Global FDI strongly attracted to good rule of law

Source: Dollar (2015).

Chinese ODI is similar to FDI overall in that it is attracted to larger markets and to natural resource wealth. For ODI, the attraction to larger markets is a bit weaker than for FDI, and the attraction to natural resources is a bit stronger; but basically Chinese investment is similar to other investment. Where Chinese ODI is different is that it is uncorrelated with the index of property rights and the rule of law (Figure 9.3). There is actually a slightly negative relationship between how much ODI a country receives and economic governance, but it is not statistically significant. It would be accurate to say that Chinese ODI appears indifferent to the governance environment.

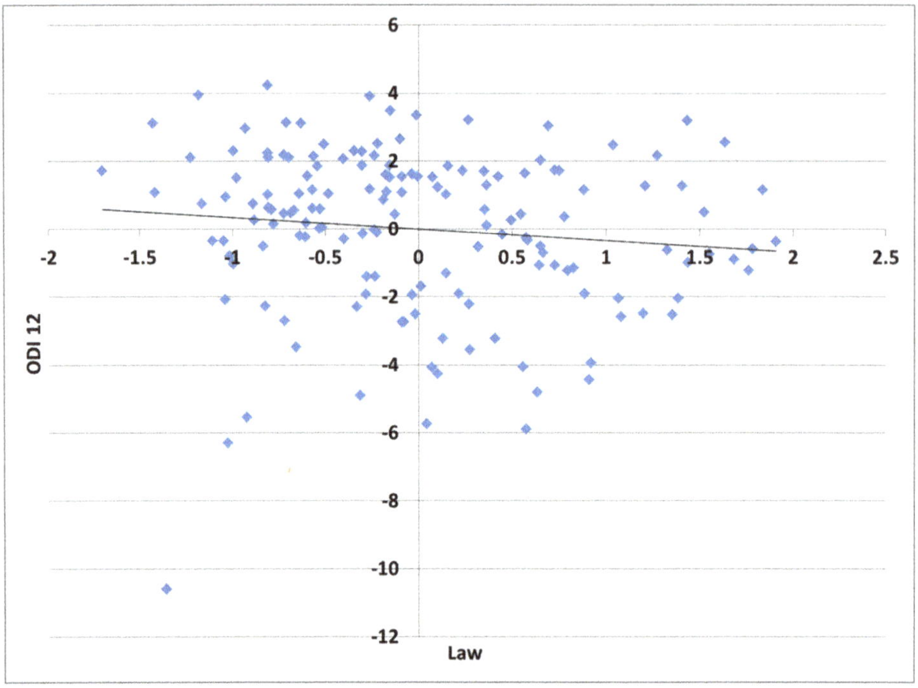

Figure 9.3 Chinese ODI uncorrelated with rule of law

Source: Dollar (2015).

This feature of Chinese investing can be illustrated through some specific examples. In Africa, the largest destination for Chinese investment is South Africa, which has some of the better governance indicators on the continent. But there is also significant Chinese investment in Angola, Democratic Republic of the Congo and Sudan, all of which have poor governance indicators. In Latin America, the largest destination for Chinese investment is Brazil, which is among the better half of the region's countries in terms of rule of law. But there is also significant investment in Argentina, Ecuador and Venezuela. If Latin American countries are divided in half on the basis of rule of law in 2014, 85 per cent of the stock of total FDI is in the better-governed half. For Chinese ODI, slightly more than half is in the poorly governed group. The pattern is similar for lending from the China EXIM Bank and the CDB. Venezuela is the largest recipient in Latin America of loan commitments from the Chinese banks, while Brazil is the second-largest borrower.

The point is not that China is seeking out the poor governance environments. It is a major investor in the well-governed countries that are the largest recipients of FDI globally. But it does appear to be indifferent to the governance environment to the extent that it is making major investments in weak governance environments where other investors fear to tread. There are a number of plausible explanations for this pattern of investment. Many of the large investments from China are made by state enterprises. On the one hand, they do not feel the same pressure as private firms to earn good returns on their investments. (It is a clear empirical regularity that state enterprises are less productive and profitable than private ones within China, so it makes sense that this would be the same abroad.) On the other hand, their investments in poor governance environments are often part of state-to-state deals and they may feel insulated from the local economic environment.

It is also the case that China is a relative newcomer on the global investment scene and Chinese firms may have underestimated the risks involved in some investments. There is evidence that some natural resource investments in poor governance environments are turning out badly. In the case of Democratic Republic of the Congo, China's $6 billion 'minerals for infrastructure' deal was signed in 2007. Chinese firms Sinohydro Corp and China Railway Group Limited agreed to build roads and hospitals in exchange for a 68 per cent stake in the Sicomines copper and cobalt mine—one of the largest in Africa. China's state-run EXIM Bank and smaller Chinese banks put up $3 billion for infrastructure plus a further $3 billion to develop Sicomines, with all the loans to be repaid with mining profits. Yet, eight years on, production from the mine has been delayed as a result of crippling power shortages, suffocating bureaucracy and corruption (Ross 2015). The main lesson from the project is that investing in one of Africa's most chaotic countries is a messy and frustrating business.

In Angola, Sinopec invested in six deepwater oilfields in cooperation with the Angolan state oil group, Sonangol, from 2004 to 2013. The investment has turned into a black hole that has swallowed funds from Sinopec without generating any commercial return. In March 2015, auditors sent by the National Audit Office to screen financial statements of Sinopec International Petroleum and Production, Sinopec's overseas investment arm, found that investments made in the five oilfields during 2008–13 have amounted to about $10 billion and that poor performance, exaggerated oil reserve estimates and sharp declines in international oil prices will lead to a majority of the investment going down the drain (Ning et al. 2015). In the case of Venezuela, China has also had to renegotiate loan terms in favour of Venezuela because the country was unable to service the original loan once the price of oil fell.

China's pattern of global investment raises two policy issues, one for China and one for the world. First, from China's point of view, is it getting the best return on its investments? Chinese state enterprises, by definition, are playing with the people's money. If they waste tens of billions of dollars in poor investments, that is a real loss for China. It makes sense that China is emerging as a major global investor at this point in its development because investment opportunities within the country are diminishing and the rapid ageing of the population has reduced domestic growth prospects. Earnings on overseas investments could help China finance its public pension system and the safety net more broadly. So it is in Chinese people's interest to have sound management of overseas investment. Based on the domestic experience, the more of the investment that comes through the private sector, the better. A study of the small and medium-sized Chinese enterprises investing in Africa, which are mostly private firms, found interesting differences to the big state-to-state deals. The small and medium-sized firms are not investing in natural resource extraction. Most investments are in services, and a significant number are in manufacturing. The manufacturing investment is influenced by the local endowments of capital and skilled labour, which is consistent with profit-maximising investment (Chen et al. 2015).

From a global point of view, there is the question of whether China's state-to-state financing is sustaining poor governance in some countries. The projects in the worst governance environments may not be returning economic benefits, but China's money is going somewhere. In some countries, Chinese funding is likely supporting corrupt political elites and helping them maintain their hold on power. In the case of Venezuela, for example, in the absence of Chinese finance, the government would have had little choice but to turn to the International Monetary Fund (IMF) and other traditional sources of finance in exchange for policy reforms to stabilise the economy and restore growth.

Environmental and social safeguards

A second issue raised by China's emergence as a major global investor concerns environmental and social safeguards. China is a major funder of mining and infrastructure projects. Such projects normally carry significant environmental risks and often involve the involuntary resettlement of large numbers of people. So far, China has been reluctant to subscribe to any international standards for environmental and social safeguards. Its position is that it follows the laws and regulations of the host country. This is a reasonable point of view, consistent with China's general position that countries should not interfere in each other's internal affairs. The problem, however, is that the implementation of environmental and social regulations is often weak, especially in the countries with weak governance.

Private financial institutions from Western countries have generally subscribed to international environmental and social standards under the rubric of the 'Equator Principles' (EP). The principles are:

> [A] *risk management framework, adopted by financial institutions, for determining, assessing and managing environmental and social risk in projects.* It is primarily intended to provide a minimum standard for due diligence to support responsible risk decision-making. Currently, 83 Equator Principles Financial Institutions (EPFIs) in 36 countries have officially adopted the EP, covering over 70 percent of international Project Finance debt in emerging markets. (Equator Principles Association 2011)

Large Chinese banks such as the China EXIM Bank and CDB have not been willing to join. Only one small Chinese bank, the Industrial Bank, has joined so far.

The multilateral development banks (MDBs) that fund infrastructure in the developing world have even more stringent standards. Led by the World Bank, these standards have been developed since the 1990s, primarily in response to pressure from civil society groups in wealthy countries. The safeguards are an area of tension between the rich countries that fund the multilateral banks and the developing countries that borrow from the banks. This tension is captured in a 2015 study by the Intergovernmental Group of Twenty-Four, which was established in 1971 to coordinate the positions of developing countries on monetary and development issues:

> One aspect of the business practices of the World Bank and major RMDBs that has a particularly strong impact on infrastructure investment is environmental and social safeguard policies. Safeguards comprise procedures and restrictions on different types of lending operations meant to 'safeguard' the project from having negative impacts on the environment and social groups. Safeguards were first instituted at the World Bank in the 1990s, and the other major RMDBs [regional multilateral development banks] followed suit in subsequent years. The World Bank's safeguards are still considered the most comprehensive and rigorous, but the safeguards of the [ADB: Asian Development Bank], IADB [Inter-American Development Bank], and AfDB [African Development Bank] have been gradually tightened over the years such that the differences between them are relatively small, particularly on the hot-button issues of environmental assessment and resettlement.
>
> As a project undergoes the initial screening process, MDB staff members determine whether it triggers any of the MDB's applicable safeguards. Should that be the case, a separate series of special requirements must be followed before the loan can be approved and disbursed. The most frequently triggered safeguards in the case of the World Bank relate to environmental assessment and involuntary resettlement, and most frequently affect investment projects in the transportation, energy, and urban sectors. The required procedures are extraordinarily detailed and specific, and in many cases (notably, the World Bank's IBRD [International Bank for Reconstruction and Development] and IDA [International Development Association]) extremely difficult for borrowers and

> even staff to fully understand. Requirements often include time-consuming, lengthy studies to be undertaken by third-party experts (usually at the government's cost), lengthy consultations with affected parties (sometimes including unelected non-governmental organizations), extensive mitigations measures, and lengthy mandatory prior public disclosure and comment periods during which time the project cannot move ahead. These requirements supersede whatever national laws may be in place in the borrowing country—a particularly troubling point of principle for many borrowing countries, beyond the practical impacts of safeguards. (Humphrey 2015: 19)

It is fair to say that these procedures developed by the World Bank are the gold standard of environmental and social safeguards in infrastructure projects. However, they have had a number of unintended consequences. It has become time-consuming and expensive to undertake infrastructure projects with the World Bank and, as a result, developing countries have turned to other sources of funding. Infrastructure was the original core business of the World Bank, accounting for 70 per cent of lending in the 1950s and 1960s. That has steadily declined to about 30 per cent in the 2000s. Looked at another way, all of the MDBs together provided about $50 billion of infrastructure financing in 2013—well under 1 per cent of total infrastructure spending in developing countries. Hence, the multilateral banks have developed gold-plated standards, but they apply to only a tiny fraction of investment.

Given this situation, the emergence of China as a major funder of mining and infrastructure projects has been welcomed by most developing countries. China is seen as more flexible and less bureaucratic. It completes infrastructure projects relatively quickly so that the benefits are seen sooner. However, China's approach of relying on the recipient country's own laws and regulations also has its risks. In Gabon, Sinopec was found exploring for oil in Loango National Park before any environmental impact study had been undertaken. Several Chinese-funded infrastructure projects on the continent will have large environmental consequences, including the Kongou Dam in Gabon, the Bui Dam in Ghana and the Lower Kafue Gorge Dam in Zambia. All these cases call for careful balance of development needs with environmental risks.

This issue of environmental and social safeguards was a key factor in the brouhaha around the founding of the Asian Infrastructure Investment Bank (AIIB). China proposed the new bank partly in response to its frustration with the slow reform of existing institutions, including the IMF, World Bank and ADB. The new bank is also a way for China to put its excess savings to use through a multilateral format, to complement (and perhaps provide some competition with) its bilateral efforts. The United States opposed the effort, primarily out of concerns about governance, including the issue of environmental and social safeguards. Other major Western nations, such as the United Kingdom, Germany, France and Australia, all chose to fight these battles from the inside.

The AIIB has promulgated environmental and social policies that, on paper, are similar to the principles embodied in World Bank safeguards: environmental and social assessments to analyse risks; public disclosure of key information in a timely manner; consultation with affected parties; and decision-making that incorporates these risks. The AIIB approach, however, differs from that of the World Bank by avoiding detailed prescriptions for how to manage the process. My own experience in the World Bank was that the application of safeguards created two problems. First, the detailed regulations—literally hundreds of pages—inevitably made implementation slow and bureaucratic. Second, management tended to be very risk-averse so that the response to problems was often additional study at extra expense. Developing countries have learned not to take complicated, risky projects to the existing banks, when in fact those are exactly the projects where the world would benefit the most from the assistance of multilateral institutions.

The AIIB's website indicates that its environmental and social guidelines should be implemented 'in proportion to the risk'. The AIIB's leadership hopes that the bank can meet international standards but be more timely and cost-effective. This is largely a matter of implementation and it will take experience on the ground and time to see if the effort is a success. The AIIB is the first major multilateral bank in which developing countries have the majority of the shareholding, so it follows that the preferences of the bank will align more with developing than developed countries. This could be a very positive innovation: since most investment and growth now take place in developing countries, it would be more efficient if development bank activities reflected the preferences of those countries. If the AIIB's activities can put pressure on the World Bank and the ADB to streamline their procedures and speed up their infrastructure projects, this would be a positive change to the global system that emanated from China.

Reciprocity

Most of the major investing countries in the world are developed economies; in addition to making direct investments elsewhere, they tend to be very open to inward investment. China is unusual in that it is a developing country that has emerged as a major investor. China itself is an important destination for foreign investment and opening to the outside world has been an important part of its reform program since 1978. However, China's policy is to steer FDI to particular sectors. In general, it has welcomed FDI into most but not all of manufacturing. However, other sectors of the economy are relatively closed to FDI, including mining, construction and most modern services. It is not surprising that China is less open to FDI than developed economies such as the United States. But it is also the case that China is relatively closed among developing countries.

The Organisation for Economic Co-operation and Development (OECD) calculates an index of FDI restrictiveness for OECD countries and major emerging markets. The index is for overall FDI restrictiveness and also for restrictiveness by sector. The measure covers various investment restrictions, the most important of which is equity caps on how much of a domestic enterprise can be owned by a foreign investor. Figure 9.4 shows the restrictiveness index in 2014 for the whole economy and some major industries for Brazil, Russia, India, China and South Africa (the BRICS). Overall, Brazil and South Africa are highly open and similar to advanced economies, with measures around 0.1 (on a scale of 0 = open and 1 = closed). India and Russia are less open, with overall measures around 0.2. China is the most closed, with an index above 0.4.

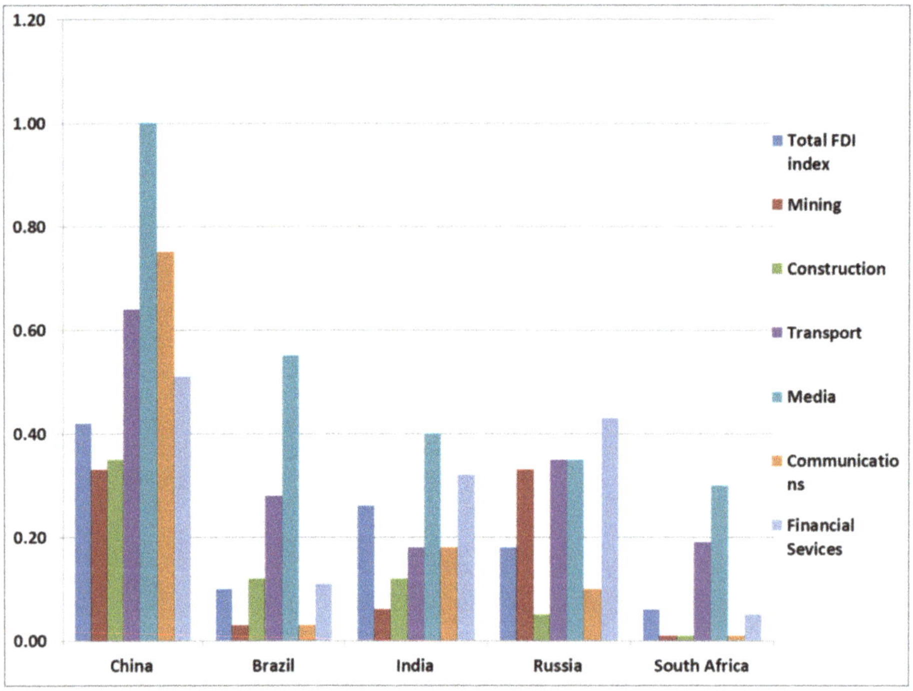

Figure 9.4 China is the most closed of the BRICS* countries (FDI restrictiveness index, 2014)

* BRICS = Brazil, Russia, India, China and South Africa
Source: Kalinova et al. (2010).

The sectors highlighted are some of the more closed ones in China. China's restrictiveness index in mining is 0.33, compared with an average of 0.11 for the other four; in communications, 0.75 compared with 0.08; in financial services, 0.51 to 0.23; and so on. Some of the key sectors in which China is investing abroad—such as mining, infrastructure and finance—are relatively closed at home.

This lack of reciprocity creates problems for China's partners. China has the second-largest market in the world. In these protected sectors, Chinese firms can grow unfettered by competition and then use their domestic financial strength to develop overseas operations. In finance, for example, China's four state-owned commercial banks operate in a domestic market in which foreign investors have been restricted to about 1 per cent of the market. The four banks are now among the largest in the world and are expanding overseas. China's monopoly credit card company, Union Pay, is similarly a world leader based on its protected domestic market. A similar strategy applies in mining and telecommunications.

This lack of reciprocity creates an uneven playing field. A concrete example is the acquisition of the US firm Smithfield by the Chinese firm Shuanghui. In a truly open market, Smithfield, with its superior technology and food-safety procedures, may well have taken over Shuanghui and expanded into the rapidly growing Chinese pork market. However, investment restrictions prevented such an option, so the best way for Smithfield to expand into China was to be acquired by the Chinese firm. Smithfield chief executive officer Larry Pope said the deal would preserve 'the same old Smithfield, only with more opportunities and new markets and new frontiers'. No Chinese pork would be imported to the United States, he said, but rather, Shuanghui desired to export American pork to take advantage of growing demand for foreign food products in China due to recent food scandals. Smithfield's existing management team is expected to remain intact, as is its US workforce (Chapman 2013).

The United States does not have much leverage with which to level the playing field. It does have a review process for acquisitions of US firms by foreign ones. The Committee on Foreign Investment in the United States (CFIUS) is chaired by the US Treasury Department and includes US economic agencies (the Department of Commerce and the Office of the US Trade Representative) as well as the Departments of Defence and Homeland Security. By statute, CFIUS can only examine national security issues involved in an acquisition. It reviewed the Smithfield deal and let it proceed because there was no obvious national security issue. CFIUS only reviews around 100 transactions per year and the majority of them proceed. This system reflects the US philosophy of being very open to foreign investment.

China's policies create a dilemma for its partners. Taking those policies as given, it would be irrational for economies such as the United States to limit Chinese investments. In the Shuanghui–Smithfield example, the access to the Chinese market gained through the takeover makes the assets of the US firm more valuable and benefits its shareholders. Assuming that the firm really does expand into China, the deal will then benefit the workers of the firm as well. It would be even better, however, if China opened up its protected markets so that such expansions could take place in the most efficient way possible. In some cases, that will be Chinese firms acquiring US ones, but, in many other cases, it would involve US firms expanding into China.

This issue of getting China to open its protected markets is high on the policy agenda of the United States and other major economies. The United States has been negotiating with China over a bilateral investment treaty (BIT) that would be based on a small negative list—that is, there would be a small number of agreed sectors that remain closed on each side—but otherwise, investment would be open in both directions. So far, however, negotiations on the BIT have been slow. It is apparently difficult for China to come up with an offer that includes only a small number of protected sectors. And there are questions as to whether the US Congress would approve an investment treaty with China in the current political environment, even if a good one were negotiated.

How is Chinese investment likely to evolve?

To the extent that Chinese investment differs from global norms and practices, there are three possible paths forward: 1) Chinese investment could become more typical; 2) global practices could shift in the Chinese direction; or 3) China could remain at odds with the rest of the world. This section speculates that we may see some combination of all three options.

First, when it comes to investment in poor governance environments, China is likely to evolve in the direction of current investment norms—that is, to favour better governance environments. Part of China's motivation for investing in countries such as Venezuela and Democratic Republic of the Congo was to access natural resources. In the 2000s, China's growth model was very resource intensive and global prices for most commodities were rising. That made it tempting to look for resources, even in risky environments; however, that has all changed this decade. A lot of new supply has come on line in sectors such as oil and gas, iron and copper. Meanwhile, China's growth model is shifting away from resource-intensive investment towards greater reliance on consumption. Consumption consists primarily of services, which are less resource intensive. As a result of these shifts in supply and demand, commodity prices have come down and China's import needs have diminished. Also, as noted earlier, the investments in poor governance countries are not working out well. As Chinese people demand a better return on state-backed investments abroad, it is likely that China will pull back on the resource investments in countries with poor governance. At the same time, many Chinese private firms are looking to invest abroad in a wide range of sectors, and those investments are heading to the United States, other advanced economies and emerging markets with relatively good governance, as is the case with global investment in general.

Concerning environmental and social safeguards for infrastructure projects, China has identified an issue that resonates with other developing countries. The World Bank and other MDBs have been imposing environmental and social standards that reflect the preferences of rich-country electorates. Developing countries have been voting with their feet and have turned away from those banks as important sources of infrastructure financing. In general, they welcome Chinese financing of infrastructure. Developing countries' response to the proposal for a new infrastructure bank, the AIIB, was particularly strong. Asian countries that are not particular friends of China—such as India, Indonesia and Vietnam—were quick to sign up to the effort. The AIIB's attempt to develop workable safeguards to address environmental and social risks without the long delays and high costs of existing MDB practices is an important innovation. This is an interesting example of where China may end up modifying global norms to make them align better with developing-country preferences. It is unfortunate that the United States and Japan have chosen to remain aloof from the effort.

The third issue identified in this chapter—reciprocity—should be an easy one for China. There is ample evidence that big state enterprises are less productive than private firms in China. Many of the sectors that remain closed are service sectors such as finance, telecommunications, transportation and media—all dominated by large state enterprises. With the shift in China's growth model, these service sectors are now the fast-growing part of the economy, while industry is in relative decline. It will be easier for China to maintain a healthy growth rate if it opens these sectors to international competition, in the same way that it opened manufacturing in an earlier era. And talk of opening these sectors can be found throughout party documents, such as the third plenum resolution. However, actual progress in opening under the new leadership has been slow. It may be difficult for China to commit to any bold opening in the next few years as it grapples with adjustment of its growth model and as it prepares for a political transition in 2017.

It will be natural for a new US administration to take a hard look at United States–China economic relations, especially the emergence of China as the largest net creditor. The massive outflow of capital from China is a new phenomenon that was not on the radar screen eight years ago. Furthermore, attitudes in the United States towards China are hardening, and it will be tempting to take a harsher stance on each of the three investment issues analysed here. But taking a hard line across the board would be a mistake as the three issues are evolving in different ways.

First, it is annoying that China is providing finance to regimes with poor governance, some of which are a thorn in the side of the United States. However, there is not much the United States can do about this. And the main destinations for Chinese investment are the same advanced, capitalist countries on which other investors focus. It is likely that Chinese investments in the poor governance environments will continue to do poorly.

Second, on infrastructure investment, China has clearly tapped into an important sentiment in the developing world that infrastructure is key to growth and that private finance and existing development banks are not sufficient. Part of the problem is that the existing banks are not large enough; a second issue is that they have turned away from infrastructure as a core business. On this issue, the smart thing for the United States would be to find a way to say 'yes' to China's standing offer to join the AIIB. More importantly, given the United States' leadership role in the World Bank and regional banks, it should accelerate the governance reform that would strengthen developing countries' shares and roles. If the next president of the World Bank were a successful reformer from the developing world, that would be a powerful statement and a real change. More developing-country voices in the existing development banks are likely to result in their getting back into infrastructure in a major way.

The issue of lack of reciprocity between China's investment openness and the US system is the most worrisome of the trends. A new president will have to take a serious look at the CFIUS process and the enabling legislation and consider what combination of carrots and sticks would accelerate the opening of China's markets. In terms of sticks, the United States could consider amendment to the CFIUS legislation that would limit acquisitions by state enterprises from countries with which the United States does not have a BIT. In terms of carrots, the best move for the United States is to approve the Trans-Pacific Partnership (TPP) and implement it well so that there is deeper integration among like-minded countries in the Asia-Pacific. Success in this will encourage China to open further and eventually meet the high standards set by the TPP. Greater investment openness is part of China's own reform plan but it clearly needs incentives to make real progress.

References

Chapman, M. (2013), China's Shuanghui buying Smithfield Foods for about $4.72 billion, taking company private, *Associated Press*, 29 May.

Chen, W., Dollar, D. and Tang, H. (2015), *Why is China investing in Africa? Evidence from the firm level*, Washington, DC: Brookings Institution.

Dollar, D. (2015), *United States–China two-way direct investment: Challenges and opportunities*, Washington, DC: Brookings Institution.

Donnan, S. (2016), Capital flight from China worse than thought, *Financial Times*, 20 January. Available from: ft.com/intl/cms/s/0/ae4dee44-bf34-11e5-9fdb-87b8d15baec2.html#axzz46Ns84ERl.

Equator Principles Association (2011), *The Equator principles*. Available from: equator-principles.com/.

Humphrey, C. (2015), *National development banks and infrastructure provision: A comparative study of Brazil, China, and South Africa*, Infrastructure Finance in the Developing World Working Paper Series, Washington, DC: Intergovernmental Group of Twenty-Four on Monetary Affairs and Development.

Kalinova, B., Palerm, A. and Thomsen, S. (2010), OECD's FDI Restrictiveness Index: 2010 Update, OECD Working Papers on International Investment, 2010/03, OECD Publishing. Available from: dx.doi.org/10.1787/5km91p02zj7g-en.

Kaufmann, D. and Kraay, A. (2015), *Worldwide governance indicators*, Washington, DC: The World Bank. Available from: info.worldbank.org/governance/wgi/index.aspx#home.

Ministry of Commerce of China (2014), Statistical Bulletin of China's Outward Foreign Direct Investment. Available from: hzs.mofcom.gov.cn/article/date/201510/20151001130306.shtml.

Ning, Y., Kaixi, H. and Yanwen, Y. (2015), Businessman linked to Sinopec's Angola deals said to face probe, *Caixin Online*, 14 October. Available from: english.caixin.com/2015-10-14/100862966.html.

Ross, A. (2015), China's 'infrastructure for minerals' deal gets reality-check in Congo, *Reuters*, 9 July. Available from: reuters.com/article/2015/07/09/us-congodemocratic-mining-china-insight-idUSKCN0PI1UB20150709.

10. Getting Rich after Getting Old: China's demographic and economic transition in dynamic international context

Lauren Johnston, Xing Liu, Maorui Yang and Xiang Zhang[1]

Introduction

When incomes and living standards rise, households tend towards having fewer children, inducing a fall in the population growth rate. This is a pattern evident in the historical development of many countries once they have progressed beyond the Malthusian poverty trap (Day and Dowrick 2004). The resulting transition produces population ageing—a process whereby the proportion of old people within the total population increases (ILO 2009).

In developing Asia in the post–Global Financial Crisis period, the speed of population ageing is among the biggest, if not the biggest, medium-term structural challenges (Park et al. 2012: xiii). The advent of ageing on such a scale is unprecedented. Population ageing affects considerably how economies behave (Stephenson and Scobie 2002). Changes affect aggregate economic and demographic characteristics, including the relative number of people who are dependent or working age, capacity for work, productivity, income distribution and investment. (Clark et al. 1978: 920).

Ageing of the population is typically measured with one or more of the following indicators:

1. greater than 7 per cent of the population aged over 65
2. less than 30 per cent of the population aged under 14
3. the ratio of old and young—as defined by (1) and (2)—exceeding 0.3
4. a median age more than 30 (Siegel 1980).

1 Lauren Johnston is a Research Fellow at the Melbourne Institute of Applied Economic and Social Research, Faculty of Business and Economics, University of Melbourne. Email: lauren.johnston@unimelb.edu.au. Xing Liu, Maorui Yang and Xiang Zhang are Research Fellows at the China Center for Health Economic Research, National School of Development, Peking University. The authors wish to thank Professors Ross Garnaut and Gordon Liu for their helpful comments on an early draft of this chapter, and also a 2015 Dyason Fellowship awarded by the University of Melbourne to support this research collaboration.

The first is the most commonly used simple indicator of population ageing and is used to empirically define an ageing population herein.

In 2014, there were 590 million people aged over 65 in a global population of 7.26 billion people—some 8.1 per cent (World Bank 2015). China's population has been classified as 'ageing' since 2000, the year the population share of those aged 65 and older reached 7 per cent. By 2014, this share had reached 9.2 per cent, or 130 million people in the total Chinese population of 1.36 billion (World Bank 2015). More than one-third of countries now host ageing populations. Figure 10.1 highlights the spatial distribution of ageing across countries in 2014 and shows there is much variation (İmrohoroğlu 2007: 148).

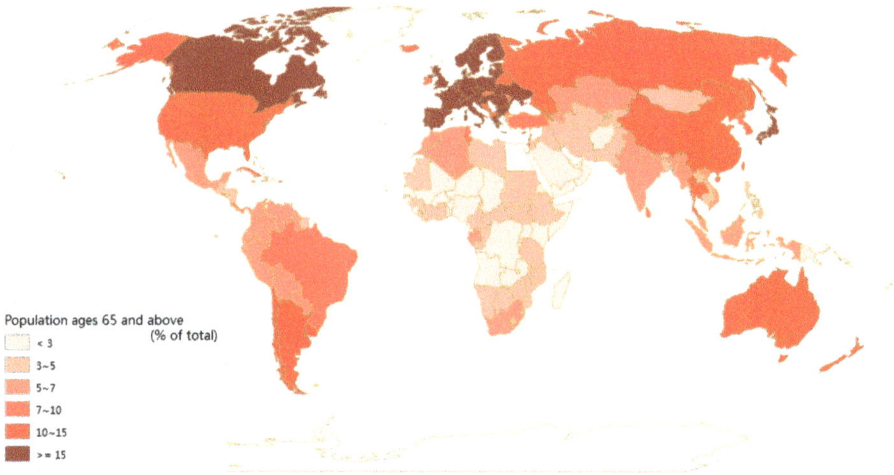

Figure 10.1 Share of population aged 65 years and older, 2014

Sources: World Bank (2015); UN (2015).

National ageing population intensity and regional density are highest in the high-income countries of Western Europe, North America and North-East Asia (Figure 10.1). Populations that were first to age among these countries are broadly shaded a dark red in Figure 10.1, and were typically developed economically before becoming 'old'. Many of the 48 countries that have joined the 'ageing' group since 1960, however, especially in East Asia, were developing countries when they reached the ageing threshold (World Bank 2015). Each 'ageing' country faces a unique mix of ageing-related challenges (Park et al. 2012: xiv), reflecting differences in behaviour across individuals and countries over the life cycle, combined with an increase in the relative number of older people (Clark et al. 1978: 949).

Studies of population ageing are divided roughly into three categories. Studies of:

- macroeconomic problems related to the decline in the workforce due to ageing
- social security systems, with many looking at pension systems
- the microeconomics of the labour market—for example, employment of the elderly, competition with younger workers, the female workforce and immigrant workers (Onofri 2004).

A prescient empirical study falling into the first category, published some two decades before China's population crossed into the 'ageing' category, predicted that China would face the challenge of ageing before its economy reached high-income per capita levels of gross domestic product (GDP) (Wu 1986).

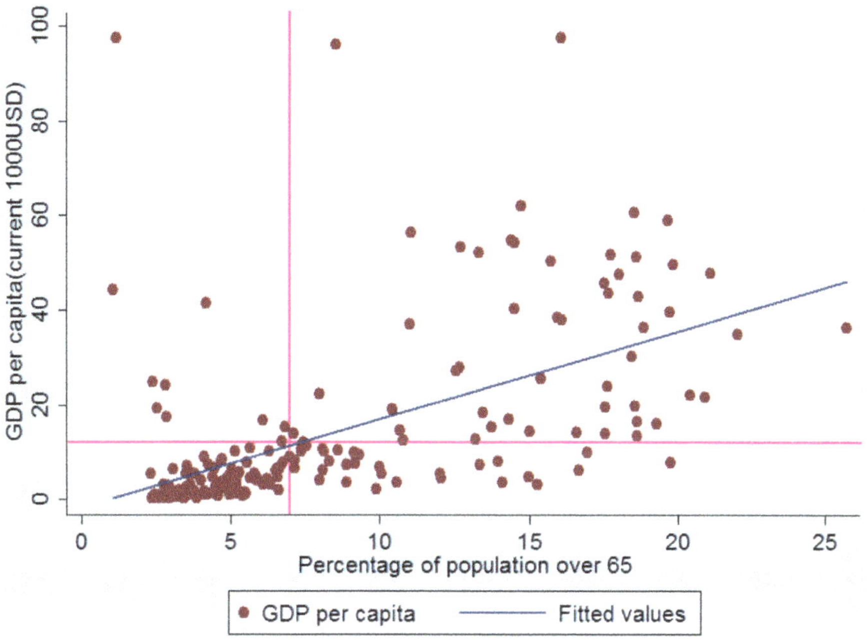

Figure 10.2 Population ageing share and income per capita, 2014

Source: World Bank (2015).

Figure 10.2 places countries into one of four categories, depending on the proportion of old people in the population and GDP per capita. China is placed in the less densely populated bottom right-hand rectangle—among countries with a share of population aged 65 and over above 7 per cent that in 2014 also had an income below the high-income threshold of $12,616 current international dollars (World Bank 2015). Wu (1986) argued that carrying such an elderly dependency weight at an early stage of development—a pattern he described as 'getting old before rich' (GOBR)—would inhibit China from joining the high-income developed group of countries. Wu (1986) focused on China. Here, we draw attention to the fact that other economies confront variants of the same challenge.

Cai and Wang (2007: 86) summarise the risk China's 'premature' ageing may bring in terms of the fact that loss of labour factor endowment advantages arrives ahead of new advantages in capital-intensive and technology-intensive industries (Cai 2010). The importance relates to the relationship between population and capital, which is explained in the Solow growth model. In Solow, where n, the rate of growth of the total workforce (L), becomes negative, capital (K) per worker (k) increases due to the decrease in L. This causes increases in wages and growth in output (Y) per worker (y), but fewer workers as a proportion of the population. Whether the shift in output per worker is greater or less than the shift in the workers' share of the population is exogenously determined.

Using a Solow framework, Wang et al. (2004) find that population ageing in China could affect economic growth via labour supply, the savings rate (through population ageing inducing changes in both consumption and savings) and through a slower rate of technological advancement. Hu et al. (2012) adopt a Solow growth model to reach similar conclusions using provincial-level panel data. Golley and Tyers (2012) use active workforce statistics rather than working-age population figures to estimate that China will enjoy a demographic dividend through to 2030. In general, however, cross-country studies of China's relative ageing challenges are few. Moreover—and remarkably given that GOBR is a relative concept—there are few studies that have explored China's ageing relatively, notable recent exceptions being the World Bank (2015) and Park et al. (2012).

Thirty years since Wu (1986), this chapter re-examines China's ageing challenge around the GOBR notion. For the first time in the literature, to our knowledge, this includes an extension of Wu's framework (1986) to the full four-state comparative framework that is implicit in the GOBR idea. The goal here is twofold:

1. To create a framework that places China's ageing challenge in an international context.
2. To draw greater attention to diversity among ageing populations and to their economic context, with various implications for policy.

China is just one of many countries navigating the process of economic development under GOBR conditions. It also identifies a prospectively useful reference point: several middle-income countries with ageing populations have in recent years successfully transitioned from being 'poor' to being 'rich'. Our analysis suggests that China's chances of making a successful transition to high-income status after growing old may be better than Chinese consensus has expected. China's 'fear of ageing' (Calvo and Reinhart 2002) may have prepared it well, but it could also be reducing the focus on positive opportunities attached to its ageing–wealth nexus, such as being able to define more sustainable ageing-related entitlements. Importantly, our results also infer that, in the absence of oil wealth, recent experience is that countries are more likely to move from middle into high per capita income status after entering the 'old' category.

The rest of this chapter is structured as follows. The second section describes the basic empirical measures of China's ageing population. The third section presents an extension of Wu (1986) using a transitions matrix approach. The fourth section compares economic structure across GOBR countries. The final section discusses the contents of this survey and proposes areas for future research.

Population ageing in China: Empirical survey

This section presents an overview of China's ageing-related indicators, including the total fertility rate, life expectancy and population share of those aged 65 and over, and the concept of 'ageing duration'. The section also defines and discusses issues in China's total, youth and elderly dependency ratios. The total fertility rate refers to the expected number of children a woman who survives to the end of the reproductive age span will have during her lifetime if she experiences given age-specific rates of childbirth (UNDATA 2016).

Table 10.1 Basic ageing population empirics, China

	Total fertility rate*	Life expectancy at birth (years)	Share of population aged 65 and over (% of total)	Number of people aged 65 and over
1980	2.7	67	4.5	44,155,575
1990	2.5	69.5	5.3	60,164,805
2000	1.5	72.1	6.7	84,597,215
2010	1.7	74.9	8.2	109,691,810
2014	1.6	75.8	9.2	125,512,840

* Excludes data for Hong Kong SAR, Macau SAR and Taiwan.
Source: World Bank (2015).

Table 10.1 presents selected ageing population indicators over recent decades. The data show that China's total fertility rate fell by nearly half in the last two decades of the past century, before lifting a little, and life expectancy increased by nearly a decade over three decades. These developments underlie the rise in the population share of people aged over 65, from 4.5 to 9.2 per cent. Home to the world's largest population, China is now also home to the world's largest stock of old people—some 125 million in 2014. By population share of people aged 65 and over, however, China's rank was just 65th in the same year (World Bank 2015). In other words, China is an outlier in the number but not the share of old people.

A commonly used empirical indicator is the dependency ratio, which is defined as the ratio of population aged 0–14 years and 65 years and over per 100 people aged 15–64. The United Nations uses a medium fertility variant to calculate the total dependency ratio, alongside child and elderly dependency ratios (UN 2002). China's total dependency ratio declined rapidly over the last quarter of the past century, providing a substantial 'demographic dividend' (Figure 10.3). In China's case, it is calculated that for every 1 per cent fall in the dependency ratio resulting from an expanding workforce share, GDP per capita increased by 0.115 per cent (Cai 2010).

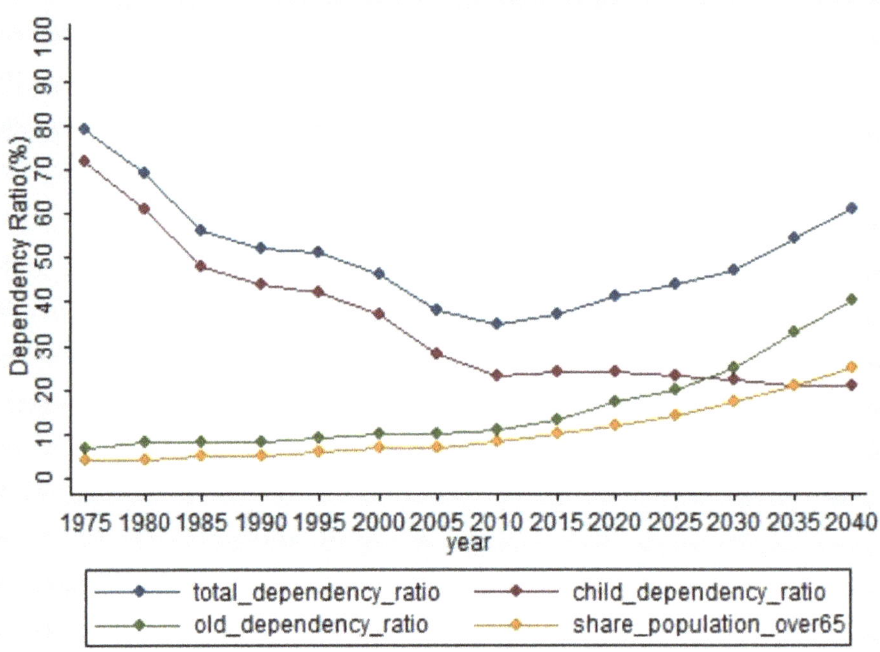

Figure 10.3 Total, child and elderly dependency ratios, China

Source: UN (2015).

A halt in the decline of the total dependency ratio reflects the end of the main demographic dividend (Minami 1968, cited in Cai 2010). The Lewis model reflects a related concept focused on how the incremental transfer of surplus labour from low productivity rural areas into higher productivity urban and industrial sectors drives industrialisation via growth in average productivity and total output (Garnaut 2010). Eventually, however, the surplus rural labour dries up—a point known as the Lewis turning point. As illustrated in Figure 10.3, in China this happened about 2009 (Garnaut 2010: 8). The proximity of the arrival of the Lewis turning point to the onset of population ageing varies between countries. Recent family planning policies cause the two turning points to be unusually close in China. This compounds the rate of increase in labour scarcity and wage pressures, and increases the challenges of the transition to a new growth model.

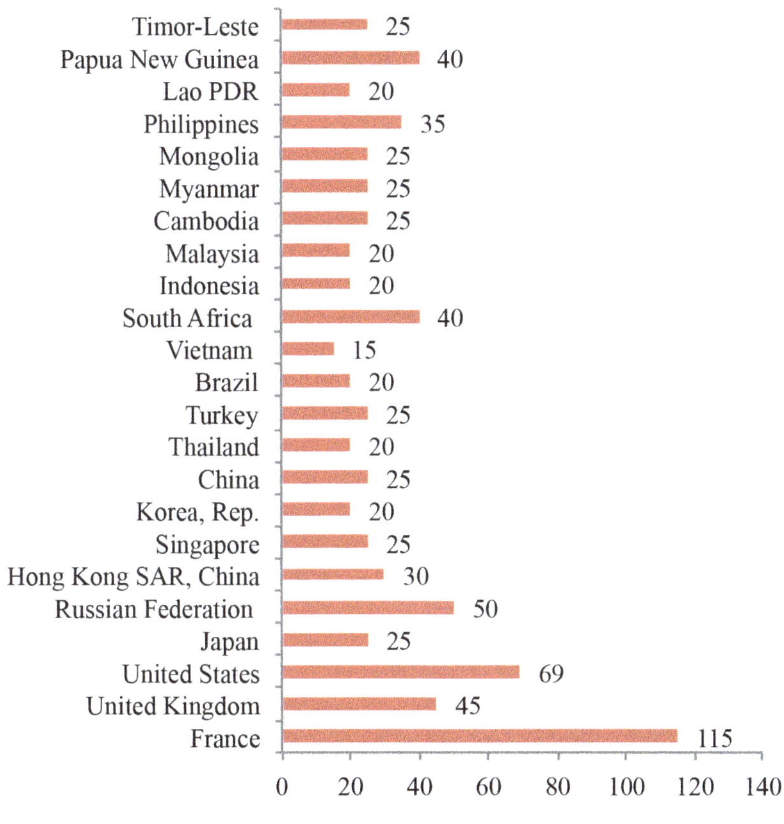

Figure 10.4 Years taken for ageing share to increase from 7 to 14 per cent of population

Note: Countries reaching 7 per cent the earliest are at the bottom of the graph, with countries ageing later at the top.

Sources: World Bank (2016).

China's geographically differentiated labour market means, however, that the end of the demographic dividend is less of a 'turning point' and more of a 'turning period' during which wages will rise as labour becomes scarce (Garnaut 2010: 6).

Several factors can shift the length of the 'turning period' including the speed of ageing and educational attainment. The ease with which the transition to a new steady state built on higher productivity and higher wages occurs relates to the efficiency of institutions. The time these institutions have had to prepare for managing the consequences of ageing populations is partly a function of the speed of the demographic transition.

A particular feature of contemporary global population ageing is its increasing speed (Lutz et al. 2008). While, for example, it took France more than a century for the percentage of people aged 65 and over to increase from 7 per cent to 14 per cent of the total population, the equivalent ageing transition is now happening within a generation in some less-developed countries (Powell and Cook 2009: 390) (Figure 10.4). East Asia and the Pacific are now ageing faster than any region in history, with nearly all middle-income countries in the region currently in or about to experience a process of rapid population ageing. Figure 10.4 illustrates the point. While it took France, for example, 115 years to shift from having 7 per cent of the population aged 65 and over to 14 per cent, Vietnam has taken just 15 years to do the same. In other words, and in parallel with the region's economic transformation, demographic transitions that took some 100 years in founding Organisation for Economic Co-operation and Development (OECD) countries are happening in 20–25 years in some middle-income countries (World Bank 2015).

In the Chinese literature, Wu and Du (2006) note the importance of 'ageing duration', which is defined as the length of time a country has been classified as having an ageing population. They argue that China's ageing challenge should only be compared with that of countries with a similar ageing duration. Their argument relates to fears that countries with a short ageing duration have had little time to prepare and, in the case of developing countries, this is compounded by the lesser availability of resources per capita (Park et al. 2012: 9).

The experience of China and other East Asian countries can be contrasted with that of countries with a long 'ageing duration'—notably, those in Western Europe, where 'wealth duration' is long: 'getting old after getting rich' (GOAR). In GOAR countries, it is more likely that the entitlements of the old—having been defined over a long period when they represented a smaller share of the population and when life expectancy after retirement was some decade shorter than today—will turn out to be unsustainable in modern conditions. The relative 'fear of ageing' (Calvo and Reinhart 2002) in newly ageing developing economies (GOBR), especially China, would seem to be misplaced. The GOBR countries may be better placed than others to install fiscally sustainable retirement policies.

The channels through which population ageing affects a population's productive power, consumption patterns and investment and political behaviours require more study (Eisele 1974: 77). This chapter offers a simple extension of Wu (1986) to elaborate China's prospects for a smooth transition to high-income status after getting old. This draws attention to the possibility that structural risks attached to ageing in rich countries may require more attention in policy development. The next section revisits and extends Wu (1986).

Extended Wu demographic-income framework

Extended Wu framework

The GOBR (Wu 1986) notion has served as a reference point in the academic literature in China for three decades. Despite being an implicitly comparative idea, Wu's logic has not been developed within the ageing income framework that it implies.

Table 10.2 Extrapolated Wu framework

		Population	
		Old	**Young**
GDP per capita	High (rich)	Ageing after rich (RO)	Rich and youth-filled (RY)
	Low/middle (poor)	Ageing before rich (PO)	Poor and youth-filled (PY)

RO = 'rich and old'
PO = 'poor and old'
RY = 'rich and young'
PY = 'poor and young'

Table 10.2 outlines the three parallel states that are implied by 'getting old before getting rich' (Wu 1986): 'getting old after getting rich' (Johnston 2012), 'rich and youth-filled' and 'poor and youth-filled'. That China falls into the 'poor–old' (PO) category is empirically established in the Chinese literature (see sections one and two of this chapter).

Table 10.3 Selected countries, extended Wu framework, 2014

		Population	
		Old	Young
GDP per capita	High (rich)	Australia, Chile, Hong Kong SAR, Korea Rep., Israel, Italy, Poland Russia, Singapore, Slovenia, USA, Uruguay	Bahrain, Brunei, Equatorial Guinea, Kuwait, Qatar, Seychelles, Saudi Arabia, UAE
	Low/middle (poor)	Brazil, Argentina, China, Lebanon, Mauritius, Panama, Romania, Sri Lanka, Thailand, Turkey, Ukraine	Ecuador, Egypt, India, Indonesia, Kenya, Libya, Malaysia, Mexico, South Africa, Vietnam

In Table 10.3, the country examples presented are from a population study listed in Appendix Table A11.1. Economies were classified into the extended Wu framework using the empirical definition of aged used throughout this chapter: a 7 per cent or higher population share of those aged 65 and over. The definition of 'rich' refers to the World Bank's high-income classification of gross national income (GNI) per capita of more than $12,616 current international dollars in 2014.

The overall distribution of countries between the four categories over time (see Appendix Table A11.1) can be summarised simply as follows. The rich and old (RO) are mostly OECD countries. Poor and old (PO) countries are mostly 'transitional economies'—Eastern European countries and China—or countries stuck in the 'middle-income trap' such as Brazil and Peru. Rich and youth-filled (RY) countries are mostly members of the Organization of the Petroleum Exporting Countries (OPEC). Finally, poor and youth-filled (PY) countries are most of the world's low-income countries and selected middle-income countries. The average share of the population aged 65 and over in RO countries is 16 per cent, compared with 11 per cent for PO countries (Appendix Table A11.2). RY countries are younger on average than PY countries: 3.4 per cent compared with 4.1 per cent. The relative average per capita income gap between PY and PO countries also appears to be substantial. This relates to the 'poor' category covering both low and middle-income economies. This point will be further explored below.

The numbers by category are presented in Table 10.4 in selected years. Note that China became an ageing population in 2000. In general, the data suggest that populations are shifting from young to old at a faster rate than they are shifting from poor to rich. In 1990, of 172 countries, 59 were old (34 per cent) and 53 rich (31 per cent). By 2014, the share of rich countries remained at 31 per cent, but the share of old countries had increased to 47 per cent.

Table 10.4 Countries by category, selected years*

Category	1990		2000		2010		2014	
	No.	%	No.	%	No.	%	No.	%
RO	31	18.0	37	19.9	46	24.6	46	25.7
PO	17	9.9	30	16.1	29	15.5	28	15.6
RY	17	9.9	8	4.3	11	5.9	9	5.0
PY	107	62.2	111	59.7	101	54.0	96	53.6
Total	172	100	186	100	187	100	179	100
Old	59	30.1	69	35.2	81	41.1	85	43.4
Rich	53	29.1	53	26.5	63	32.0	56	30.3

* Countries with missing values: 45 in 1990; 32 in 2000; 31 in 2010; 40 in 2014.

In the next section, we explore this movement more directly using a transition matrix analysis. In 2014, China was one of 28 countries confronting the GOBR challenge. There were 31 such countries in 2010. Some countries are moving between the groups over time. Further study of those transitions and the important institutions and policies underlying them, especially in the case of a successful transition from the PO to the RO category—China's contemporary economic goal—could offer useful insight for Chinese policymakers.

Extended Wu framework transition matrix

To explore country transitions within our extended Wu framework, we retain our definition of 'old' as a 7 per cent share in population of those aged 65 and older, and of 'rich' as the World Bank's high-income classification. We take the World Bank high-income classification in current international dollars over time as follows: GDP per capita of more than $6,000 in 1990, $9,361 in 2000, $11,906 in 2010 and $12,616 in 2014. These intervals are selected so as to understand China's ageing in international context, as China moved into the 'old' category in 2000 and 2014 was the most recent year with widely available data.

Data are sourced entirely from the World Bank's *World development indicators* (2015). In 1990, 45 countries dropped from the country list because they missed one or both of the population or income data points. In 2000, that number was 31, 30 in 2010 and 38 in 2014. Countries also fell out of the sample if they were affected by conflict (for example, Iraq dropped from 2000, and Eritrea and Syria from 2014). Similarly, many of the countries emerging from the former Soviet Union had sufficient data to enter the study only in 2000 and not in 1990. As we are interested mainly in the share of countries moving between categories at different intervals, for the purpose of this chapter we decided to use the sample available at each interval rather than keeping a consistent sample throughout.

Table 10.5 Transition matrix, 1990–2014 (number of countries)

		2014			
	Category	RO	PO	RY	PY
1990	RO	29	0	0	0
	PO	5	11	0	0
	RY	4	0	6	3
	PY	2	14	2	84

RO = 'rich–old'
PO = 'poor–old'
RY= 'rich–young'
PY = 'poor–young'

Table 10.5 sets out a transition matrix T, a 4*4 matrix, where element $T_{i,j}$ represents the number of countries grouped into category *i* in 1990, and into category *j* in 2014. Countries that did not change categories between the two intervals are located along the left–right diagonal line. The matrix reveals that no 'RO' country shifted between groups over the reference period. That is, all countries in the sample that were 'rich and old' in 1990 remained in the RO group in 2014. Most of the PY group also stayed poor and young.

Table 10.6 Transition matrix, 1990–2014 (percentage form)

		2014			
	Category	RO	PO	RY	PY
1990	RO	100	0	0	0
	PO	31	69	0	0
	RY	31	0	46	23
	PY	2	14	2	82

Source: Authors' own calculations using World Bank (2015) data.

Table 10.6 presents the percentages attached to the transitions of Table 10.5. The data show that the most likely transition is, in fact, from PO to RO—the very transition China is trying to make. Some 31 per cent of the 1990 PO group had transitioned to the RO group by 2014, and 69 per cent remained in the PO group. That is, the transition to high per capita incomes appears to be more probable from a base of population ageing than from a young population. China's GOBR challenge may be easier to achieve than feared.

On the other hand, more than half the 1990 PO group remained in the PO category nearly one-quarter of a century later, by 2014. Ageing is certainly not in and of itself a route to wealth. Moreover, 14 per cent of the countries in the 1990 PY group transitioned to the PO category by 2014. In the absence of oil wealth, getting old is still more probable than getting rich.

The 'poor' category is crude because it spans a wide array of economies—from dynamic upper–middle-income economies to least-developed economies. In the next step, we disaggregate the 'poor' category into 'low', 'middle' and 'upper' middle-income bands. The GNI per capita thresholds used for this were: in 1990, $545, $2,200 and $6,000; in 2000, $760, $3,030 and $9,361; in 2010, $975, $3,855 and $11,906; and, in 2014, $1,035, $4,085 and $12,616 (World Bank 2015).

Table 10.7 Disaggregated transition matrix, 1990–2014 (number of countries)

			2014						
	Population		Old			Young			
		Income	High	Upper-middle	Lower-middle	High	Upper-middle	Lower-middle	Low
1990	Old	High	29	0	0	0	0	0	0
		Upper-middle	4	5	0	0	0	0	0
		Lower-middle	1	3	3	0	0	0	0
	Young	High	4	0	0	6	3	0	0
		Upper-middle	2	5	0	1	7	0	0
		Lower-middle	0	5	1	0	16	23	2
		Low	0	1	1	1	0	14	22

Table 10.7 presents the transitions between ageing and income groups where the 'poor' category is disaggregated into upper-middle, lower-middle and low-income groups. A total of five countries that were already old in 1990 moved into the high-income group, one from lower-middle income and four from upper–middle-income country status. These countries offer a precedent for the transition China now seeks to make—from a middle-income economy with an ageing population to a high-income country with an ageing population.

Table 10.8 Countries by transition

1990		2014		
Income	**Demography**	**Income**	**Demography**	**Country**
Low	Young	Lower-middle	Young	Bangladesh, Ghana, India, Kenya, Kiribati, Lao PDR, Mauritania, Nicaragua, Nigeria, Pakistan, Sudan, Tajikistan, Vietnam, Zambia
		Lower-middle	Old	Sri Lanka
		Upper-middle	Old	China
		High	Young	Equatorial Guinea
Lower-middle	Young	Low	Young	*Comoros, Zimbabwe*
		Upper-middle		Azerbaijan, Colombia, Dominican Republic, Ecuador, Fiji, Jordan, Kazakhstan, Maldives, Namibia, Paraguay, Peru, Samoa, Suriname, Tonga, Turkmenistan
			Old	Albania, El Salvador, Lebanon, Thailand, Tunisia
	Old	High	Old	Poland
		Upper-middle		Belarus, Jamaica, Romania
Upper-middle	Young	High	Old	Chile, Trinidad and Tobago
		Upper-middle		Brazil, Costa Rica, Mauritius, St Vincent and the Grenadines, Turkey
	Old	High	Old	Czech Republic, Russian Federation, Slovakia Republic, Uruguay
High	Young	Upper-middle	Young	*Gabon, Iraq, Libya*
		High	Old	Bahamas, Korea Rep., Macau SAR (China), Singapore

Note: Countries with average per capita incomes that have transitioned to lower income groups are in italics.

Source: Authors' own calculations using World Bank (2015).

Table 10.8 elaborates ageing and income group transition by country across the years 1990 to 2014. These pathways have not previously been analysed. The data show that China has, since 1990, been alone in its transition pathway—from a low-income and young country to an upper-middle income and old country. Several countries have made different transitions—for example, Albania, El Salvador, Lebanon, Thailand and Tunisia have transitioned from lower-middle income and youth-filled to upper-middle income and old. Belarus, Jamaica and Romania were already old in 1990, and transitioned from lower-middle income to upper-middle income and old. Brazil, Costa Rica, Mauritius, Saint Vincent and the Grenadines and Turkey, on the other hand, transitioned from youth-filled to old without a shift between income groups.

It is also interesting to draw parallels between China and the countries that have recently transitioned to the 'rich' category. Among them, Equatorial Guinea, an oil-rich state in Africa, is alone in not also having moved to an ageing population. Two countries managed the transition from upper-middle income and youth-filled to high-income and old: Chile and Trinidad and Tobago. In 1990, Poland was already 'old', but managed to transition from lower-middle income to high income by 2014.

The countries that have already successfully transitioned from upper-middle income to high income status with an ageing population—the transition China seeks to make—are Uruguay, Czech Republic, Russian Federation and the Slovakia Republic. By comparison, the final row of Table 10.8 highlights that China's East Asian neighbours have populations that recently entered the 'ageing' category, while having already joined the high-income club: South Korea, Macau SAR (China) and Singapore. These countries are cases of GOAR. In other words, in earlier years it was common to transition into the high-income category from a youthful population base, but this pattern appears to be shifting towards one in which an ageing population is a more likely lift-off point. Lessons for China's transition can be drawn from both sets of experiences.

Getting rich after getting old: Comparisons

Factors associated with a successful transition from middle to high per capita income include a relatively high level of secondary and tertiary education and a relatively high share of high-technology products within exports (Eichengreen et al. 2014). Cai (2012) argues that for China to avoid the middle-income trap it must: 1) transform economic growth to a consumption-driven pattern; 2) shift labour-intensive industries to central and western regions of the country; and 3) speed up technological catch-up. The current Five-Year Plan (FYP) broadly addresses these challenges.

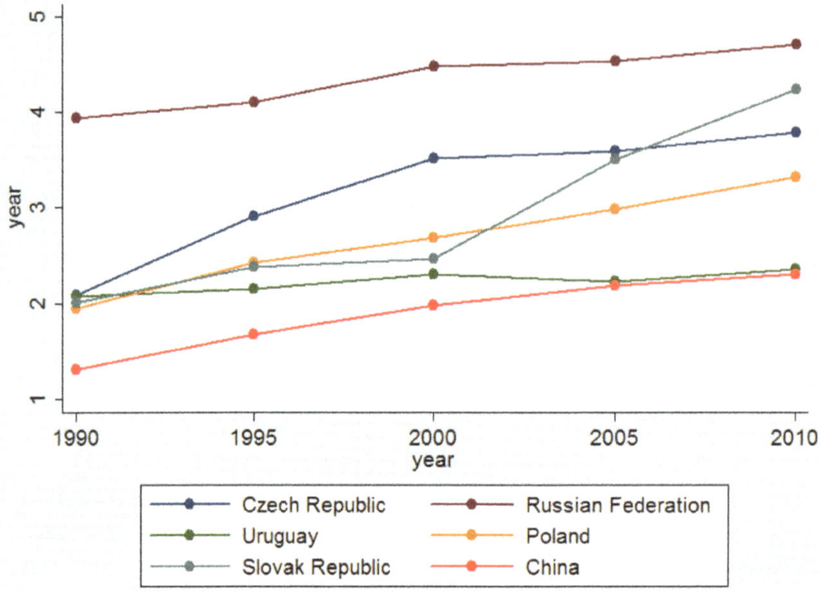

Figure 10.5 Average total years of secondary schooling, age 15+, total, in China compared with countries that were PO before RO

Source: Barro and Lee (2013).

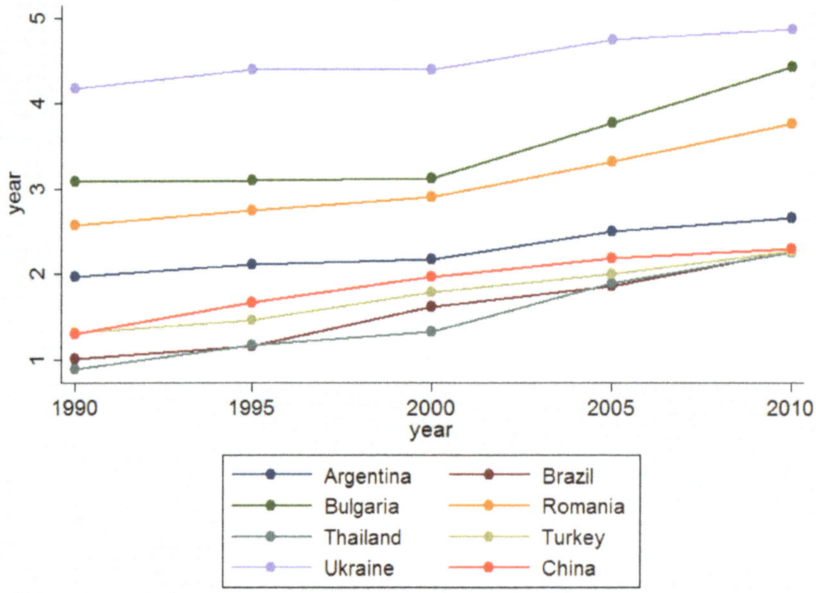

Figure 10.6 Average total years of secondary schooling, age 15+, total, in China compared with countries remaining in a PO state

Source: Barro and Lee (2013).

With regard to Eichengreen et al.'s (2014) contention that high education levels are the first necessary factor for successful transition to high per capita income, average years of secondary schooling remain low in China compared with countries that have recently succeeded in moving from the middle-income to the high per capita income group (Figure 10.5). Under the Thirteenth FYP, China is, however, increasing efforts to popularise high school education. A recent World Bank report (2016: 11) suggests that there is reason for cautious optimism about rising education rates in East Asia, with increasingly educated cohorts being better prepared than previous generations for the prospect of longer working lives. For China to avoid becoming stuck in the middle-income stage, these efforts will need to increase not only high school and university education levels, but also education quality. For example, rural labourers transferring to urban areas are often insufficiently qualified to fill available vacancies, while many university graduates cannot find jobs (Cai and Wang 2007). In general, China must ensure that its diminished number of young have abundant human capital so as to safeguard their ability to learn as they age (Cai 2012).

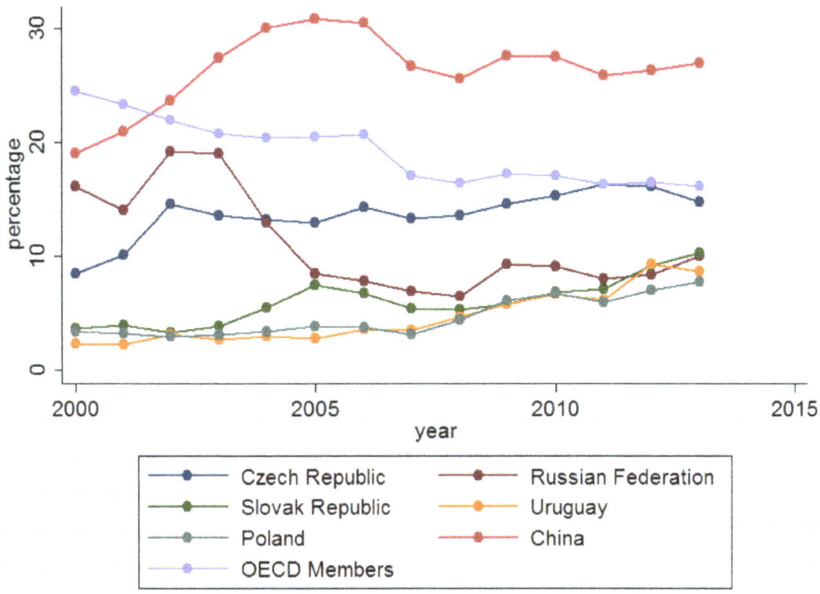

Figure 10.7 High-tech exports as a percentage of manufactured exports in China compared with countries that were PO before RO and OECD average

Source: World Bank (2015).

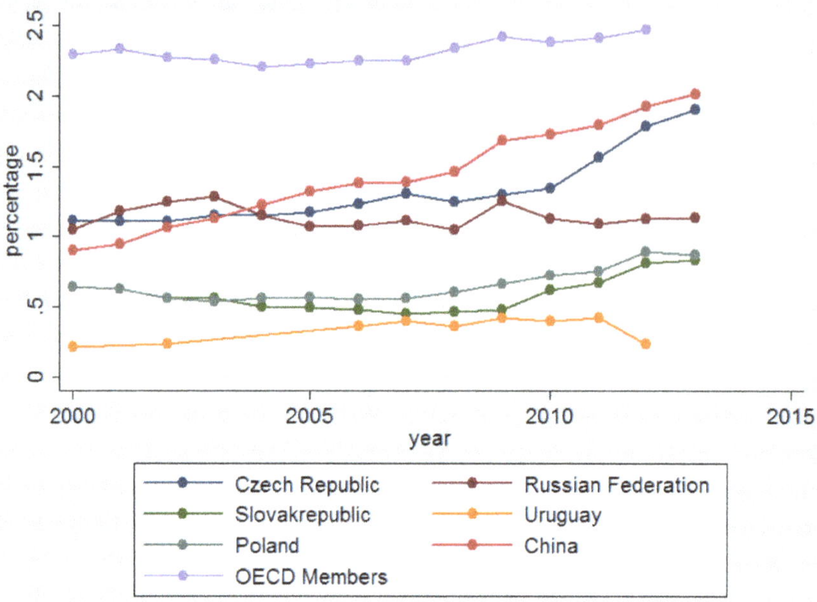

Figure 10.8 Research and development expenditure as a percentage of GDP in China compared with countries that were PO before RO and OECD average

Source: World Bank (2015).

With regard to Eichengreen et al.'s (2014) second necessary factor for successful income transition—a relatively high share of high-technology products within exports—China is in fact a positive outlier in terms of having high levels of manufactured exports and high investment in high-tech industries, even compared with the OECD. It has been so since soon after joining the World Trade Organization in 2001 (Figure 10.7). Such are the scale and success of China's high-tech exports that they are found to have displaced other middle-income country competitor exports, including those of India, Brazil and Mexico as well as Malaysia, Thailand and Vietnam (Pham et al. 2016). Using research and development (R&D) expenditure as a percentage of GDP to serve as an indicator of the potential to export such products in future. China has already surpassed the level of R&D expenditure of all countries that recently realised high per capita incomes while also having an ageing population (Figure 10.8).

These simple comparisons suggest that China may have a reasonable chance of navigating from PO to RO, as have Uruguay, the Czech Republic, the Russian Federation and the Slovakia Republic since 1990. Further, as other countries in East Asia and other regions seek to make the same transition in future, China's potentially more imminent success or failure will set an important precedent—

that a declining total fertility rate and rising life expectancy in the early phase of a development transition need not inhibit advanced economic development and, in fact, could even support it.

Discussion

For three decades, Chinese policymakers have sought to best utilise China's now fading demographic dividend. That effort built on fears about the adverse economic development effects of the premature arrival of the turning point at which the national workforce share begins to decline. Underlying these fears was the fact that China, unlike its North-East Asian neighbours, would get old before getting rich—the related pressures of which on output per person would inhibit transition to high-income livelihoods.

This chapter returned to the starting point of those fears: a 1986 paper by Renmin University demographer Wu Canping. In a first in the literature, it has extended Wu's (1986) idea of getting old before getting rich to the full four-state framework that it implies. In so doing, we shed a different but related light on China's ageing population challenge. For example, we identified that China is just one of some 30 countries that is getting old before it gets rich. Also, in recent years among countries without oil wealth, the developing countries with ageing populations were the ones most likely to ascend into the high-income group. China aims to do the same. If it succeeds, it will join the four identified countries that have already achieved this progression since 1990: Uruguay, the Czech Republic, the Russian Federation and the Slovakia Republic.

In addition to drawing comparative attention to China's relative transition prospects given its income and ageing conditions, this chapter draws attention to issues around the potential for ageing populations to have very divergent economic effects—in two countries that happen to have the same share of aged population (and the same ageing rate) but are otherwise fundamentally different. In this vein, the 'old' across countries are endogenously systematically different in terms of, for example, relative pension entitlements, share of asset ownership, accrued entitlements and access to publicly funded services through retirement. In addition, the broader macroeconomic conditions around ageing populations also vary—for example, with respect to accumulated public debt per capita and whether there is a rising or falling share of national income accruing to the working-age population. Importantly, too, older populations in different countries enjoy very different relative political powers that can be employed to preserve their benefits. As Wu (1986) implicitly found, ageing population economics extend far beyond a simple linear function of the share of the population aged over 65.

Here we hope to have encouraged a more nuanced understanding of the broader economic and political economy context of China's ageing population challenge. By implication, this also serves similarly for other countries. For all countries with an ageing population it is important to heed the additional driver of population ageing after increasing life expectancy and decreasing fertility rates: past variations in birth and death rates (Bloom et al. 2010). The population cohort born in China before the implementation of strict family planning in the late 1970s is an example. The baby boom that resulted from increased fertility in rich countries after World War II is another. These examples reflect the demographic ebb and flow and its non-synchronicity across countries (İmrohoroğlu 2007).

The specific contribution of Wu (1986) here and in the case of China was to highlight the importance of the timing of the demographic ebb and flow around national wealth accumulation and to factor the appropriate consequences into intergenerational economic planning. In China, the population is getting old before getting rich. By comparison, Japan, South Korea and most of the rest of the OECD had relatively young populations when they became rich.

In practice, this difference means that even were China to enter the high-income grouping soon, its large numbers of aged people would nonetheless have lived the majority of their lives as residents of a poor country—and their benefits are likely to have accumulated accordingly. By comparison, the emerging large cohort of those aged over 65 in rich countries has spent most of their lifespan relatively well placed economically, domestically and internationally—so much so that some researchers have voiced fears that this will lead to 'a self-centred generation just sucking down all the resources' (Dychtwald 1999, cited in Bloom et al. 2010).

In this context and to our knowledge, there are no studies directly comparing the potentially very divergent economic consequences of population ageing in GOBR versus GOAR economies. It is possible this missing more nuanced approach to ageing populations and economics research risks conceptually underestimating the potential ageing risks in rich-country democracies, and similarly miscalculating the ageing challenges confronting China and other GOBR economies. Cai (2012), for example, has pointed out that China has room to utilise the gap between it and developed countries to sustain economic growth. In contrast, OECD countries face population ageing amid the uncertainty of pushing the economic frontier while also affording the much more extensive old age dependency entitlements that the older cohort in these populations has accumulated.

In China's case, Li (2006) fears that the time when the youth dependency rate exceeds the elderly dependency rate (around 2030) will morph China into an 'ageing society'. Understanding these fears could be supported by further, parallel investigation of a newer, herein raised, notion of an 'ageing economy'. Development of the concept would seek to capture the dynamic economic consequences of the relative share of the economy accruing to the less economically active population aged over 65, and estimate the dynamic economic impact accordingly. This would vary across countries according to the factors discussed herein, and would help to form a useful indicator of the risks that ageing populations may pose to the dampening of economic activity—right at a time when the opposite is required to sustain related costs.

Conclusion

For more than three decades, China has been actively preparing for population ageing around the idea that it will get old before getting rich. In the related debate both within and outside China, it has consistently been assumed that China's ageing population conditions are uniquely adverse. In this chapter, we studied China's ageing in a cross-country context and identified that China is an outlier only for the total number, but not for the proportion, of its elderly people. It is not, however, alone in 'getting old before getting rich', and nor has that challenge proven insurmountable in recent history. We herein identified four countries that got rich after getting old. China seeks to achieve the same.

Towards that goal, it would be timely to explore more deeply whether there are in fact advantages to getting old before getting rich—and to make the most of them. Chinese researchers have, for example, highlighted that China is still experiencing catch-up growth to support its transition with an ageing population. China also has relative freedom to define its ageing population entitlements in an ageing context. Against expectation, this could be the foundation for their sustainability. GOAR countries, in comparison, must manage ageing populations amid legacy ageing institutions that were shaped in a period of high relative wealth but much smaller ageing population shares and shorter life expectancies. GOBR countries such as China may in fact experience circumstances of much easier political economy and fiscal sustainability in which to manage the ageing demographic transition.

China's government has set a goal that by about 2020, the country's per capita income will reach high-income levels—set in 2014 at more than $12,736 per capita. China's GDP per capita in 2014 was $7,590. China's ability to navigate that transition smoothly over the coming decades will depend on how it can increase output per worker despite a declining workforce share and while losing its wage-related advantages. Via education and technological upgrading in particular, and in its long-standing frontier coastal economic environments, so far, China is broadly succeeding.

Importantly, China's prospects for getting rich after getting old—like those of the other countries in the same stage of demographic/income transition—may also be enhanced through a more nuanced and dynamic understanding of the factors underlying such transitions over time. A more dynamic understanding of the impact of ageing populations on economies is also likely to be facilitated by a deliberate separation of the demographic notion of an ageing population from the economic context and dynamic effects of ageing populations. It may not be that an ageing population explicitly slows growth, but rather that this happens when an ageing population is positioned to induce effects that instead become symptomatic of the more dynamic and worrying nascent notion of an 'ageing economy'.

Further research is required. Studies that can better identify the prospectively divergent economic impacts of different ageing populations may better inform not only policymaking in developing countries with ageing populations, but also rich countries navigating the different yet potentially no less ominous challenges of getting old after getting rich. More research in this direction may in fact serve to support enhanced growth in both.

References

Barro, R. J. and Lee, J. W. (2013), A new data set of educational attainment in the world, 1950–2010, *Journal of Development Economics*, 104: 184–198.

Bloom, D. E., Canning, D. and Fink, G. (2010), Implications of population ageing for economic growth, *Oxford Review of Economic Policy*, 26(4): 583–612.

Cai, F. (2010), Demographic transition, demographic dividend, and Lewis turning point in China, *China Economic Journal*, 3(2): 107–119.

Cai, F. (2012), The coming demographic impact on China's growth: The age factor in the middle-income trap, *Asian Economic Papers*, 11(1): 95–111.

Cai, F. and Wang, M. (2007), How will population aging affect economic growth?, *China Economist*, [English edn], (1): 86–94.

Calvo, G. and Reinhart, C. (2002), Fear of floating, *Quarterly Journal of Economics*, 107(2) (May): 379–408.

Clark, R., Kreps, J. and Spengler, J. (1978), Economics of aging: A survey, *Journal of Economic Literature*, 16(3): 919–962.

Day, C. and Dowrick, S. (2004), Ageing economics: Human capital, productivity and fertility, *Agenda: A Journal of Policy Analysis and Reform*, 11(1): 3–20.

Eichengreen, B., Park, D. and Shin, K. (2014), Growth slowdowns redux, *Japan and the World Economy*, 32: 65–84.

Eisele, F. R. (ed.) (1974), Political consequences of aging, *Annals of the American Academy of Political and Social Sciences*, 415 (September).

Garnaut, R. (2010), Macro-economic implications of the turning point, *China Economic Journal*, 3(2): 181–190.

Golley, J. and Tyers, R. (2012), Demographic dividends, dependencies, and economic growth in China and India, *Asian Economic Papers*, 11(3): 1–26.

Guillermo, A., Carmen, R. and Guillermo, C. (2002), Fear of floating, *The Quarterly Journal of Economics*, 117(2): 379–408. doi: 10.1162/003355302753650274.

Hu, A., Liu, S. and Ma, Z. (2012), Population aging, population growth and economic growth: Evidence from China's provincial panel data, *Population Research*, 36(3): 14–26.

İmrohoroğlu, A. (2007), Consequences of demographic change for rates of returns to capital, and the distribution of wealth and welfare: A comment, *Journal of Monetary Economics*, 54(1): 88–91.

International Labour Organization (ILO) (2009), Ageing societies: The benefits, and the costs, of living longer, *World of Work*, 67 (December). Available from: ilo.org/global/publications/magazines-and-journals/world-of-work-magazine/articles/WCM_041965/lang--en/index.htm.

International Monetary Fund (IMF) (2015), *World economic outlook: Uneven growth—Short and long-term factors*, April, Washington, DC: IMF. Available from: imf.org/external/pubs/ft/weo/2015/01/index.htm.

Johnston, L. (2012), Getting old after getting rich: Comparing China with Japan, *East Asia Forum*, 22 December. Available from: eastasiaforum.org/2012/12/22/getting-old-after-getting-rich-comparing-china-with-japan/.

Li, J. (2006), Is China getting old before getting rich?, *Population Research*, 30(6): 23–37.

Lutz, W., Sanderson, W. and Scherbov, S. (2008), The coming acceleration of global population ageing, *Nature*, 451(7179): 716–719.

Minami, R. (1968), The turning point in the Japanese economy, *The Quarterly Journal of Economics*, 82(3): 380–402.

Onofri, P. (2004), *The economics of an ageing population*, Cheltenham, UK: Edward Elgar.

Park, D., Lee, S. H. and Mason, A. (eds) (2012), *Aging, economic growth, and old-age security in Asia*, Cheltenham, UK: Edward Elgar.

Pham, C. S., Nguyen, X., Sgro, P. and Tang, X. (2016), Has China displaced its competitors in high-tech trade?, *World Economy*, 1(2016). doi: 10.1111/twec.12390.

Powell, J. L. and Cook, I. G. (2009), Global ageing in comparative perspective: A critical discussion, *International Journal of Sociology and Social Policy*, 29(7–8): 388–400.

Sanderson, W. C. and Scherbov, S. (2007), A new perspective on population aging, *Demographic Research*, 16(2): 27–58.

Siegel, J. S. (1980), On the demography of aging, *Demography*, 17(4): 345–364.

Stephenson, J. and Scobie, G. (2002), *The economics of population ageing*, No. 02/04, Wellington: New Zealand Treasury.

UNDATA (2016), Total fertility rate, *Glossary*, UNDATA. Available from: data.un.org/Glossary.aspx?q=total+fertility+rate.

United Nations (UN) (1956), *The aging of populations and its social and economic implications*, Population Studies No. 26, New York: United Nations.

United Nations (UN) (2002), *World population ageing: 1950–2050*, Department of Economic and Social Affairs, New York: United Nations. Available from: un.org/esa/population/publications/worldageing19502050/pdf/7introduction.pdf.

United Nations (UN) (2015), *World population prospects: The 2015 revision*, Population Division, Department of Economic and Social Affairs, New York: United Nations.

United Nations Population Fund (UNFPA) (2015), *Demographic dividend*, New York: UNFPA. Available from: unfpa.org/demographic-dividend.

Wang, D., Cai, F. and Zhang, X. (2004), Saving and growth effects of demographic transition, *Population Research*, (5): 2–11.

World Bank (2015), *World development indicators*, Washington, DC: The World Bank. Available from: data.worldbank.org/data-catalog/world-development-indicators.

World Bank (2016), *Live long and prosper? Aging in East Asia Pacific*, Washington, DC: The World Bank. Available from: openknowledge.worldbank.org/bitstream/handle/10986/23133/9781464804694.pdf.

Wu, C. (1986), *Discussions on population ageing*, Shenyang: Liaoning People's Publishing House.

Wu, C. and Du, P. (2006), *Population ageing in China: Changes and challenges*, Beijing: China Population Publishing House.

Appendix 10.1

Table A10.1 Country allocation by extended Wu framework typology, 2014

Country	1990	2000	2005	2010	2014
Afghanistan			4	4	4
Albania	4	2	2	2	2
Algeria	4	4	4	4	4
Andorra		3	3	3	3
Angola	4	4	4	4	4
Antigua and Barbuda	1	1	1	1	1
Argentina	2	2	2	2	2
Armenia	4	2	2	2	2
Aruba		1	1	1	1
Australia	1	1	1	1	1
Austria	1	1	1	1	1
Azerbaijan	4	4	4	4	4
Bahamas, The	3	3	3	3	1
Bahrain	3	3	3	3	3
Bangladesh	4	4	4	4	4
Barbados	1	1	1	1	1
Belarus	2	2	2	2	2
Belgium	1	1	1	1	1
Belize	4	4	4	4	4
Benin	4	4	4	4	4
Bhutan	4	4	4	4	4
Bolivia	4	4	4	4	4
Bosnia and Herzegovina		2	2	2	2
Botswana	4	4	4	4	4
Brazil	4	4	4	4	2
Brunei Darussalam	3	3	3	3	3
Bulgaria	2	2	2	2	2

Country	1990	2000	2005	2010	2014
Burkina Faso	4	4	4	4	4
Burundi	4	4	4	4	4
Cape Verde	4	4	4	4	4
Cambodia		4	4	4	4
Cameroon	4	4	4	4	4
Canada	1	1	1	1	1
Caribbean small states	4	4	2	2	2
Central African Republic	4	4	4	4	4
Chad	4	4	4	4	4
Channel Islands		1	1	1	1
Chile	4	2	2	1	1
China	4	4	2	2	2
Colombia	4	4	4	4	4
Comoros	4	4	4	4	4
Congo, Dem. Rep.	4	4	4	4	4
Congo, Rep.	4	4	4	4	4
Costa Rica	4	4	4	2	2
Cote d'Ivoire	4	4	4	4	4
Croatia		2	1	1	1
Cuba	2	2	2	2	2
Cyprus	1	1	1	1	1
Czech Republic	2	2	1	1	1
Denmark	1	1	1	1	1
Djibouti	4	4	4	4	4
Dominican Republic	4	4	4	4	4
Ecuador	4	4	4	4	4
Egypt, Arab Rep.	4	4	4	4	4
El Salvador	4	4	4	2	2
Equatorial Guinea	4	4	3	3	3
Eritrea		4	4	4	4
Estonia		2	1	1	1
Ethiopia	4	4	4	4	4
Fiji	4	4	4	4	4
Finland	1	1	1	1	1
France	1	1	1	1	1

Country	1990	2000	2005	2010	2014
French Polynesia	3	3	3	3	1
Gabon	3	4	4	4	4
Gambia, The	4	4	4	4	4
Georgia	2	2	2	2	2
Germany	1	1	1	1	1
Ghana	4	4	4	4	4
Greece	1	1	1	1	1
Grenada	2	2	2	2	2
Guatemala	4	4	4	4	4
Guinea	4	4	4	4	4
Guinea-Bissau	4	4	4	4	4
Guyana	4	4	4	4	4
Haiti		4	4	4	4
Honduras	4	4	4	4	4
Hong Kong SAR, China	1	1	1	1	1
Hungary		2	1	1	1
Iceland	1	1	1	1	1
India	4	4	4	4	4
Indonesia	4	4	4	4	4
Iran, Islamic Rep.	4	4	4	4	4
Iraq	3		4	4	4
Ireland	1	1	1	1	1
Israel	1	1	1	1	1
Italy	1	1	1	1	1
Jamaica	2	2	2	2	2
Japan	1	1	1	1	1
Jordan	4	4	4	4	4
Kazakhstan	4	4	2	4	4
Kenya	4	4	4	4	4
Kiribati	4	4	4	4	4
Korea, Rep.	3	1	1	1	1
Kosovo				4	4
Kuwait	3	3	3	3	3
Kyrgyz Republic	4	4	4	4	4
Lao PDR	4	4	4	4	4

Country	1990	2000	2005	2010	2014
Latvia		2	2	2	1
Lebanon	4	2	2	2	2
Lesotho	4	4	4	4	4
Liberia	4	4	4	4	4
Libya	3	4	4	3	4
Lithuania			2	1	1
Luxembourg	1	1	1	1	1
Macau SAR, China	3	1	1	1	1
Macedonia, FYR	2	2	2	2	2
Madagascar	4	4	4	4	4
Malawi	4	4	4	4	4
Malaysia	4	4	4	4	4
Maldives	4	4	4	4	4
Mali	4	4	4	4	4
Malta	1	1	1	1	1
Mauritania	4	4	4	4	4
Mauritius	4	4	4	2	2
Mexico	4	4	4	4	4
Micronesia, Fed. States	4	4	4	4	4
Moldova	2	2	2	2	2
Mongolia	4	4	4	4	4
Montenegro		2	2	2	2
Morocco	4	4	4	4	4
Mozambique	4	4	4	4	4
Myanmar					4
Namibia	4	4	4	4	4
Nepal	4	4	4	4	4
Netherlands	1	1	1	1	1
New Caledonia	3	3	3	1	2
New Zealand	1	1	1	1	1
Nicaragua	4	4	4	4	4
Niger	4	4	4	4	4
Nigeria	4	4	4	4	4
North America	1	1	1	1	1
Norway	1	1	1	1	1

Country	1990	2000	2005	2010	2014
Pakistan	4	4	4	4	4
Panama	4	4	4	4	2
Papua New Guinea	4	4	4	4	4
Paraguay	4	4	4	4	4
Peru	4	4	4	4	4
Philippines	4	4	4	4	4
Poland	2	2	2	1	1
Portugal	1	1	1	1	1
Puerto Rico	1	1	1	1	1
Qatar	3	3	3	3	3
Romania	2	2	2	2	2
Russian Federation	2	2	2	2	1
Rwanda	4	4	4	4	4
Samoa	4	4	4	4	4
Sao Tome and Principe		4	4	4	4
Saudi Arabia	3	4	3	3	3
Senegal	4	4	4	4	4
Serbia		2	2	2	2
Seychelles	4	2	1	2	3
Sierra Leone	4	4	4	4	4
Singapore	3	1	1	1	1
Slovakia Republic	2	2	1	1	1
Slovenia		1	1	1	1
Small states	4	4	4	4	4
Solomon Islands	4	4	4	4	4
Somalia	4				
South Africa	4	4	4	4	4
South Asia	4	4	4	4	4
South Sudan				4	4
Spain	1	1	1	1	1
Sri Lanka	4	4	4	2	2
St Lucia	2	2	2	2	2
St Vincent and the Grenadines	4	4	2	4	2
Sudan	4	4	4	4	4
Suriname	4	4	4	4	4

Country	1990	2000	2005	2010	2014
Swaziland	4	4	4	4	4
Sweden	1	1	1	1	1
Switzerland	1	1	1	1	1
Syrian Arab Republic	4	4	4	4	4
Tajikistan	4	4	4	4	4
Tanzania	4	4	4	4	4
Thailand	4	4	2	2	2
Timor-Leste		4	4	4	4
Togo	4	4	4	4	4
Tonga	4	4	4	4	4
Trinidad and Tobago	4	4	1	1	1
Tunisia	4	4	2	2	2
Turkey	4	4	4	2	2
Turkmenistan	4	4	4	4	4
Uganda	4	4	4	4	4
Ukraine	2	2	2	2	2
United Arab Emirates	3	3	3	3	3
United Kingdom	1	1	1	1	1
United States	1	1	1	1	1
Uruguay	2	2	2	1	1
Uzbekistan	4	4	4	4	4
Vanuatu	4	4	4	4	4
Venezuela, RB	4	4	4	3	3
Vietnam	4	4	4	4	4
West Bank and Gaza		4	4	4	4
Yemen, Rep.	4	4	4	4	4
Zambia	4	4	4	4	4
Zimbabwe	4	4	4	4	4

Note: Blank cells mean there are no data for the country.

Table A10.2 Population over-65 years descriptive statistics: Year and ageing transition category

Population over 65		1990	2000	2010	2014
Rich and old	Mean	12.62	13.11	14.59	15.99
	Std.	2.46	3.20	3.59	3.98
	Max.	17.78	18.07	22.94	25.71
	Min.	8.05	7.08	7.20	7.12
Rich and youth-filled	Mean	3.77	3.15	3.16	3.41
	Std.	1.80	1.80	1.96	2.14
	Max.	6.71	5.95	6.95	6.83
	Min.	1.17	1.06	0.69	1.04
Poor and old	Mean	9.81	11.42	10.85	11.08
	Std.	1.85	2.90	3.52	3.52
	Max.	13.16	16.58	18.37	19.73
	Min.	7.20	7.07	7.03	7.15
Poor and youth-filled	Mean	3.77	4.00	4.09	4.12
	Std.	0.99	1.22	1.27	1.27
	Max.	6.69	6.93	6.80	6.76
	Min.	2.21	1.91	2.27	2.31

Table A10.3 GDP per capita descriptive statistics: Year and ageing transition category

GDP per capita		1990	2000	2010	2014
Rich and old	Mean	19,202.64	23,591.87	35,669.88	37,153.97
	Std.	8,476.86	10,059.05	20,076.97	21,141.06
	Max.	38,332.15	48,826.55	102,863.10	97,363.09
	Min.	6,325.24	10,094.76	11,938.22	12,735.92
Rich and youth-filled	Mean	11,926.88	20,472.37	27,683.47	35,187.51
	Std.	5,521.09	7,835.89	17,566.21	27,479.56
	Max.	2,7989.3	34,207.54	70,870.23	97,518.61
	Min.	6,250.64	12,579.60	11,933.78	15,359.18
Poor and old	Mean	2,395.36	3,390.68	6,259.35	7,189.90
	Std.	898.73	2,262.03	2,814.76	3,001.91
	Max.	4,318.77	7,669.27	11,379.24	12,568.57
	Min.	972.09	354.00	1,631.54	2,233.77
Poor and youth-filled	Mean	1,032.69	1,451.07	2,631.43	2,950.55
	Std.	930.25	1,629.32	2,493.88	2,773.73
	Max.	5,265.50	8,808.88	11,124.00	12,270.39
	Min.	98.03	124.05	214.88	255.04

11. Testing Bubbles: Exuberance and collapse in the Shanghai A-share stock market

Zhenya Liu, Danyuanni Han and Shixuan Wang

Introduction

When a stock market bubble bursts, it can trigger financial crises that spread to the real economy. New and selectively complicated time-series methods are emerging that allow for better understanding of bubbles. In this chapter, we use the sup augmented Dickey–Fuller test (SADF) test developed by Phillips et al. (2011) and the generalised sup augmented Dickey–Fuller test (GSADF) test developed by Phillips et al. (2013) to identify bubbles in the Shanghai A-share stock market; the tests can also track a bubble's origination and termination dates. To our knowledge, this is the first time in the literature that the SADF and the GSADF have been applied to this stock market.

The study of speculative bubbles is a topic of long-standing interest in economics research. Many researchers have proposed various testing methods to analyse these dynamics from multiple perspectives. Lehkonen (2010) used the duration dependence test to examine weekly and monthly stock prices in China, and found that bubbles for Mainland China's stock markets are observable in weekly but not in monthly data. This result suggests that duration-dependent tests might not be appropriate for identifying bubbles in Mainland China. Yu et al. (2013) suggested combining the variance decomposition method with the dynamic autoregression method to obtain a measure of bubble risk. Unfortunately, their test methodology process is very tedious, which is not generally supported by economists.

Phillips et al. (2013) successfully developed a new test methodology for detecting multiple bubbles in continuous time- and date-stamping cycles, the GSADF, which is a generalised version of the SADF. The GSADF improves the flexibility of the rolling window of the SADF test. This improvement makes the test relatively suitable for multiple bubble phenomena with both a nonlinear structure and a break mechanism. Their method succeeded in correctly identifying famous episodes of exuberance and collapse over the period from January 1871 to December 2010 using Standard & Poor's (S&P) 500 stock market data.

Such results suggest that the SADF and GSADF tests are potentially more powerful in identifying the exuberance and collapse of multiple bubbles in the Shanghai A-share stock market than other test methodologies, and we therefore adopt these methods in this chapter. The chapter is organised as follows: section two reviews the literature on bubble test methodologies. Section three provides an overview of the theoretical model. Section four introduces the model specifications and date-stamping strategies behind the SADF and GSADF tests. Section five discusses the testing data. The empirical testing results of the SADF and GSADF tests are reported in section six. Section seven analyses the evolution of each periodically collapsing bubble in the Shanghai A-share stock market, and section eight provides a conclusion.

Literature review

The concept of a rational bubble was originally proposed by Blanchard (1979a) based on his work using an overlapping generations model. If the elasticity of the current price with respect to the next period's expected price is smaller than one unity, there should exist a forward solution that takes the stationarity requirement into account, and so the rational expectation solution is conditional on the relationship between the current price and the expected future price (Blanchard 1979a). Blanchard (1979b) subsequently constructed models for detecting speculative bubbles that adopted rational expectation assumptions. Flood and Garber (1980) published the completed rational expectations model for testing the first existence of a price-level bubble. As required by the rational expectations model, bubbles appear when the current price is determined mainly by the change in the expected market price. The rational expectations model here becomes the theoretical basis for measuring market bubbles. In this way, Blanchard and Watson (1982) explain rational bubbles as the deviation of asset prices from the fundamental value by use of a dynamic forecasting model, which follows from the fact that speculative bubbles are not ruled by rational behaviour, even though rational behaviour has a real effect on market fundamentals and also modifies the behaviour of prices (Blanchard and Watson 1982). But with the interference of irrationality variables, it is not easy to find a high-power procedure to test rational stock market bubbles.

In general, most econometric methodologies that seek to detect bubbles rely on rational expectations theories and are differentiated by varying testing techniques. These different techniques, however, produce diametrically opposing results. Two different variance bounds tests (Shiller 1981; West 1987) reached the same conclusion: rejecting the null hypothesis of no bubbles. But Diba and Grossman (1988a) consider that mixed testing results produced by a cointegration test probably reflect the low power of the tests rather than the presence of explosive rational bubbles in stock prices. Diba and Grossman (1988a) and Flood and Hodrick (1990) concur that the rejection of a no-bubbles hypothesis cannot be used to confirm the existence of bubbles, because the composite null hypothesis in fact already contains bubbles—because bubbles are expected to emerge gradually, hence a variance bounds test is not well suited for testing for bubbles. Another problem is that the test methods proposed by Shiller (1981), West (1987) and Diba and Grossman (1988a) are also restricted to linear testing. But through Monte Carlo simulation, Evans (1991) finds that popular linear testing strategies cannot detect periodically collapsing bubbles since highly nonlinear periodically collapsing bubbles usually do not have integration and cointegration properties. Evans's (1991) findings served to inspire further work towards constructing nonlinear testing models for successfully detecting periodic bubble collapses.

Taylor and David (1998) proposed a bubble test based on non-cointegration test. Ahmed et al. (1999) use a vector autoregression model to examine nonlinearities in stock market movement in 10 Pacific Rim countries and districts, although they do not offer certainty that the estimated fundamentals are correct. After learning from the existing test failure, Wu (1997) proposes that if a bubble can be treated as an unobserved state vector in the state-space model, the Kalman filter technique should easily detect market bubbles. Using S&P 500 stock market data, Wu (1997) explains many of the stock price deviations of the bull and bear markets of the twentieth century. Hall et al. (1999) suggest use of a generalised Dickey–Fuller (DF) test procedure that makes use of a class of Markov regime-switching models to achieve a nonlinear testing methodology. This method works because when the ADF regression parameters are allowed to switch values among different regimes, the ADF formulation will match the dynamic changing process of periodically collapsing bubbles. Kang (2010) opts for the smooth threshold autoregressive (STAR) model to identify bubbles in China's stock market. The empirical results show that the nonlinear motion of bubbles tracked by the STAR model closely links with real stock market volatility. Kang (2010) also acknowledges, however, that the STAR model cannot cope perfectly with nonlinear and asymmetrical dynamics of bubbles in China's stock markets.

More recently, Phillips et al. (2011) use a forward recursive right-sided unit root test to solve the issue proposed by Diba and Grossman (1988a). They conduct the DF statistics sequentially for date-stamping the origination and termination dates of bubbles. This new testing procedure is called the SADF test. Using the SADF test, Phillips et al. (2011) successfully document all explosive bubbles on the Nasdaq stock market in the 1990s. In the Monte Carlo experiment, the SADF test exhibits powerful superiority in detecting periodically collapsing bubbles among all tests from the study of Homm and Breitung (2012). Phillips et al.

(2014) again express confidence in the recursive right-tailed ADF test, given its use in detecting mildly explosive or sub-martingale behaviour in the data as a form of market diagnostic alert.

Phillips et al. (2013) developed the GSADF test, which has an econometric detection mechanism similar to the SADF test, as both rely on a recursive right-tailed ADF unit root test to detect periodically collapsing bubbles. The difference is that the SADF test has a relatively fixed window width with an identified starting point and changeable end point, while the GSADF test extends sample data coverage by a feasible rolling window size so as to overcome the weakness of the SADF test. This modification is very important. The SADF test is only able to identify a single bubble because of the fixed starting point design. The GSADF test design expands the detection range so that it is able to identify all episodes of exuberance and collapse in multiple bubbles. The GSADF test is, at this stage in the literature, likely to be the most advanced bubble detection strategy, which we will use for the Shanghai A-share stock market. We elaborate further in section four.

Theoretical model background

This section presents the basic theoretical background to models of bubble detection. Under the assumption of rational expectations and efficient markets, Lehkonen (2010) allows for deviations of stock prices from fundamental values, which are actually caused by rational rather than irrational traders. Blanchard and Watson (1982), Diba and Grossman (1988a) and Flood and Hodrick (1990) agree that deviation between the stock price and the fundamental value is a product of rationality-driven bubbles, and hence the size of the deviation is equivalent to the size of the bubble.

Under the efficient market hypothesis, the market will realise a 'no-arbitrage equilibrium' at a time when the expected return on risky assets is equal to the yield demanded by investors. We assume that the stock price at time t is P_t and the stock dividend at time t + 1 is D_{t+1}. Then, R_{t+1} is the return of an asset at time t + 1 and is influenced by the changes in stock price and dividend. We thus have Equation 11.1.

Equation 11.1

$$R_{t+1} = \frac{P_{t+1} - P_t + D_{t+1}}{P_t} = \frac{P_{t+1} + D_{t+1}}{P_t} - 1$$

Under rational expectations (Equation 11.2).

Equation 11.2

$$E_t(R_{t+1}) = r_{t+1}$$

In Equation 11.2, E_t denotes expectations mathematically given the information set at time t; r_{t+1} is equal to the time-varying required rate of return (Equation 12.3).

Equation 11.3

$$P_t = \frac{E_t(P_{t+1} + D_{t+1})}{1 + r_{t+1}}$$

Equation 11.3 implies that the current stock price is equal to the sum of expected future prices and dividends at time t + 1 divided by the required return rate. Using the iterative solution method, we can then solve the fundamental value of the asset under the equilibrium condition (Equation 12.4).

Equation 11.4

$$P_t^* = \sum_{i=1}^{\infty} \frac{E_t(D_{t+i})}{\prod_{j=1}^{i}(1+r_{t+j})}$$

From this, we can derive a new formula containing a bubble variable (Equation 12.5).

Equation 11.5

$$P_t = P_t^* + B_t$$

In Equation 11.5, B_t is the rational price bubble and $B_t = E_t(B_{t+1})/(1+r_{t+1})$. Equation 11.5 demonstrates that bubble factor, B_t, drives the stock price, P_t, to deviate from the fundamentals, P_t^*. On average, this bubble factor discounts at the required rate of return, r_{t+1}. Flood and Hodrick (1990) rewrite the bubble equation as Equation 11.6.

Equation 11.6

$$B_{t+1} = B_t * (1 + r_{t+1}) + \breve{B}_{t+1}$$

In Equation 11.6, $\breve{B}_{t+1} = B_{t+1} - E_t(B_{t+1})$. B_t is a stock price bubble and $\breve{B}_{t+1}$ reflects innovation in the bubble, which has a mean of zero.

In the rational speculative bubble model, Blanchard and Watson (1982) describe the formation and bursting process of bubbles as follows (Equation 11.7).

Equation 11.7

$$B_{t+1} = \begin{cases} \frac{(1 + r_{t+1})B_t}{\pi} + u_{t+1} & \begin{pmatrix} prob = \pi \\ prob = 1 - \pi \end{pmatrix} \\ u_{t+1} \end{cases}$$

From the above mathematical expressions, we can observe that the bubble factor, B_t, grows at a fixed rate with probability π and collapses with probability $1 - \pi$, back to the initial value, u_{t+1}, where u_{t+1} is a random variable with a mean of zero. If the bubble does not collapse, investors can realise a return of r_{t+1}, which equates compensation and risk values. In other words, when investors want to be compensated for overpayment (over the fundamental price) by future appreciation of the bubble component, the bubble component must be positive.

When rational bubbles occur in the stock market, this will induce market exuberance or financial crash. Phillips et al. (2013) conclude that financial exuberance derives from pricing errors or the deviation of stock price in response to fundamentals. In the literature, there are two conditions resulting in market exuberance. In the view of Phillips et al. (2013), the first condition is that market exuberance arises from behavioural factors and the second condition relates to the fact that fundamentals themselves might be highly sensitive to changes in the discount rate; its high sensitivity therefore forces the increases in the price to mimic the inflation of a bubble.

Evans (1991) believes that the standard linear test methodology fails to identify periodically collapsing bubbles in empirical testing, and that only nonlinear bubble detection models can avoid the aforementioned mistakes. Since then, Evans (1991) has suggested describing periodically collapsing bubbles in the following way (Equation 11.8).

Equation 11.8

$$B_{t+1} = (1 + r)B_t u_{t+1} \; if \; B_t \leq \alpha$$
$$B_{t+1} = [\delta + \pi^{-1}(1 + r)\theta_{t+1} * (B_t - (1 + r)^{-1}\delta)]u_{t+1} \; if \; B_t > \alpha$$

In Equation 11.8, δ and α are positive parameters with $0 < \delta < (1 + r)\alpha$, u_{t+1} is an exogenous independently and identically distributed positive random variable with $E_t u_{t+1} = 1$ and identically distributed Bernoulli process (independent of u), which takes the value 1 with probability π and 0 with probability $1 - \pi$, where $0 < \pi \leq 1$. If $B_t \leq \alpha$, the bubble will continually grow at a mean rate $(1 + r)$. But if $B_t > \alpha$, the bubble will rapidly increase at an explosive rate, $\pi^{-1}(1 + r)$, and it has a probability of $1 - \pi$ to collapse in each period. Once a bubble bursts, it drops back to the mean value, δ, and the process begins again. Hence, the evolution of bubbles is cyclical and recursive. Moreover and briefly, when π

is close to 1, the unit root test can locate the existence of a bubble. When π gradually becomes smaller, the unit root test loses its detection power, owing to the fact that when π contracts, the explosiveness of bubble component B_t becomes less significant. At this moment, the unit root test no longer works.

To effectively detect the explosiveness of a bubble using a unit root test, Phillips et al. (2011) adopt the recursive regression technique and the right-sided unit root test. These are more useful for detecting mild explosiveness or sub-martingale behaviour than the left-sided unit root test. The SADF test (Phillips et al. 2011) can directly test the stock price without calculating the fundamentals and rapidly capture the origin and terminus of multiple bubbles. In the light of the SADF test, Phillips et al. (2013) modify the test model to improve the flexibility and accuracy of test methodology. This new test methodology is referred to as the generalised sup ADF (GSADF) test. In the next section, the model specifications and date-stamping strategies of the SADF and GSADF tests will be introduced in detail.

Model specifications and date-stamping strategies of the SADF and GSADF tests

Model specifications

For the asset pricing equation for detecting financial bubbles, here we adopt the same equation as Phillips et al. (2013) (Equation 11.9).

Equation 11.9

$$P_t = \sum_{i=0}^{\infty}\left(\frac{1}{1+r_f}\right)^i E_t(D_{t+i} + U_{t+i}) + B_t$$

In Equation 11.9, P_t is the after-dividend price, D_t is the dividend, R_f is the risk-free interest rate and B_t is the bubble factor. Equation 11.9 is equivalent to Equation 11.4 and Equation 11.5, plus a new variable, U_t, denoting the unobservable fundamentals. We know that B_t satisfies the sub-martingale property, as follows (Equation 11.10).

Equation 11.10

$$E_t(B_{t+1}) = (1 + r_f)B_t$$

If there is no bubble at time t, $B_t = 0$, thus we have Equation 11.11.

Equation 11.11

$$P_t = \sum_{i=0}^{\infty}\left(\frac{1}{1+r_f}\right)^i E_t(D_{t+i} + U_{t+i}).$$

The degree of non-stationarity of the asset price is decided by the D_t and U_t. When U_t is at I (1) and D_t is stationary after differencing, empirical evidence of explosive behaviour in asset prices may be used to conclude the existence of bubbles (Phillips et al. 2013).

There is general agreement that bubble phenomena can occur during periods of market exuberance and collapse. Disagreement, however, centres on how to measure and predict the bubble. The SADF and GSADF tests measure the bubble based on the price–dividend ratio. Their derivation processes are taken from the model specification of Campbell and Shiller (1988).

Here we first take the logarithm of Equation 11.3 (Equation 11.12).

Equation 11.12

$$p_t = \kappa + \rho p_{t+1} + (1-\rho)d_{t+1} - r_{t+1}$$

Here, $\kappa = -\log(\rho) - (1-\rho)\log(1/\rho - 1)$. Note that $\rho = 1/[1 + e^{\overline{p-d}}]$ with $\overline{p-d}$ as the average price–dividend ratio. Variables p_t, d_t and r_t are natural logarithmic values of P_t, D_t and R_t. Solving Equation 11.12 by forward iteration and taking expectations yields Equation 11.13, which includes the logarithm of the price–dividend ratio (Equation 11.13).

Equation 11.13

$$p_t - d_t = \frac{\kappa}{1-\rho} + \sum_{i=0}^{\infty} \rho^i E_t(\Delta d_{t+1+i} - r_{t+1+i}) + \lim_{i\to\infty} \rho^i E_t(p_{t+i} - d_{t+i})$$

When we set $p_t^f = \frac{\kappa}{1-\rho} + \sum_{i=0}^{\infty} \rho^i E_t(\Delta d_{t+1+i} - r_{t+1+i})$ as the fundamental component and $b_t = \lim_{i\to\infty} \rho^i E_t(p_{t+i} - d_{t+i})$ as the rational bubble component, we arrive at Equation 11.14.

Equation 11.14

$$p_t - d_t = p_t^f + b_t$$

Further, $E_t(b_{t+1}) = \frac{1}{\rho} b_t = [1 + \exp(\overline{p - d})] b_t$, with $g = [1 + \exp(\overline{p - d})] > 0$. And the logarithm of the bubble component has the growth rate g.

In the absence of a bubble component, condition $b_t = 0$, since $p_t = d_t + p_t^f$. From the equation of p_t^f, we can obtain Equation 11.15.

Equation 11.15

$$d_t - p_t = -p_t^f = -\frac{\kappa - r}{1 - \rho} - \sum_{i=0}^{\infty} \rho^i E_t(\Delta d_{t+1+i})$$

When p_t^f is ruled out from stock price p_t, the residual component should be stationary. If the residual part is non-stationary, this indicates there is a bubble in p_t.

When explosive bubbles are presented (that is, $b_t \neq 0$), p_t is determined by b_t, irrespective of whether d_t is an integrated process I (1) or a stationary process I (0) (Phillips et al. 2011). In other words, the stock price follows a non-stationary process. Thus, the dynamics of $p_t - d_t$ are determined by p_t^f and b_t. If the variables in p_t^f have stationary process I (0), there is only b_t remaining with a relationship with the explosiveness in $p_t - d_t$. That means a test for the explosive behaviour of $p_t - d_t$ is also a test for the bubble component b_t.

Although the SADF and GSADF tests share a common testing variable, the price–dividend ratio, the difference between them is at the rolling window setting. The basic idea behind the GSADF test is specifically to change the rolling window widths, first, by forward recursive progression, and then get the SADF test sequence, and, last, to find the maximum value from its SADF test sequence and compare this with the corresponding SADF critical value to decide whether to reject the null hypothesis. Phillips et al. (2013) assume a random walk (or, more generally, a martingale) process with an asymptotically negligible drift. The form is written as Equation 11.16.

Equation 11.16

$$y_t = cT^{-\lambda} + \theta y_{t-1} + u_t, u_t \sim i.i.d. N(0, \sigma^2), \theta = 1$$

In Equation 11.16, c is constant, $\lambda > 1/2$ serves as a localising coefficient that controls the magnitude of the drift and T is the sample size with $T \to \infty$. Obviously, this equation is a unit root procedure without a trend item, but with a gradually disappearing intercept.

If the initial sample proportion of the recursive approach is r_0 and the total sample is T, the test sample size is expressed as $t = \lfloor Tr_0 \rfloor$, where $\lfloor \cdot \rfloor$ takes the integer part of the input variable. From the first observation, Phillips et al. (2011) set the recursive right-sided unit root test with sample data to $t = \lfloor Tr \rfloor$. The SADF test relies mainly on recursive calculations of the ADF statistics with a fixed starting point and a changeable width window. Suppose that r_1 is the starting point of the test and r_2 is the end point, $r_w = r_2 - r_1$ is the window size of the regression. The empirical model is defined as Equation 11.17.

Equation 11.17

$$\Delta y_t = \alpha_{r_1}^{r_2} + \beta_{r_1}^{r_2} y_{t-1} + \sum_{i=1}^{k} \psi_{r_1,i}^{r_2} \Delta y_{t-i} + \varepsilon_t$$

In Equation 11.17, k is the lag order and $\varepsilon_t \sim i.i.d.(0, \sigma_{r_1,r_2}^2)$. $ADF_{r_1}^{r_2}$ denotes the ADF statistic value (t-value) of the equation.

The SADF test requires a repeated ADF test on a forward expanding sample sequence. The test result obtained is the sup value of the corresponding ADF statistics sequence (Phillips et al. 2013). Under this model specification, the starting point is fixed at r_0; in contrast, the end point, r_2, can freely expand from r_0 to 1. The SADF statistic can be written as Equation 11.18.

Equation 11.18

$$SADF(r_0) = \sup_{r_2 \in [r_0, 1]} ADF_0^{r_2}$$

The GSADF test is distinct from the SADF test in that it allows the starting point and the end point to change simultaneously. Therefore, the starting point, r_1, can vary within the range $[0, r_2 - r_0]$ and the size of window width, r_w, also flexibly shifts within the bounds of r_1 and r_2. Since this modification extends the range of subsample data, the GSADF test is more accurate for detecting multiple bubbles than the SADF test. The GSADF test is defined as follows (Equation 11.19).

Equation 11.19

$$GSADF(r_0) = \sup_{\substack{r_2 \in [r_0, 1] \\ r_1 \in [0, r_2 - r_0]}} \{ADF_{r_1}^{r_2}\}$$

The asymptotic GSADF distribution might be affected by the smallest window width, r_0, according to the limit theory of the SADF test. As a result, the starting point, r_0, is determined by T, which is the total number of sample observations.

Phillips et al. (2013) summarise the negative relationship between r_0 and T. If T is small, r_0 needs to be large enough to ensure there are enough observations for adequate initial estimation. If T is large, r_0 can be set as a smaller number so that the test does not miss any opportunity to detect an early explosive episode.

Data-stamping strategies

We summarise the data-stamping strategies used by Phillips et al. (2011, 2013) for the SADF test and the GSADF test.

To detect bubbles, an information set is defined as $I_{[T_r]} = \{y_1, y_2, \ldots, y_{[T_r]}\}$. In the current information set, $I_{[T_r]}$, this could include multiple bubbles, a single bubble or no bubble. Phillips et al. (2011) propose a backward SADF test on $I_{[T_r]}$ to enhance the accuracy of bubble detection and to avoid pseudo stationary behaviour. The backward SADF test has the same arithmetical logic as the GSADF test, except for having a different test direction. Specifically, the backward SADF test chooses a fixed end point at r_2, which is the opposite of the forward SADF test, which sets a fixed starting point of r_0. To this end, the starting point of the backward SADF test becomes a changeable point varying from 0 to $r_2 - r_0$. The backward SADF statistic can accordingly be defined as Equation 11.20.

Equation 11.20

$$BSADF_{r_2}(r_0) = \sup_{r_1 \in [0, r_2 - r_0]} \{ADF_{r_1}^{r_2}\}$$

If $BSADF_{r_2}(r_0)$ is bigger than the corresponding critical value of the standard ADF statistic at time Tr_2, this time point, denoted by Tr_e, is identified as the start date of a bubble. If, after time $\lfloor T\hat{r_e} \rfloor + \log(T)$, is smaller than the critical value of the standard ADF statistic, this is the termination date of the bubble denoted by $\lfloor T\hat{r_f} \rfloor$. Phillips et al. (2011) impose a condition that the duration of a bubble should be longer than a slowly varying quantity, $L_T = \log(T)$. The condition nicely excludes short-term volatility in the fitted autoregressive coefficient and takes the data frequency into consideration (Phillips et al. 2013). From the above discussion, we can thus use the following formulations to represent the origination and termination times of a bubble (Equations 12.21 and 12.22).

Equation 11.21

$$\hat{r_e} = \inf_{\mathrm{r}_2 \in [\mathrm{r}_0, 1]} \left\{r_2 \colon ADF_{r_2} > cv_{r_2}^{\beta_T}\right\}$$

Equation 11.22

$$\hat{r_f} = \inf_{r_2 \in [\hat{r_e} + \log(T)/T, 1]} \left\{ r_2 : ADF_{r_2} < cv_{r_2}^{\beta_T} \right\}$$

In these equations, $cv_{r_2}^{\beta_T}$ is the 100*(1- β_T)% critical value of the ADF statistic based on $\lfloor Tr_2 \rfloor$ observations.

Similarly, when Equation 11.20 relaxes the limitation of supremum value r_2, in this way, r_2 has a feasible range from r_0 to 1. We obtain the date-stamping strategy of the GSADF test (Equation 11.23).

Equation 11.23

$$GSADF(r_0) = \sup_{r_2 \in [r_0, 1]} \left\{ BSADF_{r_2}(r_0) \right\}$$

The explosiveness observation of bubbles for the GSADF test is based on the backward SADF statistic, $BSADF_{r_2}(r_0)$. Phillips et al. (2013) assume that the interval time between the origination date and the termination date is $\lfloor T\hat{r_e} \rfloor + \delta \log(T)$, where δ is a frequency dependent parameter. The estimated equations of the bubble period under the GSADF test are Equations 12.24 and 12.25.

Equation 11.24

$$\hat{r_e} = \inf_{r_2 \in [r_0, 1]} \left\{ r_2 : BSADF_{r_2}(r_0) > scv_{r_2}^{\beta_T} \right\}$$

Equation 11.25

$$\hat{r_f} = \inf_{r_2 \in [\hat{r_e} + \delta \log(T)/T, 1]} \left\{ r_2 : BSADF_{r_2}(r_0) < scv_{r_2}^{\beta_T} \right\}$$

Formally, $scv_{r_2}^{\beta_T}$ is the 100 (1- β_T)% critical value of the SADF statistic on the basis of $\lfloor Tr_2 \rfloor$ observations. The significance level, β_T, has an opposite approach with the sample size, T. If T goes to zero, the significant level, β_T, moves to infinity. If the sample size, T, approaches infinity, β_T goes to zero.

The data

The empirical data employed are the price index of the Shanghai A-share stock market and the dividend yield of the 1,061 listed companies in the Shanghai A-share stock market. The frequency of our data is monthly. Before 2000, most companies listed on the Shanghai A-share stock market did not pay out dividends, so these data are unavailable. Hence, the sample period starts from January 2000 to July 2015. Specifically, the monthly dividend yield time series of the Shanghai A-share stock market is calculated by summing the dividend yields of 1,061 listed companies. Then, the price–dividend ratio time series is calculated to reflect the relationship between the asset price and market fundamentals. All data are downloaded from *Datastream*.

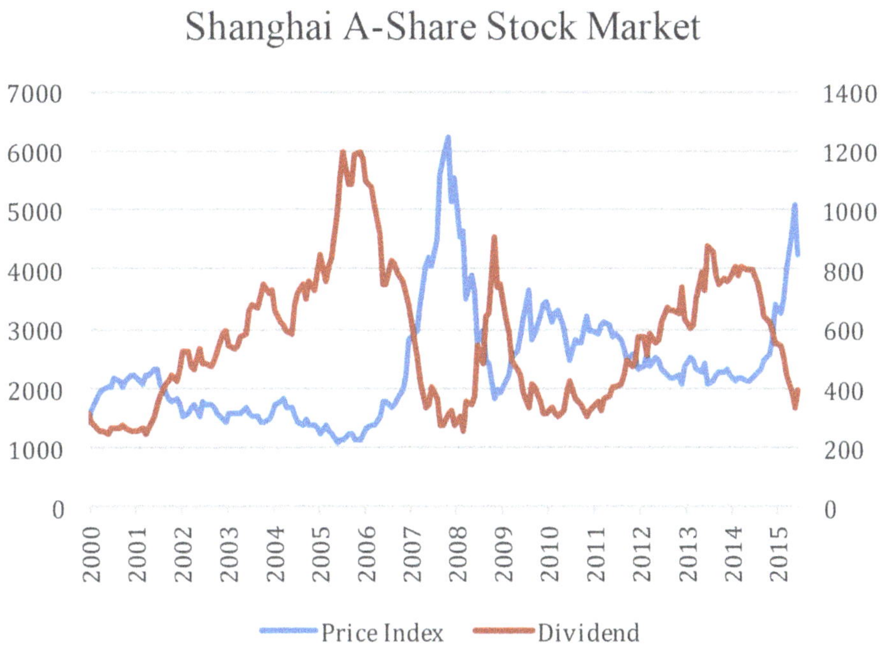

Figure 11.1 Time series of the price index (left axis) and dividend yield (right axis) of the Shanghai A-share stock market

Source: Datastream.

In Figure 11.1, there are two series. The blue line denotes the evolution of the price index. Primarily, the Shanghai A-share stock price index was stable from January 2000 to January 2006 and rose suddenly to 6,395.75 points on 16 October 2007, before rapidly dropping to 2,000 points in September 2008. After experiencing this period of volatility, the A-share market maintained a period of relatively stable fluctuation for six years, and began to enter another period of rapid increase in October 2014. The red line represents the dividend yield and shows a pattern that is generally opposite to that of the blue line. When the stock price increases, the dividend yield decreases, and vice versa.

Figure 11.2 Price–dividend ratio of the Shanghai A-share market

Source: Datastream.

Figure 11.2 displays our testing data, the price–dividend ratio of the Shanghai A-share market, from January 2000 to July 2015. Generally, the Shanghai A-share price–dividend ratio fluctuated dramatically during our sample period. Before 2006, it gradually decreased and then abruptly jumped more than 20 in 2007. After the Global Financial Crisis in 2008, the price–dividend ratio contracted sharply to around three. During 2009–12, it fluctuated between 4 and 11, and started to climb again until 2014.

Empirical testing of the SADF and GSADF tests

The SADF test

Using Eviews 8.0 software, we apply the SADF test to price–dividend ratio time series. The results are presented in Table 11.1.

Table 11.1 Critical values of the SADF test

		Statistics	P-value
SADF		2.815	0.035
Test critical values	*99% level*	7.373	
	95% level	2.232	
	90% level	1.672	

Notes: Critical values of the SADF test are calculated from a Monte Carlo simulation with 2,000 replications (sample size 187). The initial window size is four.

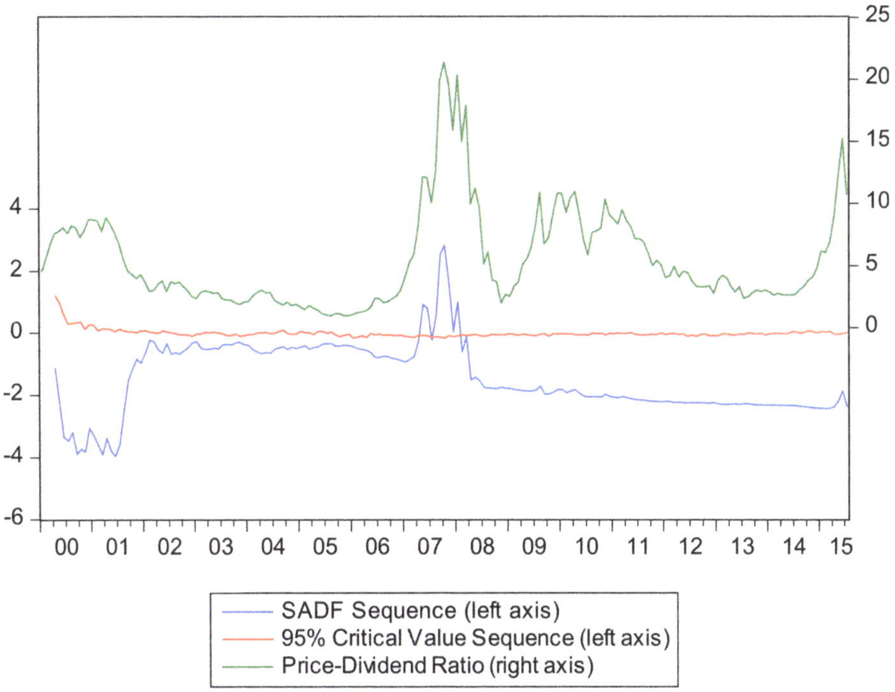

Figure 11.3 Date-stamping bubble periods in the Shanghai A-share modified price–dividend ratio: The SADF test

Source: Datastream.

Table 11.1 shows that the SADF statistic value, 2.815, is greater than the critical values at the 95 per cent and 90 per cent confidence levels. This indicates that we cannot reject the null hypothesis below a 95 per cent confidence level and, in other words, that the Shanghai A-share stock market is characterised by periodic bubbles. From Figure 11.3, it is evident that the blue line exceeds the red line, which indicates one periodic collapsing bubble occurred from March 2007 to February 2008.

The GSADF test

We applied the GSADF test to the price–dividend ratio (Table 11.2).

Table 11.2 Critical values of the GSADF test

		Statistics	P-value
GSADF		35.735	0.011
Test critical values	*99% level*	36.403	
	95% level	14.180	
	90% level	10.080	

Notes: Critical values of the GSADF test are calculated from a Monte Carlo simulation with 2,000 replications (sample size 187). The initial window size is four.

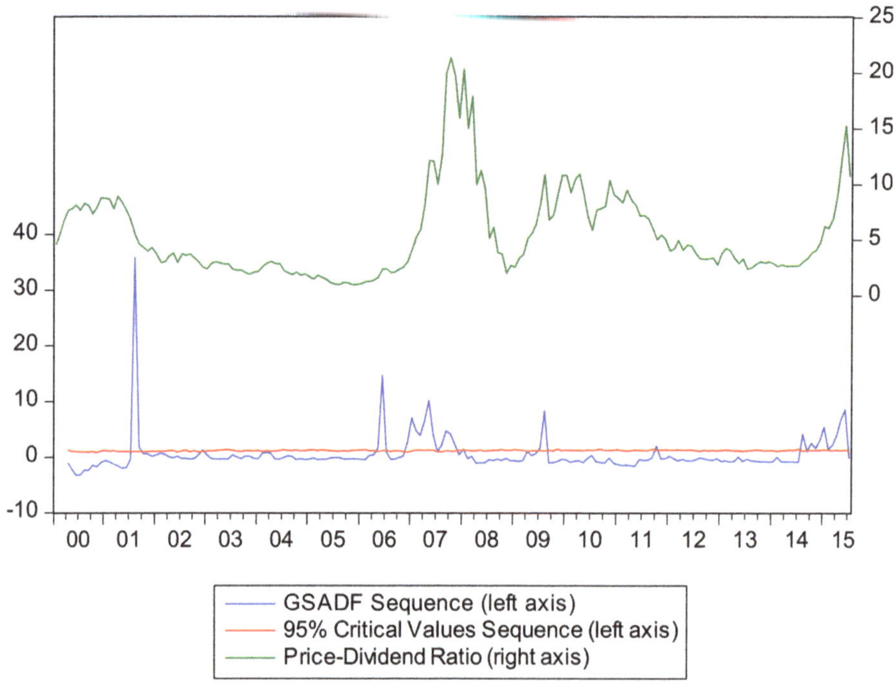

Figure 11.4 Date-stamping bubble periods in the Shanghai A-share modified price–dividend ratio: The GSADF test

Source: Datastream.

From Table 11.2, we see that the GSADF statistic obtained from sample data is 35.74, which is bigger than the two critical values at the 5 per cent and 10 per cent significance levels. Thus, we can reject the null hypothesis of no bubbles. And, in fact, Figure 11.4 clearly shows there were three periodically collapsing bubbles between January 2000 and July 2015.

The bubble between June and September 2001 had the shortest duration, which was possibly the result of media attention, government intervention or some other factor. Particularly, this bubble increase arose from positive news published by the China Securities Regulatory Commission (CSRC) that the B-share stock market was to officially open to domestic investors from February 2001. With the encouragement of this policy, the Shanghai and Shenzhen stock indexes rose together. The later collapse was also provoked by media reports—but this time, by bad news. The CSRC announced the issuance of a listed company management approach and a plan to reduce state-owned shares. This cycle of exuberance and collapse was therefore entirely manipulated by the CSRC, embodying the characteristic of a 'policy market'. Given there were no serious consequences, it is possible for the CSRC to deliberately guide this volatility. In the next section, to make our analysis more meaningful, we neglect the small, short bubble and focus on two significant periodically collapsing bubbles—namely, the subprime mortgage crisis bubble (October 2006 – January 2009) and the new bubble period (May 2014 – July 2015).

Analysis of the exuberance and collapse of multiple bubbles

The subprime mortgage crisis bubble period (October 2006 – January 2009)

Under the impetus of expectations of renminbi appreciation and the share-split reform policy, the Shanghai A-share stock market began a slow upward trend in the first half of 2006. By June 2006, the stock price had already risen to the critical 1,700 points level. As the stock market had just bailed out a bear market at that time, the A-share index maintained around 1,700 points for three months. Starting in October 2006, easing monetary policy and looser credit policy created a large amount of liquid and ideal funds, which helped to instigate a flood of investment in the stock market. The Shanghai A-share stock market provided an appealing investment channel for domestic individual investors. Consequently, the Shanghai A-share index kept increasing strongly and finally broke through 6,000 points in November 2007. In fact, in 2006 and

2007, the Shanghai A-share stock price grew by as much as 80 per cent every year. For comparison, in same period, the S&P 500 stock price increased by only about 20 per cent.

Table 11.3 compares the monthly growth rates of the Shanghai A-share price index and the S&P 500. The Shanghai A-share price index is much more volatile than the S&P 500 and generally had a much higher monthly growth rate during this bubble period. It shows that the Shanghai A-share price index maintained an average monthly growth rate of 8.5 per cent, and the highest growth rate reached was 27.4 per cent, in January 2007. The highest stock price, in November 2007, was 4.1 times the lowest point, which was in May 2006. The price-to-earnings (PE) ratios of many stocks were over 100 per cent. Such a high PE ratio requires a stronger earnings growth rate and a higher return on equity (ROE). Typically, a ROE sits at around 10 per cent, but the average ROE of Shanghai A-share listed companies is only 6.9 per cent. From the perspective of the PE ratio and the ROE, the stock price has greatly deviated from the listed companies' fundamental value.

Table 11.3 Shanghai A-share price index and S&P 500 and their monthly growth rates

Period (first day of month)	Shanghai A-share price index	Monthly growth rate (%)	S&P 500	Monthly growth rate (%)
May-06	1,511.7	-	1,305.2	-
Jun-06	1,769.6	17.1	1,285.7	–1.5
Jul-06	1,784.5	0.8	1,280.2	–0.4
Aug-06	1,682.5	–5.7	1,270.9	–0.7
Sep-06	1,720.5	2.3	1,311.0	3.2
Oct-06	1,840.3	7.0	1,331.3	1.5
Nov-06	1,949.8	6.0	1,367.8	2.7
Dec-06	2,208.9	13.3	1,396.7	2.1
Jan-07	2,815.1	27.4	1,418.3	1.5
Feb-07	2,926.8	4.0	1,445.9	1.9
Mar-07	2,937.8	0.4	1,403.2	–3.0
Apr-07	3,418.7	16.4	1,424.6	1.5
May-07	4,035.1	18.0	1,486.3	4.3
Jun-07	4,197.1	4.0	1,536.3	3.4
Jul-07	4,027.1	–4.1	1,519.4	–1.1
Aug-07	4,510.8	12.0	1,465.8	–3.5
Sep-07	5,587.3	23.9	1,474.0	0.6
Oct-07	5,827.7	4.3	1,547.0	5.0
Nov-07	6,209.4	6.6	1,508.4	–2.5

Source: Datastream.

To reduce the risk of a stock market crash, Chinese regulatory authorities imposed policies that sought to reduce the explosiveness of bubbles in the stock market. For example, the People's Bank of China (PBC) has raised the renminbi deposit reserve rate 10 times since the beginning of 2007. That year, the statutory deposit reserve rate increased from 9 per cent to 13 per cent. However, the rising deposit reserve rate did not decrease excessive liquidity in the stock market. A large volume of hot money continued to flow into the Shanghai A-share stock market, driving the stock price continuously up. Besides currency appreciation supporting the value of the renminbi-denominated A-share stock market, the price increases were driven largely by expectations of renminbi appreciation. Compared with other investor markets, the stock market has provided a relatively quick and easy way to make money, especially due to the low barriers to entrance and exit.

At the end of 2007, global financial turbulence caused major international stock markets to fall sharply. From November 2007 to January 2009, the Shanghai A-share stock price fell 224.8 per cent, from 6,209 points to 1,911 points, and so set an international milestone as the largest-ever such share price decline in history. That is, the burst of the periodically collapsing bubble was without precedent. With limitations on short selling, the stock price reveals mainly good news, such as the split-share reform and the expectation of renminbi appreciation. When the hidden bad news was released comparatively suddenly, stocks didn't just drop—they dropped heavily (Chen and Zhang 2009).

The new bubble period (May 2014 – July 2015)

The GSADF test helped us to identify a second periodically collapsing bubble that was already forming in early 2014. On the last trading day of 2013, the Shanghai A-share price index closed at 2,116 points. This was the fourth consecutive year that the Shanghai A-share stock market ended lower than it had started. From May 2014, it had started to rise again and, from mid-2014 to June 2015, the A-share stock price grew from 2,121 points to 5,056 points, or 138.3 per cent.

There are several sources of this recent rally. First, after the subprime crisis, China retained a steady economic growth rate, while the growth rate of many economies, especially high-income ones, fell significantly during the crisis and have not recovered. This climate of higher macroeconomic growth has provided favourable conditions for the rise of the A-share index. Meanwhile, the PBC, as China's central bank, has, since the subprime crisis, imposed policies for monetary easing and to encourage loose credit (Song et al. 2015). Such policies increased market liquidity, which helped the A-share stock market rebound. Additionally, the CSRC introduced new policies in 2014, including reform of the securities issuance system, approving the issuance of preferred stock and opening Shanghai–Hong Kong Stock Connect—all of which helped to boost confidence in the stock market.

The Shanghai A-share stock price had climbed to 5,166 points by mid-June 2015, and many individual investors hoped it would return to 6,000 points as in 2007. But, by 19 June, the Shanghai A-share market had fallen below 4,500 points to close at 4,478 points; the weekly decline was as high as 13.32 per cent, making this the biggest weekly decline since 2008. Until 3 July, the Shanghai A-share market continued to fall, closing at 3,686 points.

These trends are similar to those during the burst of the previous periodically collapsing bubble, though there are some new characteristics. The problem of an overly high PE ratio is particularly prominent. The PE ratio of the Shanghai A-share stock market was up 22 times by June. In general, a high PE ratio represents high valuation. If there is not a proper ROE matching the PE ratio, the Shanghai A-share stock market should, with high probability, fall. Again, the newly opened stock accounts in the first half of 2015 were close to those of 2007. Under China's high-leverage stimulus, herding behaviour drives many institutional investors to sell their shares. When the stock index falls, the leveraged funds might be required to liquidate.

The two periodically collapsing bubbles identified by the GSADF test have many similarities in their formation, development and bursting phases. Bubbles often appear when a stock market has sufficient liquidity. Initially, the existence of a bubble promotes the value of the stock market. Thereafter, a high PE ratio and turnover rate and some irrational behaviour induce the bubble to gradually inflate until it is out of control. Ultimately, bad news or a sudden market crisis will rapidly puncture the bubble and destroy the false prosperity of the stock market.

Conclusion

Our study using the GSADF test confirms the two prominent episodes of exuberance and collapse in the Shanghai A-share stock market, while the SADF test finds only a single bubble. The empirical test results, in other words, suggest that the GSADF test is, in practical terms, better than the SADF test to detect multiple bubbles.

The evolution of the periodically collapsing bubbles are analysed in depth. The first bubble revolves around the subprime mortgage crisis between October 2006 and January 2009. The second is a more recent bubble, extending from May 2014 to July 2015. These have many common characteristics in terms of the process of bubble formulation, development and the bursting phase, such as a high PE ratio, high turnover and some irrational behaviour.

In sum, this chapter confirms two bubbles in the Shanghai A-share stock market retrospectively using the GSADF test. The use of these results for understanding past bubbles in the Shanghai A-share stock market is significant and meaningful; however, this method can only be employed to identify previous bubbles. Further research may wish to explore methods to predict future bubbles.

References

Ahmed, E., Rosser, J. B. and Uppal, J. Y. (1999), Evidence of nonlinear speculative bubbles in Pacific-Rim stock markets, *The Quarterly Review of Economics and Finance*, 39(1): 21–36.

Blanchard, O. J. (1979a), Backward and forward solutions for economies with rational expectations, *The American Economic Review*, 69(2): 114–118.

Blanchard, O. J. (1979b), Speculative bubbles, crashes and rational expectations, *Economics Letters*, 3(1979): 387–389.

Blanchard, O. J. and Watson, M. W. (1982), *Bubbles, rational expectations and financial markets*, NBER Working Paper Series No. 945, Cambridge, Mass.: National Bureau of Economic Research.

Campbell, J. Y. and Shiller, R. J. (1988), The dividend–price ratio and expectations of future dividends and discount factors, *The Review of Financial Studies*, 1(3): 195–228.

Chen, G. J. and Zhang, Y. J. (2009), Heterogeneous beliefs, short sale restriction and China's stock market plunge phenomenon research, *Finance Research*, 346(4): 80–91.

Diba, B. T. and Grossman, H. I. (1988a), Explosive rational bubbles in stock prices?, *The American Economic Review*, 78(3): 520–530.

Diba, B. T. and Grossman, H. I. (1988b), The theory of rational bubbles in stock prices, *The Economic Journal*, (98): 746–754.

Evans, G. W. (1991), Pitfalls in testing for explosive bubbles in asset prices, *The American Economic Review*, 4(81): 922–930.

Flood, R. P. and Garber, P. M. (1980), Market fundamentals versus price level bubbles: The first tests, *Journal of Political Economy*, 88(4): 745–770.

Flood, R. P. and Hodrick, R. J. (1990), On testing for speculative bubbles, *Journal of Economic Perspectives*, 4(2): 85–101.

Gurkaynak, R. S. (2008), Econometric tests of asset price bubbles: Taking stock, *Journal of Economic Surveys*, 22(1): 166–186.

Hall, S. G., Psaradakis, Z. and Sola, M. (1999), Detecting periodically collapsing bubbles: A Markov-switching unit root test, *Journal of Applied Econometrics*, (14): 143–154.

Homm, U. and Breitung, J. (2012), Testing for speculative bubbles in stock markets: A comparison of alternative methods, *Journal of Financial Econometrics*, 10(1): 198–231.

Hu, C. S. and Wang, Y. F. (2013), Noise trading and stock returns: Evidence from China, *China Finance Review International*, 3: 301–315.

Kang, Z. Y. (2010), Chinese stock market bubbles test based on STAR model, *Academic Monthly*, 42(12): 83–89.

Lehkonen, H. (2010), Bubbles in China, *International Review of Financial Analysis*, (19): 113–117.

Phillips, P. C. B., Shi, S. P. and Yu, J. (2013), *Testing for multiple bubbles: Historical episodes of exuberance and collapse in the S&P 500*, Economics & Statistics Working Paper Series No. 4, July, Singapore: Singapore Management University.

Phillips, P. C. B., Shi, S. P. and Yu, J. (2014), Specification sensitivity in right-tailed unit root testing for explosive behaviour, *Oxford Bulletin of Economics and Statistics*, 76(3): 315–333.

Phillips, P. C. B., Wu, Y. and Yu, J. (2011), Explosive behavior in the 1990s Nasdaq: When did exuberance escalate asset values?, *International Economic Review*, (52): 201–226.

Shiller, R. J. (1981), Do stock prices move too much to be justified by subsequent changes in dividends?, *American Economic Review*, (71): 421–436.

Song, L., Garnaut, R., Fang, C. and Johnston, L. (2015), *China's domestic transformation in a global context*, Canberra: ANU Press.

Tan, L., Chiang, T. C., Mason, J. R. and Nelling, E. (2008), Herding behavior in Chinese stock markets: An examination of A and B shares, *Pacific-Basin Finance Journal*, (16): 61–77.

Taylor, M. P. and David, A. P. (1998), Periodically collapsing stock price bubbles: A robust test, *Economics Letters*, (61): 221–228.

West, K. D. (1987), A specification test for speculative bubbles, *The Quarterly Journal of Economics*, 102(3): 553–580.

Wu, Y. R. (1997), Rational bubbles in the stock market: Accounting for the US stock-price volatility, *Economic Inquiry*, April: 309–319.

Yu, M., Pi, D. Y. and Zhou, R. X. (2013), A study on speculative bubbles test by using variance decompositions methods in the Chinese stock market, *Economy and Management*, 27(11): 40–45.

12. Changing Patterns of Corporate Leverage in China: Evidence from listed companies

Ivan Roberts and Andrew Zurawski[1]

Introduction

Since the mid-2000s, Chinese corporate debt has risen sharply as a proportion of gross domestic product (GDP)—from around 100 per cent to over 150 per cent in 2014. By comparison, this ratio is 67 per cent in the United States and 103 per cent in Japan.[2] Historically, the ratio of debt to income has often been considered a useful indicator for assessing the risk of future banking crises (Borio and Lowe 2002; Drehmann and Juselius 2013). The rapid build-up of debt in China has therefore been increasingly flagged as a risk to financial and macroeconomic stability (Walter and Howie 2011; Pettis 2013).

The rise in corporate debt in recent years has been pronounced for state-owned firms and is frequently attributed to the credit-fuelled macroeconomic stimulus of 2008–09. According to Huang and Bosler (2014: 1), 'the debt surge [was] the result of a deliberate state-driven stimulus program to stave off economic collapse in the aftermath of the global financial crisis'. These countercyclical policies are widely thought to have favoured state-owned enterprises (SOEs) at the expense of the private sector.

In response to rising corporate and government debt, deleveraging has become an explicit focus of macroeconomic policy in China. In late 2015, the Chinese Government listed 'deleveraging' among its structural reform objectives for 2016. In the draft plan for national economic and social development that was delivered to the National People's Congress in 2016, the National Development and Reform Commission (NDRC) observed that 'the debt ratios of enterprises are ... rising; illegal fundraising is becoming more frequent; and hidden financial risks are mounting' (NDRC 2016: 20). The Governor of the People's Bank of China (PBC), Zhou Xiaochuan, has emphasised that to manage overall indebtedness, 'the key is to address the excessive corporate leverage ratio' (PBC 2016).

1 The authors are from Economic Group. The views expressed in this chapter are those of the authors and should not be attributed to the Reserve Bank of Australia.

2 These estimates are based on data provided by BIS (2016) and individual country GDP data.

This chapter examines trends in the capital structure of more than 2,000 mainland-listed Chinese non-financial companies over the past 15 years and the firm-level drivers of leverage decisions. The patterns in this panel are not necessarily representative of the much larger non-listed corporate sector, for which we lack similarly disaggregated data. Specifically, the total debt accumulated by our sample of listed companies accounts for less than 10 per cent of the broad credit stock in China.[3] There are also reasons to think that listed firms are special, because, for example, they are likely to be among the better performing mainland firms and have greater access to bank credit and bond or equity finance. Even so, growth in listed company debt or total liabilities has tracked aggregate credit growth reasonably closely in recent years. In addition, certain measures of indebtedness, such as the ratio of listed company debt to earnings, have moved in a manner that is consistent with aggregate estimates of the corporate debt ratio for the Chinese economy.

Nonetheless, a careful examination of listed company data reveals a more nuanced picture than that embodied in conventional narratives surrounding the build-up of debt in China. Our analysis confirms that the leverage of listed state-owned or state-controlled companies ('state firms') has risen relative to that of private firms since the late 2000s. This has been accompanied by a sharp decline in the operating performance of state firms over the same period relative to private firms. The relative trends in leverage for state- and private-listed firms are especially apparent for the broader measures of leverage that account for rising non-debt liabilities, such as accounts payable and advance receipts. Yet we find that parts of the private sector (particularly firms that have listed since 2008) have also contributed to the rise in leverage. While state firms have continued to account for the bulk of listed company leverage, there is some evidence of deleveraging among the more highly leveraged of these firms. Moreover, the rising share of corporate sector assets in private hands has also contributed to a sizeable shift in the distribution of the increase in listed company leverage towards private firms during the past few years.

By industry, the pattern that emerges highlights the importance of the real estate and construction industries, and particularly state firms in those industries, in driving the rise in corporate leverage since the late 2000s. In part, this reflects the increasing weight of real estate and construction firms, as measured by the proportional value of their assets, in our listed company sample. Outside of the real estate and construction industries, state firms have, in net terms, subtracted from the increase in leverage. By comparison, in manufacturing and services, private firms have tended to contribute positively to the increase in total leverage.

3 We estimate 'broad credit' by subtracting net equity issuance from the PBC's 'total social financing' aggregate, which includes bank loans, undiscounted bank acceptances, entrusted loans (intercompany loans in which a bank acts as an agent) and loans made by trust companies.

To consider the determinants of leverage at a more disaggregated level, we estimate a range of static and dynamic panel models to help explain leverage among Chinese-listed firms. We augment these models with additional dummy variables to control for macroeconomic influences on corporate leverage. In so doing, we update and extend earlier studies of Chinese corporate leverage that use smaller, shorter panels (Chen 2004; Qian et al. 2009).

The results from static fixed-effects models highlight a negative relationship between leverage and profitability and a positive correlation with firm size, collateral and industry leverage patterns as significant influences on leverage at the firm level. Consistent with the idea that the 2008–09 stimulus was disproportionately directed at state firms, these models show that state sector leverage (measured by the liabilities-to-assets ratio) increased relative to private sector leverage after 2008, when we account for firm-level determinants of capital structure. Dynamic models, which allow for leverage decisions to be correlated over time, further show that persistence in capital structure decisions at the firm level is an important driver of observed leverage behaviour. This feature, together with declining profitability among state firms and the shift in industry composition towards more highly leveraged sectors, such as real estate and construction in the wake of the stimulus, may help to explain much of the upward trend in leverage in recent years. We argue that if this is correct, sluggish adjustment in firm behaviour could make it challenging for China's corporate sector to achieve rapid deleveraging.

Our work complements recent contributions by Chivakul and Lam (2015) and Zhang et al. (2015), who use different datasets and modelling strategies to consider related questions. Employing a panel that includes Hong Kong-listed Chinese firms, Chivakul and Lam (2015) estimate pre-2009 and post-2009 static models of leverage and find that state ownership increased leverage in the post-stimulus period (consistent with our own results for static models). They also analyse the vulnerability of state-owned and private sector firms to increases in borrowing costs and emphasise the possible spillovers from financial distress in the real estate industry to the corporate sector as a whole. Zhang et al. (2015) emphasise implicit government support and widespread corporate credit intermediation as key reasons for rising indebtedness among listed state-owned firms. Using a sample of listed firms and bond issuers over the period 2009–13, they estimate the elasticity of financial assets to liabilities as a proxy for corporate credit intermediation, and find that it is higher for SOEs than for the private sector firms. By comparison, we focus on a detailed decomposition of leverage patterns by industry and firm type and explore the implications of models that allow for dynamic capital structure decisions at the level of the individual firm.

The chapter proceeds as follows. The next section discusses trends in aggregate corporate debt in China and provides a comparison with the evidence from listed companies. Section three undertakes a decomposition of listed company leverage to consider in detail the main compositional drivers after 2008. Section four describes the data and empirical strategies we use to consider the firm-level determinants of leverage, and quantifies the degree of persistence in capital structure decisions, and section five concludes.

Recent trends in Chinese corporate debt and leverage

The debt of non-financial companies in China increased rapidly in the wake of the Global Financial Crisis (GFC) and has accounted for most of the increase in economy-wide indebtedness since 2008 (Figure 12.1). Although official statistics are not available at a sectoral level, Bank for International Settlements (BIS) estimates suggest that non-financial corporations' debt grew by more than 30 per cent in year-ended terms in 2009 and that growth has averaged almost 20 per cent since 2010. Other estimates, such as official broad credit aggregates ('total social financing' adjusted for lending to households and equity issuance by corporations), show similar trends. Although there is debate regarding the extent to which lending after 2008 favoured state-owned firms rather than the private sector, bank lending to SOEs is widely assumed to have been an important driver of the rapid growth of credit during this period (Lardy 2012).

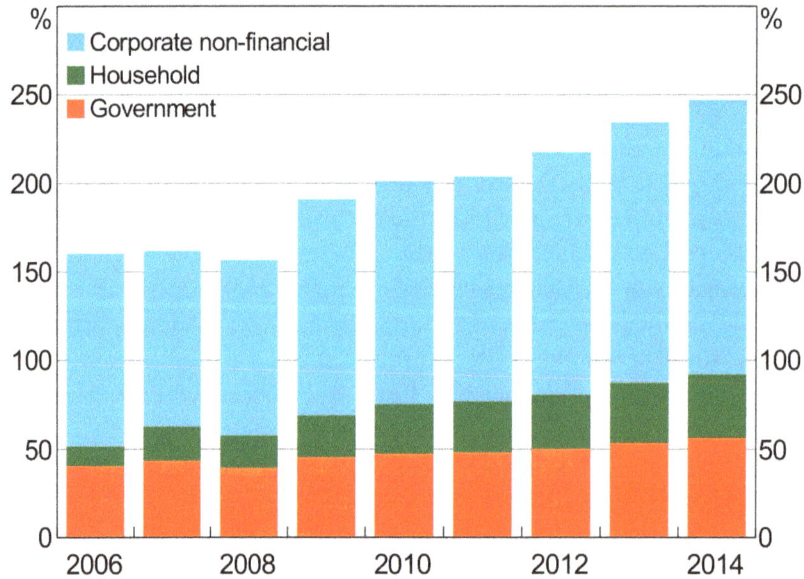

Figure 12.1 China: Ratio of debt to GDP by sector

Sources: Authors' calculations; BIS (2016); IMF (2015a).

The BIS estimates suggest that non-financial corporations' debt was slightly less than 100 per cent of GDP in 2008 and increased to more than 160 per cent of GDP by mid-2015. This has led to concerns about the sustainability of the debt build-up, with some analysts arguing that 'China has become indebted before it has become rich' (Chen 2014: 3).

A feature of China's non-financial corporate debt is that it is primarily domestically owned. Although Chinese corporations have issued foreign currency-denominated bonds in sizeable volumes in recent years, the use of cross-border funding remains relatively low, accounting for around 10 per cent of total non-financial corporate debt by the end of 2014. The low use of external funding in part reflects China's large and persistent current account surpluses and high saving rate. These features set China apart from many other emerging economies, for which foreign currency–denominated debt accounts for a sizeable share of overall corporate debt (Figure 12.2).

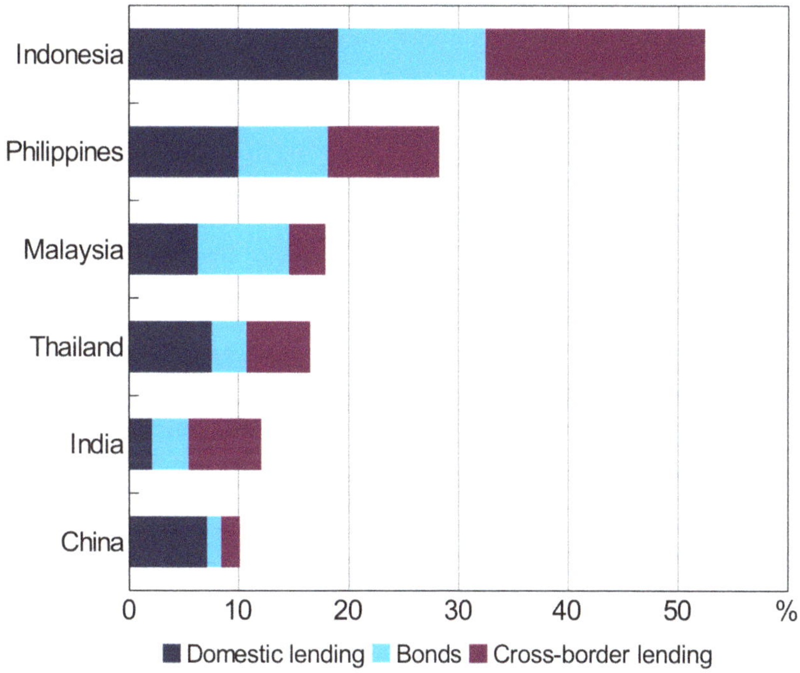

Figure 12.2 Emerging Asia non-financial corporate debt (foreign currency denominated, percentage of total), 2014

Source: IMF (2015b).

While the low use by Chinese firms of offshore funding reduces their exposure to rapid exchange rate movements, the continuous upward trend in the corporate debt to GDP ratio has been flagged as a risk to financial and macroeconomic stability by both Chinese policymakers and private sector analysts. One concern stems from the fact that, if recent trends in broad credit creation are sustained, it is unlikely that the debt-to-GDP ratio will stabilise or fall in the next one to two years. Real economic growth has been moderating, inflation pressures are subdued (exemplified by the decline in the GDP deflator in 2015) and credit growth remains strong. Official government targets tabled at political meetings in March 2016 project growth in real GDP of 6.5 to 7 per cent in 2016 and growth in the stock of total social financing—a measure of broad financing to the real economy—of 13 per cent. If these targets are realised, the upward trend in the aggregate debt-to-GDP ratio is likely to continue for at least another year. In fact, without a significant increase in nominal GDP growth, credit growth would need to fall dramatically for the current trend to be reversed.

These debt aggregates, however, reveal little about the changing composition of leverage. Even the distinction between 'non-financial corporate' debt and 'government' debt in Figure 12.1 cannot be defended too strongly, due to the importance of SOEs—centrally controlled SOEs in particular—as agents of official policy. The figures are also silent on variation at the industry level.

Evidence from industrial surveys

Official data drawn from industrial surveys provide some insight into changes in indebtedness by ownership and by industry. The National Bureau of Statistics of China (NBS) publishes aggregate data on the balance sheets of industrial, real estate and construction enterprises.[4] For comparison with the statistics corresponding to the whole economy, we calculate the ratio of total liabilities to earnings before interest and tax (EBIT) for these industries.[5] This metric similarly expresses the stock of liabilities as the ratio of an income flow and provides a gauge of how sufficient current cash flow is to service the existing stock of liabilities. Compared with the economy-wide debt-to-GDP ratio, the NBS data indicate a slight increase in the liabilities of the industrial and construction sectors relative to revenue in the past few years, alongside a particularly sharp pick-up in the same ratio for real estate post-2008 (Figure 12.3).

Another way of assessing the extent of non-financial firms' indebtedness is to measure leverage. Leverage can be defined in a variety of ways, but it is usually measured as debt or total liabilities (debt plus non-debt liabilities) as a ratio to assets or equity. Similar to the liabilities (or debt) to EBIT ratio, and all other things being equal, a higher leverage ratio can signal greater vulnerability,

4 These data are compiled from surveys of all state-owned and non–state-owned enterprises with revenue from principal business of more than RMB5 million from 1998 to 2006; from 2007, all enterprises with revenue from principal business of more than RMB5 million are also included; and since 2011, only enterprises with principal business revenue exceeding RMB20 million have been included.

5 We use total liabilities rather than debt, as figures for the latter are not available.

as this implies that a firm's reliance on external financing may exceed its ability to pay down debt principal through the sale of existing assets. Of course, increases in aggregate leverage in an economy might also reflect other factors that lead to industries with higher relative leverage becoming more important in the economy, such as changes in industry structure.

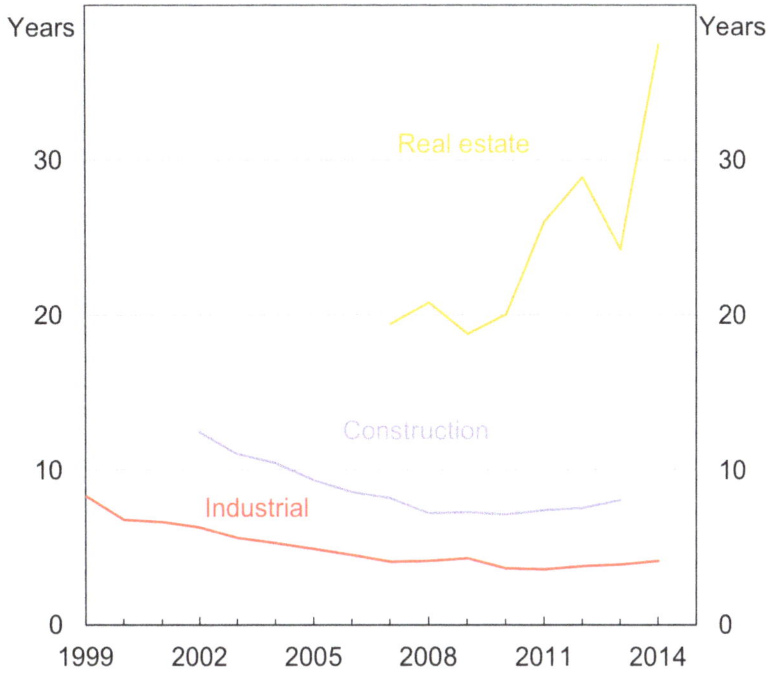

Figure 12.3 China: Liabilities by industry (ratio to EBIT)

Note: Data are available to 2015 for industrial firms, to 2014 for real estate firms and to 2013 for construction firms.

Sources: Authors' calculations; CEIC Data.

The NBS data suggest that corporate leverage, measured by the ratio of liabilities to assets, has varied by sector and by ownership (Figure 12.4). These data indicate that since the mid-2000s, leverage has generally been lower for privately owned industrial and construction firms than for state-owned or state-controlled enterprises, and that the latter have experienced rising leverage.[6] However, in the case of the real estate sector, the data suggest that state real

6 The 'state-owned and state-holding' classification is used to define SOEs in the NBS data. These are enterprises for which all assets are owned by the state or mixed ownership enterprises where the percentage of the state shareholding is larger than that of any other single shareholder. Private firms are calculated as the residual of the total less 'state-owned and state-holding'.

estate companies have reduced their leverage steadily in recent years, whereas there has been substantial growth in both the assets and the leverage of private real estate firms.

The relative increase in the leverage of state industrial firms has coincided with a deterioration in their profitability relative to private firms as measured by profits as a share of assets (Figure 12.5). For the construction and real estate industries, the data suggest that private firms have been consistently more profitable than SOEs. Private sector profitability across the sector for which data are available has fallen in recent years, but remains above the level for the broader corporate sector.

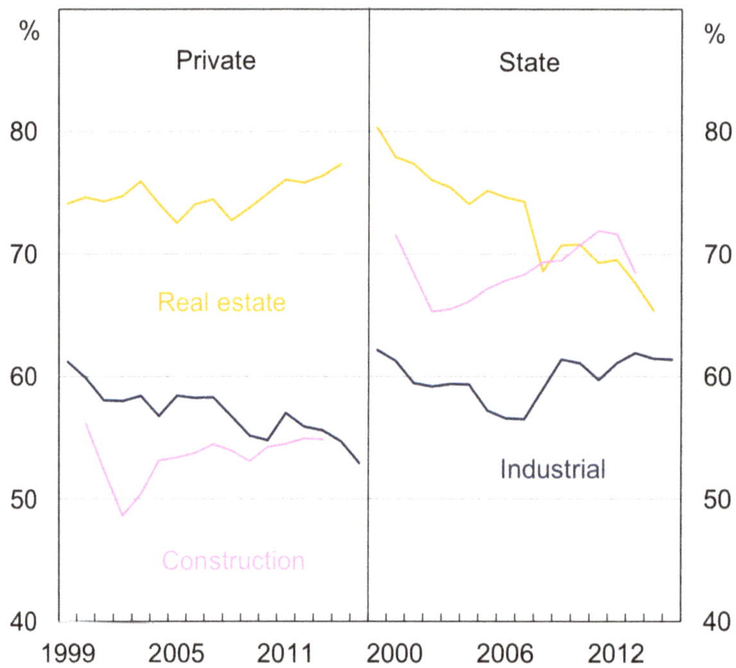

Figure 12.4 China: Corporate leverage by industry and ownership/control (ratio of liabilities to assets)

Note: Data are available to 2015 for industrial firms, to 2014 for real estate firms and to 2013 for construction firms.

Sources: Authors' calculations; CEIC Data.

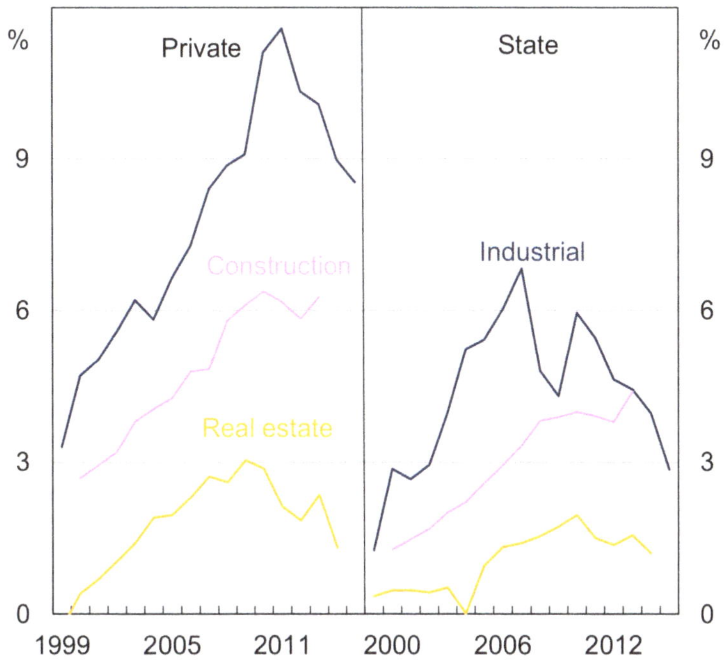

Figure 12.5 China: Return on assets by industry (profit, relative to assets)

Note: Data are available to 2015 for industrial firms, to 2014 for real estate firms and to 2013 for construction firms.

Sources: Authors' calculations; CEIC Data.

Evidence from listed companies

Official data are drawn from large surveys, but only limited disaggregated information is publicly available. In the absence of firm-level data for the broader corporate sector, listed company data can be consulted to shed light on the financing behaviour of a subset of non-financial companies. We construct our sample of listed firms by combining data from the China Securities Markets and Accounting Research Database (CSMAR) and the Wind Financial Terminal database, encompassing firms' reported balance sheet, cash flow and income statements. Our sample is a panel of more than 2,000 firms listed on the Shanghai and Shenzhen stock exchanges for the years 2000 to 2014, with estimates for 2015 based on data up to the September quarter of that year. As financial firms typically have markedly different capital structures to non-financial companies, we exclude all firms with Global Industry Classification Standard (GICS) classifications corresponding to the banking, diversified financial services, capital markets, insurance and consumer finance industries.[7] We choose a sample beginning in the 2000s to prevent our results being overly affected by reforms impacting on the corporate sector and stock markets in the 1990s and to avoid distortions due to the adoption of new generally accepted accounting principles in the late 1990s.[8] For reasons discussed in the next section, we use an unbalanced panel of listed companies for our analysis, although separate experiments suggest that the broad findings are not overly sensitive to using a balanced panel of firms.

We classify firms in the sample as state-owned or state-controlled firms ('state firms') based on whether the central State-owned Assets Supervision and Administration Commission, a local government-run asset management bureau, a local government, the Central Government or an SOE is a controlling shareholder.[9] We remove all observations for firms that have experienced an obvious shift of control from the state towards the private sector or vice versa. It is worth noting, however, that our identification is imperfect as an indicator of state influence on the listed corporate sector. The existence of pyramidal state shareholding schemes (Ding and Su 2008) means that the extent of state control can often be hard to verify. Relatedly, our methodology does not allow us to account for ostensibly 'private' firms whose chief executive officers have close political connections or whose boards are populated by current or former government bureaucrats (see Fan et al. 2007).[10]

7 We prefer the GICS classification to the China Securities Regulatory Commission's 'financial' industry classification, which only includes banks and insurance companies.

8 Qian et al. (2009) note that firms were permitted to issue new shares to raise seasoned equity (as well as rights offerings) from 2001 onwards, but our results are not sensitive to the exclusion of the year 2000 from the sample. A more serious question is whether the internationalisation of accounting standards to ensure convergence with International Financial Reporting Standards in 2006–07 had a significant effect on financial reporting at the firm level. However, the assessment of Ding and Su (2008) is that the impact is likely to have been modest due to a policy decision to allow only gradual introduction of fair value principles under the revised standards.

9 We use information on controlling shareholders provided by Wind Information Co. Ltd. Chinese official guidelines dictate that 'a controlling shareholder is one that controls 30% or more of the votes or shares, or who can elect half or more of the directors, or who can through any means effectively control the listed company' (Firth et al. 2012: 436).

10 Fan et al. (2007) find that partially privatised firms with politically connected CEOs perform worse than private firms without political connections.

For various reasons, the firms in our sample may not be representative of the wider corporate sector. The debt of listed firms has, on average, risen over time, but as of the third quarter of 2015 it accounted for only around 7.5 per cent of total social financing, while total liabilities accounted for roughly 17.5 per cent. Moreover, listed firms are likely to have greater access than the broader corporate sector to equity and bond financing channels. Nonetheless, growth in the debt and liabilities of listed firms has tracked growth in broad credit to the real economy (as measured by total social financing) reasonably closely, especially since the late 2000s (Figure 12.6).

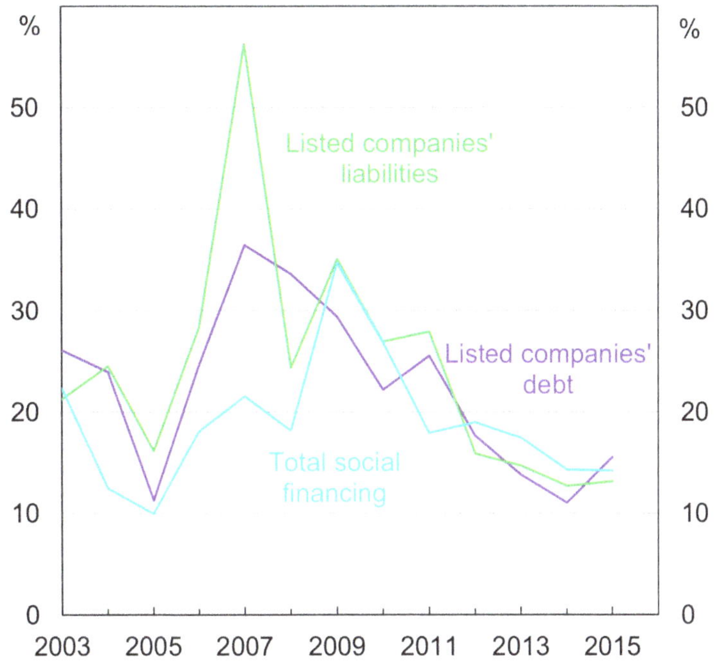

Figure 12.6 China: Annual growth of liabilities and debt

Note: Latest data are estimates based on data up to the September quarter 2015. Listed company data are for non-financial firms only.

Sources: Authors' calculations; CEIC; CSMAR; WIND Information.

If we consider listed firm liabilities and debt as a share of income (measured by EBIT), the broad pattern observed in the economy-wide debt-to-GDP ratio since the late 2000s can also be observed for these companies (Figure 12.7).[11] However, the picture for traditional leverage ratios is less straightforward (Figure 12.8). Trends in the ratio of liabilities to assets for listed companies differ by ownership/control. On average (weighted by assets), the leverage of private firms was higher than that of state firms in the early 2000s, but trended lower from 2005 to 2011 before rising again. In contrast, state firms' leverage increased steadily in the early 2000s, accelerated in the last few years of that decade and has been higher than the leverage of private firms in recent years. These trends are more striking when the distribution of leverage across companies is considered. Measures of median leverage and the leverage of the 90th percentile of listed companies indicate that private firms' leverage fell significantly over the past decade to be well below the levels of state-owned or controlled companies.

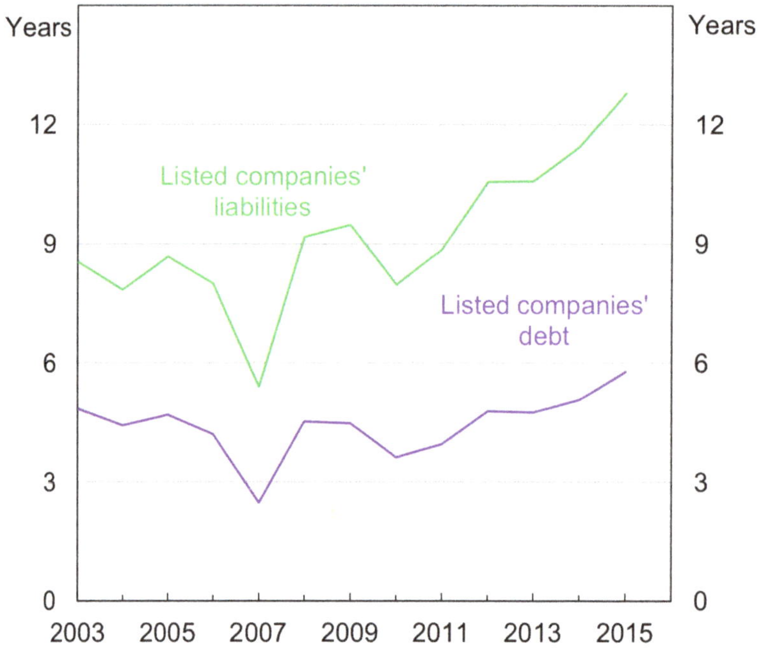

Figure 12.7 China: Liabilities and debt (ratio to EBIT, non-financial listed companies)

Note: Latest data are estimates based on data up to the September quarter 2015.

Sources: Authors' calculations; CSMAR; WIND Information.

11 We use the ratio of liabilities or debt to earnings before interest and tax (EBIT) rather than to earnings before interest, tax, depreciation and amortisation (EBITDA). Financial analysts often prefer to use EBITDA, but as data on depreciation and amortisation are unavailable or incomplete for some companies, we use EBIT instead.

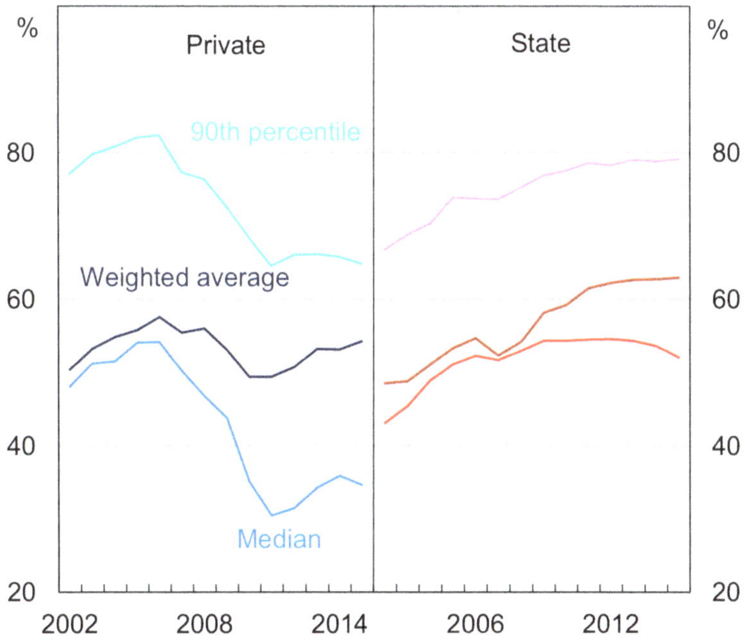

Figure 12.8 China: Liabilities-to-assets ratio of non-financial listed companies

Note: Latest data are estimates based on data up to the September quarter 2015. The weighted average leverage ratio weights each firm's liabilities-to-assets ratio by that firm's share of total listed company assets.

Sources: Authors' calculations; CSMAR; WIND Information.

When the narrower debt-to-assets ratio is used, the divergence in weighted average leverage between the private and the state sectors is less apparent, although somewhat similar patterns can be observed for the median and the 90th percentile measures (Figure 12.9). On average (weighted by assets), private firms' debt-to-assets ratios have declined, but have been only slightly below those of state firms in recent years. At the same time, compared with the liabilities-to-assets ratio, for state firms there is little evidence of an upward trend in the debt-to-assets ratio over the second half of our sample period. The difference reflects the exclusion of non-debt liabilities from the debt-to-assets ratio. In particular, accounts payable and advance receipts have both grown more strongly as a share of total liabilities for state companies than they have for private firms (Figure 12.10).

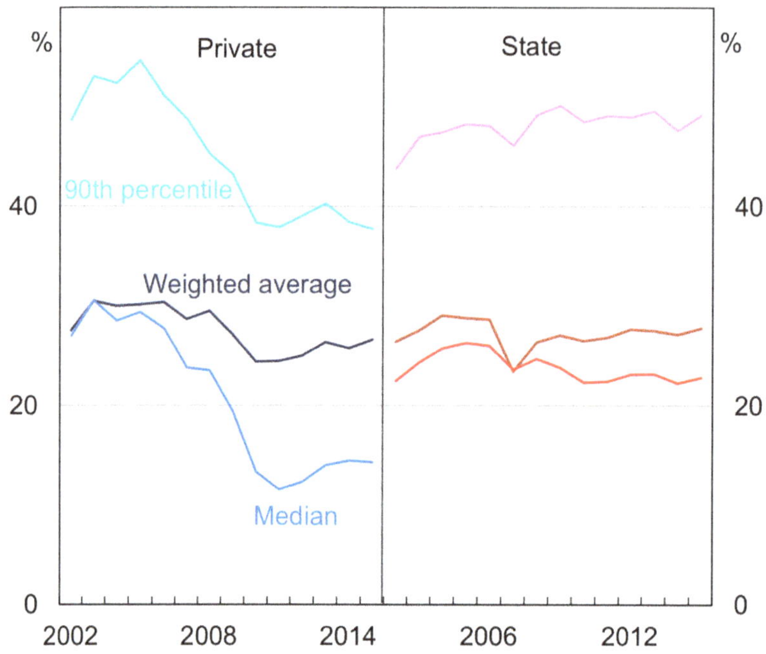

Figure 12.9 China: Debt-to-assets ratio of non-financial listed companies

Note: Latest data are estimates based on data up to the September quarter 2015. The weighted average leverage ratio weights each firm's liabilities-to-assets ratio by that firm's share of total listed company assets.

Sources: Authors' calculations; CSMAR; WIND Information.

Accounts payable can be thought of as an alternative form of short-term credit that allows firms to receive goods or services now and pay for them in the future. Although these are not interest-bearing agreements, they are typically structured so that firms receive discounts from suppliers to pay before a certain date, which can in effect give them the characteristics of debt instruments. The increase in accounts payable relative to other liabilities can be observed in several industries, but is most pronounced for the real estate industry (Figure 12.11).[12]

12 While the ratio to total liabilities has been relatively stable in the past few years for the real estate and construction industries, and has fallen for the mining industry, the median ratio of accounts payable to operating revenue has risen sharply since 2008 for all three industries. This suggests that the capacity to make payments from current sales in these industries has fallen.

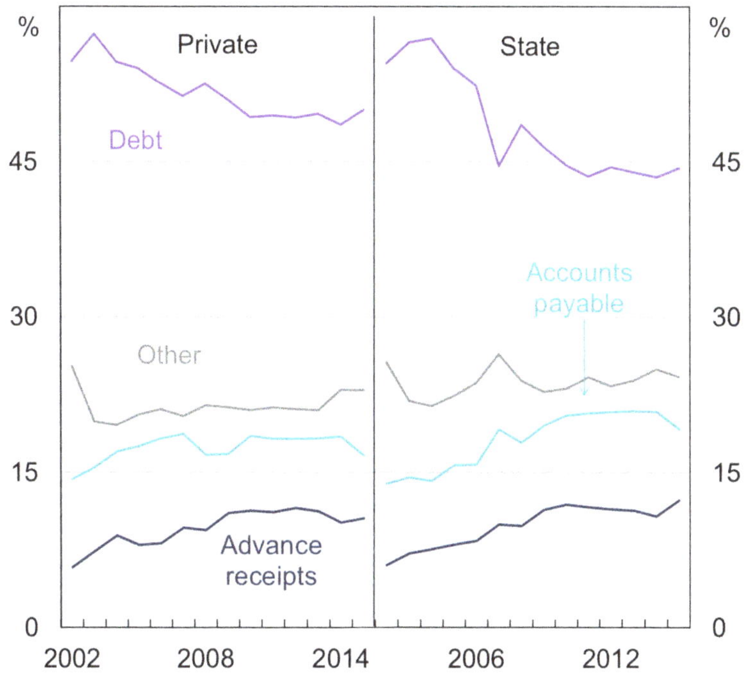

Figure 12.10 China: Composition of liabilities by ownership/control (share of total liabilities)

Note: Latest data are estimates based on data up to the September quarter 2015. All data are for non-financial listed companies.

Sources: Authors' calculations; CSMAR; WIND Information.

Advance receipts are funds received now in exchange for the provision in the future of a good or service, and could also be considered a form of credit. An example of an advance receipt is a real estate developer preselling a property that is yet to be built. This increases liabilities while generating cash. The increase in the share of advance receipts over the past 15 years has been almost entirely attributable to the real estate and construction industries, and real estate has more exclusively driven the increase since the late 2000s (Figure 12.11). It is possible the increased use of both accounts payable and advance receipts in recent years has substituted for debt. Together, they largely explain the divergences that have emerged between the liabilities-to-assets and debt-to-assets ratios.

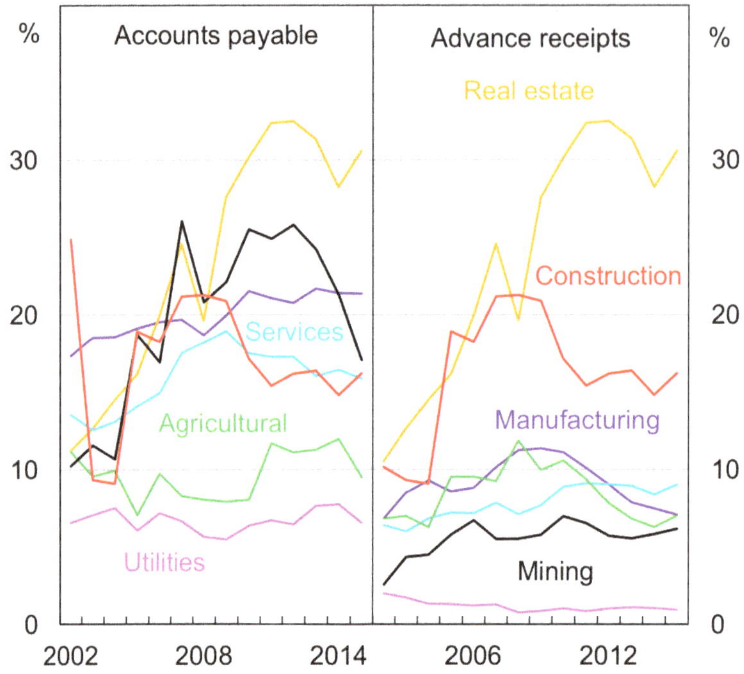

Figure 12.11 China: Composition of liabilities by industry (share of total liabilities)

Note: Latest data are estimates based on data up to the September quarter 2015. All data are for non-financial listed companies.

Sources: Authors' calculations; CSMAR; WIND Information.

It is worth noting that a rise in accounts payable as a share of liabilities can occur for many reasons and does not necessarily indicate a problem. Nonetheless, rapid or persistent increases may signify repayment difficulties for some listed companies. Similarly, for firms such as property developers, a rise in advance receipts relative to other liabilities could (as with an increase in other types of liabilities including debt) signal an increased likelihood of financial stress in the event that current funding is insufficient to meet related contractual obligations.

At the industry level, the liabilities-to-assets ratio has been consistently higher for the real estate, construction and utilities industries over the sample period. Leverage has risen noticeably since 2008 for the real estate, construction and mining industries and to a lesser extent for services industries (Figure 12.12).[13] In contrast, leverage in the manufacturing and utilities industries has eased a little since the late 2000s.[14]

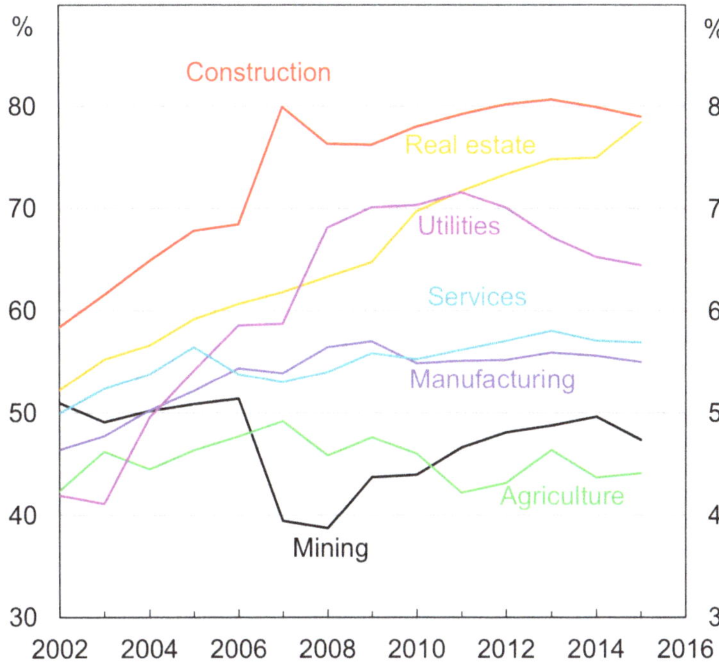

Figure 12.12 China: Leverage of non-financial listed companies by industry (ratio of liabilities to assets)

Note: Latest data are estimates based on data up to the September quarter 2015.

Sources: Authors' calculations; CSMAR; WIND Information.

Apart from debt-to-assets and liabilities-to-assets ratios, other measures of leverage that are commonly used to analyse corporate indebtedness are the debt-to-equity and liabilities-to-equity ratios (Figure 12.13). The ratio of debt to equity has followed a similar trend to the liabilities-to-assets ratio—specifically, it has increased by almost 20 percentage points since 2002. The ratio of liabilities to equity has shown an even sharper increase over the past decade, rising from

13 The measures we present for the services sector include data for the following industries: accommodation and catering; transportation and logistics; wholesale and retail trade; rental and commercial services; culture, sport and recreation; information technology (IT) and software; scientific, research and technical services; health and social work; and education.

14 In general, the trajectory of leverage for each industry is similar whether the debt-to-assets, debt-to-equity, liabilities-to-assets or liabilities-to-equity ratios are used. The upward trajectory for real estate and construction industries, relative to other industries, appears more dramatic in the case of the liabilities-to-equity ratio than for the liabilities-to-assets ratio. The leverage of the utilities industry appears noticeably higher compared with other industries if the debt-to-assets ratio is considered.

around 100 per cent in 2002 to nearly 160 per cent in 2015. The divergent trends reflect the fact that assets have grown at a faster rate than equity while debt has fallen as a share of liabilities, which is not surprising given the accounting identity between assets and the sum of liabilities and equity. As discussed above, the increase in non-debt liabilities is due to an increase in accounts payable (funds owed to other suppliers) and advance receipts (whereby firms have received payment but are yet to provide related goods or services).

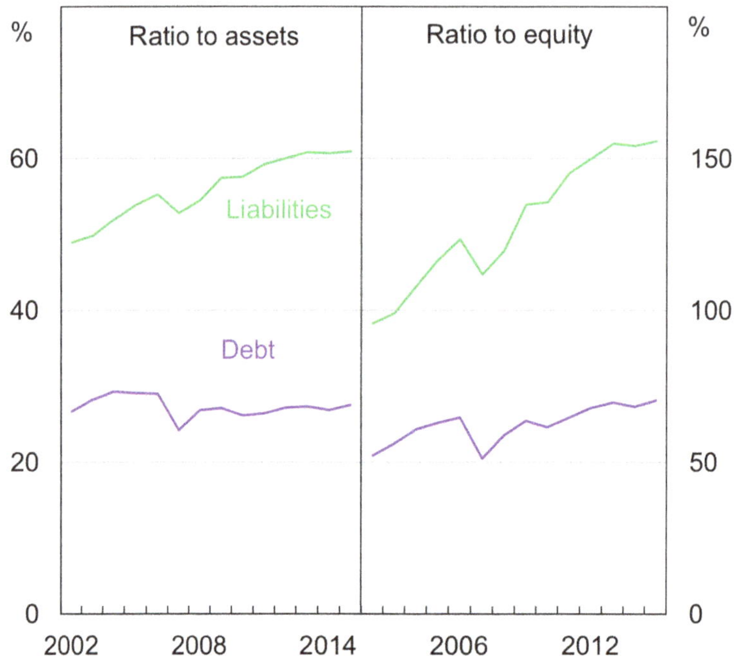

Figure 12.13 China: Measures of non-financial listed company leverage

Note: Latest data are estimates based on data up to the September quarter 2015.

Sources: Authors' calculations; CSMAR; WIND Information.

As is the case with the official industrial survey data, the divergence of leverage patterns between listed private and state companies has been accompanied by a divergence in their operating performance. Prior to 2008, listed state firms were more profitable than private firms and their operating performance, as measured by the ratio of EBIT to assets, was clearly higher (Figure 12.14). In part, this explains the finding of Chen et al. (2009), based on econometric analysis of a similar dataset up to 2004, that private firms' operating performance was inferior to that of both central government and local government-controlled SOEs. More recent data, however, highlight the dramatic reversal that occurred after 2008. Since 2009, private firms have instead experienced a sustained improvement in profitability relative to state firms, while the operating performance of the latter has fallen in both relative and absolute terms. This pattern is generally also apparent at the industry level.[15]

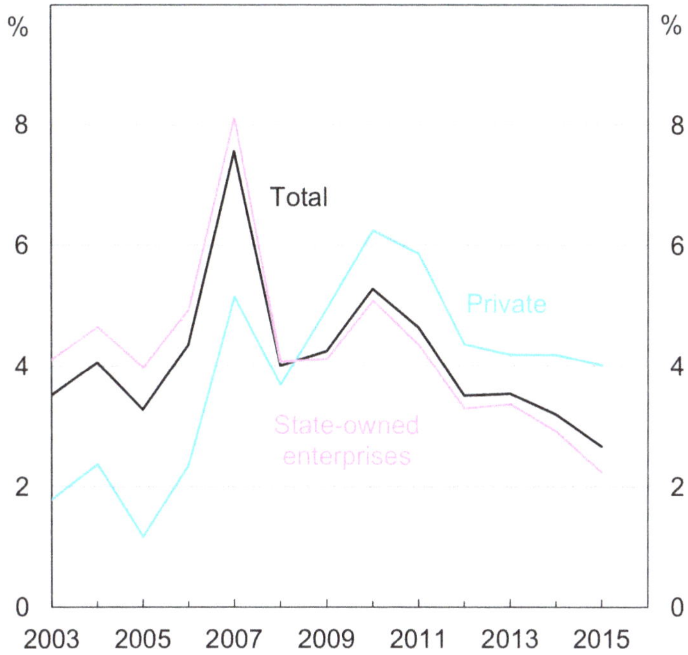

Figure 12.14 China: Return on assets of non-financial listed companies (net profit, ratio to assets, per cent)

Note: Latest data are estimates based on data up to the September quarter 2015.

Sources: Authors' calculations; CSMAR; WIND Information.

In summary, aggregate trends in listed company data indicate that leverage has increased for state firms in absolute terms and also relative to private firms since the stimulus of 2008–09. This was, moreover, accompanied by a simultaneous deterioration in their relative operating performance. However, another feature of our sample is that, while state-owned or controlled companies (based on our definitions) constitute the bulk—about three-quarters—of non-financial listed company assets, private firms appear to have accounted for a rising share of assets since the late 2000s.[16] The relative increase in private sector assets has

15 An exception is the utilities industry, in which the operating performance of state firms has improved relative to private firms in recent years.

16 These estimates differ from Chivakul and Lam (2015), who find that around two-thirds of the assets of listed firms are under state ownership or control, although they also find that the state share has fallen in recent years.

been broad-based across most major asset types.[17] As the next section shows, a consequence of this compositional shift is that the private sector has been responsible for a larger proportion of the change in listed company leverage than average leverage ratios for state and private firms would suggest.

Decomposing listed company leverage

To clarify the sources and composition of rising listed company leverage since the late 2000s, we use a simple arithmetic decomposition to calculate contributions to leverage by firm ownership/control and by industry. To do this, we exploit the following identity (Equation 12.1).

Equation 12.1

$$L_t = \frac{\sum_i l_{it}}{\sum_i a_{it}} = \sum_i \frac{l_{it}}{a_{it}} \cdot \frac{a_{it}}{\sum_i a_{it}}$$

In Equation 12.1, L_t is the total liabilities-to-assets ratio for our sample at time t; l_{it} corresponds to the liabilities of a subset of firms, i, at time t; and a_{it} corresponds to the assets of the same subset, i, at time t (for example, i could refer to different industries or firm ownership types).

We focus on the liabilities-to-assets ratio because narrower measures, such as the debt-to-assets ratio, exclude the striking rise in non-debt liabilities since the early 2000s. Although it is more common in the corporate finance literature to use the debt-to-assets ratio, broader leverage ratios have been used in several recent studies of Chinese corporate behaviour (Li et al. 2009; Yu 2013; Chivakul and Lam 2015).[18]

Tables 12.1 and 12.2 consider how the liabilities-to-assets ratio has been affected by compositional change in ownership or control of listed companies, and the relative importance of old and new firms in driving leverage. Table 12.1 shows leverage ratios calculated for state and private firms. For both state and private firms, we show the leverage ratios for a 'matched sample' of firms that were continuously listed between 2008 and 2015 and the remaining firms, which were listed for part of that same period (net new entrants to the sample). For firms that were listed for the period 2008–15, we also consider the leverage of firms

17 Growth since 2008 has been faster for private than for state firms in the case of cash, net accounts receivable, net prepayments, net inventories, equity, net fixed assets and net intangible assets. Growth in net long-term equity investment has been faster for state firms.

18 Recent history also suggests that non-debt liabilities have been an important aspect of leverage in China. A feature of the macrofinancial challenges faced by Chinese authorities in the late 1990s was a rise in inter-enterprise liabilities (often described as 'triangular debt'), which typically took the form of unpaid bills owing from state-owned to private firms (Lardy 1998: 40–41).

that already displayed 'high' leverage in 2008 and of those firms whose leverage was lower. For the latter comparison, we define 'high' leverage as a liabilities-to-assets ratio of 0.75 (75 per cent). This compares with a median leverage ratio of a little less than 0.5 in our sample. Having calculated these leverage ratios, Table 12.2 multiplies each by their weight (the proportional share of assets due to each category) to compute contributions of each category to aggregate leverage for the listed company sample.[19]

Table 12.1 Leverage by firm ownership/control

	Liabilities-to-assets ratio (per cent)			Average annual change (percentage points)
	2008	**2012**	**2015**	**2008–15**
State-owned or controlled	***54.2***	***62.2***	***62.9***	***1.2***
Matched sample (2008–15)	54.2	61.2	61.8	1.1
Leverage > 0.75 in 2008	*82.5*	*79.6*	*77.3*	*–0.7*
Leverage ≤ 0.75 in 2008	*48.4*	*57.2*	*58.4*	*1.4*
Net new entry (2008–15)[a]	70.0	69.2	69.4	–0.1
Private	***56.0***	***50.7***	***54.2***	***–0.3***
Matched sample (2008–15)	56.0	58.3	60.7	0.7
Leverage > 0.75 in 2008	*88.6*	*70.8*	*69.5*	*–2.7*
Leverage ≤ 0.75 in 2008	*52.3*	*56.9*	*59.7*	*1.1*
Net new entry (2008–15)[a]	24.6	36.5	45.5	3.5

[a] For comparison with later leverage ratios and consistency with the annual average change calculation, the leverage ratio for 2009 is given in the first column.

Sources: Authors' calculations; CSMAR; WIND Information.

The decomposition shows that state-owned or controlled firms accounted for the majority of listed company leverage in the period after 2008. The bulk of this leverage was due to firms that were already listed in 2008, although firms listed since 2008 (or delisted) have accounted for an increasing share. Overall, the leverage of state firms increased steadily over this period, while the leverage of private firms declined for a time before picking up again after 2011 (Table 12.1). However, the value of assets in private hands increased relative to the value of state sector assets. This is what accounts for the modest fall in the state sector's share of leverage since 2008 (Table 12.2).

19 We do not exclude outliers from the sample when performing this exercise, as we do for the econometric exercises in the next section. Applying outlier correction strategies, such as censoring leverage on the unit interval or excluding firms whose leverage exceeds a certain threshold, makes a modest quantitative difference and virtually no qualitative difference to the results.

Table 12.2 Compositional change in leverage by firm ownership/control

	Share of total liabilities-to-assets ratio (per cent)			Change (percentage points)
	2008	2012	2015	2008–15
State-owned or controlled	***84.7***	***83.8***	***79.2***	**-5.6**
Matched sample (2008–15)	84.7	72.0	66.1	–18.6
Leverage > 0.75 in 2008	*22.0*	*16.4*	*14.9*	*-7.1*
Leverage ≤ 0.75 in 2008	*62.8*	*55.5*	*51.2*	*-11.6*
Net new entry (2008–15)	0.0	11.8	13.0	13.0
Private	**15.3**	**16.2**	**20.8**	**5.6**
Matched sample (2008–15)	15.3	12.1	13.4	–1.8
Leverage > 0.75 in 2008	*2.4*	*1.5*	*1.6*	*-0.9*
Leverage ≤ 0.75 in 2008	*12.8*	*10.7*	*11.9*	*-0.9*
Net new entry (2008–15)	0.0	4.1	7.4	7.4

Sources: Authors' calculations; CSMAR; WIND Information.

The data suggest that, on average, firms with leverage ratios exceeding 0.75 in 2008 deleveraged over the subsequent seven years (most prominently in the case of private firms). This parallels the finding that the leverage of the ninetieth percentile of the listed company distribution declined after 2008 for private companies and was relatively stable for state firms (see section two). In contrast, there is evidence that firms with lower leverage than this in 2008 'leveraged up', on average, although the weight of these firms in the sample (the proportional value of their assets) fell by a greater amount, resulting in a declining contribution to overall leverage.[20] The leverage of net new entrants to the sample of state firms was relatively stable over the 2009–15 period, but the weight of these firms in the sample increased sharply, leading them to account for a rising share of total listed company leverage. Net new private entrants, in contrast, saw rapid average annual growth in leverage. When combined with their rising weight in the sample, this also resulted in them accounting for an increasing share of overall leverage.

20 An analysis of the *incidence* of firms with leverage within certain ranges delivers slightly different findings, as it does not take into account the weight of each firm in terms of its share of total assets in the listed company sample. Since 2008, the majority of firms (between 86 and 90 per cent) have had leverage ratios equal to or less than 0.75. The proportion of these firms in the sample declined between 2008 and 2013 and has subsequently increased. Within this group, the share of firms in the 0.25–0.5 range fell and the share in the 0.5–0.75 range rose between 2008 and 2013—a trend that reversed after 2013. The proportion of firms with leverage above 0.75 has fallen since 2013.

While Table 12.2 summarises the contributions of different types of firms to the overall *level* of leverage, a similar decomposition can also be used to consider contributions to the *change* in leverage (Equation 12.2).

Equation 12.2

$$\Delta L_t = \sum_i \left(\frac{l_{it}}{a_{it}} \cdot \frac{a_{it}}{\sum_i a_{it}} - \frac{l_{it-1}}{a_{it-1}} \cdot \frac{a_{it-1}}{\sum_i a_{it-1}} \right)$$

Looking at contributions of each type of firm to the overall leverage, it is apparent that state firms accounted for the bulk of the increase in leverage between 2008 and 2012, but subsequently subtracted from growth in leverage (Table 12.3). The further increase in leverage since 2012 can thus be attributed mainly to private firms. Deleveraging by highly leveraged firms (especially state firms) subtracted significantly from the rise in leverage over the 2008–15 period. In net terms, new entrants to the sample contributed strongly to growth in leverage. New listed state firms accounted for most of the increase between 2008 and 2012, but new private firms accounted for the bulk of the increase in leverage thereafter.

Table 12.3 Contributions to the change in leverage by firm ownership/control

	Contribution to change in total liabilities-to-assets ratio (percentage points)		**Cumulative (percentage points)**
	2008–12	**2012–15**	**2012–15**
Total	**5.5**	**0.9**	**6.4**
State-owned or controlled	***4.1***	***-2.1***	***2.1***
Matched sample (2008–15)	-3.0	-2.9	-5.9
Leverage > 0.75 in 2008	*-2.1*	*-0.8*	*-2.9*
Leverage ≤ 0.75 in 2008	*-0.9*	*-2.1*	*-3.0*
Net new entry (2008–15)	7.1	0.9	7.9
Private	***1.4***	***3.0***	***4.4***
Matched sample (2008–15)	-1.0	0.9	-0.1
Leverage > 0.75 in 2008	*-0.5*	*0.1*	*-0.4*
Leverage ≤ 0.75 in 2008	*-0.6*	*0.8*	*0.3*
Net new entry (2008–15)	2.4	2.1	4.5

Sources: Authors' calculations; CSMAR; WIND Information.

In summary, although the leverage of state firms increased and the leverage of private firms fell overall, the more highly leveraged private and state firms deleveraged (most prominently in the case of private firms). Virtually all other categories of firms experienced an increase in leverage, and the rising weight of private firms in the sample resulted in them accounting for an increasing share of total leverage. Indeed, private firms have accounted for much of the increase in leverage since 2008 and particularly over the past few years.

Table 12.4 Leverage by industry

	Liabilities-to-assets ratio			Average annual change (percentage points)
	2008	2012	2015	2008–15
Real estate	***63.3***	***73.3***	***78.4***	***2.2***
State-owned or controlled	63.4	73.2	78.5	2.2
Private	62.9	73.6	78.0	2.1
Construction	***76.3***	***80.1***	***78.9***	***0.4***
State-owned or controlled	76.5	80.9	79.8	0.5
Private	72.8	63.4	64.6	–1.2
Manufacturing	***56.4***	***55.2***	***55.1***	***–0.2***
State-owned or controlled	57.7	60.5	60.4	0.4
Private	52.0	45.2	46.9	–0.7
Utilities	***68.1***	***70.1***	***64.4***	***–0.5***
State-owned or controlled	68.4	70.5	64.7	–0.5
Private	60.8	57.4	56.8	–0.6
Mining	***38.7***	***48.1***	***47.4***	***1.2***
State-owned or controlled	38.6	48.1	47.3	1.2
Private	50.6	45.0	50.0	–0.1
Services	***53.7***	***57.0***	***57.0***	***0.5***
State-owned or controlled	53.6	57.7	57.2	0.5
Private	54.2	53.9	56.4	0.3
Other	***51.2***	***56.9***	***59.1***	***1.1***
State-owned or controlled	45.9	61.8	62.7	2.4
Private	59.4	44.5	52.7	–1.0

Sources: Authors' calculations; CSMAR; WIND Information.

At the industry level, the increase in leverage since 2008 has been concentrated in the real estate, construction, mining and services industries (Table 12.4). Over this period, firms in the real estate and construction industries have had persistently higher leverage than firms in other industries. The observed increases in leverage have been more pronounced for state firms than for private companies. Modest deleveraging has been apparent for the manufacturing and utilities sectors, partly offsetting the above trends. Yet the rapid growth of assets in real estate and construction has noticeably boosted the share of the total liabilities-to-assets ratio accounted for by these two industries (Table 12.5).

Table 12.5 Compositional change in leverage by industry

	Share of total liabilities-to-assets ratio (per cent)			Change (percentage points)
	2008	2012	2015	2008–15
Real estate	***7.4***	***9.6***	***13.9***	**6.5**
State-owned or controlled	5.5	6.9	9.8	4.4
Private	2.0	2.7	4.1	2.1
Construction	***8.0***	***16.7***	***16.9***	***8.8***
State-owned or controlled	7.6	16.1	16.1	8.4
Private	0.4	0.6	0.8	0.4
Manufacturing	***35.6***	***32.5***	***32.0***	***–3.6***
State-owned or controlled	28.0	23.4	21.3	–6.7
Private	7.6	9.1	10.7	3.1
Utilities	***10.9***	***8.9***	***7.9***	***–3.0***
State-owned or controlled	10.6	8.6	7.6	–2.9
Private	0.3	0.2	0.2	–0.1
Mining	***17.1***	***15.3***	***12.3***	***–4.8***
State-owned or controlled	17.0	15.1	12.0	–5.0
Private	0.1	0.2	0.3	0.2
Services	***15.8***	***13.2***	***12.6***	***–3.2***
State-owned or controlled	14.2	11.0	9.5	–4.7
Private	1.6	2.2	3.1	1.6
Other	***5.1***	***3.8***	***4.4***	***–0.7***
State-owned or controlled	1.8	2.7	2.8	0.9
Private	3.3	1.1	1.6	–1.7

Sources: Authors' calculations; CSMAR; WIND Information.

Table 12.6 Contributions to the change in leverage by industry

	Contribution to change in total liabilities-to-assets ratio (percentage points)		Cumulative (percentage points)
	2008–12	2012–15	2008–15
Total	**5.5**	**0.9**	**6.4**
Real estate	***1.7***	***2.7***	***4.4***
State-owned or controlled	1.2	1.8	3.0
Private	0.6	0.9	1.4
Construction	***5.6***	***0.3***	***5.9***
State-owned or controlled	5.5	0.2	5.6
Private	0.2	0.1	0.3
Manufacturing	***0.1***	***0.0***	***0.1***
State-owned or controlled	–1.2	–1.0	–2.3
Private	1.3	1.1	2.4
Utilities	***–0.6***	***–0.5***	***–1.2***
State-owned or controlled	–0.6	–0.5	–1.1
Private	–0.1	0.0	0.0
Mining	***–0.2***	***–1.7***	***–1.8***
State-owned or controlled	–0.2	–1.7	–1.9
Private	0.0	0.1	0.1
Services	***–0.7***	***–0.3***	***–0.9***
State-owned or controlled	–1.1	–0.8	–2.0
Private	0.5	0.6	1.0
Other	***–0.5***	***0.4***	***–0.1***
State-owned or controlled	0.6	0.1	0.7
Private	–1.1	0.3	–0.8

Sources: Authors' calculations; CSMAR; WIND Information.

If we decompose the *change* in leverage, a similar picture is revealed (Table 12.6). State-owned or controlled real estate and construction firms have accounted for the bulk of the increase in leverage, although private firms in these industries also contributed. All other major industry categories with the exception of manufacturing have subtracted from the increase since 2008. Outside the real estate and construction industries, private firms have tended to make a positive contribution to the change in leverage, particularly in manufacturing and services industries, while state firms have generally made a negative contribution.

The decomposition of listed company leverage helps identify the broad categories of firms that have underpinned rising leverage since the late 2000s. It shows that certain industries (especially real estate and construction) have been important drivers of the pick-up in leverage and that firms in these industries have typically been more highly leveraged than other firms. Second, it indicates that state firms were the key drivers of this increase in the immediate aftermath of the 2008–09 stimulus, but also that private firms have made a larger contribution to the rise in leverage in the past few years. While the decomposition does not shed light on the drivers of leverage at the firm level, it suggests that the industry to which a firm belongs and its ownership/control are likely to be important. To consider these issues in more depth, in the next section we model the capital structure decisions of listed firms using a similar dataset.

Modelling Chinese-listed company leverage

In the corporate finance literature, two main hypotheses have typically been considered in the analysis of firms' capital structure choices. The trade-off theory holds that optimal leverage is attained when the marginal tax benefit of higher leverage equals the marginal potential cost of financial distress. The theory predicts that firms will therefore set a target debt-to-value ratio. Assuming that there are costs of adjustment, they will move towards this target gradually (Flannery and Rangan 2006). In contrast, the pecking order theory predicts that, in an environment of asymmetric information between owners and managers, firms will prefer internal to external funds and debt to equity if external financing is required (Donaldson 1961; Myers 1984).[21]

In the case of China, Chen's (2004) panel study of Chinese-listed firms fails to find evidence for either hypothesis, but characterises capital structure decisions as following a 'modified pecking order' rule. More recent work, by Huang and Song (2006) and Qian et al. (2009), has tended to find more support for the trade-off theory. Qian et al. (2009) present evidence that a firm's current leverage ratio is strongly correlated with that in the previous period, which is consistent with sluggish adjustment to some 'target' leverage ratio.

21 Firms prefer debt to equity because the agency cost is higher for equity. The market may misprice equity if new investors are less well informed than current shareholders with access to private information. Underpricing by the market allows new investors to capture more of the net present value (NPV) of the project than current shareholders, leading to the project being rejected even if the NPV is positive (Harris and Raviv 1991).

Models and data

We consider both static and dynamic panel approaches to modelling the leverage of listed firms, using annual firm-level data for nearly 2,500 firms from 2000 to 2015. The basic static, fixed-effects model of leverage is specified as Equation 12.3.

Equation 12.3

$$L_{it} = \alpha + \boldsymbol{X}_{it}\beta + \boldsymbol{Z}_t\gamma + \mu_i + \eta_{it}$$

In Equation 12.3, L_{it} is the leverage ratio of firm i in year t, X_{it} is a vector of time-varying, firm-level explanatory variables and Z_t is a vector of additional determinants of leverage that vary over time but are the same for all firms. In our model, this vector consists of several time dummy variables. The firm fixed effect is given by μ_i, and η_{it} is the error term.

Static models may be incorrectly specified if firms' capital structure choices reflect their past borrowing behaviour as well as their current external finance needs. Flannery and Rangan (2006) argue that firms in the United States target a long-run leverage ratio (which itself might depend on pecking order or other considerations) and that a firm will converge to its long-run target gradually. This can be modelled as Equation 12.4.

Equation 12.4

$$L_{it} - L_{it-1} = \lambda(L^*_{it} - L_{it-1}) = \lambda\left(\delta + \boldsymbol{X}_{it}\tau + \boldsymbol{Z}_t\theta + \varphi_i + \omega_{it}\right) - \lambda L_{it-1}$$

In Equation 12.4, target leverage, L^*_{it}, depends on the same standard static determinants of leverage included in Equation 12.3, and where $0 < \lambda < 1$ is the speed of adjustment. Adding lagged leverage to both sides yields Equation 12.5.

Equation 12.5

$$L_{it} = \upsilon + (1 - \lambda)L_{it-1} + \boldsymbol{X}_{it}\phi + \boldsymbol{Z}_t\psi + \xi_i + v_{it}$$

In Equation 12.5, $\phi = \lambda\tau$ and $\psi = \lambda\theta$. A standard fixed-effects model can be used to estimate λ. However, it is poorly equipped to model the dynamics of adjustment to the target leverage, because the lagged dependent variable will be correlated with the firm fixed effects and therefore estimated coefficients will be biased (Nickell 1981). As a result, many recent studies, including Qian et al. (2009), have used dynamic panel specifications, estimated using the difference generalised method of moments (GMM) estimator (Holtz-Eakin et al. 1988;

Arellano and Bond 1991). This approach transforms Equation 12.5 by taking first differences and thereby removing the unobserved firm fixed effects (Equation 12.6).

Equation 12.6

$$\Delta L_{it} = (1 - \lambda)\Delta L_{it-1} + \boldsymbol{\Delta X}_{it}\phi + \boldsymbol{\Delta Z}_{t}\psi + u_{it}$$

To address the endogeneity of lagged dependent variables with respect to the fixed effects, the difference GMM estimator uses lagged levels of the dependent and explanatory variables as instruments. Including lagged levels of explanatory variables in the instrument set allows for the possibility that some regressors are endogenous. This is appealing in the context of corporate finance, as many balance sheet variables are likely to be codetermined rather than exogenous.

However, Blundell and Bond (1998) find that the difference GMM estimator has poor finite sample properties when the lagged levels of the series are only weakly correlated with subsequent first differences, as is often the case with persistent autoregressive processes. They make an assumption that first differences of the instruments are uncorrelated with the fixed effects, and this increases the number of possible instruments. Their system GMM estimator involves a system of two equations, using lagged differences as instruments for the original levels equation and lagged levels as instruments for the difference equation.[22] Flannery and Hankins (2013) show that this alternative estimator performs better than difference GMM in a range of circumstances for leverage regressions, using simulated US-listed company data. As the system GMM estimator may be preferable to the difference GMM estimator, and neither method is necessarily superior to the other, in this chapter we consider the results of both approaches and compare them with the results of the fixed-effects regression to make an assessment of the drivers of leverage decisions at the firm level.

The leverage measure we employ for our regressions is the liabilities-to-assets ratio. The covariate regressors ($\boldsymbol{X}_{it}$) we use in our estimation are profitability, the market-to-book ratio, collateral, the non-debt tax shield, firm size and industry median leverage. The variables we consider are similar to those used in most previous studies (Table 12.7).

22 A controversial assumption regarding initial conditions, which allows the additional moment conditions to be exploited, is that the difference of the lagged dependent variable in the first period is uncorrelated with the error in the subsequent period.

Table 12.7 Data summary

Series[(a)]	Number	Mean	Median	Standard deviation
Leverage	26,235	0.46	0.46	0.25
Profitability	24,945	0.05	0.05	0.15
Market-to-book	21,351	2.44	1.93	1.92
Collateral	26,235	0.26	0.22	0.18
Non-debt tax shield	25,602	0.02	0.02	0.02
Size	26,235	21.66	21.49	1.29

[(a)] Leverage refers to the book liabilities-to-assets ratio; profitability refers to EBIT divided by total assets; the market-to-book ratio refers to book liabilities plus the market value of equity divided by the book value of total assets; collateral refers to the ratio of fixed assets to total assets; non-debt tax shield refers to depreciation divided by total assets; and size refers to the natural logarithm of total assets (denominated in local currency).

Sources: Authors' calculations; CSMAR; WIND Information.

Profitability is measured as EBIT divided by total assets.[23] The pecking order theory predicts that firms will prefer to finance projects with retained earnings rather than debt, and hence implies a negative relationship with profitability (Myers and Majluf 1984). More profitable firms may also use their profits to pay down debt. An alternative view is that creditors will be more willing to lend to firms with stronger cash flows, as higher earnings imply greater capacity to meet debt payments. However, the aggregate comparisons in section two suggest a negative correlation between leverage and profitability.

The market-to-book ratio of assets (or price-to-book ratio) is commonly used in the literature as a proxy for growth opportunities. This ratio may be associated with either higher leverage (due to greater demand for external funds to realise these opportunities) or lower leverage (if these earning opportunities reduce the need for or incentive to take on additional debt).

To proxy firms' overall debt-raising capacity and available collateral, in the form of tangible assets, we use the ratio of fixed assets to total assets.

As a proxy for the non-debt tax shield, we use depreciation expense divided by total assets. The non-debt tax shield reduces the incentive for firms to prefer debt financing as a means of obtaining interest reductions when filing tax returns.

23 The rationale for scaling variables by total assets is to control for differences in firm size.

The log of the book value of total assets measures firm size. Larger firms may be lower-risk debtors, with reduced probability of bankruptcy, leading them to take on higher leverage. An alternative (pecking order) view is that older and larger firms may have had greater opportunities to retain earnings.[24]

We use median industry leverage as an additional variable in our analysis, to control for capital structure characteristics at the industry level. Frank and Goyal (2009) argue that this variable may act as a proxy for several determinants of leverage, including regulatory factors.[25] The decomposition in section three highlights the significance of real estate and construction industries in driving aggregate leverage patterns, which suggests a role for industry-level leverage in influencing leverage decisions at the firm level.

An implication of the analysis in the previous two sections is that state or private ownership/control has been an important factor in driving leverage outcomes. This is especially the case in the aftermath of the large fiscal-monetary stimulus that was introduced by the authorities in late 2008 and implemented over the subsequent few years. Several observers have seen the stimulus as symbolic of a fundamental shift in government policy, returning to a model of directed lending favouring SOEs (for a summary of these arguments, see Lardy 2012: 11–13). To consider this hypothesis at the firm level, we augment our specifications with a number of dummy variables. First, we augment each specification with a step dummy equal to zero in 2008 and earlier years and equal to one from 2009 onwards ('post-2008 dummy'). We specify a break in 2009 to allow for the change in the aggregate financing environment experienced by firms following the introduction of the stimulus.[26] Second, to measure the differential effects on state and private firms, we interact this variable with a dummy variable ('state') indicating firm ownership/control (equal to unity if a firm is state owned or controlled). In addition to the above regressors, we include a set of year dummy variables to control for exogenous annual variation affecting all firms. Collectively, the various time dummy variables form the vector Z_t.

A number of listed companies in our dataset exhibit very unusual leverage behaviour, resulting in very large liabilities-to-assets ratios. This mainly reflects some firms having negative book values for equity at certain points in time, potentially arising from financial distress, which is consistent with the book

24 We experimented with the inclusion of firm age as well, but this variable proved to be insignificant in our specifications.

25 Some studies also use proxies for earnings volatility, but we exclude this variable, as it is difficult to measure with precision in a short time series.

26 We also experimented with including an additional variable measuring growth in the stock of aggregate bank, non-bank and off balance sheet financing, using data on the national stock of trust loans, entrusted loans and undiscounted bank accepted bills, compiled from net flows published by the PBC. However, our main results were not meaningfully affected by the inclusion of this variable.

leverage ratios taking on values larger than one. Strategies commonly used in the literature to deal with outliers include censoring the leverage ratio on the unit interval, deleting certain percentiles of the leverage distribution and Winsorisation (for examples, see Byoun 2008; Flannery and Rangan 2006; Lemmon et al. 2008). For our main results, we exclude all firms that experience a liabilities-to-assets ratio in excess of five during the sample period. The reason for admitting firms with leverage ratios greater than unity into the sample is that the non-standard features and unusual values of the leverage distribution are in part what we are trying to explain. However, the key results are not particularly sensitive to censoring on the unit interval (see Appendix 12.1, Table A12.2).

Finally, it is worth noting that we do not use a matched sample of firms for our main set of results. In principle, using a matched sample could bias our results by ignoring compositional change (in particular, the changing relative shares of private and state firms) over the sample period. Against this consideration, it is possible that *not* using a matched sample could introduce bias due to firm exit and entry over the sample period. Reassuringly, our results are not especially sensitive to whether or not a matched sample is used. Supplementary matched sample results are shown in Appendix 12.1 (Table A12.1).

Results

The results are displayed in Table 12.8. The static (fixed effects) regression results given in Column 1 suggest that a firm's leverage is negatively correlated with profitability and positively correlated with firm size, collateral, the market-to-book ratio and industry median leverage, controlling for other factors.[27] The correlation with the non-debt tax shield is insignificant.

Interacting the post-2008 dummy with the ownership dummy, we detect evidence that state ownership increased the liabilities-to-assets ratios of listed companies in the post-2008 period by around 4 percentage points relative to private firms (compared with a median leverage ratio, after excluding outliers, of 45.6 per cent). This suggests that state firms increased their leverage *relative* to private firms after 2008 by a magnitude exceeding that which could be expected based on normal drivers of leverage decisions at the microeconomic level. However, if firms' leverage decisions are dynamic and persistent over time, the implications of static models may be misleading.

27 We focus on fixed effects rather than random effects as the latter is rejected by a Hausman (1978) test. Chivakul and Lam (2015) present results from a random effects model. Similar to our own results from static models, their results support the hypothesis that state ownership had a positive effect on leverage in the post-2008 period.

Table 12.8 Determinants of the liabilities-to-assets ratio[(a)]

Variable	Fixed effects (1)	Difference GMM (2)	System GMM (3)
Leverage(–1)		0.76*** (0.04)	0.83*** (0.12)
Profitability	–0.41*** (0.11)	–0.51*** (0.14)	–0.52 (0.43)
Market-to-book ratio	0.01*** (0.00)	0.01*** (0.00)	0.01 (0.00)
Collateral	0.12*** (0.04)	–0.01 (0.04)	–0.01 (0.04)
Non-debt tax shield	0.68 (0.59)	0.01 (0.89)	–0.18 (0.81)
Size	0.07*** (0.01)	0.03* (0.01)	0.03** (0.01)
Industry median	0.29*** (0.04)	0.23*** (0.03)	0.23*** (0.09)
Post-2008 dummy	0.01 (0.01)	–0.01 (0.02)	–0.02 (0.04)
State			–0.06 (0.16)
State × post-2008 dummy	0.04*** (0.01)	–0.01 (0.01)	–0.01 (0.08)
Constant	–1.21*** (0.14)		–0.50* (0.26)
Observations	21,285	16,832	19,191
Firms	2,444	2,172	2,323
Hausman test[(b)]	0.00		
Serial correlation[(c)]		0.57	0.51

(a) Standard errors in parentheses.

(b) p-value for Hausman test of null hypothesis that individual effects are adequately modelled by a random effects model.

(c) p-value for Arellano and Bond (1991) test for second-order serial correlation.

*** significant at the 1 per cent level

** significant at the 5 per cent level

* significant at the 10 per cent level

Notes: The regressions include a set of year dummy variables (not reported). Standard errors are heteroscedasticity consistent and adjusted. In the case of dynamic panel models, robust standard errors are estimated using the procedure described by Windmeijer (2005).

Source: Authors' calculations.

Columns 2 and 3 of Table 12.8 indicate that some of the variables that are significant in the static regression become insignificant when we allow firm leverage decisions to be correlated over time. This is not entirely surprising, as some of the information about static firm-level determinants of leverage that we observe in the results for the fixed-effects model is already summarised by the lagged dependent variable in the dynamic models. In fact, for several determinants of leverage, the results are quite robust to changes in specification. As in the fixed-effects model, the difference GMM specification finds that leverage displays a significant negative correlation with profitability and is positively correlated with the market-to-book ratio, firm size and industry median leverage, accounting for other factors.[28] The system GMM model finds firm size and industry median leverage to be significant, but profitability and the market-to-book ratio become insignificant even though they display similar coefficients to those found in the difference GMM specification.[29] Collateral is found to be insignificant in both models.

Estimates for the interaction between the post-2008 dummy and the ownership dummy diverge from the findings of the static fixed-effects model. The sign of the coefficient on this interaction is reversed but it is insignificant. To check the robustness of this finding, we re-estimated the above models over different periods, with starting periods ranging from 2002 to 2004 and end periods ranging from 2010 to 2015. The results are robust to these variations (see Table A12.3 in Appendix 12.1). Qualitatively similar findings are also found for a matched sample of firms listed since 2000 (see Table A12.1 in Appendix 12.1).

These results suggest that when we control for persistence in leverage, the leverage of state firms relative to private firms after 2008 is not significantly higher than would be predicted based on standard static determinants of capital structure. The change in the coefficient on the interaction term and its significance reflect the transformation of the relationship from levels to changes and also the inclusion of a lagged dependent variable (that is, the shift from Equation 12.3 to Equation 12.6). As the lagged dependent variable already captures differences in prior leverage behaviour between state and private firms, it reduces the ability of the interaction term to detect a significant change in behaviour over and above standard static determinants of leverage.

In both of the dynamic models, the coefficient on lagged leverage is significant, suggesting that a firm's past leverage has an important bearing on current capital structure decisions. The implied speed of adjustment to a hypothetical target leverage ratio is around 24 per cent per annum for the difference GMM model and around 17 per cent for the system GMM model. This suggests an

28 In these specifications, profitability, the market-to-book ratio and collateral are treated as potentially endogenous, and hence second lags of these variables are used as instruments.

29 Profitability is found to be significant and negative in the matched sample specification (see Appendix 13.1).

approximate half-life of 2.5 to 3.7 years. Our estimate of the speed of adjustment is remarkably similar to that estimated by Qian et al. (2009) for the debt-to-assets ratio using a smaller and older sample of firms, who find an adjustment speed of 18.5 per cent per year.[30] This is much slower than adjustment speeds derived for listed firms in the United States by Flannery and Rangan (2006), who estimate an adjustment speed of 34 per cent per annum in a fixed-effects model (which uses an instrumental variable correction for lagged leverage) and 52 per cent using a difference GMM model.

Overall, the results from our models suggest that, controlling for other factors, a firm's lagged leverage ratio, its size, its profitability and the median leverage of the industry to which it belongs are all helpful in explaining its capital structure decisions. The coefficients on profitability, firm size, the market-to-book ratio and industry median leverage are fairly similar across the three different specifications. The results, combined with the findings of our decomposition of listed company leverage in section three, suggest some reasons for the increase in leverage since the late 2000s. In particular, it is possible that persistence in firm-level leverage behaviour, combined with deteriorating state sector profitability and a compositional shift of listed company assets towards industries such as real estate and construction that display higher average leverage, accounts for much of the upward trend in leverage in recent years. The decomposition in section three indicates that state firms account for the majority of the increase in the leverage of the real estate and construction industries since 2008, although private firms in these industries have also contributed positively to overall leverage.

The fact that some of the most highly leveraged private and state firms have shown signs of deleveraging in the past few years (see section three) could signal a gradual shift towards lower 'target' leverage ratios. Yet if recent trends continue, rising leverage in parts of the private sector and the tendency for more recently listed firms to contribute positively to overall leverage could be counteracting forces. The sustained upward trend in debt and leverage in China is widely perceived by analysts and commentators as a potential precursor to a disruptive financial event or crisis. Should rising leverage eventually result in financial instability that forces an abrupt deleveraging in the corporate sector, it is unlikely that listed companies would be immune. However, if the process of deleveraging proves to be more orderly than this, and if capital structure decisions are highly persistent, as suggested by our model-based estimates, the process of deleveraging for listed firms is likely to be gradual.

30 The speed of adjustment is also robust to estimation over different sample periods, such as those shown in Table A13.3 (Appendix 13.1).

Concluding remarks

The rapid build-up in corporate leverage in China since the late 2000s has fuelled concerns about the potential risks for financial stability and growth. Discussions of leverage in China often emphasise the role played by stimulus policies during the GFC in driving up the indebtedness of SOEs. This chapter examines the leverage of a small component of the broader Chinese corporate universe—non-financial companies listed on mainland public exchanges—to obtain a more granular picture of how leverage patterns have evolved in recent years, particularly since the late 2000s.

Our analysis supports the view that state-owned or state-controlled firms have led the rise in corporate leverage, and that these firms have seen a corresponding deterioration in operating performance relative to private firms since the stimulus period. As the bulk of listed company assets are controlled or owned by state entities, state firms continue to account for the lion's share of overall leverage. However, this broad picture masks considerable heterogeneity at a more disaggregated level.

On the one hand, there is evidence of deleveraging among some of the more highly leveraged private and state firms. On the other hand, the rising share of listed company assets in private hands and pockets of increasing private sector leverage (especially firms that have entered the sample since 2008) mean that the private sector has accounted for a greater share of the increase in listed company leverage than average leverage ratios for state and private firms might suggest. By industry, real estate and construction firms have contributed the most to the pick-up in leverage, while utilities, mining and services firms have subtracted overall. Private firms have tended to contribute positively to the increase in leverage since 2012, particularly in manufacturing and services industries.

Results from fixed-effects panel regressions of leverage on key firm-level determinants point to a negative association between leverage and profitability and a positive correlation with firm size, collateral and industry leverage patterns. Dynamic models, which allow for leverage decisions to be serially correlated, further indicate that persistence in capital structure decisions at the firm level is an important feature of observed leverage behaviour. It is possible that this characteristic, combined with weaker state-sector profitability and a shift in industry composition towards more highly leveraged sectors such as real estate and construction in the wake of the government's 2008–09 stimulus, explains much of the upward trend in leverage over recent years. If this is correct, and true for non-listed companies as well, sluggish adjustment in firm behaviour could make it challenging for China's corporate sector to achieve rapid deleveraging.

References

Arellano, M. and Bond, S. (1991), Some tests of specification for panel data: Monte Carlo evidence and an application to employment equations, *Review of Economic Studies*, 58: 277–297.

Bank for International Settlements (BIS) (2016), *Long series on credit to the private non-financial sector*, Online database, Bank for International Settlements, Basel. Available from: bis.org/statistics/credtopriv.htm.

Blundell, R. and Bond, S. (1998), Initial conditions and moment restrictions in dynamic panel data models, *Journal of Econometrics*, 87: 115–143.

Borio, C. and Lowe, P. (2002), Asset prices, financial and monetary stability: Exploring the nexus, BIS Working Paper No. 114, Basel: Bank for International Settlements.

Byoun, S. (2008), How and when do firms adjust their capital structures toward targets?, *Journal of Finance*, 108(6): 2069–3096.

Chen, G., Firth, M. and Xu, L. (2009), Does the type of ownership control matter? Evidence from China's listed companies, *Journal of Banking and Finance*, 33: 171–181.

Chen, J. (2004), Determinants of capital structure of Chinese-listed companies, *Journal of Business Research*, 57: 1341–1351.

Chen, L. (2014), The future history of China's deleveraging, *Gavekal Dragonomics*, July.

Chivakul, M. and Lam, W. R. (2015), *Assessing China's corporate sector vulnerabilities*, IMF Working Paper No. WP/15/72, Washington, DC: International Monetary Fund.

Ding, Y. and Su, X. (2008), Implementation of IFRS in a regulated market, *Journal of Accounting and Public Policy*, 27: 474–479.

Donaldson, G. (1961), *Corporate debt capacity: A study of corporate debt policy and the determination of corporate debt capacity*, Cambridge, Mass.: Harvard Business School.

Drehmann, M. and Juselius, M. (2013), *Evaluating early warning indicators of banking crises: Satisfying policy requirements*, BIS Working Paper No. 421, Basel: Bank for International Settlements.

Fan, J. P. H., Wong, T. J. and Zhang, T. (2007), Politically connected CEOs, corporate governance and post-IPO performance in China's newly partially privatized firms, *Journal of Financial Economics*, 84: 300–357.

Firth, M., Malatesta, P. H., Xin, Q. and Xu, L. (2012), Corporate investment, government control, and financing channels: Evidence from China's listed companies, *Journal of Corporate Finance*, 18: 433–450.

Flannery, M. J. and Hankins, K. W. (2013), Estimating dynamic panel models in corporate finance, *Journal of Corporate Finance*, 19: 1–19.

Flannery, M. J. and Rangan, K. P. (2006), Partial adjustment toward target capital structures, *Journal of Financial Economics*, 79: 469–506.

Frank, M. Z. and Goyal, V. K. (2009), Capital structure decisions: Which factors are reliably important?, *Financial Management*, 38: 1–37.

Harris, M. and Raviv, A. (1991), The theory of capital structure, *Journal of Finance*, 46: 297–355.

Hausman, J. A. (1978), Specification tests in econometrics, *Econometrica*, 46: 1251–1271.

Holtz-Eakin, D., Newey, W. and Rosen, H. S. (1988), Estimating vector autoregressions with panel data, *Econometrica*, 56: 1371–1395.

Huang, S. G. H. and Song, F. M. (2006), The determinants of capital structure: Evidence from China, *China Economic Review*, 17: 14–35.

Huang, Y. and Bosler, C. (2014), *China's debt dilemma: Deleveraging while generating growth*, Paper, 18 September, Beijing: Carnegie Endowment for International Peace. Available from: carnegieendowment.org/2014/09/18/china-s-debt-dilemma-deleveraging-while-generating-growth.

International Monetary Fund (IMF) (2015a), *People's Republic of China, Article IV consultation*, IMF Country Report No. 15/234. Available from: imf.org/external/pubs/ft/scr/2015/cr15234.pdf.

International Monetary Fund (IMF) (2015b), *Global Financial Stability Report: Vulnerabilities, Legacies and Policy Challenges – Risks Rotating to Emerging Markets*, October 2015: 12. Available from: imf.org/External/Pubs/FT/GFSR/2015/02/pdf/text.pdf.

Lardy, N. (1998), *China's unfinished economic revolution*, Washington, DC: Brookings Institution.

Lardy, N. (2012), *Sustaining China's economic growth after the Global Financial Crisis*, Washington, DC: Institute for International Economics.

Lemmon, M. L., Roberts, M. R. and Zender, J. F. (2008), Back to the beginning: Persistence and the cross-section of corporate capital structure, *Journal of Finance*, 118(4): 1575–1607.

Li, K., Yue, H. and Zhao, L. (2009), Ownership, institutions and capital structure: Evidence from China, *Journal of Comparative Economics*, 37(3): 471–490.

Myers, S. (1984), The capital structure puzzle, *Journal of Finance*, 39: 575–592.

Myers, S. and Majluf, N. (1984), Corporate financing and investment decisions when firms have information that investors do not have, *Journal of Financial Economics*, 13: 187–221.

National Development and Reform Commission (NDRC) (2016), *Report on the implementation of the 2015 Plan for National Economic and Social Development and on the 2016 Draft Plan for National Economic and Social Development*, Beijing: NDRC. Available from: online.wsj.com/public/resources/documents/NPC2016_NDRC_English.pdf.

Nickell, S. (1981), Biases in dynamic models with fixed effects, *Econometrica*, 49: 1417–1426.

People's Bank of China (PBC) (2016), Transcript of Governor Zhou's Xiaochuan's press conference, Beijing, 10 March. Available from: pbc.gov.cn/english/130721/3029330/index.html.

Pettis, M. (2013), *Avoiding the fall: China's economic restructuring*, Washington, DC: Carnegie Endowment for International Peace.

Qian, Y., Tian, Y. and Wirjanto, T. S. (2009), Do Chinese publicly listed companies adjust their capital structure toward a target level?, *China Economic Review*, 20: 662–676.

Walter, C. E. and Howie, F. J. T. (2011), *Red capitalism: The fragile financial foundations of China's extraordinary rise*, Singapore: John Wiley & Sons.

Windmeijer, F. (2005), A finite sample correction for the variance of linear efficient two-step GMM estimators, *Journal of Econometrics*, 126: 25–51.

Yu, M. (2013), State ownership and firm performance: Empirical evidence from Chinese listed companies, *China Journal of Accounting Research*, 6: 75–87.

Zhang, W., Han, G., Ng, B. and Chan, S. (2015), *Corporate leverage in China: Why has it increased fast in recent years and where do the risks lie?*, Working Paper No. 10/15, Hong Kong: Hong Kong Institute for Monetary Research.

Appendix 12.1: Supplementary regression results

Table A12.1 Determinants of the liabilities-to-assets ratio: Matched sample[(a)]

Variable	Fixed effects (1)	Difference GMM (2)	System GMM (3)
Leverage(–1)		0.78*** (0.03)	0.83*** (0.03)
Profitability	–0.37*** (0.11)	–0.39*** (0.13)	–0.43*** (0.13)
Market-to-book ratio	0.01** (0.01)	0.01*** (0.00)	0.00 (0.00)
Collateral	0.06 (0.04)	–0.05 (0.04)	–0.04 (0.04)
Non-debt tax shield	0.67 (0.61)	–0.23 (0.52)	0.26 (0.81)
Size	0.06*** (0.01)	0.01 (0.64)	0.02*** (0.01)
Industry median	0.28*** (0.05)	0.21*** (0.04)	0.19*** (0.05)
Post-2008 dummy	–0.03* (0.02)	0.02* (0.01)	0.02 (0.01)
State			0.02 (0.04)
State × post-2008 dummy	0.07*** (0.01)	–0.01 (0.01)	–0.01 (0.01)
Constant	–1.01*** (0.19)		–0.47*** (0.10)
Observations	11,685	10,028	10,899
Firms	839	787	839
Hausman test[(b)]	0.00		
Serial correlation[(c)]		0.45	0.39

[(a)] Standard errors in parentheses.

[(b)] p-value for Hausman test of null hypothesis that individual effects are adequately modelled by a random effects model.

[(c)] p-value for Arellano and Bond (1991) test for second-order serial correlation

*** significant at the 1 per cent level

** significant at the 5 per cent level

* significant at the 10 per cent level

Notes: The regressions include a set of year dummy variables (not reported). Standard errors are heteroscedasticity consistent and adjusted. In the case of dynamic panel models, robust standard errors are estimated using the procedure described by Windmeijer (2005).

Source: Authors' calculations.

Table A12.2 Determinants of the liabilities-to-assets ratio (censored on unit interval)[(a)]

Variable	Fixed effects (1)	Difference GMM (2)	System GMM (3)
Leverage(–1)		0.75*** (0.28)	0.81*** (0.05)
Profitability	–0.51*** (0.02)	–0.17* (0.09)	–0.25 (0.63)
Market-to-book ratio	–0.00 (0.00)	0.01*** (0.00)	0.00 (0.00)
Collateral	0.11*** (0.02)	0.02 (0.02)	0.02 (0.05)
Non-debt tax shield	–0.43*** (0.14)	–0.87 (0.22)	–0.98** (0.42)
Size	0.09*** (0.00)	0.05*** (0.01)	0.02*** (0.01)
Industry median	0.19*** (0.03)	0.24*** (0.03)	0.23*** (0.07)
Post-2008 dummy	–0.01 (0.01)	–0.01 (0.01)	–0.02 (0.04)
State			–0.03 (0.11)
State × post-2008 dummy	0.02*** (0.01)	–0.01 (0.01)	–0.01 (0.01)
Constant	–1.49*** (0.11)		–0.44*** (0.08)
Observations	20,197	15,934	18,183
Firms	2,353	2,091	2,232
Hausman test[(b)]	0.00		
Serial correlation[(c)]		0.96	0.99

(a) Standard errors in parentheses.

(b) p-value for Hausman test of null hypothesis that individual effects are adequately modelled by a random effects model.

(c) p-value for Arellano and Bond (1991) test for second-order serial correlation.

*** significant at the 1 per cent level

** significant at the 5 per cent level

* significant at the 10 per cent level

Notes: The regressions include a set of year dummy variables (not reported). Standard errors are heteroscedasticity consistent and adjusted. In the case of dynamic panel models, robust standard errors are estimated using the procedure described by Windmeijer (2005).

Source: Authors' calculations.

Table A12.3 Sample sensitivity: Coefficient on state × post-2008 dummy[(a)]

Sample	Fixed effects	Difference GMM	System GMM
2000–15	0.04***	–0.01	–0.01
2001–15	0.04***	–0.01	–0.01
2002–15	0.04***	–0.01	–0.01
2003–15	0.04***	–0.01	–0.01
2004–15	0.04***	–0.01	–0.00
2000–14	0.04***	–0.01	–0.01
2000–13	0.04***	–0.01	–0.01
2000–12	0.03***	–0.01	–0.01
2000–11	0.03***	–0.01	–0.01
2000–10	0.02**	–0.01	–0.01

[(a)] Standard errors in parentheses.

*** significant at the 1 per cent level

** significant at the 5 per cent level

* significant at the 10 per cent level

Notes: Standard errors are heteroscedasticity consistent and adjusted. Windmeijer (2005) robust standard errors are used for dynamic panel models.

Source: Authors' calculations.

Part II: Resources, Energy, the Environment and Climate Change

13. Evaluating Low-Carbon City Development in China: Study of five national pilot cities[1]

Biliang Hu, Jia Luo, Chunlai Chen and Bingqin Li

Introduction

China was responsible for 25 per cent of global carbon dioxide emissions in 2012 (Liu 2015). This followed the passing of key milestones in the previous decade. From 2007, China's per capita carbon dioxide emissions exceeded the world average and it has become the world's largest contributor to annual carbon dioxide emissions, with the burning of fossil fuels and cement production being two important emission sources. According to World Bank research (Hu 2013), cities hold more than 65 per cent of global wealth, consume more than 65 per cent of global energy and emit some 70 per cent of greenhouse gases (GHGs). Reducing urban carbon dioxide emissions is considered to be key to reducing overall emissions, within which transforming cities into 'low-carbon cities' is seen as an important policy tool (Bao et al. 2008; Feliciano and Prosperi 2011).

China's urbanisation rate increased from 17.9 per cent in 1978 to 56.1 per cent in 2015. Under the Thirteenth Five-Year Plan (FYP), China's urbanisation rate is set to increase to 60 per cent by 2020. Fast economic growth and rapid development of urban centres have, however, already caused many environmental problems, including environmental degradation and air and water pollution, and this has drawn the increasing attention of the public (Li 2013; Gu et al. 2011). The pressure to reduce carbon dioxide emissions and so help achieve sustainable development is mounting both internationally and domestically.

In early 2008, the Ministry of Construction of China and the World Wide Fund for Nature (WWF) introduced the 'Low-Carbon City' pilot schemes in Shanghai and Baoding in Hebei province (near Beijing, and located in an area known as China's 'Power Valley'). In 2010, such schemes were formally endorsed by the National Development and Reform Commission (NDRC 2010). The main aims of

1 This chapter is part of the research arising from 'The Key Research Project of The National Social Science Fund of China on China New Urbanization: A five dimensional integration development approach' (14ZDA035).

the pilot low-carbon city programs are to develop low–carbon dioxide emission industries, to establish a GHG emission data collection and management system and to encourage residents to adopt green and low-carbon consumption patterns and lifestyles. According to the NDRC document, this endorsement meant that five provinces (Guangdong, Liaoning, Hubei, Shanxi and Yunnan) and eight cities (Tianjin, Chongqing, Shenzhen, Xiamen, Hangzhou, Nanchang, Guiyang and Baoding) would enter the national low-carbon pilot scheme. A second batch of pilots entered the scheme in 2012, bringing to 36 the total number of cities involved (NDRC 2012).

One of the key challenges raised by observers of the pilot cities is that so far, despite strong public and government support and sound individual examples, no clear set of indicators exists to definitively measure the overall outcomes of low-carbon city projects (Hu and Li 2016). This is not to say that specific initiatives are not important, as they may well contribute to the reduction of carbon dioxide emissions, but producing an overall evaluation of related projects in China could shed light on how low-carbon city initiatives have contributed to overall carbon dioxide emission levels.

This chapter develops a low-carbon city evaluation system to assess the performance of five pilot low-carbon city projects in China. Section two discusses and introduces the principles and the main indictors for evaluating the performance of low-carbon cities, including the methodology used herein. Section three uses the indicators to evaluate the performance of five national pilot low-carbon cities in China. The final section summarises the findings and provides policy suggestions based on our findings.

Low-carbon cities in China

Despite the number of low-carbon city pilots in China, there is no clear definition of what such a city is, with the implementation process also being used to shape the meaning of the concept for each city. As suggested in the name, the low-carbon city initiative is meant to reduce the carbon dioxide emissions of cities. What complicates the endeavour is that Chinese cities vary greatly in their economic structure and environmental resources and their capacity to reduce carbon dioxide emissions. Cities therefore need to develop local strategies to fit their own circumstances (Li 2013). Introducing a universal standard for all cities to enforce would be unacceptable and could also suffocate local innovation.

As a result of these difficulties, the policy process is a two-way one: 1) the Central Government sets the overall target, as in the Twelfth FYP, to reduce the carbon intensity per unit of gross domestic product (GDP) by 17 per cent (Li and Wang 2012); and 2) local governments are held accountable for achieving the target.

Local governments must come up with low-carbon development strategies to align with the aggregate target, which can be achieved by different means (Baeumler et al. 2012).

Given that China is urbanising rapidly, the intention is to reduce carbon dioxide emissions not in absolute terms, but in relative terms—that is, to combine economic development with carbon dioxide emission goals. In the low-carbon city initiatives, cities focus on cutting their carbon intensity (carbon dioxide emissions per unit of GDP) (Huang 2011) and adopt strategies to highlight their own advantages. The volume of carbon emissions, therefore, is used only as a reference.

To some extent, the pilots can be perceived as a form of field research. Through the practices of each city, policymakers can collect firsthand information on the effectiveness of a range of local strategies. However, such an approach also faces a challenge: how to assess the actual performance of cities carrying out various experiments. This chapter tries to address this challenge by designing a method by which to measure the performance of low-carbon cities.

Evaluation of the performance of low-carbon cities

To evaluate the performance of low-carbon cities, it is important to have a set of measureable indicators. This is a challenge both for China and for the rest of the world. The existing evaluation practices follow two approaches. One is to use a single indicator—for example, total carbon dioxide emissions, per capita carbon dioxide emissions, per capita residential consumption carbon dioxide emissions, per unit of land carbon dioxide emissions, carbon dioxide emissions intensity or the growth rate of carbon dioxide emissions. The advantage of this method is that it is clear and straightforward. It targets carbon dioxide emissions directly. However, even if it can be viewed as a composite indicator, this approach has been criticised for oversimplification and the risk of narrowing understanding of the issues (Weidema et al. 2008; Pulselli et al. 2015). Further, low-carbon cities are not just about lowering carbon dioxide emissions. More importantly, the concept also embraces sustainable development, which tries to strike a balance between economic development, environmental protection and efficient use of natural resources and energy.

The second, and more popular, approach to evaluating low-carbon cities is to create a set of indicators. This approach captures multiple dimensions of the performance of a low-carbon city and thus takes a broader approach than the first one. This approach can therefore also reflect the level of sustainable development of a low-carbon city. One such popular model is the Driving

Force-Pressure-State-Impact-Response (DPSIR) model (Carr et al. 2007), which classifies economic, social, resource and environmental indicators into five categories: driving forces, pressure, state, impact and response. The advantage of this model is that it reveals the reciprocal relationship between the environment and economic activity, and also provides feedback via the status of resources and the environment on the potential impacts of human activities (Shao and Ju 2010; Wang 2013). To achieve this, the selection of indicators should be comprehensive. Examples include economic factors, such as per capita GDP, and demographic factors, such as population growth rate and the rate of urbanisation. The multivariate context makes it difficult to isolate drivers, not to mention generating targeted policies. Given that we want to produce targeted policy suggestions, we opt not to use DPSIR for our analyses.

Another popular approach is the Stochastic Impact by Regression on Population, Affluence and Technology (STIRPAT) model (York et al. 2003; Fan et al. 2006; Gabrielsen and Bosch 2003), which is developed from the Impact, Population, Affluence and Technology (IPAT) model. There are modified versions of the basic STIRPAT framework with which to evaluate the levels of low-carbon city development. These indicators take into account economic, social, environmental, resources and energy, technology and residential consumption. In this chapter, we adapt the STIRPAT model to analyse the performance of low-carbon cities in China.

The low-carbon city development index: Indicator selection

Our evaluation framework includes five low-carbon city dimensions: economic growth, energy consumption, urban construction, government support and residential consumption. Seventeen specific indicators are selected based on the STIRPAT model. Our choice is adapted according to the *China green development index report 2012*, produced by the School of Economics and Resource Management of Beijing Normal University (Li and Pan 2015). This is widely regarded in China as the seminal annual report in this field. Figure 13.1 illustrates the evaluation framework, the five indicators and sub-indicators, on which we elaborate next.

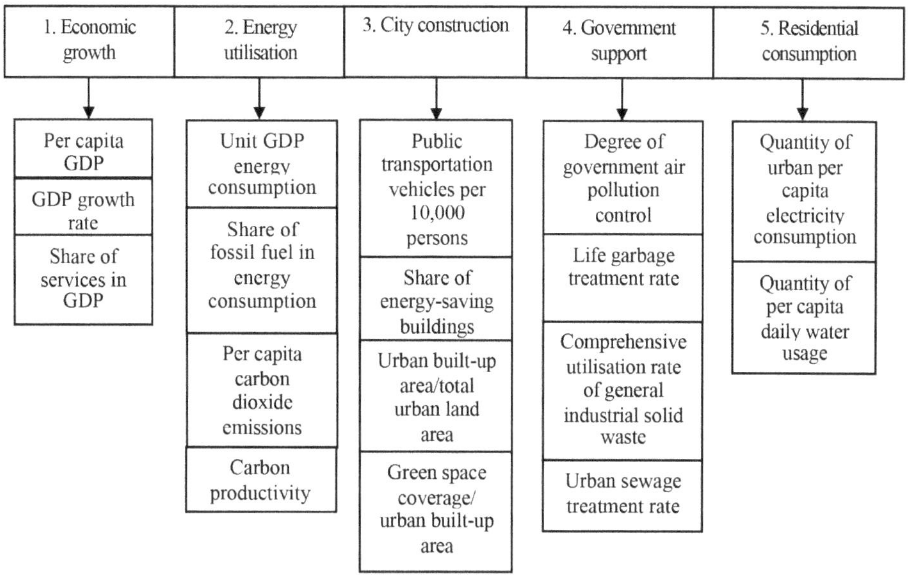

Figure 13.1 An indicator for the performance of cities in the 'low-carbon city' program

Source: Authors' own design.

Figure 13.1 shows the framework we use to measure five different aspects of performance. A composite indicator is calculated according to the performance of each city indicator. The composite indicator thus offers an overall assessment. For example, a city may have achieved a high level of economic growth; however, this outcome might be compromised by its poorer performance in terms of energy consumption.

With regard to the first indicator, economic growth, existing research shows that three economic factors are related to carbon dioxide emissions: the level of economic development (Selden and Song 1994; Stern and Common 2001), the rate of economic growth (Soytas and Sari 2009; Zhang and Cheng 2009) and the share of the services sector (Golove and Schipper 1997; Casler and Blair 1997). We selected three proxy indicators for these three economic factors: 1) GDP per capita—the level of economic development; 2) GDP growth rate—economic growth; and 3) the services sector's share of GDP in total GDP—economic structure.

The second indicator, energy utilisation, includes indicators for both energy consumption and carbon dioxide emissions. We choose unit GDP energy consumption and fossil fuels' share of energy consumption to measure energy consumption. Unit GDP energy consumption is measured as the total quantity of energy consumption divided by GDP. The higher the value of this indicator, the more energy will be used to produce a unit of GDP, thus having a negative impact on low-carbon city development. Fossil fuels' share of energy consumption is measured as the quantity of fossil fuels consumed divided by the total quantity of energy consumed. Because fossil fuels produce large carbon dioxide emissions, we consider that a high share of fossil fuels in total energy consumption will compromise the city's overall performance.

To capture total carbon dioxide emissions, we use the quantity of carbon dioxide emissions generated by industrial enterprises' energy consumption as the total quantity of a city's carbon dioxide emissions. We select two measures of carbon dioxide emissions. The first is per capita carbon dioxide emissions, measured as the total quantity of carbon dioxide emissions divided by the total population of a city, which subtracts from the level of low-carbon city development. The second measure is carbon productivity, measured as GDP divided by the total quantity of carbon dioxide emissions, which associates positively with the level of low-carbon city development. To measure carbon dioxide emissions, we include in our analyses coal, charcoal, four fuel products (petrol, kerosene, diesel and oil) and natural gas. We first convert the quantity of each type of energy into tonnes of standard coal equivalent (tce) and then multiply the quantity of tce by the carbon dioxide emissions index to generate the quantity of carbon dioxide emissions (see Table 13.1).

Table 13.1 Standard coal equivalent conversion index and carbon dioxide emissions index of energy categories

Energy categories	Standard coal equivalent conversion index (tce/tonne)	Carbon dioxide emissions index (carbon dioxide tonne/tce)
Coal	0.71	0.76
Charcoal	0.97	0.86
Petrol	1.47	0.55
Kerosene	1.47	0.57
Diesel	1.46	0.59
Burning oil	1.43	0.62
Natural gas	1.27	0.45

Sources: Standard coal conversion index is from NDRC (2008); IPCC (2006).

The third indicator, urban construction, includes four sub-indicators: 1) the number of public transportation vehicles per 10,000 people as a proxy for the coverage of public transportation; 2) the share of energy-saving buildings; 3) the green coverage rate of built-up areas, which represents the urban construction aspect and is positively associated with the level of low-carbon city development; and 4) the share of built-up areas in total urban land area. Poor performance in these indicators means that the overall performance is compromised.

The fourth indicator, government support, is important because it reflects the fact that low-carbon city development is more difficult to achieve without active government support. It is included as a dimension for evaluation to stress the important role government can play in developing low-carbon cities, and to reflect the effect of government actions on city environmental controls. We choose four sub-indicators for this dimension: the degree of government air pollution control (measured as the number of days with air quality above grade two); the life garbage treatment rate; the comprehensive utilisation rate of general industrial solid waste; and the urban sewage treatment rate. When a city performs well in these four sub-indicators, this should also contribute positively to its overall performance.

The fifth indicator in our study, residential consumption, is captured by two sub-indicators: urban per capita electricity consumption and urban per capita daily water usage. These two sub-indicators contribute negatively to the indicator.

Allocating weights

There are two leading methods for assigning weights to selected indicators: subjective allocation and objective calculation. In this study, we adopt the subjective allocation approach. We invited 10 experts[2] with outstanding research achievements in this area to allocate weight to each indicator. Based on the resulting scores, the weight for economic growth is 20 per cent, 31 per cent for energy utilisation, 21 per cent for urban construction, 19 per cent for government support and 9 per cent for residential consumption. The details of weight allocations are presented in Table 13.2.

2 We would like to thank Professor Xiaoxi Li, Professor Weibin Lin, Professor Yongsheng Lin and Professor Yanting Zheng from Beijing Normal University; Professor Faqi Shi from the National Bureau of Statistics; Professor Zuojun Li from the Development Research Centre of the State Council; Professor Yulong Shi and Professor Changyun Jiang from the Macroeconomic Academy of the State Development and Reform Commission; and Professor Zhixiong Du and Professor Yuanhong Zhang from the Chinese Academy of Social Sciences, for their help in allocating weight to each of the indicators.

Table 13.2 Low-carbon city development evaluation indicators and weights

	Dimension		Indicator	Unit	Impact	Weight (%)*
Level of low-carbon city development	Economic growth (20%)	Level of economic development	Per capita GDP	RMB	Positive	6
		Economic growth	GDP growth rate	%	Positive	5
		Economic structure	Share of services in GDP	%	Positive	9
	Energy utilisation (31%)	Energy utilisation	Unit GDP energy consumption	tce/RMB10,000	Negative	8
			Share of fossil fuels in energy	%	Negative	9
		Carbon dioxide emissions	Per capita carbon dioxide emissions	tonne/person	Negative	7
			Carbon productivity	RMB10,000/tonne	Positive	7
	City construction (21%)	Transportation	Public transportation vehicles per 10,000 people	Unit	Positive	6
		Construction	Share of energy-saving buildings	%	Positive	6
		Land utilisation	Urban built-up area/total urban land area	%	Negative	4
			Green space coverage/total built-up area	%	Positive	5
	Government support (19%)	Results of government control and treatment	Degree of government air pollution control	%	Positive	6
			Life garbage non-harmful treatment rate	%	Positive	5
			Comprehensive utilisation rate of general industrial solid waste	%	Positive	4
			Urban sewage treatment rate	%	Positive	4
	Residential consumption (9%)	Consumption level	Quantity of urban per capita electricity consumption	1,000 watt/person	Negative	5
			Quantity of per capita daily water usage	litre/person	Negative	4

Note: The 10 experts are required to allocate a weight score to each indicator. The overall weight shown in the right-hand column is an average of all the weight scores given by all 10 experts. The total score for the 17 indicators is one. The weight scores of all indicators in one dimension are added together to generate the dimension weight scores shown in parentheses in the left column 'Dimension'.

Source: Authors' own design.

Calculating the index

Because different indicators are measured in different units, when calculating the low-carbon city development index (LCCDI), our first step is to use the following equations to calculate the standard value for all indicators.

Equation 13.1

$$A' = \frac{A - MinA}{MaxA - MinA}$$

Equation 13.2

$$A' = \frac{MaxA - A}{MaxA - MinA}$$

In Equations 13.1 and 13.2, A' is the standard value, A is the original value, $MaxA$ is the maximum value and $MinA$ is the minimum value of an indicator. The standard value of A' ranges from zero to one. Equation 13.1 is for the positive indicators and Equation 13.2 is for the negative indicators.

Second, based on the results from the above equations, we can use Equation 13.3 to calculate the score for each of the five dimensions and the total score of the LCCDI for a city.

Equation 13.3

$$LCCDI = \sum_i^n w_i \times A'$$

In Equation 13.3, w_i is the weight of indicator i. Based on the score calculated from Equation 13.3, we can compare the levels of low-carbon development for each city. The higher the value of the index, the higher is the level of low-carbon development.

Evaluating low-carbon city development

For this study, we select five cities—Tianjin, Shenzhen, Hangzhou, Nanchang and Baoding—from the national pilot low-carbon city program. Shenzhen is a special economic zone, which still had a basic agrarian economy in the 1980s, but is today host to high and new technology industries, financial services and modern logistics and cultural industries. Hangzhou is in one of China's richest per capita provinces, Zhejiang, and is a famous tourist city. Its high and new technology industries are growing rapidly. Baoding, in contrast, is a less-developed, historical city in northern China. The city is increasingly host to heavy industries being relocated from Beijing and Tianjin. As a result, it is one of the most polluted cities in China. The rate of growth of Nanchang, in Jiangxi Province, has picked up in recent years and it is considered to have great potential for future development. Table 13.3 shows the basic information for the five selected cities.

Table 13.3 Basic information for the selected five cities, 2013

City	Per capita GDP (RMB10,000)	Land area (10,000 sq km)	Urbanisation rate (%)	Unit GDP energy consumption (tce/RMB10,000)	Green coverage rate of built-up areas (%)
Tianjin	9.96	1.19	82.01	0.64	34.93
Shenzhen	13.69	0.20	100.00	0.48	45.07
Hangzhou	9.46	1.66	74.90	0.56	40.23
Nanchang	6.47	0.74	69.83	0.60	42.41
Baoding	2.55	2.22	42.93	0.25	40.36

Sources: NBS (2014b, 2014f); Statistics Bureau of Shenzhen City (2014); Tianjin Municipal Statistics Bureau (2014); Nanchang Municipal Statistics Bureau (2014); Statistical Bureau of Baoding (2014).

Based on the LCCDI outlined in section two, we calculated the level of low-carbon city development for the eight national pilot low-carbon cities designated by the NDRC in 2010. Here we first evaluate the total level of low-carbon city development and then the level of each dimension of low-carbon city development for the five selected representative cities.

Evaluating the overall level of low-carbon city development

The low-carbon city development indices for the five selected cities for the period 2010–13 are presented in Table 13.4.

As Table 13.4 shows, during the period 2010–13, the average LCCDI score for Shenzhen was 0.71—the highest among the five cities. Hangzhou ranked second, with a score of 0.51, followed by Nanchang (0.49), Tianjin (0.49) and Baoding (0.41). However, because the level of low-carbon development for Shenzhen is far higher than that for the other four cities, it raised the average level of low-carbon development and, as a result, the levels of low-carbon development for the other four cities are all below the average. It is important to note that even in Hangzhou, a world-famous tourist city, low-carbon development is at a relatively low level. Moreover, many Chinese cities have even lower levels of low-carbon development, which suggests there is plenty of room for improvement for China's overall levels of low-carbon city development.

Table 13.4 LCCDI and ranking of the five selected cities

	Four-year average		2010		2011		2012		2013	
City	**Score**	**Ranking**	**Score**	**Ranking**	**Score**	**Ranking**	**Score**	**Ranking**	**Score**	**Ranking**
Shenzhen	0.71	1	0.75	1	0.73	1	0.71	1	0.67	1
Hangzhou	0.51	2	0.46	4	0.49	3	0.59	2	0.49	2
Nanchang	0.49	3	0.50	3	0.48	4	0.56	3	0.44	3
Tianjin	0.49	4	0.51	2	0.50	2	0.55	4	0.40	4
Baoding	0.41	5	0.39	5	0.41	5	0.41	5	0.41	5
Average	**0.52**	**n/a**	**0.52**	**n/a**	**0.52**	**n/a**	**0.56**	**n/a**	**0.48**	**n/a**

n/a not applicable

Sources: The data used to calculate the indices are from NBS (2011a–g, 2012a–g, 2013a–g, 2014a–g); Statistics Bureau of Shenzhen City (2011, 2012, 2013, 2014); Nanchang Municipal Statistics Bureau (2011, 2012, 2013, 2014); Tianjin Municipal Statistics Bureau (2011, 2012, 2013, 2014); Statistical Bureau of Baoding (2011, 2012, 2013, 2014).

It is also important to observe that Shenzhen's score has been declining over time, falling from 0.75 in 2010 to 0.68 in 2013. In contrast, Hangzhou's low-carbon development has been improving over time, moving from fourth place in 2010 to second place in 2013. The scores for Nanchang and Tianjin have been fluctuating over time, but are consistently lower than the average. Baoding's ranking has been last for all four years and shows no apparent improvement.

In terms of geographic locations, Shenzhen and Hangzhou, ranking first and second, are in China's south-eastern coastal region. Nanchang, in third place, is in the central region, while Tianjin and Baoding, in fourth and last place, are in the north of the country. Therefore, the level of low-carbon development of Chinese cities presents an apparent declining trend from the cities in the south to the cities in the north. One reason could be the coal intensity of steel production in cities like Baoding in the northern region. However, the most important reason may be because the overall economic and social development levels in the south, especially in the south-eastern cities, are higher than those of northern cities. Cities in the south-eastern region also have more advantages in terms of technology, capital, human resources and city infrastructure development, which in turn facilitate rapid industrial restructuring and technological upgrading, especially in improving energy efficiency and reducing the emissions of high carbon dioxide-emitting industries. This also reveals that, in the process of pursuing city development, the 'low-carbon' development model is practical and necessary to achieve the goals of sustainable city development, including economic growth, good industrial structure, city construction and environmental protection. Therefore, 'low-carbon' is not only a goal but also the means by which to achieve sustainable development.

Evaluating the level of low-carbon city development by dimensions

Tables 13.5–9 present the scores for low-carbon city development by the five dimensions for each of the five cities.

Table 13.5 Economic growth

	Four-year average		2010		2011		2012		2013	
City	**Score**	**Ranking**	**Score**	**Ranking**	**Score**	**Ranking**	**Score**	**Ranking**	**Score**	**Ranking**
Shenzhen	0.15	1	0.15	1	0.15	1	0.16	1	0.17	1
Hangzhou	0.14	2	0.14	2	0.15	2	0.13	2	0.13	2
Nanchang	0.11	3	0.10	3	0.11	3	0.11	4	0.11	3
Tianjin	0.08	4	0.07	4	0.06	4	0.12	3	0.07	4
Baoding	0.01	5	0.02	5	0.01	5	0.01	5	0.01	5
Average	**0.52**	**n/a**	**0.52**	**n/a**	**0.52**	**n/a**	**0.56**	**n/a**	**0.48**	**n/a**

Sources: NBS (2011a–g, 2012a–g, 2013a–g, 2014a–g); Statistics Bureau of Shenzhen City (2011, 2012, 2013, 2014); Nanchang Municipal Statistics Bureau (2011, 2012, 2013, 2014); Tianjin Municipal Statistics Bureau (2011, 2012, 2013, 2014); Statistical Bureau of Baoding (2011, 2012, 2013, 2014).

Table 13.6 Energy utilisation

	Four-year average		2010		2011		2012		2013	
City	**Score**	**Ranking**	**Score**	**Ranking**	**Score**	**Ranking**	**Score**	**Ranking**	**Score**	**Ranking**
Shenzhen	0.29	1	0.31	1	0.31	1	0.31	1	0.24	1
Nanchang	0.18	2	0.20	2	0.16	2	0.21	3	0.15	3
Baoding	0.16	3	0.14	4	0.12	5	0.21	4	0.15	2
Hangzhou	0.15	4	0.13	5	0.13	4	0.22	2	0.12	4
Tianjin	0.15	5	0.16	3	0.13	3	0.20	5	0.10	5
Average	**0.52**	**n/a**	**0.52**	**n/a**	**0.52**	**n/a**	**0.56**	**n/a**	**0.48**	**n/a**

Sources: NBS (2011a–g, 2012a–g, 2013a–g, 2014a–g); Statistics Bureau of Shenzhen City (2011, 2012, 2013, 2014); Nanchang Municipal Statistics Bureau (2011, 2012, 2013, 2014); Tianjin Municipal Statistics Bureau (2011, 2012, 2013, 2014); Statistical Bureau of Baoding (2011, 2012, 2013, 2014).

Table 13.7 Urban construction

	Four-year average		2010		2011		2012		2013	
City	**Score**	**Ranking**	**Score**	**Ranking**	**Score**	**Ranking**	**Score**	**Ranking**	**Score**	**Ranking**
Shenzhen	0.11	1	0.11	1	0.11	1	0.11	1	0.11	1
Hangzhou	0.07	2	0.07	2	0.06	2	0.07	2	0.06	2
Nanchang	0.06	3	0.06	3	0.06	3	0.06	3	0.06	3
Tianjin	0.04	4	0.04	4	0.04	5	0.05	4	0.04	5
Baoding	0.03	5	0.03	5	0.05	4	0.02	5	0.04	4
Average	**0.52**	**n/a**	**0.52**	**n/a**	**0.52**	**n/a**	**0.56**	**n/a**	**0.48**	**n/a**

Sources: NBS (2011a–g, 2012a–g, 2013a–g, 2014a–g); Statistics Bureau of Shenzhen City (2011, 2012, 2013, 2014); Nanchang Municipal Statistics Bureau (2011, 2012, 2013, 2014); Tianjin Municipal Statistics Bureau (2011, 2012, 2013, 2014); Statistical Bureau of Baoding (2011, 2012, 2013, 2014).

Table 13.8 Government support

	Four-year average		2010		2011		2012		2013	
City	**Score**	**Ranking**	**Score**	**Ranking**	**Score**	**Ranking**	**Score**	**Ranking**	**Score**	**Ranking**
Hangzhou	0.14	1	0.13	3	0.14	3	0.15	1	0.15	2
Shenzhen	0.14	2	0.14	1	0.15	2	0.12	2	0.15	1
Nanchang	0.13	3	0.13	2	0.15	1	0.12	3	0.12	3
Baoding	0.12	4	0.11	4	0.13	4	0.09	4	0.12	4
Tianjin	0.09	5	0.11	5	0.11	5	0.09	5	0.06	5
Average	**0.52**	**n/a**	**0.52**	**n/a**	**0.52**	**n/a**	**0.56**	**n/a**	**0.48**	**n/a**

Sources: NBS (2011a–g, 2012a–g, 2013a–g, 2014a–g); Statistics Bureau of Shenzhen City (2011, 2012, 2013, 2014); Nanchang Municipal Statistics Bureau (2011, 2012, 2013, 2014); Tianjin Municipal Statistics Bureau (2011, 2012, 2013, 2014); Statistical Bureau of Baoding (2011, 2012, 2013, 2014).

Table 13.9 Residential energy consumption

	Four-year average		2010		2011		2012		2013	
City	**Score**	**Ranking**	**Score**	**Ranking**	**Score**	**Ranking**	**Score**	**Ranking**	**Score**	**Ranking**
Baoding	0.09	1	0.09	1	0.09	1	0.09	1	0.09	1
Tianjin	0.07	2	0.07	2	0.08	2	0.08	2	0.07	2
Nanchang	0.04	3	0.04	3	0.05	3	0.05	3	0.04	3
Hangzhou	0.04	4	0.03	5	0.04	4	0.04	4	0.04	4
Shenzhen	0.02	5	0.04	4	0.01	5	0.01	5	0.01	5

Sources: NBS (2011a–g, 2012a–g, 2013a–g, 2014a–g); Statistics Bureau of Shenzhen City (2011, 2012, 2013, 2014); Nanchang Municipal Statistics Bureau (2011, 2012, 2013, 2014); Tianjin Municipal Statistics Bureau (2011, 2012, 2013, 2014); Statistical Bureau of Baoding (2011, 2012, 2013, 2014).

A summary of these results is provided, in descending order of levels of low-carbon development.

Shenzhen

Shenzhen has the highest level of low-carbon development of the five sampled cities. It ranks first for economic growth, energy utilisation and urban construction, and second for government support. Shenzhen, however, ranks last in residential energy consumption, which is the weakest link in its low-carbon development.

Hangzhou

Hangzhou's level of low-carbon development places it second among the five sampled cities. It is ranked first for government support, but comes in fourth for energy utilisation and residential energy consumption.

Nanchang

The level of Nanchang's low-carbon development ranks third among the five sampled cities. Of the five dimensions of low-carbon development, Nanchang has relatively low scores for economic growth, city construction and residential energy consumption, but relatively high scores for energy utilisation and government support. Across the period 2010–14, the rankings of the five dimensions of low-carbon development in relative terms are all declining over time.

Tianjin

Tianjin's overall level of low-carbon development is low despite the fact that the city has relatively high levels of economic development. Tianjin measures relatively well for economic growth and residential energy consumption, but scores lower for urban construction and government support.

Baoding

The overall level of Baoding's low-carbon development is very low, ranking it last among the five sampled cities. Of the five dimensions of low-carbon development used herein, Baoding has the highest score in residential energy consumption, but the lowest scores in economic growth and city construction. It also has relatively low scores for energy utilisation and government support. In other words, Baoding has a long way to go to achieve low-carbon development.

Conclusion and policy suggestions

This chapter has used a multiple indicator system to evaluate the level of low-carbon city development in five selected pilot low-carbon development cities in China. The evaluation model includes five dimensions: economic growth, energy utilisation, city construction, government support and residential consumption. We invited experts to allocate weights to each of the 17 indicators and calculated the score for each of the five dimensions and the total score for the LCCDI for the eight national pilot low-carbon cities for the period 2010–13. Based on the calculated scores, we evaluated the level of low-carbon city development for five selected cities. The main findings are as follows.

First, the low-carbon development and economic growth of a city do not form a 'zero-sum' relationship. 'Low-carbon' and 'development' can be achieved simultaneously. This study reveals that the levels of economic development and low-carbon development in the southern Chinese cities are higher than those in the central and northern cities. This implies that 'low-carbon' and 'development' can go hand-in-hand, and that China and other countries can achieve a 'win-win' situation for both environmental protection and economic development. Therefore, in the process of implementing new urbanisation, and promoting economic and social development, a low-carbon development model can serve as a way to save resources while also achieving economic growth, which offers China a feasible path forward.

Second, the overall level of low-carbon development of the five cities is not high, and has shown little apparent improvement over the period 2010–13. Among the five cities, only Shenzhen—one of China's most economically advanced cities—has a relatively high level of low-carbon development, with a score above 0.7, while the other four cities all present relatively low levels. This reveals that after a number of years' implementation of low-carbon development, including energy saving and emissions reduction policies and interventions promoted by the government, there is no apparent improvement in the level of low-carbon development in the national pilot low-carbon cities. This also implies that there is room for improvement in low-carbon development in Chinese cities.

Third, geographically, the level of low-carbon city development is higher in the south than in the north. Shenzhen and Hangzhou scored the highest, followed by Nanchang in the central region, while the northern cities of Tianjin and Baoding present much lower low-carbon development indicators.

Fourth, there is heterogeneity between the five cities across the selected five dimensions. For example, Shenzhen has the highest overall level of low-carbon development among the five cities, but it scores the lowest for residential consumption. Tianjin has a relatively low overall score, but scores relatively high for economic growth. Baoding has the lowest score for the overall level of low-carbon development, but has a relatively high score for energy utilisation and the highest score for residential consumption. This suggests that cities may increase the level of low-carbon city development more effectively by targeting the weakest link.

Based on these main findings, we offer several policy suggestions to help promote the future development of low-carbon cities in China.

First, energy saving and emissions reduction measures are the most important tasks for future low-carbon development and China's urbanisation program. The key to realising energy savings and reducing emissions is to increase the efficiency of energy utilisation, adjust the energy structure, encourage related innovation and adoption and increase utilisation of less carbon-intensive energy sources. On the one hand, renewable sources such as solar, wind and tidal energy are carbon-free and can directly reduce carbon dioxide emissions if they are substituted for non-renewable fossil fuel–based energy sources, which also produce serious environmental pollution. On the other hand, the key to increasing energy efficiency is to upgrade, develop and extend low-carbon technology in a time-efficient manner. Currently, low-carbon technologies in China include mainly solar energy to generate electricity (photovoltaics), carbon capture and storage technology, green lighting (light-emitting diodes), and so on (Wang 2011). However, because China started developing low-carbon technology relatively late, its overall level of such technology is relatively low. Therefore, China should adopt and incorporate advanced low-carbon technology from abroad. This would help not only to reduce carbon dioxide emissions, but also to push forward innovation and the development of renewable energy technology, energy saving and emissions reduction technology and clean coal technology.

Second, on the one hand, government can use subsidies, taxation and concessional financing to encourage enterprises through the research and development process or to introduce low-carbon technology and increase its application share in production and consumption. For high energy consumption industries such as transportation and construction, the government should further encourage enterprises to accelerate industrial structural adjustment and upgrading. On the other hand, government should strengthen institutions and laws governing the low-carbon economy—for example, by operationalising a carbon trading and carbon finance market; improving taxation relating to the development of the low-carbon economy; implementing low-carbon economy laws and regulations; and better regulating and governing the construction and development of low-carbon cities.

Third, China should pay great attention to the development of strategic new industries, one of the main characteristics of which is low consumption of energy and resources. This is also among the targets for low-carbon development under the urbanisation policy. Of the seven strategic new industries promoted by the Chinese Government,[3] energy saving and environmentally friendly industries, new energy industries and the new energy car industry directly reflect the goal of low-carbon development. Compared with traditional heavy manufacturing industries, the new-generation information and communication technology industry, biology industry, high-end equipment manufacturing industry and new materials industry are also resource-saving industries. As they develop, these strategic new industries will promote the upgrading of the local industrial structure and fundamentally change local economic development. From the perspective of low-carbon and sustainable development, developing strategic new industries provides a clear direction for the future development of Chinese cities.

Fourth, China should allow the market to allocate resources and promote low-carbon development under the umbrella of new urbanisation. It is important to gradually establish market-oriented low-carbon mechanisms—for example, through developing carbon emissions trading rights and carbon finance. China has created carbon dioxide emission trading exchanges in Shenzhen, Tianjin, Guangzhou, Hubei and Chongqing, and the Beijing environment exchange and Shanghai environment and energy exchange. However, the carbon trading quantity of these exchanges remains very low compared with those of developed countries in Europe and North America. The operation mechanism also needs to be improved.

Fifth, raising public awareness of and encouraging low-carbon consumption are also important for low-carbon city development. Currently, residents' poor understanding of low-carbon behaviour is the weakest link in the low-carbon city development chain in China. It is little understood, for example, that low-carbon consumption does not have to be synonymous with reductions in quality. It must be communicated effectively that low-carbon development can improve people's quality of life. It will take a relatively long time to increase awareness of low-carbon consumption and change traditional consumption behaviour. Government should therefore make great efforts to publicise the significance of low-carbon residential consumption and encourage the public to gradually adopt a low-carbon consumption lifestyle, thus contributing to low-carbon and sustainable city development.

3 The seven strategic new industries proposed by the Chinese Government are energy saving and environmentally friendly industries, new generation information and communication technology industries, biology industries, high-end equipment manufacturing industries, new energy industries, new materials industries and new energy car industries.

References

Baeumler, A., Ijjasz-Vasquez, E. and Mehndiratta, S. (eds) (2012), *Sustainable low-carbon city development in China*, Washington, DC: World Bank Publications.

Bao, J., Miao, Y. and Chen, F. (2008), Low carbon economy: Revolution in the way of human economic development, *China Industrial Economics*, 4: 153–160.

Carr, E., Wingard, P., Yorty, S., Thompson, M., Jensen, N. and Roberson, J. (2007), Applying DPSIR to sustainable development, *International Journal of Sustainable Development & World Ecology*, 14(6): 543–555.

Casler, S. and Blair, P. (1997), Economic structure, fuel combustion, and pollution emissions, *Ecological Economics*, 22(1): 19–27.

Fan, Y., Liu, L., Wu, G. and Wei, Y. (2006), Analysing impact factors of CO_2 emissions using the STIRPAT model, *Environmental Impact Assessment Review*, 26(4): 377–395.

Feliciano, M. and Prosperi, D. (2011), Planning for low carbon cities: Reflection on the case of Broward County, Florida, USA, *Cities*, 28(6): 505–516.

Gabrielsen, P. and Bosch, P. (2003), *Environmental indicators: Typology and use in reporting*, Copenhagen: EEA.

Golove, W. and Schipper, L. (1997), Restraining carbon emissions: Measuring energy use and efficiency in the USA, *Energy Policy*, 25(7): 803–812.

Gu, C., Hu, L., Zhang, X., Wang, X. and Guo, J. (2011), Climate change and urbanization in the Yangtze River Delta, *Habitat International*, 35(4): 544–552.

Hu, B. (2013), On the new urbanisation path with six integrated dimensions, *Guangming Daily*, 28 June.

Hu, M. and Li, A. (2016), Between vision and reality: China low carbon city development, *Financial Times* [Chinese], 3 April. Available from: ftchinese.com/story/001066469?full=y.

Huang, H. (2011), The China environment yearbook. Volume 5. State of change: Environmental governance and citizens' rights, [Book review], *China Review International*, 18(2): 253–256.

Intergovernmental Panel on Climate Change (IPCC) (2006), *IPCC guidelines for national greenhouse gas*, London: Cambridge University Press.

Li, B. (2013), Governing urban climate change adaptation in China, *Environment and Urbanization*, 25(2): 413–427.

Li, J. and Wang, X. (2012), Energy and climate policy in China's twelfth five-year plan: A paradigm shift, *Energy Policy*, 41: 519–528.

Li, X. and Pan, J. (2015), *China green development index report 2012*, New York: Springer.

Liu, Z. (2015), *China's carbon emissions report 2015*, Cambridge, Mass.: John F. Kennedy School of Government, Harvard University.

Nanchang Municipal Statistics Bureau (2011), *Nanchang statistical yearbook 2011*, Beijing: China Statistics Press.

Nanchang Municipal Statistics Bureau (2012), *Nanchang statistical yearbook 2012*, Beijing: China Statistics Press.

Nanchang Municipal Statistics Bureau (2013), *Nanchang statistical yearbook 2013*, Beijing: China Statistics Press.

Nanchang Municipal Statistics Bureau (2014), *Nanchang statistical yearbook 2014*, Beijing: China Statistics Press.

National Bureau of Statistics (NBS) (2011a), *China city construction statistical yearbook 2011*, Beijing: China Statistics Press.

National Bureau of Statistics (NBS) (2011b), *China city statistical yearbook 2011*, Beijing: China Statistics Press.

National Bureau of Statistics (NBS) (2011c), *China energy statistical yearbook 2011*, Beijing: China Statistics Press.

National Bureau of Statistics (NBS) (2011d), *China statistical yearbook on environment 2011*, Beijing: China Statistics Press.

National Bureau of Statistics (NBS) (2011e), *China statistical yearbook 2011*, Beijing: China Statistics Press.

National Bureau of Statistics (NBS) (2011f), *Hangzhou statistical yearbook 2011*, Beijing: China Statistics Press.

National Bureau of Statistics (NBS) (2011g), *Statistical bulletin of national economic and social development 2011*, Beijing: China Statistics Press.

National Bureau of Statistics (NBS) (2012a), *China city construction statistical yearbook 2012*, Beijing: China Statistics Press.

National Bureau of Statistics (NBS) (2012b), *China city statistical yearbook 2012*, Beijing: China Statistics Press.

National Bureau of Statistics (NBS) (2012c), *China energy statistical yearbook 2012*, Beijing: China Statistics Press.

National Bureau of Statistics (NBS) (2012d), *China statistical yearbook on environment 2012*, Beijing: China Statistics Press.

National Bureau of Statistics (NBS) (2012e), *China statistical yearbook 2012*, Beijing: China Statistics Press.

National Bureau of Statistics (NBS) (2012f), *Hangzhou statistical yearbook 2012*, Beijing: China Statistics Press.

National Bureau of Statistics (NBS) (2012g), *Statistical bulletin of national economic and social development 2012*, Beijing: China Statistics Press.

National Bureau of Statistics (NBS) (2013a), *China city construction statistical yearbook 2013*, Beijing: China Statistics Press.

National Bureau of Statistics (NBS) (2013b), *China city statistical yearbook 2013*, Beijing: China Statistics Press.

National Bureau of Statistics (NBS) (2013c), *China energy statistical yearbook 2013*, Beijing: China Statistics Press.

National Bureau of Statistics (NBS) (2013d), *China statistical yearbook on environment 2013*, Beijing: China Statistics Press.

National Bureau of Statistics (NBS) (2013e), *China statistical yearbook 2013*, Beijing: China Statistics Press.

National Bureau of Statistics (NBS) (2013f), *Hangzhou statistical yearbook 2013*, Beijing: China Statistics Press.

National Bureau of Statistics (NBS) (2013g), *Statistical bulletin of national economic and social development 2013*, Beijing: China Statistics Press.

National Bureau of Statistics (NBS) (2014a), *China city construction statistical yearbook 2014*, Beijing: China Statistics Press.

National Bureau of Statistics (NBS) (2014b), *China city statistical yearbook 2014*, Beijing: China Statistics Press.

National Bureau of Statistics (NBS) (2014c), *China energy statistical yearbook 2014*, Beijing: China Statistics Press.

National Bureau of Statistics (NBS) (2014d), *China statistical yearbook on environment 2014*, Beijing: China Statistics Press.

National Bureau of Statistics (NBS) (2014e), *China statistical yearbook 2014*, Beijing: China Statistics Press.

National Bureau of Statistics (NBS) (2014f), *Hangzhou statistical yearbook 2014*, Beijing: China Statistics Press.

National Bureau of Statistics (NBS) (2014g), *Statistical bulletin of national economic and social development 2014*, Beijing: China Statistics Press.

National Development and Reform Commission (NDRC) (2008), *National standard of the People's Republic of China, GB/T 2589-2008, General principles for calculation of total production energy consumption*, Beijing: NDRC.

National Development and Reform Commission (NDRC) (2010), *Notice for carrying out low-carbon pilot schemes at provincial and city levels*, Beijing: NDRC. Available from: gov.cn/zwgk/2010-08/10/content_1675733.htm.

National Development and Reform Commission (NDRC) (2012), *Circular on the second batch of national pilot low-carbon provinces and low-carbon cities*, Beijing: NDRC. Available from: ccchina.gov.cn/nDetail.aspx?newsId=28162&TId=60.

Pulselli, F., Coscieme, L., Neri, L., Regoli, A., Sutton, P., Lemmi, A. and Bastianoni, S. (2015), The world economy in a cube: A more rational structural representation of sustainability, *Global Environmental Change*, 35: 41–51.

Selden, T. and Song, D. (1994), Environmental quality and development: Is there a Kuznets curve for air pollution emissions?, *Journal of Environmental Economics and Management*, 27(2): 147–162.

Shao, C. and Ju, M. (2010), Studies of low-carbon city indicator system based on the DPSIR model, *Ecological Economics*, 10: 95–99.

Soytas, U. and Sari, R. (2009), Energy consumption, economic growth, and carbon emissions: Challenges faced by an EU candidate member, *Ecological Economics*, 68(6): 1667–1675.

Statistical Bureau of Baoding (2011), *Baoding statistical yearbook 2011*, Beijing: China Statistics Press.

Statistical Bureau of Baoding (2012), *Baoding statistical yearbook 2012*, Beijing: China Statistics Press.

Statistical Bureau of Baoding (2013), *Baoding statistical yearbook 2013*, Beijing: China Statistics Press.

Statistical Bureau of Baoding (2014), *Baoding statistical yearbook 2014*, Beijing: China Statistics Press.

Statistics Bureau of Shenzhen City (2011), *Shenzhen statistical yearbook 2011*, Beijing: China Statistics Press.

Statistics Bureau of Shenzhen City (2012), *Shenzhen statistical yearbook 2012*, Beijing: China Statistics Press.

Statistics Bureau of Shenzhen City (2013), *Shenzhen statistical yearbook 2013*, Beijing: China Statistics Press.

Statistics Bureau of Shenzhen City (2014), *Shenzhen statistical yearbook 2014*, Beijing: China Statistics Press.

Stern, D. and Common, M. (2001), Is there an environmental Kuznets curve for sulfur?, *Journal of Environmental Economics and Management*, 41(2): 162–178.

Tianjin Municipal Statistics Bureau (2011), *Tianjin statistical yearbook 2011*, Beijing: China Statistics Press.

Tianjin Municipal Statistics Bureau (2012), *Tianjin statistical yearbook 2012*, Beijing: China Statistics Press.

Tianjin Municipal Statistics Bureau (2013), *Tianjin statistical yearbook 2013*, Beijing: China Statistics Press.

Tianjin Municipal Statistics Bureau (2014), *Tianjin statistical yearbook 2014*, Beijing: China Statistics Press.

Wang, H. (2013), Review of DPSIR framework, *Guidance of Economic Research*, 19: 4–5.

Wang, W. (2011), Studies on status, problem and development mode of China's low-carbon technology, *China Soft Technology*, 12: 84–91.

Weidema, B., Thrane, M., Christensen, P., Schmidt, J. and Løkke, S. (2008), Carbon footprint, *Journal of Industrial Ecology*, 12(1): 3–6.

York, R., Rosa, E. and Dietz, T. (2003), STIRPAT, IPAT and ImPACT: Analytic tools for unpacking the driving forces of environmental impacts, *Ecological Economics*, 46(3): 351–65.

Zhang, X. and Cheng, X. (2009), Energy consumption, carbon emissions, and economic growth in China, *Ecological Economics*, 68(10): 2706–2712.

14. Issues and Prospects for the Restructuring of China's Steel Industry

Haimin Liu and Ligang Song

Introduction

China's steelmaking capacity has expanded rapidly over the reform period and especially since the beginning of the twenty-first century. The scale of that expansion is unprecedented in the history of industrialisation in Europe, North America and East Asia. This is a result of the fact that the rapid growth of the Chinese economy was driven by an investment-led growth model centring on the development of heavy industries such as machinery and transport equipment manufacturing, and also an unprecedented scale of urbanisation with associated demand for housing and infrastructure such as roads, railways, ports, airports and utilities.

China's annual production of crude steel reached 804 million tonnes in 2015, 6.3 times higher than the total production in 2000. It accounts for nearly 50 per cent of the total global steel output, rising from only 15 per cent of the total at the end of the previous century. This follows from China becoming the largest steel producer in the world two decades ago, in 1996.

The rapid expansion of the industry induced a parallel increase in demand for iron ore, leading to soaring prices for iron ore on world markets. In the Asian market, the price of iron ore increased from US$13.8/t in 2003 to US$96.8/t in 2014, after peaking at US$187.2/t in 2011 (Hurst 2015). These dramatic shifts in iron ore prices underscore the so-called super resource boom in the period 2003–13. During this decade, the Chinese steel industry consumed more than 60 per cent of total global production of iron ore. Its dependency on imported iron ore (the ratio between imports and domestic production) also reached unprecedented levels.

The rapid expansion in the domestic production of steel products transformed China into a net exporter of steel products in 2006, and it is now the largest exporter of those products in the world. China exported more than 100 million tonnes of steel products to the world market in 2015—50 per cent larger than the entire amount of steel produced in the United States the same year (Sanderson 2015). These exports have helped to ease overcapacity pressures in China's domestic industrial sector. At the same time, rising dependence on global sales has increased related trade tensions with other steel-producing countries. In 2015, there were 37 cases relating to antidumping and anti-subsidy launched against China by major steel-producing countries.

Since the onset of the Global Financial Crisis (GFC) in 2008, China's annual economic growth rate has progressively slowed. The steel industry is prone to cyclical changes alongside other industries including cement and aluminium, which means that the sector has become trapped in a cycle of excess capacity. In turn, in 2014–15, the price of steel products continuously hit new lows, adding enormous pressure to domestic industrial restructuring. Having earlier lingered around breakeven point, the members of the China Iron and Steel Association (CISA)—namely, large and medium-sized steel enterprises—have as a whole incurred huge losses. Dozens of enterprises have stopped operating or will be forced into bankruptcy, highlighting the urgency for restructuring and reform of the industry.

In recent years, the focus in the restructuring of China's steel industry has been mainly on reducing the quantity of production and increasing the industry's overall technical standards. For example, the government encouraged enterprises to remove obsolete and old-fashioned equipment, to limit building new capacity, to increase exports, to develop new steel production structures via production of higher value-added products and to expand overseas projects by carrying out more foreign direct investment. These reform and restructuring measures have, however, not helped the steel industry to exit a difficult period. Instead, the overriding structural problems in the industry have deepened.

At the end of 2015, the Central Government proposed and started implementation of a strategy of 'supply-side reforms' that aimed to improve and restructure supply-side aspects of China's economy. This represents an important shift in policy focus towards dealing with the underlying structural challenges facing the economy, compared with the greater focus on demand expansion of earlier policy. Within the steel industry, the main objective of supply-side reforms is to address excess capacity through various reform measures including shutting some steel mills. In January 2016, the State Council promulgated the 'Advice on addressing excessive capacity and relieving hardship for the steel industry', which specifically proposed that steelmaking capacity in China should be reduced by 100–150 million tonnes in the next five years.

There is evidence also that the root causes of the problems currently facing the industry are not exclusively or even chiefly related to issues of production quantity and technology used, but rather to the operating mechanisms of the industry itself—in particular, the dual ownership structure of China's steel industry, which sees it divided roughly equally between state-owned and private companies. In the state-owned steel sector, there have been various market failures, including the inefficient market allocation of resources and lagging ownership reforms, plus local governments' blind strategy approaches to industry expansion that worsened the problem of overcapacity and have transformed many enterprises into 'zombie enterprises' (Liu 2013a).

It is clear that the Chinese steel industry has no choice but to further restructure and address this 'zombie companies' issue. This will only happen by deepening reform that is supported by public policy, including in terms of relocating and retraining workers whose employment may be adversely affected. Only in this way can the steel industry ultimately get back on track towards more sustainable future development.

This chapter reviews the performance of China's steel industry by analysing the underlying drivers of its recent rapid development; identifies the key challenges facing the industry amid the economic slowdown, including the causes of deteriorating performance and overcapacity; and finally, offers an outlook for the industry that could result from current restructuring programs.

Twenty-first-century expansion and performance of China's steel industry

Steel production in China witnessed explosive growth in the decade after 2000. China's rapidly growing economic size underpinned huge growth in demand for steel products, which gave impetus to the rapid growth and expansion of the industry (Song and Liu 2012). Accompanying the increase in the scale of the industry were several concurrent structural shifts. In 2006, China shifted from being a net importer of steel to become a net exporter of steel products (Table 14.1). Also in 2006, China replaced Japan as both the biggest steel-exporting country and the biggest net steel-exporting country in the world.

A decade on, the latest available data (Table 14.1) reveal that Chinese imports of steel equivalent dropped to 13.9 million tonnes in 2015, from the historic peak of 45.6 million tonnes in 2003. Exports of steel equivalent in the same period increased to 120 million tonnes, up from 8.9 million tonnes. The self-sufficiency ratio of steel in China exceeded 100 per cent in 2005, and had increased to 115 per cent by 2015, as shown in the last column of Table 14.1.

Table 14.1 China's steel production, trade and self-sufficiency ratios, 2000–15 (million tonnes)

Year	Steel production in the world	Steel production in China	China's share (%)	Crude steel equivalent of imports	Crude steel equivalent of exports	Apparent consumption of crude steel	Self-sufficiency (%)
2000	847.7	128.5	15.2	22.2	11.8	138.9	92.5
2001	850.4	151.6	17.8	26.8	7.8	170.6	88.8
2002	904.1	182.4	20.2	30.9	7.2	206.1	88.5
2003	969.9	222.3	22.9	45.6	8.9	259.0	85.8
2004	1,068.9	282.9	26.5	35.1	21.3	296.7	95.4
2005	1,147.9	355.8	31.0	28.8	29.0	355.5	100.1
2006	1,250.1	421.0	33.7	20.0	54.6	386.4	108.9
2007	1,348.1	489.7	36.3	18.1	72.9	434.9	112.6
2008	1,343.4	512.3	38.1	16.6	64.3	464.6	110.2
2009	1,238.8	577.1	46.6	23.3	26.2	574.2	100.5
2010	1,433.4	638.7	44.6	18.1	45.4	611.4	104.4
2011	1,538.0	701.9	45.6	17.2	52.0	667.2	105.2
2012	1,560.1	731.1	46.9	14.9	59.3	686.6	106.5
2013	1,650.3	822.0	49.8	15.5	66.3	771.2	106.6
2014	1,670.1	822.7	49.3	15.2	97.2	740.8	111.1
2015	1,622.8	803.8	49.5	13.9	119.6	698.1	115.1

Sources: Authors' own calculations based on the data from World Steel Association, CISA, National Bureau of Statistics (NBS) and China Customs data.

Table 14.1 highlights recent increases in domestic consumption of steel, which triggered massive investment in the industry by both the state and the private sectors, which in turn produced continually increasing volumes of steel above domestic demand, until 2015, when production levels began to fall. Domestic consumption, as Table 14.1 also shows, peaked two years before this decline in production, at 771 million tonnes in 2013. That year China produced 822 million tonnes of steel. The mismatch between peak domestic consumption and peak domestic production exacerbated overcapacity problems when, in 2015, domestic consumption declined to 698 million tonnes but domestic production did not adjust smoothly in response. Instead, domestic production stayed at 803 million tonnes. And, because over 2013–15 China accounted for nearly half of global total steel production, these numbers have in turn impacted on world steel markets (OECD 2016).

In addition to these production and consumption trends, a recent structural shift in China's steel industry means that the steel products it produces have improved in terms of both quality and variety. Table 14.2 provides data on total production, trade, apparent consumption and the self-sufficiency ratio for different varieties of steel products. Almost all varieties had, by 2015, achieved at least 100 per cent self-sufficiency. In some product areas, including rails and wheels, steel bars, medium plates, galvanised sheets (strip), seamless tubes and coated sheets (strip), there are severe overcapacity problems, as measured by very high self-sufficiency ratios. Steel companies have naturally turned to international markets and sold more than 100 million tonnes of related products in 2015. This raises questions about China's competitiveness in steel products on the world market and reactions to it by other steel-producing countries such as increasing antidumping cases against China's steel exports.

China's steel products are competitive on world markets mainly as a result of economies of scale and technical progress, as well as improvement in equipment, meaning that steel production processes are more efficient in terms of energy, water and other resource consumption per unit of output. This follows from the fact that over the past decade the Chinese Government adjusted its industrial policies in ways that led to the closure of outdated steel plants. For example, firms with iron-smelting production capacity of less than 120 million tonnes and steel smelting capacity below 90 million tonnes were forced to close. By 2016, almost all small blast furnaces (those smaller than 400 cu m) and all small steel-smelting equipment (less than 30 tonnes capacity) had been closed.

Table 14.2 Production, foreign trade, consumption and self-sufficiency ratio by steel product category, China, 2015 (million tonnes)

Steel varieties	Production	Exports	Imports	Apparent consumption	Self-sufficient rate (%)
Total finished steel	779.5	112.4	12.8	679.9	114.7
Rail & wheel	4.8	0.8	0.0	4.1	119.2
Large section	14.4	0.9	0.3	13.7	104.7
M&S section	56.6	4.3	0.0	52.3	108.2
Steel bar	71.3	31.4	0.5	40.4	176.7
Rebar	204.3	0.2	0.0	204.1	100.1
Wire rod	147.2	12.3	0.6	135.5	108.6
Ultra-thick plate	7.7	0.1	0.1	7.7	100.2
Heavy plate	25.4	0.1	0.3	25.7	99.0
Medium plate	40.2	7.5	1.3	34.0	118.4
MT wide strip	123.3	15.3	1.5	109.6	112.6
HR wide sheet (strip)	62.0	0.2	0.8	62.5	99.1
CR wide sheet (strip)	83.8	6.0	2.8	80.7	105.4
HR narrow strip	63.6	0.2	0.1	63.5	100.2
CR narrow strip	13.5	0.2	0.2	13.5	99.9
Galvanised sheet (strip)	52.1	11.4	3.0	43.7	119.2
Coated sheet (strip)	8.1	7.1	0.2	1.2	684.3
Electrical sheet	8.8	0.4	0.5	8.9	99.1
Seamless tube	28.6	4.5	0.2	24.2	118.0
Welded tube	69.7	4.7	0.2	65.1	107.0
Others	38.0	0.7	0.0	37.3	101.8

Sources: Calculated using data from NBS, China Customs.

In addition to closing small-scale production sites, energy saving and emission reduction technologies have been widely adopted. Examples include top-pressure recovery turbine technology (a device used in generating electricity at differential pressures inside a blast furnace), gas recycling, dry quenching, dry dust removal and water recycling, as well as the adoption of sulphur removal from sintering machines. The comprehensive energy consumption of the CISA members dropped accordingly, from 0.9 tonnes of standard coal equivalent (tce) in 2000 to 0.6 tce in 2015. Freshwater consumption per tonne of steel produced also dropped sharply, from 30 cu m to 3.3 cu m over 2000–15. Finally, sulphur dioxide emissions dropped from 4.5 kg/t in 2001 to 0.9 kg/t in 2015.

The eruption of the GFC in 2008 marked an inflexion point for the Chinese economy. The worldwide economic slowdown reduced demand for China's exports at the same time as structural change within the Chinese economy was producing rising wages that were also eroding China's export competitiveness. In response, in 2009 China implemented a large-scale fiscal stimulus package that was effective in stimulating the economy for a while, but was ultimately unable to sustain the earlier role of fixed-asset investment in driving China's growth. The economic growth rate has fallen annually since 2012.

It was inevitable that the steel industry—a pillar of China's industrial and fixed-asset investment sectors—would be adversely affected. In 2015, output of crude steel in China reached 804 million tonnes, reflecting a year-on-year fall of 2.3 per cent. This was the first production decline since 1982. The same year, China's apparent consumption of steel was 698 million tonnes, reflecting a year-on-year fall of 5.8 per cent.

The fall in steel production has inevitably also affected the prices of raw materials that are fundamental to steel production, such as iron ore and coking coal. Prices for steel and related materials, as well as industry profits, have decreased dramatically. In 2015, the 100 or so large steel enterprises with CISA membership—which together account for 76 per cent of crude steel output in China—achieved sales revenue of RMB2.9 trillion. This reflects a year-on-year fall of 19 per cent. Profits were, however, in negative territory, reaching minus RMB64.5 billion, of which losses attributable to steel businesses were more than RMB10 billion, and the share of loss-making enterprises was 51 per cent.

This is the background that has made it necessary to dramatically restructure the Chinese steel industry. The next section provides more discussion on how the problems associated with the steel industry have been created, due especially to the changing market environment as well as problems of state-owned enterprises (SOEs) in relation to governments. The section thereafter discusses reform issues.

Market failures, homogeneous competition and poor industry performance

Steel has been a central pillar of China's rapid growth story. It has, however, also been a source of problems, ranging from its adverse environmental impacts to problems associated with the continued dominance of the state sector. The latter is a core part of the restructuring strategy for the industry. Before discussing the reform of SOEs in restructuring, we first clarify the fundamental factors that are driving declining profits in the steel industry.

Some of the challenges facing the steel industry have in recent years been attributed to its declining profits owing to the high price of imported iron ore (Liu 2013a). This is associated with the view that the three mining giants of BHP, Rio Tinto and Vale eroded the profit margins of the steel industry by taking advantage of their monopoly position (Hurst 2015). In general, however, the changing trends in the iron ore price and changes in CISA member profitability since 2000 appear to have little correlation. The iron ore price, for example, was below US$30 per tonne from 2000 to 2003, while the profits of CISA members increased from nearly zero to about 7 per cent—a rate higher than the average levels of the manufacturing and mining industries across the same period. Moreover, after 2003, the iron ore price increased continuously until peaking at US$190 per tonne monthly in 2011, while the profit rate of CISA members was retained within the normal range of 6–8 per cent (Figure 14.1). Since the economic slowdown, however, the iron ore cost, insurance and freight price has fallen continuously, to below US$40 per tonne at the end of 2015. This is the equivalent of just one-quarter of the earlier peak price. The profitability of the steel industry has not improved, but has in fact incurred overall losses from an early base of low profits. This may suggest that rising iron ore prices are not directly related to falling profits in the steel industry.

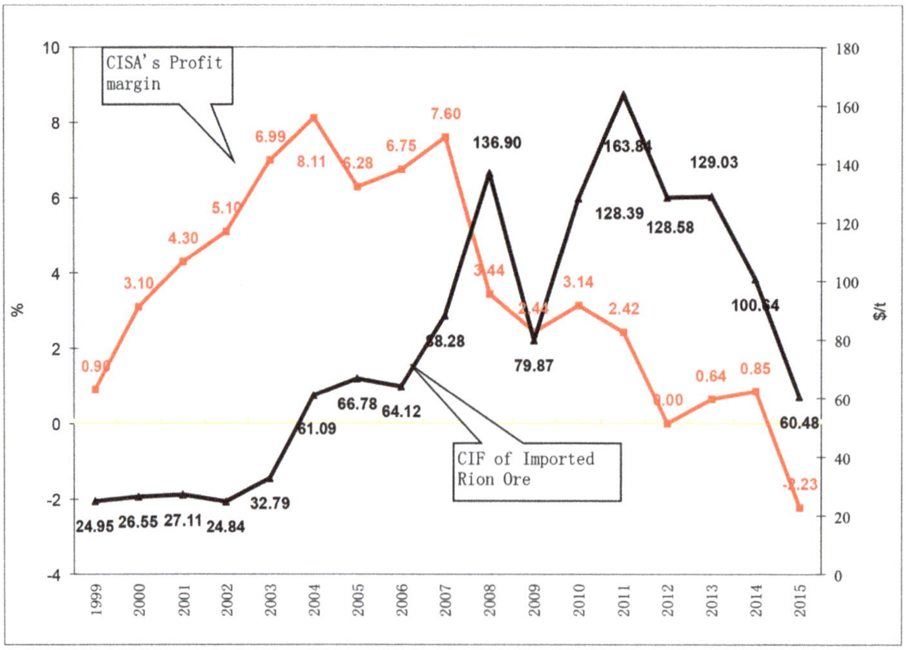

Figure 14.1 Changing profit margins of CISA members versus iron ore prices, 1999–2015 (per cent and US$/t)

Sources: Data taken from CISA, China Customs.

There is another view in industry circles that the reduction of demand and resulting excess capacity are the core drivers of declining steel industry profits (Liu 2013a). This view may not hold true, however, as within the same industrial environment, the profit rate of large enterprises lags far behind that of the small enterprises in the industry. Data from 2015 illustrate the point. Smelting and pressing processing enterprises for ferrous metals that are above the designated size[1] realised profits of RMB52.6 billion at the same time as CISA members incurred total losses of RMB64.5 billion, with the latter accounting for some two-thirds of the total steel production in China (Table 14.3). This suggests that SOEs are responsible for a disproportionate share of financial losses in the steel industry.

Table 14.3 Profitability of steel enterprises

	NBS: Smelting and pressing processing enterprises for ferrous metals above designated size (about 10,000 firms)		CISA members: 100 large and medium-sized steel enterprises	
	Total profits	Profit margin (%)	Total profits	Profit margin (%)
2012	1,229	1.73	–7.6	0.00
2013	1,695	2.22	228.86	0.64
2014	1,647	2.20	304.44	0.85
2015	52.55	0.81	–645.34	–2.23

Sources: Data taken from CISA and NBS.

In an efficient and fully competitive market, fluctuations in raw material prices and final demand changes will be transmitted through the changes in the supply–demand relationship and resulting market prices. Steel products are an industrial necessity with extremely low demand elasticity. Changes in the demand volume are therefore unlikely to affect the supply–demand relationship much in a normal circumstance. The emphasis in dealing with such a relationship should be placed on adjustments to the supply side. In this view, the marginal producer plays a vital role in acting as an adjusting or regulating mechanism in influencing market outcomes. In responding to changes in the supply–demand relationship and in product prices, marginal producers will decide whether to enter into or suspend operations. If this type of regulating mechanism works smoothly and effectively, as in a free market system, the market allows for average profits that are just sufficient to keep firms operating efficiently, while inefficient firms will exit.

1 These enterprises, which were included in the national statistics, had annual sales income of RMB20 million or more. There were about 10,000 such enterprises at the end of 2014, including those engaging in further processing of steel.

In a highly capital-intensive, continuous thermal energy consuming and mass employee-driven industry such as steel production, it is technically and socially difficult for the marginal producer to stop and start operations as readily as the logic of an economic model implies. In reality, there are certain obstacles to exit that make it difficult to replicate pure market conditions, as would be reflected by a near instant market-oriented self-readjustment or regulation.

In recent years in China's steel industry, the annual average losses of a number of enterprises have exceeded RMB1,000 per tonne. These losses, however, may be much higher if viewed in terms of monthly operations, and where each product type and order are examined. For some enterprises, the losses have even exceeded the sum of depreciation, wages and interest—yet these firms have continued production.

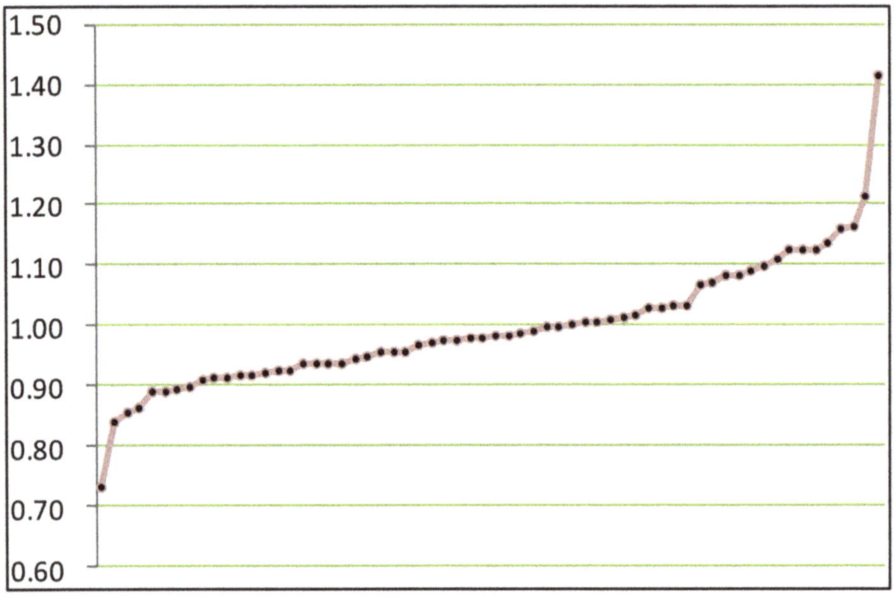

Figure 14.2 CISA members' cost rates, 2015 (cost of sales over total sales)

Note: The vertical axis represents cost of sales/total sales and the horizontal axis represents steel companies.

Source: Data taken from CISA, including only integrated steel mills.

Figure 14.2 indicates that the selling costs for almost half of the enterprises in China's steel industry exceeded their selling prices in 2015. In other words, their gross profits are negative. In addition to the costs of manufacturing, there are costs for pending sales, including general administration and financial expenses. Accounting for those additional costs would drive the ratio even higher for some firms.

Assuming an effective market mechanism, the average price line (selling price/selling cost) should approximate 1.2, as indicated in Figure 14.2. The average price line, however, just slightly exceeds 1.0 (the ratio is 1.0). The difference between the two is attributable mainly to the marginal producers who suffer losses but continue to produce anyway. Marginal producers—mostly large SOEs—drag down average industry profits by incurring huge losses. These firms also dump their excess production on to the market, pushing down steel prices and pulling up the prices of steelmaking inputs.[2] This prevents more efficient firms from making normal profits. This is the basic situation confronting the steel industry. The solution is clear: inefficient enterprises must exit the market.

Another reason for the severe losses in the steel industry is homogeneous competition—that is, companies are producing similar products and compete with each other to sell them in the markets. There are some 500 enterprises with steel metallurgy capacity in China. In Hebei province, where one-quarter of the national steel capacity is based, there are 120 steel enterprises, many of which produce the same type of steel products. The market environment in which these firms operated changed in 2010, when the iron ore market worked around a long-term contract pricing mechanism.

Under the old model, especially in its later period, the long-term price contract system saw prices in general increase dramatically, but contracts were sold to different enterprises at different prices. In particular, large enterprises (typically SOEs) enjoyed privileged access to cheap long-term contracts or owned iron ore mines themselves, meaning their cost of acquiring iron ore was relatively low. Across the first half of 2008, the average price for imported iron ore for SOEs, for example, was RMB500 per tonne lower than that for small private enterprises, which were forced to buy more expensive iron ore at spot-market prices. This certainly constituted a very different cost curve for operators in China's steel market. On the other hand, although small and medium-sized enterprises produced steel with relatively higher material costs, these enterprises enjoyed some advantages, including lower labour costs, more flexible management and being more sensitive to market signals in that once they suffered a certain level of losses, they could suspend production or even exit the industry. In other words, if we assume that the steel industry is dominated by private enterprises, the market clearing mechanism will work more effectively, leading to a more efficient allocation of resources.

2 It should be noted that this type of overshoot may be common in capital-intensive industry—adjustment to changed market conditions takes time and does not go smoothly, even with all private players in a competitive market.

The long-term contract pricing mechanism for iron ore ended in 2010, and since then the price has declined significantly. At the same time, China's commodities market has matured in the range of financial instruments available. China has, for example, successively developed a futures market, spot market and e-commerce systems for finished and semifinished steel products as well as for steelmaking raw materials, including iron ore, coking coal, coke and ferrous alloys. With these mechanisms in place, domestic steel producers enjoy more channels through which to buy raw materials. In addition, large steel mills no longer have access to cheaper iron ore. As a result, the cost difference for raw materials among different enterprises is shrinking and in some cases has even been eliminated. This situation has put enterprises on a more equal footing in terms of their cost competitiveness, especially between SOEs and private enterprises. On the competitive market, with more homogeneous steel products being produced and sold, all enterprises tend to take 'positive cash flow' as the shutdown point, meaning that all would suffer losses where losses arose. This is the background to the fact that the entire Chinese steel industry is making a loss at the moment.

Market failures and the rigidity of SOEs' operations

At present, within China's steel industry, a number of marginal producers are not responding to market signals and are not exiting the industry. These enterprises can in fact operate into the long term while making continuous losses. It is, however, impossible for them to do so without financial support from external sources, such as governments. This is especially the case for SOEs. Private enterprises, on the other hand, usually do not enjoy this kind of external support. They usually suspend production when their losses reach a certain level because they cannot sustain them. For example, when steel market product prices declined greatly in late 2015, about 30 private steel enterprises in northern China suspended production, including a large steel mill named Songting Steel with annual output of 5 million tonnes. The extent of their losses was, in fact, far lower than that of some large SOEs, who continued production.

Three types of support enable SOEs to maintain production at a loss for a long time: 1) government subsidies; 2) support from a superior group of enterprises (through direct subsidy, interest-free loans or provision of loan guarantees); and 3) loans from a state-owned bank. These conditions have made SOEs much less sensitive to profit changes and other market signals. For example, when the market environment and profits deteriorated, these marginal producers became 'zombie enterprises'—firms that are reliant on external support for survival. Such enterprises have operational indicators that include long-term losses, no hope of stopping those losses and insolvency. Therefore, SOEs, with their rigid operating mechanisms, are in fact the main cause of market failures in the steel industry.

This view can also be demonstrated by comparison of the distribution characteristics of the rate of profit (sales) of 42 industrial and mining industries in China. For industries whose proportion of state-owned capital is low or close to zero, average selling profit rates are distributed intensively in the narrow range of 5–10 per cent (Figure 14.3). With increasing use of state-owned capital, the distribution of profit rates scatters. For example, the rates of profit for petroleum, mining and tobacco enterprises with a high degree of monopoly are higher than average, but industries with a high proportion of state-owned capital and no monopolistic position, such as ferrous and nonferrous metals and coking, have observably lower profit rates (Liu 2013b).

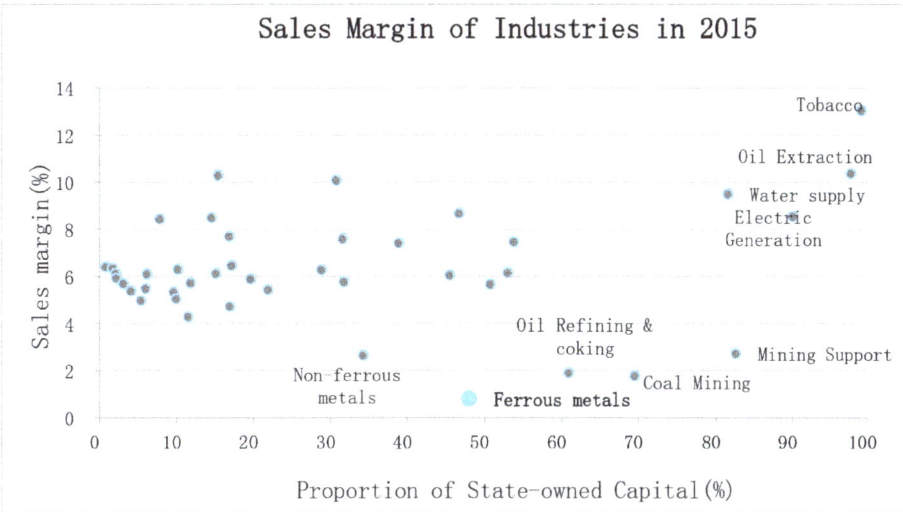

Figure 14.3 Sales margin versus proportion of state-owned capital, 2015 (per cent)

Sources: Data taken from NBS.

The Chinese steel industry comprises SOEs and private enterprises. Until 2015, there were 27 large steel SOEs (including group companies that owned many steel mills). Their collective steel output was 353 million tonnes, which accounted for 44 per cent of China's total steel output. The remaining output is attributed to the more than 400 private steel mills (70 of them CISA members) whose steel metallurgy capacity accounts for the remaining 56 per cent of China's total steel output.

Although losses are happening across the board, data for the past few years indicate that losses are arising disproportionately within large enterprises, especially large SOEs. Among the top 10 enterprises with losses in 2015, nine were SOEs (Liu 2015). Table 14.4 outlines descriptive data on the comparative performance of SOEs and private enterprises (that are CISA members) in the steel industry for 2015.

Table 14.4 Comparison of performance between SOEs and private enterprises, 2015 (RMB)

	Profits on steel business (RMB billion)	Loss per tonne of finished steel	General administration per tonne of finished steel	Financial cost per tonne of finished steel
Total	**-77.9**	**177.27**	**102.28**	**98.10**
SOE	-72.7	228.38	116.67	110.9
Private*	-5.2	42.69	64.37	64.40

* Private enterprises here are only those which are CISA members.
Sources: Data taken from CISA.

The high cost of labour is one direct reason for the poor efficiency of SOEs. According to a 2014 survey of CISA members, the average steel output per worker for private steel enterprises is 514 tonnes per annum; for SOEs, it is just 270 t/p.a. The average wage for an SOE steel mill worker (including social insurance) is RMB5,094 per month, which is 1.34 times that for a private enterprise employee, whose per capita wage is RMB3,807 a month. In other words, in SOEs, each tonne of steel incurs a RMB227 human cost—2.6 times greater than for a private enterprise, where the equivalent cost is only RMB89. Table 14.4 also shows that the total management cost per tonne of finished steel in SOEs is nearly double that of CISA members.

Complex organisational layering is a common problem among SOEs. Data disclosed by the media in recent years show that the actual number of staff in SOEs is often double the number required. For example, at a forum held in Taiyuan, capital of Shanxi province, on 23 February 2016, at which Chinese Premier Li Keqiang was a speaker, the President of Taiyuan Steel Co. Ltd reported to the Premier that there were 50,000 employees in his enterprise, but only 20,000 were needed. Later, Wuhan Steel Group declared that it planned to reduce staff numbers from 80,000 to 30,000 employees, on the basis of maintaining the original production scale. Anshan Steel Group, the oldest steel enterprise in China, also plans to reduce its 160,000-strong workforce to about 100,000.

Not only are SOEs planning to downsize, but there is also a trend in the industry towards a greater share of output being produced by the private sector (Figure 14.4). Specifically, the share has risen from only 9.8 million tonnes in 2000, accounting for just 7.7 per cent of the nation's total steel output in that year, to 450 million tonnes in 2015—56 per cent of total steel output.

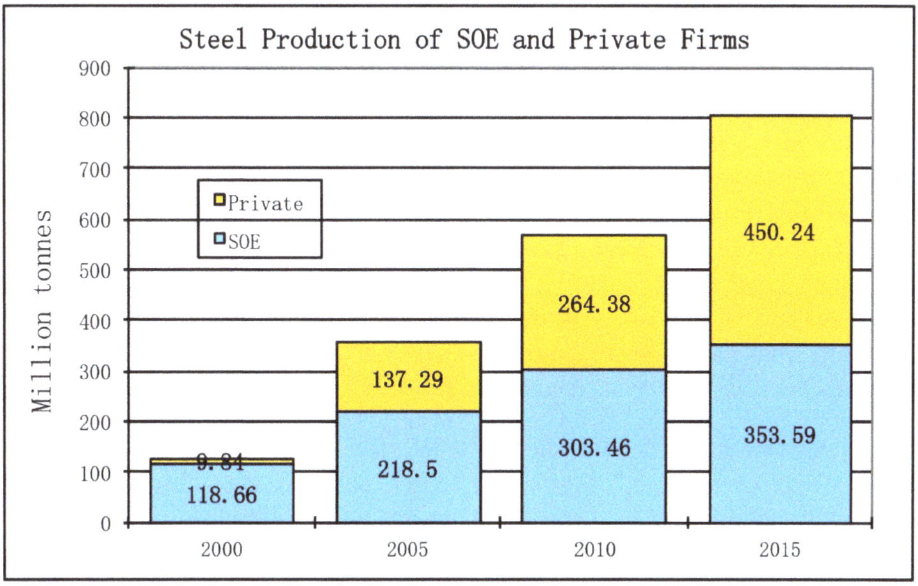

Figure 14.4 Comparison of SOE and private enterprise steel production, 2000–15 (million tonnes)

Sources: Data taken from CISA and NBS.

The rising role of private steel enterprises in the industry can be attributed to two factors, the first of which is privatisation of SOEs. Firms that were once state-owned but are now in private hands include Nanjing Steel Co. Ltd, Pingxiang Steel Co. Ltd, Nanchang Steel Co. Ltd, Jiyuan Steel Co. Ltd and Fushun Steel Co. Ltd. The second factor is the expansion in scale of newly built, privately owned and run enterprises (Liu 2015).

Nationally, the Chinese Government has issued a plan that will encourage a decline in steel production capacity from 150 to 100 million tonnes over the next five years. It is estimated that 500,000 workers from the industry could lose their jobs under the plan. Given that enterprises that will retain current capacity might still reduce their workforce, the actual number of workers losing their jobs could be even higher. The province of Hebei will be especially affected.

Despite several rounds of enterprise reform carried out in the past (Song 2015), the problem of redundancies associated with SOEs remains a key outstanding issue. If SOEs had employed workers according to need in the past 10 years, the task of reallocating workers from the industry may not present as dramatically as it now does, but a policy of 'securing jobs' has been deeply entrenched in the running of SOEs. Leaders of SOEs as well as local governments have tended to tolerate losses rather than risk dismissing staff, which would generate an alternative—and noisier—problem on the social front. Moreover, there is a pervasive view that not dismissing staff assumes social responsibility, justifying loss-making conformity under the banner of the equity principle.

The second reason for the poor efficiency of steel SOEs is their heavy debt burden. It can be seen from Table 14.4 that the financial cost assumed for each tonne of steel in an SOE is nearly twice that for private enterprise. On the surface, this could appear to be inconsistent with the idea that it is easier for SOEs than for private companies to gain low-interest loans from state-owned commercial banks. In fact, this is precisely the reason why SOEs tend to accumulate more debt—because they face 'soft budget constraints'. In turn, SOEs in China's steel industry have, year after year, suffered heavy financial losses.

A third reason for the poor efficiency of SOEs is that compared with private sector firms, SOEs face a relatively high level of direct and operational intervention by local government. Owing to the structure of China's government performance examination, local officials are highly motivated to increase tax revenues, expand employment and maintain social stability. When the demand for steel was high, local governments rushed to develop their own steel industry without paying much attention to environmental protection, geographical location or product quality. This led to the rapid expansion of steel production capacity in the SOE sector, in spite of repeated Central Government orders to reduce the scale of steel production.

The fourth political economy explanation for poor steel industry efficiency also has an economic geography component. Among large steel enterprises incurring heavy financial losses, a disproportionate share is located in China's inland areas, where access to raw materials such as iron ore means depending almost entirely on imports. And, compared with Chinese provinces that are proximate to seaports such as Hebei, inland industries must then have the imported materials freighted by domestic railway, ship or road transportation. And, not only are these steel mills paying more for inputs, but also their steel production usually outstrips local demand, meaning some of these producers sell more than half of their product back to China's more economically dynamic coastal regions—sales that again involve high transportation costs. Such enterprises are unlikely to have the capacity to make a profit even if their management is very efficient.

Such SOE-led market failures have had industry-wide and also upstream and downstream effects, and so far the industry has been incapable of overcoming the disadvantage of homogeneous competition. The main reason for this is that the operational purpose of SOEs and of private enterprises is fundamentally different. Private enterprises are pursuing maximum returns on capital, while SOEs hold on to the value derived when 'everyone has a secure job'. In seeking mergers and industry reorganisation, it has been difficult to align these worlds.

It has also been difficult to realise the so-called mixed ownership model sought by the government. Another reason is the negative impact on firms' financial positions as a result of reorganisation among SOEs. When a competitive enterprise merges with an uncompetitive one, the former immediately bears the burden of providing support to the latter, often over an extended period. The scale of the challenges adopted by competitive steel industry firms in merging with uncompetitive firms means that the concentration ratio of the Chinese steel industry has never realised the targets set by various plans and industrial policies (Liu 2015). On the contrary, the concentration has been in decline (Figure 14.5).

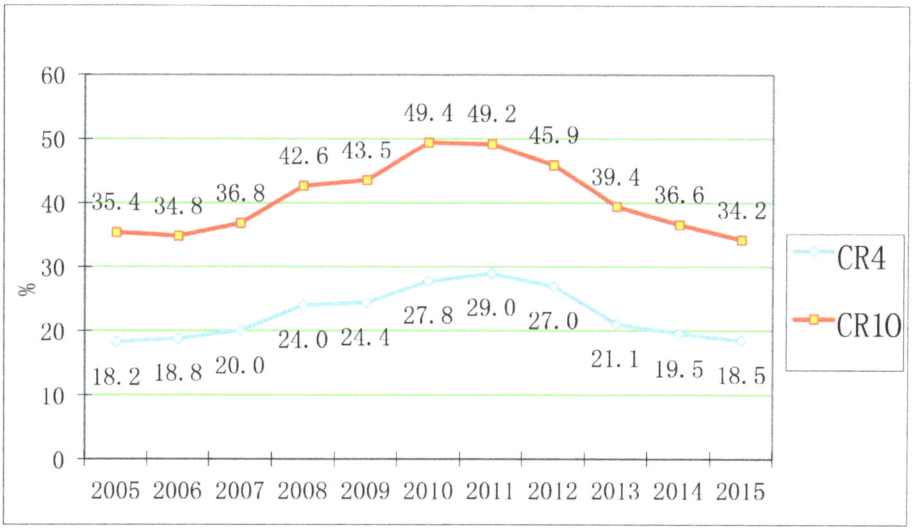

Figure 14.5 Concentration ratio of the steel industry, 2005–15 (per cent)

Note: CR4 and CR10 stand for the ratios of top 4 and top 10 companies' output to total outputs respectively.

Sources: Data taken from CISA and NBS.

The outlook for the reform and restructuring of China's steel industry

First, a factor that will inevitably and significantly shape steel industry dynamics in coming years is the reality that China's steel consumption appears to have passed its peak. Specifically, 2013 was the highest year by far of apparent steel consumption. That year, 772 million tonnes were demanded—equivalent to 569 kg per capita and more than twice the world average (234 kg) for that year. In 2014 and 2015, China's steel consumption per capita decreased annually, by 4.6 and 5.9 per cent respectively.

As Figure 14.6 shows, however, China's per capita steel consumption remains above the world average, at 511 kg for 2015—placing China above most developed countries in North America and the European Union. Interestingly, China's consumption levels are roughly comparable with those of high-end industrial manufacturers, such as Germany and Japan, and still lower than those of smaller but developed industrial countries such as South Korea and the Czech Republic (Figure 14.6).

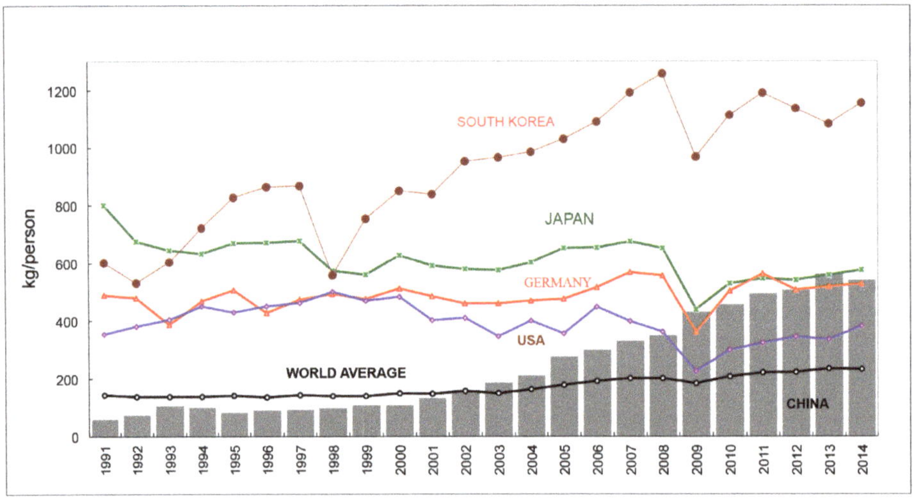

Figure 14.6 Apparent steel use per capita of major economies, 1991–2014 (kg per person)

Source: World Steel Association (2005–15).

Historical experience shows that steel consumption in most industrialised countries follows the 'life cycle' steel industry rule: its trajectory often has a strong correlation with the economy's development stage, speed of growth, economies of scale and domestic industrial structure. The United States, Japan and France reached their peak levels of per capita steel consumption of 711 kg, 802 kg and 485 kg, respectively, in 1973. Germany's peak arrived a few years earlier, in 1970, when per capita steel consumption reached 660 kg.

Researchers of China's steel industry and foreign research institutions have for some years been trying to forecast China's own 'peak' steel consumption level. Studies have forecast that China will complete its industrialisation by about 2020 and total steel consumption will then peak at 0.8 to 1 billion tonnes (McKay et al. 2010). As steel consumption has fallen along with the slowdown in the economy in the past two years, some observers have suggested that China has already reached peak steel consumption, in 2013, and that declines will continue for some years. Others, however, disagree with this conclusion (Liu 2016).

The average of these views means that, at best, there will be limited if any room for further growth in steel consumption in China. Some analysts, however, believe that China's steel consumption will stay on a 'high platform' for a long time (Xu 2016). This will depend on the industrial path that China's economy takes in the years ahead. For example, despite the negative impact of the GFC on selective industrialised economies, steel consumption has remained continuously high over a long period. In South Korea, consumption even appears to have significantly increased with per capita steel consumption reaching 1,113kg in 2015.[3] Considering that China has not yet completed its industrialisation, its gross domestic product (GDP) per capita was less than US$8,000 in 2015 and the urbanisation rate had reached only 56 per cent in the same year, it seems China still has some distance to go before reaching the industrialisation levels of a developed country. It is therefore difficult to confidently predict the direction of the steel industry.

Also, importantly, average national statistics for China hide the great imbalance in economic development across the country. In first-tier cities such as Beijing, Shanghai, Tianjin and Guangzhou's frontier city of Shenzhen, GDP per capita stands at about US$17,000. For several of China's less-developed provinces, however, GDP per capita was just over US$4,000 in 2015. Such an unbalanced pattern enables the steel consumption curve to change in a gradual fashion. This will necessitate managing the previously mentioned geographic cost factors attached to inland steel production.

Thanks to modern technical gains that may reduce metal intensities in further industrialisation, China may never reach the historical per capita steel consumption peaks of the United States and Japan. But, owing to the factors discussed herein, we predict that for the time being there will be a relatively slow and incremental decline in consumption. At the same time, one cannot rule out the possibility for China to reach a new peak in steel consumption on per capita terms in future. First, the efficiency gains resulting from the current economic rebalancing and restructuring could generate new impetus for growth and thus demand for steel consumption. Second, the economic catching up by those inland regions could generate new demand for steel products. Third, China may increase its exports of those goods that have high metal intensities such as machinery and automobiles in the future.[4]

Second, measures adopted by the Central Government to limit total steel production capacity may not be effective in the short term. In turn, the problem of overcapacity could persist for some time. In recent years, the Central Government has repeatedly called for the expansion of new steel production

3 World Steel Association, 2016.

4 China's 'One Belt and One Road' strategy could be another factor in increasing future demand for steel.

capacity to be limited. New steelmaking projects, such as Baosteel's project in Zhanjiang, WISCO's Fangchenggang project and the Shandong Steel Group project in Rizhao, have required investors to prove the principle of 'equal or decrement replacement'. This means they have to close an equal or greater amount of existing and less technically advanced capacity before being allowed to operationalise new facilities.

In general, however, there is much uncertainty about whether such principles are being adhered to. It is difficult for the Central Government to effectively monitor big industry when there are hundreds of steel mills. Existing competitive enterprises may, for example, expand their production capacity by replacing smaller furnaces with bigger ones. Local governments benefit from the capacity expansion and have little incentive to limit their investments in steel capacity. For these reasons, it may be reasonable to fear that excess steel capacity in China will not change significantly regardless of future steel consumption levels.

Third, SOE reforms necessitate fundamentally changing the management and governance systems and operating mechanisms of these enterprises. Helping the Chinese steel industry to exit its 'winter' is not simply a matter of adjusting the supply and demand imbalance, but also requires solving the problem of market failure (or, to a great extent, 'government failure') by ensuring that SOEs become truly competitive in the steel market. This transition will take time and will depend on how fast the general package of market-oriented reforms also shifts the broader economy.

The story is not, however, entirely bleak. There are some favourable factors for achieving reform targets sooner than expected. First, there exist superior SOE and state-owned bank 'group companies' within local governments. These have been suffering from the endless transfer of finance to 'zombie enterprises' and are therefore eager for a change to the status quo. Second, zombie enterprises that have accrued heavy debts or have become insolvent may not survive long without external support, and therefore may have no choice but to finally exit the market. Third, the Central Government has arranged tens of billions of renminbi in funds to solve the unemployment problems that will be caused by removing zombie enterprises from the steel market.

These challenges and the need for change arise within a complex broader environment of political economy reform—for example, the question of how to address the contradiction between the special political status (or privileges) of SOEs and the principles of fair market competition. There is so far no established guiding principle for solving this contradiction, and the experience of other large economies transitioning to large-scale privatisation shows this problem should be approached with care. How to ensure SOEs practise effective self-governance is another unresolved challenge that ultimately hinges on how much the government is willing to overhaul the relationship between the state and markets. There are no certain solutions to these problems, but the sheer scale of loss-making by some SOEs has become financially unsustainable. It is estimated that some firms will need to exit the industry permanently and some will likely be privatised through merger and acquisition (M&A) or by selling assets to private enterprises.

In turn, M&A activities in the industry may be expected to accelerate as the reform program deepens. The declining net assets of disadvantaged enterprises provide opportunities for mergers and reorganisation at low cost for more competitive enterprises. Local governments and shareholders of loss-making enterprises are increasingly less likely than previously to resist M&A. Steel industry market concentration is therefore expected to increase greatly in coming years. By restructuring within and between domestic regional markets, a monopolistically competitive market structure can be formed within the steel industry. The resulting curbing of the price war will be the main means of enhancing competition and also of deepening product division and improving the quality and profitability of the steel industry as a whole. As a result, the industry in the medium term is expected to recover to a normal level of profitability.

References

China Custom Statistics (various years), China Custom, Beijing, China. Available at: china-trade-research.hktdc.com/business-news/article/Fast-Facts/China-Customs-Statistics/.

China Iron and Steel Association (CISA) Statistics (various years), China iron and Steel Association, Beijing, China.

Hurst, L. (2015), China's impact on global iron ore market, PhD thesis, Crawford School of Public Policy, The Australian National University, Canberra.

Liu, H. (2013a), Analysis and suggestions on the lower profitability of China's steel industry, *China Steel*, 2013(10): 11–18.

Liu, H. (2013b), Looking for the antidote to the excess capacity in the steel industry, *China Metallurgical News*, 20 June.

Liu, H. (2015), How to break the deadlock of M&A in China's steel industry, *China Metallurgical News*, 10 June.

Liu, H. (2016), Demand side, supply side: The key is to reform supply side, *China Steel Focus*, 2016(1): 34–36.

McKay, H., Sheng, Y. and Song, L. (2010), China's metal intensity in comparative perspective, in R. Garnaut, J. Golley and L. Song (eds), *China: The next twenty years of reform and development*, 73–98, Canberra and Washington, DC: ANU Press and Brookings Institution Press.

National Bureau of Statistics (NBS) (2015), *China statistical yearbook 2015*, Beijing: China Statistics Press.

Organisation for Economic Co-operation and Development (OECD) (2016), *Excess capacity in the global steel industry and the implications of new investment projects*, Paris: OECD. Available from: oecd-ilibrary.org/docserver/download/5js65x46nxhj.pdf?expires=1463020168&id=id&accname=guest&checksum=A59B9DA06B0EA68A8DF241517C7A35B0.

Sanderson, H. 2015, China steel exports climb over 100m tonnes, *The Financial Times*, 9 December. Available from: ft.com/intl/cms/s/0/7700d728-9e8f-11e5-8ce1-f6219b685d74.html#axzz48c9W7m5j.

Song, L. (2015), State and non-state enterprises in China's economic transition, in G. C. Chow and D. H. Perkins (eds), *Routledge handbook of the Chinese economy*, 182–207, London and New York: Routledge.

Song, L. and Liu, H. (2012), Steel industry development and transformation in China: An overview, in L. Song and H. Liu (eds), *The Chinese steel industry's transformation: Structural change, performance and demand on resources*, 1–16, Cheltenham, UK: Edward Elgar.

World Steel Association (2005–15 [yearly issues]), *Steel Statistical Yearbook*, Brussels: World Steel Association.

World Steel Association (2016), *Steel Statistical Yearbook*, Brussels: World Steel Association.

Xu, X. (2016), Will China's steel consumption substantially drop after reaching the peak level?, *China Metallurgical News*, 2 March.

15. Divergent Industrial Water Withdrawal and Energy Consumption Trends in China: A decomposition and sectoral analysis

Can Wang and Xinzhu Zheng[1]

Introduction

Water and energy are indispensable inputs to modern economies. Currently in China, however, these are both under threat. China's per capita quantity of fresh water is only one-quarter of the global average. The fact those resources are spatially distributed unevenly across the country exacerbates the shortage problem, especially in arid and densely populated parts of northern China. Ominously, at the same time, China faces an energy crisis relating to the dominance of coal in the energy consumption structure and high external energy dependence in general.

From 2000 to 2014, when national water use declined at an annual rate of 0.8 per cent, energy consumption rose at an annual rate of 8.1 per cent. Generally, however, these two variables move in the same direction and show a roughly linear relationship (Figure 15.1).

Changes in water use and energy consumption are sensitive to some common driving factors. Rapid economic growth and population increase will increase demand for water and energy, while technological improvement can curb the increase. Simultaneously, structural adjustment of production will effect water use and energy consumption. In turn, changes in water use and energy consumption will interact with one another.

1 This research was funded jointly by the National Natural Science Foundation of China (No. 71273153 and No. 71525007) and Tsinghua–Rio Tinto Research Center for Resources, Energy and Sustainable Development.

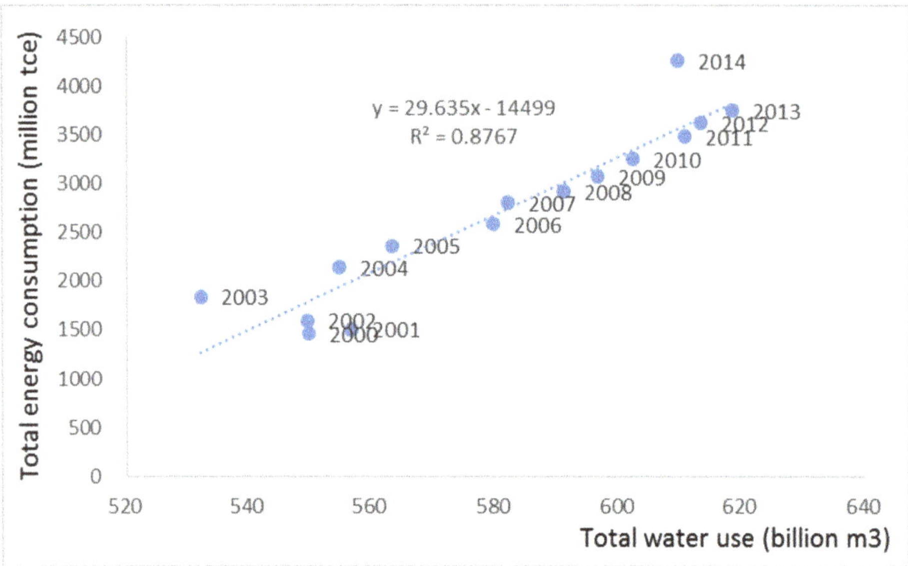

Figure 15.1 Relationships between national water use and energy consumption, 2000–14

Source: Authors' work drawn from MWR (2002–14), NBS (2014b).

Sustainable development requires concurrent management of water and energy resources. Effective control of both requires understanding of the contributions of the common driving factors that produce changes in water use and energy consumption. Studies have explored the effects of these driving factors on energy consumption or on water use. To our knowledge, however, few studies have reviewed and explained changes in water use and energy consumption together, towards the goal of identifying the correlations between these two indicators. This study therefore conducts an investigation into these driving factors, with the main focus being a quantitative comparison of how they contribute to water use and energy consumption simultaneously, and an exploration of the interactions to facilitate integrated water and energy management.

Specifically, we investigate changes in freshwater use and energy consumption across 36 industrial sectors in China. The time frame for the analysis is 2007–12, and this is further divided into two periods: 2002–07 and 2007–12. The latter period serves to distinguish the influence of the Global Financial Crisis (GFC) of 2008. Decomposition methods are used to analyse the drivers of economic growth, population growth, structural adjustment and resource efficiency. Moreover, a deeper analysis of the contribution of individual industrial sectors to these drivers is quantitatively evaluated. The results of that decomposition analysis demonstrate the importance of understanding the interrelated factors that drive change in freshwater use and energy consumption. Future policy in this area should heed the need for integrated water and energy management.

It is noted that withdrawal and consumption are two aspects of water usage, and this study focuses on the former. According to the United States Geological Survey, 'withdrawal' is defined as the amount of water removed from the ground or diverted from a surface water source for use, while 'consumption' refers to the part of water withdrawn that is lost to evaporation or transpiration, incorporated into products or crops or otherwise removed from the immediate water environment (Kenny et al. 2009). The remainder of this chapter is organised as follows: section two provides a literature review on related decomposition analyses; section three introduces the methodology and data sources for the analysis; section four presents the decomposition results of industrial water withdrawal and energy consumption, including the contributions of individual industrial sectors to the driving factors; while section five concludes with the main findings of this study and offers policy recommendations.

Literature review

The focus of a recent proliferation of studies has been on the sources of change in energy consumption (Ma 2014), energy intensity (Zeng et al. 2014), carbon dioxide emissions (Zhang and Da 2015; Jiang et al. 2015), carbon dioxide intensity (Liu et al. 2015) and emissions of air pollutants (Guan et al. 2014; Liu and Wang 2013; He 2010). The samples for such studies are global (for example, Lan et al. 2016; Peters and Hertwich 2008), national (for example, Cansino et al. 2016; Feng et al. 2015) and regional (for example, Kang et al. 2014; Lu et al. 2015). Zeng et al. (2014) quantitatively investigated the changing contribution of five driving factors to China's energy intensity fluctuation during 1997–2007. Feng et al. (2015) evaluated the driving factors affecting the decline of carbon dioxide emissions from fossil fuels during 2007–13 in the United States. They found that economic recession was the dominant driver of the decline, rather than the shift from coal to natural gas. Ma (2014) explored the driving factors of a country's changing energy consumption at the multi-fuel, multi-sector and multi-region level. Additional studies have paid attention to the decomposition analysis of interregional embodied carbon flows. Jiang et al. (2015), for example, focused on the virtual carbon flows among eight regions in China and found that trade balance and energy intensity are determining factors.

As China is the largest manufacturer in the world and its industry is energy intensive, large volumes of studies have used decomposition analysis to study the related industrial energy consumption and carbon dioxide emissions. Zha et al. (2009) used a sample comprising 36 industry subsectors in China to investigate what specific factors drive energy intensity in the country. They also provided the contribution degree of subsectors to the structure and intensity effects during 1993–2003. Hasanbeigi et al. (2013) provided retrospective and prospective decomposition analyses of energy use in the Chinese manufacturing sector. Zhao et al. (2014) compare the energy consumption and energy intensity of Japanese and Chinese manufacturing industries at the sectoral level. Wu and Huo (2014) analyse the effectiveness of energy conservation policies in China through the study of energy efficiency impacts in the industrial and transport sectors. Liu et al. (2007) have analysed the change in China's industrial carbon dioxide emissions over the period 1998–2005 using the logarithmic mean Divisia index (LMDI) method. Ouyang and Lin (2015) provided a similar study in the period 1991–2010. Yan and Fang (2015) focus on energy-related carbon dioxide emissions from Chinese manufacturing for the period 1993–2011 and explore the mitigation potential based on scenario analyses. Liu et al. (2015) analyse the change in carbon intensity in China's industrial sector over the period 1996–2012 using the Divisia index decomposition method, and also identified the contribution of individual subsectors. Apart from industrial energy consumption and carbon dioxide emissions, there are also some studies analysing China's industrial air pollutant emissions. For example, Fujii et al. (2013) analyse the changes in emissions of air pollutants in 10 Chinese industrial sectors from 1998 to 2009, and illustrate the impact of the elimination policy on air pollution management.

Compared with studies of energy use and related environmental impacts, those investigating factors contributing to change in water use are comparatively few. Duarte et al. (2014) decomposed global water use over the entire twentieth century to project future water use trends. Zhang et al. (2012) focused on Beijing's water challenges and conducted a decomposition analysis for both the internal and the external water footprints over the period 1997–2007. The results shed light on strategies to combat the challenge.

Few studies simultaneously explore two or more indicators. One exception is Kopidou et al.'s (2016) study, which explored common trends in and drivers of carbon dioxide emissions and employment. To our understanding, this literature review implies that our study is an original one, as it compares the effects of driving factors on both industrial energy consumption and water withdrawal. As in the case of the studies mentioned, the decomposition results of this study are intended to review past performance to facilitate a future integrated management approach to water and energy resources.

Methodology and data

Driving factors

The contributions of four driving factors—economic scale, structural adjustment, resource intensity and population growth—to water withdrawal and energy consumption are explored in this study. This follows from the logic that economic and population growth can stimulate both increased freshwater withdrawal and energy consumption. Structural shifts in production are seen as an important pathway for tackling environmental and energy issues in China (State Council of China 2011). In fact, given the scale of the dual challenge of water and energy conservation, retuning the industrial structure is unavoidable. A structural shift to energy-efficient but water-intensive sectors is expected to alleviate the energy crisis and related air pollution, but will put greater pressure on water resources. Resource intensity is another important factor driving changes in water withdrawal and energy consumption. Resource intensity is defined as the water withdrawal or energy consumption per unit of value added in each industrial sector.

Methodology

There are two main methods for undertaking decomposition analysis at the sectoral level: index decomposition analysis (IDA) and structural decomposition analysis (SDA). The similarities and differences between IDA and SDA were introduced in the literature by Hoekstra and van den Bergh (2003) and Su and Ang (2012). The decomposition analysis adopted in this study is the LMDI method (Ang and Zhang 2000; Ang 2015)—a frequently used IDA method.

In the LMDI model, industrial freshwater withdrawal can be given by Equation 15.1.

Equation 15.1

$$W = \sum_i W_i = \sum_i f_i s_i e P = \sum_i \frac{W_i}{Q_i}\frac{Q_i}{Q}\frac{Q}{P}P$$

In Equation 15.1, W is total industrial freshwater withdrawal; W_i is the freshwater withdrawal of sector i; f_i is the water intensity of sector i, defined as the ratio of freshwater withdrawal in sector i (W_i) to its value added (Q_i); s_i is the share of sector i in total industrial output, defined as the ratio of value added in sector i (Q_i) to the total industrial value added (Q); e is the industrial value added per capita, defined as the ratio of total industrial value added (Q) to national population (P); and P is national population.

The changes in industrial freshwater withdrawal (ΔW) from the base year, 0, to year t are decomposed into the changes driven by four effects: 1) the water intensity effect (Δf); 2) the production structure effect (Δs); 3) the economic scale effect (Δe); and 4) the population effect (ΔP) (Equation 15.2).

Equation 15.2

$$\Delta W = W_t - W_0 = \Delta f + \Delta s + \Delta e + \Delta P$$

The changes caused by each driving factor can be calculated by Equation 15.3.

Equation 15.3

$$\Delta f = \sum_i L(W_i^t, W_i^0) \times \ln(f_i^t / f_i^0)$$

$$\Delta s = \sum_i L(W_i^t, W_i^0) \times \ln(s_i^t / s_i^0)$$

$$\Delta e = \sum_i L(W_i^t, W_i^0) \times \ln(e^t / e^0)$$

$$\Delta P = \sum_i L(W_i^t, W_i^0) \times \ln(P^t / P^0)$$

In this, the logarithmic mean of total industrial water withdrawal is given by Equation 15.4.

Equation 15.4

$$L(W_i^t, W_i^0) = (W_i^t, W_i^0)/(\ln W_i^t - \ln W_i^0)$$

The decomposition method for industrial energy consumption is similar. Industrial energy consumption can be given by Equation 15.5.

Equation 15.5

$$E = \sum_i E_i = \sum_i f'_i s_i e P = \sum_i \frac{E_i}{Q_i} \frac{Q_i}{Q} \frac{Q}{P} P$$

In this equation, E is total industrial energy consumption; E_i is the energy consumption of sector i; f'_i is the energy intensity of sector i, defined as the ratio of energy consumption in sector i (E_i) to its value added (Q_i); s_i is the share of sector i in total industrial output, defined as the ratio of value added in sector i (Q_i) to total industrial value added (Q); e is industrial value added per capita, defined as the ratio of total industrial value added (Q) to national population (P); and P is national population.

Changes in industrial energy consumption (ΔE) from the base year, 0, to year t are decomposed into the changes driven by four factors: 1) the water intensity effect (Δf); 2) the production structure effect (Δs); 3) the economic scale effect (Δe); and 4) the population effect ($\Delta P'$) (Equation 15.6).

Equation 15.6

$$\Delta E = E_t - E_0 = \Delta f' + \Delta s' + \Delta e' + \Delta P'$$

The changes caused by each driving factor can be calculated by Equation 15.7.

Equation 15.7

$$\Delta f' = \sum_i L(E_i^t, E_i^0) \times \ln(f'^t_i / f'^0_i)$$

$$\Delta s' = \sum_i L(E_i^t, E_i^0) \times \ln(s_i^t / s_i^0)$$

$$\Delta e' = \sum_i L(E_i^t, E_i^0) \times \ln(e^t / e^0)$$

$$\Delta P' = \sum_i L(E_i^t, E_i^0) \times \ln(P^t / P^0)$$

The logarithmic mean of total industrial water withdrawal is given by Equation 15.8.

Equation 15.8

$$L(E_i^t, E_i^0) = (E_i^t, E_i^0)/(\ln E_i^t - \ln E_i^0)$$

Data sources

This study's focus is on 36 secondary industrial sectors in China, covering energy production and supply and manufacturing. The water production and supply sector is excluded from the discussion due to the data limitations. Data on the value added for each sector in 2002 and 2007 come from the annual

China industrial economy statistical yearbook (NBS various years). The data for value added for each sector in 2012 come from China's *Input–output table* for 2012 (NBS 2012). The current industrial value added was deflated into 2002 constant prices. The energy consumption data were cited from the 2014 *China energy statistical yearbook* (NBS 2014a). Data for freshwater withdrawal in industrial sectors were taken from the *Annual statistical report on the environment in China* (MEP various years). The computational problems with the zero values of the variables given in the logarithmic form are overcome by replacing the zero values with a small positive number, referring to Ang and Choi's (1997) study. Convergence results are obtained as the positive number approaches zero.

Results and discussion

Declining water withdrawal and growing energy consumption

Over the period 2002–12, industrial water withdrawal in China decreased by 27.5 per cent (MEP various years). Using the methodology outlined above, we calculate that, driven by economic growth, freshwater withdrawals (yellow bars in Figure 15.2) in 2002–07 increased by 60.9 per cent. Population growth (purple bars in Figure 15.2) further pushed up freshwater withdrawals, by 2.7 per cent; however, the overall level of industrial water withdrawals in the period decreased, by 6.1 per cent. This is a result of changes in water intensity (–58.6 per cent) and in production structure (–11.1 per cent). A similar situation occurred between 2007 and 2012. The decreases in water intensity and production structure offset the increases caused by economic growth and population growth and led to declining water withdrawals.

Unlike the declining trend for industrial freshwater withdrawals, industrial energy consumption in China increased significantly over the same period (Figure 15.3). Our calculations identify a sharp acceleration of 137.9 per cent in industrial energy consumption across 2002–12. The only factor helping to curb increasing industrial energy consumption was falling energy intensity. There were different but related trends around the GFC of 2008. In the five years before the GFC, industrial energy consumption increased by 88.5 per cent. The downward influence of energy intensity (–18.8 per cent) was overwhelmed by the upward influence of changes in economic growth (+88.3 per cent), population growth (+3.9 per cent) and production structure (+14.1 per cent). In the five years after the onset of the GFC, the more substantial effect of the decrease in energy intensity (–73.5 per cent) slowed the growth of industrial energy consumption. However, the downward influence of energy intensity still cannot offset the upward influence of economic growth (+87.9 per cent), population growth (+2.7 per cent) and production structure adjustment (+9 per cent).

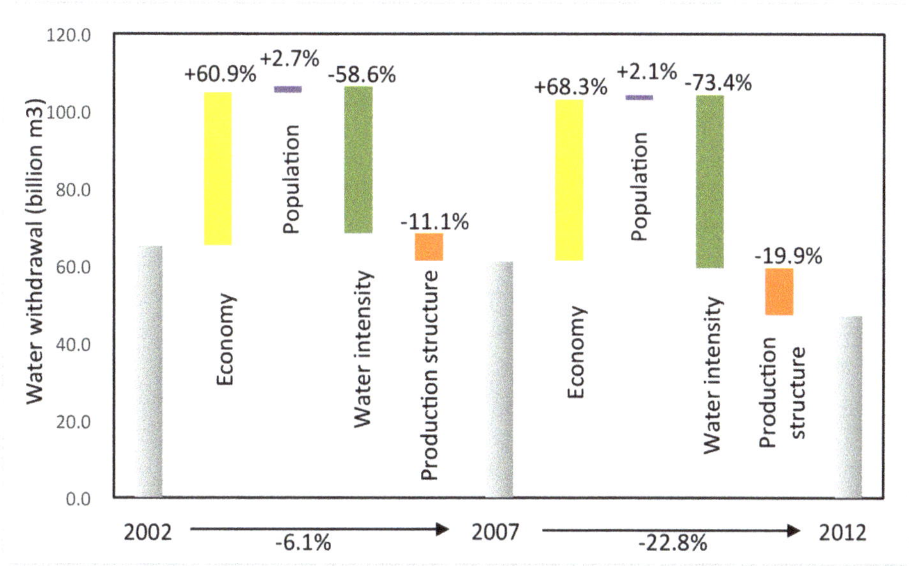

Figure 15.2 Decomposition results for changes in industrial freshwater withdrawals, 2002–12

Source: Authors' work.

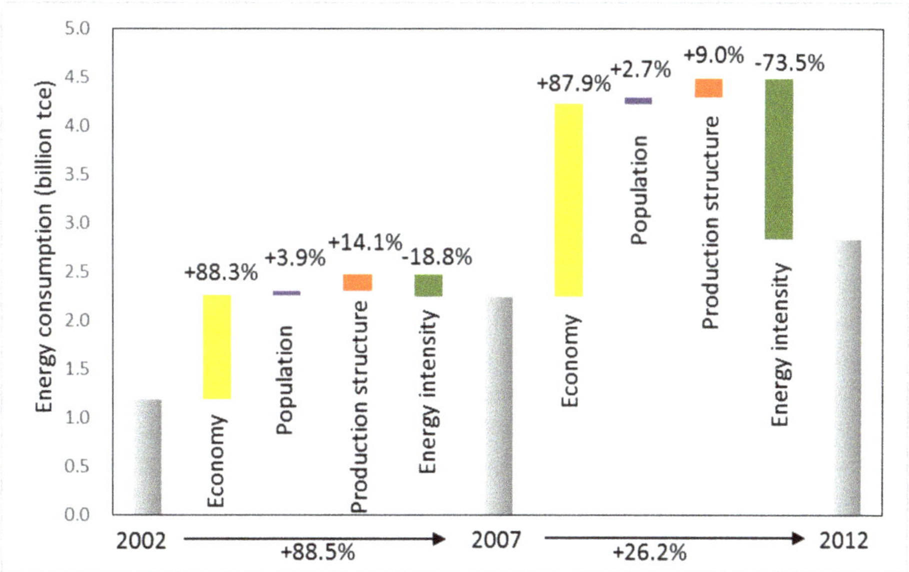

Figure 15.3 Decomposition results for changes in industrial energy consumption, 2002–12

Source: Authors' work.

Comparison of the driving factors of these two indicators identifies several noteworthy findings. In the period 2002–12, economic development served as the dominant factor driving the increase in both industrial freshwater withdrawal and energy consumption. Falls in intensity were the primary driver curbing the growth of industrial freshwater withdrawals and energy consumption. Importantly, the reason for the divergent trends between water withdrawal and energy consumption is that the improvement in water efficiency exerted more influence than the improvement in energy efficiency over the past decade. The reduction effect of improvements in water efficiency exceeded the promotion effect of economic growth and so decreased overall freshwater withdrawals. This optimistic situation did not, however, emerge for energy consumption. Instead, the downward effect of declining energy intensity was insufficient to offset the increasing effect caused by economic growth—due mainly to the energy intensiveness of industry in China.

Mutually related economic growth and resource efficiency

These results illustrate that the water efficiency effect overwhelmed the economic growth effect, producing a decline in water withdrawals, while the opposite happened to industrial energy consumption. Although the prevailing patterns in changes to water withdrawal and energy consumption were divergent, there is a common theme in that the two dominant driving factors—economic scale and resource intensity—interacted mutually in terms of the degree of contribution at the subsector level. The degrees of contribution of individual industrial sectors to each driving factor are provided in Figure 15.4.

Across the entire sample period, the increase in energy consumption caused by economic growth occurred mainly in four sectors: smelting and pressing of ferrous metals, non-metal mineral production, chemical production and the smelting and pressing of nonferrous metals. These sectors also contributed significantly to the decrease in energy intensity (26.6 per cent, 13.7 per cent, 13.7 per cent and 10.2 per cent, respectively) (Figure 15.4a). The increase of freshwater withdrawals that was caused mainly by economic growth arose mainly from the electricity/heating supply sector. This sector is also the main contributor to the falling water intensity of production (56.1 per cent). That is, across the period 2002–12, the sectors whose production scales accelerated significantly also demonstrated the most obvious improvement in energy or water intensity. These sectoral decomposition results illustrate that those sectors experiencing economic growth made the most effort to improve resource efficiency (Figure 15.4b). This finding is consistent with Kopidou et al.'s (2016) study, which explored the common trends and drivers of carbon dioxide emissions and employment.

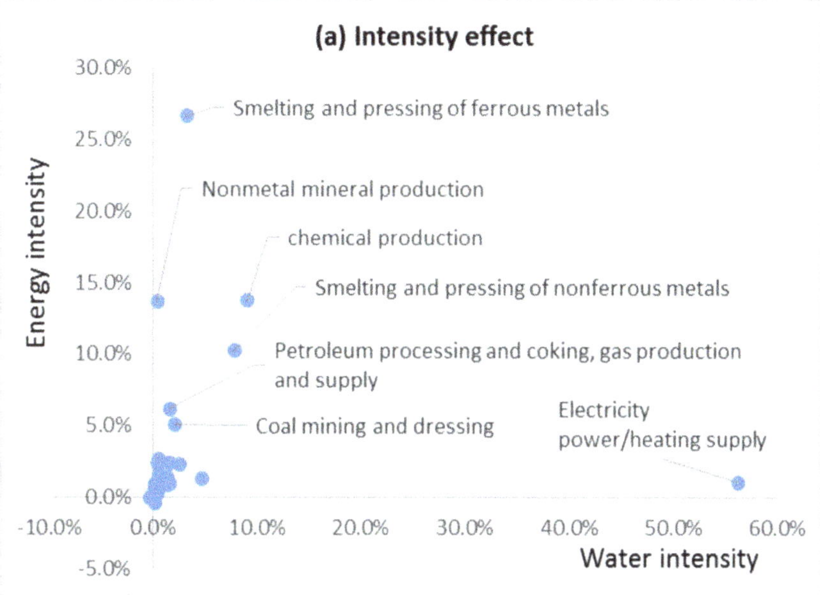

Figure 15.4a Degree of contribution of individual industrial sectors to the resource intensity effect

Source: Authors' work.

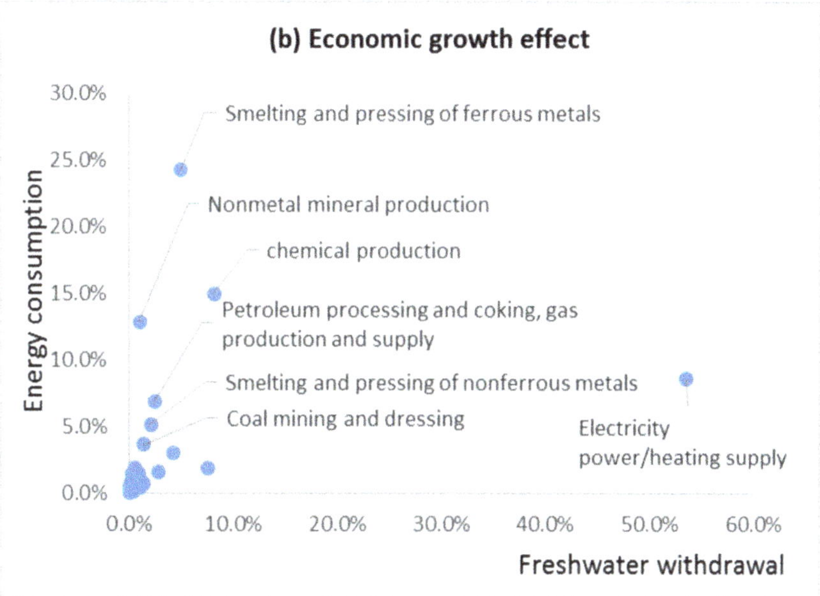

Figure 15.4b Degree of contribution of individual industrial sectors to the economic growth effect

Source: Authors' work.

Divergence of structural shifts in water and energy use

Divergence between the driving effects of production structure on freshwater withdrawal and energy consumption was observed in the period 2002–12 (Figures 15.2 and 15.3) in this study. Increases in industrial freshwater withdrawals were inhibited by adjustment of production structure, while industrial energy consumption was increased.

The reason for this divergence is illustrated by further decomposition results at the sectoral scale (Table 15.1). For structural adjustment, the share of 17 industrial sectors in total production fell, including in selective water-intensive industries, including electricity/heating supply, paper printing, textile manufacturing and beverage manufacturing. At the same time, the share of the other 19 sectors increased. The increasing proportion of selected energy-intensive industries—such as smelting and pressing of ferrous metals, smelting and pressing of nonferrous metals and coalmining and dressing—is the main contributor to the expansion of industrial energy consumption and freshwater withdrawal. The fact that industrial production turned out to be more water efficient but remained energy intensive suggests China should continuously adjust its industrial structure.

Exploration of selected industrial sectors

In this study, selected industrial sectors are highlighted as the biggest contributors to the increase of both freshwater withdrawal and energy consumption. These include the smelting and pressing of ferrous metals sector and the non-metal mineral production sector. Moreover, for the electricity/heating supply and the smelting and pressing of nonferrous metals sectors, although their energy consumption increased significantly, they were the primary contributors to the decrease of industrial freshwater withdrawals. Based on the multisectoral decomposition results for industrial freshwater withdrawal and energy consumption (Table 15.1), this section will provide detailed analysis of the contributions of highlighted subsectors.

Table 15.1 Sectoral decomposition results for industrial freshwater withdrawal and energy consumption, 2002–12

Industrial sectors	Decomposition results of industrial water withdrawal (million tonnes)					Decomposition results of industrial energy consumption (million tce)[1]				
	Δf	ΔS	ΔE	ΔP	Total	Δf'	ΔS'	ΔE'	ΔP'	Total
Smelting and pressing of ferrous metals	–2,716.1	891.5	4,064.6	143.0	2,383.0	–499.1	169.7	736.9	26.2	433.7
Chemical production	–7,519.2	697.9	6,638.5	245.1	62.3	–257.2	43.4	454.6	16.2	257.0
Non-metal mineral production	–288.8	228.0	793.1	26.8	759.0	–256.7	93.1	391.1	13.9	241.4
Electricity/heating supply	–46,554.1	–21,485.9	43,487.9	1,660.0	–22,892.1	–19.3	–140.0	260.5	9.4	110.7
Smelting and pressing of nonferrous metals	–6,457.2	1,636.8	1,667.9	66.5	–3,085.9	–192.2	136.0	157.2	5.6	106.6
Petroleum processing and coking, gas production and supply	–1,307.4	35.7	1,971.5	71.1	770.9	–115.3	5.7	207.1	7.4	104.9
Coal mining and dressing	–1,735.9	794.0	1,143.0	41.7	242.9	–94.9	79.4	110.7	3.9	99.2
Textiles	–952.0	–1,327.0	3,471.3	125.1	1,317.5	–22.1	–34.8	90.4	3.2	36.7
Rubber and plastic products	–108.2	–30.4	209.2	7.6	78.2	–10.6	–6.4	43.7	1.5	28.2
Metal products	–1,101.4	78.8	763.7	28.6	–230.2	–25.2	5.7	43.2	1.5	25.3
Ordinary equipment	–426.6	142.9	226.3	8.5	–49.0	–50.2	29.0	40.8	1.5	21.0
Transportation equipment	–587.9	–74.6	519.0	19.4	–124.1	–14.5	–5.4	39.0	1.4	20.5
Electronic and telecommunications equipment	236.7	–214.2	496.9	17.0	536.4	0.9	–11.2	27.6	1.0	18.3
Food processing	–2,150.2	536.6	2,306.9	83.4	776.7	–43.1	11.2	48.1	1.7	18.0
Electrical equipment and machinery	–2.0	–23.2	135.6	4.7	115.0	–5.3	–3.7	25.0	0.9	16.9
Ferrous metals mining and dressing	–1,363.0	1,297.9	624.9	21.9	581.7	–45.2	40.9	19.6	0.7	16.1
Paper	–3,942.6	–2,077.5	6,223.3	228.9	432.1	–23.7	–18.9	55.7	2.0	15.0
Non-metals mining and dressing	–435.5	149.0	207.9	7.8	–70.7	–29.2	19.8	21.3	0.8	12.6
Timber processing, bamboo, cane, palm and straw production	–143.3	61.4	90.5	3.3	11.8	–15.7	11.2	15.5	0.5	11.5

Industrial sectors	Decomposition results of industrial water withdrawal (million tonnes)					Decomposition results of industrial energy consumption (million tce)[1]				
	Δf	ΔS	ΔE	ΔP	Total	Δf'	ΔS'	ΔE'	ΔP'	Total
Pharmaceutical manufacturing	–309.0	–319.3	841.9	30.6	244.2	–5.4	–9.0	23.9	0.9	10.3
Special equipment	–297.3	46.9	186.1	7.0	–57.4	–18.5	5.9	21.1	0.8	9.3
Other metals mining and dressing	–1,083.9	608.7	800.3	28.7	353.8	–15.4	9.7	12.8	0.5	7.6
Food production	–1,299.9	–61.4	996.4	37.4	–327.4	–17.0	–1.3	24.0	0.9	6.5
Beverage production	–279.5	–377.2	1,155.0	41.4	539.7	–8.6	–6.9	20.7	0.7	6.0
Textiles, clothing, shoes, hats manufacturing	–22.8	–78.8	215.1	7.7	121.2	–1.8	–4.0	10.9	0.4	5.6
Garments and other fibre production, leather, furs, feather and related production	–163.0	–30.1	365.3	13.0	185.2	–0.1	–0.4	4.6	0.2	4.3
Handicraft manufacturing and other manufacturing products, waste collection, separation, processing and treatment	–146.7	–115.6	114.0	4.4	–143.9	7.6	–25.8	20.3	0.7	2.8
Printing	–18.6	–8.1	30.7	1.1	5.1	–2.0	–1.2	5.0	0.2	2.0
Waste resources and recycling of waste materials	–191.4	144.7	39.0	1.5	–6.3	–5.3	5.8	1.3	0.0	1.9
Educational and sports goods production	–9.5	9.4	20.5	0.7	21.2	–3.3	1.3	3.6	0.1	1.7
Instruments, meters, cultural and office machinery	–234.1	1.6	122.7	4.8	–105.0	–2.1	–0.6	3.9	0.1	1.4
Furniture manufacturing	–26.7	12.1	20.1	0.7	6.2	–3.1	1.6	2.7	0.1	1.3
Gaseous fuels production and supply	–162.3	62.2	77.3	2.9	–20.0	–16.8	7.7	9.5	0.4	0.8
Tobacco processing	–44.4	–54.1	68.9	2.6	–27.0	–1.7	–3.0	3.8	0.1	–0.7
Chemical fibre manufacturing	–788.5	–317.8	831.3	31.3	–243.7	–19.5	–10.9	27.2	1.0	–2.2
Petroleum and natural gas extraction	–336.9	–188.5	467.5	17.4	–40.6	–44.4	–22.6	56.8	2.1	–8.1

[1] tce = tonnes of standard coal equivalent

Electricity/heating supply sector

From 2002 to 2012, the electricity/heating supply sector contributed the most to the decrease in industrial freshwater withdrawals. The cumulative decrease in freshwater withdrawals by this sector over the period was 22.9 billion cubic metres. Economic growth in the sector initially increased freshwater withdrawals by 43.5 billion cu m, but water intensity improvements served to reduce the withdrawals dramatically ($\Delta f = -46.6$ billion cu m). Although the economic effect made a substantial additional contribution to the increase of freshwater withdrawals in the electricity/heating supply sector, improvements in efficiency offset this upward influence and served to decrease freshwater withdrawals. It was also observed that the electricity/heating supply sector made the greatest contribution to the adverse effects of production structure on energy consumption. Although economic growth also significantly increased energy consumption ($\Delta E' = +62.5$ million tonnes of standard coal equivalent, or tce), the curbing effect of improved energy intensity could not compensate for the otherwise increased consumption over 2002–12. Thus, energy consumption in the electricity/heating supply sector increased by 11.5 million tce in that period.

Smelting and pressing of ferrous metals

In total, across all industries and over the period 2002–12, the smelting and pressing of ferrous metals sector contributed the most to increases in both industrial energy consumption and industrial water withdrawal. Significant increases in both production scale and industrial proportion, alongside only a marginal fall in energy intensity, caused a 338.33 million tce increase in energy consumption in the sector. At the same time, all three of the driving factors studied herein, including water intensity, had additive effects on the increase of water withdrawals, leading to an increase in withdrawals of 3.3 billion tonnes over 2002–07. Over the second five-year interval, however, the energy and water intensities of this sector improved significantly. The energy efficiency improvement in the iron and steel sector in that period largely compensated for the additive influence of economic growth, meaning that the overall increase in energy consumption was only 95.4 million tce. These considerable efficiency improvements were also seen in relation to freshwater withdrawal in this sector. During 2002–07, increased water intensity in the iron and steel sector served to increase freshwater withdrawals, while during 2007–12, water intensity decreased dramatically and inhibited freshwater withdrawals.

Other industrial sectors

Aside from the considerable increase in energy consumption in the smelting and pressing of ferrous metals sector, large energy consumption growth also occurred in the following sectors: coalmining and dressing, smelting and pressing of nonferrous metals, chemical production and petroleum processing and coking, gas production and supply. Energy consumption in these sectors was, however, curbed somewhat by the energy intensity effect. But energy efficiency improvements were not enough to offset the additive effect of economic growth. The energy intensity effect improved in the second interval of our study, but the inhibitive effect on energy consumption was limited. Meanwhile, freshwater withdrawals in these sectors did not demonstrate obvious changes, because water efficiency improvement almost offset the effect of economic growth.

Conclusion

This study sought to understand the drivers of water and energy consumption in China towards facilitating the evolution of integrated water and energy management. Focusing on 36 secondary industrial sectors, and covering energy production and supply and manufacturing, the study explored the driving factors behind recent changes in industrial water withdrawal and energy consumption in China. A decomposition analysis using the LMDI method was adopted and applied to the period 2002–12, which was itself subdivided into two five-year periods that pivot around the potential impact of the GFC in 2008. The main findings are as follows:

1. Declining water withdrawal and growing energy consumption in Chinese industrial sectors were observed over the period 2002–12. Decomposing these trends identified that economic development served as the dominant additive factor driving the increase of both industrial freshwater withdrawal and industrial energy consumption. Declining energy intensity of production was the primary driver helping to curb that rate of growth. The different trends in water withdrawal and energy consumption are explained by the fact that in the past decade water efficiency improvement has exerted a more obvious effect than energy efficiency improvement. The reduction effect of water efficiency improvement exceeded the promotion effect of economic growth, serving to reduce overall freshwater withdrawals. Such an optimistic situation did not emerge vis-a-vis energy consumption.
2. Although the prevailing pattern of change in water withdrawal and energy consumption diverged, the common factors of economic scale and resource intensity interacted with one another. Sectors experiencing economic growth were more active in improving resource efficiency. Over the entire period, the increase in energy consumption caused by economic growth occurred mainly in four sectors: smelting and pressing of ferrous metals; non-metal mineral production; chemical production; and smelting and pressing of nonferrous metals. These four sectors also contributed significantly to the decrease in energy intensity of production (26.6 per cent, 13.7 per cent,

13.7 per cent and 10.2 per cent, respectively). In parallel, the sectors in which there was an increase in freshwater withdrawal induced by economic growth were mainly those related to the electricity/heating supply sector, which is also the main contributor to falling water intensity of production (56.1 per cent).

3. Divergence between the driving effects of production structure on freshwater withdrawal and energy consumption was observed during the sampling period. The fact that industrial production was found to be increasingly water efficient but also highly energy intensive suggests China should continue to adjust its industrial structure.
4. Some industrial sectors are highlighted due to the significance of their contributions to changes in industrial water withdrawal and industrial energy consumption. For example, the smelting and pressing of ferrous metals sector contributed the most to the increase in both industrial energy consumption and industrial water withdrawal. The electricity/heating supply sector played a significant role in curbing the intensity of industrial water withdrawal in China.

Despite the interaction identified herein between water use and energy consumption in China, at present national policies for water and energy are determined separately. Given the importance of sustainable development and, in particular, the fragility of China's highly degraded water supplies, this chapter addresses the need to better integrate water and energy resource management in the country. Future research could further support the implementation of integrated management by exploring the trade-offs and synergies of various policies and technological alternatives.

References

Ang, B. W. (2015), LMDI decomposition approach: A guide for implementation, *Energy Policy*, 86: 233–238.

Ang, B. W. and Choi, K. H. (1997), Decomposition of aggregate energy and gas emission intensities for industry: A refined Divisia index method, *The Energy Journal*, 18(3): 59–73.

Ang, B. W. and Zhang, F. Q. (2000), A survey of index decomposition analysis in energy and environmental studies, *Energy*, 25(12): 1149–1176.

Cansino, J. M., Román, R. and Ordóñez, M. (2016), Main drivers of changes in CO_2 emissions in the Spanish economy: A structural decomposition analysis, *Energy Policy*, 89: 150–159.

Duarte, R., Pinilla, V. and Serrano, A. (2014), Looking backward to look forward: Water use and economic growth from a long-term perspective, *Applied Economics*, 46(2): 212–224.

Feng, K., Davis, S. J., Sun, L. and Hubacek, K. (2015), Drivers of the US CO_2 emissions 1997–2013, *Nature Communications*, 6: 7714.

Fujii, H., Managi, S. and Kaneko, S. (2013), Decomposition analysis of air pollution abatement in China: Empirical study for ten industrial sectors from 1998 to 2009, *Journal of Cleaner Production*, 59: 22–31.

Guan, D., Su, X., Zhang, Q., Peters, G. P., Liu, Z., Lei, Y. and He, K. (2014), The socioeconomic drivers of China's primary PM2.5 emissions, *Environmental Research Letters*, 9(2): 024010.

Hasanbeigi, A., Price, L., Fino-Chen, C., Lu, H. and Ke, J. (2013), Retrospective and prospective decomposition analysis of Chinese manufacturing energy use and policy implications, *Energy Policy*, 63: 562–574.

He, J. (2010), What is the role of openness for China's aggregate industrial SO_2 emission? A structural analysis based on the Divisia decomposition method, *Ecological Economics*, 69(4), 868–886.

Hoekstra, R., and van den Bergh, J. C. (2003), Comparing structural decomposition analysis and index. *Energy economics*, 25(1): 39–64.

Jiang, Y., Cai, W., Wan, L. and Wang, C. (2015), An index decomposition analysis of China's interregional embodied carbon flows, *Journal of Cleaner Production*, 88: 289–296.

Kang, J., Zhao, T., Liu, N., Zhang, X., Xu, X. and Lin, T. (2014), A multi-sectoral decomposition analysis of city-level greenhouse gas emissions: Case study of Tianjin, China, *Energy*, 68: 562–571.

Kenny, J. F., Barber, N. L., Hutson, S. S., Linsey, K. S., Lovelace, J. K. and Maupin, M. A. (2009), Estimated use of water in the United States in 2005, *United States Geological Survey Circular*: 1344.

Kopidou, D., Tsakanikas, A. and Diakoulaki, D. (2016), Common trends and drivers of CO_2 emissions and employment: A decomposition analysis in the industrial sector of selected European Union countries, *Journal of Cleaner Production*, 112: 4159–4172.

Lan, J., Malik, A., Lenzen, M., McBain, D. and Kanemoto, K. (2016), A structural decomposition analysis of global energy footprints, *Applied Energy*, 163: 436–451.

Liu, L., Fan, Y., Wu, G. and Wei, Y. (2007), Using LMDI method to analyze the change of China's industrial CO_2 emissions from final fuel use: An empirical analysis, *Energy Policy*, 35(11): 5892–5900.

Liu, N., Ma, Z. and Kang, J. (2015), Changes in carbon intensity in China's industrial sector: Decomposition and attribution analysis, *Energy Policy*, 87: 28–38.

Liu, Q. and Wang, Q. (2013), Pathways to SO_2 emissions reduction in China for 1995–2010: Based on decomposition analysis, *Environmental Science & Policy*, 33: 405–415.

Lu, Q., Yang, H., Huang, X., Chuai, X. and Wu, C. (2015), Multi-sectoral decomposition in decoupling industrial growth from carbon emissions in the developed Jiangsu Province, China, *Energy*, 82: 414–425.

Ma, C. (2014), A multi-fuel, multi-sector and multi-region approach to index decomposition: An application to China's energy consumption 1995–2010, *Energy Economics*, 42: 9–16.

Ministry of Environmental Protection (MEP) (various years), *Annual statistical report on the environment in China*, Beijing: China Environmental Science Press.

Ministry of Water Resources (MWR) (2002–2014), *China Water Resources Bulletin*, [in Chinese], Beijing: China Waterpower Press.

National Bureau of Statistics (NBS) (various years), *China industrial economy statistical yearbook*, Beijing: China Statistics Press.

National Bureau of Statistics (NBS) (2012), *Input–output table*, Beijing: China Statistics Press. Available from: data.stats.gov.cn/ifnormal.htm?u=/files/html/quickSearch/trcc/trcc01.html&h=740.

National Bureau of Statistics (NBS) (2014a), *China energy statistical yearbook*, Beijing: China Statistics Press.

National Bureau of Statistics (NBS) (2014b), *China Statistical Yearbook*, [in Chinese], Beijing: China Statistics Press.

Ouyang, X. and Lin, B. (2015), An analysis of the driving forces of energy-related carbon dioxide emissions in China's industrial sector, *Renewable and Sustainable Energy Reviews*, 45: 838–849.

Peters, G. P. and Hertwich, E. G. (2008), CO_2 embodied in international trade with implications for global climate policy, *Environmental Science & Technology*, 42(5): 1401–1407.

State Council of China (2011), *Comprehensive work plan for energy conservation and emission reduction during the 'Twelfth Five-Year Plan' period*, Beijing: State Council. Available from: gov.cn/zwgk/2011-09/07/content_1941731.htm.

Su, B., and Ang, B. W. (2012), Structural decomposition analysis applied to energy and emissions: some methodological developments. *Energy Economics*, 34(1): 177–188.

Wu, L. and Huo, H. (2014), Energy efficiency achievements in China's industrial and transport sectors: How do they rate?, *Energy Policy*, 73: 38–46.

Yan, X. and Fang, Y. (2015), CO_2 emissions and mitigation potential of the Chinese manufacturing industry, *Journal of Cleaner Production*, 103: 759–773.

Zeng, L., Xu, M., Liang, S., Zeng, S. and Zhang, T. (2014), Revisiting drivers of energy intensity in China during 1997–2007: A structural decomposition analysis, *Energy Policy*, 67: 640–647.

Zha, D., Zhou, D. and Ding, N. (2009), The contribution degree of sub-sectors to structure effect and intensity effects on industry energy intensity in China from 1993 to 2003, *Renewable and Sustainable Energy Reviews*, 13(4): 895–902.

Zhang, Y. and Da, Y. (2015), The decomposition of energy-related carbon emission and its decoupling with economic growth in China, *Renewable and Sustainable Energy Reviews*, 41: 1255–1266.

Zhang, Z., Shi, M. and Yang, H. (2012), Understanding Beijing's water challenge: A decomposition analysis of changes in Beijing's water footprint between 1997 and 2007, *Environmental Science & Technology*, 46(22): 12373–12380.

Zhao, Y., Ke, J., Ni, C. C., McNeil, M., Khanna, N. Z., Zhou, N., Fridley, D. and Li, Q. (2014), A comparative study of energy consumption and efficiency of Japanese and Chinese manufacturing industry, *Energy Policy*, 70: 45–56.

16. Beyond Trees: Restoration lessons from China's Loess Plateau

Kathleen Buckingham

Introduction

China has the highest afforestation rate in the world, resulting in an increase in forest cover of 9 per cent over the past 30 years (Wellesley 2014). This is not for reasons of altruism. Since 2000, China has emerged as the main processing hub for the world's forest sector. China is now the world's largest importer and consumer of wood-based products (Hoare 2015). Yet historical forest loss has made China one of the most forest-deficient countries in the world, with a national forest cover of 22 per cent, compared with the global average of 31 per cent (FAO 2012). Tree loss, moreover, is just the tip of the iceberg. China is also one of the most water-stressed countries on the planet, having 21 per cent of the world's population, but only 6 per cent of its freshwater (Wong 2013). Sustainability of both water resources and land affects the population and the economy.

As a country with a population of more than 1.3 billion people and given the above constraints, China is among those countries facing the highest adverse risk levels around climate change (Department of Climate Change 2015). Historical deforestation, land conversion, overgrazing and mining have left landscapes particularly vulnerable. Devastating floods, desertification and sandstorms have forced China to take action to restore its land, particularly when considering increased threats from climate change and the need for food and natural resource security (World Bank 2006).

To combat these compounding issues, China will need increased crop productivity, resource use efficiency and environmental protection (Fan et al. 2012). To facilitate disaster preparedness, the Chinese Government has made significant financial investments to restore degraded areas. Restoration refers to the long-term process of regaining ecological functionality and enhancing human well-being across deforested or degraded landscapes. Restoration is a key tool to mitigate disasters arising from degradation and to protect natural resources (Buckingham et al. 2016).

Policy is therefore essential to protect land and resources facing adverse impacts from climate change, development and population pressure. At the United Nations Framework Convention on Climate Change (UNFCCC) Conference of Parties (COP21) in Paris in December 2015, countries across the globe committed to create a new landmark international climate agreement: to keep global temperature increase below 2°C (3.6°F) and to pursue efforts to limit it to 1.5°C (BBC 2015). Countries publicly outlined what post-2020 climate actions they intend to take under a new international agreement. These are known as their 'intended nationally determined contributions' (INDCs).

Of course, forests have a key role to play in carbon sequestration. China's INDCs related to forestry aspire to increase forest carbon stocks by 4.5 billion cubic metres. This implies an increase in forest cover of 50–100 million hectares (124–247 million acres) of forest, or about two to four times the size of the United Kingdom. This amount of forest would create a roughly 1 gigatonne carbon sink, equivalent to stopping tropical deforestation for almost a full year or taking 770 million cars off the road. This is on top of significant progress already made: China increased its tree cover by 49 million ha (121 million acres) between 1990 and 2010 (Frazen et al. 2015).

China's INDCs plan promotes afforestation, voluntary tree planting, protection of natural forests and restoration of forest and grassland from farmland. Controls intend to be implemented to mitigate sandification for areas in the vicinity of Beijing and Tianjin and desertification, to reduce soil erosion and enhance water reserves (Department of Climate Change 2015). Prior to the INDCs, nationally, China invested about US$100 billion in six forestry programs, which covered more than 97 per cent of China's counties and targeted 76 million ha of land for afforestation (Cao et al. 2010a). In 1999, the Chinese Government launched 'Grain for Green' (Tang et al. 2013), one of the world's largest conservation programs. Grain for Green consisted of projects and practices designed to curb soil erosion, increase the amount and variety of natural vegetation in the landscape and introduce more sustainable land management practices. The program included a payment for ecosystem services that directly engaged millions of rural households in project implementation (Lu et al. 2012).

Most recently, the Thirteenth Five-Year Plan (FYP) put forward in 2016 aims to enhance and complete a series of national geographic databases for natural resources, including one for forests. Key data include forecasts—for example, that the national forest coverage rate is expected to reach 23.04 per cent and forest carbon storage volume will reach 9.5 billion tonnes by 2020. In addition, the plan identifies four key areas of focus in forestry: 1) policy and institutional reform; 2) forest resource conservation; 3) forest quality and efficiency improvement (for restoration); and 4) forest management, protection and innovation. First, state-owned forest areas will be reformed to promote government, public institutions, enterprises and management in a streamlined manner with more efficient state-owned forest management agencies. Second, natural forests, forest resources and wetlands will be conserved and protected and a rare and endangered species national park established. Third, the pace of afforestation will be accelerated with the aim to strengthen forest management, improve the quality of forest resources and national timber reserves as well as develop the forest economy, forest tourism and nurseries for restoration. Last, the government aims to strengthen forest protection through prevention and control of forest fires and pests using scientific and technological innovation in forestry. China's forestry database platform was launched in February 2016 (Xinhua Net 2015).

Part of the solution to maintaining forest stocks, increasing forest quality and allowing for restoration involves logging bans. Part of the Central Government's Thirteenth FYP includes a ban on commercial logging of natural forests in state-owned plantations by the end of 2016.[1] The first such pilot was a ban on all commercial logging of natural forests in key forest zones in north-eastern China's Heilongjiang province in April 2014 (Hoare 2015). Heilongjiang has historically produced over 30 per cent of China's domestic log supply (Sun et al. 2016). The forestry component of the Thirteenth FYP and this new logging ban are essential to maintain the country's demand for timber. Some 49.94 million cu m of natural forest are presently logged each year. Since more than half of China's timber demand is met by imports, it is also important that controls be put in place to ensure the legality of timber resources being sourced from abroad (Jie 2015). At present, it is estimated that exports destined for China make up half of all the global trade in illegal wood-based products (Hoare 2015). There is speculation that the vision for a greener China may end up exporting environmental damage to other, more vulnerable countries through sourcing timber from beyond China (Thiel and Sun 2016).

It is too early to speculate on the outcomes of new legislation and how the international INDCs will affect national policies, both of which have significant implications for forest reserves. However, lessons have been learnt from existing land degradation across China. Some of the most acute crises triggering strengthening resolve to restore degraded land relate to sandstorms that hit downwind urban areas. A particularly highly publicised case, soil erosion in the Loess Plateau, contributed to massive sandstorms that periodically choked Beijing during the 1980s and 1990s, including the infamous 'Black Wind' of

1 The ban will be completed nationwide by 2017. This is an extension of a program that was started in 1998, which aimed to allow forests to recover from decades of overlogging and to help restore forest ecosystems and their resilience. The halt of commercial logging in state-owned natural forests in Heilongjiang province started on 1 April 2014. The extension of the ban in April 2015 covered all natural forests across north-eastern China and Inner Mongolia and the government plans for further expansions to all other state-owned natural forests, including those in the 14 provinces not currently covered by the National Forest Protection Program (Sun et al. 2016).

1993 (Qian and Quan 2002). It is no surprise that the first World Bank Loess Plateau project started a year later. Soil erosion was so severe that the plateau contributed more than 90 per cent of the total sediment entering the Yellow River (Chen et al. 2007). Furthermore, a large amount of once cultivated land had to be abandoned in the Loess Plateau due to soil degradation, resulting in economic losses of approximately US$1.28 billion over recent decades and an unprecedented threat to food security (Chen et al. 2007).

Loess Plateau: A case study

The Loess Plateau in north-central China is a large, hilly, semi-arid region roughly the size of Afghanistan. Thousands of years of farming, which intensified during the Cultural Revolution, left the former grasslands degraded and eroded. Food production was down, waterways filled with silt and air in faraway cities suffered from sandstorms born on the Loess Plateau. The fact that the local population had reached some 50 million people made the problems worse. Something had to be done.

In 1994 a restoration effort began. Two Loess Plateau watershed rehabilitation projects were implemented in 48 counties across Shanxi, Shaanxi and Gansu provinces and the autonomous region of Inner Mongolia (Liu and Hiller 2016). One the one hand, some observers may not consider the restoration of these 1,100 watersheds within the Loess Plateau a strict case of 'forest landscape restoration', due to the use of extensive afforestation (introduction of trees on lands not historically forested). On the other hand, the restoration effort—or bid to restore ecosystem functionality—did exhibit a number of the features and key success factors of forest landscape restoration (Hanson et al. 2015). Importantly, these generate insights for other forest and landscape restoration initiatives and lessons for future projects (Hanson et al. 2015).

Given the significance of the Loess Plateau and also of the restoration effort, the latter was chosen as one of 16 forest landscape restoration case studies worldwide for a large forestry review project by the World Resources Institute (WRI) (Hanson et al. 2015).

Via literature review and expert interviews, each of the 16 case studies was analysed in search of common features of restoration success and failure. Three common themes for successful restoration were identified (Hanson et al. 2015):

- *A clear motivation.* Decision-makers, landowners and/or citizens were inspired or motivated to restore forests and trees in landscapes.
- *Enabling conditions in place.* A sufficient number of ecological, market, policy, social and/or institutional conditions were in place to create a favourable context for forest landscape restoration.

- *Capacity and resources for sustained implementation*. Capacity and resources existed and were mobilised to implement forest landscape restoration on a sustained basis on the ground.

Within each of the three themes, relevant historical examples point to a number of factors that, when present—either already naturally or because people have taken steps to create them—increase the likelihood that restoration will be successful. The key success factors are summarised in Table 16.1, in the 'Restoration Diagnostic'.

Table 16.1 Key success factors for forest landscape restoration

Theme	Feature	Key success factor
Motivate	Benefits	• Restoration generates economic benefits
		• Restoration generates social benefits
		• Restoration generates environmental benefits
	Awareness	• Benefits of restoration are publicly communicated
		• Opportunities for restoration are identified
	Crisis events	• Crisis events are leveraged
	Legal requirements	• Law requiring restoration exists
		• Law requiring restoration is broadly understood and enforced
Enable	Ecological conditions	• Soil, water, climate, and fire conditions are suitable for restoration
		• Plants and animals that can impede restoration are absent
		• Native seeds, seedlings, or source populations are readily available
	Market conditions	• Competing demands (e.g., food, fuel) for degraded forestlands are declining
		• Value chains for products from restored area exists
	Policy conditions	• Land and natural resource tenure are secure
		• Policies affecting restoration are aligned and streamlined
		• Restrictions on clearing remaining natural forests exist
		• Forest clearing restrictions are enforced
	Social conditions	• Local people are empowered to make decisions about restoration
		• Local people are able to benefit from restoration
	Institutional conditions	• Roles and responsibilities for restoration are clearly defined
		• Effective institutional coordination is in place
Implement	Leadership	• National and/or local restoration champions exist
		• Sustained political commitment exists
	Knowledge	• Restoration "know how" relevant to candidate landscapes exists
		• Restoration "know how" transferred via peers or extension services
	Technical design	• Restoration design is technically grounded and climate resilient
		• Restoration limits "leakage"
	Finance and incentives	• Positive incentives and funds for restoration outweigh negative incentives
		• Incentives and funds are readily accessible
	Feedback	• Effective performance monitoring and evaluation system is in place
		• Early wins are communicated

Source: Hanson et al. 2015.

The diagnostic was developed as a structured method for identifying which key success factors for restoration are already in place, which are partially in place and which are missing within a country or landscape that has restoration opportunities. It is a qualitative tool and is intended as a way to help decision-makers and restoration supporters rapidly focus their efforts on the most important factors to get in place before large amounts of human, financial or political capital are invested. When applied periodically every few years once a restoration effort is under way, the diagnostic can help implementers adjust and refine their policies and practices as a means of adaptive management.

A few caveats are important to note. First, no case example exhibited every single key success factor. Thus, it appears that a landscape need not have *every* key success factor in place for restoration to succeed. Second, no single factor appears to be necessary or sufficient for restoration success; a combination is needed. However, some key success factors appear to be particularly important for restoration via natural regeneration (for example, ecological and market conditions), while others are particularly important for active restoration (for example, clear tenure). Third, some of the key success factors are interrelated and can have effects on other factors. For instance, performance monitoring is a key success factor for implementation that, in turn, can further motivate restoration when monitoring is used to widely communicate emerging successes and benefits of restoration (Hanson et al. 2015).

Recognising key success factors

Motivating factors

The Chinese Government became motivated to pursue restoration of the Loess Plateau due to several factors. As with many examples of large-scale restoration, including cases in South Korea and Ethiopia (see Hanson et al. 2015), crisis was the principal trigger to resolve to restore the Loess Plateau, with sandstorms in the late twentieth century hitting downwind urban areas. Decision-makers recognised that landscape restoration would provide a number of economic, social and environmental benefits. Economically, it would improve food security and diversify income generation opportunities, particularly for poor rural communities (Tsunekawa et al. 2014). In the Loess Plateau, funding from the World Bank and the Chinese Government helped restore 4 million ha of land, reportedly more than doubling the incomes of local farmers, reducing erosion by 100 million tonnes of sediment annually, reducing flood risk and dramatically increasing grain production. Socially, it aimed to strengthen household stability and reduce migration to cities. Environmentally, restoration aimed to improve soil health, reduce erosion, ensure cleaner water and sequester carbon (Lu et al. 2012).

Enabling conditions

Several enabling conditions were in place to facilitate restoration in the Loess Plateau—namely, ecological, policy and market conditions. First, ecological conditions: via the Grain for Green program, factors prohibiting the recovery of natural vegetation were removed. In particular, prohibiting grazing in areas designated for restoration resulted in a 99 per cent increase in vegetation cover in those areas (Cao et al. 2011).

Second, policy conditions: clearing restrictions and land rights played important roles. After 1999, for instance, the government banned the cutting of trees and crop-growing on slopes and withdrew permission for unrestricted grazing in the region. The imposed grazing ban became a cornerstone of the strategy to reverse soil degradation in the Loess Plateau area and to re-establish natural vegetation (Hiller and Guthrie 2011). Just as importantly, the bans were enforced. Combined with replanting of vegetation, these bans allowed the perennial vegetation cover to increase from 17 per cent of the region to 34 per cent by the mid-2000s (World Bank 2007b). In addition, the government granted local people the opportunity to take out low-cost land leases to restore fields, followed by the opportunity to acquire land rights such that commodities or payments for ecosystem services derived from a tract of land belonged to them (World Bank 2007a). Further, the Rural Land Contracting Law of 2003 provided security for land users. While farmland use contracts are valid for 30 years, those for grassland extend to 30–50 years and for forest land to 30–70 years (Zhao et al. 2014).

Finally, market conditions: there were value chains for products from restored areas. Originally, the effort to motivate cooperation from local farmers focused on fruit trees and vegetables, with a small amount of payments for ecosystem services. However, what farmers asked for most during the first phase of the World Bank effort was help with new livestock enterprises. Much of the second phase of the World Bank project became a livestock project, with successful introduction of Kashmiri sheep (confined) for wool, dairy cattle (confined) and lots of planting in difficult areas for biomass harvest. Both of these livestock activities were new in the area, made possible by the new biomass being generated through restoration. The success of the new labour-intensive, high-value livestock enterprises based on better biomass management are what will likely determine the future of the Loess Plateau. Loess provides an important example of why forest and agricultural restoration are highly synergistic (C. Delgado, personal communication, 3 September 2015).

Implementation factors

During the restoration period, capacity and resources for implementation came into place that facilitated restoration, including leadership, knowledge and technical design and funds and incentives. Regarding leadership, the Chinese Government and the World Bank demonstrated sustained commitment to Loess Plateau restoration, particularly through the Grain for Green policy from the late 1990s (Hiller and Guthrie 2011).

Regarding knowledge and technical design, in partnership with the World Bank, the Chinese Government created a restoration plan that included both technical design and capacity development. The technical design component included activities focusing on terracing, afforestation, orchards, grasslands, sediment control dams, irrigation, grazing and gully control. The capacity development component included activities focusing on training, research and technology transfer (World Bank 2003). Integrated watershed management practices created water-harvesting structures and ensured continuous vegetative cover through large-scale reafforestation, grasslands regeneration and agroforestry methods (EEMP 2013).

Regarding funds and incentives, the Loess Plateau restoration project had significant project financing: a budget of approximately US$500 million over the period 1994–2005. Finance included direct Chinese Government expenditures and World Bank loans. This finance fuelled subsidies that made converting degraded farmland into trees and other vegetation economically viable for farmers. Subsidies included US$122/ha for seeds and seedlings and a payment for ecosystem services of US$49/ha per year lasting for two to eight years (World Bank 2006).

Challenges to sustainability

The positive impacts of the Loess Plateau restoration project have received a lot of attention. Many ecological and social benefits have been recognised (World Bank 2006; Ferwerda 2012; Tsunekawa et al. 2014). Policy change and enforcement were essential to this success, especially in stopping grazing and controlling land use change.

According to the World Bank, in some places in the Loess Plateau, local farmers saw their incomes double, erosion was reduced by 100 million tonnes of sediment annually, there was a reduction in flood risk and grain production dramatically increased. However, these results also brought costs. The speed of China's effort was possible only by using single species or minimally diverse plantings, and local communities were often unable to enjoy the benefits of restored forests. While in some areas restoration has protected land from desertification and brought better rural livelihoods, in others, trees have grown slowly and some are already dying. Chinese experts readily admit trees were sometimes planted in arid regions better suited to grass. This has led to a growing desire to 'green China naturally' (Cao et al. 2011).

The Loess Plateau's performance against several key success factors highlights what may become challenges to the long-term sustainability of the region's restoration, including awareness, finance and incentives, ecological conditions and technical design.

In terms of awareness, the benefits of restoration and soil conservation currently may not be sufficiently understood by all relevant local populations and local officials (Chen et al. 2007; Lu et al. 2012). This lack of awareness may be due—at least in part—to the top-down nature of the project's design and decision-making. More local participation and engagement could address this information asymmetry. Most farmers—both inside and outside project areas—participated in the project activities, but sometimes they were mandated to do so by the government. Thus, while participation rates were high, the local sense of ownership of project processes and plans could have been higher (Hiller 2012).

Regarding finance and incentives, a survey of farmers in the region indicated that 56 per cent would recultivate sloping land once the subsidies cease in 2018 (Chen et al. 2007; Jiao et al. 2012). Furthermore, some researchers have argued that the eight-year payment for ecosystem services is too short: the subsidies stop before the land generates a high enough yield and before robust markets for products from the restored landscape have developed. For example, apricot trees take time to bear enough fruit to provide an economic return (Chen et al. 2007). Given that the cities downstream (for example, Beijing) are large and have an interest in reducing sandstorms, increased water quality and reduced flooding of the Yellow River, perhaps payment from urban dwellers to rural dwellers is warranted (Hiller 2012). Furthermore, Cao et al. (2009) noted that transferring state property to private ownership alone is not enough of an incentive for residents to protect and restore the land (Cao et al. 2010c). Because most of the program's plots are in impoverished regions of China, the ban on logging and open grazing has led to severe shrinkage in the parts of the economy that were based on forest resources and open livestock grazing. In some regions, inadequate compensation or alternative livelihoods were available (Cao et al. 2010a).

Besides donor funding, the private sector has an important stake in restoration. Popularising the danger to the food industry (of toxins, additives and bioaccumulation), coupled with the environmental needs for restoration, can be leveraged to motivate industry to engage in restoration efforts. For example, outside the Loess Plateau in southern China, Danone, a multinational food products corporation, is piloting projects with 'dynamic farming' techniques from Australia. Danone is piloting financial models that allow the farmers to see the impact of restoration on their business: one that allows them to switch to native Chinese fir instead of non-native, rapid-growing Eucalyptus, one that provides competitive prices in the high-end honey market and one that proves that mandarins can be farmed without high chemical input (Buckingham 2015). Working at small scale will not solve the problem of degradation, however, engaging the private sector to facilitate restoration of landscapes will help identify restoration as a necessity.

Regarding ecological conditions, in some parts of the plateau, non-native tree species were planted in an area more suited to grasses. Furthermore, an adequate supply of high-quality tree and shrub seedlings was lacking due to inadequate incentives for timely delivery. For example, performance targets were not aligned with in-the-field success, as nursery objectives were to transplant all seedlings regardless of quality. As a result, many of the trees planted were unable to survive drought years and about one-third had to be replaced. The situation marginally improved towards the end of the project due to the agricultural reforms of 2002, which established some private nurseries. Nonetheless, farmers and government officials maintain that the supply of high-quality seedlings is a challenge (World Bank 2007a).

Some technical features of the Loess Plateau project have come under scrutiny. One area is afforestation, which has been accepted as an important strategy for preventing soil erosion on the plateau. Increasingly, however, Chinese scientists are debating the long-term sustainability of afforestation in such a semi-arid environment (Jiao et al. 2012). The total survival rate of trees in the Loess Plateau has been low in some areas. For instance, 400,000 Chinese pine trees were planted in northern Shaanxi, but only 25 per cent survived (Chen et al. 2007). Managers often prefer short-lived species that offer attractive short-term gains, but landscape regeneration involving the species mix needed for sustainability is typically a long-term process (Cao et al. 2010b, 2011).

Another area of scrutiny is climate resilience. Some researchers have raised questions about the resilience of the project's technical design in light of the regional climate having a warming and drying trend. Within the context of climate change, large-scale afforestation on Loess soils could increase the severity of water shortages (Cao et al. 2007) owing to increased evapotranspiration from trees. In addition, if trees do not grow adequately, they will be unable to control runoff and soil erosion (Chen et al. 2007). Because of poor species/site pairing, excessive tree planting (Cao et al. 2007) and poor management, in some areas tree plantations have grown well initially but later die due to water shortages (Chen et al. 2007). Vegetation restoration strategies, therefore, need to be tailored to the water availability and other ecological conditions of the region (Chen et al. 2010; Cao et al. 2011). For instance, restoration designs could rely less on pine plantations, favour tree species with more drought resistance and utilise shrubs and alternative vegetation better adapted to the ecological conditions (Cao et al. 2007; Chen et al. 2007; Jiao et al. 2012).

It is easy to blame restoration mistakes on poor science, but that underplays the importance of culture. The open, semi-arid landscape of the Loess Plateau is home to the Hui ethnic people and is peppered with mosques. This landscape is very different from the cultural ideal of the Han ethnic people who make up 92 per cent of China's population and dominate its political and cultural life.

China has worked hard to create a sense of national unity, making Mandarin (the language of the Han people) the country's common language, in 1912. In 1949, Chairman Mao Zedong decreed that all of China would operate on Beijing time, even though the country spans five time zones. Nature, however, will not be bound by our sense of order. It is important to consider what land managers could learn from the Hui people's historical relationship with their landscape. The trees planted on the Loess Plateau were biological settlers, foreigners to the arid landscape. The settler trees also represent the migration of a cultural perspective. While the introduction of non-native plants attracts scientific and public attention, the cultural perspective is often overlooked. Cultural bias can be difficult to perceive; as the Chinese poem states, it is difficult to see the situation when you are deeply involved: you can't see the forest for the trees.

The restoration of the Loess Plateau is unmatched in scale, yet the allure of non-native species to engineer a desired outcome in the landscape is common globally. We need to understand the biophysical and cultural factors to build on the indigenous ecological and cultural memory of the landscape. With changing climate and increasing populations, we need to restore landscapes to ensure the resilience of ecosystem services in the twenty-first century, recognising that cultural diversity is as important as biodiversity in restoration decisions (Buckingham et al. 2014).

Looking forward: Restoration strategy for rehabilitating severely degraded areas

The Loess Plateau has gained much attention for overgrazing, farming and tree planting. Yet, China's land use challenges transcend issues of land utilisation towards arguably more destructive degradation: mining. To successfully restore land, strategies need to go beyond narrow tree and afforestation programs to the need to implement ecologically sustainable land cover to protect soil quality. A sobering report by the Ministry of Environmental Protection (MEP) highlighted the extent of soil degradation, which renders one-fifth of China's soil fallow—a consequence of exposure to heavy metal contaminants (MEP 2014; Patel 2014). This is largely due to mining activities.

There are more than 9,000 large and medium-sized mines and 26,000 small mines in China (Li et al. 2014). Mineral resources play a key role in Chinese economic development. There are 171 varieties of mineral resource in China, accounting for 12 per cent of total global mineral resources (Hu et al. 2010). Soils surrounding mining areas are seriously polluted by heavy metals emitted from mining activities. This kind of pollution not only degrades the quality of the atmosphere, water bodies and food crops, but also threatens the health and well-being of animals and humans by way of the food chain, particularly through bioaccumulation. Soil pollution by heavy metals poses high carcinogenic and non-carcinogenic risks to the public, especially to those living in the most severely polluted regions (Hu et al. 2010).

The Loess Plateau area is home to a significant amount of mining activities, which further threaten the landscape. Open-cast coalmines are primarily located in the environmentally vulnerable regions of north-western China, such as Shanxi province, Inner Mongolia, Gansu, Ningxia and Shaanxi province (Zhang et al. 2015). Large areas of degraded mining land remain barren, preventing agricultural, social and economically sustainable development in affected areas. As land is in short supply in China—exacerbated by the rapidly expanding population—it is now policy to restore or reclaim land degraded by mining (Miao and Marrs 2000). Policy mandates that the ecological environment of 45 per cent of historical abandoned mines must be rehabilitated, and the environment of 30 per cent of polluted mining areas should be restored. New mines are required to restore 100 per cent of their land (Hu et al. 2010).

Extensive grasslands like those within the Loess Plateau are being converted globally. Grasslands are being lost to agriculture, tree plantations, mining and urban development and degraded by invasive species, poorly managed domestic livestock, altered fire regimes, elevated atmospheric carbon dioxide and nitrogen deposition (Veldman et al. 2015a). Tree planting, fire suppression and exclusion of native or domestic grazers are suitable restoration strategies in deforested landscapes. However, interventions such as these can have negative consequences when applied to biomes such as grasslands, savannas and open canopy woodlands. There needs to be a clear distinction between 'reafforestation' (planting trees on deforested land) and 'afforestation' (converting historically non-forested lands to forests or tree plantations) to ensure sustainable restoration strategies (Veldman et al. 2015b).

To facilitate sustainable landscape restoration, lessons from the Loess Plateau case study should be learned and mistakes not repeated. A thorough assessment needs to be conducted to understand the landscape opportunities and challenges for China at specific landscape scales. The restoration diagnostic can be utilised as one part of a toolkit developed by the International Union for Conservation of Nature (IUCN) and the WRI, known as the Restoration Opportunities Assessment Methodology (ROAM). Since mining restoration and rehabilitation are now mandated, ROAM can assist in facilitating the development of a restoration strategy. The methodology would help avoid some of the pitfalls that led to unsustainable restoration practices in the Loess Plateau.

The methodology involves stakeholder consultation to identify opportunity mapping, cost–benefit analysis, enabling conditions and financial and investment options (IUCN and WRI 2014). First, adequate local stakeholder consultation on local landscapes and climate could provide important information to feed into mapping of opportunities and perceived challenges. Landscape opportunity mapping needs to be conducted to understand which vegetation types are suitable to the ecological conditions. This may be trees, but alternatively may be grasslands, shrubs or other vegetation depending on the topography, rainfall and soil types. Conducting a diagnostic will enable stakeholders to gauge the key success factors that are in place and not in place and create the foundations for a restoration strategy. Much needs to be done to adequately facilitate and monitor restoration strategies. However, there is a pressing need in China to develop participatory restoration strategies in critically degraded landscapes to ensure sustainable development.

References

British Broadcasting Corporation (BBC) (2015), COP21 climate change summit reaches deal in Paris, *BBC News*, 13 December. Available from: bbc.com/news/science-environment-35084374.

Buckingham, K. (2015), Duck-rice, honey-bees and mandarins, China Policy Institute Blog, Nottingham, UK: University of Nottingham. Available from: blogs.nottingham.ac.uk/chinapolicyinstitute/2015/05/18/duck-rice-honey-bees-and-mandarins/.

Buckingham, K., DeWitt, S. and Laestadius, L. (2016), The global restoration initiative, in I. Chabay, M. Frick and J. Helgeson (eds), *Land restoration: Reclaiming landscapes for a sustainable future*, 483–496, Atlanta: Elsevier.

Buckingham, K., Laestadius, L., Padovezi, A. and Covell, P. (2014), Taking culture into account in restoring China's Loess Plateau, WRI Blog, Washington, DC: World Resources Institute. Available from: wri.org/blog/2014/12/taking-culture-account-restoring-china%E2%80%99s-loess-plateau.

Cao, S., Chen, L. and Zhu, Q. (2010a), Remembering the ultimate goal of environmental protection: Including protection of impoverished citizens in China's environmental policy, *Ambio*, 39: 439–442.

Cao, S., Chen, L., Shankman, D., Wang, C., Wang, C., Wang, X. and Zhang, H. (2010b), Excessive reliance on afforestation in China's arid and semi-arid regions: Lessons in ecological restoration, *Earth-Science Reviews*, 104: 240–245.

Cao, S., Chen, L., Xu, C. and Liu, Z. (2007), Impact of three soil types on afforestation in China's Loess Plateau: Growth and survival of six tree species and their effects on soil properties, *Landscape and Urban Planning*, (83): 208–217.

Cao, S., Sun, G., Zhang, Z., Chan, L., Feng, Q., Fu, B., McNulty, S., Shankman, D., Tang, J., Wang, Y. and Wei, X. (2011), Greening China naturally, *Ambio*, 40(7): 828–831.

Cao, S., Wang, X., Song, Y., Chen, L. and Feng, Q. (2010c), Impacts of the Natural Forest Conservation Program on the livelihoods of residents of northwestern China: Perceptions of residents affected by the program, *Ecological Economics*, 69(2010): 1454–1462.

Cao, S., Xu, C., Chen, L. and Wang, X. (2009), Attitudes of farmers in China's northern Shaanxi province towards the land-use changes required under the Grain for Green project, and implications for the project's success, *Land Use Policy*, 26(2009): 1182–1194.

Chen, L., Wang, J., Wei, W., Fu, B. and Wu, D. (2010), Effects of landscape restoration on soil water storage and water use in the Loess Plateau region, China, *Forest Ecology and Management*, 259: 1291–1298.

Chen, L., Wei, W., Fu, B. and Lu, Y. (2007), Soil and water conservation on the Loess Plateau in China: Review and perspective, *Progress in Physical Geography*, 31: 389–403.

Department of Climate Change (2015), Enhanced actions on climate change: China's intended nationally determined contributions, 30 June, Beijing: Department of Climate Change, National Development and Reform Commission of China. Available from: www4.unfccc.int/submissions/INDC/Published%20Documents/China/1/China's%20INDC%20-%20on%2030%20June%202015.pdf.

Environmental Education Media Program (EEMP) (2013), *Loess Plateau watershed*, 5 August, Environmental Education Media Program. Accessible from: eempc.org/loess-plateau-watershed-rehabilitation-project/.

Fan, M., Shen, J., Yuan, L., Jiang, R., Chen, X., Davies, W. J. and Zhang, F. (2012), Improving crop productivity and resource use efficiency to ensure food security and environmental quality, *China Journal of Experimental Botany*, 63(1): 13–24.

Ferwerda, W. (2012), *Organizing ecological restoration by partners in business for next generations*, IUCN Commission on Ecosystem Management, Rotterdam: Rotterdam School of Management, Erasmus University.

Food and Agriculture Organization (FAO) (2012), *State of the world's forests*, Rome: Food and Agriculture Organization of the United Nations.

Frazen, T., Song, R., Stolle, F. and Henderson, G. (2015), A closer look at China's climate plan (INDC), WRI Insights Blog, Washington, DC: World Resources Institute. Available from: wri.org/blog/2015/07/closer-look-chinas-new-climate-plan-indc.

Guan, L., Sun, G. and Cao, S. (2011), China's bureaucracy hinders environmental recovery, *Ambio*, 40: 96–99.

Hanson, C., Buckingham, K., DeWitt, S. and Laestadius, L. (2015), *Restoration diagnostic*, Washington, DC: World Resources Institute.

Hiller, B. T. (2012), Sustainability dynamics of large-scale integrated ecosystem rehabilitation and poverty reduction projects, PhD thesis, University of Cambridge, Cambridge.

Hiller, B. T. and Guthrie, P. M. (2011), Phased large-scale approaches to integrated ecosystem rehabilitation and livelihood improvement: Review of a Chinese case study, *Agricultural Science Research Journal*, 1(3): 50–63.

Hoare, A. (2015), *Tackling illegal logging and the related trade: What progress and where next?*, A Chatham House Assessment, London: Chatham House.

Hu, R., Liu, J. and Zhai, M. (2010), *Mineral resources science in China: A roadmap to 2050*, Beijing: Chinese Academy of Sciences.

International Union for Conservation of Nature (IUCN) and World Resources Institute (WRI) (2014), *A guide to the Restoration Opportunities Assessment Methodology (ROAM): Assessing landscape restoration opportunities at the national or sub-national level*, Working Paper (Road-test edition), Gland, Switzerland: IUCN.

Jiao, J., Zhang, Z., Bai, W., Jia, Y. and Wand, N. (2012), Assessing the ecological success of restoration by afforestation on the Chinese Loess Plateau, *Restoration Ecology*, 20(2): 240–249.

Jie, K. (2015), China to launch natural forest logging ban in 2016, *Global Times*, 4 December. Available from: globaltimes.cn/content/956510.shtml.

Li, R., Liu, G., Xie, Y., Qinke, Y. and Liang, Y. (2002), Ecosystem rehabilitation on the Loess Plateau, in T. R. McVicar, R. Li, J. Walker, R. W. Fitzpatrick and C. Liu (eds), *Regional water and soil assessment for managing sustainable agriculture in China and Australia*, 358–365, ACIAR Monograph 84, Canberra: Australian Centre for International Agricultural Research.

Li, Z., Ma, Z., van der Kuijp, T. J., Yuan, Z. and Huang, L. (2014), A review of soil heavy metal pollution from mines in China: Pollution and health risk assessment, *Science of the Total Environment*: 843–853.

Liu, J. D. and Hiller, B. T. (2016), A continuing inquiry into ecosystem restoration: Examples from China's Loess Plateau and locations worldwide and their emerging implications, in I. Chabay, M. Frick and J. Helgeson (eds), *Land restoration: Reclaiming landscapes for a sustainable future*, Atlanta: Elsevier.

Lu, Y., Fu, B., Feng, X., Zeng, Y., Liu, Y., Chang, R., Sun, G. and Wu, B. (2012), A policy-driven large scale ecological restoration: Quantifying ecosystem services changes in the Loess Plateau of China, *PLoS ONE*, 7(2): 1–10.

Miao, Z. and Marrs, R. (2000), Ecological restoration and land reclamation in open-cast mines in Shanxi Province, *China Journal of Environmental Management*, 59: 205–215.

Ministry of Environmental Protection (MEP) (2014), Environmental Protection and the Ministry of Land and Resources issued nationwide survey of soil pollution bulletin, 17 April, Beijing: MEP. Available from: mep.gov.cn/gkml/hbb/qt/201404/t20140417_270670.htm.

Patel, K. (2014), China's food security dilemma, World Policy Blog, 4 June, New York: World Policy Institute. Available from: worldpolicy.org/blog/2014/06/04/chinas-food-security-dilemma.

Qian, W. and Quan, L. (2002), Variations of the dust storm in China and its climatic control, *Journal of Climate*, 15: 1216–1229.

Sun, X., Canby, K. and Liu, L. (2016), China's logging ban in natural forests: Impacts of extended policy at home and abroad, *Forest Trends Information Brief*, March.

Tang, Q., Bennett, S. J., Xu, Y. and Li, Y. (2013), Agricultural practices and sustainable livelihoods: Rural transformation within the Loess Plateau, China, *Applied Geography*, 41: 15–23.

Thiel, A. and Sun, X. (2016), China's logging ban impacts not just its own forestry industry, but others around the world as well, Forest Trends Blog, March. Available from: forest-trends.org/blog/2016/03/14/chinas-logging-ban/.

Tsunekawa, A., Liu, G., Yamanaka, N. and Du, S. (eds) (2014), *Restoration and development of the degraded Loess Plateau, China*, Tokyo: Springer Japan.

Veldman, J. W., Buisson, E., Durigan, G., Fernandes, G. W., Le Stradic, S., Mahy, G., Negreiros, D., Overbeck, G. E., Velman, R. G., Zaloumis, N. P., Putz, F. E. and Bond, W. J. (2015a), Toward an old-growth concept for grasslands, savannas, and woodlands, *Frontiers in Ecology and the Environment*, 13(3): 154–162.

Veldman, J. W., Overbeck, G. E., Negreiros, D., Mahy, G., Le Stradic, S., Fernandes, G. W., Durigan, G., Buisson, E., Putz, F. E. and Bond, W. J. (2015b), Tyranny of trees in grassy biomes, *Science Insights*, 347(6221): 484–485.

Wellesley, L. (2014), *Trade in illegal timber: The response in China*, A Chatham House Assessment, London: Chatham House.

Wong, G. (2013), *China's war on water scarcity: Gridlines*, London: PricewaterhouseCoopers.

World Bank (2003), *Implementation completion report on a credit in the amount of SDR 106.3 million (US$150 million equivalent) to the People's Republic of China for a Loess Plateau watershed rehabilitation project*, Washington, DC: The World Bank.

World Bank (2006), *Implementation completion report on a loan in the amount of SDR 36.9 million (US$50 million equivalent) to the People's Republic of China for the second Loess Plateau watershed rehabilitation project*, Washington, DC: The World Bank. Accessible from: www-wds.worldbank.org/external/default/WDSContentServer/WDSP/IB/2006/01/20/000011823_20060120152438/Rendered/PDF/34612.pdf.

World Bank (2007a), *Project performance assessment report, People's Republic of China, second Loess Plateau watershed rehabilitation project and Xiaolangdi multipurpose project and Tarim Basin project*, Washington, DC: The World Bank. Available from: www-wds.worldbank.org/external/default/WDSContentServer/WDSP/IB/2007/10/31/000020953_20071031102004/Rendered/PDF/41122.pdf.

World Bank (2007b), *Restoring China's Loess Plateau*, Washington, DC: The World Bank. Available from: worldbank.org/en/news/feature/2007/03/15/restoring-chinas-loess-plateau.

World Bank (2010), *Rehabilitating a degraded watershed: A case study from China's Loess Plateau*, Washington, DC: World Bank Institute.

Xinhua Net (2015), China's 13th national plan areas of focus, [in Chinese], *Xinhua Net*, 7 October. Available from: news.xinhuanet.com/fortune/2015-10/07/c_1116746981.htm.

Zhang, L., Bai, K., Wang, M. and Karthikeyan, R. (2015), Basin-scale spatial soil erosion variability: Pingshuo opencast mine site in Shanxi Province, Loess Plateau of China, *Natural Hazards*, 80(2): 1231–1230. doi: 10.1007/s11069-015-2019-9.

Zhao, Y., Wen, T., Yan, J., Sit, T., Yang, S. and Xia, F. (2014), *Land governance in China: Historical context and critical junctures of agrarian transformation*, International Land Coalition Framing the Debate Series, Rome: International Land Coalition.

17. Policies and Measures to Transform China into a Low-carbon Economy

ZhongXiang Zhang[1]

Introduction

China's Thirteenth Five-Year Plan period (2016–20) marks a shift in the focus of China's economic priority from a war against poverty to a war against pollution. Domestically, the drivers of the shift include the dense smog that frequently shrouds Beijing and other areas, and steeply rising oil imports that have raised concerns about a range of environmental problems, health risks and energy security. In addition, domestic concerns for climate stability have reinforced international pressure for China to play an ambitious part in the global effort to combat global climate change. In other words, for the sake of national and international interests, China can no longer continue along its conventional path of encouraging economic growth at the expense of the environment.

Chinese leaders have for some years been aware of the environmental challenges the country faces. In November 2012, the Eighteenth National Congress of the Central Committee of the Communist Party of China adopted a general policy of establishing an 'ecological civilisation'. This places ecological goals at the same level of priority as existing policies on economic, political, cultural and social development—and emphasises that the values of an ecological civilisation will be embedded in all aspects of economic development.

With the grand vision of creating an ecological civilisation in place, the issue becomes how China will deal with the environmental costs of energy consumption needed to fuel economic growth, especially the impact of climate change. This presents a tremendous climate policy dilemma, not only for China but also for the world given the scale of China's emissions and dynamic economy. This is true even in the context of the current slowdown of the Chinese economy, for even though the rate of China's growth has slowed, the incremental additions of this level of growth are still significant at the global level.

1 ZhangZX@tju.edu.cn. This chapter has benefited from comments by Yannick Ringot. The views expressed here are those of the author and do not necessarily reflect the views of the grant provider (National Natural Science Foundation of China under grant no. 71373055). The author bears sole responsibility for any errors and omissions.

Against this background, this chapter discusses China's energy and environmental goals and policies and the measures undertaken, and draws some concluding remarks from the discussion. The next section outlines China's energy and environmental goals, while the third section highlights 10 mitigation policies and measures being implemented to limit China's contribution to climate change. The final section summarises the significance of the goals and policies outlined and discusses the related challenges for the future.

Energy and environmental goals

Between 1980 and 2000, China achieved a quadrupling of its gross domestic product (GDP) with only a doubling of energy consumption (Zhang 2003). Based on the trends of these two decades, the US Energy Information Administration (EIA 2004) estimated that China's carbon dioxide emissions would not catch up to the world's then largest carbon emitter, the United States, until 2030. China's energy use, however, surged after the turn of the century, almost doubling between 2000 and 2007. Despite similar rates of economic growth as in the previous two decades, the rate of growth in energy consumption during this period more than doubled. As a result, China became the world's largest emitter of carbon dioxide in 2007 (IEA 2007). To reverse this underlying trend, China, for the first time, incorporated an input constraint into its five-year economic planning. Specifically, the government required that during the Eleventh FYP period (2006–10), energy use per unit of GDP should be cut by 20 per cent (State Council 2006).

Zhang (2000a, 2000b) envisioned that it would be about 2020 when China could make a voluntary commitment to reduce total greenhouse gas (GHG) emissions per unit of GDP. Zhang estimated that around or beyond that year, a combination of a targeted carbon intensity level and an emissions cap at the sector level would be the most stringent commitment. It was only just before the Copenhagen summit in 2009 that China pledged to cut its carbon intensity by 40–45 per cent relative to 2005 levels by 2020. Although this was consistent with China's long-standing opposition to absolute emission caps—on the grounds that such limits would restrict economic growth—this marked a point of departure from China's long-standing position on its own climate-related actions. Importantly, then prime minister Wen Jiabao made it clear at Copenhagen that China's pledges were 'unconditional and they are not dependent on the reduction targets of other nations' (Watts 2009). The Twelfth FYP (2011–15) adopted a carbon intensity target as a domestic commitment for the first time. Under the target, energy intensity was required to be cut by

16 per cent nationwide (10–18 per cent across provinces) and carbon intensity by 17 per cent nationwide (10–19.5 per cent across provinces) relative to 2010 levels.

While this unilateral commitment pointed to China's determination to further decouple its energy use and carbon dioxide emissions from economic growth, it raised the issue of whether the pledge was truly ambitious or just 'business as usual' (for example, Qiu 2009; Carraro and Tavoni 2010). To give perspective to China's climate pledge, Zhang (2011a, 2011b, 2011c) examined whether it was as challenging as the energy-saving goals set in the Eleventh FYP blueprint and asked the following: 1) Would these goals drive emissions below the projected baseline levels; 2) would China fulfil its part of a coordinated global commitment to stabilise the concentration of GHG emissions at the level set as the target of the international community; and 3) was China's pledge conservative, leaving room for further increases. A balanced analysis of China's climate pledge suggested that the proposed carbon intensity target did not represent business as usual, as some Western scholars (for example, Levi 2009) have argued. On the other hand, the target might not have been hugely ambitious. Given that China was already the world's largest emitter of carbon dioxide, and its share in total global emissions was continuing to rise, even a few additional percentage point reductions in its carbon intensity would translate into significant global emissions reductions. It would be hard but not impossible for China to increase its proposed carbon intensity reduction target. Zhang (2011a, 2011b, 2011c) suggested that China aim for a 46–50 per cent cut in its carbon intensity for the period 2006–20. Achieving this type of goal would put its absolute emissions reductions very much within the Intergovernmental Panel on Climate Change's recommended level for developing countries.

As shown in Table 17.1, China plans both to strengthen and to extend its commitments to 2030. Under the joint China–United States climate statement announced by Chinese President Xi Jinping and US President Barack Obama in November 2014 (and formally released on 25 September 2015), China committed to cap its carbon emissions by about 2030,[2] to try to peak early and to increase the share of non-fossil fuels in primary energy consumption to about 20 per cent by 2030 (White House 2014). These commitments were officially incorporated into China's 'intended nationally determined contributions' submission, dated 30 June 2015 (NDRC 2015). In addition, China pledged to reduce the carbon intensity of its economy by 60–65 per cent by 2030 compared with 2005 levels. In March 2016, the National People's Congress, China's parliament, approved the aim to cut energy intensity by 15 per cent and carbon intensity by 18 per cent relative to 2015 levels by 2020 as part of the Thirteenth

2 How China's carbon emissions are likely to develop or at what level they will finally peak are still open questions.

FYP (State Council 2016). If these goals were realised, China would overshoot its pledge made in Copenhagen, and the eventual outcomes would very much fall within the range envisioned in Zhang (2011b, 2011c).

Table 17.1 China's energy and environmental goals, 2006–30

Time frames	Target goals
11th FYP (2006–10)	Cut energy use per unit of GDP by 20 per cent relative to 2005 levels (actually achieved: 19.1 per cent); cut sulphur dioxide emissions by 10 per cent; close small thermal power plants with total cumulative capacity of 50 GW (actually achieved: 76.8 GW); through the 'Top 1,000 Enterprises Energy Conservation Action Program', save a cumulative 100 million tonnes of standard coal equivalent (tce) (actually achieved: 150 million tce).
12th FYP (2011–15)	Cut energy intensity by 16 per cent (10–18 per cent across provinces) and carbon intensity by 17 per cent (10–19.5 per cent across provinces) relative to 2010 levels; cut sulphur dioxide emissions by 8 per cent and emissions of nitrogen oxides by 10 per cent; through the '10,000 Enterprises Energy Conservation Low Carbon Action Program', save a cumulative 250 million tce.
13th FYP (2016–20)	Cut energy intensity by 15 per cent and carbon intensity by 18 per cent relative to 2015 levels; set an absolute limit for energy consumption of 5 billion tce; cut carbon intensity by 40–45 per cent relative to 2005 levels and have alternative energy sources meet 15 per cent of national energy consumption, with an installed capacity of 200 GW for wind power and 100 GW for photovoltaics.
Year 2030	Cap carbon emissions around 2030 and make best efforts to peak early; increase the share of non-fossil fuels to about 20 per cent and reduce carbon intensity by 60–65 per cent compared with 2005 levels.

Mitigation policies and measures

The burning of coal is responsible for the overwhelming majority of China's total emissions of dust, sulphur dioxide, nitrogen oxides and carbon dioxide, and has given rise to unprecedented environmental pollution and health risks across the country (Zhang 2007a, 2011b; CCCCPPRP 2014). Cutting carbon intensity to meet climate commitments by 2020 is closely linked to reining in energy consumption in general, and coal consumption in particular. The timing of China's coal-use peak is thus crucial to determining when its carbon emissions will peak, and to realising the goal of an ecological civilisation.

Capping coal consumption requires not only enhanced efforts in key energy-consuming sectors, but also unprecedented regional coordination, especially among more developed and severely polluted regions. The 'Atmospheric Pollution Prevention Action Plan' (State Council 2013) sets more stringent concentration targets for hazardous particles for more developed areas, with the Beijing–Tianjin–Hebei region, Yangtze River Delta and Pearl River Delta required to cut levels by 25 per cent, 20 per cent and 15 per cent by 2017 relative to 2012 levels, respectively. Coal consumption in these more advanced and severely air polluted regions should thus be reduced in absolute terms in the Thirteenth FYP period. The key challenge of China's Thirteenth FYP is therefore to undertake concerted measures that ensure the peaking of coal consumption during the period of the Plan. It is estimated that this would lead to carbon dioxide emissions peaking between 2025 and 2030, and coal's share in the total energy mix falling below 50 per cent in 2030 (Wang 2014; Zhang 2014c).

Under the Eleventh and Twelfth FYPs, China implemented a variety of energy-saving and pollution-reduction programs and initiatives, along with supporting economic and industrial policies and measures (Zhang 2015c). Flagship initiatives include but are not limited to the 'Top 1,000 Enterprises Energy Conservation Action Program', the '10,000 Enterprises Energy Conservation Low Carbon Action Program', mandatory closures of small power plants combined with construction of larger and more efficient units, and a low-carbon city development pilot program. In the meantime, the government is making great efforts to promote widespread use of renewable energy, set energy prices at appropriate levels and reform resource taxes while also harnessing market forces to genuinely transform China into a low-carbon economy.

The Top 1,000 Enterprises Energy Conservation Action Program

Industry accounts for about 70 per cent of China's total energy consumption. To achieve China's 2010 goal of reducing energy intensity by 20 per cent, the government put much effort into changing the pattern of industrial growth. China explored industrial policies that encourage technological progress, strengthen pollution controls and promote industrial upgrading and energy conservation. On energy saving, it established the Top 1,000 Enterprises Energy Conservation Action Program in April 2006, involving 1,008 enterprises in nine key energy-supplier and energy-consumer industrial subsectors. Each enterprise consumed at least 180,000 tonnes of standard coal equivalent (tce) in 2004 and together they accounted for 33 per cent of national and 47 per cent of industrial energy consumption. The program aimed to save 100 million tce cumulatively during the Eleventh FYP (2006–10) (NDRC 2006).

Although there are areas that still require improvement (Price et al. 2010), in November 2009, the National Development and Reform Commission (NDRC 2009b) reported that the program had realised energy savings of 106.2 million tce by the end of 2008, thus reaching its goal two years ahead of schedule. In September 2011, the National Development and Reform Commission (NDRC) estimated that the Top 1,000 program would achieve total energy savings of 150 million tce during the Eleventh FYP (NDRC 2011a).

The 10,000 Enterprises Energy Conservation Low Carbon Action Program

To help meet the energy saving and carbon intensity reduction goals of the Twelfth FYP (2011–15), in December 2011, the NDRC and 11 other Central Government organisations introduced the 10,000 Enterprises Energy Conservation Low Carbon Action Program—an expansion of the Top 1,000 program. The enlarged program involved 16,078 enterprises, including industrial and transportation operations that in 2010 consumed 10,000 tce or more and entities in other sectors that consumed at least 5,000 tce. Together, these enterprises consumed at least 60 per cent of the nation's energy that year. The program aimed to save a cumulative 250 million tce during the period 2011–15 (NDRC 2012).

In December 2013, the NDRC reported the 2012 performance results for the 10,000 Enterprises program. Of 14,542 enterprises examined, 3,760 (25.9 per cent) had exceeded their energy-saving targets; 7,327 (50.4 per cent) had comfortably fulfilled their energy-saving goals; 2,078 (14.3 per cent) had basically fulfilled their energy-saving goals; and 1,377 (9.5 per cent) had failed to meet their targets. The program achieved total energy savings of 170 million tce during 2011–12—equivalent to 69 per cent of the total energy-saving goal of the Twelfth FYP (NDRC 2013b).

Mandatory closure of small power plants while building larger, more efficient units

The NDRC established a series of incentives to shut small, inefficient power plants. Feed-in tariffs for small plants were lowered. Power companies were given the option to build new capacity to replace retired capacity. Plants designated for closure were given electricity generation quotas that could be used to continue operations for a limited time or sold to larger plants (Williams and Kahrl 2008; Schreifels et al. 2012; Zhang 2010a, 2011b, 2015c).

These incentive-based policies helped the government surpass its 2006–10 goal of closing small thermal power plants with total capacity up to 50 GW. By the end of 2008, the sum of small plant capacity closed had reached 34.2 GW, compared with just 8.3 GW decommissioned during the period 2001–05 (NDRC 2008). By the end of the first half of 2009, the total capacity of decommissioned smaller and older units had increased to 54 GW, exceeding the 50 GW target 18 months ahead of schedule. By the end of 2010, the total capacity of decommissioned smaller and older units had increased to 76.8 GW—more than the entire power capacity of the United Kingdom and almost 10 times the total capacity decommissioned during 2001–05 (Zhang 2015c).

Regarding the construction of larger, more efficient and cleaner units, by the end of 2012, 75.6 per cent of fossil fuel–fired units had capacities of 300 MW or more, compared with 42.7 per cent in 2000 (Zhu 2010; NDRC 2013a). The combined effect of shutting small, inefficient power plants and building larger, more efficient ones saw the average grams of standard coal consumed per kilowatt hour (gce/kWh) in electricity generated decline to 326 gce/kWh by 2012—a 12.8 per cent reduction compared with the 2005 level of 374 gce/kWh (CEC 2011; CEC and EDF 2012; Zhang 2015c).

As the Chinese economy enters the 'new normal', the policy of building more efficient coal-fired power plants is being supplanted by restrictions on all-new coal generation facilities. On 23 March 2016, the National Energy Administration ordered 13 provincial governments to stop issuing approvals for such plants until the end of 2017. It also directed 15 provinces to cease the construction process for new coal-fired power plants that had already been approved. This was a result mainly of changed market conditions for coal-fired power utilities, which face a greater threat of asset writedowns and prospective asset stranding due to displacement by renewable energy sources, falling utilisation rates and lower than expected demand for electricity (China Carbon Forum 2016).

Supportive economic policies

Economic policies have been designed to encourage technological progress and to strengthen pollution control so China can meet its goals for energy saving and environmental control. To support the 'Ten Energy-Saving Projects' plan, launched by the NDRC in July 2006 and aimed at helping to meet the 2010 energy-saving goal of cutting energy intensity, the Central Government in August 2007 began to offer financial incentives of RMB200 to enterprises in eastern areas and RMB250 to those in central and western China for every tonne of standard coal equivalent saved annually. Such payments were made to enterprises with energy metering and measuring systems that could document energy savings of at least 10,000 tce through energy-saving technical transformation projects (Ministry of Finance and NDRC 2007). In July 2011, these rewards were increased to RMB240 for enterprises in the east and RMB300 for others for every tonne of standard coal equivalent saved per year. Concurrently, the minimum threshold for total energy savings from energy-saving technological transformation projects was lowered to 5,000 tce from the previously required 10,000 tce (Ministry of Finance and NDRC 2011).

Since 1997, when the World Bank introduced the concept of energy management companies (EMCs) to China, the government has also pushed forward this mechanism to promote energy savings. The system awards EMCs RMB240 for every tonne of standard coal equivalent saved, with additional compensation of no less than RMB60 for every tonne of standard coal equivalent saved by local governments (State Council 2010). China had only three EMCs in 1998. By 2005, that number had increased to more than 80, and to more than 800 by 2010. As a result of these incentives and the increasing number of firms to which they apply, the total annual energy savings by EMCs increased to 13 million tce by 2010—up from 600,000 tce in 2005 (NDRC 2011b).

When China reformed its tax system in 1994, it introduced an excise tax (levied at the time of purchase) to provide an incentive for sales of energy-efficient cars. The tax rate, adjusted over time, increases with the size of a car's engine. Excise tax on a car with an engine of less than 1 L was set at 1 per cent of its value, whereas a 4 L engine would be taxed at 40 per cent of the car's value (Zhang 2011b). From the beginning of October 2015 to the end of 2016, the purchase tax on cars with an engine of 1.6 L or less was halved. Renewable energy-fuelled cars, such as electric, hybrid and fuel-cell cars, are exempt from purchase taxes until the end of 2017.

In January 1998, the Chinese Government mandated that new coal-fired units must come equipped with a flue-gas desulphurisation (FGD) facility and that plants built before 1998 had until 2010 to begin the process of retrofitting an FGD facility. Other policies to promote FGD-equipped power plants include imposition of an on-grid tariff incorporating desulphurisation costs, giving FGD-equipped plants priority in grid connection and allowing them to operate longer than plants without desulphurisation capacity. All the while, the capital cost of FGD has fallen significantly, making it cheaper to install such facilities (Zhang 2010a, 2011b, 2015c).

As a result of these policies, newly installed desulphurisation capacity in 2006 alone was greater than the combined total over the previous 10 years, and had reached 30 per cent of total installed thermal (mostly coal-fired) capacity. Coal-fired power units installed with FGD increased from 53 GW in 2005 to 630 GW by 2011. The same year, the proportion of coal-fired units with FGD rose to 90 per cent of total installed thermal capacity—up from just 13.5 per cent in 2005 (CEC and EDF 2012; Zhang 2015c). By the end of 2009, China had reduced its sulphur dioxide emissions by 13.1 per cent compared with its 2005 levels,[3] and had met its 2010 target of a 10 per cent cut one year ahead of schedule (Zhang 2010a, 2011b).

3 The reduction in sulphur dioxide emissions could be even larger than that achieved so far if the installed FGD facilities were running continuously and reliably. FGD costs are estimated to account for about 10 per cent of power generation costs, there is a lack of staff trained in operating and maintaining the FGD facilities and a lack of government enforcement, which means many power plants do not operate an FGD facility, even if one is installed. Ministry of Environmental Protection field inspections in early 2007 found that less than 40 per cent of the installed FGD facilities were running continuously and reliably (Xu et al. 2009; Zhang 2015c).

The use of renewable energy

The Chinese Government initially supported solar energy through 'Golden Sun' investment subsidies (Zhang 2011b). After years of simply taking advantage of overseas orders to drive down the cost of manufacturing solar panels, a solar power market was created, with the establishment of solar power feed-in tariffs in July 2011. By comparison, wind power had benefited from bidding-based tariffs since 2003 (Zhang 2010a, 2011b). In August 2009, however, this supportive policy for wind power was replaced with feed-in tariffs. Under the new policy, four areas were designated for wind energy development based on the quality of wind energy resources and conditions for engineering construction (NDRC 2009a). On-grid tariffs were set accordingly as benchmarks for wind power projects.

China is not only setting ambitious renewable energy goals, but is also making dramatic efforts to meet these goals. In terms of committing finance, as far back as 2009 China's renewable energy investments of US$39.1 billion exceeded the United States' US$22.5 billion—knocking it from the top spot for the first time in five years. China consolidated its lead in 2010, with US$54.4 billion in renewable energy investments. Germany moved into second place that year, with investments in renewables of US$41.2 billion, pushing the United States to third place, with US$34 billion.

China's investments as a share of GDP are more striking again. In 2010, renewable energy investments reached 0.55 per cent of GDP, meaning that China's relative domestic investment was more than double that of the United States, at 0.23 per cent. With an installed capacity of 103.4 GW, in 2010, China overtook the United States (total installed capacity of 58 GW) for the first time to lead in total renewable energy capacity (Pew Charitable Trusts 2011). China aims now to increase total installed wind power capacity to 200 GW by 2020 and to implement a green dispatch system to favour renewable power generation in the electricity grid. However, since it can take months for wind turbines to be connected to the power grid, China needs to substantially improve both its power grids, including through introduction of smart grids, and the planning and coordination of the development and construction of wind power. That is, as wind farms are built, new transmission lines should be constructed at the same time. Moreover, given the scaled-up wind power capacity planned for 2020, China should already be placing more emphasis on companies ensuring flow of power into the grid rather than just on meeting capacity generation goals (Zhang 2010a, 2011b, 2014b).

Low-carbon city development pilot program

In China, cities are responsible for more than 60 per cent of total energy consumption. Their contribution to energy usage and resulting carbon dioxide emissions is expected to increase given the target urbanisation rate of 65 per cent by 2030. Cities will therefore play an increasingly greater role in shaping energy demand and carbon dioxide emissions. They are crucial to China meeting its 2020 carbon intensity reduction target of 40–45 per cent relative to 2005 levels and the target of peak carbon emissions around 2030.

China began experimenting with low-carbon city development in five provinces and eight cities on 19 July 2010. The experiment was expanded to a second batch of 29 provinces and cities on 5 December 2012. All of these pilot cities and provinces are making efforts towards: 1) strengthening industrial restructuring and technological upgrading; 2) improving the energy mix and energy efficiency; 3) prioritising the use of public transport; 4) promoting efficient public transport systems; and 5) optimising the urban landscape (Wang et al. 2013). In the process, these cities have, however, confronted a variety of problems and challenges (Wang et al. 2013), including but not limited to the absence of sound carbon accounting systems, lack of low-carbon specific evaluation systems, insufficient government–enterprise interactions and excessive budget dependence on land concessions. While these are areas that need improvement, there are encouraging signs that the low-carbon pilot program is moving in the right direction.

An NDRC evaluation revealed that in 2012, 10 provinces of the two batches of pilots had successfully reduced their carbon intensity by 9.2 per cent compared with their 2010 level and compared with the national average of 6.6 per cent (NDRC 2014a). In addition, all pilot provinces and cities have set 2030 or earlier as the target for the carbon dioxide emissions peak even though this was not mandated by the Central Government at the time the pilot programs were launched. Shanghai and Suzhou are among the 15 pilot provinces and cities that have set 2020 as the year for their peak in carbon dioxide emissions. Ningbo, a key industrial port city in Zhejiang province, set its peak emission target as 2015.

The practices and ambitions of the pilot regions have set good examples for keeping emissions under control and making positive contributions to overall low-carbon development in China. Zhang (2011b, 2011c) has argued that China's GHG emissions could peak between 2025 and 2032 or around 2030. The efforts of China's low-carbon pilot cities may contribute to the country reaching peak carbon emissions sooner than planned.

Getting the energy prices right

To have the market play a decisive role in allocating resources requires getting energy prices right, so both producers and consumers of energy receive clear signals. The overall trend in China's energy pricing reform since 1984 has been to move away from prices set exclusively by the Central Government and towards a more market-oriented pricing mechanism. The pace and scale of the related reforms differ across energy products (Zhang 2014c).

Reform of electricity tariffs has lagged particularly far behind. The government retains control over electricity tariffs, which has complicated the implementation of a pilot carbon-trading scheme in the power sector. Introduction of emissions trading, however, will offer impetus to power pricing reforms to allow the pass-through of carbon costs in the electricity sector. For this reason, power pricing should be a key area for reform in the Thirteenth FYP.

Natural gas prices are an additional area in pressing need of reform. Given China's coal-dominated energy mix, increasing the share of cleaner fuels, such as natural gas, has been considered the key option for achieving the twin goals of meeting energy needs and improving environmental quality. In this way, in December 2011, the government adopted a new pricing mechanism in Guangdong province and in the Guangxi Zhuang Autonomous Region (NDRC 2011c). Under the new mechanism, pricing benchmarks were selected and pegged to prices of alternative fuels generated by market forces to establish a price linkage between natural gas and alternative fuels. Gas prices at various stages would then be adjusted accordingly. The pilot schemes in Guangdong and Guangxi point to a move in the direction of establishing a market-oriented natural gas pricing mechanism. Under the Thirteenth FYP, China should heed the lessons learned from the two pilot schemes and identify the kinds of adjustments and improvements that are needed in terms of the choice of alternative fuels and selection of a pricing reference point to implement the Guangdong and Guangxi pilot reform programs successfully across the entire country (Gao et al. 2013; Zhang 2014c).

Resources tax reform

Even were energy price reform to be comprehensively undertaken, energy prices still would not fully reflect the cost of production in terms of the entire value chain of resource extraction, production, use and disposal. Combined with a pressing need to avoid the wasteful extraction and use of resources, getting energy prices right requires that China reform its current narrow coverage and level of resource taxation (Zhang 2014c, 2015c). At present, resource tax is levied on crude oil and natural gas according to revenue (ad valorem) rather than volume—a practice that began in Xinjiang on 1 June 2010 and was applied nationwide from 1 November 2011. This is a first step in the right direction. Beginning on 1 December 2014, China broadened these reforms to include coal by levying a tax on coal based on revenue. The Task Force on Green Transition in China of the China Council for International Cooperation on Environment and Development (CCICED 2014) recommends that a higher resource tax be imposed on fossil fuels, with tax rates raised to at least 10 per cent, but preferably 15 per cent, for domestic and imported coal and to 10–15 per cent for domestic and imported oil by 2025. This will also help to increase local governments' revenue, as well as providing them with an incentive not to focus on economic growth alone (Zhang 2010a, 2011b).

Environmental taxes

The introduction of environmental taxes to replace current charges for sulphur dioxide emissions and chemical oxygen demand has been discussed in academic and policy circles in China for some time. A draft tax law on environmental protection was released for public comment in June 2015 (Legislative Affairs Office of the State Council 2015), but the timing of its revision and eventual passage into law is unknown. Accordingly, the date for implementation has not been set. Clearly, however, the sooner environmental taxes are imposed in the Thirteenth FYP, the better. This is expected to be no later than 2020. Other countries' experiences with environmental taxes suggest that these are best initially levied at low rates and in limited scope, with their levels then increasing over time (Andersen and Ekins 2009; Zhang 2011b; Zhang and Baranzini 2004). Moreover, environmental taxes should be shared taxes, with the majority of the revenue going to local governments (Tian and Xu 2012; Zhang 2016). Given that China has not yet levied environmental taxes, in terms of timing it may be better to introduce them as part of the Thirteenth FYP—not least because such a distinction will enable the country's additional efforts towards carbon abatement to be disentangled from the broader energy-saving and pollution-cutting programs.

Pilot carbon-trading schemes

In October 2011, the NDRC approved seven pilot carbon-trading schemes: in the national capital, Beijing, the business hub of Shanghai, the sprawling industrial municipalities of Tianjin and Chongqing, the manufacturing centres of Guangdong and Hubei provinces and Shenzhen.[4] These pilot regions were

4 See Zhang (2015a, 2015b) for detailed discussion of the features and compliance rates of pilots and their transition to a nationwide scheme.

deliberately selected for their varying stages of development and capacity to design tailored schemes. These pilot schemes have features in common, but vary considerably in their approach to issues such as sectoral coverage, allocation of allowances, price uncertainty and market stabilisation, the potential market power of dominant players, use of offsets and enforcement and compliance (Zhang 2015a, 2015b).

Beijing, Guangdong, Shanghai, Shenzhen and Tianjin launched their first trading schemes before the end of 2013. The remaining two schemes, Hubei and Chongqing, began trading on 2 April and 19 June 2014, respectively, marking the start of the pilot scheme as a whole. As shown in Table 17.2, the compliance rate in the 2014 cycle improves markedly. For example, in Beijing, 257 entities had not complied by the deadline set for the 2013 cycle, but only 14 entities had failed to do so for the 2014 cycle. Overall, for the 2014 cycle, four pilot schemes had a 100 per cent compliance rate and two had an almost 100 per cent compliance rate. In 2013, in contrast, only Shanghai had realised full compliance. Chongqing, however, had an approximately 70 per cent compliance rate one month after the deadline. The path forward from pilots to a national scheme is expected to be a bumpy but ultimately successful one.

Table 17.2 Compliance rates of seven carbon-trading pilot schemes for the 2014 compliance cycle (per cent)

	Measured against entities[a]	Measured against allowances[b]
Beijing	100 (97.1)	100
Chongqing	..	..
Guangdong	100 (98.9)	100 (99.97)
Hubei	100.0	100.0
Shanghai	100 (100)	100 (100)
Shenzhen	99.69 (99.4)	100 (99.7)
Tianjin	99.1 (96.5)	..

.. not available

[a] Share of the total number of entities that meet their compliance obligations in the total entities covered in a given carbon trading pilot.

[b] The total combined allowances of entities that meet their compliance obligations as a percentage of the total allowances allocated in a given carbon trading pilot.

Note: Numbers in parentheses are for the 2013 compliance cycle.

In the joint China–United States climate change statement, China announced that it would launch a national emissions trading scheme (ETS) by 2017. Initially, the national ETS will cover eight sectors: petrochemicals, power generation, metallurgy, nonferrous metals, building materials, chemicals, papermaking and aviation. The threshold for an entity to be part of the national scheme has been set at 10,000 tce annually. It is expected that initially the national ETS will cover about 10,000 entities, with an estimated market size of 2–3 billion tonnes of carbon dioxide equivalent emissions. Following a three-year pilot phase, a nationwide carbon market will become fully functional after 2019 (DCCNDRC 2015; Zhang 2015a, 2015b; NDRC 2016).

It appears the management of the national ETS is being instituted at two levels. First, the Central Government will be in charge of setting national rules for, among other things, the coverage and scope of the ETS, uniform standards for measurement, reporting and verification (MRV), the allocation of allowances and the rules for compliance across provinces or equivalent. Second, provincial governments will be assigned responsibility for implementation and enforcement of the rules. This includes, but is not limited to, identifying the entities covered and determining their emissions, calculating the amount of free allowances to the entities covered and, once approved by the Central Government, distributing these allowances to the entities and implementing compliance rules. Provincial governments, however, are also to be allowed to set rules that are stricter than the national rules. For example, they could increase the coverage of sectors and the scope of entities and have even stricter allocation rules for allowances (NDRC 2014b).

There will be a number of challenges, of which two are highlighted below. First, to create reliable allowances that are comparable across sectors and regions, it will be important to ensure that all emissions data are properly measured, reported and verified. For that, national ETS legislation needs to be established to provide uniform guidelines for and methodologies on the design and operation of the ETS and enforcement of MRV, including penalties for noncompliance. Such legislation would also define allowances as financial assets and environmentally credible reductions.

The second and most thorny issue is the allocation of allowances in the national ETS because this involves dealing with unused allowances from the seven pilot markets. It is estimated that, by the time of the national launch, the seven pilot markets will have accumulated 50–100 million tonnes of surplus allowances (Carbon Pulse 2015). Ruling out banking of these allowances into the national scheme would likely cause regional carbon prices to crash towards zero, but allowing all or some of the units to be carried forward, while maintaining their value, would risk burdening the national market with a sizeable oversupply on its launch. But there are other options. One is to consider a conversion mechanism that would allow pilot allowances to be eligible in the national market, but at a discounted value. A conversion rate would depend on the degree of overallocation and the price levels in the market from which they originated, giving surplus allowances from highly overallocated pilot areas a higher discount rate than those from markets with much smaller surpluses.

Another option is to allow pilot permits to be used, but only for a portion of the allowances carried forward each year and for a limited period. The option announced by Shanghai's government on 9 May 2016 is very much along this line (SMDRC 2016). A third option is to link the level of allowances with bankable surplus allowances from each pilot region. This will allow allowances from the pilot carbon markets to be banked in the national ETS, but at the expense of reduced allocation levels in that region. Which option prevails will depend on the outcome of intense negotiations between the Central Government, regional governments and industry over how to treat up to 100 million tonnes of unused allowances from the seven pilot markets in the national ETS. This could have a huge bearing on the success of the world's biggest carbon market.

Conclusion

The need to improve the quality of the environment has been elevated to unprecedented importance internationally. In China's case, this is demonstrated by the fact that in 2013 nearly every Chinese city monitored for pollution failed to meet state standards. In March 2014, Chinese Premier Li Keqiang told 3,000 delegates in China's national legislature that the country would 'declare war against pollution as we declared war against poverty' (State Council 2014). If China's internationally recognised accomplishments in reducing poverty can be considered any kind of predictor, there is some credibility to prospects of winning the fight against pollution.

In line with public acknowledgement at the highest levels of China's government that the country faces an environmental crisis, attempts are being made to cut coal consumption in absolute terms in severely polluted regions, and to take unprecedented steps to keep energy consumption and carbon emissions under control in key energy-consuming industries and cities in the context of government decentralisation and unprecedented urbanisation. Steps are also being taken to strengthen and expand flagship programs and initiatives, alongside parallel supportive economic policies, and to increase the widespread use of renewable energy. Moreover, given that many environmental issues have a cross-border nature, neighbouring regions—such as the Beijing–Tianjin–Hebei region and the Yangtze and Pearl river deltas—are now increasingly acting collectively rather than independently. These coordinated efforts should significantly increase their effectiveness in combating pollution.

Governments at all levels are now taking broad approaches to tackling environmental issues. While having relied mostly on administrative measures to date, China now realises that while these can be effective, they are often not efficient. In turn, China's government is increasingly harnessing market forces to foster reduced energy consumption and to cut the emissions of carbon dioxide and other conventional pollutants—and to genuinely induce the shift to a low-carbon, green economy. Market-based instruments include but are not limited to moving away from central government energy pricing and towards a more market-oriented pricing mechanism; reforming the current narrow coverage of resource taxation; shifting the resource tax to being levied ad valorem rather than by volume; experimenting with seven pilot carbon-trading schemes and undertaking preparation for the transition to a nationwide scheme; and implementing a system for chargeable use of resources and ecological compensation.

Meeting the domestic emissions intensity reduction goals for 2020 and the absolute commitments for 2030 will require significant economic restructuring and technological upgrading. Carbon emissions reduction provides a variety of ancillary benefits, such as reductions in conventional air pollutants and associated health risks. This creates new impetus for structural economic reforms to maximise synergies between climate change mitigation efforts and structural economic reforms. These synergies could be further enhanced by capping nationwide coal consumption to realise peak consumption in the Thirteenth FYP period and a peak in carbon dioxide emissions during 2025–30.

To that end, China needs to put in place new policies and measures while strengthening and expanding existing flagship programs and initiatives. It needs supportive economic policies that can genuinely induce the creation of a low-carbon economy across the entire country. China's current pilot carbon trading schemes have made encouraging progress. A well-designed, well-implemented and well-operated national carbon scheme is expected to play a crucial role in helping China meet its carbon-control targets.

References

Andersen, M. S. and Ekins, P. (eds) (2009), *Carbon-energy taxation: Lessons from Europe*, New York: Oxford University Press.

Carbon Pulse (2015), Scrap over unused allowances could prove vital for China's carbon market, *Carbon Pulse*, 10 November. Available from: carbon-pulse.com/11675/.

Carraro, C. and Tavoni, M. (2010), Looking ahead from Copenhagen: How challenging is the Chinese carbon intensity target?, *VOX*, 5 January. Available from: voxeu.org/index.php?q=node/4449.

China Carbon Forum (2016), *Insights: China's coal power stranded assets challenge*, April, Beijing: China Carbon Forum.

China Coal Consumption Cap Plan and Policy Research Project (CCCCPPRP) (2014), *Contributions of coal use to air pollution in China*, October, Beijing: Natural Resources Defense Council China Program. Available from: nrdc.cn/coalcap/console/Public/Uploads/2014/12/30/AirPollutionContribution.pdf.

China Council for International Cooperation on Environment and Development (CCICED) (2014), *Evaluation and prospects for a green transition process in China*, CCICED Task Force Report, December, Beijing. Available from: cciced.net/encciced/policyresearch/report/201504/P020150413497198320874.pdf.

China Electricity Council (CEC) (2011), *Annual development report of China's power industry, 2011*, Beijing: China Electricity Council.

China Electricity Council (CEC) and Environmental Defense Fund (EDF) (2012), *Studies on pollution cutting in China's power industry*, Beijing: China Electricity Council.

China Securities Journal (2015), 13th FYP sketches out reform roadmap, top-level design becoming clear, *China Securities Journal*, 14 August. Available from: news.xinhuanet.com/finance/2015-08/14/c_128127689.htm.

Department of Climate Change of National Development and Reform Commission (DCCNDRC) (2015), On the basic conditions and work plan to promote the establishment of a nationwide carbon emissions trading market, *China Economic & Trade Herald*, (1): 15–16.

Energy Information Administration (EIA) (2004), *International energy outlook, 2004*, Washington, DC: US Energy Information Administration.

Gao, M., Wang, Z., Wu, Q. and Yang, Y. (2013), Natural gas pricing mechanism reform and its impacts on future energy options in China, *Energy and Environment*, 24(7–8): 1209–1228.

Graham-Harrison, E. (2009), Snap analysis: China happy with climate deal, image dented, *Reuters*, 18 December. Available from: reuters.com/article/idUSTRE5BI0DH20091219.

International Energy Agency (IEA) (2007), *World energy outlook 2007*, Paris: International Energy Agency.

Legislative Affairs Office of the State Council of China (2015), *A circular on call for public comments on 'Environmental Protection Law of the People's Republic of China (draft)'*, 10 June, Beijing: State Council of China.

Levi, M. (2009), *Assessing China's carbon-cutting proposal*, 30 November, New York: Council on Foreign Relations.

Miliband, E. (2009), The road from Copenhagen, *The Guardian*, 20 December. Available from: guardian.co.uk/commentisfree/2009/dec/20/copenhagen-climate-change-accord.

Ministry of Finance and National Development and Reform Commission (NDRC) (2007), *A circular on interim measures for fund management of financial incentives for energy-saving technical transformation*, 10 August, Beijing: NDRC.

Ministry of Finance and National Development and Reform Commission (NDRC) (2011), *A circular on measures for fund management of financial incentives for energy-saving technical transformation*, 21 June, Beijing: NDRC.

National Bureau of Statistics (NBS) (2015), *Statistical communiqué on the 2014 national economic and social development of China*, 26 February, Beijing: China Statistics Press.

National Development and Reform Commission (NDRC) (2006), *The top 1,000 enterprises energy conservation action program*, NDRC Environment and Resources No. [2006]571, 7 April, Beijing: NDRC.

National Development and Reform Commission (NDRC) (2008), *China had decommissioned fossil fuel-fired small plants with a total capacity of 25.87 GW since 1 January 2006*, 14 July, Beijing: NDRC.

National Development and Reform Commission (NDRC) (2009a), *A circular on improving on grid feed-in tariffs for wind power*, 22 July, Beijing: NDRC.

National Development and Reform Commission (NDRC) (2009b), *Performance of the thousand enterprises in 2008*, NDRC Proclamation No. [2009]18, 16 November, Beijing: NDRC.

National Development and Reform Commission (NDRC) (2011a), *The thousand enterprises exceeded the energy-saving target during the 11th five-year plan period*, 14 March, Beijing: NDRC.

National Development and Reform Commission (NDRC) (2011b), *Rapid development of energy service industry: Energy saving and pollution cutting during the 11th five-year period in retrospect*, 8 October, Beijing: NDRC.

National Development and Reform Commission (NDRC) (2011c), *A circular on pilot reform on natural gas pricing mechanism in Guangdong Province and Guangxi Zhuang Autonomous Region*, NDRC Price No. [2011]3033, 26 December, Beijing: NDRC.

National Development and Reform Commission (NDRC) (2012), *List and energy-saving targets of the ten thousand enterprises committed to energy-saving and low-carbon activities*, NDRC Proclamation No. [2012]10, 12 May, Beijing: NDRC.

National Development and Reform Commission (NDRC) (2013a), *China's policies and actions for addressing climate change*, November, Beijing: NDRC.

National Development and Reform Commission (NDRC) (2013b), *Energy conservation performance of the 10,000 enterprises*, Circular No. [2013]44, 25 December, Beijing: NDRC.

National Development and Reform Commission (NDRC) (2014a), *Promoting low-carbon development pilot to press forward a change in the model of economic development*, 14 February, Beijing: NDRC.

National Development and Reform Commission (NDRC) (2014b), *The interim administrative measures for emissions trading*, 10 December, Beijing: NDRC.

National Development and Reform Commission (NDRC) (2015), *Enhanced actions on climate change: China's intended nationally determined contributions*, 30 June, Beijing: NDRC. Available from: www4.unfccc.int/submissions/INDC/Published%20Documents/China/1/China's%20INDC%20-%20on%2030%20June%202015.pdf.

National Development and Reform Commission (NDRC) (2016), *A circular on key tasks to launch a national carbon emission trading market*, 11 January, Beijing: NDRC. Available from: sdpc.gov.cn/gzdt/201601/t20160122_772150.html.

Pew Charitable Trusts (2011), *Who's winning the clean energy race? 2010 edition: G-20 investment powering forward*, March, Philadelphia: Pew Charitable Trusts. Available from: pewenvironment.org/uploadedFiles/PEG/Publications/Report/G-20Report-LOWRes-FINAL.pdf.

Price, L., Wang, X. and Yun, J. (2010), The challenge of reducing energy consumption of the top-1000 largest industrial enterprises in China, *Energy Policy*, 38: 6485–6498.

Qiu, J. (2009), China's climate target: Is it achievable?, Nature, 462: 550–551.

Schreifels, J., Fu, Y. and Wilson, E. J. (2012), Sulfur dioxide control in China: Policy evolution during the 10th and 11th five-year plans and lessons for the future, *Energy Policy*, 48: 779–789.

Shanghai Municipal Development and Reform Commission (SMDRC) (2016), *A circular on issues related to carrying forward surplus allowances in Shanghai carbon trading pilot phase*, 9 May, Shanghai: SMDRC. Available from: shdrc.gov.cn/xxgk/cxxxgk/23507.htm.

State Council of China (2006), The outline of the eleventh five-year plan for national economic and social development of the People's Republic of China, *China Network*, 16 March.

State Council of China (2010), *A circular of the National Development and Reform Commission and other departments to speed up the implementation of energy management contracts to promote the energy service industry*, 2 April, Beijing: State Council of China.

State Council of China (2013), *Atmospheric pollution prevention action plan*, September, Beijing: State Council of China.

State Council of China (2014), Report on the work of the government delivered at the Second Session of the Twelfth National People's Congress on 5 March, Beijing: State Council of China.

State Council of China (2016), *The outline of the 13th five-year plan of national economic and social development of the People's Republic of China*, March, Beijing: State Council of China. Available from: 219.233.30.70/cache8/97/62/78/64/5f/52/0b/7b/79/35/b9/41/c5/51/77/50/P020160318576353824805.pdf.

The Economist (2009), Climate change after Copenhagen: China's thing about numbers, *The Economist*, 2 January: 43–44.

Tian, S. and Xu, W. (2012), On the distribution of environmental tax revenue in China, *Public Finance Research*, (12): 18–21.

Wang, C., Lin, J., Cai, W. and Zhang, Z. X. (2013), Policies and practices of low carbon city development in China, *Energy and Environment*, 24(7–8): 1347–1372.

Wang, E. (2012), NDRC determined the second batch of 29 pilot low-carbon provinces and cities, *21st Century Business Herald*, 3 December.

Wang, L. (2014), China's coal consumption peaks at 4100 mt in 2020, *Economic Information Daily*, 5 March. Available from: finance.chinanews.com/ny/2014/03-05/5910245.shtml.

Watts, J. (2009), China 'will honour commitments' regardless of Copenhagen outcome, *The Guardian*, 18 December. Available from: guardian.co.uk/environment/2009/dec/18/china-wen-jiabao-copenhagen.

White House (2014), *US–China joint announcement on climate change*, 11 November, Washington, DC: US Government.

Williams, J. H. and Kahrl, F. (2008), Electricity reform and sustainable development in China, *Environmental Research Letters*, 3(4): 1–14.

Xu. Y., Williams, R.H. and Socolow, R.H. (2009), China's rapid deployment of SO_2 scrubbers, *Energy & Environmental Science*, 2(5): 459–465.

Zhang, Z. X. (2000a), Can China afford to commit itself to an emissions cap? An economic and political analysis, *Energy Economics*, 22(6): 587–614.

Zhang, Z. X. (2000b), Decoupling China's carbon emissions increases from economic growth: An economic analysis and policy implications, *World Development*, 28(4): 739–752.

Zhang, Z. X. (2003), Why did the energy intensity fall in China's industrial sector in the 1990s? The relative importance of structural change and intensity change, *Energy Economics*, 25(6): 625–638.

Zhang, Z. X. (2007a), China is moving away from the pattern of 'develop first and then treat the pollution', *Energy Policy*, 35: 3547–3549.

Zhang, Z. X. (2007b), China, the United States and technology cooperation on climate control, *Environmental Science and Policy*, 10(7–8): 622–628.

Zhang, Z. X. (2009), *Climate commitments to 2050: A roadmap for China*, East–West Dialogue No. 4, Honolulu: East–West Center. Available from: eastwestcenter.org/fileadmin/stored/pdfs/dialogue004.pdf.

Zhang, Z. X. (2010a), China in the transition to a low-carbon economy, *Energy Policy*, 38: 6638–6653.

Zhang, Z. X. (2010b), Copenhagen and beyond: Reflections on China's stance and responses, in X. Labandeira and E. Cerdá (eds), *Climate change policies: Global challenges and future prospects*, Cheltenham, UK: Edward Elgar.

Zhang, Z. X. (2011a), Assessing China's carbon intensity pledge for 2020: Stringency and credibility issues and their implications, *Environmental Economics and Policy Studies*, 13(3): 219–235.

Zhang, Z. X. (2011b), *Energy and environmental policy in China: Towards a low-carbon economy*, New Horizons in Environmental Economics Series, Cheltenham, UK: Edward Elgar.

Zhang, Z. X. (2011c), In what format and under what timeframe would China take on climate commitments? A roadmap to 2050, *International Environmental Agreements: Politics, Law and Economics*, 11(3): 245–259.

Zhang, Z. X. (2012a), Effective environmental protection in the context of government decentralization, *International Economics and Economic Policy*, 9(1): 53–82.

Zhang, Z. X. (2012b), Who should bear the cost of China's carbon emissions embodied in goods for exports?, *Mineral Economics*, 24(2–3): 103–117.

Zhang, Z. X. (2014a), China needs an international agreement on climate change, *China Reform*, (4): 101–102.

Zhang, Z. X. (2014b), China's energy and environmental issues and policy, in G. C. Chow and D. H. Perkins (eds), Routledge *h*andbook of the Chinese *e*conomy, London and New York: Routledge.

Zhang, Z. X. (2014c), Energy prices, subsidies and resource tax reform in China, *Asia and the Pacific Policy Studies*, 1(3): 439–454.

Zhang, Z. X. (2015a), Carbon emissions trading in China: The evolution from pilots to a nationwide scheme, *Climate Policy*, 15(S1): S104–S126.

Zhang, Z. X. (2015b), Crossing the river by feeling the stones: The case of carbon trading in China, *Environmental Economics and Policy Studies*, 17(2): 263–297.

Zhang, Z. X. (2015c), Programs, prices and policies towards energy conservation and environmental quality in China, in S. Managi (ed.), *Handbook of environmental economics in Asia*, London and New York: Routledge.

Zhang, Z. X. (2016), Policy plus market: 'Two hands' jointly paint green China, *China Economic Report*, (2): 44–46.

Zhang, Z. X. and Baranzini, A. (2004), What do we know about carbon taxes? An inquiry into their impacts on competitiveness and distribution of income, *Energy Policy*, 32(4): 507–518.

Zhu, X. R. (2010), China Electricity Council released data on fossil fuel-fired power plants in 2009, *China Energy News*, 19 July. Available from: paper.people.com.cn/zgnyb/html/2010-07/19/content_572802.htm.

18. Managing Economic Change and Mitigating Climate Change: China's strategies, policies and trends

Fergus Green and Nicholas Stern[1]

Introduction

The year 2015 marked a turning point in China's role in both contributing to and responding to global climate change. As we illustrate in this chapter, China's coal consumption fell significantly in 2015; history will likely show that it peaked in 2013–14. That downturn in coal consumption is a consequence of profound change in Chinese economic activity and also in government strategy and policy across a wide range of issues that extend far beyond a narrow understanding of 'climate policy'. The purpose of this chapter is to explain these changes and to trace their implications for climate change mitigation in China, especially over the next decade.

To do so, we analyse both demand-side and supply-side factors affecting greenhouse gas (GHG) emissions. While the business and economic communities have made much of the changes and challenges relating to China's economic activity in the period since 2014, most of those in the climate policy world have focused primarily on policies and investments affecting the energy supply mix, attending much less to the effects of wider economic changes on China's demand for energy. Yet the relationships between overall economic activity, industrial composition, the government's economic strategy and policies and energy demand form a key part of the story of China's turnaround on climate change. The first part of the chapter is therefore dedicated to a discussion of the demand side. As well as explaining the underlying factors and mechanisms at play, we draw on recent data and policy announcements to forecast the direction of key, climate-relevant demand-side trends over the next decade and consider some of the risks and opportunities that could arise over this period.

The second part of the chapter turns to the supply side—again focusing on energy and industry. In this section, we discuss China's targets, policies and investments with regard to both energy supply and GHG emissions per se.

1 The authors are grateful to Patrick Curran for his guidance and support in preparing this article, and to Lauren Johnston for constructive comments on the penultimate draft.

We also consider recent developments in the electricity and heavy industry sectors and draw on these to forecast key trends, risks and opportunities over the coming decade. This section of the chapter brings us more squarely into the domain of 'climate policy' as traditionally conceived, though we stress that, even here, China's actions must be understood as products of disparate (yet convergent) motivations, of which mitigating climate change is only one.

The chapter concludes with a brief discussion of some implications of our analysis for China and for global efforts to mitigate climate change.

The demand side: Patterns in growth and energy consumption

Previous editions of this book series have drawn attention to the change in China's growth model that has begun to occur in recent years. The previous growth model was characterised by rapid, 'catch-up' growth in gross domestic product (GDP) frequently registering double-digit rates, very high savings and investment rates, exceptionally low proportions of expenditure on domestic consumption, high profit shares of income and a strong export orientation (Garnaut et al. 2013, 2014). In the period 2000–13, China also made huge investments in heavy manufacturing industries such as steel and cement production—which consume large amounts of electricity and direct fossil fuel inputs—and in the expansion of coal-fired power generation to supply electricity to those industries (CCICED 2014; Guan et al. 2014). A further wave of investment in infrastructure, building construction and heavy industry was stimulated by the government's response to the drop in Chinese exports caused by the Global Financial Crisis of 2007–08.

This model of growth brought with it benefits such as job creation and poverty reduction; however, there is now widespread recognition within China that this model is neither sustainable nor desirable due to a combination of its economic, financial, social, local environmental and global climate impacts, which have been much discussed elsewhere (see, for example, Green and Stern 2016: 3–4).

The economic and financial legacies of the old model include widespread excess capacity in the construction and heavy industry sectors, diminishing returns on capital investment, weak productivity growth and mounting debt-related problems (CCICED 2014; IMF 2015; Pettis 2013). These problems have become acute at a time when China has also faced a difficult external economic environment. Further, it is approaching a Lewis turning point (Lewis 1954) in relation to the allocation of labour in the process of growth as the working-age population begins to decline and the large pools of 'surplus' labour migrating from the countryside to urban areas begin to dry up, putting upward pressure on wages and signalling the beginning of the end of the low-wage export-oriented manufacturing dimension of China's growth model (Das and N'Diaye 2013; Garnaut and Song 2006; Huang and Cai 2014). In short, the main drivers of the old model—capital investment focused on construction, infrastructure and heavy industry, along with cheap labour and low value-added exports—are slowing or, in some sectors, going into reverse.

These changes in economic activity have been met with the articulation and, increasingly, implementation of a new economic strategy by China's current generation of leaders (CCCP 2013; State Council 2013; Zhang 2014; and see Kuijs 2015). Together, the changes in activity and strategy add up to a new model of growth (Garnaut et al. 2013; cf. Hu 2015). This 'new normal' is understood in Chinese policymaking circles as involving a shift towards economic growth of a higher quality but lower rate, with a particular emphasis on four sub-themes: *services*, *innovation*, *reduced inequality* and *environmental sustainability* (see Green and Stern 2016: 4–5). These themes feature strongly in China's Thirteenth Five-Year Plan (FYP), released in March 2016.

The nature, scale and pace of change in China's economy, and their implications for energy demand, can be gleaned from an analysis of recent Chinese economic data and associated dynamics from the period 2014–15, especially when these are compared with the period of growth from 2000 to 2013, in which there was a strong focus on heavy industry.

Demand-side change: GDP, energy intensity and energy consumption

The extent of change on the demand side over the past two to three years is illustrated by Figures 18.1–18.3, showing, respectively, growth rates in China's: 1) GDP; 2) energy intensity of GDP (which exhibits negative growth); and 3) total primary energy consumption (PEC) (which is the product of GDP and energy intensity).

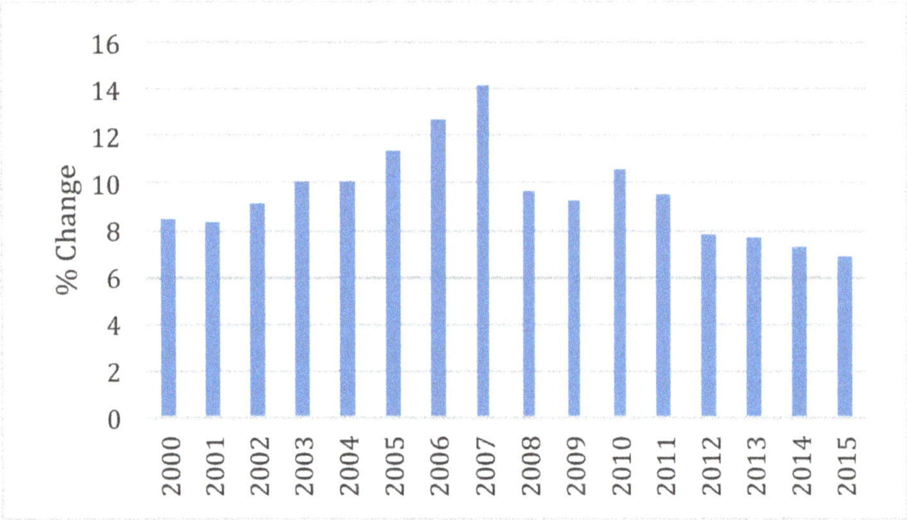

Figure 18.1 Chinese GDP growth rates, 2000–15

Sources: World Bank (2016); NBS (2016).

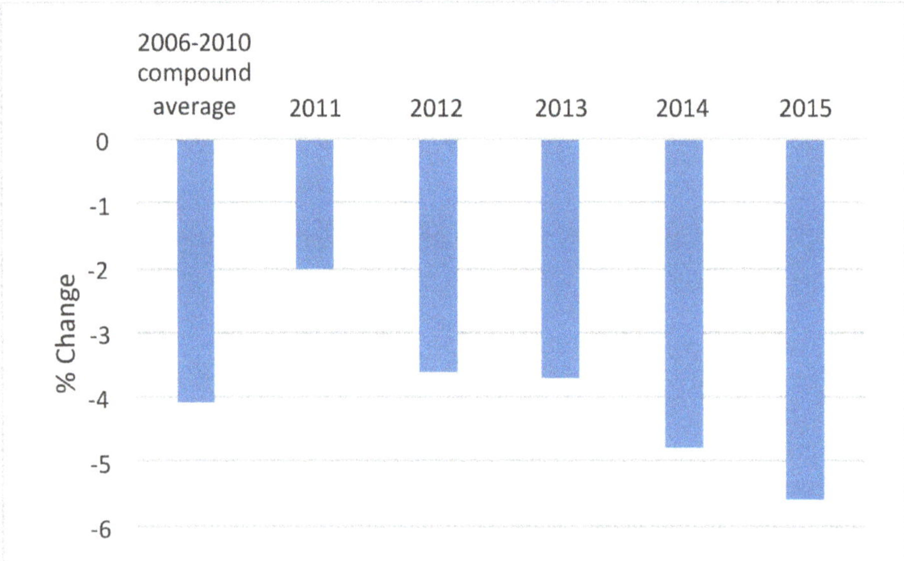

Figure 18.2 Growth rates in Chinese energy intensity of GDP, 2006–15

Sources: Data for 2011–15 from NBS (2016); 2006–10 compound average computed from aggregate 19.1 per cent reduction reported for the period of the Eleventh FYP (see, for example, Lewis 2011).

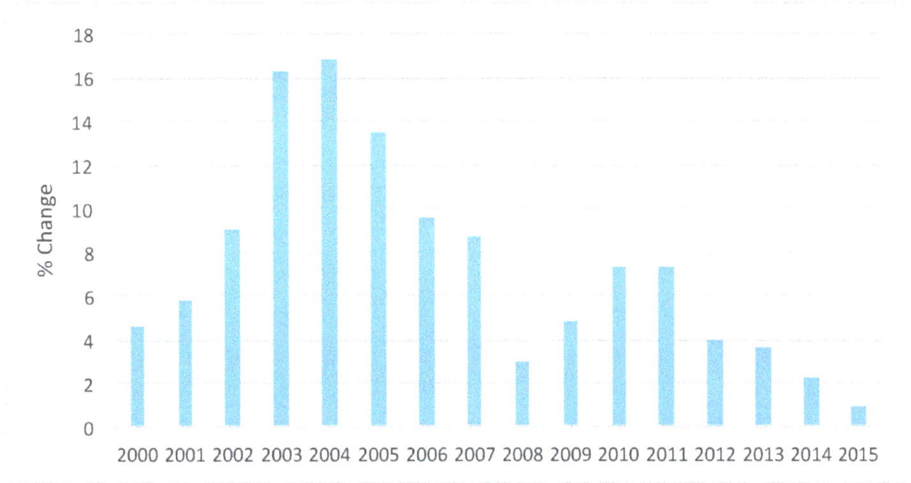

Figure 18.3 Chinese PEC growth rates, 2000–15

Sources: NBS (2015a, 2016).

The data in Figure 18.1 show GDP growth falling from an average of 10.5 per cent per annum over the period 2000–10 to below 7 per cent in 2015 (6.9 per cent, according to official statistics; NBS 2016).[2] This falling growth rate is explained by the combination of (predominantly structural) factors discussed above, albeit partly offset by faster growth in domestic consumption and tertiary production, which are at the heart of the 'new normal' model (IMF 2015; NBS 2016).

This change in economic structure also helps to explain why the annual decline in the energy intensity of GDP has actually accelerated over the past two years at the same time as GDP growth has slowed (Figure 18.2). Central to understanding this dynamic is the relationship between industry and GDP, given that industry is a very large consumer of energy within China's economy. Under the old growth model, industry[3] expanded rapidly, ultimately accounting for 44 per cent of GDP in 2013—an exceptionally high level compared with countries at similar levels of development (Grubb et al. 2015; Xu et al. 2014). As the share of industry in an economy declines relative to the household, commercial and transport sectors, the energy requirement of economic activity tends to fall (Grubb et al. 2015; Schafer 2005). This appears to be what is now happening in China, and this in turn is putting downward pressure on the energy intensity of GDP (Green and

2 Many forecasters using alternative methods think China's growth in 2015 was significantly lower. See, for example, the average of forecasts by experts using alternative methods produced by Consensus Economics (cited in Wolf 2015).

3 Industry here includes 'basic industrial production (e.g. mining and materials production) and manufacturing industry, and the energy and emissions also associated with these sectors' use of electricity' (Grubb et al. 2015: S34).

Stern 2016). Changes in output from the steel and cement industries, which are especially energy intensive, over the past two years illustrate the scale and speed of the decline in energy-intensive economic activity in China. Whereas steel and cement production grew at a compound average annual rate of more than 15 per cent and 10 per cent, respectively, during the period of heavy industrial growth between 2000 and 2013, output in both sectors contracted in 2015—crude steel by more than 2 per cent and cement by more than 5 per cent, year-on-year (NBS 2016).

These structural changes affecting the composition of GDP have occurred on top of an ongoing trend of energy efficiency improvement within industries. Beginning with the Eleventh FYP (2006–10), China has introduced and expanded a range of targets and policies to improve energy conservation within industry and other economic sectors (see Song et al. 2015). Macro-level targets to reduce the energy intensity of GDP were primarily intended to guide intra-industry energy conservation efforts. During the Eleventh FYP, energy intensity decreased by 19 per cent relative to the 2005 baseline—just shy of the government's 20 per cent target (Lewis 2011). Energy efficiency efforts were expanded throughout the Twelfth FYP, contributing to that plan's 16 per cent energy intensity reduction target (relative to 2010) being easily beaten—by more than 3 percentage points.[4]

The most important policies for improving energy efficiency have been the 'Top 1,000 Enterprises Energy Conservation Action Program' (later expanded into the 'Top 10,000 Enterprises' program), which provides for energy conservation within energy-intensive state-owned enterprises (SOEs), and the Energy Conservation Law (revised in 2007), which provides a legal basis for the systematic monitoring, evaluation and enforcement of energy conservation performance.

The top enterprises program requires managers of SOEs to achieve targeted energy savings. The main means through which targets are implemented in China's planning system is by subdividing national targets and allocating them to provincial and local officials and to managers of SOEs, who are held accountable for achieving them through a system of performance monitoring and evaluation known as the Target Responsibility System. Crucially, personnel evaluations under this system are tied to job promotion within the Communist Party, meaning officials and SOE managers have strong incentives to achieve their targets. Different targets have different evaluative weights and, historically,

4 As discussed above, these targets also capture changes in the balance of energy-intensive and non-energy-intensive activities within overall economic activity, which helped especially to reduce energy intensity during the later stages of the Twelfth FYP (see Figure 18.2). The energy intensity decline across the Twelfth FYP was calculated using data from NBS (2016).

economic growth targets have been privileged over environmental targets. However, this is gradually changing and, indeed, the National Development and Reform Commission (NDRC) has deemed the abovementioned SOE energy conservation targets essential (or 'veto') targets, meaning failure to achieve them is deemed to result in an automatic failure for the entire performance review (see, for example, State Council 2007). Accordingly, China's energy conservation system has had a strong incentive effect at the industry level, driving improvements in industrial energy efficiency (Zhao and Ortolano 2010). Some evidence of gaming—undetected by inadequate verification processes—has been observed (Zhao et al. 2015). The system of energy conservation targets and associated accountability mechanisms for subnational government officials have been found to have strengthened the institutional arrangements and government capacity for improving energy performance at the local level (Li et al. 2013).

In sum, the combined effect of changes in the growth rate and composition (and hence energy requirements) of economic activity in China and policy-driven improvements in energy efficiency within industries has been a dramatic slowdown in the growth of China's total PEC—from a compound annual rate of more than 8 per cent per year between 2000 and 2013 to less than 1 per cent year-on-year in 2015 (Figure 18.3).

The demand-side in the medium term: Trajectory, risks and opportunities

Looking forward over the next decade or so, how are these factors affecting energy demand likely to evolve? What are the key opportunities and risks? And how could policy respond effectively to these? We first consider GDP growth and the structure of the economy, and then turn to energy efficiency.

It is likely that the recent decline in the overall growth rate in Chinese economic activity marks the beginning of a long-term structural trend (see, for example, IMF 2015; Hu 2015; Johansson et al. 2013; Pettis 2013; Pritchett and Summers 2014). Two key mechanisms (which are related) can be discerned here. The first—to use language popular over the past few years in China—reflects a Lewis turning point, as discussed above, associated with a running down of 'surplus' labour, combined with a slowing of the 'catch-up' growth, which was fuelled by industrial investment, cheap labour and urbanisation (such slowing in growth associated with these processes has been experienced by a number of developing countries) (Das and N'Diaye 2013; Garnaut and Song 2006; Green and Stern forthcoming; Huang and Cai 2014).

The second has more to do with the dynamics of savings and investment in China. As discussed above, the very high investment share of GDP in China is likely to be unsustainable and there are large debt-related vulnerabilities in China's financial sector. Thus, China's investment rate is likely to fall significantly, one way or another, over the next decade (Pettis 2013); there will be a rise in the consumption share, especially of services. Because it is likely, as reflected in the experience of other countries, to be more difficult to obtain very high growth rates from consumption expansion and productivity improvements, compared with the past strong driver of investment in capital stock, this structural transition will entail slower GDP growth for China (though it would significantly improve living standards) (Green and Stern 2016).

In addition to affecting the rate of growth, this structural transition will continue to reduce the energy requirements of China's economic activity in the manner discussed above (Green and Stern 2016). While relative growth in the household, transport and commercial sectors will increase the energy demand from these sectors, such increases are for the foreseeable future likely to be strongly outweighed by the decline in energy demand associated with the shift away from industry, which we expect to continue (Grubb et al. 2015). In particular, we expect to see further declines in heavy industry sectors, with excess capacity such as steel and cement, especially in the near term, as the government prioritises 'supply-side policy' and 'capacity management', and as production in these sectors is restructured and rationalised during the Thirteenth FYP (regarding steel, see, for example, Bloomberg News 2016a, 2016c).

A smooth and successful transition to China's new economic model is far from guaranteed. Success will depend on increasing domestic consumption and on greatly improving productivity—especially of capital—as investment rates fall (Stern 2011; Green and Stern forthcoming). Moreover, obtaining these outcomes will require domestic policy reforms, which will entail transitional costs and political-economic challenges in declining sectors and affected regions (see, for example, Green and Stern 2014, 2016). The alternative to successful transition to the new model is not 'continuation of the old model', as this is effectively impossible (at least in any sustainable sense over the medium to long term) and surely undesirable, for the reasons presented earlier. The unfortunate alternative potential outcome associated with trying to avoid the new model (or something similar) is a sharper decline in growth followed by stagnation (for discussion, see Pettis 2013). Although a degree of stimulus directed towards the drivers of the old model of growth could boost GDP growth of the energy-intensive kind in the short term, it would do so at the cost of sustainable growth in the longer term, as it would undermine much needed efforts towards policy reform, productivity improvement and sustainable debt management (IMF 2015; Green and Stern 2016).

There are much better ways than credit-fuelled stimulus of the construction and heavy industry sectors for China to maintain strong aggregate demand and low unemployment through the transition to the new model. One is to increase per capita government spending on provision of social services (education, health care, pensions, welfare support) and to expand coverage to the full resident populations of cities (not merely registered residents). Second, the government could expand specific forms of transitional social protection—such as job retraining and structural adjustment assistance—to facilitate structural change, equip workers with skills in growing economic sectors and reduce the financial impact of transition, especially on workers and affected communities. A third response is to incentivise a redirection in investment towards decarbonisation of the economy, environmental clean-up, pollution reduction and energy and resource efficiency (see further Green and Stern forthcoming). Each of these areas does indeed feature strongly in the Thirteenth FYP. While many of these (education, skills, environmental services and so on) might be classified as consumption (public or private) in conventional terms of accounting, they could—and, in our view, should—be seen as investments in human and natural capital.

The future rate of decline in energy intensity depends also on continued improvements in energy efficiency—that is, within industries. There are several reasons recent improvements are likely to continue at (at least) a similar rate to those of recent years: China remains far from the energy efficiency frontier (Baeumler et al. 2012; Hove et al. 2015); the energy efficiency frontier is likely to expand rapidly in the next decade as countries increasingly decarbonise their energy sectors; energy conservation policy, which yields multiple economic, environmental, social and geopolitical benefits, remains a key policy focus for government, as evidenced in the Thirteenth FYP;[5] and China has relatively successful systems and policies in place to incentivise and monitor energy conservation improvements (as discussed above), which can be strengthened and built on.

Against this must be weighed a number of risks on the energy efficiency front. One is that energy efficiency improvements slow within the heavy industries experiencing structural stagnation or decline. Another is that the fast-growing household and commercial sectors will lead to rapid growth in energy demand for vehicles, buildings and appliances. In each of these cases, there is a critical role for policy—from factor pricing to regulated standards and from urban planning to government procurement—to ensure or encourage high and continuously improving standards of efficiency in new capital stock (for example, buildings,

5 For example, the 'use of energy and resources more efficiently' is a key component under the 'Promoting green, circular, and low-carbon development' major task of the plan.

vehicles and appliances) and the efficient retrofitting of existing building stock and industrial facilities (Green and Stern 2014; Hove et al. 2015; World Bank and DRC 2014).

Overall, in light of forecast slower growth, the changing structure of economic activity and continued energy efficiency improvements, we anticipate only modest growth in China's PEC over the next decade—of less than 2 per cent per annum, based on what are arguably conservative assumptions across each of these dimensions (see Green and Stern 2016: Section 4). Being less conservative, one can see how a continuation of patterns from 2014–15 could lead to a scenario in which GDP growth averages 5–6 per cent and annual reductions in energy intensity also average 5–6 per cent over the next decade. Under this scenario, the range of PEC growth could be centred on zero. This would imply that every tonne of carbon dioxide per unit of energy saved on the supply side would translate into an equivalent absolute reduction in carbon dioxide.

The supply side: Beyond peak coal

We now turn to analysing policies and trends on the energy supply side. We begin by looking at measures relating to the diversification of China's energy supply and at the outcomes that have been achieved in terms of the energy production and electricity generation mix. We then consider China's main targets and policies aimed at reducing GHG emissions per se. Finally, we consider the outlook on the energy supply side over the decade ahead and discuss some potential issues and challenges.

Diversification of China's energy supply: Motivations, measures and outcomes

Coal has long been the dominant source of energy consumed in China, accounting for around two-thirds of PEC in 2014 (NBS 2015a). Between 2000 and 2013, Chinese coal consumption grew at a compound average rate of more than 8 per cent per year (NBS 2015a). By the end of that period, China was consuming half of the coal consumed in the entire world.

Over the past decade or so, China has for various reasons increasingly sought to diversify its energy supply (Boyd 2012). The first motivation is energy security. After China's energy consumption increased dramatically in the first half of the 2000s (during which time the energy intensity of GDP actually increased for a brief period), energy security became a more important issue for Chinese policymakers (Baghat 2010; Boyd 2012). As China became increasingly dependent on imported fossil fuels in the subsequent decade—for example, China is a large importer of oil and gas, and it became a net coal importer in 2009—it became increasingly exposed to international energy prices. This exposure poses not only geopolitical risks for China, but also economic risks:

> Compared to developed economies, China's economy is more exposed to price volatility in the global energy market due to its fossil fuel dominated energy structure and high proportion of secondary industry. Sectors of the economy with high exposure to price risk account for about 20% of GDP, several times higher than that in the developed economies. (Global Commission on the Economy and Climate 2014, p. 1)

Accordingly, energy security has remained high on the government's policy agenda.

A second motivating factor behind China's energy supply diversification is the strategic development of innovation-oriented manufacturing industries in renewable and nuclear energy, for which considerable government support has been provided. During the 2000s, China began strongly supporting the development of its wind (Dai et al. 2014; Wang et al. 2012), solar photovoltaics (Zhang et al. 2014) and nuclear (World Nuclear Association 2016) industries. While there have been ups and downs, China has had considerable success in developing internationally competitive companies with innovative capabilities in these industries (Nahm and Steinfeld 2014). As noted earlier, as China transitions to its new growth model, it needs, and indeed aspires, to rely more on productivity improvements, innovation and higher value-added sectors for its industrial growth. In this context, it has identified low/zero-carbon electricity generation, advanced electricity grid infrastructure and clean transportation industries (including the energy efficiency technologies and services sector and 'new energy vehicles', among others) as key sources of future industrial growth and has targeted these for ongoing state support (Xinhua 2015; ERI 2015; Nahm and Steinfeld 2014; Ng et al. 2016).

A third motivation for diversifying the energy supply—and one that has increased rapidly in salience since the latter part of the previous decade—has been to combat China's worsening levels of air pollution, especially in its coastal megacities (Sheehan et al. 2014). A fourth motivation for diversification is to contribute to the mitigation of climate change (Boyd 2012).

These diverse motivations have resulted in a complex web of targets, policies and state investments (for simplicity, we will refer to these collectively as 'measures') aimed at diversifying China's energy supply away from coal.

These include, first, various measures aimed at expanding the supply of 'non-fossil' (renewable and nuclear) power generation and expanding the supply of natural gas in power generation, industry and buildings. The government has set overall targets for the non–fossil fuel share of PEC of 15 per cent by 2020 and 20 per cent by 2030, as well as absolute capacity targets for individual energy sources. It has also introduced various support mechanisms to encourage wind and solar power production,[6] nuclear energy[7] and innovation in each of these areas (Andrews-Speed 2012). As the electricity mix has diversified towards increasing amounts of variable (wind and solar) and invariable (nuclear) generation in more diverse geographic locations—and in anticipation of future such expansions—the government has also encouraged the expansion of high-voltage electricity transmission networks and the development of energy storage (especially pumped hydro sites and a battery storage industry) (Garnaut 2014; Mathews and Tan 2014).

As air pollution reduction has become a more urgent priority in recent years, government energy policy has increasingly expanded beyond attempts to increase the relative shares and absolute levels of non-coal energy sources to encompass direct controls on coal production and consumption (Sheehan et al. 2014). For example, in 2013, pursuant to its Air Pollution Prevention and Control Plan (State Council 2013), the government established coal caps in nine provinces and cities that together account for 30 per cent of China's coal consumption (Song et al. 2015). In the key economic regions that are heavily affected by air pollution—Beijing–Tianjin–Hebei, Yangtze River Delta and Pearl River Delta—the plan prohibits the building of new coal-fired power plants and seeks to remove some heavy industry from these regions. This set of measures extends well beyond longer-standing (and ongoing) measures to improve the efficiency of China's coal-fired power generation fleet by replacing the least-efficient and highest-polluting plants with larger and more efficient ones (Mai and Feng 2013).

Efforts to reduce coal consumption in industry, which accounts for about half of China's total coal consumption, are also under way. The downward pressure on industrial coal use resulting from falling steel and cement output (discussed above) is being compounded by trends within these industries to substitute away from emissions-intensive production processes, such as by using electric arc furnaces using recycled scrap steel.[8]

The results of all these and other measures can be measured partly in terms of expansion in non-coal energy capacity (see Figure 18.4). For example, China installed a record-breaking amount of wind and solar power in 2015 (more than 30 GW and 18 GW, respectively), as well as 18 GW of hydro-electric and 6 GW of nuclear power.

6 These include, for example, the Renewable Energy Law (introduced in 2005 and subsequently amended), feed-in tariffs for distributed solar rooftop installations and provincial renewable energy deployment quotas (Chu 2015).

7 Including setting wholesale prices (World Nuclear Association 2016).

8 Ross Garnaut (Personal communication, 12 March 2015).

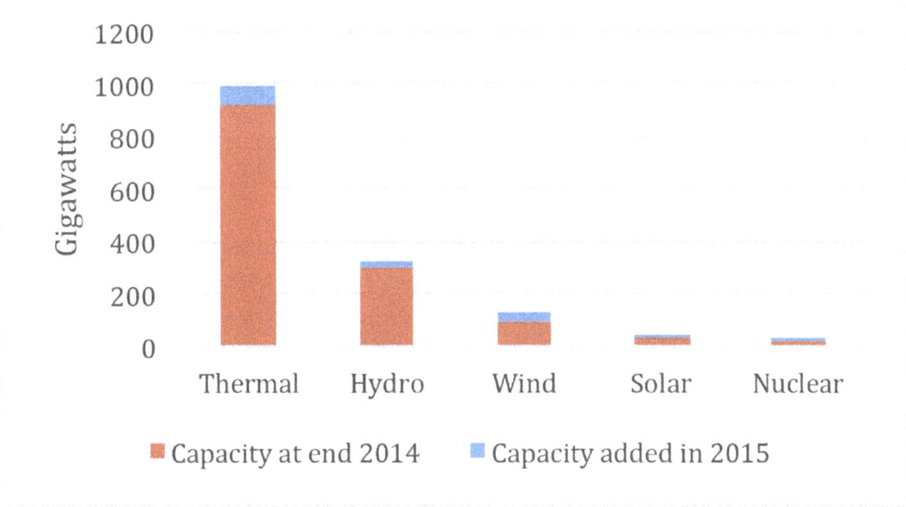

Figure 18.4 Electricity generation capacity in China by source

Sources: Data for 2015 total capacity from NBS (2016); capacity additions in 2015 inferred from difference between NBS (2016) data and 2014 data from China Electricity Council (2015); 'thermal' category includes coal, gas, biomass, cogeneration and wastes and is not disaggregated in Chinese statistics; the 'total' figure is as reported in NBS (2016) and is, for reasons that are not clarified, greater than the sum of the components also reported therein.

The non-coal energy capacity expansions of recent years have also contributed greatly to changes in China's electricity generation mix, such that coal-fired power generation has fallen for the past two years as generation from other sources has expanded (see Green and Stern 2015; NBS 2016; Plumer 2016). These shifts in the electricity market, along with changes in industrial energy consumption, add up to a profound change in China's overall energy supply mix (Figure 18.5).

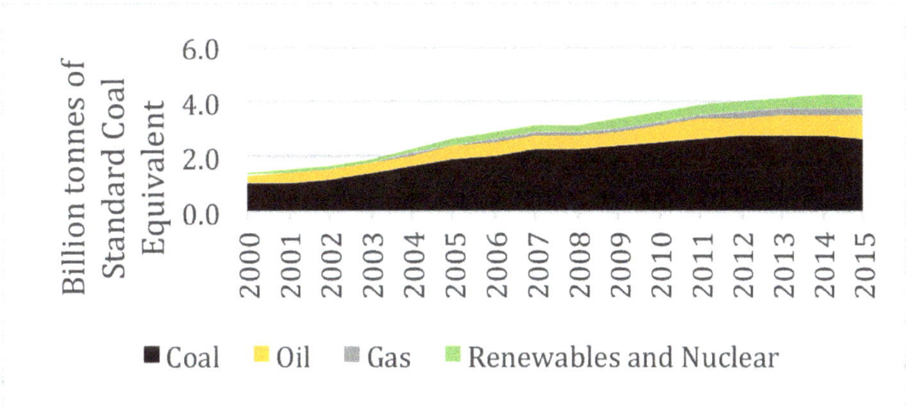

Figure 18.5 Total PEC by source

Sources: NBS (2015a, 2016).

In 2014–15, these changes in the energy supply mix combined with the dramatic slowdown in energy demand growth to cause a remarkable turnaround in China's coal consumption (see Figure 18.5). Measured in terms of energy content, China's coal consumption was flat in 2014[9] (NBS 2015a; EIA 2015)[10] and in 2015 it fell by more than 3 per cent, according to preliminary estimates (NBS 2016). After compound annual growth in coal consumption of more than 8 per cent per year between 2000 and 2013, this turnaround is remarkable. The rapid change is also reflected in coal production and import data for 2014 and 2015; coal production fell 2.5 per cent in 2014 and a further 3.3 per cent in 2015, and coal imports fell 10.9 per cent in 2014 and 29.9 per cent in 2015 (NBS 2015b, 2016). Because the decline in China's coal consumption is caused by a combination of forces on the demand and supply sides that are overwhelmingly structural, it is likely, in our view, that China will never again consume as much coal as it did in 2013–14. In other words, history will likely show that 2013–14 marked the peak in Chinese coal consumption.[11]

Measures to reduce GHG emissions per se

All of the strategies, policies and other changes discussed so far affect GHG emissions in a more or less indirect way, through their effect on energy-intensive economic activity or the energy supply mix. In addition, China has introduced a number of measures aimed at reducing GHG emissions per se. We focus here on two such measures: China's targets for reducing the carbon dioxide intensity of GDP and the associated governance arrangements, and carbon emissions trading.

9 When measured in terms of physical tonnage, coal consumption fell by 2 per cent in 2014 (EIA 2015). The difference between the energy content (standard coal equivalent, SCE) and physical tonnage measurements reflects the increase in the average quality (hence energy content) of coal burned in China in 2014. Preliminary statistics from China's National Bureau of Statistics (NBS 2015b) had earlier estimated a 2.9 per cent decline in coal consumption in SCE terms in 2014, before changes in average energy content were factored in.

10 China's National Bureau of Statistics (NBS 2015a) reported an increase of less than 0.06 per cent in the consumption of coal in SCE terms in 2014 compared with 2013. The figures cited here take into account the upward revisions to China's historical coal consumption made by China's statistical agencies following the five-year economic census, which took place in 2013. The census put China's coal data on a surer footing.

11 While there has been considerable attention paid to anomalies and revisions in China's recent historical coal data up to the end of 2013 (Buckley 2015; Wilson 2015; Wynn 2015), the 2014 and 2015 data are likely to be relatively accurate owing to changes in calculation methods made following China's five-year economics census in 2013. The 2014–15 data, moreover, are consistent with wider market trends, most relevantly in thermal electricity generation (for which data are more reliable due to metering) and in heavy industry sectors such as steel and cement, discussed above (see China Shenhua Energy Company Limited 2015: 14–15; Green and Stern 2015). Accordingly, it is highly unlikely that the 2014–15 coal data misrepresent the general picture over this period: flattening and then falling coal consumption, production and imports.

China has, since its Twelfth FYP (2011–15), adopted targets to reduce the carbon dioxide intensity of GDP, expressed against a 2005 baseline. The targets initially set were to achieve a 17 per cent reduction by 2015—which it has achieved—and a 40–45 per cent reduction by 2020.[12] The Thirteenth FYP includes a target of reducing the carbon dioxide intensity of GDP by 18 per cent over the course of the plan—that is, by 2020—compared with 2015 levels. This equates to a 50 per cent reduction on 2005 levels, implying a strengthening of the 2020 target compared with the original 40–45 per cent target, a recognition that China will likely 'far surpass' the latter target (Xie, quoted in King 2016).[13]

China's carbon dioxide intensity reductions have occurred largely because of the economic factors and policy measures already discussed in this chapter. Relatively little progress has been made in developing robust systems for incentivising subnational governments and SOEs to reduce carbon dioxide intensity per se, especially when compared with the efforts that have gone into energy conservation and non-coal energy expansion. Determining the achievement of carbon dioxide intensity targets at the micro level requires not only granular data on economic activity but also a detailed system for the monitoring, reporting and verification (MRV) of carbon dioxide emissions at a scale relevant to the performance evaluation—for example, at a provincial scale for provincial officials and at a facility and enterprise scale for enterprises. Establishing such systems is a major task in any country; it is enormous in a country as large and administratively complex as China. While ongoing efforts are being undertaken to improve carbon dioxide MRV mechanisms, comprehensive systems are still lacking. For example, despite the inclusion of the carbon dioxide intensity target in the Twelfth FYP, it was not until August 2014 that the NDRC released the implementation plan for the evaluation of performance against this target. Many provinces have not implemented provincial versions of the Implementation Plan and, as of 2015, the NDRC had not done any formal assessment of progress made by provinces in achieving targets.

Robust facility-level and enterprise-level MRV systems for GHGs are but one of many institutional prerequisites for an effective carbon emissions trading scheme (ETS),[14] which is the other key measure China has introduced to mitigate GHG emissions per se.

12 Aggregate carbon dioxide emissions can be inferred from economic activity and energy data, without the need for facility and enterprise-level carbon dioxide data.

13 However, on our forecasts, even the strengthened target is likely to be beaten (Green and Stern 2016: Section 4).

14 Such systems are necessary to determine the annual emissions produced by a facility or enterprise, and hence determine the liability of the facility operator or enterprise owner to acquire (and, at the end of a compliance period, surrender to the relevant regulator) carbon permits in respect of their emissions.

Seven Chinese pilot ETSs—covering two provinces and five major cities—were established during 2013–15. By design, the features of the schemes vary (as do the economic characteristics of the regions themselves). The schemes were established as policy experiments to generate useful lessons and build capacity on the basis of which a national ETS could be developed during the Thirteenth FYP (Zhang 2015).

Ex ante analyses of the expected barriers to effective ETS operation in China (Baron et al. 2012; Jiang 2013; Kong and Freeman 2013; Lo 2013; Lo and Howes 2014; Shen 2013; Teng et al. 2014; Zhang et al. 2014), early ex post facto analyses of the operation of the pilot schemes (Jotzo and Löschel 2014; Lo 2015; Yu and Lo 2015; Shen 2014; Zhang 2015) and expert survey data (de Boer et al. 2015) identify a wide range of major challenges and barriers to the effective development and implementation of such schemes in China. These barriers and challenges include technical complexities concerning issues of institutional design, such as transparent, specific and comprehensive legal provisions for cap-setting, allowance allocation, MRV, liability and enforcement; technical and organisational matters such as the establishment of robust emissions measurement and reporting systems, registries and exchanges and regulatory agencies for market oversight; institutional and political challenges concerning complementary electricity market reform; incongruent cultures and incentive structures among the relevant business sectors; excessive state intervention in market operations; and incomplete regulatory institutions.

Notwithstanding these barriers and challenges, China's Thirteenth FYP confirms that a national ETS will be established, including the release of regulations and oversight systems, and will build on the current pilot schemes (Reklev 2016a). At the time of writing, key officials had foreshadowed the start of the national ETS in the second half of 2017 (Reklev 2016b). The provinces and regions will reportedly be allocated individual intensity targets that add up to the national 18 per cent carbon dioxide intensity reduction goal, and these provincial targets will then be allocated to industries in covered sectors, which include petrochemicals, chemicals, building materials, iron and steel, non-ferrous metals, paper production, electricity generation and aviation (Reklev 2016a). The government's preference appears to be to determine allocations on the basis of sectoral emissions intensity benchmarks, so as to mitigate the risk of overallocation that comes with allocations based on absolute emissions targets (Reklev 2016b).

The barriers and challenges identified above—many of which have afflicted ETS experiments in advanced developed countries—will likely constrain the contribution that China's planned national ETS will be able to make to its wider climate mitigation effort for the foreseeable future. The rollout of the national ETS scheme may well benefit that wider effort indirectly, just as the pilot schemes have likely done (see Kong and Freeman 2013), including through capacity building, improvement of MRV systems and increased awareness of mitigation opportunities and strategies among Chinese firms and government officials. More substantively, structuring the scheme to focus on intra-industry carbon intensity improvements (as appears to be the preferred direction) may help with ongoing efforts to improve energy efficiency within heavy industries during an expected difficult period for such industries (Green and Stern 2016). Nonetheless, the barriers and challenges to the MRV and trading of carbon dioxide emissions suggest that other new supply-side measures may be worth considering as means to achieve rapid climate change mitigation. We have argued in the past that a combination of direct regulation and upstream taxation of fossil fuels, especially coal, would likely be relatively effective and efficient in the Chinese context (Green and Stern 2014, 2015).

In sum, despite the intense interest of the international climate policy community in China's carbon dioxide intensity targets and nascent carbon trading schemes, these measures have in fact played very little role in the radical shift in China's emissions trajectory that has occurred over the past few years (Green and Stern 2016). Moreover, while the importance of these measures is likely to grow over the next decade, we nonetheless think that they will remain less important than the other factors we discuss in this chapter, on both the demand side (discussed earlier) and the supply side. We now turn to the main drivers on the supply side over this future period.

Energy supply over the medium term: Transformation without growth?

Over the next decade, we expect continued transformation of China's energy supply, albeit with much uncertainty about the pace of change. We focus here on the electricity and transport sectors.

As discussed earlier, we forecast relatively flat demand for electricity over the next decade. This will create a new dynamic: whereas previously China's investments in non-coal capacity have supplied incremental demand, now new supply will be competing for dispatch in a relatively static market, intensifying competition for market share.

On the one hand, we expect China's expansion of non-coal and non–fossil fuel electricity generation capacity to continue apace, driven by the same motivations identified earlier: energy security, air pollution reduction, industrial modernisation and climate change mitigation. 'Greening' is a central theme of the Thirteenth FYP, which encompasses support for new energy industries, green cities, green finance, modern energy systems, clean energy innovation and controlling GHG emissions. In this context, and as more detailed plans and policies for the energy sector over the coming period are developed, we expect state support for financing, manufacturing, deploying, researching and developing zero-emissions electricity generation sources and associated infrastructure and technologies (for example, grid infrastructure and energy storage) to be prioritised and strengthened (see also PBC and UNEP 2015; Kuijs 2015).

Moreover, China's technology-specific absolute targets for capacity expansion in renewable energy have been consistently revised upwards by energy planning agencies as costs have plummeted and the industries have grown (Jiang 2014; Reed 2015). We expect these trends to continue as China and the world move increasingly decisively away from fossil fuels, resulting in the achievement, and possibly raising, of targets for solar and wind energy (currently 150–200 GW and 250 GW, respectively). Hydro-electric capacity is likely to expand over the next five years, though constraints on appropriate sites are likely to limit expansion beyond that time. China's highly ambitious targets for nuclear energy and gas may not be met, yet we still expect large build-outs of nuclear and gas-fired electricity capacity (for more detailed discussion, see Green and Stern 2015: 36–39; World Nuclear Association 2016). The continued expansion of non-coal energy infrastructure plays to China's institutional strengths in engineering, manufacturing and mobilising infrastructure finance, and its strong track record in this area provides reasons for optimism about future potential. Favourable international market, technology and financing trends in the renewable energy sector, buoyed by the recent Paris Agreement, should complement China's expansion.

On the other hand, ensuring that China's growing zero-carbon and low-carbon electricity sources are able to achieve their full potential for reducing the carbon intensity of electricity generation will require China to overcome a number of institutional and political hurdles that are likely to prove more challenging. A key set of institutional reform priorities involves marketisation and pricing reforms in the electricity sector. Fossil fuel production and electricity production currently enjoy a range of subsidies and are pervasively undertaxed (CCICED 2014), putting renewable energy in particular at a competitive disadvantage. A key priority is to remove subsidies for, and increase taxes on, fossil fuels, especially coal, so that prices for these pollution-intensive commodities more closely reflect their full social costs.[15] Additionally, reforms to the electricity sector are needed to ensure that prices paid by consumers and to generators fully reflect these social costs and to ensure therefore that the lowest-carbon,

15 We have advocated a rising coal tax as a highly efficient and administratively effective measure that would be well suited to China's institutional context (Green and Stern 2014, 2015; see also CCICED 2014).

lowest-pollution sources of generation are given priority in electricity dispatch arrangements (so-called green dispatch). At an administrative level, these reforms are likely to be technically challenging in a country that has had limited experience of effective externality taxation and market-based regulation.

The political challenges of enacting and implementing these reforms are likely also to be formidable. In a flat market for electricity, altering pricing and dispatch arrangements to favour zero-carbon and low-carbon energy sources will mean that the existing coal-fired power generation fleet will see its annual hours of operation continually falling in absolute terms (as has already happened over the past two years). In fact, individual coal-fired generators would see their generating hours fall even more precipitously: the continuing wasteful expansion in coal-fired generation capacity means that the coal fleet will be expanding at the same time as its share of a flat electricity market is falling (Myllyvirta et al. 2015; Spencer 2016). These trends are likely to intensify ongoing conflict among generators and system operators over dispatch priority (which determines which generators get paid)—conflicts that in 2014–15 led to high rates of wind and solar 'curtailment' and more coal than necessary being consumed (The Economist 2014).

Ultimately, transforming an electricity sector that has great overcapacity and not growing substantially (and possibly not growing at all or even shrinking) will be a complex political-economic task that requires managing the decline of an entire industry associated with coal. That will involve stranding assets on a large scale, leaving millions of people in need of alternative employment and, in some communities, removing the main source of economic activity (this applies not only to coal industries, but also to steel, cement and other heavy industries that were central to the old model of growth). Managing this 'degrowth' aspect of China's energy transformation will require a proactive strategy from the government across each of these dimensions. Encouragingly, the Central Government has given strong indications in this direction. 'Supply-side reform' and reducing overcapacity are key themes of the Thirteenth FYP. In the coal and steel industries specifically, the government has announced targets to close large amounts of excess production capacity, imposed a three-year moratorium on new coalmine approvals and set up funds to support coal and steel industry restructuring and the redeployment of millions of coal and steel workers (Bloomberg News 2016b, 2016c). Monitoring—and indeed supporting—this essential transition should be a major focus of the international research and policy communities in the years ahead.

Turning to the transport sector, the outlook for China is perhaps more uncertain. On the one hand, slowing GDP growth and heavy industrial activity will continue to put downward pressure on oil demand, as they did in 2014–15, to the point that diesel fuel consumption decreased in 2015 (Olson and Spegele 2016).

On the other hand, oil consumption growth will be driven by rising demand from household and commercial transportation as these sectors grow, consistent with the shift to the new growth model. Yet projections of the future vehicle stock vary enormously (see Gambhir et al. 2015). The low global oil price will likely increase oil demand, though the government has moved to impose a price floor on crude oil of US$40 a barrel, which will be reflected in petrol prices, mitigating the consumer demand response (Bloomberg News 2016a). There are also many supply-side variables that complicate forecasting, including the potential for disruptive technological innovation in 'new energy vehicles'—such as electric, hybrid and autonomous vehicles—a market that China is itself already building through supportive policy, and which it has made a strong focus of the Thirteenth FYP (Ng et al. 2016).

On balance, it seems most likely that oil demand will grow over the coming decade in China, albeit more slowly than over the previous decade, and more slowly than has been projected by major international forecasters in recent years (see Coulter 2015; Olson and Spegele 2016).

Overall, it appears likely that the transformation of China's energy sector will continue and strengthen over the next decade. We expect coal to continue to decline in absolute terms and as a share of PEC, renewable energy to grow rapidly, nuclear and gas to grow steadily and oil to grow moderately.

Conclusion

From this analysis of economic and policy factors on the demand and supply sides of China's energy transition, we conclude that China's net emissions over the next decade will grow only very slowly—and will peak sometime during this period (for an illustrative scenario, see Green and Stern 2016: Section 4). It is not beyond the realm of possible outcomes that carbon dioxide emissions, which appear to have fallen in 2015 (Boren 2016; Peters and Korsbakken, cited in Plumer 2016), will continue to fall gradually over this period, which would imply that 2014 was China's peak year for carbon dioxide emissions. The actual scenario will depend on the extent to which risks such as those discussed in this chapter arise and can be effectively mitigated.

Ultimately, whatever the exact trajectory turns out to be, it is clear that the outlook for China's carbon dioxide emissions has changed radically over the past few years. This is welcome news for the global effort to mitigate climate change. If China's emissions were to continue rising at rates similar to those of the first decade of this century, it would make it extremely difficult for global warming to be restrained to less than 2°C above pre-industrial levels—the conventionally agreed global climate mitigation goal (Boyd et al. 2015; Green and

Stern 2015: 14–18). The emerging outlook for China's emissions trajectory, in contrast, suggests that a mitigation pathway of less than 2°C is more feasible than previously expected.

The analysis presented in this chapter also has implications for China's international climate change diplomacy, and for global climate policy more generally. China played a crucial role in the successful negotiation of a new international climate change agreement in Paris in December 2015. The Chinese Government's general attitude and approach to global climate change mitigation during the Paris process were flexible and constructive, and its own specific policy pledges, including to peak its carbon dioxide emissions by 2030, were more stringent than in past negotiations. The analysis presented here sheds light on the domestic, structural drivers of this constructive turn in China's international climate diplomacy. The domestic economic and policy trends we have identified gave the government confidence that the country could achieve its pledged targets and that major steps by other countries to decarbonise the world economy would align with China's short- to medium-term economic interests, not just its long-term interest in avoiding catastrophic climate change.

In fact, if the analysis in this chapter is correct, China's official target to peak its carbon dioxide emissions by 2030 is likely to be substantially beaten, as are its other 2030 targets for non–fossil fuel energy and carbon dioxide intensity of GDP (see also Green and Stern 2016: Section 4). This probability highlights the virtue of the 'dynamic' climate governance model embodied in the Paris Agreement, whereby countries are required to update their pledges with more ambitious targets and policies over time. China is likely to be in a strong position to strengthen its commitment ahead of the first five-year revision period in 2020.

Achieving the ultimate, long-term objective of the Paris Agreement with a reasonable probability will require all countries, including China, to reduce their emissions rapidly towards net zero global emissions within the second half of this century. The challenge for China now is therefore one of avoiding a 'long plateau' in emissions by implementing reforms that will enable it simultaneously to achieve growing prosperity and rapidly falling emissions after the carbon dioxide peak (whenever it occurs). Given the various social, environmental, economic and financial reasons China has for moving rapidly to a clean, low-carbon, less resource-intensive, services-oriented economy—quite independently of mitigating climate change—these objectives are highly complementary.

References

Andrews-Speed, P. (2012), *The governance of energy in China: Transition to a low-carbon economy*, Basingstoke, UK: Palgrave Macmillan.

Baeumler, A., Ijjasz-Vasquez, E. and Mehndiratta S. (eds) (2012), *Sustainable low-carbon city development in China*, Washington, DC: The World Bank.

Baghat, G. (2010), China's energy security: Challenges and opportunities, *The Journal of Social, Political, and Economic Studies*, 35: 137–166. Available from: jspes.org/online.html.

Baron, R., Aasrud, A., Sinton, J., Campbell, N., Jiang, K. and Zhuang, X. (2012), *Policy options for low-carbon power generation in China*, Paris: OECD & IEA.

Bloomberg News (2016a), Crude stopped falling at $40 a barrel for Chinese consumers, *Bloomberg News*, 18 January. Available from: bloomberg.com/news/articles/2016-01-18/oil-prices-stopped-falling-at-40-a-barrel-for-chinese-consumers.

Bloomberg News (2016b), China puts coal production capacity on chopping block, *Bloomberg News*, 5 February. Available from: bloomberg.com/news/articles/2016-02-05/china-puts-1-billion-tons-of-coal-capacity-on-chopping-block.

Bloomberg News (2016c), China expects 1.8 million coal, steel layoffs on capacity cuts, *Bloomberg News*, 29 February. Available from: bloomberg.com/news/articles/2016-02-29/china-expects-1-8-million-coal-steel-layoffs-on-capacity-cuts.

Boren, Z. D. (2016), China's fossil fuel emissions fall for the second year running, *Energy Desk*, 29 February. Available from: energydesk.greenpeace.org/2016/02/29/china-coal-fall-the-sequel/.

Boyd, O. (2012), *China's energy reform and climate policy: The ideas motivating change*, Centre for Climate Economics and Policy Working Paper 1205, Canberra: The Australian National University.

Boyd, R., Stern, N. and Ward, B. (2015), *What will global annual emissions of greenhouse gases be in 2030, and will they be consistent with avoiding global warming of more than 2°C?*, Policy Paper, London: Grantham Research Institute on Climate Change and the Environment and Centre for Climate Change Economics and Policy. Available from: lse.ac.uk/GranthamInstitute/publication/what-will-global-annual-emissions-of-greenhouse-gases-be-in-2030-and-will-they-be-consistent-with-avoiding-global-warming-of-more-than-2c/.

Buckley, C. (2015), China burns much more coal than reported, complicating climate talks, *The New York Times*, 3 November. Available from: nytimes.com/2015/11/04/world/asia/china-burns-much-more-coal-than-reported-complicating-climate-talks.html?_r=0.

Central Committee of the Communist Party of China (CCCP) (2013), *Decision on major issues concerning comprehensively deepening reforms*, 15 November, Beijing: CCCP. Available from: news.xinhuanet.com/politics/2013-11/15/c_118164235.htm. English version available from: english.people.com.cn/90785/8525422.html.

China Council for International Cooperation on Environment and Development (CCICED) (2014), *Evaluation and prospects for a green transition process in China*, CCICED Task Force Report, Beijing: CCICED. Available from: cciced.net/encciced/policyresearch/report/201504/P020150413497198320874.pdf.

China Electricity Council (2015), *China power industry situation and prospects*, 10 March, Beijing: China Electricity Council. Available from: cec.org.cn/yaowenkuaidi/2015-03-10/134972.html.

China Shenhua Energy Company Limited (2015), *Third quarterly report for the year 2015*, Beijing: China Shenhua Energy Company Limited. Available from: iis.quamnet.com/media/IRAnnouncement/1088/EN_US/002345329-0.PDF.

Chu, J. (2015), *RE 100: China's fast track to a renewable future*, Beijing: The Climate Group. Available from: theclimategroup.org/_assets/files/RE100-China-analysis.pdf.

Coulter, T. (2015), China's fuel demand to peak sooner than oil giants expect, *Bloomberg News*, 1 April. Available from: bloomberg.com/news/articles/2015-04-01/china-s-fuel-demand-to-peak-sooner-than-oil-giants-expect.

Dai, Y., Zhou, Y., Xia, D., Ding, M. and Xue, L. (2014), *The innovation path of the Chinese wind power industry*, Bonn: German Development Institute/Deutsches Institut für Entwicklungspolitik. Available from: die-gdi.de/discussion-paper/article/the-innovation-path-of-the-chinese-wind-power-industry/.

Das, M. and N'Diaye, P. (2013), *Chronicle of a decline foretold: Has China reached the Lewis turning point?*, IMF Working Paper 13/26, Washington, DC: International Monetary Fund. Available from: imf.org/external/pubs/ft/wp/2013/wp1326.pdf.

de Boer, D., Roldao, R. and Slater, H. (2015), *2015 China carbon pricing survey*, Beijing: China Carbon Forum. Available from: chinacarbon.info/wp-content/uploads/2015/09/2015-China-Carbon-Pricing-Survey-EN.pdf.

Energy Information Administration (EIA) (2015), *Recent statistical revisions suggest higher historical coal consumption in China*, Washington, DC: Energy Information Administration. Available from: eia.gov/todayinenergy/detail.cfm?id=22952.

Energy Research Institute (ERI) (2015), *China 2050 high renewable energy penetration scenario and roadmap study: Executive summary*, April, Beijing: National Development and Reform Commission. Available from: efchina.org/Attachments/Report/report-20150420/China-2050-High-Renewable-Energy-Penetration-Scenario-and-Roadmap-Study-Executive-Summary.pdf.

Gambhir, A., Tse, L. K. C., Tong, D. and Martinez-Botas, R. (2015), Reducing China's road transport sector CO_2 emissions to 2050: Technologies, costs and decomposition analysis, *Applied Energy*, 157: 905–917. doi: 10.1016/j.apenergy.2015.01.018.

Garnaut, R. (2014), China's role in global climate change mitigation, *China and World Economy*, 22(5): 2–18. doi: 10.1111/j.1749-124X.2014.12081.x.

Garnaut, R. and Song, L. (2006), *The turning point in China's economic development*, Canberra: ANU E Press/Asia Pacific Press.

Garnaut, R., Song, L. and Cai, F. (2013), China's new strategy for long-term growth and development, in L. Song, R. Garnaut and F. Cai (eds), *China: A new model for growth and development*, pp. 1–16, Canberra: ANU E Press.

Garnaut, R., Song, L. and Cai, F. (2014), Reform and China's long-term growth and development, in L. Song, R. Garnaut and F. Cai (eds), *Deepening reform for China's long-term growth and development*, pp. 3–26, Canberra: ANU Press.

Global Commission on the Economy and Climate (2014), *China and the new climate economy: China case study—Executive summary*, Beijing: Tsinghua University. Available from: newclimateeconomy.net/sites/default/files/china-nce-exec-summary-eng_reduced_1.pdf.

Green, F. & Stern, N. (forthcoming), *A new development model for China: Turning points for growth, urbanisation and environment*, Policy Paper, London: Grantham Research Institute on Climate Change and the Environment and Centre for Climate Change Economics and Policy.

Green, F. and Stern, N. (2014), *An innovative and sustainable growth path for China: A critical decade*, Policy Paper, London: Grantham Research Institute on Climate Change and the Environment and Centre for Climate Change Economics and Policy. Available from: lse.ac.uk/GranthamInstitute/publication/an-innovative-and-sustainable-growth-path-for-china-a-critical-decade/.

Green, F. and Stern, N. (2015), *China's 'new normal': Structural change, better growth, and peak emissions*, Policy Brief, London: Grantham Research Institute on Climate Change and the Environment and Centre for Climate Change Economics and Policy. Available from: lse.ac.uk/GranthamInstitute/wp-content/uploads/2015/06/China_new_normal_web1.pdf.

Green F. and Stern, N. (2016), China's changing economy: Implications for its carbon dioxide emissions, *Climate Policy*, 16 March. Available from: tandfonline.com/doi/full/10.1080/14693062.2016.1156515.

Grubb, M., Sha, F., Spencer, T., Hughes, N., Zhang, Z. and Agnolucci, P. (2015), A review of Chinese CO_2 emission projections to 2030: The role of economic structure and policy, *Climate Policy*, 15(S1): S7–S39. doi: 10.1080/14693062.2015.1101307.

Guan, D., Klasen, S., Hubacek, K., Feng, K., Liu, Z., He, K., Geng, Y. and Zhang, Q. (2014), Determinants of stagnating carbon intensity in China, *Nature Climate Change*, 4(11): 1017–1023. Available from: doi.org/10.1038/nclimate2388.

Hove, A., Enoe, M. and Gordon, K. (2015), *China's next opportunity: Sustainable economic transition*, Beijing: Paulson Institute.

Hu, A. (2015), Embracing China's 'new normal': Why the economy is still on track, *Foreign Affairs*, 94(3): 8–12. Available from: foreignaffairs.com/articles/china/2015-04-20/embracing-chinas-new-normal.

Huang, Y. and Cai, F. (2014), *Debating the Lewisian turning point in China*, London: Routledge.

International Monetary Fund (IMF) (2015), *People's Republic of China: Staff report for the 2015 Article IV consultation*, Washington, DC: International Monetary Fund. Available from: imf.org/external/pubs/ft/scr/2015/cr15234.pdf.

Jiang, K. (2014), China's CO_2 emission scenario toward 2 degree global target, Presentation to Victoria University Conference on Abrupt Change in China's Energy Path: Implications for China, Australia and the Global Climate, Melbourne, 26 June. Available from: vu.edu.au/sites/default/files/cses/pdfs/Kejun_2014_China's_CO2_emission_scenario.pdf.

Jiang, X. (2013), The rise of carbon emissions trading in China: A panacea for climate change?, *Climate and Development*, 6(2): 111–121.

Johansson, Å., Guillemette, Y., Murtin, F., Turner, D., Nicoletti, G., de la Maisonneuve, C., Bagnoli, P., Bousquet, G. and Spinelli, F. (2013), *Long-term growth scenarios*, Economics Department Working Papers No. 1000, Paris: Organisation for Economic Co-operation and Development. Available from: search.oecd.org/officialdocuments/publicdisplaydocumentpdf/?cote=ECO/WKP(2012)77&docLanguage=En.

Jotzo, F. and Löschel, A. (2014), Emissions trading in China: Emerging experiences and international lessons, *Energy Policy*, 75: 3–8.

King, E. (2016), China will 'far surpass' 2020 climate target, says top envoy, *Climate Home*, 24 February. Available from: climatechangenews.com/2016/02/24/china-will-far-surpass-2020-climate-target-says-top-envoy/.

Kong, B. and Freeman, C. (2013), Making sense of carbon market development in China, *Carbon & Climate Law Review*, 7(3): 194–212.

Kuijs, L. (2015), Plan aims to balance growth with reform, *China Daily* [USA], 4 November. Available from: usa.chinadaily.com.cn/.

Lewis, A. (1954), Economic development with unlimited supplies of labour, *The Manchester School*, 22: 139–191.

Lewis, J. (2011), *Energy and climate goals of China's 12th Five-Year Plan*. Arlington, Va.: Pew Centre on Global Climate Change. Available from: c2es.org/docUploads/energy-climate-goals-china-twelfth-five-year-plan.pdf.

Li, H., Zhao, X., Ma, L. and Qi, Y. (2013), Policy implementation: Energy conservation target responsibility system, in Y. Qi (ed.), *Annual review of low-carbon development in China*, pp. 78–150, Beijing: Social Sciences Academic Press.

Lo, A. Y. (2013), Carbon trading in a socialist market economy: Can China make a difference?, *Ecological Economics*, 87: 72–74.

Lo, A. Y. (2015), Challenges to the development of carbon markets in China, *Climate Policy*, 16(1): 109–124.

Lo, A. Y. and Howes, M. (2014), Powered by the state or finance? The organization of China's carbon markets, *Eurasian Geography and Economics*, 54(4): 386–408.

Mai, Y. and Feng, S. (2013), Increasing China's coal-fired power generation efficiency: The impact on carbon intensity and the broader Chinese economy to 2020, Paper presented to State Information Centre and National Development and Reform Commission Workshop, Beijing.

Mathews, J. and Tan, H. (2014), Manufacture renewables to build energy security, *Nature*, 513: 166–168.

Myllyvirta, L., Shen, X. and Lammi, H. (2015), *Is China doubling down on its coal power bubble?*, Beijing: Greenpeace East Asia. Available from: greenpeace.org/eastasia/publications/reports/climate-energy/climate-energy-2015/doubling-down/.

Nahm, J. and Steinfeld, E. S. (2014), Scale-up nation: China's specialization in innovative manufacturing, *World Development*, 54: 288–300. Available from: doi.org/10.1016/j.worlddev.2013.09.003.

National Bureau of Statistics (NBS) (2015a), *China Statistical Yearbook 2015*, Beijing: China Statistics Press.

National Bureau of Statistics (NBS) (2015b), *Statistical communiqué of the People's Republic of China on the 2014 national economic and social development*, Beijing: National Bureau of Statistics. Available from: stats.gov.cn/english/PressRelease/201502/t20150228_687439.html.

National Bureau of Statistics (NBS) (2016), *Statistical communiqué of the People's Republic of China on the 2015 national economic and social development*, Beijing: National Bureau of Statistics. Available from: stats.gov.cn/english/PressRelease/201602/t20160229_1324019.html.

Ng, S., Mabey, N. and Gaventa, J. (2016), *Pulling ahead on clean technology: China's 13th Five Year Plan challenges Europe's low carbon competitiveness*, Briefing Paper, London: E3G. Available from: e3g.org/docs/E3G_Report_on_Chinas_13th_5_Year_Plan.pdf.

Olson, B. and Spegele, B. (2016), China slowdown stokes fears of peak oil demand, *The Wall Street Journal*, 25 January. Available from: wsj.com/articles/china-slowdown-stokes-fears-on-peak-oil-demand-1453736237.

People's Bank of China (PBC) and United Nations Environment Programme (UNEP) (2015), *Establishing China's green financial system*, Final Report of the Green Finance Task Force, April, Nairobi: UNEP. Available from: unep.org/inquiry/PBC/tabid/1060068/Default.aspx.

People's Republic of China (PRC) (2015), *Enhanced actions on climate change: China's intended nationally determined contributions*, New York: UNFCCC. Available from: www4.unfccc.int/submissions/INDC/Published%20Documents/China/1/China's%20INDC%20-%20on%2030%20June%202015.pdf.

Pettis, M. (2013), *Avoiding the fall: China's economic restructuring*, Washington, DC: Carnegie Endowment for International Peace.

Plumer, B. (2016), The real war on coal is happening in China right now, *Vox*, 6 March. Available from: vox.com/2016/3/6/11168914/china-peak-coal.

Pritchett, L. and Summers, L. H. (2014), *Asiaphoria meets regression to the mean*, NBER Working Paper No. 20573, Cambridge, Mass.: National Bureau of Economic Research. Available from: nber.org/papers/w20573.

Reed, S. (2015), China raises its targets for renewable energy, *The New York Times*, 8 December. Available from: nytimes.com/interactive/projects/cp/climate/2015-paris-climate-talks/china-raises-its-targets-for-renewable-energy.

Reklev, S. (2016a), China sets 18% carbon intensity reduction target by 2020, *Carbon Pulse*, 5 March. Available from: carbon-pulse.com/16618/.

Reklev, S. (2016b), China national ETS launch likely in second half of 2017, *Carbon Pulse*, 15 March. Available from: carbon-pulse.com/17057/.

Schafer, A. (2005), Structural change in energy use, *Energy Policy*, 33: 429–437.

Sheehan, P., Cheng, E., English, A. and Sun, F. (2014), China's response to the air pollution shock, *Nature Climate Change*, 4(5): 306–309. Available from: doi.org/10.1038/nclimate2197.

Shen, W. (2014), Chinese business at the dawn of its domestic emissions trading scheme: Incentives and barriers to participation in carbon trading, *Climate Policy*, 15(3): 339–354.

Shen, Y. (2013), Moving steadily or great leap forward? The emerging carbon market in China, *Deakin Law Review*, 18(2): 233–270.

Song, R., Dong, W., Zhu, J., Zhao, X. and Wang, Y. (2015), *Assessing implementation of China's climate policies in the 12th 5-year period*, September, Working Paper, Washington, DC: World Resources Institute.

Spencer, T. (2016), Chinese coal? What does it mean for the Paris Agreement?, *IDDRI Blog*, 12 February, Paris: Institute for Sustainable Development and International Relations. Available from: blog-iddri.org/en/2016/02/12/chinese-coal-what-does-it-mean-for-the-paris-agreement/.

State Council of the People's Republic of China (State Council) (2007), *Implementation plan for the performance evaluation system of energy consumption per unit of GDP*, Beijing: State Council of the People's Republic of China.

State Council of the People's Republic of China (State Council) (2013), *Air pollution prevention and control plan*, Beijing: State Council of the People's Republic of China.

Stern, N. (2011), Raising consumption, maintaining growth and reducing emissions: The objectives and challenges of China's radical change in strategy and its implications for the world economy, *World Economics*, 12(4): 13–34.

Teng, F., Xin W. and Lv, Z. (2014), Introducing the emissions trading system to China's electricity sector: Challenges and opportunities, *Energy Policy*: 1–7.

The Economist (2014), Generational shift, *The Economist*, 25 October. Available from: economist.com/news/china/21627626-china-developing-clean-sources-energy-problem-getting-them-used-generational-shift.

Wang, Z., Qin, H. and Lewis, J. (2012), China's wind power industry: Policy support, technological achievements, and emerging challenges, *Energy Policy*, 51: 80–88.

Wilson, R. (2015), Peak coal in China? Not so fast, *Carbon Counter Blog*, 27 February. Available from: carboncounter.wordpress.com/2015/02/27/peak-coal-in-china-not-so-fast/.

Wolf, M. (2015), Why worries about China make sense, *Financial Times*, 25 August. Available from: ft.com/cms/s/0/edd707ba-4a56-11e5-9b5d-89a026fda5c9.html??ftcamp=crm/email//nbe/FirstFTEurope/product#axzz3jgMhxWRg.

World Bank (2016), *GDP growth (annual %)*, Washington, DC: The World Bank. Available from: data.worldbank.org/indicator/NY.GDP.MKTP.KD.ZG.

World Bank and Development Research Centre of the State Council, People's Republic of China (DRC) (2014), *Urban China: Toward efficient, inclusive, and sustainable urbanization*, Washington, DC: The World Bank.

World Nuclear Association (2016), *Nuclear power in China*, London: World Nuclear Association. Available from: world-nuclear.org/information-library/country-profiles/countries-a-f/china-nuclear-power.aspx.

Wynn, G. (2015), China's carbon emissions: Did they really fall in 2014?, *Responding to Climate Change*, 16 February. Available from: rtcc.org/2015/02/16/chinas-carbon-emissions-did-they-really-fall-in-2014/#sthash.eIHJOsEd.dpuf.

Xinhua (2015), 'Made in China 2025' plan unveiled, *Xinhua*, 19 May. Available from: chinadaily.com.cn/bizchina/2015-05/19/content_20760528.htm.

Xu, X., Zhao, T., Liu, N. and Kang, J. (2014), Changes of energy-related GHG emissions in China: An empirical analysis from sectoral perspective, *Applied Energy*, 132: 298–307. doi: 10.1016/j.apenergy.2014.07.025.

Yu, X. and Lo, A. Y. (2015), Carbon finance and the carbon market in China, *Nature Publishing Group*, 5(1): 15–16.

Zhang, D., Karplus, V. J., Cassisa, C. and Zhang, X. (2014), Emissions trading in China: Progress and prospects, *Energy Policy*, 75: 9–16.

Zhang, G. (2014), Comprehensively deepen reforms to promote sustainable and healthy development of the economy and society, Speech at the 15th China Development Forum, Beijing, 23 March. Available from: cpc.people.com.cn/n/2014/0324/c64094-24714056.html.

Zhang, S., Andrews-Speed, P. and Ji, M. (2014), The erratic path of the low-carbon transition in China: Evolution of solar PV policy, *Energy Policy*, 67: 903–12.

Zhang, Z. (2015), Carbon emissions trading in China: The evolution from pilots to a nationwide scheme, *Climate Policy*, 15(S1): S104–S126.

Zhao, X. and Ortolano, L. (2010), Implementing China's national energy conservation policies at state-owned electric power generation plants, *Energy Policy*, 38(10): 6293–6306.

Zhao, X., Li, H. and Wu, L. (2015), Enterprise-level energy savings targets in China: Compliance, weaknesses, and the way forward, Unpublished ms.

19. Issues in Greening China's Electricity Sector

Xiaoli Zhao

Introduction

China's electric power generating industry has developed rapidly since the reform era began in 1978 (Figures 19.1 and 19.2). The average annual growth rates of installed power capacity and power generation were 7.8 per cent and 7.9 per cent respectively from 1978 to the end of the last century. This meant that from 1996 China was ranked second in the world for both installed power capacity and power generation. By 2011 China's power generation had exceeded that of the United States, to make China the largest power generator in the world (BP 2015). Installed power generation capacity reached 1,247 GW by the end of 2013, thus also exceeding the United States, according to the *Electric power construction industry annual report 2013* (China Electric Power Construction Enterprise Association 2014). By 2014, power generation had reached 5,649 terawatt-hours (TWh), accounting for 24 per cent of the global total (BP 2015), and installed capacity had reach more than 1,360 GW—22.66 per cent of the global total (China Renewable Energy Society 2015).

The characteristics of China's resource endowments mean it presently relies predominantly on coal. Total installed thermal power capacity increased from 39.84 GW in 1978 to 915.69 GW in 2014. Thermal power generation increased from 211.9 TWh in 1978 to 4,233.73 TWh the same year. Over the past 36 years, installed thermal capacity and power generation have grown the fastest amid China's power mix, in terms of both installed capacity and power generation. By 2014, installed thermal power capacity and power generation accounted for some 70 per cent and 75 per cent, respectively, of the totals. Those shares, and the high scale of production in China, have in turn brought serious environmental externalities.

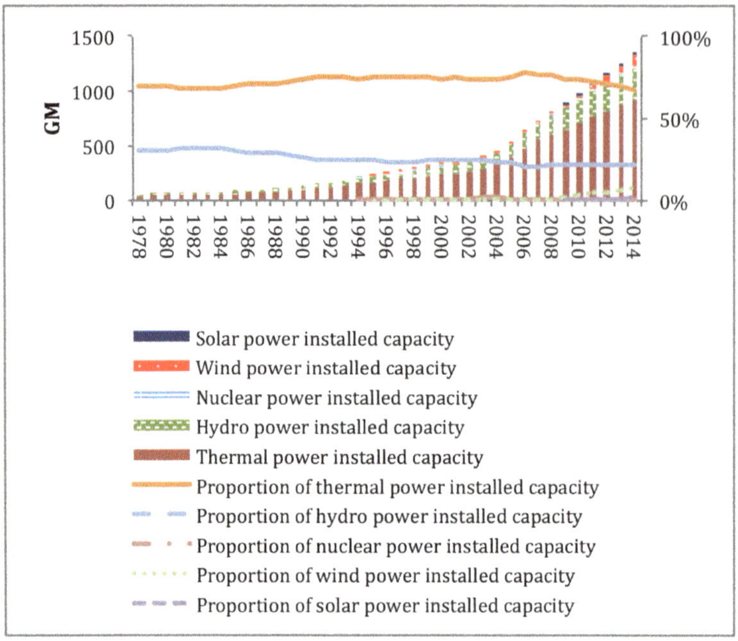

Figure 19.1 Power installed capacity mix in China

Sources: China Electricity Council (2014); NBS (1978–2014).

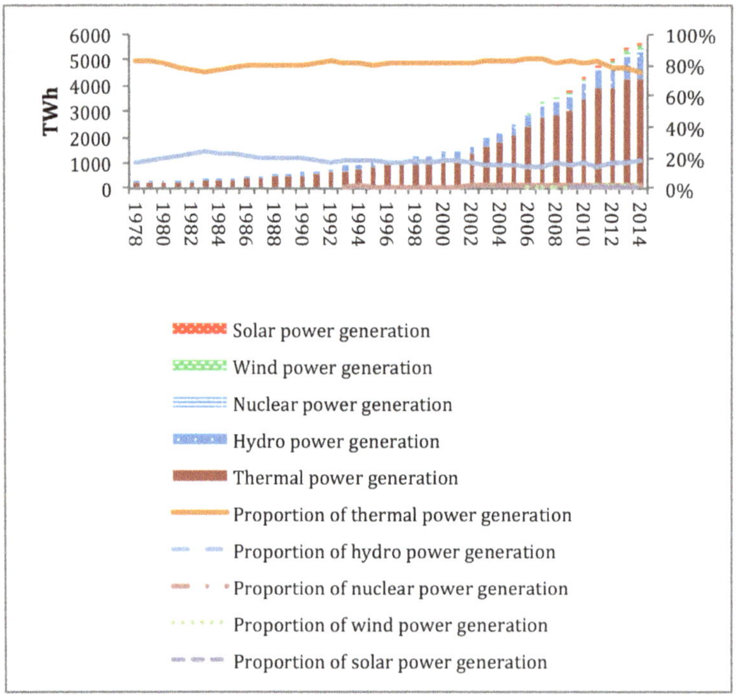

Figure 19.2 China's power generation mix

Source: NBS (1978–2014).

Figure 19.3 shows the share of carbon dioxide emissions for each industrial sector in China. In 2014, the power industry's emissions accounted for half of all carbon dioxide emissions in China. Figure 19.4 shows the changes in three pollutant emissions from China's power industry—smoke dust, nitrogen oxides and sulphur dioxide—and their respective shares in total industrial emissions. As a result of increasing power demand and production, sulphur dioxide emissions from China's power industry in 1999–2006 have fluctuated, from 7.4 million tonnes in 1999 to 13.2 million tonnes in 2006. The rise of sulphur dioxide emissions has been curbed by desulphurisation technology, which was prioritised under the Eleventh Five-Year Plan (FYP). The leading method China uses to achieve this is limestone-gypsum wet desulphurisation (92 per cent), which is accepted practice across a wide range of applications, with a desulphurisation rate, on average, above the 95 per cent level. Accordingly, sulphur dioxide emissions began to drop in 2006, from 13.2 million tonnes to 6.8 million tonnes by 2014.

At the same time, China's broader thermal power emission standards have become increasingly strict, via the *Thermal Power Plant Air Pollution Emission Standards GB13223-1996* and up to *GB13223-2011*, with the aim of reducing the environmental footprint of the industry. As a result, dust emissions decreased from 4.7 million tonnes in 1998 to 980,000 tonnes in 2014 (MEP 1998–2014), supported by improvements in power plant dust removal technology and efficiency. The industry accounted for 39 per cent of total industrial dust emissions in 1998 but only 16 per cent in 2014 (MEP 1998–2014). On the other hand, nitrogen oxide emissions from the thermal power industry increased from 3.6 million tonnes in 1998 to 10.7 million tonnes in 2011. Since the implementation of the Twelfth FYP, there appears to have been a decline to 7.8 million tonnes in 2014. The total emissions of sulphur dioxide, nitrogen oxides and dust rose from 16.4 million tonnes in 1998 to 22.4 million tonnes in 2006, followed by a marked decline to 13.4 million tonnes in 2014.

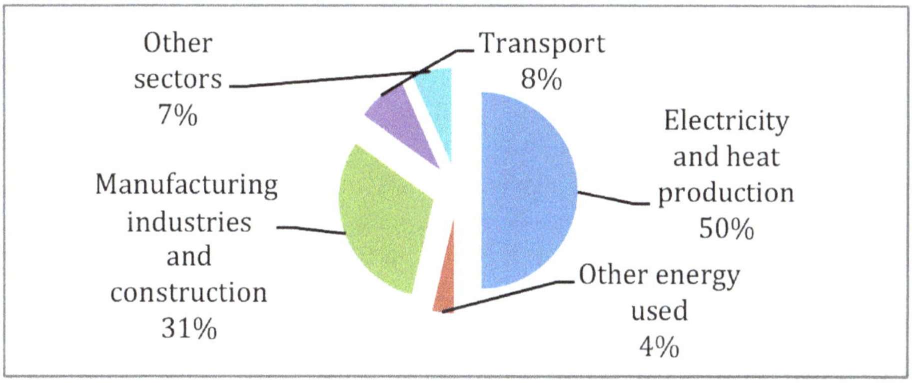

Figure 19.3 Carbon dioxide emissions of various sectors in China

Note: 'Other energy used' includes emissions from petroleum refining, the manufacture of solid fuels, coalmining, oil and gas extraction and other energy-producing industries.

Source: IEA (2014).

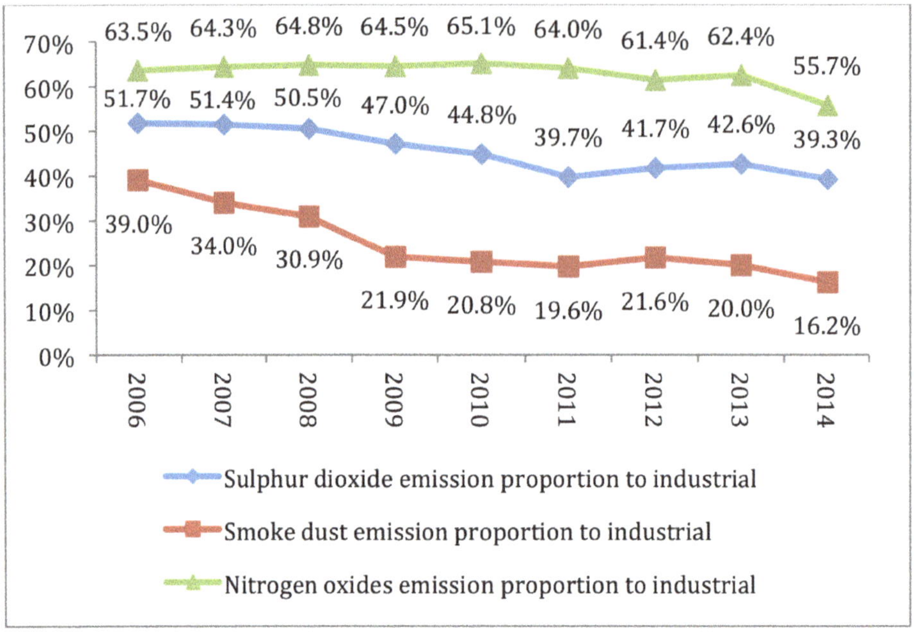

Figure 19.4 Pollutant emissions from China's thermal power generation and their proportion in total industrial emissions

Note: The emissions of sulphur dioxide, nitrogen oxides and dust from the power industry accounted for 34.61 per cent, 13.53 per cent and 37.69 per cent of the national total, respectively, in 2014.

Source: MEP (1998–2014).

Figure 19.5 shows the sulphur dioxide and nitrogen oxides emissions from China's power industry and the US power industry. The nitrogen oxide emissions from China's power industry exceeded those in the United States in 2001, and its sulphur dioxide emissions exceeded those in the United States in 2005. According to the data in Figure 19.6, the carbon dioxide emissions of China's power industry exceeded those of the United States in 2009. According to BP (2015) statistics, however, this transition took place in 2006, which is also when China became the world's largest emitter of carbon dioxide.

The reasons for China's power industry emissions exceeding those of the United States are twofold. First, China's power generation levels reached 5,650 TWh in 2014 (China Electricity Council 2014), compared with 3,880 TWh in the United States (EIA 2014). Second, coal-fired power generation accounts for about 75 per cent of total power generation in China (China Electricity Council 2014)—a much higher share than in the United States, where it is only about 40 per cent (EIA 2014).

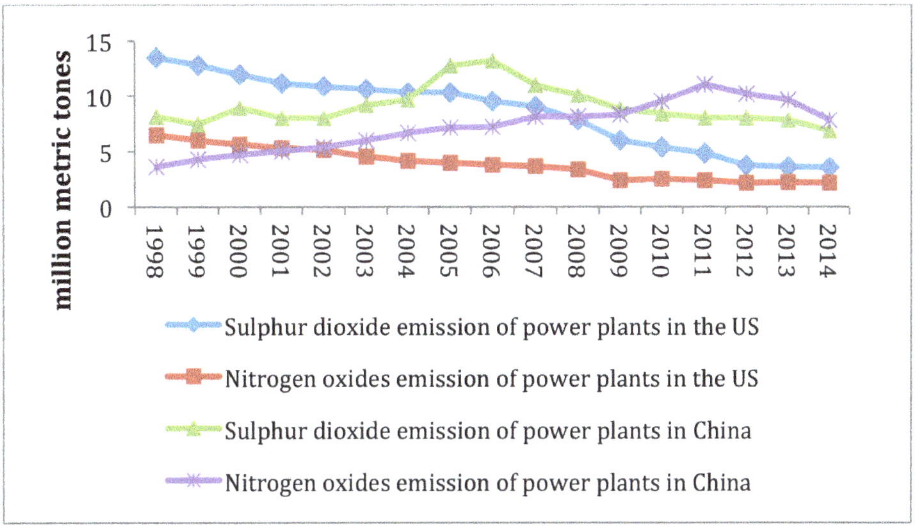

Figure 19.5 Comparison of sulphur dioxide and nitrogen oxide emissions from Chinese and American power industries, 1998–2014

Sources: EIA (1998–2014); MEP (1998–2014).

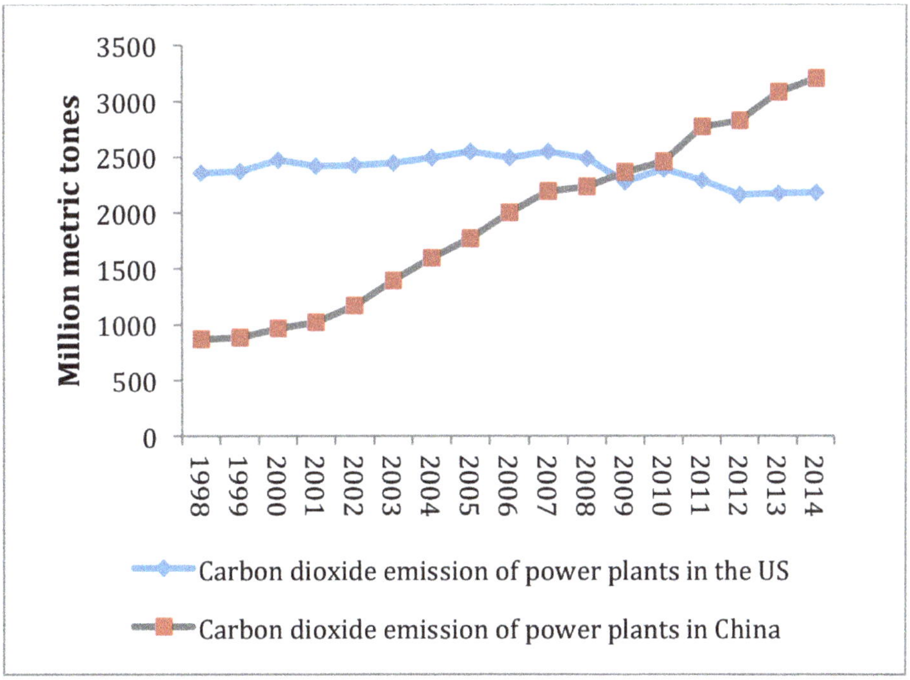

Figure 19.6 Comparison of carbon dioxide emissions from Chinese and American power industries, 1998–2014

Source: EIA (1998–2014); China's carbon dioxide emissions are calculated using data from NBS (1978–2014, 1998–2014a).

Assessing the external environmental cost of China's electricity sector

We use a choice experiment (CE) approach to quantitatively evaluate the external environmental cost of China's coal-based power generation.

The CE approach offers a promising opportunity to measure various environmental economic values as it is concerned with modelling choices that vary across a range of characteristics rather than relying on estimated willingness to pay (WTP) for a single option (Ku and Yoo 2010). CE formats have also been applied to a wider range of environmental problems (for example, Adamowicz et al. 1994; Carlsson and Martinsson 2001; Shrestha and Alavalapati 2004). Moreover, a key advantage of the CE approach compared with an alternative method for evaluating external environmental value, the contingent valuation method, is the ability to elicit the marginal value of attributes of the good or service (Hanley et al. 2002). This is useful because many policies are concerned with changing attribute levels, rather than losing or gaining the environmental good as a whole.

In our CE design, we selected four attributes and the relative levels of each one (Table 19.1). This includes three environmental attributes—reduction of carbon dioxide emissions, of PM2.5 (the particulate matter standard for dust emissions) and of acid rain (sulphur dioxide and nitrogen oxide emissions)—and a price attribute, which is defined as the WTP in terms of environmental improvements at the cost of increasing households' monthly electricity bills. The levels of the price attribute were decided through a pre-test and in consultation with an expert at the University of Western Australia. The lower bound is RMB0 and the upper bound is RMB25 per month.

Table 19.1 Description of attributes and levels

Attribute	Description	Level
CO_2	Percentage reduction of carbon dioxide emissions	1–5% (low) 6–10% (medium) 11–20% (high)
PM2.5	Air quality level, corresponding to percentage reduction of dust emissions	Excellent air quality Good air quality Light pollution Moderate pollution Heavy pollution (status)
Acid rain	Distribution of acid rain, corresponding to percentage reduction of sulphur dioxide and nitrogen oxides	No acid rain Light acid rain Moderate acid rain Relatively severe acid rain Heavy acid rain
Bill	Increase in monthly electricity bill	RMB0, RMB5, RMB10, RMB15, RMB25

Survey data were collected from 600 questionnaires containing six choice sets per respondent. There were three types of questionnaires, and 18 sets in total. After removing the incomplete questionnaires, 411 were suitable for analysis, yielding 2,466 observation points (411 effective respondents × six choice sets).

Sampling was distributed across the eastern (145 samples with 35.28 per cent), western (99 samples with 24.09 per cent) and central (167 samples with 40.63 per cent) parts of China, including urban and rural areas. There were 170 samples from urban areas and 241 from rural areas, accounting for 41.36 per cent and 58.64 per cent respectively of the total. The sample was randomly selected so as to reflect a broad population range in terms of education levels, different ages and different income levels.

Among the important elements in the questionnaires were the various alternatives, which were designed by combining the four attributes given in Table 19.1 based on the different levels of attributes. To solve the key problem encountered in CE information overload—that is, too many alternatives with too many complex attributes—we applied the orthogonal main effects design to reduce the number of possible combinations of attributes. The orthogonal main effects design was implemented using the SPSS software 19.0, and 18 choice sets were selected. Previous literature (for example, Susaeta et al. 2011; Lee and Yoo 2009) and expert recommendation informed our decision for each respondent to fill up to a maximum of four to six choice sets. We divided the 18 choice sets into three questionnaires—Questionnaire 1, Questionnaire 2 and Questionnaire 3—each with six choice sets. An example of the choice sets is presented in Table 19.2.

Table 19.2 Choice set examples

Attribute	Plan 1	Plan 2	Plan 3	Status quo
PM2.5	Good	Excellent	Excellent	Moderate pollution
Acid rain	None	None	Light	Relatively severe
Carbon dioxide	6~10%	1~5%	6~10%	0
Bill	RMB25	RMB25	RMB25	0
Please choose	Plan 1	Plan 2	Plan 3	Status quo

Random utility theory (McFadden 1986) is the principle theory for evaluating environmental externalities. The basic indirect utility for respondent n to choose alternative j in choice set t can be expressed mathematically according to Train (2009) and McFadden (1973) (Equation 19.1).

Equation 19.1

$$U_{njt} = V_{njt} + \varepsilon_{njt} \forall j, t$$

In Equation 19.1, U_{njt} is decomposed into a deterministic component, V_{njt}, and a stochastic component ε_{njt}. V_{njt} is the utility of respondent *n* when he/she chooses alternative *j* in choice set *t*. Furthermore, if $U_{nit} > U_{njt}$ for all $i \neq j$ in choice set *t*, the respondent will choose alternative *i* over *j*. Moreover, V_{njt} can be expressed as Equation 19.2

Equation 19.2

$$V_{njt} = V(X_{njt}, S_n) \forall j, t$$

In Equation 19.2, X_{njt} is a vector comprising the attributes associated with environmental quality and S_n is a vector comprising the socioeconomic attributes of respondents.

The random utility model can be transformed between different classes of choice models by varying assumptions about the distribution of the error term (van der Kroon et al. 2014). If the distribution of the error term, ε_{njt}, is assumed to be independently and identically distributed, extreme value distribution for all *i*, the function of choice probability can be expressed as Equation 19.3.

Equation 19.3

$$P_{nit} = \frac{\exp(V_{nit})}{\sum_j \exp(V_{njt})}$$

Equation 19.3 describes the multinomial logit (MNL) model, which is the most widely used choice model (Train 2009). It is also the most basic of the choice models. The MNL model without interactions is therefore employed as the first step in the analysis.

To explain preference heterogeneity and WTP variations among individuals, it is necessary to consider some individual specific variables (socioeconomic, attitude and experience) (Lim et al. 2014). We applied three different econometric models (MNL, MNL with interaction and random parameters logit: RPL) to analyse respondents' preferences when facing environmental improvement alternatives.

Following Hanemann (1983, 1984), the marginal WTP is specified as Equation 19.4.

Equation 19.4

$$MWTP_{attribute} = -(\beta_{attribute} / \beta_{cost})$$

In Equation 19.4, $\beta_{attribute}$ is the coefficient attached to each environmental attribute, which in this study includes carbon dioxide emission reduction, PM2.5 emission reduction and acid rain reduction. β_{cost} is the coefficient of the bill/cost attribute.

We estimate the marginal WTP of each of the three attributes—PM2.5, acid rain and carbon dioxide—along with the 95 per cent confidence intervals estimated using the procedure proposed by Krinsky and Robb (1986). The marginal WTP of each attribute represents the marginal rate of substitution between the cost and each environmental attribute. The marginal WTP can be estimated by taking the average over the sample distribution of $WTP_{attribute}$ coefficients.

Beyond the marginal WTP estimations for individual environmental attributes, this is also needed to estimate the compensation surplus or welfare change in three future scenarios that are compared with the base of the status quo. We calculated the amount of money required to reach a higher level of environmental quality by comparing the utility of any alternative option with the reference alternative. This is called total WTP, which was calculated as in Equation 19.5 (Hanemann 1984).

Equation 19.5

$$TWTP = -(1 / \beta_{cost})[\ln \sum \exp(V_1) - \ln \sum \exp(V_0)]$$

In Equation 19.5, β_{cost} is the estimated coefficient of cost, V_1 represents the utility of any alternative option and V_0 represents the utility of the reference alternative.

Finally, we obtain the results for the external environmental cost of China's coal-based power generation, which show that respondents have a WTP for the improvement of environmental quality. All the marginal WTPs are significantly positive, indicating that respondents assigned positive values to thermal power environmental improvement. Taking the RPL model results as an example (Table 19.3), the marginal WTP per household for improving PM2.5 levels from moderate pollution (status quo) to excellent air quality, good quality and light pollution is RMB13.3, RMB10.1 and RMB6 per month, respectively. For acid rain levels to shift from severe acid rain to no acid rain, light acid rain and moderate acid rain the WTPs are RMB18.5, RMB13.6 and RMB12.2 per month, respectively; and for carbon dioxide to move from no emission reduction to high emission reduction (11~20 per cent emission reduction), medium emission reduction (6~10 per cent) and light emission reduction (1~5 per cent) is RMB10.8, RMB9.8 and RMB7.2 per month, respectively.

Table 19.3 Marginal WTP values for MNL, MNL with interactions and RPL

	MNL	MNL with interactions	RPL
PM2.5(Excellent)	16.258*** (12.064, 20.453)	16.105*** (11.850, 20.359)	13.282*** (5.356, 21.207)
PM2.5(Good)	15.7793*** (11.188, 20.371)	15.516*** (11.148, 19.885)	10.110*** (3.193, 17.027)
PM2.5(Light)	5.983*** (1.618, 10.348)	5.894*** (1.788, 10.000)	5.982*** (1.608, 10.356)
No acid rain	17.612*** (10.310, 24.914)	17.614*** (10.625, 24.602)	18.452*** (9.120, 27.785)
Light acid rain	12.580*** (4.986, 20.173)	12.694*** (5.435, 19.952)	13.628*** (6.098, 21.157)
Moderate acid rain	10.254** (2.279, 18.228)	10.124** (2.232, 18.016)	12.178*** (3.993, 20.363)
CO_2 reduction (11%~20%)	9.727*** (4.604, 14.849)	10.011*** (4.935, 15.088)	10.757*** (5.037, 16.477)
CO_2 reduction (6%~10%)	9.010*** (4.082, 13.939)	9.078*** (4.345, 13.810)	9.836*** (4.565, 15.108)
CO_2 reduction (1%~5%)	5.136** (0.729, 9.544)	5.269** (1.036, 9.501)	7.223*** (2.084, 12.362)

** significant at the 5 per cent level
*** significant at the 1 per cent level

Adding up the above estimates, the total WTP for improvements that reach the best-case scenario from the status quo is a monthly amount of RMB40. To equate this to thermal power generation scales, we refer to data from the National Energy Administration (NEA 2015), which suggest the average electricity consumption of a Chinese resident is 6,928 TWh per year. According to the *China family development report* (National Health and Family Planning Commission 2014), there were 430 million households in China in 2014; hence, annual electricity consumption per household is 1,611 kWh per year or 134 kWh per month. From these numbers, we can estimate the total WTP for improvement to the best-case scenario is RMB0.30 per kWh. This indicates that the external cost of thermal power generation in China is RMB0.30/kWh.

To ensure these results are credible, we need to make a theoretical and standard empirical validity check.

The theoretical validity check tests the consistency between the results in this study and the results expected according to theory. According to the data for residential electricity consumption in 2014 (6,928 TWh) and the number of households (430 million), the average electricity consumption for each household in China can be calculated (134 kWh in 2014). Meanwhile, we know that the residential electricity fee in China is about RMB0.6/kWh; hence, the average monthly household electricity fee in 2014 was RMB80.4. According to this study's results, however, respondents are willing to pay an extra RMB40 to reduce the environmental impacts of electricity generation. Since the premium accounts for about 50 per cent of the total electricity fee per month, it is consistent with the theoretical anticipated scope (no more than 50 per cent).

Empirically, we can also compare our results with those of similar studies. Mahapatra et al. (2012) calculated the environmental cost of thermal power plants in India using a dose-response model. The result was an external cost of RMB0.26/kWh, which is lower than but close to our result. Georgakellos (2010) evaluated the environmental cost of thermal power plants in Greece based on the Ecosense LE method, and found an external cost of RMB0.26/kWh, which is also close to our result. The European Commission (1995) used the ExternE method to calculate the environmental cost of thermal power plants in the European Union, and identified a range of RMB0.23~0.34/kWh. The International Energy Agency analysed the environmental cost of various kinds of power generation in 19 countries and found the environmental cost of thermal power plants is RMB0.20~0.45/kWh. Our result is within the scope of these studies.

The environmental footprint of China's electricity market reform

China's electric utility industry can be characterised by two major reform stages. During the first stage, from 1949 to 1984, the industry (like other energy industries) was treated simply as a means to an end—in other words, as a subordinate sector whose goal was to support the development of the downstream industrial sector. As a result, the performance of the industry itself, and improvements in its management efficiency, received little attention. In general, a highly centralised administrative mechanism was deemed suitable given those instrumental aims.

Stage one of China's market: 1949–84

Within this era, four critical phases can be identified that had a great impact on the management of China's power generation and distribution. The first occurred in the 1950s, when the Soviets had a major influence on the country, leading to a highly centralised administrative mechanism that would dominate the sector for years to come. The second was the disastrous Great Leap Forward period, from 1958 to 1960, during which the Chinese Government required vast increases in iron and steel production, and energy consumption increased rapidly. The third key phase was the Cultural Revolution, from 1966 to 1976, during which China's economic development was largely blocked and energy demand increased more slowly. The fourth phase was the market reform era that began in 1978. From this time on, China's economy embarked on a rapid development path, but power supply shortages, until the mid-1980s, became increasingly severe.

Throughout the first stage of China's industrialisation phase following opening and reform, electricity prices were held below average costs of production (Huang 2009). This meant it was impossible for the sector to finance its own investment, which ultimately seriously hindered the industry's development. Under the socialist economy of this period, industry and employment were organised around work units (*danwei*), which paid for the electricity used not only at work, but also in the *danwei* housing where workers lived. Electricity was considered an entitlement and, as a result of the very low electricity price, people used power profligately. In a parallel with the government-supplied water pouring out of the taps, which was also essentially unpriced, electricity was simply there to be freely used.

In the mid-1980s, power shortages became so common as to have serious negative impacts on industrial production, and on citizens' living standards. Rationing was implemented and homes and places of work were required to minimise their use of power during the day so that factories would have sufficient power. By the late 1980s, even in large cities, students were often unable to read in university libraries in the late afternoon due to power shortages.

Stage two of China's market: Reform

To mitigate the huge imbalance between the quantity of electricity being demanded at below-cost prices and the generating capacity available, from the mid-1980s, the Chinese Government issued a series of important regulatory policies. In 1985, it issued two policy documents entitled 'Interim provision on promotion fund-raising for electricity investment and implementing multiple electricity prices' and 'The measures of implementing multiple electricity prices'. The two policies, the major elements of which are outlined in Ma and He (2008), broadly succeeded in solving the electricity generation shortage. In fact, by the mid-1990s and over the first decade of the twenty-first century, China experienced a surplus in electricity supply (Huang 2009). This was due partly to the rapid growth in supply unleashed by parallel and new investment policies and partly to the fall in electricity demand instigated by the East Asian

Financial Crisis in 1997. Regardless, the excess supply led to strict control of electricity investment by the Chinese Government from 1998 to 2001, which in turn resulted in a renewed electricity supply shortage in 2002 (Huang 2009).

The new period of limited supply was, however, short-lived. The breakup in 2002 of the vertical monopoly held by the State Power Corporation (SPC) prompted a second investment rush in electricity generation in China. In December 2002, the SPC was dismantled and five large mutually autonomous power generation corporations were established. The competition for resources between the five corporations greatly accelerated investment in power capacity in 2003, as can be seen in Figure 19.7.

With rapid growth in electricity capacity, the supply shortage was mitigated to some extent; however, it was not resolved completely until 2011 because of a related shortage in the supply of coal. In sum, during the second half of the twentieth century, China's centralised management of the electricity system led to severe problems in the allocation of energy resources, as would be predicted by standard price theory. By 1985, persistent shortages had instigated various reforms that helped to bring forth new generation capacity. Nevertheless, the continued reliance on government-controlled prices rather than markets led to dramatic swings from power shortages to excess supply and back again.

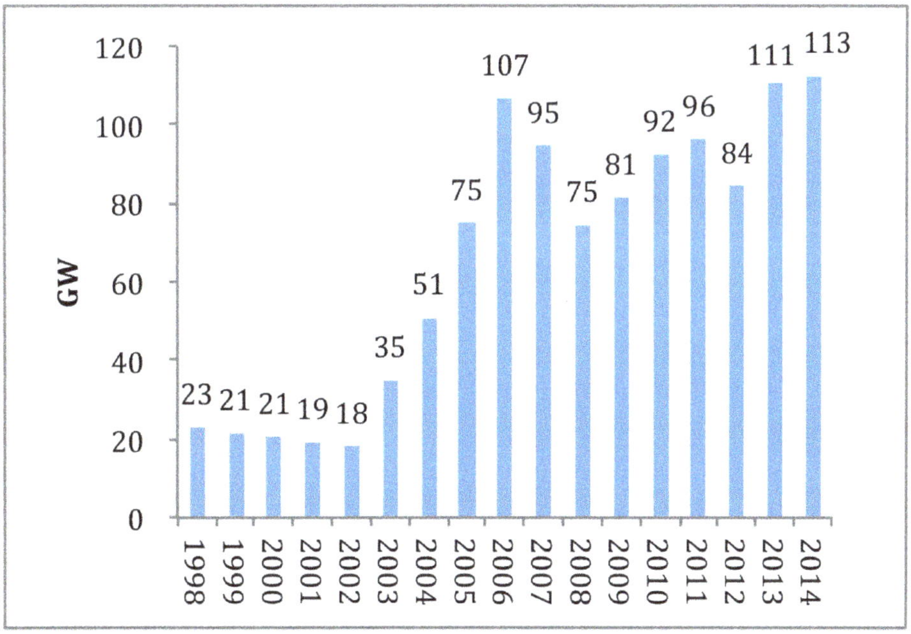

Figure 19.7 Additional power capacity added each year in China

Source: China Electricity Council (2014).

Electricity price reform and its impact on the environment

To resolve the serious shortage pre-1985 in electricity supply, the Chinese Government implemented a pricing system for new power plants under the 'capital and interest price' (in 1985) and 'operation period price' (in 1996) initiatives. The two prices are cost-plus regulation prices (or rate of return prices). Under such mechanisms, profit was guaranteed, greatly encouraging investment in power generation plants. On the other hand, new plants were opportunistic by overstating their cost to get a higher grid price. Moreover, most plants built during that period were high in cost and low in energy efficiency, and thus created serious environmental pollution. Under the capital and interest pricing mechanism, the investment costs could be recovered in a short time. Most investors chose to construct small units because of the lower capital requirements and simpler approval procedures, even though small units were low in efficiency. By the end of 1996, the average thermal power unit capacity was only 46 MW (Ren 2002). More specific data from the China Electricity Council show that by the end of 2014 thermal power unit capacity above 300 MW accounted for about 77.7 per cent of total thermal power capacity; units above 600 MW accounted for 41.5 per cent; and most units with less than 100 MW capacity had been shut to improve energy efficiency.

The Chinese Government has created a yardstick power price (similar to a fixed power price), characterised by a capped power price, since 2004. Up to this point, there had been growing support among both academics and policy practitioners for price-cap regulation as an alternative to rate-of-return regulation in the relative regulatory policy discussions (Baumol and Sidak 1994). Joskow (1991) argued that incentive mechanisms aimed at promoting efficient (and cleaner) supply had focused on 'yardstick' comparisons for specific components of electricity costs.

Electricity investment reform and its impact on the environment

The 'Interim provision on promotion fund-raising for electricity investment and implementing multiple electricity prices' policy document was issued in 1985. Part of its aim was to encourage various investors—including private, local government and foreign investors—to access electric power generation plants. Through this policy and to induce more investment in power generation, the Chinese Government allowed a very high rate of return on power generation plants (Ma and He 2008). Specifically, the rate of return for foreign investors was 13–18 per cent and even 20 per cent (Ou et al. 2009)—much higher than the average at that time.

The most significant in-principle contribution of the 1985 investment reforms was to attract vast capital for power plant construction in a short time. One specific and remarkable effect of this reform, in principle and efficiency, would be the construction of the Ertan Hydropower Station, which started in 1991 and was completed in 2000. Investors in Ertan included the State Development Investment Corporation, Sichuan Investment Group Corporation and Sichuan Electric Power Corporation. The other prominent hydropower station in China is also the largest hydro project in the world: the Three Gorges Project. Much of the investment for this came from the public via the issuing of bonds and stock.

From the mid-1980s, such investments saw a rapid increase in total generating capacity. Within a decade severe shortages in power supply had been nearly eliminated—but only temporarily. Moreover, the economic losses caused by power shortages in the years up to the mid-1990s were huge. In 1993, $27.6 billion of industrial value added was estimated to have been lost to power shortages—the equivalent of 7 per cent of gross domestic product (Li and Dorian 1995). Rapid growth in power generation investment from the mid-1990s, in contrast, prevented the continuation of such huge losses.

Unfortunately, to circumvent complicated central government approval processes and also to minimise risk, the most commonly implemented power generation plants had a capacity of no more than 200 MW. Large-scale generation plants, of 600 MW or more capacity, made up the smallest share of new plants before the mid-1990s (Figure 19.8). From this perspective, the reforms in 1985, while spurring necessary investments in the sector, had a negative impact on the scale-related environmental and economic efficiencies of the industry.

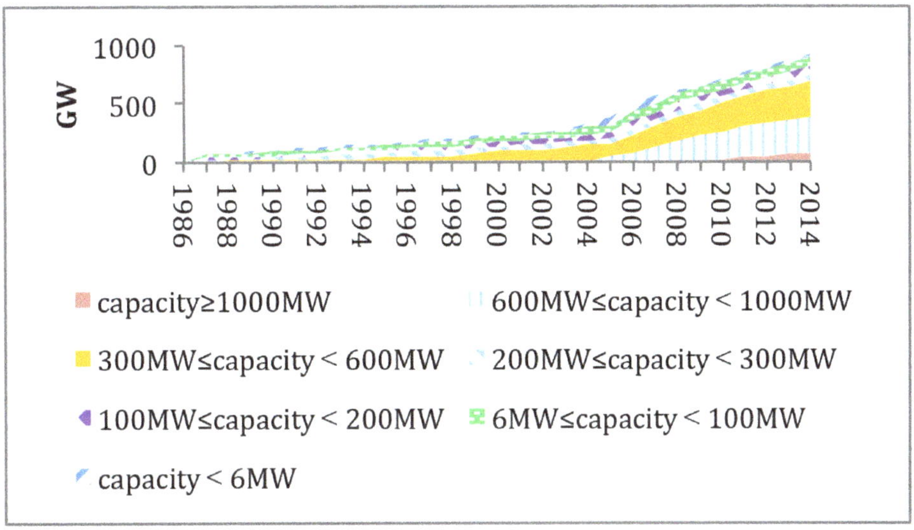

Figure 19.8 Change in size of thermal power generating units

Source: China Electricity Council (2014).

Vertical monopoly reforms and their environmental impact

In 2002, the SPC was dismantled and five big independent power generation corporations were set up: Huaneng Group, Datang Group, Huadian Corporation, Guodian Corporation and Power Investment Corporation. Their assets came from the disbanded SPC and they have been totally independent of the State Grid Corporation since 2003. This end to the vertical monopoly of the sector had the effect of promoting a second wave of investment in power generation in China. From 2003 to 2007, new power plants were established at a rapid rate.

Another reason for ending the vertical monopoly in 2002 was that the efficiency of China's electricity utility had already improved greatly. Alongside those efficiency gains, China's electricity sector had also shifted towards cleaner production. The power plants built after 2002 were mostly large-scale generation units (Figure 19.7). Figure 19.9 shows that since 1997, China's sulphur dioxide emissions from the electric power industry have decreased rapidly, particularly after 2005. These changes are attributed to two factors, the first of which was policy. China's electricity reform after the mid-1990s attached greater importance to the improvement of efficiency (quality) than to increasing power supply (quantity). The second factor was the corporate pursuit of profit. With the enforcement of a yardstick grid price and also competition, corporations with higher efficiency received the greatest benefits. Energy efficiency in power generation has since improved remarkably.

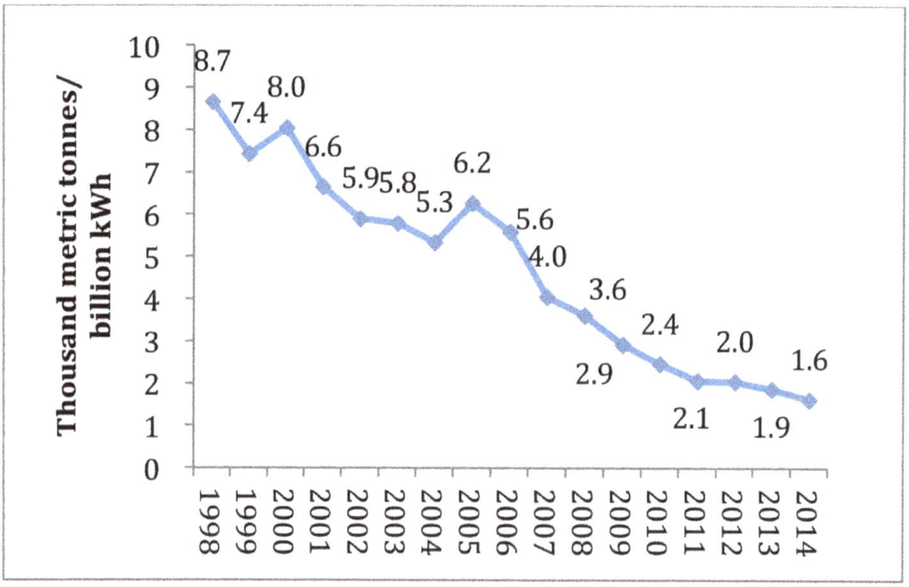

Figure 19.9 Sulphur dioxide emissions from the thermal electric power industry in China

Source: MEP (1998–2014).

China's environmental regulation and its impact on power industry carbon dioxide emissions

China's environmental regulation policies

China has a long history of strong, centralised government, so most of its environmental regulations follow a command-and-control approach. Regulations relating specifically to improving energy efficiency include 'The notice on several issues of improving China's energy efficiency' in 1979, 'The notice on progressively setting up the evaluation institute of integrated energy consumption' in 1980 and 'The specific requirements of energy saving for industrial and mining enterprises and cities (trial)' in 1981.

With regard to environmental protection, *The Managerial Guidelines for Standards of Environmental Protection in China* were promulgated in 1983. This set standards for air, water and soil quality and also for pollutant discharge and environmental monitoring. In the 1990s, as concerns about environmental protection increased, the regulators of China's power sector and other pollution-intensive industries paid more attention to pollutant control. For example, in 1991 China published *Standards for Air Pollutant Discharge from Thermal Power Plants GB13223-1991*, which was revised in 1996, 2003 and 2011. This is a performance-based regulation and the latest revision established several standards for pollutant discharge, including for the upper limit for soot emissions of 30 mg per cubic metre; 100 mg/cu m for sulphur dioxide emissions from newly installed boilers; 200 mg/cu m for sulphur dioxide from existing boilers; 100 mg/cu m for nitrogen oxides; and 0.03 mg/cu m for mercury and its compounds. Technology-based regulations were also ratified during this time to curb pollution from the power industry. For example, 'The division program of acid rain and SO_2 control zones', published in January 1998, required all thermal plants under construction and in future to install desulphurisation facilities (Li and Colombier 2011).

Although not a primary approach, market-based regulation (MBR) was also developed to promote environmental protection in the power industry. For example, in 1982, 'The interim measures on pollution charges' stipulated that firms should pay RMB40 for every tonne of sulphur dioxide or nitrogen oxide emissions above specified standards, and RMB3–10 per thousand cubic metres of sulphuric acid mist, lead and mercury exceeding specified standards. This is a typical pollution charge system. Meanwhile, government subsidies (GSs) were often implemented by increasing the regulated electricity prices. For example, to support power industry desulphurisation and denitrification, China increased the tariff by RMB15/MWh in 2004 and by RMB8/MWh in 2013.

Although these subsidies were not sufficient to cover all pollution abatement costs (Wang et al. 2012), they serve as important economic support for corporate efforts to reduce sulphur dioxide and nitrogen oxide emissions.

In addition to pollution charges and subsidies, two market-based policies have been implemented or attempted: the Clean Development Mechanism (CDM) and the cap and trade system. To promote the development of the CDM, the Chinese Government promulgated 'The operation and management measures of CDM projects (trial)' in 2004. That same year, the first CDM project, the HuiTengXiLe wind farm in Inner Mongolia, began operation. China's CDM projects focus mainly on the power industry. By the end of 2010, renewable energy sector CDM projects accounted for 71 per cent of the total approved projects (Yang et al. 2011).

As for cap and trade, under the Eleventh FYP (2006–10), the Chinese Ministry of Environmental Protection (MEP) prioritised the promotion of key pollutant emission trading rights. The MEP specifically selected eight provinces and provincial-level municipalities—Jiangsu, Zhejiang, Tianjin, Hubei, Hunan, Shanxi, Inner Mongolia and Chongqing—as pilot areas for sulphur dioxide emission rights trading. In practice, however, there has been little substantial voluntary trading of sulphur dioxide emission rights. The majority of the few transactions that have occurred have been government facilitated. As for the trading of carbon dioxide emission rights, the first pilot program was set up in Shenzhen in June 2013. By the end of April 2014, six provincial entities had followed in Shenzhen's footsteps: Shanghai, Beijing, Tianjin, Chongqing, Guangdong and Hubei. The trading volume of carbon dioxide emissions, however, accounts for only a limited proportion of national carbon dioxide emissions.

In sum, command-and-control regulation (CCR) still dominates the environmental regulation of China's power industry, although MBR and government subsidy (GS) are rising in prominence. In general, different types of environmental regulations may have different influences on corporate efficiency and environmental performance. In the following subsections, I empirically analyse the impact of various policy shifts in China on the corporate efficiency and environmental performance of the country's power plants. From the results, I offer policy suggestions for promoting the sustainable development of China's power industry with consideration of environmental issues.

Sample and data collection

The data were collected from two major sources: *Electric power industry statistics compiled* (China Electricity Council 2014) and my study group's survey of power plant managers (Table 19.4). China Electricity Council (2014) provides information on power capacity and coal consumption for 2011 and 2012. To the best of our knowledge, plant-level employee numbers are not publicly available. Therefore, we estimated the number of employees based on the labour quota used in the power industry. Specifically, we followed the 'Labour force quota for thermal power plants' (SPC 1998), the 'Labour force quota for general thermal power plants' and the 'Labour force quota for new thermal power plants' (China Huadian Group Corporation 2008) to estimate employee numbers across all power plants. Three factors play significant roles in this estimation: power plant capacity, when the power plants were established and the capacity of each unit within a power plant. Labour force information in the questionnaire survey was also collected. Specifically, in the questionnaire, respondents were asked to allocate their power plant into one of four capacity-related categories: less than 100 employees, 100–500 employees, 501–2,000 employees and more than 2,000 employees. Labour force information from the survey is used in the regression analyses.

The survey, conducted in 2012, involved questionnaires being sent to 308 power plants in 22 of China's 31 provinces. The sample covers power plants across most regions of China (Figure 19.10). Moreover, the sample covers various sized power plants (Figure 19.2) and all five power corporations. Hence, the sample covers the full range of power plant types in China.

To ensure survey accuracy, the related literature was reviewed (for example, Milliman and Prince 1989; Liu 2009). In addition, we interviewed nine leaders from the China Guodian Corporation, the China Huadian Corporation and the China State Grid Energy Research Institute specialising in issues related to energy savings and emission reductions. Their suggestions and comments helped us refine our questionnaire.

The survey asked plant managers to assess their perceived influence from three policy perspectives—CCR, MBR and GS (the items for capturing the three types of policies are shown in Appendix Table A19.1)—and to note when the power plant was established.

To measure the perceived influence of CCR, MBR and GS, we developed a set of questions using the Likert scale (Likert 1932), which is the most commonly used method for perception measurements (Zhao et al. 2015). Oaster (1989) indicated that a seven-point scale showed the highest reliability. Therefore, the seven-point Likert scale is used in this study.

Table 19.4 Variables and the data sources

	Variable description	Variable name	Data source
Dependent variables	Efficiency change	EF	Calculated by author
	Carbon dioxide emissions	CO_2	Calculated by author
Independent variables	Command-and-control regulation	CCR	Questionnaires
	Market-based regulation	MBR	Questionnaires
	Government subsidy	GS	Questionnaires
Other variables	Power capacity	PC	China Electricity Council (2014)
	Number of employees	SC	Questionnaires and calculated by author
	Power plant age	T	Questionnaires
	Coal consumption	CC	China Electricity Council (2014)
	Power generation	PG	China Electricity Council (2014)

The survey was conducted in two formats: through email and through on-the-spot surveys. Firms were selected according to existing contacts and the questionnaires were distributed to leaders of these firms responsible for making strategy and other management decisions. The second method was an on-the-spot survey. Survey opportunities provided by training courses for leading power firm cadres (who come from all over China) at the North China Electric Power University were also maximised. The topics of these courses focused on firm strategy and management issues. Hence, participants were leaders responsible for making strategy and other management decisions in their firms.

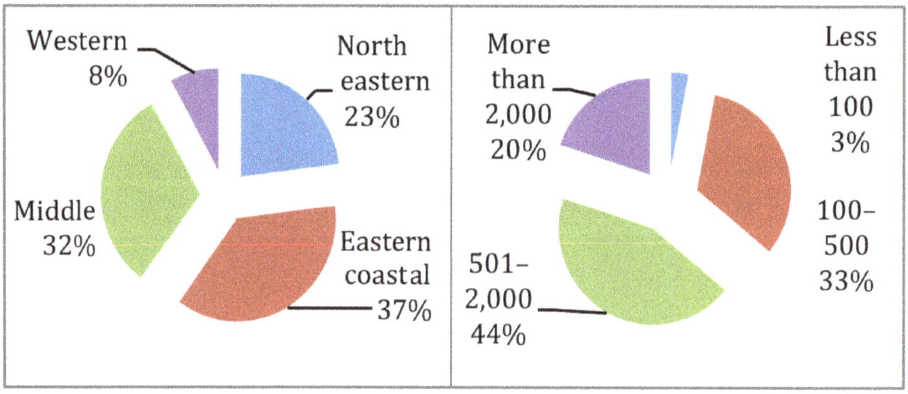

Figure 19.10 Region and size distribution of sampled power plants

Source: Created by the author.

Questionnaires were deemed invalid mainly if there was a non-response to a significant portion of the survey questions or all questions had the same answer. In total, 172 were returned and 137 were valid (for a 55.84 per cent response rate and 79.65 per cent validity rate). Fortunately, invalid questionnaires were randomly distributed across firms, implying that invalid questionnaires do not bring a systematic bias into the evaluation.

Carbon dioxide emissions

Power plant-level carbon dioxide emissions data are not publicly available. We estimated this data based on the method recommended by the Intergovernmental Panel on Climate Change (IPCC). We specifically calculated the carbon dioxide emissions for 137 power plants in China, a selection of which is outlined in Table 19.5.

Table 19.5 The carbon dioxide emissions of sampled power plants

Summary statistics	Carbon dioxide emissions (thousands of tonnes)	Power generation (100 GWh)	Carbon dioxide emissions from power generation (thousands of tonnes/100 GWh)
Mean	8,095.08	56.58	171.64
Median	4,512.29	33.7	140.53
Std dev.	13,371.58	101.10	160.92

Types of environmental regulation

In line with the existing research (for example, Milliman and Prince 1989; Liu 2009; Blind 2012), our chapter categorises environmental regulations into three types: CCR, MBR and GS. CCR is mandatory and allows managers very little freedom. Previous studies (Walley and Whitehead 1994; Liu 2009; Testa et al. 2011) and expert interviews indicate that it is logical to focus on five types of CCR: emission standards, fines, supervision, environmental assessment systems and production technology standards (Appendix Table A19.1). We specifically asked managers to assess the extent to which they were strongly influenced by these five types of regulation.

MBR, meanwhile, sends market signals and firms have flexibility to decide the appropriate level of pollution abatement in response to these signals. Based on previous research (Magat 1979; Downing and White 1986; Milliman and Prince 1989; Walley and Whitehead 1994) and interviews with experts who are familiar with the power industry in China, we focused on three types of marked-based environmental policies: tax credits (tax-exempt financing, one type of GS), CDM and emissions trading systems (Appendix Table A19.1). We asked managers to assess the extent to which they were strongly influenced by these three types of policies.

The model

We construct the model for environmental regulations on carbon dioxide emissions as follows (Equation 19.6).

Equation 19.6

$$CO_2 = \alpha + \beta_1 CCR + \beta_2 MBR + \beta_3 GS + \beta_4 PC + \beta_5 T + \beta_6 CCR * GS + \beta_7 MBR * GS \\ + \beta_8 SC + \beta_9 AP * SC + \beta_{10} MBR * SC + \beta_{11} CCR * SC + \varepsilon$$

In Equation 19.6, *PC* represents power capacity; *T* is the age of the power plant; *SC* is power plant size; and ε captures other factors that affect efficiency but do not correlate with explanatory variables in the model.

We included age, size and power demand in our regression analyses as control variables. Joskow and Schmalensee (1987) pointed out that the technical profile of generation units, such as age and size, could be potentially significant factors affecting efficiency. Hence, we introduced the age of a power plant into our model and defined it as the calendar year minus the year of initial operation. As for size, we divided enterprises into two groups: power plants with 500 or fewer employees are defined as medium or small enterprises, and those with more than 500 employees are defined as large ones. We coded the size variable as a binary: zero for medium or small enterprises and 1 for large enterprises.

The literature has highlighted that power demand has an impact on carbon dioxide emissions (Declercq et al. 2011; Zhao et al. 2013). We used power capacity to measure this. One notable feature of China's power market is its rapid upgrading due to increasing pressure for energy conservation and emissions reduction, at the same time as increasing power demand. The situation is prominently reflected in the 'build large and shut down the small' policy implemented across China's power industry in the late 1990s. In this context, the focus is on replacing small power units with large ones, which has resulted in capacity change at the plant level in line with increasing power demand. As a result, we chose power capacity as one of our control variables.

Findings

Table 19.6 presents the results of our regression analysis. These suggest that CCR has no significant impact on the dependent variable, carbon dioxide emissions. This may be due to the fact that China's command-and-control environmental regulations on power plants focus primarily on the installation of desulphurisation and denitrification equipment, as well as on the emissions standards for sulphur dioxide, soot and nitrogen oxides. To date, no command-and-control policies for carbon dioxide emissions reduction exist.

Table 19.6 also shows that the coefficients for market-based and government subsidy policies are negative and statistically significant, which tells us that power plants that perceive a strong influence from market-based policies and subsidies have lower carbon dioxide emissions intensity than others.

Table 19.6 Impact of environmental regulations on power plants' carbon dioxide emissions

Variable	Coefficient	Std. error	t-Statistic	Prob.
CCR	0.3623	0.4606	0.7865	0.4335
MBR	–1.0118***	0.3211	–3.1517	0.0022
GS	–1.1396***	0.3241	–3.5163	0.0007
CCR•GS	–0.1529	0.2468	–0.6195	0.5370
MBR•GS	–0.1193	0.1965	–0.6070	0.5453
TIME	0.0433***	0.0105	4.1315	0.0001
PC	0.0162***	0.0021	7.5493	0.0000
SC	2.5187***	0.3867	6.5126	0.0000
CCR•SC	–0.4317	0.5454	–0.7916	0.4306
MBR•SC	0.7416*	0.4019	1.8454	0.0681
GS•SC	1.1480***	0.4032	2.8476	0.0054
C	5.1898***	0.0237	219.1719	0.0000
R-squared	0.2734			
Adjusted R-squared	0.1884			
F-statistic	3.2160			
Prob. (F-statistic)	0.0009			

*** significant at the 1 per cent level
* significant at the 10 per cent level

It is interesting to find that, generally, larger power plants have a higher carbon dioxide emissions intensity than smaller ones. More importantly, the impact of market-based environmental policies and subsidies was somewhat smaller for larger power plants than for small ones. In this study, we measured power plant size by the number of employees. Power plants with more employees, in general, had a longer history. With old facilities, higher carbon dioxide emissions intensity is common, as is the difficulty of lowering emissions in response to market-based environmental policies or subsidies. This is consistent with the time coefficient, which was statistically positive and showed that older power plants have a higher carbon dioxide emissions intensity.

Conclusion: China's electric power industry's green future

China faces a great challenge to improve the quality of its environment while maintaining economic growth at a relatively high level. China's electric power sector is both highly energy and highly emission intensive, especially given the ongoing domination of coal-fired power stations. Greening China's power industry is crucial to realising the national goals for 'green' economic development. From this study, we know that power market reform and environmental regulation play significant roles in the promotion of energy efficiency and emissions mitigation in China's power industry. We found particularly that MBR has an important impact on efficiency improvement and carbon dioxide emissions reduction among China's power plants.

The Chinese Government has realised that expanding market-oriented mechanisms can play an important role in effective distribution of resources, and also in strengthening the role of MBR in the environmental regulations governing the power sector. China has implemented cap and trade for carbon dioxide emissions in seven pilot provinces and cities; however, some improvements should be made to help the system function better. For example, further study is required into how to rationally identify the carbon emission factor, which is crucial for measuring carbon dioxide emissions and deciding the trading amount. Another challenge is to appropriately determine a carbon dioxide emissions quota for power generators. This is critical for controlling the risk of buying carbon dioxide emission rights for some coal-based plants. In sum, MBR in China's power industry is still at a nascent stage, and we need to pay more attention to the use of this type of policy instrument in developing future regulation instead of relying solely on CCR.

Concurrently, China's policymakers need to coordinate different policy instruments. One of the significant characteristics of China's power sector is that most enterprises are government-owned. Moreover, CCR is still an essential instrument with which to guide power enterprises in green development. It would be interesting and pertinent for scholars and policymakers in China to explore how to better coordinate MBR and CCR to improve future outcomes.

Finally, to promote the green development of China's power industry, improving the share of renewable energy generation is crucial. China's renewable energy generation share in total power generation is currently limited, although this capacity has increased rapidly since 2006. Nonetheless, by 2015, the wind power and solar power generation proportions in total power generation were only 3.3 per cent and 0.70 per cent respectively.[1] Improving the proportion of renewable energy in the power generation mix and reducing dependence on coal should therefore be the choice for China's future power development strategy. To realise such a strategy, again, both MBR and CCR should be coordinated to construct a flexible power system that is suitable for large-scale renewable energy integration, thus promoting continuous greening of China's electric power industry.

References

Adamowicz, W., Louviere, J. and Williams, M. (1994), Combining revealed and stated preference methods for valuing environmental amenities, *Journal of Environmental Economics and Management*, 26(3): 271–292.

Aragón-Correa, J., Hurtado-Torres, N., Sharma, S. and García-Morales, V. J. (2008), Environmental strategy and performance in small firms: A resource-based perspective, *Journal of Environmental Management*, 86(1): 88–103.

Baumol, W. J. and Sidak, J. G. (1994), *Toward competition in local telephony*, Cambridge, Mass.: The MIT Press.

Blind, K. (2012), The influence of regulations on innovation: A quantitative assessment for OECD countries, *Research Policy*, 41(2): 319–400.

BP (2015), *Statistical review of world energy*, London: BP.

Brian, S. (1995), Firm-level responses to government regulation: Theoretical and research approaches, *Journal of Management*, 21(3): 495–514.

Carlsson, F. and Martinsson, P. (2001), Do hypothetical and actual marginal willingness to pay differ in choice experiments: Application to the valuation of the environment, *Journal of Environmental Economics and Management*, 41(2): 179–192.

1 Data source: The report on the current development situation of China's wind and solar power issued by the National Energy Commission (not available for public distribution).

China Electricity Council (2014), *Electric power industry statistics compiled*, Beijing: China Electricity Council.

China Electric Power Construction Enterprise Association (2014), *Electric power construction industry annual report 2013*, Beijing: China Electric Power Construction Enterprise Association.

China Huadian Group Corporation (2008), *Labour force quota for new thermal power plants*, Beijing: China Huadian Group Corporation.

China New Energy Chamber of Commerce (2015), *Proceedings of the 9th China New Energy International Forum*, Beijing, 15–16 April. Available from: docin.com/p-1467494284.html.

China Renewable Energy Society (2015), *Global new energy development report*, Beijing: China Renewable Energy Society.

Declercq, B., Delarue, E. and William, D. (2011), Impact of the economic recession on the European power sector's CO_2 emissions, *Energy Policy*, 39(3): 1677–1686.

Downing, P. B. and White, L. J. (1986), Innovation in pollution control, *Journal of Environmental Economics and Management*, 13(1): 18–29.

Energy Information Administration (EIA) (2014), *Electric Power Annual*. Available from: www.eia.gov/electricity/annual/.

European Commission (1995), *Externalities of energy*, 6.01.0.10/66 (KOSTEN), Brussels: European Commission.

Georgakellos, D. A. (2010), Impact of a possible environmental externalities internalisation on energy prices: The case of the greenhouse gases from the Greek electricity sector, *Energy Economics*, 32(1): 202–209.

Greene, D. L., Patterson, P. D., Singh, M. and Li, J. (2005), Feebates, rebates and gas-guzzler taxes: A study of incentives for increased fuel economy, *Energy Policy*, 33(6): 757–775.

Hanemann, W. M. (1983), Marginal welfare measures for discrete choice models, *Economics Letters*, 13: 129–136.

Hanemann, W. M. (1984), Welfare evaluations in contingent valuation experiments with discrete response, *American Journal of Agricultural Economics*, 66: 332–341.

Hanley, N., Mourato, S. and Wright, R. E. (2002), Choice modelling approaches: A superior alternative for environmental valuation?, *OECD Economic Surveys*, 15(3): 435–462. doi: 10.1111/1467-6419.00145.

Hitchens, D., Clausen, J., Trainor, M., Keil, M. and Thankapan, S. (2003), Competitiveness, environmental performance and management of SMEs, *Greener Management International*, 44: 45–57.

Huang, S. Zh. (2009), Review and forecast of Chinese electricity price reform. *Journal of Price Theory and Practice*,5: 11–14.

International Energy Agency (IEA) (2014), *CO_2 emissions from fuel combustion*, Paris: IEA.

Joskow, P. L. (1991), The role of transaction cost economics in antitrust and public utility regulatory policies, *Journal of Law Economics and Organization*, 7: 53–83.

Joskow, P. and Schmalensee, R. (1987), The performance of coal-burning electric generating units in the United States: 1960–1980, *Journal of Applied Economics*, 2(2): 85–109.

Kaiser, H. F. (1974), An index of factorial simplicity, *Psychometrika*, 39(1): 31–36.

Krinsky, I. and Robb, A. L. (1986), On approximating the statistical properties of elasticities, *Review of Economics & Statistics*, 68(4): 715–719.

Ku, S.-J. and Yoo, S.-H. (2010), Willingness to pay for renewable energy investment in Korea: A choice experiment study, *Renewable & Sustainable Energy Reviews*, 14(8): 2196–2201.

Lee, J.-S. and Yoo, S.-H. (2009), Measuring the environmental costs of tidal power plant construction: A choice experiment study, *Energy Policy*, 37: 5069–5074.

Li, B. and Dorian, J. (1995), Change in Chinese power sector, *Energy Policy*, 23(7): 619–626.

Li, J. and Colombier, M. (2011), Economic instruments for mitigating carbon emissions: Scaling up carbon finance in China's building sector, *Climate Change*, 107: 567–591.

Likert, R. (1932), A technique for the measurement of attitudes, *Archives of Psychology*, 140: 5–53.

Lim, S. Y., Lim, K. M. and Yoo, S.-H. (2014), External benefits of waste-to-energy in Korea: A choice experiment study, *Renewable & Sustainable Energy Reviews*, 34: 588–595.

Liu, Y. (2009), Investigating external environmental pressure on firms and their behavior in Yangtze River Delta of China, *Journal of Cleaner Production*, 17(16): 1480–1486.

Ma, C. B. and He, L. (2008), From state monopoly to renewable portfolio: Restructuring China's electric utility, *Energy Policy*, 36: 1697–1711.

Magat, W. A. (1979), The effects of environmental regulation on innovation, *Law and Contemporary Problems*, 43(1): 4–25.

Mahapatra, D., Shukla, P. and Dhar, S. (2012), External cost of coal based electricity generation: A tale of Ahmedabad city, *Energy Policy*, 49: 253–265.

McFadden, D. (1973), Conditional logit analysis of qualitative choice behavior, in P. Zarembka (ed.), *Frontiers in Econometrics*, 105–142, New York: Academic Press.

McFadden, D. (1986), The choice theory approach to market research, *Marketing Science*, 5(4): 275–297. Milliman, S. R. and Prince, R. (1989), Firm incentives to promote technological change in pollution control, *Journal of Environmental Economics and Management*, 17(3): 247–265.

Ministry of Environmental Protection (MEP) (1998–2014 [yearly issues]), *Annual statistic report on environment in China*, Beijing: MEP. Available from: mep.gov.cn/zwgk/hjtj/.

National Bureau of Statistics (NBS) (1978–2014 [yearly issues]), *China statistical yearbook*, Beijing: China Statistics Press.

National Bureau of Statistics (NBS) (1998–2014a [yearly issues]), *China energy statistical yearbook*, Beijing: China Statistics Press.

National Bureau of Statistics (NBS) (1998–2014b [yearly issues]), *China statistical yearbook on environment*, Beijing: China Statistics Press.

National Energy Administration of China (NEA) (2015), *Statistics of China's electric power consumption 2015*, Beijing: National Energy Administration of China. Available from: power.in-en.com/html/power.

National Health and Family Planning Commission (2014), *China family development report 2014*, Beijing: China Population Publishing House. Available from: rkcbs.net/Web/c_0000000100020002/d_0260.htm.

Oaster, T. R. F. (1989), Number of alternatives per choice point and stability of Likert type scales, *Perceptual and Motor Skills*, 68: 549–550.

Ou, X., Xiliang, Z., Shiyan, C. and Qingfang, G. (2009), Energy consumption and GHG emissions of six biofuel pathways by LCA in People's Republic of China, *Applied Energy*, 86(1): S197–208.

Ren, J. (2002), *Price regulation of China's public utility*, January, Beijing: Economic and Management Press.

Shrestha, R. K. and Alavalapati, J. R. R. (2004), Valuing environmental benefits of silvopasture practice: A case study of the Lake Okeechobee watershed in Florida, *Ecological Economics*, 49(3): 349–359.

SPC (1998), *Labour force quota for thermal power plants*, Beijing: State Power Corporation.

Susaeta, A., Lal, P., Alavalapati, J. and Mercer, E. (2011), Random preferences towards bioenergy environmental externalities: A case study of woody biomass based electricity in the southern United States, *Energy Economics*, 33: 1111–1118.

Testa, F., Iraldo, F. and Frey, M. (2011), The effect of environmental regulation on firms' competitive performance: The case of the building and construction sector in some EU regions, *Journal of Environmental Management*, 92(9): 2136–2144.

Train, K. (2009), *Discrete choice methods with simulation*, 2nd edn, New York: Cambridge University Press.

US Energy Information Administration (EIA) (1998–2014, [yearly issues]), *Electric power annual*, Washington, DC: EIA. Available from: eia.gov/electricity/annual/.

van der Kroon, B., Brouwer, R. and van Beukering, P. J. H. (2014), The impact of the household decision environment on fuel choice behavior, *Energy Economics*, 44: 236–247.

Walley, N. and Whitehead, B. (1994), It's not easy being green, *Harvard Business Review*, 72(3): 46–52.

Wang, Z. X., Pan, L., Yang, F. and Liu, J. (2012), Thinking on the achievements and problems of energy conservation and emissions reduction for the power industry in China during the 11th Five-Year Plan, [in Chinese], *Journal of Environmental Engineering Technology*, 2(2): 81–89.

Yang, Z. H., Ju, M. T., Zhou, Y. P. and Wang, Q. (2011), Clean development mechanism and construction of carbon trading market in China, [in Chinese], *China Population, Resources and Environment*, 21(8): 118–123.

Zhao, X. L., Ma, Q. and Yang, R. (2013), Factors influencing CO_2 emissions in China's power industry: Co-integration analysis, *Energy Policy*, 57: 89–98.

Zhao, X., Yin, H. and Zhao, Y. (2015), Impact of environmental regulations on the efficiency and CO_2 emissions of power plants in China, *Applied Energy*, 149: 238–247.

Appendix 19.1

Appendix Table A19.1: Descriptive Statistics of Manager Perceptions of Environmental Regulations

	Items	Mean	SD	Corrected item-total correlat.	α value	Cumulative variance[1]
CCR	Emission standards	4.38	1.687	0.678	0.887	68.990%
	Fines	4.53	1.778	0.752		
	Supervision	4.87	1.726	0.793		
	ESS[2]	5.04	1.750	0.712		
	PTS[3]	5.01	1.646	0.701		
MBR	Tax credits	4.42	1.827	0.500	0.766	82.312%
	CDM	4.34	2.016	0.729		
	Cap &trade	4.04	2.054	0.574		
GS	Subsidy for new technological R&D	3.72	2.135	0.903	0.941	89.543%
	Subsidy for new technical production	3.87	2.050	0.897		
	Preferential loan guarantees	3.84	2.166	0.942		

[1] If the value of the cumulative variance is more than 60%, it is within the scope of what can be considered acceptable (Kaiser 1974).

[2] ESS: environmental assessment system.

[3] PTS: production technology standards.

20. Urban Density and Carbon Emissions in China

Jianxin Wu, Yanrui Wu and Xiumei Guo[1]

Introduction

As the world's largest emitter of carbon dioxide, China faces enormous carbon abatement challenges. These challenges are concentrated in cities, which account for the largest share of energy consumption in China. One estimate for 2006 suggested that some 84 per cent of China's total commercial energy use occurred in urban areas (Dhakal 2009).

In economic theory, ideas from new economic geography suggest that urban agglomeration can lead to economies of scale, technological progress and transaction cost reduction—and therefore lower energy consumption and lower carbon dioxide emissions. Moreover, the spatial distribution of population and economic activities is a key factor influencing energy consumption and carbon dioxide emissions, including the distribution of people within and between urban clusters.

As the hubs of most of the energy consumption in the world's largest carbon emitter, cities in China are fundamental to addressing global and domestic energy-related challenges. Analysis of the relationship between carbon dioxide emissions and the spatial distribution of urban populations and economic activities therefore also has important policy implications for China's national urbanisation policy.

That urbanisation policy has instigated a process of rapid relocation that has seen more than 20 million people move from rural areas to urban areas annually over the past decade. This was supported by the implementation of preferential regional development programs and industry relocation policies. As these policies can affect the spatial distribution of population and economic activities, they may also have significant environmental consequences.

1 Work on this chapter was supported by the China National Natural Science Foundation (1333007, 71473105), China National Social Science Foundation (15ZDA054) and a BHP Billiton Visiting Professorship (University of Western Australia). The first draft was completed while Jianxin Wu was visiting the UWA Business School. We also thank Lauren Johnston and Ligang Song for helpful comments.

International institutions and national governments have long considered the idea of developing compact cities as an approach for reducing energy consumption and greenhouse gas (GHG) emissions (Gaigné et al. 2012). One assumption is that compact cities are less dependent than others on private vehicle use, which leads to lower energy consumption and lower carbon dioxide emissions. A recent theoretical and empirical literature highlights the mechanisms by which urban density affects the environment through the level of commuting (Brownstone and Golob 2009; Glaeser and Kahn 2010; Gaigné et al. 2012). Some household-level research also finds strong evidence in developed country samples that urban population density is negatively related to energy use for commuting (Brownstone and Golob 2009; Glaeser and Kahn 2010; Cirilli and Veneri 2014; Lee and Lee 2014). However, many authors argue that the impact of urban density on carbon dioxide emissions is a complicated issue (Gaigné et al. 2012; Borck and Pflüger 2013; Larson and Yezer 2014). The aggregate effect of urban density on carbon dioxide emissions remains indeterminate. As researchers debate whether compact cities perform better than dispersed ones in terms of energy efficiency, environmental policymakers may safely adopt a comprehensive urban-wide approach to such efficiency, instead of considering just the effects of commuting or transport.

In this chapter, we aim to conduct a comprehensive empirical examination of the relationship between urban density and carbon dioxide emissions. In doing so, we believe we make three contributions to the literature. First, the full panel data for China's prefecture-level and above (PAA) cities used here allow us not only to newly control for time-invariant omitted variables that may distort the cross-sectional estimates, but also to avoid possible sample selection biases associated with the partial samples and household survey samples used in most existing studies. Second, we examine the impact of urban density on carbon dioxide emissions through three mechanisms: intra-city commuting, transport and the entire urban system. Third, our empirical results suggest that compact cities are more environmentally friendly than dispersed ones. However, we also find that denser cities in China depend more on public commuting and therefore create more carbon dioxide emissions through intra-city commuting.

The remainder of the chapter is organised as follows: the second section presents a brief literature review; the third section describes the data and variables; the fourth section reports some stylised facts about Chinese urban population density; the fifth section discusses the empirical analysis and results; and the sixth section concludes and offers some policy implications.

Literature review

Since transport accounts for a large and growing share of energy consumption and GHG emissions, a large body of empirical literature has focused on the effects of urban density on GHG emissions from transport, particularly in the case of intra-city commuting. Holden and Norland (2005) use household survey data from eight residential areas in the Greater Oslo region in Norway, and find that compact cities tend to be 'greener' than dispersed ones in terms of energy use for housing and transport. Similarly, Muñiz and Galindo (2005) use data for 163 metropolitan municipalities in Barcelona, Spain, and find that denser central areas have lower energy consumption from commuting than those on the periphery. Based on a Californian subsample from the 2001 US National Household Travel Survey, Brownstone and Golob (2009) find that a decrease in housing density by 1,000 units per square mile (2.6 sq km) (40 per cent) results in an increase of 1,200 miles (1,930 km) driven (4.8 per cent) and 65 more gallons (246 L) (5.5 per cent) of fuel used per household per year. Regarding the effects of residential density on fuel usage, increased mileage leads to a difference of 45 gallons (170 L), with the remaining 20 gallons (76 L) relating to vehicle choice. Lee and Lee (2014) find that doubling population-weighted urban density is associated with a reduction in carbon dioxide emissions from household travel and residential energy consumption, by 48 per cent and 35 per cent, respectively. Cirilli and Veneri (2014) use a cross-sectional dataset of the 111 largest Italian urban areas in 2001 and find that smaller, more compact cities are associated with lower carbon dioxide emissions per commuter. Most of these studies rely on cross-sectional, household-based survey data.

The availability of data for carbon dioxide emissions in cities across countries enables one strand of the literature to examine the effects of urban density on other pollutants (such as sulphur dioxide, nitrogen dioxide and particulate matter). Hilber and Palmer (2014) use panel data for 75 cities in 45 countries and find that increasing both vehicle and population densities can significantly reduce air pollution concentration in city centres. The negative effect of car density on pollution is due to the association of car density with decentralisation of residential and economic activities. Their results show that the impact of private vehicles on pollutant emissions is substantially more complicated than expected. Sarzynski (2012) uses a sample of 8,038 cities worldwide in 2005 and finds that compact cities are significantly correlated with lower aggregate pollutant emissions.

Transport accounts for 20 per cent of GHG emissions in the EU15 countries and 30 per cent in the United States (OECD 2008). In China's PAA-level cities, according to our estimation, the transport sector accounts for approximately 18 per cent of carbon dioxide emissions. Although transport plays an important role in energy consumption and carbon dioxide emissions, other factors also contribute to GHG emission levels and cannot be neglected. Recent studies have also tried to investigate the impacts of urban compactness on carbon dioxide emissions by using a more general framework. Larson and Yezer (2014) develop an urban simulation model using endogenous population, housing supply and demand and commuting. The simulation results show no significant effect on energy consumption of city size and population density. In a more general equilibrium framework, Gaigné et al. (2012) develop a model of an urban system with two cities and theoretically find that households in denser cities are not necessarily more environmentally friendly. Higher population density may reduce carbon dioxide emissions generated by commuting, but can increase the emissions because of the relocation of economic activities due to changes in prices, wages and land rents. In other words, the increase in compactness is environmentally desirable only if the intercity and intra-urban distribution of economic activities remains the same. Compactness, therefore, may not mitigate carbon dioxide emissions when one accounts for the possible relocation of activities within and between cities in response to a higher population density and its associated consequences. Unlike Larson and Yezer (2014) and Gaigné et al. (2012), Borck and Pflüger (2013) develop a new economic geography model that accounts for comprehensive pollutant emissions that arise from commuting within cities, intercity goods transport, production of manufacturing and agricultural goods and residential energy use. They find that city size has an ambiguous effect on pollution. However, these results are based on theoretical analyses or simulations and empirical research is therefore required to verify these hypotheses.

Another strand of research has tried to investigate the effect of urban layout and planning on carbon dioxide emissions in developing countries—China, in particular. Chen et al. (2008) use data from 45 large cities to analyse the costs and benefits of urban compactness from an environmental perspective, and conclude that population density in many Chinese cities is generally less than the critical density level that may maximise the environmental quality of a city. Liu et al. (2014) construct indicators of carbon dioxide economic efficiency (the ratio of gross domestic product to total carbon dioxide emissions) and carbon dioxide social efficiency (the ratio of a social welfare measure to total carbon dioxide emissions). Using panel data from 30 Chinese cities, they find that urban compactness is positively related to carbon dioxide economic efficiency, but negatively correlated with carbon dioxide social efficiency. Qin and Wu (2015) examine data from 25 provinces in China over the period 1998–2008 and find a nonlinear relationship between carbon dioxide emissions and urban concentration. More specifically, they found that as the degree of urban concentration increases, carbon dioxide emission intensity first increases and then declines. They attribute this bell-shaped relationship between carbon dioxide emission intensity and urban concentration to the interplay of economies of scale, technological change, institutional reform and associated changes in industrial composition. Jenks and Burgess (2000) use cases from developing countries to highlight the sustainable characteristics of compact cities; however, this strand of research is always limited by small sample sizes.

In general, due to data constraints, most existing research is based on cross-sectional household survey data from developed countries, particularly cities in the United States and Europe. This type of research has three potential limitations. First, cross-sectional data neglect technology and structural changes over time, which may radically reduce carbon dioxide emissions that arise from certain types of energy consumption. Industry composition and the structure of energy consumption in cities can also change over time. Advocates of the environmental Kuznets curve argue that as income grows, pollution first increases and then declines due to structural change and adoption of clean technologies (Stern 2014). The decline may be driven by other factors such as the enforcement of environmental regulations, increased environmental awareness and education and probably the relocation of polluting industries. Second, studies that use household data consider only carbon dioxide emissions that result from consumption, neglecting emissions from the production side. Yet carbon dioxide emissions arising from the production process account for a large share of total emissions. Therefore, neglecting carbon dioxide emissions from production may lead to significantly biased results and incorrect policy implications. Third, in developed countries, private vehicles are the predominant mode of transport, while in developing countries, public transportation modes such as buses and taxies are popular. According to Zheng et al. (2011), private cars account for only a very small proportion of energy use in China.

Most empirical studies adopt cross-sectional household data because economic data are not collected and reported at the city level in developed countries (Au and Henderson 2006). Fortunately, the Chinese Government regularly collects and reports economic data at the city level, which provide a unique database for city-level analysis. This chapter aims to analyse the impacts of urban density on carbon dioxide emissions from intra-city commuting, transport and the entire urban system.

Data and variables

Our data are drawn from a series of official publications by China's National Bureau of Statistics (NBS). The three major sources are the *China city statistical yearbook* (NBS 2008–12a), *China urban construction statistical yearbook* (NBS 2008–12e) and *China statistical yearbook* (NBS 2008–12c). As of 2011, there were 287 cities in China at the PAA level. As most data for Lhasa city are not available, our panel dataset uses 286 of the 287 cities for the period 2007–11.

Energy consumption

Because our estimation of carbon dioxide emissions is based on energy consumption, we need first to estimate energy consumption. In this chapter, we consider four major sources of energy consumption: electricity, coal gas and liquefied petroleum gas, transportation and heating. The *China city statistical yearbook* provides original annual data for electricity and coal gas and liquefied petroleum gas in each city.

As part of the welfare system, centralised heating systems provide winter heating in northern Chinese cities (those north of the Huai River), between 15 November and 15 March. Small and medium-sized industrial boilers burn coal to provide this heating. Data for central heating at the city level can be obtained from the *China urban construction statistical yearbook*. We adopt a 70 per cent thermal efficiency rate according to the Chinese National Standard *GB/T 15317-2009 Monitoring and testing for energy saving of coal fired industrial boilers*. With data for heat values, thermal efficiency and average low calorific value (20,908 kJ/kg), we can easily estimate coal consumption for winter heating in each city.

Transport accounts for a large share of energy consumption in cities. Unfortunately, no energy consumption data for transport are directly available at the city level. The *China city statistical yearbook* does, however, provide detailed freight traffic (t-km) and passenger traffic (passenger-km) data for road, railway, waterway and aviation. The *China statistical yearbook* provides data for all types of energy consumption in the transport sector. Li et al. (2013) report the types of energy consumption corresponding to different modes of transport. Thus, we can calculate the energy intensity of each transportation mode. With data for the city-level freight traffic, passenger traffic and the energy intensity of each transportation mode, we can also estimate the energy consumption by the transport sector in each city. Finally, consumption by these four transport types is converted to tonnes of standard coal equivalent (tce) using the standard conversion factors published in the *China energy statistical yearbook*.

Carbon dioxide emissions

Aggregate carbon dioxide emissions and carbon dioxide emissions from the transport sector

The estimation of carbon dioxide emissions is based on the energy consumption data discussed in the preceding section. Therefore, we estimate carbon dioxide emissions as follows (Equation 20.1).

Equation 20.1

$$Emissions_{co2} = \delta_1 * Transport + \delta_2 * Electricity + \delta_3 * Heating + \delta_4 * Fuel$$

In Equation 20.1, δ_i (i = 1, 2, 3 and 4) is the conversion factor. The computation of carbon dioxide emissions generated by the transport sector is similar to that of energy consumption. Carbon dioxide emissions from fuel and heating can be estimated using the consumption statistics for coal gas, liquefied petroleum gas and heating coal, using relevant conversion factors. The carbon dioxide emission conversion factors in this chapter are drawn from the Intergovernmental Panel on Climate Change guidelines (IPCC 2006).

As different Chinese cities use different natural resources to produce electricity, the electricity conversion factor differs significantly across regions. China's state power grid comprises six regional power grids. Fortunately, in recent years, the baseline emission factors for each regional power grid have been estimated and reported by the National Coordination Committee on Climate Change. As electricity transmitted through a regional power grid is substitutable (Glaeser and Kahn 2010), we use regional baseline emission factors to convert electricity consumption into carbon dioxide emissions in each region.

Carbon dioxide emissions generated by intra-city commuting

In China, intra-city commuting includes buses, taxies, private vehicles and metro systems (railway). As of 2011, nine cities ran metros (Beijing, Shanghai, Guangzhou, Shenzhen, Tianjin, Nanjing, Shenyang, Chengdu and Wuhan), but only three ran a metro during the period of this study (2002–11): Beijing, Shanghai and Guangzhou. The remaining six cities introduced metros very late in our sample period and most had only one line in operation. The data for private vehicles in PAA-level cities are not available for China, and Zheng et al. (2011) estimated that private vehicles account for only a small proportion of public transport. We therefore assume that the contribution of metros and private vehicles to intra-city commuting is relatively small. Following Zheng et al. (2011), we use intra-city public transportation (buses and taxies) as a replacement for intra-city commuting. The number of buses and taxies in each city is available in the *China city statistical yearbook*. Fuel consumption (gasoline and diesel) is calculated according to Chinese National Standard *JT 711-2008 Limits and measurement methods of fuel consumption for commercial vehicle for passenger transportation*. Carbon dioxide emissions from gasoline and diesel consumption during commuting can be estimated by using conversion factors from the IPCC guidelines (2006).

Dependent variables

The objective of this chapter is to examine the impacts of urban density on carbon dioxide emissions from intra-city commuting, transport and the entire urban system. Therefore, we use the following dependent variables: commuting-related per capita carbon dioxide emissions (CPCCEs), transport-related per capita carbon dioxide emissions (TPCCEs) and urban system-related per capita carbon dioxide emissions (UPCCEs).

Explanatory variables

Urban density

Following the literature in the field, we use urban residential population per square kilometre in a city as a proxy for urban density (denoted as *density*). As high population density can reduce the mean commuting distance, the impact of urban density on CPCCEs is expected to be negative. However, as argued by some authors (for example, Gaigné et al. 2012; Borck and Pflüger 2013; Larson and Yezer 2014), the impacts of urban density on carbon dioxide emissions generated by the transport sector and the entire urban system are complicated. Therefore, the effects of urban density on TPCCEs and UPCCEs are ambiguous.

Income level

We use gross city product (GCP) per capita in a city as a proxy for income level (denoted as ln(*income*)). As increases in income levels may lead to greater production and consumption of goods and services, it is expected that income levels will be positively related to carbon dioxide emissions.

Energy intensity

Energy intensity (energy consumption per unit of real GCP, denoted as *energyintensity*) is always the standard proxy for heterogeneity and variation in technological progress in environmental studies (for example, Auffhammer and Carson 2008; Du et al. 2012). It is expected that energy intensity will be positively related to carbon dioxide emissions.

Industry structure variables

Industry structure variables are measured by the income shares of secondary and tertiary industries, denoted as *Sec_Share* and *Ter_Share*, respectively. Industry composition may affect carbon dioxide emissions in two ways. First, industries differ greatly in terms of their direct energy consumption and carbon dioxide emissions. For example, secondary industries usually produce more carbon dioxide emissions than agricultural and tertiary industries. Second, secondary industries are more capital intensive and thus create more carbon dioxide emissions through cargo transport. Conversely, tertiary industries are more labour intensive and thus produce more carbon dioxide through passenger transport. Therefore, the output shares of secondary and tertiary industries are included to capture possible variations in industry compositions across cities over time.

Trade openness

We use the ratio of the total value of foreign trade to GCP in a city as a proxy for trade openness (denoted as *openness*). The relationship between foreign trade and carbon dioxide emissions is widely discussed in the literature (Halicioglu 2009; Lin and Sun 2010; Ren et al. 2014). Firms may get clean production technology from foreign trade; however, the export of energy-intensive products may increase domestic carbon dioxide emissions. Therefore, the aggregate effects of foreign trade on carbon dioxide emissions remain ambiguous.

Foreign direct investment

Considering that China is one of the largest host countries in the world for foreign direct investment (FDI), we include FDI (denoted as *FDIY*) as a control variable in our specification. The variable is measured by the ratio of actually utilised FDI to GCP in a city. The relationship between FDI and carbon dioxide emissions is associated with the 'pollution haven' theory, which says that high-emission foreign firms from developed countries with stringent environmental regulations may be attracted to developing countries with weak environmental regulations (Kellenberg 2009). Empirical evidence for this effect is, however, mixed.

Urban population density in this chapter is calculated by actual residential population rather than population recorded through the *hukou* (household registration) system. Data for actual residential population and foreign trade volume are drawn from the *China statistical yearbook for regional economy* (NBS 2008–12d), while data for jurisdiction, nominal GCP and FDI are obtained directly from the *China city statistical yearbook* (NBS 2008–12a). The nominal GCP is deflated using a province-specific gross regional product (GRP) deflator, with 2007 as the base year. The province-specific GRP deflator is drawn from the *China statistical yearbook* (NBS 2008–12c). Table 20.1 shows the descriptive statistics for major variables and reveals substantial heterogeneity across cities.

Table 20.1 Descriptive statistics for all variables

Variable	Mean	Std dev.	Min.	Max.
UPCCEs (tonnes per capita)	2.640	4.156	0.067	48.137
TPCCEs (tonnes per capita)	0.397	0.399	0.033	3.474
CPCCEs (tonnes per capita)	0.047	0.074	0.001	1.228
density (people per sq km)	413.3	311.800	4.700	2,565.100
income (RMB10,000 per capita)	1.869	2.314	0.163	32.066
energyintensity (tonnes per RMB1,000)	0.306	0.257	0.059	2.871
Sec_share	0.481	0.116	0.090	0.910
Ter_share	0.358	0.081	0.086	0.853
openness	0.278	0.779	0.000	26.970
FDIY (FDI/GCP)	0.027	0.031	0.000	0.420

Source: Authors' own calculations.

Stylised facts about Chinese urban population density

China has experienced rapid urbanisation in the past few decades. The country has a scarcity of arable land relative to the rest of the world. For example, in 2011, per capita arable land in China was approximately 1,023 sq m, roughly 40.9 per cent of the global average of 2,500 sq m. The Chinese Government has therefore implemented stringent land regulation policies throughout the urbanisation process, a consequence of which is a continuous increase in urban population density.

Figure 20.1 presents changes in average urban population density from 2007 to 2011. Among China's three main regions, the eastern cities have much higher average urban population density than the central and western cities. According to the classification in the *China statistical yearbook* (NBS 2008–12c), we can divide cities into five types according to population: small cites (less than 500,000), medium–small cities (500,000 – 1 million), medium-sized cities (1–2 million), large cities (2–4 million) and megacities (more than 4 million). We find that urban population density is highly correlated with city size (Figure 20.2). The average urban population density of megacities is 6.11 times that of small cities. In China, the best public services—such as education, health care and public facilities—are in large cities due to the concentration of administrative power. This leads to further concentration of population in large cities and, therefore, a trend of increasing urban population density in China is expected in coming decades.

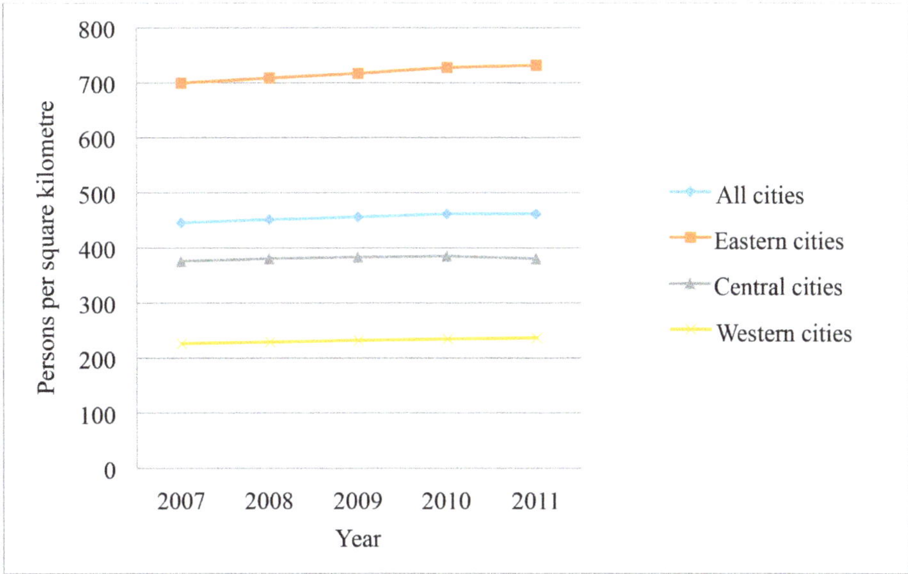

Figure 20.1 Evolution of urban density, 2007–11

Note: The unit for urban density is the number of people per square kilometre.

Source: Authors' own work.

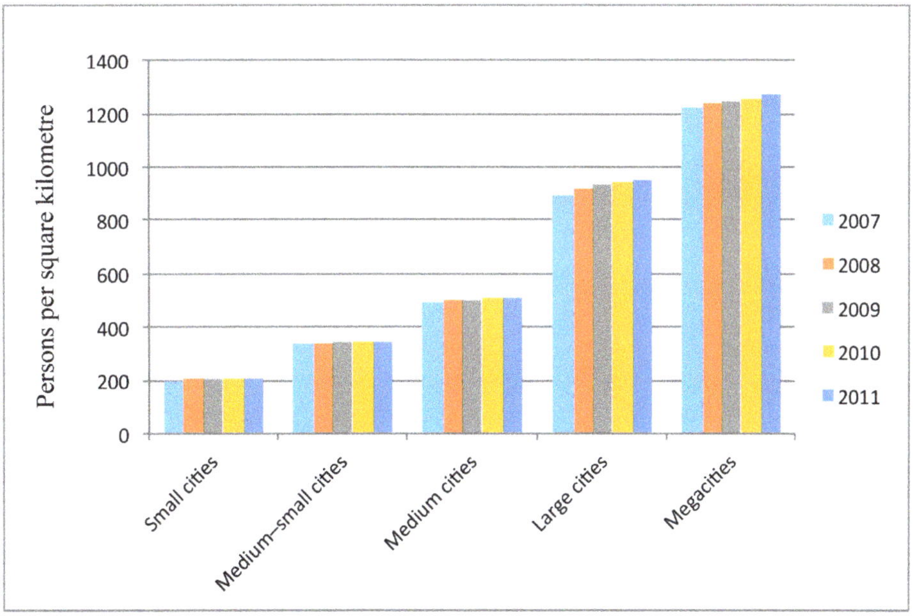

Figure 20.2 City size and urban density, 2007–11

Note: The unit for urban density is the number of people per square kilometre.

Source: Authors' own work.

Empirical analysis

To investigate the impact of urban density on carbon dioxide emissions in China, we estimate Equation 20.2.

Equation 20.2

$$PCCEs_{i,t} = \varphi_0 + \varphi_1 density_{i,t} + Z_{i,t}\beta + \eta_i + T_t + \varepsilon_{i,t}$$

In Equation 20.2, $density_{i,t}$ represents the natural logarithm of people per square kilometre in a city. $Z_{i,t}$ denotes a vector of control variables, including income level, energy intensity, capital intensity, industry structure, trade openness and FDI; ϕ_0 is a constant, ϕ_1 is a scalar and β is a vector of parameters. The variable η_i captures city fixed effects, which are used to control for unobserved, time-unvarying city characteristics; T_t is a year fixed effect used to control for unobserved, time-varying exogenous shocks that are common to all cities; and $\varepsilon_{i,t}$ is the error term.

Several specifications are considered for each of the PCCEs representing intra-city commuting, the transport sector and the urban system (Tables 20.2–20.4), respectively. Column 1 in each of the tables presents the pooled ordinary least squares (OLS) specification. However, the OLS estimation may be biased due to a lack of controls for possible time-unvarying city characteristics and time-varying year fixed effects. Therefore, we include city fixed effects in column 2, and then both city fixed effects and year fixed effects in column 3. Hausman tests are applied to check the fitness of the specifications. To deal with the possible problem of endogeneity, the generalised method of moments (GMM) is applied and the results are reported in column 4 as a further robustness check.

Urban density and CPCCEs

The regression results for intra-city commuting are reported in Table 20.2. It is found that urban density has a negative and statistically significant coefficient (column 1). This finding suggests that carbon dioxide emissions from intra-city commuting are lower in more densely populated cities. However, this result may be biased due to the lack of controls for various city characteristics. As shown in columns 2 and 3 of Table 20.2, the results reverse completely after controlling for city fixed effects. The estimation results in column 2 are overall reasonably consistent with those in column 3. The coefficient of urban density is positive and significant at the 1 per cent level, implying that higher urban density is associated with greater per capita carbon dioxide emissions from public commuting. Despite the differences in intra-city commuting modes, this result contrasts with the findings of previous studies (Brownstone and Golob 2009; Glaeser and Kahn 2010; Cirilli and Veneri 2014) based on household vehicle use data from developed countries. One possible reason is that urban residents in China are more dependent on public mass transport in bigger and denser cities, while in smaller and more dispersed cities, people depend more on bicycles and motorbikes. Our fixed effect estimation results for CPCCEs are consistent with the theoretical argument that an increase in population density may generate higher per capita carbon dioxide emissions from public commuting (Gaigné et al. 2012). However, in the GMM specification (column 4), the coefficient of urban density is not statistically significant, despite still being positive.

The coefficient of ln(*income*) is positive in all specifications but significant at the 1 per cent level only in column 2 in Table 20.2, indicating the existence of a positive relationship between CPCCEs and income levels. The coefficient of *openness* is positive and significant in the fixed effect specifications. However, the coefficients of other control variables (*energyintensity*, *Sec_Share*, *Ter_Share* and *FDIY*) are insignificant.

Urban density and TPCCEs

The estimation results for TPCCEs are reported in Table 20.3. The coefficient of urban density is negative and significant in all four specifications for TPCCEs, which implies that higher urban population density is strongly correlated with lower carbon dioxide emissions across the entire transport network. In other words, in terms of the transport sector, denser cities are more environmentally friendly than dispersed ones. This result is quite different from that in the CPCCE estimations; given that TPCCEs include intra-city and intercity passenger and cargo transportation, this is, however, not so surprising. However, contrary estimation results between CPCCE and TPCCE equations highlight the complexity of calculating carbon dioxide emissions generated by transportation. Although some theoretical studies (for example, Borck and Pflüger 2013) have tried to include intercity goods transportation in their analysis framework, many questions remain about the relationship between urban density and carbon dioxide emissions generated by transport. Moreover, in China, empirical evidence shows that local protectionism hinders market integration (Bai et al. 2004; Poncet 2005; Lu and Tao 2009). As a result, most Chinese cities tend to be more autarkic than cities in developed countries. The fragmentation of Chinese regional markets may reduce intercity transportation, particularly in larger cities. This could partially explain why more densely populated cities generate less carbon dioxide emissions from transport in China.

In contrast with the results for the CPCCEs, in the TPCCE estimations, many control variables become significant. The positive and significant coefficient of ln(*income*) implies that the improvement in income levels is one of the major reasons for the rapid increase in carbon dioxide emissions. The coefficient of energy intensity is positive and significant at the 1 per cent level in all four specifications, indicating that energy intensity has a strong and positive impact on carbon dioxide emissions generated by the transport sector. The coefficients of *Sec_share*, *Ter_share* and *FDIY* are significant in the city fixed estimation, while the coefficients of *openness* are insignificant in all three specifications in Table 20.3.

Table 20.2 The estimation results for the determinants of CPCCEs

	(1)	(2)	(3)	(4)
density	–0.00900***	0.104***	0.105***	0.00758
	(0.00269)	(0.0233)	(0.0231)	(0.00908)
ln(*income*)	0.00824***	0.00202***	0.00147	0.00176
	(0.000728)	(0.000767)	(0.000919)	(0.00110)
energyintensity	0.00722***	0.000133	0.000171	0.000727*
	(0.000341)	(0.000355)	(0.000356)	(0.000411)
Sec_share	0.0709***	–0.00681	–0.0202	0.00624
	(0.0117)	(0.0125)	(0.0176)	(0.0183)
Ter_share	0.159***	0.00689	–0.00779	0.0235
	(0.0168)	(0.0177)	(0.0217)	(0.0320)
openness	–0.00856***	0.00648**	0.00702*	0.00420
	(0.00276)	(0.00316)	(0.00358)	(0.00446)
FDIY	0.113***	–0.00796	–0.00814	–0.0195
	(0.0314)	(0.0189)	(0.0190)	(0.0275)
CPCCEst-1				0.586***
				(0.215)
Constant	–0.0870***	–0.0112	0.00107	–0.00426
	(0.00955)	(0.0142)	(0.0172)	(0.0187)
Observations	1,430	1,430	1,430	1,144
Adjusted R^2	0.6558	0.2913	0.2961	
City fixed effect	No	Yes	Yes	
Year fixed effect	No	No	Yes	
Hausman test		350(0.00)***	353(0.00)***	
Ar(1)				0.017
Ar(2)				0.072
Sargan test				23.18(0.109)

*** denotes statistical significance at the 1 per cent level
** denotes statistical significance at the 5 per cent level
* denotes statistical significance at the 10 per cent level

Note: Robust standard errors in parentheses.

Source: Authors' own estimations.

Table 20.3 The estimation results for the determinants of TPCCEs

	(1)	(2)	(3)	(4)
density	–0.144***	–0.534***	–0.494***	–0.176***
	(0.0311)	(0.137)	(0.134)	(0.0553)
ln*(income)*	0.0420***	0.0897***	0.0450***	0.0331***
	(0.00920)	(0.0118)	(0.0153)	(0.0125)
energyintensity	0.0378***	0.0603***	0.0617***	0.0357**
	(0.00615)	(0.0173)	(0.0170)	(0.0142)
Sec_share	1.065***	1.054***	0.143	0.107
	(0.0916)	(0.214)	(0.227)	(0.223)
Ter_share	1.377***	0.535*	–0.254	0.119
	(0.153)	(0.303)	(0.312)	(0.287)
openness	–0.0171	0.0756	0.0575	0.0314
	(0.0368)	(0.0684)	(0.0736)	(0.0695)
FDIY	1.761***	0.952**	0.886**	0.324
	(0.401)	(0.409)	(0.398)	(0.505)
CPCCEst-1				0.984***
				(0.0799)
Constant	–0.774***	–0.474**	0.313	–0.171
	(0.0751)	(0.202)	(0.229)	(0.195)
Observations	1,430	1,430	1,430	1,144
Adjusted R^2	0.3784	0.2589	0.3050	
City fixed effect	No	Yes	Yes	
Year fixed effect	No	No	Yes	
Hausman test		53.71(0.00)	41.49(0.00)	
Sargan test				26.282(0.0695)
Ar(1)				P = 0.000
Ar(2)				P = 0.6115

*** denotes statistical significance at the 1 per cent level
** denotes statistical significance at the 5 per cent level
* denotes statistical significance at the 10 per cent level

Note: Robust standard errors in parentheses.

Source: Authors' own estimations.

Urban density and UPCCEs

The regression results of UPCCEs are reported in Table 20.4. Similar to the results for the TPCCE estimations, here the coefficients attached to urban density are negative and significant in all four specifications. The magnitude of the coefficients is, however, relatively larger here than in the TPCCE estimations. This could imply that the impact of urban density on carbon dioxide emissions is not restricted to the transport sector and could also come through other channels such as residential heating and airconditioning, the sharing of public facilities and so on. Together with the results observed in the preceding sections, our findings suggest that more densely populated cities in China might be less 'green' than dispersed ones with regard to intra-city commuting, but are more environmentally friendly in terms of their transport sectors and the entire urban system. These findings do not support arguments about the relationship between carbon dioxide emissions and urban density that have been proposed in some recent theoretical studies (for example, Gaigné et al. 2012; Borck and Pflüger 2013; Larson and Yezer 2014).

As expected, however, income level and energy intensity are still the key determinants of UPCCEs. Given that China's income levels will continue to increase, reduction in energy intensity would be one of the key channels by which to reduce GHG emissions.

In contrast with the results for CPCCEs and TPCCEs, here the coefficients for *Sec_share* are positive and significant in all specifications, implying that expansion of secondary industries may create more carbon dioxide emissions in cities. Similarly, the coefficient of *FDIY* is positive and significant in most specifications (columns 1–3). Considering that most FDI in China is in the manufacturing industry, this may suggest that an increase in FDI volume will lead to higher carbon dioxide emissions in cities. However, the coefficients of *Ter_share* and *openness* are insignificant in most specifications, indicating that the impacts of tertiary industries and trade openness on carbon dioxide emissions are less significant.

Table 20.4 The estimation results for the determinants of UPCCEs

	(1)	(2)	(3)	(4)
density	−1.538***	−2.249***	−2.144***	−1.562***
	(0.230)	(0.753)	(0.813)	(0.350)
ln(*income*)	0.650***	0.613***	0.542***	0.463***
	(0.0637)	(0.0955)	(0.134)	(0.0790)
energyintensity	0.855***	0.529***	0.528***	0.678***
	(0.0804)	(0.105)	(0.106)	(0.142)
Sec_share	7.653***	3.245***	2.246**	3.418*
	(0.829)	(1.234)	(1.110)	(1.996)
Ter_share	−0.527	1.659	1.283	1.716
	(1.304)	(1.863)	(1.475)	(2.298)
openness	0.435**	−0.195	−0.320	0.00835
	(0.221)	(0.291)	(0.313)	(0.196)
FDIY	2.106	3.803**	3.596**	1.970
	(1.898)	(1.766)	(1.783)	(1.649)
CPCCEst-1				0.369***
				(0.105)
Constant	−4.363***	−1.447	−0.715	−2.949*
	(0.616)	(1.285)	(1.174)	(1.703)
Observations	1,430	1,430	1,430	
Adjusted R^2	0.6623	0.6062	0.5796	
City fixed effect	No	Yes	Yes	
Year fixed effect	No	No	Yes	
Hausman test		59.72(0.000)	64.96(0.000)	
Sargan				P = 0.0000
Ar(1)				P = 0.2899
Ar(2)				P = 0.4657

*** denotes statistical significance at the 1 per cent level
** denotes statistical significance at the 5 per cent level
* denotes statistical significance at the 10 per cent level

Note: Robust standard errors in parentheses.

Source: Authors' own estimations.

Conclusion

In this chapter, we investigated the impacts of urban density on carbon dioxide emissions from intra-city public commuting, the aggregate transport sector and the aggregate urban system using a panel dataset applying to 286 Chinese cities in the period 2007–11.

The results suggest that urban population density has a negative and significant impact on carbon dioxide emissions arising from the transport sector and the aggregate urban system, but has a positive impact on carbon dioxide emissions generated by intra-city public commuting. Our results do not support arguments in some recent theoretical studies that compact cities are less environmentally friendly than dispersed ones (Gaigné et al. 2012; Borck and Pflüger 2013; Larson and Yezer 2014). Our results also highlight some significant differences in commuting patterns between China and developed countries. In particular, Chinese cities depend more on public commuting modes, whereas cities in developed countries rely more on private vehicles.

As for China, due to strict land regulations, more and more apartment towers are being constructed to accommodate the influx of rural migrants into cities that has come with the policy of rapid urbanisation. As a result of such trends, Chinese cities are much more compact than cities in most developed countries. In recent decades, increased urban density has, however, been driven mainly by land-saving policies rather than environmental concerns. But our findings suggest these compact city arrangements are positive from a carbon dioxide emissions perspective.

Broader environmental policy should, however, be based on a comprehensive assessment of various pollutants (such as sulphur dioxide, particulate matter and nitrogen dioxide) that are generated by urban systems. And to this end, studies published to date should be taken as the first step towards building a theory of ecologically and socially desirable urban systems (Gaigné et al. 2012). Our results contribute to this body of knowledge and encourage scholars, city planners and policymakers to pay greater attention to the various consequences of urban population density. The urbanisation mode we select today will have significant environmental consequences in the future, and thus should be considered as carefully as possible.

Our research findings do have some limitations. First, we acknowledge that our data are drawn from different sources, which means we were not able to distinguish directly between intra-city and intercity transport. In addition, our intra-city public commuting data excluded household vehicle usage. Given recent rapid increases in private vehicle usage in China, commuting styles could change significantly in the future and potentially displace our findings based on panel data that do not account for these methods of transport. On the other hand, although our city-level data are imperfect, they are the best data available at present. Second, our research is limited to the extent that the impacts of urban density on carbon dioxide emissions prove to be a nexus for multiple mechanisms. Future research is expected to shed light on more mechanisms and how they work.

References

Au, C. C. and Henderson, J. V. (2006), Are Chinese cities too small?, *The Review of Economic Studies*, 73(3): 549–576.

Auffhammer, M. and Carson, R. T. (2008), Forecasting the path of China's CO_2 emissions using province level information, *Journal of Environmental Economics and Management*, 55(3): 229–247.

Bai, C.-E., Du, Y., Tao, Z. and Tong, S. (2004), Local protectionism and regional specialization: Evidence from China's industries, *Journal of International Economics*, 63(2): 397–417.

Borck, R. and Pflüger, M. (2013), Green cities? Urbanization, trade and the environment, *Annual conference 2013 (Duesseldorf): Competition policy and regulation in a global economic order*, No. 79763, Heidelberg: German Economic Association.

Brownstone, D. and Golob, T. F. (2009), The impact of residential density on vehicle usage and energy consumption, *Journal of Urban Economics*, 65(1): 91–98.

Chen, H., Jia, B. and Lau, S. S. Y. (2008), Sustainable urban form for Chinese compact cities: Challenges of a rapidly urbanized economy, *Habitat International*, 32(1): 28–40.

Cirilli, A. and Veneri, P. (2014), Spatial structure and carbon dioxide (CO_2) emissions due to commuting: An analysis of Italian urban areas, *Regional Studies*, 48(12): 1993–2005.

Dhakal, S. (2009), Urban energy use and carbon emissions from cities in China and policy implications, *Energy Policy*, 37(11): 4208–4219.

Du, L., Wei, C. and Cai, S. (2012), Economic development and carbon dioxide emissions in China: Provincial panel data analysis, *China Economic Review*, 23(2): 371–384.

Gaigné, C., Riou, S. and Thisse, J. F. (2012), Are compact cities environmentally friendly?, *Journal of Urban Economics*, 72(2): 123–136.

Glaeser, E. L. and Kahn, M. E. (2010), The greenness of cities: Carbon dioxide emissions and urban development, *Journal of Urban Economics*, 67(3): 404–418.

Halicioglu, F. (2009), An econometric study of CO_2 emissions, energy consumption, income and foreign trade in Turkey, *Energy Policy*, 37(3): 1156–1164.

Hilber, C. A. and Palmer, C. (2014), *Urban development and air pollution: Evidence from a global panel of cities*, Grantham Research Institute on Climate Change and the Environment Working Paper, London: London School of Economics and Political Science.

Holden, E. and Norland, I. T. (2005), Three challenges for the compact city as a sustainable urban form: Household consumption of energy and transport in eight residential areas in the greater Oslo region, *Urban Studies*, 42(12): 2145–2166.

Intergovernmental Panel on Climate Change (IPCC) (2006), *2006 IPCC guidelines for national greenhouse gas inventories*, Geneva: Intergovernmental Panel on Climate Change. Available from: ipcc-nggip.iges.or.jp/public/2006gl/.

Jenks, M. and Burgess, R. (eds) (2000), *Compact cities: Sustainable urban forms for developing countries*, Abingdon, UK: Taylor & Francis.

Kellenberg, D. K. (2009), An empirical investigation of the pollution haven effect with strategic environment and trade policy, *Journal of International Economics*, 78(2): 242–255.

Larson, W., Liu, F. and Yezer, A. (2012), Energy footprint of the city: Effects of urban land use and transportation policies, *Journal of Urban Economics*, *72*(2): 147–159.

Larson, W. D. and Yezer, A. M. (2014), The energy implications of city size and density, *Journal of Urban Economics*, 90(November): 35–49.

Lee, S. and Lee, B. (2014), The influence of urban form on GHG emissions in the US household sector, *Energy Policy*, 68: 534–549.

Li, H., Lu, Y., Zhang, J. and Wang, T. (2013), Trends in road freight transportation carbon dioxide emissions and policies in China, *Energy Policy*, 57: 99–106.

Lin, B. and Sun, C. (2010), Evaluating carbon dioxide emissions in international trade of China, *Energy Policy*, 38(1): 613–621.

Liu, Y., Song, Y. and Song, X. (2014), An empirical study on the relationship between urban compactness and CO_2 efficiency in China, *Habitat International*, 41: 92–98.

Lu, J. and Tao, Z. (2009), Trends and determinants of China's industrial agglomeration, *Journal of Urban Economics*, 65(2): 167–180.

Muñiz, I. and Galindo, A. (2005), Urban form and the ecological footprint of commuting: The case of Barcelona, *Ecological Economics*, 55(4): 499–514.

National Bureau of Statistics (NBS) (2008–12a), *China city statistical yearbook*, Beijing: China Statistics Press.

National Bureau of Statistics (NBS) (2008–12b), *China energy statistical yearbook*, Beijing: China Statistics Press.

National Bureau of Statistics (NBS) (2008–12c), *China statistical yearbook*, Beijing: China Statistics Press.

National Bureau of Statistics (NBS) (2008–12d), *China statistical yearbook for regional economy*, Beijing: China Statistics Press.

National Bureau of Statistics (NBS) (2008–12e), *China urban construction statistical yearbook*, Beijing: China Statistics Press.

Organisation for Economic Co-operation and Development (OECD) (2008), *Highlights of the international transport forum 2008: Transport and energy*, Paris: OECD.

Poncet, S. (2005), A fragmented China: Measure and determinants of Chinese domestic market disintegration, *Review of International Economics*, 13(3): 409–430.

Qin, B. and Wu, J. (2015), Does urban concentration mitigate CO_2 emissions? Evidence from China 1998–2008, *China Economic Review*, 35: 220–231.

Ren, S., Yuan, B., Ma, X. and Chen, X. (2014), International trade, FDI (foreign direct investment) and embodied CO_2 emissions: A case study of China's industrial sectors, *China Economic Review*, 28: 123–134.

Sarzynski, A. (2012), Bigger is not always better: A comparative analysis of cities and their air pollution impact, *Urban Studies*, 49(14): 3121–3138.

Stern, D. I. (2014), *The environmental Kuznets curve: A primer*, Canberra: Centre for Climate Economics & Policy, Crawford School of Public Policy, The Australian National University.

Zheng, S., Wang, R., Glaeser, E. L. and Kahn, M. E. (2011), The greenness of China: Household carbon dioxide emissions and urban development, *Journal of Economic Geography*, 11(5): 761–792.

Index

www.ingramcontent.com/pod-product-compliance
Lightning Source LLC
LaVergne TN
LVHW070906210926
848482LV00017B/1002
9781760460341